# CAPITAL, RACE AND SPACE
## VOLUME 1

# Studies in Critical Social Sciences Book Series

Haymarket Books is proud to be working with Brill Academic Publishers (www.brill.nl) to republish the *Studies in Critical Social Sciences* book series in paperback editions. This peer-reviewed book series offers insights into our current reality by exploring the content and consequences of power relationships under capitalism, and by considering the spaces of opposition and resistance to these changes that have been defining our new age. Our full catalog of *SCSS* volumes can be viewed at https://www.haymarketbooks .org/series_collections/4-studies-in-critical-social-sciences.

# Capital, Race and Space

## Volume 1

The Far-Right from Bonapartism to Fascism

## Richard Saull

Haymarket Books
Chicago, IL

First published in 2023 by Brill Academic Publishers, The Netherlands
© 2023 Koninklijke Brill NV, Leiden, The Netherlands

Published in paperback in 2024 by
Haymarket Books
P.O. Box 180165
Chicago, IL 60618
773-583-7884
www.haymarketbooks.org

ISBN: 979-8-88890-229-5

Distributed to the trade in the US through Consortium Book Sales and
Distribution (www.cbsd.com) and internationally through Ingram Publisher
Services International (www.ingramcontent.com).

This book was published with the generous support of Lannan Foundation,
Wallace Action Fund, and the Marguerite Casey Foundation.

Special discounts are available for bulk purchases by organizations and
institutions. Please call 773-583-7884 or email info@haymarketbooks.org for more
information.

Cover design by Jamie Kerry and Ragina Johnson.

Printed in the United States.

Library of Congress Cataloging-in-Publication data is available.

*In memory of my grandmother, Josephine Saull*

∵

# Contents

# Acknowledgements

This project has its origins in a conversation with Alexander Anievas, Neil Davidson and Adam Fabry in the Marlborough Arms pub in Bloomsbury in November 2011 where we met while attending the Annual Conference of the journal *Historical Materialism*. This meeting laid the basis for a series of ongoing conversations and collaborations about the history and politics of the far-right and, in particular, how to explain its origins, development and mutations by addressing what we all saw as the neglected and under-theorized significance of international relations and geopolitics. Our conversation led to a two-day workshop held at Queen Mary, University of London in October 2012 which enriched the discussion by bringing in Nicola Short, Mark Rupert, Owen Worth, Stuart Shields and Ishay Landa and which resulted in the co-edited volume, the *Longue Durée of the Far-Right: An International Historical Sociology* (Saull et al., 2015). I owe a debt of gratitude to all the above for helping me develop my knowledge and thinking on the far-right.

Since then, I have continued to work with Alexander Anievas (Anievas and Saull, 2020, 2022) and I also co-wrote an article with Neil Davidson (Davidson and Saull, 2017). Neil sadly passed away in 2020 and I, like many others, miss him. His work on nationalism, uneven and combined development, and neoliberalism along with his encyclopaedic knowledge of Marxist theory have significantly influenced my thinking on the far-right and it is a great loss that he is no longer around to discuss these ideas. My thinking on the far-right has also benefited from discussions and collaborations with colleagues in the School of Politics and International Relations at Queen Mary. I teach a second-year undergraduate module with Ray Kiely in which the nineteenth century history of the far-right, inter-war fascism and the inter-connections between the far-right and neoliberalism all feature. We also co-edited a forum in *Critical Sociology* on 'Neoliberalism and the Right' (2017) for which we provided the introduction. I have also benefited from conversations with Jean-Francois Drolet, another colleague, and a foremost authority on Neoconservatism and the American right. My former colleague, Robbie Shilliam, has been a major influence on my thinking about race and racism and that also extends to Gurminder Bhambra and Lisa Tilley and the wider collaboration involving others that resulted in the special issue of *New Political Economy* in 2018 on 'Raced Markets'.

The most important influence on my thinking on the far-right has been Alexander Anievas. Since we worked on the *Longue Durée* volume, Alex and I have been in conversation about the history and politics of the far-right, presenting papers at conferences and organizing panels, co-writing articles as well as regularly talking on Skype given that we are separated by the Atlantic Ocean. I am very grateful to Alex for his time, friendship and his deep engagement with my work and I have also learnt a lot from his own work on uneven and combined development, inter-war Germany and British appeasement policy. He read through a very rough first draft of the manuscript (of both volumes) and the quality of the two volumes – which is for others to decide – owes a great deal to his input. I would also like to thank my partner, Liza, for providing me with love and support during the researching and writing of these two volumes and for reading through several chapters of the final draft. Writing is a solitary activity and I have been lucky to have such a wonderful and supportive partner who has also been a great sounding-board. I would also like to thank the Series Editor, David Fasenfest, for his patience and support in getting the final manuscript to the publisher.

These two volumes are dedicated to my grandmother, Josephine Saull. She died in 2018. She had been an integral part of my life for as long as I can remember. Growing up, she would visit us – my parents and brother and I – most weekends and, in some respects, she was almost an additional mother. And after my mum died when I was 18 her love, support and encouragement became even more important to me. My nan was also very supportive of me in my academic studies. I lived with her whilst I completed my Masters degree and then, later, a PhD at the LSE. I don't think that she fully understood what these studies involved – she had not benefited from a decent primary let alone a higher education – or much about my career as a university lecturer, but she always made clear to me and to others how very proud of me she was. I will be forever in her debt. I miss her deeply and hope that she knew how important she was to me.

# Prologue

This work, compromising two volumes (*Volume 1: The Far-Right from Bonapartism to Fascism* and *Volume 2: The Far-Right from Cold War to Trumpism*), provides an international historical sociology of the far-right that focuses on its origins, development, and transformations within the advanced capitalist states. Less a comparative survey of parties and movements, the work addresses the enabling conditions – socioeconomic, political, ideological and geopolitical – that have abetted the development and advance of this kind of politics from the middle of the nineteenth century up until the present day.

The existing literature on the far-right – which I examine in depth in the first chapter of *Volume 1* – is vast, incorporating work in the fields of national histories, comparative politics and the history of ideas. These literatures provide a huge reservoir of resources for understanding and explaining the history and present of the far-right, and much of my argument across both volumes draws on the contributions of these scholars. But I offer a different way of conceptualizing the far-right, with the aim of outlining an argument that explains how and why the far-right persists – and, in particular, how it is determined by 'the international'.

This is an ontological question revealed in the spatial assumptions of the methodological internalism that tends to characterise historical and contemporary work on the far-right – work in which the structures, processes and relations that make up the inter-societal connections that cut across the borders of discrete political communities are either neglected or undertheorized. Focusing on the boundary between the domestic and the international, my argument specifically addresses the ways in which the evolving character and configuration of the international political economy and geopolitics shapes the conditions of possibility of far-right politics. In what ways does the international – in its political, ideological, economic and geopolitical dimensions – enable and produce the far-right? And how does the mutating organization and character of the international contribute to its shifting ideo-political character?

In what follows I argue that the various historical instantiations of national far-right politics are always conditioned and structured by the way in which the international – in its various political, socioeconomic, ideological, and geopolitical dimensions – interacts with, conditions, and to some extent even constitutes, the domestic political contexts within which the far-right emerges and develops. That the international constitutes the ideology and politics of the far-right in both the material and the imaginary senses means that the precise ideological character of the far-right in any particular time or place is always drawn from and reflects the specific properties of the international system at that time. Thus, the unique properties of fascism as an expression of the far-right were a product of the distinct character of the international system (in relation to mass politics, capitalist imperialism, racism and the legacies of total war) in the same way that the contemporary, or neoliberal, far-right reflects the particular form, character and contradictions of the existing neoliberal international order associated with the workings of a financialized transnational capitalism, transnational political and legal governance structures, and a populist political mood connected to 'anti-politics'.

Consequently, the argument outlined across these two volumes aims to make a contribution to the developing historical-sociological literature in the fields of International Relations (IR) and International Political Economy (IPE). This literature has sought both to historicize particular aspects of international relations and, more broadly, to integrate the specific political, sociological, economic and geographical characteristics of states into the structures of an historical evolving capitalist world economy and geopolitics. This work provides the first contribution to this literature that addresses the politics of the far-right.

The methodology and argument that frames the historical analysis that follows relies on the conceptual fragments of 'uneven and combined development' (UCD), originally outlined by Leon Trotsky (Trotsky, 1962, 2008) and developed more recently by a number of other thinkers working broadly within the academic discipline of International Relations (Allinson and Anievas, 2009; Anievas, 2013, 2014; Davidson, 2006; Rosenberg, 1996, 2006, 2010, 2016). I outline the framework of UCD in the first chapter of *Volume 1*. Theorizing the historical sociology of the far-right through the lens of UCD provides a way of explaining how this particular expression of politics emerges, evolves and advances over the *longue durée* out of the contradictory dynamics of capitalist development, in which the spatial and temporal dimensions of the far-right – that are often overlooked – are properly understood and explained. Thus, we can see how the most recent political breakthroughs of the far-right in the vote for Brexit and the election of Donald Trump in 2016 reveal the workings of an ideational imaginary of the 'reproduction of the past in the present' (Saull et al., 2015: 10–11). In both cases the far-right succeeded through offering a way of addressing the crisis of the present through political messaging that drew on the reservoir of an idealized past. However, its success and appeal to specific political constituencies also relied on a connection to distinct spatial domains and social layers that are produced by the contradictory outcomes of uneven capitalist development. The temporality of the far-right is revealed, then, in specific moments of capitalist crisis when its political appeal and ideological invective gains much greater political traction than before and how such moments rely on political references to an idealized and *racialized* past that become much more powerful within such crisis conditions.

The work is organized as follows. In *Volume 1: The Far-Right from Bonapartism to Fascism*, following an Introduction, Chapter 1 provides a survey and critique of existing approaches, in which I also outline my methodology and theoretical argument, framing the historical discussions that follow. The volume then addresses the first three historical phases of the far-right. Chapter 2 focuses on its emergence as a distinct ideo-political imaginary drawing on distinct petty bourgeois social layers in the midst of the 1848–49 European Revolutions that laid the foundations for Bonapartism – an 'ideal-type' authoritarian state form of the far-right. Chapter 3 discusses the consolidation of the far-right as a subaltern, anti-system and mass-based politics that grew as a consequence of the contradictions associated with the socioeconomic transformations powered by capitalist imperialism over the last two decades of the nineteenth century up until World War I. The final chapter focuses on the rise of fascism as the 'revolution of the right' emergent from within a hyper-militarized capitalist imperialism alongside the emergence of the Soviet Union, with the associated threat of the internationalization of communist revolution, and an analysis of the political economy of Italian and German fascism and the characteristics of Nazi imperialism.

In *Volume 2: The Far-Right from Cold War to Trumpism*, the historical survey encompasses three chapters that chart the transformation of the far-right as a 'post-fascist' form of politics in the early years of the Cold War, up until the recent political advances of the far-right in Britain – specifically, England – the United States and Western Europe in a context of overlapping crises in the geopolitical organization and social reproduction of the liberal international order. Chapter 1 addresses the construction of a new liberal international order under the aegis of American hegemony in the immediate period after World War II, excavating and re-centring the various ways in which far-right, and specifically fascist legacies were crucial to the construction of a postwar order safe for private property, capital accumulation and the crushing of the radical and democratic potential bequeathed by the defeat of fascism. Chapter 2 provides an analysis of the revival of a new form of far-right politics in the 1980s and its connection to the emergence and success of the hegemonic neoliberalism within Britain and the United States that grew out of the period of systemic crisis across the advanced capitalist world in the 1970s. Chapter 3 addresses the way in which the 2007–8 North Atlantic financial crisis and the subsequent policy responses to it in the US, Britain and across the EU supercharged the fortunes of the far-right. Specifically, I will examine how and why the far-right succeeded in becoming the dominant 'anti-system' form of populism as revealed in Brexit, the election of Trump to the White House and the major advances made by far-right parties such as the League in Italy, Alternative für Deutschland (AfD) in Germany and the Front National in France. Across these two volumes, my theoretical argument – articulated more fully in the first chapter of Volume 1 – is integrated into the substantive historical analysis. My empirical focus is limited to the principal advanced liberal-capitalist powers from the mid nineteenth century. This is partly a function of the necessity of limiting the sheer length of a study like this, but also reflects the fact that these states have been the most important sites of the working-out of the contradictions of the evolving liberal modernity that is my primary concern. This geopolitical focus obviously imposes an analytical limit on my argument as it relates to the global far-right – in particular, constraining what I am able to say about the far-right across the Global South. Nonetheless, while I do not address them directly here, I hope that the argument developed in this work may be useful in explaining the far-right in these different geopolitical contexts.

# Introduction

## 1    Capital, Race and Space: An International Historical Sociology of the Far-Right

From the viewpoint of Britain, and much of the wider liberal-democratic world in 2021, the far-right appears to be on the march. The strong showings of far-right parties in recent elections in a number of countries have built on major electoral advances from the 1990s.[1] Meanwhile, the election of a far-right demagogue to the White House, and the decision by a majority of British – or more precisely English – voters to leave the European Union (EU) in 2016 signal the same trend. Much of the academic and journalistic commentary on these developments reflects a widespread sense of liberal foreboding and despair about the state of liberal democracy and the liberal international order, provoking a flurry of alerts about the possibility of the encroachment of a new fascism (Albright, 2019; Goldberg, 2018; Lilla, 2018; Mounk, 2019).

Such concerns cannot be easily dismissed. The recent advances for the far-right, with their attendant policy consequences – Britain leaving the EU, raising the prospect of the break-up of the United Kingdom; the United States embarking on a policy of trade protectionism, and appointing Supreme Court justices who threaten to entrench the policies and norms of a new reactionary right – demonstrate the real political impact of the strengthened political influence and power of the far-right. Moreover, the violence of the mob attack on the US Capitol building on 6 January 2022 – incited by Donald Trump in an attempt to prevent the constitutional transfer of power to president-elect Joe Biden – and the subsequent failure of the apparatus of the Republican

---

1    In France, Marine Le Pen, the candidate of the Front National, saw off electoral challengers from the left and right to take on the centrist, Emmanuel Macron, in the second round of the 2017 presidential election, where she gained a third of the vote. In Germany, the Alternative für Deutschland (AfD) secured 11.5 percent of the vote in the 2017 federal election, becoming the third-largest party in the Bundestag and the official opposition to the Christian-Democrat (CDU)/Social Democrat (SPD) coalition government – a quite unprecedented development for a far-right party since the war. In the 2018 Italian parliamentary elections, the League gained the largest share of votes (17.5 percent) in the right-wing coalition, which allowed it to form a coalition government with the Five Star Movement (M5S). In Austria, the Freedom Party (FPÖ) gained 26 percent of votes in the 2017 parliamentary elections, entering into government with the People's Party. In addition to these developments, the Hungarian far-right leader Viktor Orbán was returned to power in elections in 2018, and in Poland the far-right Law and Justice Party, under the leadership of Jarosław Kaczyński, has been in power since 2015.

Party to disown both Trump and his supporters indicate the possibilities for fascism within the simmering political crisis that continues to play out across the United States (see Eley, 2021). Indeed, the discourse and culture of a newly resurgent and supposedly 'post-fascist' (Traverso, 2019) far-right is never fully removed from the neo-fascist and violent fringes that make-up part of the far-right's eco-system, even if most far-right politicians tend to publicly disavow such currents and behaviour. The truth of the situation is revealed by an increased prevalence of racist abuse and violence that has tended to parallel such moments of far-right advance.

However, in recognizing this, we should not assume, as much analysis and discussion of these developments has tended to do, that these far-right political currents are in some way alien or new to the political culture of liberal democracies. Rather, the rise of the new far-right reflects a crisis within liberal democracy closely connected to the fall-out from the 2007–08 North Atlantic financial crisis. This crisis – which has two interconnected dimensions one political and the other economic – reflects a combined assault on the twin pillars of liberal democracy and liberal order. The former concerns a crisis of political representation and the functioning of the institutions of liberal democracy and associated party systems. The latter, the organization and working of capitalist markets and the livelihoods of the millions who depend on them. And the current crisis is but the latest in a history of *recurring* crises that have defined liberal-capitalist modernity since the middle of the nineteenth century.

All of these crises originated *within* the contradictory relationship between the political and economic components of liberal order – in particular, they emerged out of the nature of its international and geopolitical configuration. Further, the far-right has been a major political beneficiary of each of these crises. A general trend within the recurring crises of the liberal order is that the far-right has tended to emerge or re-emerge as a major vector of politics in response to each crisis, as one of the most significant ideological options for dealing with it. In what follows, I try to answer the question of why this is so. Why does the far-right benefit from the crises of the liberal order? What are the major factors that explain the recurring 'rise' of the far-right? The fact that the far-right, while it has changed in various ways, has not disappeared as a major political force, even as liberal democracy has been consolidated and the operations of capitalist markets have become more entrenched, is suggestive of how it is connected to and reproduced within the structures that define liberal-capitalist modernity. To some degree, then, the inner workings and various weaknesses of the liberal order are conducive to the reproduction of the far-right (Anievas and Saull, 2020; Saull, 2015b; Saull et al., 2015).

Inevitably, a key assumption that informs my argument is that existing accounts within the academic literature do not adequately answer, or in many ways even address, such questions. The literature on the far-right is enormous; the discussion of inter-war fascism and Nazism alone is huge. However, largely because of the specific historical questions that much of this literature is concerned with (such as why Hitler came to power), the historical work is conceptually limited by its focus on specific cases, rather than on the structural forces revealed by the recurring patterns they generate. It is limited also by a methodological internalism in which analytical assumptions and theoretical arguments are derived from national cases, and putatively domestic causes that are abstracted from their origins within wider inter-societal relations that take place across national borders and demonstrate the international and interactive dimensions of domestic politics.

To be clear, the historian's craft of examining particular national cases of the far-right is a necessary and important one. The knowledge developed by the work of these scholars – far too many to mention here – has contributed to major advances in our knowledge of fascist regimes and the particular contexts that have shaped their rise to power and political nature. However, these studies do not by themselves address the primary questions that concern me here regarding the enduring and recurring dimensions of the far-right: the continuities as well as the differences in its historical reproduction over the *longue durée*. Consequently, much of this literature provides few analytical tools with which to account for the persistence and recurrence of the far-right within the evolving politics of liberal democracies.

The contributions and shortcomings of the existing literature are also revealed in its various attempts to define the far-right. In the academic literatures of comparative politics and the history of ideas, much ink – perhaps too much – has been spilled in attempts to define the far-right, as well as the various other terms deployed: 'extreme', 'radical', 'populist', 'reactionary', 'anti-system', and so on (see Caiani et al., 2012; Eatwell, 2000, 2017; Hainsworth, 2008; Ignazi, 2003; Mudde, 2000, 2007; Prowe, 1994, 2004; Wodak et al., 2013).[2] Much of this definitional debate has been informed, and in some respects distorted,

---

2   In using the descriptor 'far-right' rather than the many others available in the academic literature, I mean to indicate that I see the forces and movements that I am concerned with as located on a spectrum of right-wing thought and politics, contrary to claims by scholars such as George Mosse (1999), Stanley Payne (1983) and Zeev Sternhell (1986, 1996) as to the 'left-wing' or 'socialist' character of fascism. The key ideological attributes of the far-right are connected to the right in general. Thus, 'far' reflects the relative distance along the spectrum where these parties and movements are located and is a better descriptor than the other options: 'radical' confusingly suggests a parallel with the left that is typical of analytical

by the debate on fascism. For understandable reasons, the fascist experience casts a deep shadow over the discussion of the far-right. Indeed, fascism, with its taste for revolutionary forms of political struggle and its celebration of violence, is a distinctive form of far-right politics.[3]

But fascism is not unique with respect to its ideological origins and political praxis. Its revolutionary character and penchant for violence derived from the context in which it emerged – namely, a liberal modernity already afflicted by such features: industrial total war, and the spectre and reality of international socialist revolution. Fascism is the direct progeny of such a context. Consequently, fascism intensifies and radicalizes an already-existing racialized nationalism and political authoritarianism of the far-right. Thus, as Michael Mann (2004: 1–30) has emphasized, fascism is distinguished by its racialized paramilitarism, which was itself a product of the generic militarism that characterised the capitalist-imperialist states of the era before, during and after World War I. To speak of fascism always requires an attention to its enabling conditions within the crises of liberal modernity. Consequently, the relative marginality of fascist movements in the contemporary era should be understood in relation to the very different context within which liberal-capitalist states rather than capitalist-imperial states relate to each other and reproduce themselves. It is when militarism and militarized racism reappear as defining vectors of the politics of a state that the door is (re)opened for fascism.

Discussion of the far-right over the *longue durée* – from the late nineteenth century up to the current era – obviously needs to be attentive to the particularities of the historical and international contexts within which each expression of the far-right is located. Yet, despite the significant changes in both international context and the social and political fabric of liberal states (particularly the dissolution of the social structure of lord and peasant which was

---

thinking informed by liberal political assumptions, while 'populist' tends to describe language and style, while also overlooking the specific class dimensions of the far-right.

3  An influential strand of liberal thinking on the far-right during the Cold War deployed the concept of 'totalitarianism' (see Arendt, 1968) as a catch-all term that emphasized the 'revolutionary' dimensions of fascism, and consequently implied that it was part of the same intellectual and political genus as communism because of its 'revolutionary extremism' (i.e., Hitler and Stalin were more or less the same). Furthermore, in the early years of the Cold War, a significant degree of anti-communist propaganda and discourse on the right spoke of a 'red fascism' (thanks to Alexander Anievas for alerting me to this point). The reference to 'totalitarianism' was obviously an intervention connected to the ideological imperatives of the liberal Cold War but was also about insulating conservatism and the broader right from fascism. For important critiques of these liberal positions, see Ishay Landa (2012, 2018) and Daniel Woodley (2010).

central to the nineteenth century far-right), it is possible to identify attributes and forms of political activity across time and space that characterise a singular and enduring far-right.

Like all forms of politics, the precise ideo-political content of the far-right reflects the evolving character of liberal modernity, and the specific properties of its international form at any given time. Thus, as Enzo Traverso suggests (2019: 35), what might be regarded as the 'ideological incoherence' of the far-right merely reflects a more common political phenomenon applicable to all ideo-political expressions resulting from the effects of historical social change – as revealed in the various forms that liberalism and the liberal order have taken today compared to the past – and the way in which such change is absorbed by political parties. Further, in terms of both its ideology and its activities, the far-right overlaps with other parts of the right. This is visible in its political propaganda and the ideological tropes it has been associated with – not least anti-Semitism and other forms of racism, its emphasis on naturalized hierarchies, among other things. This does not mean that the distinctions between the far-right and the traditional or conservative right are not important, but only registers the ideas that inform it, which cut across multiple political and organizational representations. Moreover, in moments of crisis the distinctions and differences between the various political articulations on the right can readily dissolve. But if the term 'far-right' means anything substantive, then the core ideas that we associate with it must cohere with the actions of the parties and movements identified with it.

I understand the far-right as a distinct ideological representation and articulation of politics and form of political agency connected to specific social layers and spaces. It has a set of ideational features that distinguish it from the broader right; but it acts upon and is conditioned by a broader set of social and political forces. Consequently, its defining attributes relate to how its distinct ideological orientation is conditioned by the evolving character of its social and political contexts, including its international context; and these factors obviously condition the specific social layers from which the far-right draws its support. For all the variety of the historical contexts that have shaped it, and despite the precise forms of crises to which it has constituted one response, the far-right is defined by a common set of features across time and space.

The far-right is an ideo-political current associated with conservatism and the right in general. Its political identity has much in common with that of the generic right, even if conservatives can sometimes be counted among its opponents. In a fundamental sense, like conservatism, the far-right is committed to upholding the traditional social, ethnic, moral and cultural bases of society in the face of the ongoing disruptive dislocations produced by an evolving liberal-capitalist modernity. Such a disposition is based on hostility to the universalizing processes within liberal modernity – linked to the flattening or erosion of the institutions and social hierarchies it regards as natural or organic, which buttress 'traditional' sociopolitical orders, anchored in family, church and nation – and especially the normative commitment to equality associated with liberal universalism. In dwelling on what is rooted in the past, and associated with fixed ideas of place and space, cultures and people are assigned organic spatial properties that tend to be linked to an idealization of the past based on a 'natural order' of hierarchy, located specifically in gender and racial relations (Caplan, 1979; De Hart, 1991), and juxtaposed with a sense of cultural despair (Mudde, 2000: 11; see also Stern, 1974).[4]

This romanticization of the past and despair at the present of the far-right – that aligns with conservatism – differentiates, however, in the conspiratorial and apocalyptic discourses that also characterise it. Thus, articulations of cultural degeneration and national decline tend to focus on blaming the actions of nefarious 'alien' forces in the national community working to weaken and subvert 'the people' from inside and outside, invoking, among others, ethnic minorities, socialists, 'globalist elites' and, especially, the figure of the Jew (Anievas and Saull, 2022: 3). Such conspiracism is a defining characteristic of the far-right over the *longue durée*, even if the dramatis personae identified as the conspirators, and their supposed objectives, may differ over time. The far-right and the traditional conservative right also tend to diverge in terms of how each expresses itself and, in particular, in how the latter tends to be more accommodating to forms of liberalizing and progressive social and political change over time.

The far-right's identification with the right more broadly means that an idealized past based on a sense of racial homogeneity and hierarchy, and traditional gender norms and family structures has provided the core of its ideological coherence over the *longue durée*, even as social and political circumstances have changed. We can detect this in the evolution of its racialized *Weltanschauung*. Thus, in a context of capitalist imperialism and generalized racism, the far-right was particularly associated with an ideology of racial supremacy connected to conquest, and in some cases extermination. Since World War II, and especially in the contemporary era – defined by the

---

4   As Sally Davison and George Shire note (Davison and Shire, 2015), immigration has been one
    of those sources of change that has triggered recurrent responses connected to each par-
    ticular wave of migrants, and reflecting a deeply embedded sense of 'self' among Europeans
    based on 'whiteness' – and the assumptions of 'natural order' and 'superiority' that has gone
    along with it – that has also provided an important source for the far-right's 'common sense'.

institutions and norms of a postcolonial liberal international order – the far-right has been conditioned by a very different racial context. Thus, for all of the racialized assumptions and limits of liberalism, the post-war era has seen social and racial advances that have significantly transformed the international and social circumstances of race relations.

One result is that, although the far-right in the past provided the loudest and most uncompromising articulation of white supremacy, biological racism and racial violence, that underpinned a wider social order of imperial domination, it is now defined by a race politics focused on a defensive separation from and expulsion of 'non-indigenous' racialized others – Muslims in particular – from inside the homeland (Mudde, 2007; Betz and Meret, 2009; Rydgren, 2007). Such politics emphasize the need to 'defend European culture' from 'alien cultural subversion and degeneration'. The contemporary far-right, like its historical forbears, is therefore defined by its racialization of both the social and the political. While this does not mean we should ignore the way in which racialized assumptions and signifiers continue to inform liberal political discourse, it is the far-right that provides an autonomous, permanent and radical repository of racism that exercises influence over *wider* political discourse well beyond the confines of the far-right. For the far-right, today as in the past, there is no overcoming of race, or of the fixed and inherited identities connected to it. Liberalism may offer a compromised anti-racist politics, but it does provide both a political space and means for contesting racism that are anathema to the far-right, especially in its avowed commitment to equality between individuals.

Another defining feature of the far-right that shows a high degree of continuity across time and space is its ambivalence towards capitalist social relations, despite the radical 'anti-capitalist' rhetoric that has sometimes been associated with far-right critiques of capitalism (Davidson, 2015; Saull, 2015a, 2015b, 2015c). Thus, today's far-right, like its past incarnations, is less preoccupied by contesting the fundamental elements of capitalism – private property, market exchange, production based on the exploitation of wage labour – than by suspicion and hostility towards its internationalizing and globalizing aspects. Here, the far-right singles out finance as the transmitter of capitalism's destabilizing and internationalizing tendencies. In particular, the obsession or fetishization of cosmopolitan financialized capitalism as reflecting capitalism in general, rather than one aspect of it, provides the basis for the perverse nature of the far-right's 'anti-capitalism' (see Postone, 2006).

This bowdlerized account of capitalism fetishizes its spatial and financial aspects because it is in these that its racialized properties appear most tangible. The encroachments – through immigration – of foreign capital and labour on the home market are thus highlighted as evidence of unfairness and racial insecurity, in a way that betrays a framing of political economy based on zero-sum assumptions about trade. This perspective is connected to an enduring 'producerism', understood as a celebration of the individual artisan or craftsman carrying out his (never her) own labour in small-scale production addressed to a local market. In this articulation of political economy, the social structure based on capital's exploitation of wage labour – and thus the core workings of capitalism – are written out of the political explanation of crises. Thus, crises are reduced to a set of racialized and spatialized conspiracies focused on particular states: Britain (or London) in the nineteenth century, the US (or Wall Street) in the twentieth, and today China or George Soros. Consequently, the overdetermining dimensions of race and space in the political economy of the far-right serve in effect to distort the core properties of capitalism, or even remove them from political contention. And this helps us understand how some strands of the far-right (neoliberal strands – see *Volume 2*) actually embrace capitalism.

In the far-right imaginary, capitalism is conceived as a cosmopolitan social dynamic essentialized in the form of big and international (monopoly) capital, that operates through the disembodied circuits of finance capital in particular. It is in the racialization of the economy, where the figure of the Jew as money-lender or the racial embodiment of finance comes to play a significant role in the far-right's political economy, producing a distinct form of racism in anti-Semitism – a racism based less on the supremacy of whites over 'racial inferiors' than on fear of the influence of the Jew, and of the effects of the cosmopolitanism that the Jew is taken to represent, on the social and racial fabric of the nation. The Jew is thus fetishized as the 'universal-cosmopolitan spectre associated with the moneyed properties of circulation' divorced from and undermining of production. The Jew reflects the 'abstract domination of capital' (Saull, 2015d: 138) untethered to land or people – Rothschild in the past, Soros today – reflecting the 'rootless universalism' of Jews (Postone, 2003, 2006; see also Bonefeld, 2004; Jacobs, 2011; Judaken, 2008).

In many respects, it is the global structure of a hegemonic capitalism that conditions the historical specificities of the political economy of the far-right and the limits of its anti-capitalism – hence the articulation of an imperialist-protectionist geopolitics during the period from 1870 to 1945, whereas the political economy of the contemporary era has been conditioned by the structural transformations wrought by neoliberalism. Yet, while the structure and dynamics of capital accumulation have changed since the nineteenth century, the central principles and tropes of far-right political economy have remained remarkably consistent.

This fact helps to explain the social constituencies that tend to support the far-right. Thus, the disappearance since the early twentieth century of the peasantry, along with the social and political power of the landlord class, reflects a significant rupture in the social bases of the far-right, some of whose historical constituents no longer exist. However, in spatial terms the concentration of support in smaller towns and the geographical periphery, and away from metropolises and areas of large-scale industrial activity, remains largely constant. The petty bourgeoisie remains an important social constituency of the far-right, by virtue of its material location within the capitalist division of labour between big/monopoly capital and organized labour. Moreover, the ideology of producerism and the anti-Semitism based on a fetishization of finance capital play a particularly strong role among small producers and employers, given their particular vulnerabilities to the difficulty of accessing secure lines of credit. Workers have always been drawn to the far-right, just as some workers have supported conservative parties; but the tendency has generally been for workers socialized into the structures and institutions of organized labour to be the least vulnerable to far-right appeals.

In this respect, there is an important distinction to be made between the demography of far-right support that includes sections of the white working class with that of the working class in general and the political subjectivities of people who sell their labour powers as *workers*. Thus, in the former the implicit racialization of class identities means that an over-emphasis on working class support for the far-right can result in a form of racial primacy in which some workers are regarded as better or more fully representing the working class in general over other parts of the working class who are not 'white' or male. And in the latter, a focus on working class support for the far-right also struggles to consider the political antagonism between the far-right and the political subjectivities of workers that are connected to and reproduced through the independent social and political institutions that workers create, such as trade unions. So, while the working class is not reducible to a membership of organized labour it is the latter that provides a collective political subjectivity to workers, and it is this that has shown itself to be the most hostile *class* disposition to the far-right.

The far-right's avoidance of any meaningful questioning of private property rights, either as a foundational basis of the social order or in relation to the exploitative nature and iniquitous consequences of relations between labour and capital, renders its supposed – and sometimes avowed – anti-capitalism highly questionable. Indeed, even in its most 'revolutionary' incarnation, during the era of the inter-war fascist states, the most radical instantiation of the far-right in power reproduced the fundamental properties of capitalism (Davidson, 2015; Tooze, 2007). Moreover, the far-right has consistently sought to weaken the collective social and political power of organized labour. Accordingly, while the far-right certainly problematizes the spatial and governance relations of a hegemonic capitalism – whether during the late-nineteenth-century belle époque, in the inter-war period, or amid globalizing neoliberalism – it also helps to generate a populist 'common sense' that erases the fundamental class character of capitalism, thus removing capitalism from any serious political contention (Anievas and Saull, 2022: 4).

The far-right's political economy is closely connected to its embrace of the possibilities that come with the mass and democratic politics associated with the weakening of the political privileges of elite layers. In this respect, the far-right articulates a populist anti-elitism that encompasses the traditional right as representative of the political elite and ruling class. Elites are attacked as out of touch, weak, corrupt and compromised by international and cosmopolitan structures. It is here that the far-right can be differentiated from conservatism where the latter is defined by a politics committed to working through and upholding existing forms of constitutional order and political representation. Instead, a populist and demagogic politics is articulated through conspiracy theories that reinforce racist tropes, including anti-Semitism in particular – given that Jews are seen as the most dangerous representatives of cosmopolitanism, and of what is now referred to across parts of the far-right as a 'cultural Marxism' associated with 'globalists'.

This populist anti-elitism, invoking the myth of a people or nation unmediated by social fractures, is counterposed to an elite that represents the constitutional, representative framework of law-making and governance.[5] So, while it suggests an embrace of 'mass politics' and participation in democratic processes, the far-right's objective is to reconfigure politics through the destruction of existing constitutional limits on executive power, enabling an authoritarian politics based on executive fiat freed from the representative and judicial constraints of a constitutional democracy. This still characterises the contemporary far-right, in spite of its formal embrace of democratic-representative politics and its efforts to distance itself from street violence and paramilitarism. This is the far-right's model of the state, today as in the past. It promotes and realizes authoritarianism through the extension of police powers and attacks on minority protections and individual rights. This represents the important distinction between the far-right and liberalism that is lost in

---

5   See Laclau (2005). Using populism to describe the far-right helps in the sense of identifying a distinct method associated with it, but it does not capture who or what the far-right is. A populist vernacular can, after all, be deployed by other political currents, including the left.

some left-wing analyses of the far-right (see Mishra, 2017; Mondon and Winter, 2020). Fascist street violence and the terroristic fascist state take such politics to an extreme – but the initial opening to such tendencies is secured through the far-right's mobilization against the liberal and representative institutions of the state.

The far-right's embrace of democracy rests on the evisceration of some of the core features of democratic processes and institutions. Democracy is reduced to the role of sanctifying the sovereignty of majoritarian power, defined as representing 'the people'. In this framing, the substantive workings of a democratic politics – whether those of parliamentary representation and the politics of negotiation, deliberation and compromise in law-making, or of civil society as representative of social and cultural plurality in the democratic process – are all marginalized or actively undermined. Instead, with sovereign power bestowed exclusively by 'the people', government becomes a means to enact the 'the will of the people' – conceived, along racial and/or ethnic lines, as a unitary entity, and uninhibited by any other source of political–legal authority or democratic legitimacy.

Thus, the return of sovereign authority to the nation state is associated with the centralization of executive power, as well as the strengthening of authoritarian tendencies and coercive apparatuses within the state through which constitutional and other limits on fulfilling the 'people's will' are bypassed. Of course, the identification of who counts as 'the people' rests on the far-right's racialization of the demos, which entails restricting the citizenship rights of racial Others, whether they are ethnic minority citizens or immigrants. Populist rhetoric about 'bringing political power back to the people' – articulated by Brexit supporters in the 2016 referendum – results, through far-right framing, in the fetishization of spatial proximity in substantiating the procedural and deliberative norms that are allowed to operate in democracy. The far-right embrace of democracy thus relies on the translation of its imaginary of the demos as racially homogenous and spatially bound. As a result, democratic politics can be transformed into authoritarianism by means of disenfranchising significant sections of the population that fall outside the far-right's racialized conception of 'the people', while at the same time the constitutional and parliamentary institutions of democracy are inexorably subverted – often by democratic means (Anievas and Saull, 2022: 10).

This account of the particular objectives and consequences of the populism of the far-right as a strategy for weakening existing liberal and democratic institutional arrangements while strengthening the authoritarian tendencies within the state connects the far-right firmly to both ruling-class forces and political elites – a paradox, given the ostensible anti-elitism of the far-right.

In contrast, much of the historical writing on the far-right, and on fascism in particular, has tended to downplay, or sometimes even deny, this connection (see Beck, 2008; Turner, 1985). And much of the comparative political science literature barely registers it as an issue worthy of consideration. Thus, while in the case of some discussions of fascism such perspectives derive from taking too seriously the rhetoric of fascist leaders and the text of fascist party programmes, in the case of comparative political science it derives from the liberal political assumptions about the organization of the state that informs much of this work.

However, as the chapters in this and the following volume will demonstrate, the history of the far-right reflects a politics defined by a close, if contradictory and sometimes antagonistic, 'embrace' of dominant social forces and elites. Indeed, over the period from the 1870s until the end of World War II, far-right forces partly constituted capitalist-imperialist ruling classes, whose social reproduction was predicated on a racialized and conflictual geopolitics closely associated with far-right political assumptions and popular mobilizations. Accordingly, the far-right was central to the reproduction of such imperialist arrangements – inside and outside of the metropole – and provided a mass basis in support of imperialism and geopolitical rivalry. Further, its connection to the ruling class was also because it provided an important popular bulwark against the socialist left; a kind of reactionary 'reserve army' which meant that the far-right had much closer connections to and opportunities to penetrate the coercive apparatus of the state than any other political current.

This disposition towards the far-right reveals the para-political dimensions of the liberal state[6] that were reproduced during the Cold War era even as liberal democracy was consolidated and far-right and fascist ideology and social forces were cast out of the post-war state after the defeat of fascism and the end of empire. Consequently, the coercive apparatuses of the liberal state have not always been aligned with its social-democratic features  and in moments of crisis this para-political dimension and the political agency of the far-right can be significant in opposition to the social and democratic institutions and impulses contained within the liberal state. Such tendencies continue to be evident, and they reinforce the class character  of the far-right as an antagonist of the organized working class and wider democratic forces within liberal democracies. Thus, while the far-right has demonstrated an enduring

---

6  It is also the case that those sections of the state dealing with population control, immigration and borders are founded on a set of social, geographical and political assumptions that, arguably, are consistent with a far-right conception of the core properties of the nation-state and of citizenship.

antagonism to the radical possibilities bequeathed by democracy and a willingness to dismantle existing liberal constitutional arrangements it has never been a social antagonist of the capitalist class or capitalist system.

# Theorizing the Far-Right over the *Longue Durée*

In this chapter I provide a critical survey of the dominant methodological framings of the scholarship on the far-right in the fields of comparative politics and the history of ideas. I then discuss Marxist perspectives on fascism, as this literature provides an important methodological and theoretical basis for my argument, which I build on in the second half of the chapter. The theoretical framework I outline below encompasses the following elements: (I) framing of the far-right in a *longue durée* temporality that suggests its coherence as a distinct ideo-political form running from the middle of the nineteenth century up to the contemporary era; (II) emphasizing the ways in which the structural qualities of capitalism centred on uneven and combined development (UCD) have provided the spatial and socioeconomic determinants of the far-right; (III) exploration of how the politics of the far-right have been constituted by the international – both as an imaginary spectre, and in relation to the way in which the evolving organization of geopolitics and international order has conditioned both the politics of the far-right and the openings for its advance; (IV) discussion of the paradoxes and contradictions of liberalism both as an institutional structure for a democratic politics – including the behaviour of liberal political forces – and political economy; and, finally (V) an exploration of the significance of race/racism as the dominant political category in the ideology of the far-right.

## 1   Situating the Study of the Far-Right

The literature on the politics of the far-right – whether in a particular national context or historical period, or concerning a specific form, most notably interwar fascism – is immense. Necessarily, my comments here can only touch the surface of many of these contributions. I shall provide a brief overview of the key elements contained within prevailing theorizations of the far-right, while at the same time outlining what I consider to be their main shortcomings. In doing so, I will identify those issues that will be developed in the second part of the chapter.

Within the existing academic literature, two core methodological perspectives dominate in work that seeks to describe and account for the character of the far-right. Work in the field of comparative political science has dominated the study of the contemporary far-right across advanced capitalist democracies (recent examples include Albertizi and McDonnell, 2008; Caiani et al., 2012; Eatwell and Goodwin, 2018; Ford and Goodwin, 2014; Hainsworth, 2008; Ignazi, 2003; Mammone et al., 2012; Mudde, 2000, 2007; Rydgren, 2013; Wodak et al., 2013). This literature tends to view the far-right as a constituent element of national party-systems – part of the traditional political party framework within the various national party systems – within which it operates, albeit a dissenting and toxic variant. In many respects, this view tends to assume the 'normalization' of the far-right, predicated on the formal acceptance by far-right parties of the general 'rules of the game' of liberal representative democracy. This assumption provides the main reasoning for the so-called 'post-fascist' quality of these parties (Ignazi, 2003; Prowe, 1994; see also Traverso, 2019: 3–19).

This broad perspective – grounded in quantitative surveys of electoral performance, voter-identification, and key policy issues centred on immigration (notably anti-Muslim racism), Euroscepticism, law and order, and 'welfare nativism' – has provided important empirical insights into who the contemporary far-right are, and what particular issues are responsible for their political advances. This work has also developed our understanding of the contemporary far-right, notably through the anatomization of the various national forms it takes, as well as identifying some of the primary reasons for both the electoral strength of far-right parties and their wider significance for political debate and policy across Western states. In emphasizing, for example, the significance of electoral and constitutional rules based on minimal thresholds for legislative representation, this work has also helped to explain the ability – and limits – of far-right parties to 'shake up' the character of politics within these states.

The ostensible objective of these analyses is to offer a robust understanding of the far-right based on a wealth of empirical data, including opinion-poll evidence, to identify which social groups vote for the far-right, or are more broadly in sympathy with their appeals, and why certain far-right parties gain especially high levels of political traction while others do not. Given this focus, such work is not particularly interested either in explaining the more enduring significance of the far-right over time or in problematizing the structural dimensions of the state and social forms, and geopolitical contexts, within which far-right parties operate. Further, given their comparative focus, such analyses have a rather under-developed and limited theorization of the international and the significance of inter-societal relations in constituting the fabric of the domestic political contexts within which each far-right party is conditioned by and operates within.[1]

A second methodological tradition in work on the far-right derives from the field of political ideas (see Eatwell, 1992a, 1996, 2003, 2004; Griffin, 1993, 2000a; see also Camus and Lebourg, 2017; Carter, 2018; Drolet and Williams, 2018). This perspective has focused on the subtleties of political taxonomy when it comes to labelling the 'far-right' – often opting for alternatives such as 'extreme', 'populist', 'radical', 'reactionary' and 'neo-fascist' – terms drawn from the examination of speeches and party documents to assess the ideological coherence of the parties and movements involved. Drawing on this material, these scholars have sought to establish the degree to which the far-right should be regarded as distinct from its counterpart identified in the analytical template based on historical fascism. This has resulted in an endless search for an 'objective' or 'minimal' definition of the far-right (see Eatwell, 1996) – the focus of something of an academic cottage industry. The result is a definition that tends to freeze, and in some respects, simplify, the far-right as a distinct ideo-political current trapping it within a specific time and place, abstracted from the wider evolving social contexts that it is located in and conditioned by. Further, this emphasis on the far-right's ideational character comes at a cost of neglecting the messier politics of the far-right as an evolving sociopolitical movement.[2]

This methodological framework has sometimes produced analytical contortions to the effect that the far-right – in its fascist incarnation, at least – can be seen as a 'revolutionary' or 'socialist' movement comparable to communism (see Griffin, 2000b; Payne, 1983; Sternhell, 1986; Thurlow, 1998), thus echoing Cold War liberalism and its deployment of the term 'totalitarianism'. This is not to suggest that fascism did not have revolutionary characteristics or effects in the ideational, political, and geopolitical spheres: clearly, it did – especially in its Nazi variant. But use of the term 'revolutionary' without careful specification of the revolutionary context from which fascism emerged – namely, a context of the threat of revolution from the socialist left, imagined

---

1  Such methodological problems also tend to characterize most singular national historical studies of the far-right. So, while such studies are, implicitly, located in a *longue-durée* framework in the sense that far-right forces are reproduced over decades and more, these national accounts do not tend to be theorized through reference to a structural context of international capitalist political economy and geopolitics, and so they also tend to be trapped within the ontological confines of methodological internalism.

2  In referring to the far-right as a 'current' I want to use this term to emphasize the flowing and over-lapping nature of political identities and movements; so though such definitional properties relate to specific political groupings these ideas or themes also seep into the political identity, language and behaviour of other (right and some centrist) political positions.

or otherwise – and of the revolutionary geopolitical challenge of the Soviet Union, too easily distorts a defining ideological element of fascism: that of its *counter*-revolutionary animus towards the left, revolutionary and non-revolutionary alike (see Neocleous, 1997; Traverso, 2019: 116–27; Woodley, 2010).

A number of criticisms can be levelled at these perspectives on the far-right. First, in the work within the field of political ideas, the far-right tends to be understood as an ideological phenomenon whereby the core ideas associated with it are, in effect, isolated and detached from not only substantive, concrete far-right movements, but also from wider capitalist socioeconomic and liberal-democratic political structures. Simply put, in much of this literature there is little recognition of the way in which ideological articulations of the far-right are: (I) problematic as evidence, in themselves, of a concrete political commitment and identity in terms of how they these movements actually behave;[3] and (II) connected to deeper and broader ideological articulations associated with the state, and with dominant socioeconomic interests. As Dave Renton suggests, fascism as an instance of the far-right should be understood and theorized as 'a particular form of mass movement, possessing a core set of ideas, and in which the ideology and movement interact' (Renton, 1999: 3; see also Mann, 2004: 1–30). The search for a consistent ideational 'essence' of such a political movement can lead to a failure to register the wider social context, political dynamics and contradictions associated with these movements. In short, the absence of a political sociology with which to contextualize the evolution and relative political significance of ideas means that the ideas are left to speak for themselves.[4]

---

3  Such a problem is particularly evident in some treatments of fascism based on an engagement with and presentation of the 'political thought' or ideas of fascist leaders such as Mussolini or Hitler. In some cases – and most notably in the case of Renzo De Felice's work (De Felice, 1977) – such ideas are presented as approximating truth statements rather than as ideologically-loaded and politically-contingent comments and responses to the moment within which they were made. Consequently, the study of these political ideas while crucial to securing a coherent basis upon which to group a party or movement as 'fascist' or 'far-right', needs to be equally cognizant of what said leaders and parties actually did, and also how their views related to and overlapped with other political currents (for example on race or political economy) and dominant social and political forces.

4  This does not mean, however, that the search for an ideational specification as to what constitutes the essence of fascism *vis-à-vis* other forms of right-wing/authoritarian dictatorship is pointless, analytically, or politically. As Trotsky (1975: 132) noted, differentiating fascism from other forms of far-right was fundamental to determining the appropriate political response to fascism, 'the wiseacres who claim that they see no difference between Brüning, and Hitler are in fact saying it makes no difference whether our organisations exist or whether they are already destroyed'.

This problem becomes deeper when one asks how far scholars should treat the ideas and words of far-right and fascist leaders not only as reflective in themselves of a consistent and coherent political vision, but also in relation to how close an association there is between them and the actions taken by the movements and states they represent. Taken at face value, the term 'socialism', connected to 'national' in the official title of the Nazi Party, suggests a commitment to the politics of socialism, which would put Nazism on the left of the political spectrum. And while Nazi propaganda – including one of its early election manifestos – was replete with anti-capitalist tropes, the practical reality of National Socialism was decidedly *anti*-socialist, as was made clear in the murderous suppression of the socialist and communist left after 1933.

The question of the relationship between the words of fascist demagogues and their actions – with all their notorious consequences – has a renewed relevance in contemporary articulations of the far-right. As Federico Finchelstein (2018) explains, the propaganda strategy of Jair Bolsonaro in his successful campaign for the Brazilian presidency in late 2018 emulated classic fascist techniques in portraying the Brazilian left as a 'Nazi threat' – despite Bolsonaro's own numerous racist and authoritarian pronouncements, including celebration of the military dictatorship of 1964–85, that cemented his identification with fascist politics. As Finchelstein reminds us, [t]his is, of course, a falsehood that comes straight out of the Nazi playbook. Fascists always deny what they are and ascribe their own features and their own totalitarian politics to their enemies' (Finchelstein, 2018).

The utterances of the far-right should be taken seriously, though with all due scepticism. But their words and ideas need to be understood and interpreted in the particular context within which they are expressed, including the audience at which they are directed. The ideas of the far-right and of fascism – including the most reprehensible ones associated with racial violence – have not gone away. But this only matters politically when those ideas are actualized, becoming material forces that condition the behaviour of significant numbers of people in determining the politics of societies – most importantly, those with close proximity to state power. Thus, without reference to a political sociology, the words and ideas of the far-right may not only be misconstrued but in a way that might also advantage the political agenda of the far-right.

Both of these prevailing approaches also tend to treat the far-right as an *autonomous* political actor, effectively detached from wider sources of social and material power connected to state agencies and ruling-class interests. This is an important consideration with respect to the ideological categorization of the far-right – and, in particular, of the rhetorical 'anti-capitalism' and anti-elitist populism typical of much of the contemporary and historical far-right. At face value, both the historical far-right (especially the 'national-Bolshevik' wing of the National Socialist German Workers Party – NSDAP) and a number of contemporary movements appear to have distinct anti-capitalist – indeed, democratic-populist – and proletarian dimensions (see Arzheimer, 2013: 83; Eatwell and Goodwin, 2018; Ford and Goodwin, 2014; Ignazi, 2003: 216). Certainly, this may be a result of the evacuation of the terrain of a socialist class politics by the established social-democratic and labourist lefts in European liberal democracies. Nonetheless, both the historical practice of fascist states and the contemporary structural connections between the popular far-right and dominant ruling-class interests, in terms of its ambivalent attitude towards neoliberalism demonstrate that the radical threat from the far-right to the interests of political elites and dominant social classes is partial at best. (Davidson, 2015; Saull, 2015a, 2015d). Indeed, as Neil Davidson noted, the far-right's framing of its political economy – and what needs to be done – rarely departs from the prevailing ideological assumptions associated with dominant political and social interests of the time (Davidson, 2015: 139–40; see also see Schivelbusch, 2006).

An additional set of objections to the dominant approaches to understanding the contemporary far-right can be identified in two more areas: (I) historicization; and (II) methodological internalism. Regarding the former, comparativist analyses in particular have tended to provide only a rather narrow historicization of the far-right. Referring to the 'return' of the far-right, these analyses note the distinctive features of the contemporary era: the socioeconomic context generated by neoliberal globalization and the political one framed by the fracturing and realignment of the left after the end of the Cold War. But they largely overlook the longer-term set of historical structures and processes out of which far-right politics have been continually reproduced as an artefact of liberal-capitalist modernity. Consequently, much of this literature struggles to explain why the contemporary far-right has come to replicate its historical predecessors while at the same time remaining significantly different from them.

The main problem with the historicizations of the far-right that have emerged from the field of political science is their inability to explain the reproduction of the far-right over time; in capturing and detailing a particular moment, the question of what preceded and succeeded it is left unexplained. This also means that the explanation of the far-right at any one time can end up exaggerating the uniqueness of that particular moment – and thus the character of the far-right – divorced from the historical structures (such as geopolitics and capitalism) within which it originated and is reproduced beyond the specificities of any particular historical moment.

There is also a tendency in much of the writing on the far-right – particularly in contemporary comparativist accounts – to use the inter-war fascist episode as a definitive historical marker against which to measure all subsequent articulations of the far-right. This is understandable given the relatively recent history of the fascist episode, and the way in which fascism appeared to encapsulate far-right politics in its purest form; but it remains historically short-sighted. First, by reifying the fascism of the inter-war period, this approach reduces the longer-term historical experience and broader significance of the far-right as a current of modern politics. Second, it serves to obscure the longer-term significance of the far-right in the constitution and evolution of liberal-democratic politics, the development of capitalism and in the framing of geopolitics and imperialism before fascism. The result is that, in the contemporary setting, the far-right is only understood as an 'extremist' threat to democratic order to the extent that it resembles fascism. This has been particularly evident in discussions of Donald Trump and 'Trumpism' following his election to the US presidency in November 2016. As the following chapters show, the far-right is not reducible to fascism, even if fascism is the most radical and crisis-induced form of far-right politics. Consequently, both before and after the inter-war fascist episode, the historical significance of the far-right goes well beyond fascism.

The methodological shortcoming of this comparativist framing is that it fails to account for how ideas associated with political factions develop over time and in different spaces. As a result, the contemporary far-right becomes detached from the historical structures – domestic and international – from which it emerged, which help to sustain it and generate its mutations. Since the contemporary far-right operates within a political and geopolitical context of neoliberalism, the fascism conditioned by the statist, authoritarian and militarist conditions of the past is unlikely to be replicated. In other words, there are 'structural aspects of the capitalist system at any time which are likely to be adopted by far-right parties: nationalism is a defining characteristic of the far-right, but nationalization is not' (Saull et al., 2015: 2).

Such limited historicization serves to obscure the long history of the far-right as a *constitutive* element within capitalist modernity that has existed as a distinct current within the politics of developing capitalist states since the mid-to-late nineteenth century, at least within Europe, and has involved a clutch of social and political movements not confined to the historical experience of fascism. This insight poses fundamental challenges of both a methodological and ontological nature to any attempt to understand the nature of the far-right. Emphasizing the long-term historical rootedness of the far-right as a political current, or pathology, within liberal-capitalist states suggests a need to identify and explain the factors that have helped to reproduce it over the *longue durée*. But any attempt to do so must apply a theoretical framework that is able to account adequately for its evolving character – given that the history of the far-right is not, thankfully, one of a constant reproduction of fascism. In many respects, the capacity of the dominant approaches to the far-right to do this are limited; indeed, in many respects, they fail to recognize the causal nature of such long-term structural factors.

The under-theorizations of capitalism and racism within both of the academic fields identified above tend to lead to key elements of *structural causation* for the far-right being overlooked. Treated as a factor to be considered as one amongst a number of causes of the far-right, the social structures of capitalism and racism are not conceptualized as hard-wired into the social and political fabric of the states and societies wherein the far-right develops. And this means that the casual properties associated with each that works to advantage the far-right within these societies is not adequately recognized. For example, the constant reconfiguration and transformation of space in terms of access to public space and the reconstitution of the relations between different spatial locales – metropole and periphery and town and country – provides an ongoing feature of capitalism that constantly reproduces a spatial backdrop ready for weaponizing by the far-right.

Further, to conceive of capitalism as a 'factor' – juxtaposed with 'culture' (see Inglehart and Norris, 2019 for a recent example) – that may explain the significance of the far-right in terms of 'economic causes' is fundamentally to misconceive the structural *social* properties of the object under consideration. Indeed, the *historical* particularities of the 'economic sphere' are a by-product of these social relations, including the appearance of distinct 'political' and 'economic' domains. In other words, capitalism is central to the reconstitution of the meaning, terrain and dynamics of the political, and it is through the social transformations and insecurities produced by it, that individual political subjectivities develop and change. And it is such disruptive and unsettling qualities that far-right populist framings of and appeals to a 'people' can secure significant political traction as an ideological means of exit from the destabilizing character of the present through calls for a return to an idealized past where individual political subjectivities are re-established and resecured.

A similar problem is also apparent in the treatment of race and racism. Again, within the comparativist political universe racism is identified – most recently in relation to anti-Muslim bigotry – as one factor among many in defining far-right ideology. What this perspective tends to overlook, however, is the way in which race and racism are fundamentally hard-wired within the sociology and political economy of the societies under consideration, to the extent that race, like class and gender, seeps into all dimensions of the social and political: it is not just one causal factor like any other from a menu of such causes. Thus, invocation of the significance of the legacy of colonization or of the Algerian war of independence in the framing of the contemporary far-right in France requires a broader recognition of race and racism as constitutive of the societies under scrutiny. Just as capitalism is not just one factor, but rather constitutes the structural socioeconomic context from which the far-right emerges and derives its political meaning so race and racism must be regarded as constitutive features of capitalist societies. To consider racism as a factor like any other (e.g., rising unemployment, disillusionment with mainstream political parties or immigration) is to misconceive the fundamentally colonial character of historical experience and societal and state formation. It is also to overlook the continuing legacies and historical residue of that colonial past across the institutions of state and society that reveal sediments of far-right ideology – even if they are not always articulated in a far-right vernacular (Balibar, 1991; Lentin, 2004; Roediger, 1991).

This brings us to the problem of the methodological internalism that dominates most work on the far-right. Thus, these studies are largely conducted within the rather abstract spatial universe of the nation-state, disembodied from its wider location in an international system and the inter-societal relations that traverse borders and, to a significant degree, shape and constitute the fabric of 'domestic' social and political institutions and relations. Such ontological assumptions result in an analytical blindness to the way in which the evolving structures and relations of the international not only provide the ideological motifs for the far-right – largely capturing each historical instantiation of different national far-rights from 'Manchesterism' in the belle epoque, Bolshevism in the inter-war and 'globalism' in the contemporary era – but also directs us to how and why the far-right is more advantaged in some historical periods rather than others.

Understanding the properties of either inter-war fascism or of the contemporary far-right therefore requires a methodological approach that is able to contextualise the far-right as a product of a national political moment that is partly reproduced through the nature of its interconnections with the wider international system of which it forms a part. The task here is not to dissolve the specificities of the national or local – borders and nations do have concrete consequences. Rather, it is to adopt a methodological perspective that can take account of the various structural dimensions of the international context in conditioning the character of the domestic. It is in this respect that such an 'international' or 'global' framing differs from that of the comparativist accounts that dominate the discussion of the contemporary far-right.

This is particularly relevant to the period of the Cold War, and to how the establishment and reproduction of a distinct kind of liberal international order across the Western world after 1945 was connected to the articulation and institutionalization of a virulent anti-communist ideological 'common sense'. What this historical period demonstrates is the mutual interconnections of domestic and international order construction, and how a particular international or geopolitical orientation facilitated a more favourable orientation to a 'post-fascist' far-right than would otherwise have been the case (see Anievas, forthcoming; Anievas and Saull, 2020, forthcoming). Such an analytical sensibility also relates to the distinct articulation of racism within the United States after 1917, and through the period of the Cold War up until the mid-1960s – something that came to complicate the realization of Civil Rights after 1945 (see Borstelmann, 2001; Seymour, 2016), and assisted the reproduction of the racialized order of Jim Crow across the south. The absence of a properly conceptualized international framing of the far-right across historical time means that the prevailing methodological perspectives are unable to provide an adequate theorization of the dynamics of the far-right – and, specifically, of how and why the particular geopolitical and political-economic configurations of the international not only shape the domestic socioeconomic and ideo-political interiors of states but also provide material advantages for far-right mobilizations.

In short, then, while much of the comparativist and history-of-ideas literatures have provided important analytical insights into the self-identification of these movements, and a range of data-sets that allow us to assess who they comprise and where they may be influential, they fall considerably short in recognizing the deeper structural causes of the far-right and how its persistence and re-emergence is a product of both historically defined socioeconomic and internationally mediated forces. My aim in the chapters that follow is thus not to erase the singularity and specificity of each national manifestation of the far-right – replacing methodological internalism with a one-dimensional externalism only serves to repeat the errors of the former, if in an inverted manner – but rather to locate the explanation of these national manifestations within an ontology where the international should be understood as constituting part of the domestic political spaces from which the far-right emerges and develops. The point is to offer a sober assessment of the political challenge and threats that the far-right poses to the social and political interests and constituencies connected to the internationalist socialist left, and thus a basis for thinking about effective political responses to this menace.

The critical points above are also applicable to those other accounts of the far-right that are particularly evident in historical literatures – whether focusing on a particular periods or countries. This is not to diminish the scholarly significance and quality of these types of contribution to the study of the far-right and fascism. Indeed, many of these studies populate and inform the present work. Rather, it is to note the inevitable limitations of certain kinds of scholarly work in addressing particular analytical questions.

## 2    Marxist Theorizations of the Far-Right

So far, my critical commentary has been limited to dominant theorizations within the academic literature that largely avoid a serious consideration of the socioeconomic dimensions of the far-right. These, mainly Marxist-informed positions[5] identify and seek to explain the primary causal drivers of the far-right/fascism as rooted in the structures, social relations and crises of capitalist political economy and the significance of class forces in the support of the far-right. In what follows I provide a commentary on some aspects of Marxist-informed analysis of the far-right:[6] where I draw on them and why, and in what ways my approach differs.

In many respects, an antipathy or neglect of socioeconomic and Marxist-informed analyses in the study of the contemporary far-right is peculiar. Thus, most of this work does recognize the importance of what are labelled as 'economic factors' in explaining the revival of the far-right (see Betz, 1994; Kitschelt, 1995; Mudde, 2007). However, this has not tended to result in serious engagement with Marxist approaches.[7] In part, this seems to be a legacy of the inter-war Comintern debates on fascism and the intrusions and problems derived from Stalinist political interference on the content and direction of

---

5    The best collection of Marxist writing on fascism remains David Beetham's (Beetham, 1983) edited volume. In addition see the following: Adamson, (1980); Adler, (1979); Bambery, (1993); Bataille and Lovitt, (1979); Bloch and Ritter, (1977); Botz, (1976); Cammet, (1967); Caplan, (1977); Ceplair, (1987); Davidson, (2015); Dülffer, (1976); Guerin, (1973); Hillach, (1979); Kitchen, (1973, 1975, 1976); Kühnl, (1972–73, 1975); Landa, (2018); Linton, (1989); Poulantzas, (1974); Rabinbach, (1974, 1977); Renton, (1999); Roberts, (2011); Rosenberg (2012); Sohn-Rethel, (1987); Trotsky, (1975); Vadja, (1972, 1976); Wistrich, (1976).

6    Dave Renton (1999: 44–53) provides a useful defence of the Marxist method as a way of theorising fascism that equally applies to the far-right in general.

7    As already noted, a number of more recent scholars of the far-right (Betz, 1994; Betz and Immerfall, 1998; Kitschelt, 1995; Oesch, 2008) have also focused on materialist explanations of the contemporary far-right, but these writers have not tended to be concerned with offering a reconstructed Marxist account of the far-right nor in relating these material factors to an evolving international political economy.

these debates.[8] It also relates to a widespread sense that because many workers embraced fascism and now, also support contemporary far-right parties and movements, an analytical framework founded upon a class analysis and which assumes certain social and political properties of the working class is, consequently, fundamentally flawed and redundant. This, I think, not only reflects an inaccurate and partial reading and assessment of the Marxist oeuvre on fascism and the far-right (see Davidson, 2015; Renton, 1999: 44–76; Saull et al., 2015; Saull, 2015a), but also mistakes the social and class content of contemporary far-right movements and the articulations of class within them.

The Marxist-informed discussion consists broadly of two sets of literature: one, concerned with the political economy of fascism and its connections to capitalist crises; and the other, work that is more concerned with the social, aesthetic, and psychological dimensions of fascism and the individual subjectivity of those particular social layers that were attracted to it. Although my main concern here will be with the former, it is worth noting the importance of this latter contribution. The key figures in this strand of Marxist thinking – Walter Benjamin (Benjamin, 2008), Ernst Bloch (Bloch, 2009), Wilhelm Reich (Reich, 1970) and the Frankfurt School writers Theodor Adorno (Adorno, et al., 1950), Max Horkheimer (Horkheimer and Adorno, 2002), Herbert Marcuse (Marcuse, 2002) and Erich Fromm (Fromm, 1994) – provided important explanations for the subjective and psychological bases of fascism. In many respects, these writers were path-breaking in their revitalization of Marxist theory through their attempts to focus on the subjective bases of class domination and hegemony (Bataille, and Lovitt, 1979). Indeed, in their focus on the importance of aesthetics and sexuality their work continues to be relevant to thinking about the contemporary far-right.[9]

---

8  Perhaps the most infamous episode concerns the co-called 'social fascism' of the Comintern's 'third period'. Identifying social democracy as the twin of fascism because of the way it, like fascism, was seen as trying to 'save' or 'reform' monopoly capitalism from its otherwise inevitable collapse. This Stalinist depiction of fascism viewed the destruction of the Weimar Republic and social democracy as a 'positive' development, as highlighted in the April 1933 April resolution of the Praesidium of the Executive Committee of the Communist International 'On the Present Situation in Germany', which stated, '[t]he establishment of an open fascist dictatorship, by destroying all the democratic illusions among the masses and liberating them from the influence of Social-Democracy, accelerates the rate of Germany's development toward proletarian revolution.'(quoted in Draper, 1969).

9  For more recent interventions that draw on this aspect of Marxist thinking see Short (2017); Toscano (2017, 2021); and Woodley, (2010: 100–104, 211–30).

In focusing on the first strand and some of the key contributions to the Comintern inter-war debate on fascism[10] I do so because these arguments were pre-occupied with addressing the kinds of questions that I am concerned with in regard to the far-right over the *longue durée*: what explains the emergence and rise of fascism/far-right; how are these movements connected to capital and state; what social layers are most attracted to them? Given the context within which these authors were writing and – for many of them, their personal involvement in anti-fascist political struggles – these contributions are infused with political as much as analytical judgements and their pre-occupation of articulating a strategy for how the international workers' movement should respond to fascism. However, both the historical context and the political concerns of these writers, do not mean that their arguments are marginal to an analysis of the contemporary far-right. And although there are limitations in this Marxist literature, there is also much to be retrieved from the inter-war debates which the discussions that follow in subsequent chapters will draw on.

My engagement with these writers is primarily concerned with identifying and developing some of their analytical insights that remain relevant and illuminating beyond the historical context and political questions that they were concerned with. So, my aim is less about trying to revive any one of these writers and their arguments as theorists of the far-right over the *longue durée* and more concerned with retrieving those elements of the Marxist theorization of fascism that will assist me in developing an understanding of the far-right as an organic feature of capitalist development in its international and geopolitical dimensions in particular.

In doing so I also aim to go beyond these accounts in two important ways. First, through differentiating between the structure of capitalism as a mode of accumulation based on the exploitation of wage labour through privatised

---

10    Renton (1999: 54–62) provides a good summary of the three distinct Marxist positions that emerged in response to the rise of fascism (in Italy): a 'left theory' particularly associated with Amadeo Bordiga, the leader of the newly founded Italian Communist Party (PCI) that saw fascism as a reactionary movement controlled by the capitalist class (an approach that came to influence later Stalinist Comintern doctrine); a 'right theory' associated with Giovanni Zibordi of the Italian Socialist Party (PSI) that understood fascism as a mass movement largely autonomous of any ruling class influence; and a 'third' or 'dialectical' approach that emerged in response to the destruction of the left in Italy and Mussolini coming to power. Initially based on Clara Zetkin's interpretation, it was developed by Antonio Gramsci, Ignazio Silone, August Thalheimer and Leon Trotsky and understood fascism as a deeply contradictory and dynamic form of politics reflected in its relationship to the bourgeoisie and hostility to the workers' movement. It is this third approach that my argument particularly engages with and draws on.

relations of market exchange, and the way in which the multiple dimensions of the international condition and facilitate such social relations. Consequently, I recognise something that a couple of more recent Marxist accounts (see Bambery, 1993 and Renton, 1999) largely overlook: that capitalist development evolves as much in its institutional, spatial, and geopolitical dimensions as it does in its material relations of production. And, further, that such changes condition the social and political effects of the crises that develop out of capitalist development. In particular, the geopolitical re-organization of capitalism under US hegemony after 1945 has been fundamental to thinking about and explaining the possibilities for far-right advance in the post-war era in a similar way that the international and geopolitical determinants of the 'social' or 'new' imperialism of the late nineteenth century was causal of the far-right at this time.

The central issue here is the need to think through the connections and evolution of *spatially uneven* regimes of capital accumulation (e.g., imperialism, Fordism, neoliberalism) to: (i) the social dislocations and crises generated by such patterns in the articulations of sets of nationally-organized class forces; and (ii) the particularities of the social mobilizations behind the far-right over the *longue durée*. The spatially-mediated reproduction and recomposition of classes is key to unlocking the social possibilities for the politics of the far-right over the *longue durée* and provides an important sociological, and geographical insight into the possibilities for the success of the far-right as a transformative mode of politics. The Marxist arguments discussed below are crucial to addressing these issues; indeed, they provide the only developed methodological and theoretical frameworks that attempt to address them.

Secondly, although I focus on the behaviour of capitalist classes as the key actors, in determining the social context in which far-right movements operate, I differ from existing Marxist accounts through singling out their causal role in creating the socioeconomic context out of which the European far-right has re-emerged from their *political* role in benefiting from and/or seeking the support of far-right movements, as a means to secure their social and political interests. In the former, it has been the commitment of ruling classes and state managers to an increasingly globalized neoliberalism (Glynn, 2006; Harvey, 2005; Panitch and Gindin, 2012; Robinson, 2004) over the last four decades or so that has provided the structural and material context that has determined the social and spatial possibilities for far the far-right. Yet, while the political economy of neoliberalism has opened up political opportunities for the far-right because the reproduction of dominant social layers remains increasingly based on globalized and liberalized circuits of production and exchange, these leading social forces and their allies in the state are much less aligned with a politics of extreme nationalism than they were in the past. The consequence of this is to limit, structurally, the possibilities of the contemporary far-right (Saull, 2015a).

This point also relates to the long-standing question that pre-occupied the inter-war Marxists (and Marx and Engels with respect to their conceptualization of the politics of the regime of Louis-Napoléon Bonaparte), as to the relationship between capital, the capitalist state and the far-right and the degree of autonomy of the far-right as a popular or mass movement from ruling class forces. In this respect, while a number of inter-war Marxists recognized the independent agency of fascist movements (see Gramsci, 1983a, 1983b; Silone, 1983; Thalheimer, 1983a, 1983b; Trotsky, 1975) they did so without fully articulating a geopolitical framing of it. Thus, they did not provide an account of the spatially (and temporally) uneven possibilities for fascist advance. Instead, they remained, in general, trapped in the 'monopoly capital'/imperialist paradigm of the time that largely closed-off the possibility of producing such an account. In the rest of the section, I spell out the continuing relevance of Marxist arguments for any theorization of the far-right.

### 2.1 Capitalism, Crisis and Fascism

Most of the inter-war Marxist contributions emphasised the singular and universal tendency of (monopoly) capitalism as the primary driver of the geopolitical conflict that gave rise to fascism. There was also a recognition amongst a number of writers as to the more varied and open possibilities resulting from capitalist development. In many respects, such a position – which was found in the writings of Antonio Gramsci, Palmiro Togliatti and Ignazio Silone in particular – reflected an understanding of the developmental logic of capitalism as 'uneven and combined'. Consequently, it was not only the working out of the logic of capitalist accumulation that was uneven but also that the spatial consequences of crises produced by such unevenness were not uniform and reflected more diverse developmental trajectories and geopolitical relations between states (Gramsci, 1983a, 1983b; Silone, 1983; Togliatti, 1983). Consequently, while these writers recognized that fascism was a generic tendency or organic feature always present within capitalism during moments of crisis, the establishment of fascist states was not an inevitable political outcome.

Nicos Poulantzas (Poulantzas, 1974; see also Kühnl, 1972–73, 1975), writing in the 1970s, developed this further by arguing that fascism was successful in some states (Germany and Italy) and not in others (Britain, France, and the United States) due to the way in which competitive struggles within a global capitalist–imperialist system filtered into the politics of each national formation (Poulantzas, 1974: 17–24). Thus, fascism was a more or less likely outcome of crisis depending on the particular location and the form of its integration into the geopolitical circuits of a hierarchical system of capitalist imperialism. This insight is significant for a general theory of the causal relationship between capitalism and fascism because it recognizes the varied political fortunes of European inter-war fascism and the variations in the relationship across different national spaces.[11]

What we can take from this is that the theorization of the relationship between capitalist development and fascism/far-right requires a recognition of the uneven and shifting spatial relations and geopolitical organization within the global capitalist economy that shape and constitute the domestic political fabric of state-society complexes that can strengthen as much as weaken the hegemonic blocs therein. Thus, these Marxist writers recognized and emphasized the *political* – ideational, institutional and agential – dimensions of Marxist political-economy that reflected a shared assumption that the causes and political success of fascism cannot be read-off from a set of purely economic or material determinations. However, it goes beyond this because of the geographically uneven nature of the crises produced from capitalist development, fascism and the far-right are likely to be a stronger force and less subject to counter-vailing tendencies in some geopolitical locales (such as Italy and Germany) than in others (Britain, the US and Scandinavia). Indeed, it was the geopolitical and structural properties of the capitalist-imperialist world economy of the time that made the likelihood of a fascist solution to the crises that both Italy and Germany confronted – if they were to remain capitalist states – much more likely than elsewhere because the existing geopolitical order cut off alternative strategies and the domestic political-institutional arrangements associated with them.

Consequently, as Michael Mann (Mann, 2004; see also Luebbert, 1991) has noted, while the specific nature of the crisis of capitalist hegemony in Italy and Germany saw liberal forces tolerate fascism as the means to secure capitalist

---

11   This is significant particularly with respect to the most important capitalist state in the inter-war era, the United States. Thus, while there were some developmental and organizational tendencies within the New Deal – the particular US response to the economic crisis triggered by the 'Wall Street crash' of October 1929 – that pointed towards fascist political economy (e.g., trade protectionism and the carving out of imperial spheres of influence and an embrace of reactionary and racist forces of the Jim Crow South – see Volume II) the New Deal also reflected the *resilience* of liberal politics and institutions even if this response was based on a social and political compromise with the racist South and an imperialist/protection shift (see Gardner, 1964 and Tooze, 2015a and the work of Ira Katznelson (2013) for the definitive account of the politics of the New Deal).

social order and deal with the threat of the radical left, other liberal states –
and Britain, Sweden, and the US in particular – did not follow this path. The
defence of bourgeois social order in moments of crisis does not, necessarily,
always entail a fascist embrace. However, the degree to which this variation in
outcomes across different liberal democracies can be explained 'internally' via
the institutional strength and support for liberal democracy within these states
(i.e., via methodological internalism) as the reason why fascism failed to get
close to capturing state power rests on ignoring the way in which the existing
international arrangements helped reinforce, if not constitute, those domestic
political spaces. Further, it was because of such international arrangements –
and the kind of hierarchical inter-societal relations that they nurtured – that
the relative security of the existing hegemonic arrangements within these
liberal states was realized. Thus, as Nicos Poulantzas (Poulantzas, 1974: 17–24)
posited, what was ultimately determining for the strength of fascism within
*particular* states was the location of their polities within a hierarchical imperial system whereby developmental late-comers were the most susceptible to
fascism in moments of systemic crisis. Such a view appropriately balances the
analytical and political weight of explanation between structural and international factors of causation with those of the domestic and contingent and, in
doing so, also qualifies the causal role of the liberal democratic credentials of
those major capitalist states that did not succumb to fascism during the inter-
war period.

Therefore, while we can fault some inter-war Marxists for failing to recognize and explain the varied developmental and political trajectories of
capitalist states in a context of systemic crisis emergent from a global geopolitical order of capitalist accumulation, this does not mean that the non-Marxist
accounts of inter-war fascism that dwell on *the differentia specifica* of particular nation-states as somehow inoculated against the fascist virus offer superior
explanations. As much as fascism cannot be reduced to the playing out of a
global *economic* logic of capitalist development, nor can it be reduced to a crisis of domestic political institutions and party competition. The potential of
the arguments of Gramsci, Silone, Togliatti and Trotsky for a general theorisation of the far-right is that they recognised the specific properties and causal
role of domestic politics. Moreover, they did so through connecting the specificities of each domestic setting to structural socioeconomic developments
at the international level thus revealing the inter-connected and inter-societal
dimensions of domestic politics associated with (i) the actions of far-right
movements on the ground; (ii) the behaviour of state leaderships and ruling
classes; and (iii) the workings of political institutions in ultimately determining the success or failure of the far-right (Saull, 2015a).

Such a structural perspective based on the causal relationship between the evolving geopolitics of capitalist development and the varied fortunes of the far-right is also intimately connected to the concepts of 'hegemony' and 'passive revolution' as articulated in the work of Antonio Gramsci in particular (Gramsci, 1971: 58, 109, 263, 1988: 192; see also, Thomas, 2009: 145–58, 159–96, 213–17, 224–8). Thus, and corroborating Poulantzas' observation above as to the varied geopolitical possibilities for fascist outcomes during periods of systemic crisis, likewise the strength, durability and legitimacy of hegemonic arrangements within nation-states and the stable reproduction of class rule also relies on the conditioning role of the existing international organization and management of capital accumulation. It is this international dimension to hegemony that may determine its precise character and the relative dialectical fusion of, and the relative influence of consent and coercion, legitimacy, and domination in the reproduction of domestic order and class rule. It is hegemony's character as an evolving process rooted in the interactions between the international and domestic that means that it requires the political agencies of the ruling class to mobilize subaltern and dissenting social layers as ongoing 'conscious, planned struggle' (Gramsci, 1971: 263). Further, because, as Gramsci noted, hegemony is a dynamic and unstable political arrangement, the socioeconomic foundations that underpin it – with regard to the integration of subaltern layers into the historical bloc and the material reproduction of the dominant class forces – require the maintenance and stability of the inter-societal arrangements upon which such hegemonic arrangements were originally founded. The strength of hegemonic order and thus the social and political limits on the possibilities for fascist advance are contingent, then, on the reproduction of particular forms of inter-societal relationships upon which the material, institutional and ideational components of hegemony are partly derived.

Complimenting the idea of hegemony is the concept of passive revolution that Gramsci utilized to explain the process by which fascism came to power in Italy as a consequence of the 'organic crisis' of hegemony (Gramsci, 1973: 210–11). Passive revolution refers to a 'molecular' process of transformation, in the hegemonic organization of class rule that results in a change in the existing composition of the ruling class through its absorption of popular counter-hegemonic forces but where the structure of capitalist social relations remains intact (see Gramsci 1971: 58, 109; Hesketh, 2017: 398, 401). Such a dialectic of 'revolutionary restoration' reveals the partial fulfilment of a revolutionary conjuncture based on a mass mobilization from below drawing on social forces outside of the historical bloc that forms the socio-political basis of hegemony. Nevertheless, the result is a restructuring of the political form of capitalist rule that emerges out of moments of crisis; it signals a ruptural point and contingent possibility for revolution, unfulfilled and conditioned by the international relations of existing hegemonic arrangements (Allinson and Anievas, 2010; Morton, 2007).

While not reducible to solely explaining far-right and fascist forms of political power transition (see Riley and Desai, 2007), the concept of passive revolution helps to specify the unique political and institutional circumstances when far-right and fascist movements gain strength, as well as the precise social, political and ideological processes through which radical political, institutional and ideological changes take place within a state when far-right forces come to access state power. Further, while noting the very different political circumstances within which the far-right attains state power, it also emphasizes the persistence of the pre-existing relations of class hierarchy and capitalist social property relations. Gramsci's concept of passive revolution was developed as a way of explaining the Risorgimento and the rise of Mussolini and, like hegemony, passive revolution is a concept that can be deployed to explain the specificities – in terms of structural context and political process – of far-right forces gaining access to state power in general over the *longue durée*.

So, although the interwar period is of course the paradigmatic era of far-right/fascist ascendency, because these two inter-connected concepts address the *generic* properties of capitalist development (see Cox, 1987; Gill and Law, 1989; Morton, 2007; Rupert, 1995) – and crises generated from within it – they are applicable to the politics of capitalist states in general, including the contemporary era. Indeed, whilst the geopolitical organization of capitalism was radically reconfigured after 1945 with a new liberal historical bloc constructed as the basis for the restoration of capitalist hegemony, this process – as I will demonstrate in Volume 2 – also involved forms of passive revolution and far-right political agency.

What the insights – originally connected to Gramsci's explanation of Italian fascism (Gramsci, 1983a, 1983b) – demonstrate, then, is the analytical utility of these Marxist concepts to an examination of the far-right over the *longue durée*. Gramsci's insights highlight how the organic tendencies within capitalist development mean that the long-term durability of the political-institutional structures and associated ideological imaginaries necessary for the reproduction of a hegemonic order are always contingent and temporary. Further, because the dialectic of capitalism contains the seeds of the next crisis – through which new political opportunities emerge – the possibilities for passive revolution and the agency of the far-right are an immanent feature of such developmental tendencies.

## 2.2     *The Social Basis of Fascism*

Much of the work of the inter-war Marxists was concerned with examining the class basis of fascism – as movement and state – and especially the relationship between dominant class interests and fascism. In this regard, there are two issues to highlight with reference to a general theorisation of the causal relationship between capitalism and politics of the far-right: (I) the social complexion of fascism, who supported or were part of the mass movement; and (II) the relationship between fascism and capital and what fascist states did in managing society and balancing conflicting social interests. This is, arguably, the key question about fascism and the far-right in general that Marxist writers have prioritized over non-Marxists and, consequently, has a significant bearing on both how we should treat the radical and anti-capitalist rhetoric and propaganda of these movements and their success in mobilizing subaltern layers.[12]

Regarding the former, Marxists have tended to identify fascism as a particular kind of 'petty-bourgeois [sic], reactionary mass movement' (Davidson, 2015: 129–30; Guerin, 1973: 41–62; Poulantzas, 1974: 237–46; Togliatti, 1983; Bambery, 1993: 62; Renton, 1999: 35–6). This class-based account of fascism has been the subject of on-going scrutiny from non-Marxists, with contrary accounts arguing that the fascist movement was built on a significant degree of support from the working class (Eatwell, 2003; Payne 1995), while other scholars give greater emphasis to fascism's trans-class identity (Mann, 2004: 20–8).[13] This is something that I will come back to later in this volume when I focus on inter-war fascism. For now, I want to comment on the way in which support for fascism was intimately connected to the dynamics and crisis moments produced from uneven capitalist development. So, while Mann (Mann, 2004) and others are correct in insisting on the multiple social layers supportive of fascism, it is also necessary to recognise the uneven and differentiated character of the social bases of fascism in terms of where and when it secured this mass trans-class support (see Hamilton, 1982; Larsen, et al., 1980) as well as the role of petty bourgeois imaginaries in the mass mobilizations of fascism. Thus, we need to recognize that the significance of the petty bourgeoisie as a basis of support for fascism goes beyond the mobilization of a distinct class layer, to include the role played by an ideology of producerism within the political

---

12     As Ignazio Silone recognized, the contradictions of fascism were that 'it mobilised a layer within society and yet could not resolve the grievances that arose from the situation that this layer found itself trapped within' (cited in Renton, 1999: 67).

13     See Kershaw (2000: 47–68) and Mann (2004: 1–30) for thorough examinations of the theoretical and empirical literature on the social basis of fascism.

economy of the far-right. That this ideology – based on the fetishization of independent work and labour and connected to the idea of an independent and self-sufficient producer juxtaposed and, at odds with, the combined monopolies of labour and capital – was not realized in the political economy of fascist states, merely highlights the need to differentiate between fascism as movement and state form.

Further, while fascists drew on support from sections of the working class this was an ideo-political mobilization that was fundamentally concerned with denying *and* destroying the ideological and political properties of independent working-class political agency. Thus, although people within certain working-class socioeconomic categories were sympathetic – sometimes joining fascist parties – this was fundamentally about disavowing the politics of a *working* class or proletarian identity. This became all the more evident if and when fascists secured political power, as one of their primary objectives was the destruction of the institutional bases of a working class politics and the key institutions (and social achievements) of organized labour and the working class.

Indeed, the differentiation between fascist movement and state is fundamentally important in accurately differentiating the social properties of fascism. In this sense, to talk about working class support for fascism or 'working class fascists' seems to rest on the evacuation of any of the social, ideological and political categories usually associated with a class politics and its dispersal or absorption into a politics of race/nation/spectacle/emotion. The point then is not to dispute that fascists secured support from people who materially reproduced themselves as workers, but rather to emphasize that the ideo-political properties of fascism rest on the destruction of the sources of class solidarity and class identity which, in effect, de-couple the material (wage labour) dimension of class from that of the social, cultural, and ideological properties of class identity. Thus, as the Marxist arguments of the inter-war period rightly insisted, this means that a fascist politics – though it might secure support from some workers – cannot *base* itself on the working class, since this would necessitate a recognition of different and antagonistic class interests and a politics that was committed to the primacy of working class interests.

In stressing the fluctuating and dynamic character of the social basis of the far-right, the inter-war Marxists correctly identified the close connections between the moments of crisis and the specificities of who supported fascism and where. Thus, Italian landlords became active supporters of fascist *squadristi* during 1920 in response to the growing socialist threat to their property rights and class power in the countryside, and farmers, the petty bourgeoisie and non-unionised workers began to be drawn towards the Nazi

Party after 1929, when the full effect of the global economic crisis began to hit the German economy. The point here, as recognised in the work of Trotsky and others (Trotsky, 1975; Togliatti, 1983), is that although fascism appealed to a trans-class constituency, it ended up drawing on *specific* social forces who were confronted with particular concerns during exceptionally intense moments of economic crisis that played out across distinct geographical locales.

This is also relevant to a general theorisation of the sociology of the far-right in that the degree to which certain social layers – in particular geographical locales and positions within the capitalist division of labour – are much more likely to support the far-right in temporally contingent moments of crisis (Saull, 2015a). It is also the case – and the empirical data tends to support this – that the sections of society that were most immune to fascism and the far-right in general are those identified by an association with the institutions and culture of organized labour (Davidson, 2015; Saull, 2015a, 2015d). Consequently, while it may be the case that class – understood as a 'social relation of production' – is insufficient to account for the social basis of fascism, in connecting class categories to the uneven character of capitalist development, we are able to identify a *logic of class* in the social mobilisations behind fascism.

The question of the social basis of fascist movements also concerns the relationship between fascists and the capitalist class, a core preoccupation of Marxist writing on fascism. However, many of the contributions to the inter-war Marxist debate on fascism failed to adequately distinguish the distinct phases in the relationship between fascism and capitalist ruling-class interests and state elites.[14] Indeed, it is important to note the more hesitant and, in some respects, hostile attitude of significant parts of the capitalist class to fascist movements before fascists came to power, after which the relationship became much more intimate (Adler, 1995; Tooze, 2007). Trotsky was one of several Marxists[15] who recognized this but such qualifications have tended to

---

14    Nicos Poulantzas's (1974) otherwise excellent analysis of fascism is seriously undermined by the fact that his temporal focus does not extend beyond the initial years of the Hitler dictatorship, which means that his account has a very underdeveloped theorization of the Nazi state and political economy. See Jane Caplan's (1977) important critique in her review of Poulantzas's work.

15    As Trotsky (1975: 265; see also Rosenberg, 2012; Sohn-Rethel, 1987; Thalheimer, 1983a, 1983b) recognized, 'the barons, the magnates of capital, and the bankers have made an attempt to safeguard their interests by means of the police and the regular army. The idea of giving up all power to Hitler, who supports himself upon the greedy and unbridled bands of the petty bourgeoisie [sic], is a far from pleasant one to them. They do not, of course, doubt that in the long run Hitler will be a submissive instrument of their domination. Yet this is bound up with convulsions, with the risk of a long and weary civil war and great expense.'

be drowned out by the Comintern debates on the idea of the fascist state as representing a form of 'monopoly capitalism'.[16] Although fascist movements did not become pawns of capital or the traditional ruling elite once invited into power, the fact that their accession to state power was not only achieved through the active involvement of ruling class interests but that such advance was a *requirement* of it, gives some indication as to the priorities and concerns for capitalists in contexts of severe economic crisis and also the social concerns, or lack thereof, of fascist states (Riley, 2004).

The shortcomings of inter-war Marxist analyses of the relationship between fascist movements and the capitalist class and political elites should not, however, lead us to overlook or downplay this sociological and political dynamic in a broader theorisation of the far-right. While the relationship between capital and fascist movements was more contingent than much of the inter-war Marxist writing tended to acknowledge (see Künhl and Rabinbach, 1975) the ultimate political success of these movements depended on the invitation to govern by these interests as the best solution for resolving the political and economic crises that these states confronted while upholding the social rule of capital. This implies that any assessment of the political fortunes of the far-right *must examine* the role of dominant social layers and state elites and, in particular, the extent to which they provide support and encouragement for the far-right and – as in the fascist episode – active political cooperation with fascist movements. However, it goes beyond this, as recognized by those Marxists such as Trotsky (1975) who theorized fascism as a distinct ideopolitical response to moments of crisis that invoke the agencies of capitalist classes – collectively and internationally – in the outbreaks of crises and the wider social and political conditions that give rise to the far-right, but also differentiates the actual behaviour of capitalist classes in the rise and coming to power of far-right movements.

## 2.3  *Bonapartism and the Fascist State*

In this final section looking at Marxist theory and the far-right I want to address the Marxist theorization of the fascist state and, in particular, the extent to which the concept of Bonapartism[17] – that Marx originally outlined in 1852

---

16    The (Comintern's) orthodox view rested on Georgi Dimitroff's 1935 definition of fascism as 'the openly terroristic dictatorship of the most reactionary, most chauvinistic and most imperialistic elements of finance-capital,' (cited in Rabinbach, 1974: 136) which also assumed that Hitler's accession to power was, in effect, organized and directed by the capitalist class.

17    There is an extensive literature on the Marxist concept of Bonapartism (see the following: Draper, 1977; Jessop, 1990; Linton, 1989; Thalheimer, 1973, 1983a, 1983b) much of

(Marx, 1934) – provides some conceptual utility in thinking about the distinct kind of political arrangements associated with far-right political regimes. In coming to power in Italy and Germany fascist movements came to transform the domestic and international political relations of each; not least in organizing their respective societies for total war. Inevitably, such re-orientations had an impact on the organizational and geopolitical arrangements within which capitalist accumulation took place within and, in some cases, had a negative impact on some sections of each country's capitalist class. The re-organization of accumulation for war was, then, a unique feature of fascism that has not historically travelled beyond this particular experience of far-right regime including those that lasted after 1945 on the Iberian Peninsula and the far-right military dictatorships that emerged in South America.

The concept of Bonapartism provides a way of explaining the reproduction of a capitalist socioeconomic order in the absence of the political rule of the representatives of the capitalist class and where the legitimating political institutions and processes of bourgeois democracy have been dismantled. Fascism reveals the fullest expression of such developments. And while short-lived in duration and dominated by war it provides us with distinct historical case studies of a particular metamorphosis or degeneration of capitalism. Although fascism remains a possible outcome emergent from within the contradictory and crisis-ridden nature of uneven capitalist development, given the historically distinct social, ideological and geopolitical circumstances that fascist states developed out of, Marx's account of Bonapartism provides a more useful analytical reference point for a generic theorization of far-right authoritarian state forms.

What then does the concept of Bonapartism refer to and in what ways might it be useful, analytically, to theorizing the far-right over the *longue-durée?* Bonapartism refers, specifically, to the state form(s) associated with, first, Napoleon Bonaparte – established by the coup d'état in 1799 (the so-called 18th Brumaire of November 9, 1799) that overthrew the Directory regime – and, secondly, that of Louis-Napoléon Bonaparte (the nephew of the former) that was

---

which focuses on and contributes to the debate on the so-called 'relative autonomy' of the capitalist state. My concern here is less with intervening in the debate on the relative autonomy of the capitalist state and more on the distinct ideo-political qualities of the Bonapartist state as it emerged in the early 1850s under the direction of Louis-Napoléon Bonaparte and in the context of a severe political and socioeconomic crisis produced from the 1848 revolution. What the concept of Bonapartist state throws up then is a form of 'ideal-type' or template of far-right infused authoritarian response and state form to overcome moments of systemic crisis.

established after the coup that overthrew the parliamentary republic in 1851, inaugurating the regime of the Second Empire. Although Bonapartism is used to refer to both forms of regime, Marx's concept of 'Bonapartist state' (Marx, 1934) was primarily concerned with the politics that established the regime of the Second Empire and the type of capitalist state that it inaugurated. The essence of this new political regime is that the capitalist class – which Marx defined as represented by the two wings of the 'Party of Order'[18] - was forced to abdicate its political privileges as a means to preserve its social power. In Marx's own words,

> [t]hus the French bourgeoisie was compelled by its class position to anni-hilate, on the one hand, the vital conditions of all parliamentary power, and therefore, likewise, of its own, and to render irresistible, on the other hand, the executive power hostile to it ... [and] by now stigmatising as '*socialistic*' what it had previously extolled as '*liberal*,' the bourgeoisie con-fesses that its own interests dictate that it should be delivered from the danger of its *own rule*; that, in order to restore tranquillity in the country, its bourgeois parliament must, first of all, be laid to rest; that, in order to preserve its social power intact, its political power must be broken.
>
> MARX, 1934: 53, 57 original emphases

Bonapartism, then, reveals a specific and crisis-driven re-organization of state and politics whereby the norms, institutions and relations of liberal represent-ative or democratic order are suspended on the altar of the maintenance of the capitalist *social* order. Consequently, the conjuncture that results in the estab-lishment of the Bonapartist state/dictatorship is one outcome of the circum-stances of a passive revolution as understood by Gramsci (Gramsci, 1971: 150, 203, 210, 227). The new political form of the capitalist state has a deformed 'mass-populist' character derived from the revolutionary crisis and counter-hegemonic popular mobilizations that Bonapartism emerges from. The state is organized around and legitimated through the charismatic leader who embodies the 'mass person' – as both alternative to the mediated character of the democratic republic and 'fulfilment' of mass desires through the mass organizations associated with the leader and *his* personal appeals and commu-nications to the masses. Yet, such political transformation and integration of

---

18      Marx labelled the two wings according to their Royalist sympathies – Bourbon/Legitimists and Orleanist/July; whereas the former tended to reflect the class interests of landed property and reactionary capital, the latter was associated with high finance and large-scale industry and trade (Draper, 1977: 393).

popular layers into the apparatuses of the state not only leaves intact the social dominance of capital but involves the destruction of the social and political organizations that contest such dominance. This is not an 'aestheticization' or 'sacralization' of politics that resembles classical fascism, but it does inaugurate a form of regime and reveals a range of features resonant with the far-right over the *longue durée*.

Bonapartism reflects a number of characteristics – in terms of the crises that produce it, the organization of the state and its class relations – that could be seen to reveal an ideal-typical form of far-right state in the following ways. First, the specific confluence of an internationally-framed political and economic crisis of the state-society complex that provides the context and *strategic necessity* for a kind of Bonapartist political intervention. Such crises are systemic in that they appear to present a fundamental threat to an existing way of life and social order. The substance of what amounts to an existential crisis of the twin – political and economic – features of liberal order reveal themselves in: (a) the breakdown of the basic workings of the capitalist market order in terms of the productive and profitable investment of the factors of production, as evidenced in falls in production, unemployment and profits, i.e., an inability of the market to internally reproduce itself or return to a state of 'equilibrium'; and (b) politically, in two senses: (I) in the inability of the existing representative/parliamentary system to deal with revolutionary challenges (i.e., how to manage the political threat from the working class); and (II) the inability of existing political representatives to construct a class alliance as a new basis for the political hegemony of capital.

The issue that Bonapartism responds to is how the existing  bourgeois political-institutional framework and associated representative vehicles are unable to secure a popular mandate or legitimacy for rule. As Derek Linton (1989: 105–6) notes, Bonapartism emerges out a context of the defeat of the working-class revolutionary offensive, and the inability of existing or traditional political representatives to secure a political or electoral mandate to carry out necessary tasks. And it develops out of a collective resignation and fear across the representatives of the bourgeoisie as to what is politically possible within existing political institutions and the ideology of bourgeois hegemony. It is such a context and political assessment which moves the bourgeoisie to seek a political resolution to the crisis of rule based on alternative institutional arrangements that necessitate the destruction of parliamentary democracy and the embrace of a new constitutional order that can secure a fresh political basis for the securing of bourgeois social rule based on a new historical bloc founded upon the integration of subaltern classes.

Secondly, the reconfiguration of the state and its administrative-coercive apparatus. In many respects this re-arrangement – such that the coercive and authoritarian dimensions of the state are over-developed vis-à-vis the other parts – can be seen as immanent to the liberal state (see Tomba, 2013) and reflected in liberal political thought with the recognition of the need to 'provide for the negation of the workings of liberal institutional arrangements in order to ensure the continued existence of bourgeois society' (Franz Neumann cited Rabinbach, 1974: 132). This political authoritarianism, however, serves a singular purpose – that of stamping out any further possibilities of working-class resistance to the social order and the new political arrangements. It is this development that provides the political resolution of the crisis that brought Bonapartism into being. Bonapartism reveals the coercive inner core of the state where force is much more evident in the realization of capital's social rule. It is no longer a hegemonic kind of order premised on the balance between 'coercion and consent' in Gramsci's iteration with the emphasis on the former (Gramsci, 1971: 169–70) but, rather, a decoupling and supervision of the state over civil society with the suspension of any democratic supervision over the state's executive and coercive power. It is the end point of that which is immanent within the liberal constitutional order in terms of the resolution of social conflict and the preservation of a social order based on private property. This 'relative autonomy' sees the 'primacy of politics' over civil society and the wider milieu of capitalist production and exchange but not its overthrow.[19]

Consequently, it is the executive organs of the state and, in many respects, the executive office-holder; the personification of power and authority that is revealed in Bonapartism. While this remains a question of degree – both in terms of the levels of charisma[20] and the power that the office-holder deploys – it is fundamentally about rule by fiat at the cost of representative deliberation and the appearance of a direct and unmediated connection between executive authority and the ruled. In this sense, this political arrangement is no mere dictatorship over society but rather an arrangement where the leader is in direct communication with the masses via the institutions of the mass

---

19    Tim Mason's (1968) work provides the definitive account of this in the Marxist theorization of the Nazi state. For an excellent discussion of the debate over the nature of the Nazi state within Marxist theory see Rabinbach (1974).

20    Louis-Napoléon was ridiculed by Marx (and others) but his rhetoric and posturing – although vague, contradictory, and theatrical – managed to secure widespread democratic appeal including amongst the poor, petty bourgeoisie, and peasantry. The particular charisma of Donald Trump (and Boris Johnson) – and the critical commentary on it – echoes the way in which Bonaparte secured mass appeal.

party that permeate and, in effect, take over the state. The capitalist state is not abolished, nor is the *ancien régime* reconstituted but rather, the state becomes 'massified' and more authoritarian through the permeation of the populist and authoritarian ideology and personnel of the mass movement.

Thirdly, the primary objective of Bonapartism is the disciplining and smashing of autonomous sources of political organization and resistance. Necessarily, this focuses on the political institutions of the working class and wider civil society. It is here where ideology plays a significant role in the nature of the state and attempts to craft a new form of national unity as the basis for the new political dispensation. Thus, in the rhetoric and propaganda associated with both Bonapartist-infused movements and states, there is a combined anti-capitalist and anti-socialist rhetoric with a particular emphasis on *order* and overcoming chaos and stasis. This does have material effects; the economy is re-organized, and the autonomous privileges of capital are clipped. Capitalists are directed towards certain political and geopolitical goals connected to a nationalist and geopolitically-oriented re-ordering of priorities. But this 'state capitalism' does not abolish the capitalist labour process, indeed it provides an ideo-political reinforcement of the exploitation of wage labour and profits continue to flow to capitalists. Capitalists also remain responsible for how they produce.

The change is in the wider *political* economy within which these processes and relations play out. Capitalist production is explicitly politicized but given that this is now – under the Bonapartist form – legitimized around national greatness and the re-vitalization of the nation, it has a new-found and mass-based form of social and political legitimacy that the previous liberal-democratic political arrangements struggled to confer. Such framing produces a nationalist capitalism that approximates the classical template of the vertical integration of 'monopoly capital' based on the fusion of industrial and finance capital oriented towards imperialist forms of competition and geopolitical rivalry. It also connects to the far-right ideology of producerism which not only fixates on localized production but also fetishizes individual over collective labour located within a social universe where the 'social monopoly' of organized labour has been abolished.

This brings us to the fourth and final dimension of the Bonapartist type – the deployment and direction of the state to overcome the economic crisis. The political economy of the French Second Empire under Louis-Napoléon Bonaparte provides the template here. The state becomes an innovator and promoter of economic change and modernization through directing capital and encouraging it with monopoly privileges particularly in infrastructure developments. These changes are negligible in terms of economic development, growth, and employment (Draper, 1977: 404–5), as well as charting a way out of crisis, but they rest on a hierarchical corporatism: autonomous workers organizations are dismantled, and the political power of any organized labour is dissolved, and workers are integrated into compliant, state-based representative arrangements. However, the political economy of Bonapartism is no return to the *status quo ante*. Indeed, the resources and power of the state are deployed to boost and direct economic activity – hence the idea of 'state capitalism' or, at least a more politically-directed framework of capitalist development – while maintaining the fundamentals of the capital-labour relationship and the reinforcement of the real subsumption of labour to capital.

The characterization of the Bonapartist type of state offers a way of making sense of the political and geopolitical responses to capitalist social crises involving far-right mobilizations 'from below'. Arguably, the Bonapartist model provides the *generic* prototype for a far-right form of political economy and state. Although the geopolitical context and social organization of capitalist development has changed significantly since the time when Marx drafted his comments on Bonapartism, his and subsequent Marxist writing – most notably on the character of the fascist state – pose the most useful questions for thinking about the political legitimacy of capitalism in contexts of social and political crises and stasis. Further, in connecting the Bonapartist state to the political particularities of the far-right, Bonapartism captures many of the ambiguities and contradictions in the far-right's relationship to both capital and the liberal and democratic features of the state, or the nature of political rule, administration, and legitimacy in a context of mass democracy.

In many respects, Bonapartism reflects a conjunctural moment emergent from profound crises that permits an extraordinary reconstitution of the internal mechanics and relations within the capitalist state. It also amounts to a reconfiguration of the social relations of capitalism and the relationship between the capitalist class and state elites that is mediated by mass or democratic/popular veneer provided by the far-right. It is this aspect of Bonapartism, specifically, that has a relevance for the far-right over the *longue durée* including explanations of the significance of the contemporary far-right in the politics of liberal democracies. Moreover, this does not need to be read or understood in functionalist terms; this is not about 'far-right dupes' for capital – the histories of the French Second Empire and the inter-war fascist regimes should be enough to demonstrate that. Instead, the contradictory dimensions within Bonapartism and the immanent possibilities within such state forms for outright fascism, as Thalheimer (1983a,1983b) and Trotsky (1975) recognized in their different ways, are also suggestive of the instabilities within it. This is evident with respect to the overcoming of the capitalist crisis out of which it originates and in facilitating a longer-term stability in its international and geopolitical arrangements that are associated with hegemony and the restoration of secure and stable forms of capital accumulation.

## 3 An Alternative Theoretical Framework – Capital, Race and Space

In this section I aim to build to on the critical commentary above to map out the main co-ordinates of an alternative theorization of the far-right that will frame and direct the more historically-focused discussion that follows in the subsequent chapters. As already indicated, I see the far-right as a constituent or pathology within the modern political condition associated with the twin transformations unleashed by a liberal-capitalist modernity which took a definitive shape in the latter part of the nineteenth century. In short, my perspective on the far-right conceptualizes it as a *longue durée* form of ideo-political agency and subjectivity shaping – if in spatially and temporally uneven ways – the political content and direction of modern political development (see Saull, et al., 2015).

The starting point for the structural conditions – socioeconomic, political, and geopolitical – that have come to characterize the *longue durée* – emerged in the middle of the nineteenth century and were given a conjunctural and concrete expression in the European Revolutions of 1848–9, which is the subject of the next chapter. Consequently, it is not only – as I will demonstrate in the following chapters – that the ideo-political character of far-right parties and movements bear high levels of similarity from this period up to the present day. It is also the case that the enabling conditions, or causes, are also replicated in recuring conjunctures of crises derived from the contradictory inter-connections between and reproduction of the same structural forces that gave birth to the far-right in the middle of the nineteenth century.

This temporal framing directly relates to the sociological analysis that I offer, which is particularly concerned with identifying and explaining the ways in which the shifting international and geopolitical arrangements through which the social relations of capitalism are organized and the associated politics that liberal order(s) are partly constituted by, define the politics of the far right. In emphasizing this, I am not granting an explanatory *primacy* to geopolitics or the 'international,' rather, I am calling attention not only to a neglected dimension within the theorization and ontology of the far-right, but also stressing how the workings – as well as contradictions and crises – of capitalist development are conditioned by the broader spatial and political context within which such developments occur and are *politically* mediated by. The theoretical framing that follows below is organized around four thematics: the spatial politics derived from uneven and combined capitalist development; the conditionalities of the international and geopolitics; the antinomies of liberalism and, finally, the master signifier of race in the ideology of the far-right.

### 3.1      *Uneven and Combined Development and the Pathologies of Capital*

In framing my theorization of the far-right over the *longue durée* I analytically privilege structural factors associated with capitalist transformation and development. This raises the question of the interaction and significance of the 'general' and 'particular' or the 'structural' and 'conjunctural' in the theorization of the far-right and how best to explain, conceptually, the developmental tendencies of capitalism across time and space and how and why such pathologies help foster far-right forms of politics. To address this, I draw on Trotsky's remarks on the 'uneven' and 'combined' character of capitalist development, as a way of providing a conceptual account of the long-term developmental processes within capitalism.

Trotsky's rather fragmented account of 'uneven and combined development' or UCD (see Trotsky, 1962, 2008; see also Knei-Paz 1978) has, over the last ten-to-twenty years, been taken up by several scholars working within the field of International Relations, led by Justin Rosenberg in particular (Rosenberg, 1996, 2006, 2010, 2016).[21] Much of this debate – which has focused on trying to offer an alternative systemic and materialist account of the international as an alternative to neorealism – does not concern me here (see Callinicos, 2007; Callinicos and Rosenberg, 2008). Rather, my engagement with UCD relates to how the key social characteristics and developmental tendencies within the historical social process of capitalist development usefully combines with a *longue durée* perspective in accounting for the enduring properties of the far-right across time and space. Further, the analysis offered here builds on a growing range of detailed conjunctural analyses that have deployed UCD as a way of emphasizing the explanatory significance of the structural or organic tendencies within capitalism whilst, at the same time, avoiding subsuming these tendencies within the historical and spatial specificities of the case under consideration (see, in particular, Allinson and Anievas 2010; Anievas, 2013, 2014; Davidson 2006, 2009; Green, 2012; Matin, 2007; Saull, 2015b). Let me unpack a framing of the far-right through UCD in  more detail. What do the two terms

---

21      See the following on-line list of sources in the disciplinary field of International Relations (IR) that have utilized and developed UCD as an analytical tool: https://unevenandcomb ineddevelopment.wordpress.com/.

'unevenness' and 'combined' refer to and how do they connect to thinking about and explaining the history and politics of the far-right?

I take uneven development to refer to two aspects, organic tendencies, or pathologies within capitalism. The first, which is not reducible to the epoch of capitalist modernity is the recognition of multiplicity or spatial plurality in the consideration of the history of human development. What this means is that because there has always existed more than one type of society, indeed a plurality across the earth, the developmental patterns (or rates of growth) of each of these societies will be different revealing development as both multilinear and uneven. This is a fundamental challenge to methodological internalism not only because of the analytical falsehood of singularity and separation but also because any study of the sociological or political dynamics of a particular or singular historical society is, necessarily, a study of its inter-societal dimensions (Rosenberg, 2006). Indeed, from this we can assume that the international was and is, to varying degrees, constitutive of the development of any one particular state-society complex and its division of labour.

What is of more interest is the second dimension which goes beyond the ontology of multiplicity and refers to the historical specificities of how unevenness is reproduced within capitalism. For Trotsky and subsequent UCD theorists capitalism has distinct socioeconomic *and* spatial properties that produce historically distinct political effects on those societies that are brought within its social orbit. Both Lenin (Lenin, 2010) and Trotsky's theorization of uneven development, then, provided a reformulation of Marx and Engels' earlier understanding; most famously outlined in the *Communist Manifesto* which suggested the universalizing and homogenizing consequences of the global expansion and productive consequences of capitalism. In Neil Smith's (2006, 2008) formulation, uneven capitalist development rests on how the fundamental accumulation drives of capitalism – the search for and the creation of (exchange) value conditions the organization of geographical space. Thus, at the same moment in time, capitalism creates value in some spaces through utilizing and exploiting the factors of production (and especially labour) to produce commodities to realize profit whilst, at the same time, neglecting or removing productive capacity (capital) from other geographical zones (Smith, 2006: 190). Further, in the ceaseless and relentless quest for value through the competition between capitalist firms there exists a propulsion or tendency towards the equalization of profit as firms respond to competition – revealed in the higher levels of profitability of other firms – through altering production relations and the labour process; a tendency that is never fully realized. The outcome of these developmental drives is a persistent and relentless production of unevenness – in the geographical distribution and concentration of capitalist economic activities and a consequential inequality as some areas, regions and states grow and develop through the localized and temporal concentrations of capital, whilst others do not. This is a *permanent and unresolvable* contradiction of capitalism that continually reproduces spatial tensions in its geopolitical organization pulling at the social and political fabric of capitalist nation-states (Harvey, 2006a, 2006b) upon which the far-right is nurtured and thrives.

However, the significance of uneven development goes beyond these spatial arrangements. What fundamentally defines these processes is that they are disruptive, dislocating and destabilizing for existing social and political structures and the ideological imaginaries associated with them. It is not just that the relationship between town and country is reconfigured or that between a metropolis and provinces, but that, in a world geopolitically organized around separate nation-state jurisdictions, it has significant geopolitical implications and especially in moments of crisis. Thus, what has characterized the history of capitalism as uneven development has been its *political and geopolitical consequences* with state-political authorities trying to manage this unevenness through a range of diplomatic, legal, administrative, and coercive mechanisms to ensure that the unevenness works to their political benefit or to minimise its deleterious political effects. Consequently, understanding capitalist development as uneven in material and spatial terms inevitably invokes geopolitical questions as to the competition rivalry and conflict in managing these processes and the political solutions offered to mitigate the crises that they produce and the possible conflicts inherent within them. Indeed, as Anievas and Nişancioğlu (2015: 45) stress, 'such relations of unevenness [create] structural competitive conditions between societies themselves – "the whip of external necessity".'

While capitalist development – understood as the competitive search for value and accumulation through the employment of the factors of production and the exploitation of wage labour – produces uneven and unequal forms of economic development, necessarily, it invokes a political and geopolitical framing of it because the (geo)political organization of space is directly implicated in these processes. Thus, capital does not penetrate into a political vacuum – a *tabula rasa* – but rather into a set of pre-existing social and political arrangements and geopolitical co-ordinates that are in place within the capital social relation in terms of a legal and geopolitical framework that allows and protects such processes; encapsulated in their representation as taking place within the 'private' or 'economic' spheres (see Teschke, 2003). It also means that although the political and geopolitical determinants of capitalist development are a part of capitalism, they are not reducible to it, and they are also subject to change. And this political-institutional or geopolitical autonomy is highly relevant to theorizing the far-right because these different institutional and geopolitical arrangements have variable consequences for producing the kinds of political contexts more favourable to the far-right.

What follows, inevitably, from the unevenness of capitalist development is the emergence, over time, of new forms of capitalist spatial relations – within and across nation-states – and, correspondingly, new forms of geopolitical hierarchy whereby the complexion, relations and rivalries between great powers are mediated via capitalist development. Indeed, it is the outcomes of capitalist development that, in effect, determine the arrangements of geopolitical order and the character of hegemony. This stems from the material and political benefits of development – of being first or being 'more advanced' and richer than other state-society complexes – and it is through such hierarchies that, in some cases, weaker, less developed societies may come to be dominated by the more advanced society, or at least some social or traditional social interests within it (e.g., landlords and peasants in particular). The distinct historical quality provided by the unevenness of capitalist development – and the geopolitical hierarchies that are a result of it – necessarily, then, mean that political questions and challenges emerge as to how state-society complexes need to be organized and mobilized to meet the competitive challenges enforced by the 'whip of external necessity'. This has been a key determinant of the far-right and has come in a number of ways: (I) as a defensive reaction against external competition/inequality reflected in calls for protection from external competition and a more aggressive form that seeks to geopolitically challenge the more advanced or dominant power through the invocation of nationalism in particular; and (II) internal political scapegoating or 'Othering' centred on targeting ethnic minorities and 'alien' political ideas that are depicted as 'disloyal' or allied to external foes.

This idea of unevenness also has an important temporal dimension. For Trotsky such temporal variation of multi-linearity reflected the uneven developmental trajectories and logics that existed at any one moment: reflected in the different 'stages' of development in comparing late nineteenth century Paris with Moscow and Moscow with the artic region of Russia etc. However, the work of Ernst Bloch (Bloch, 1977; see also Rabinbach, 1977) in particular offers a more developed consideration of temporal unevenness and its political consequences. Bloch sums up this temporal unevenness, what he terms as nonsynchronousity as,

> [n]ot all people exist in the same Now. They do so only externally, by virtue of the fact that they may all be seen today. But that does not mean that they are living at the same time with others.
> BLOCH 1977: 22

Further, he states,

> [people] carry earlier things with them, things which are intricately involved. One has one's times according to where one stands corporeally, above all in terms of classes. Times older than the present continue to effect older strata; here it is easy to return or dream one's way back to older times.
>
> BLOCH, 1977: 22

For Bloch uneven development realizes the incorporation or co-existence of pasts – based on myth, historical attachment, aesthetics etc – with the present, but in which such reproductions of the past are differentiated across different classes playing a more significant role in some classes than in others; Bloch singles out the peasantry in particular. And this also operates ideologically amongst individuals and groups in a way that is not reducible to the material or socioeconomic/class position of the people who may become attached to such ideological imaginaries. This provides an important and recurring political resource for the far-right because this reproduction of the past, or its ideological lingering, continues to exercise influence on political subjectivities, including those social layers who have no lived experience or connection to these pasts and when that past cannot be recreated.

Anson Rabinbach (1977) develops Bloch's comments on the non-synchronous character – which we can take to be as the temporal or historical unevenness of the present – of capitalism. For Rabinbach, Bloch introduces how, within capitalism there exists a 'real lack of historical continuity within and among classes' which produces a 'dissonance of "specific modes of being" ... [that results in] the *authentic* nonsynchronism of the peasantry and rural life' because the 'romanticized image ... is not purely mythological ... but corresponds to the actual conditions of life' but which also extends to other (urbanized) social strata in a less authentic manner given that it is further removed from their actual and lived material experience (Rabinbach, 1977: 6 emphasis added). Bloch contrasts the asynchronous romantic anti-capitalist imaginary of the past held by peasants and some urbanized social layers with the 'synchronism of modern life' as reflected in the 'authentic' class consciousness of the proletariat and the technocratic consciousness of capitalist elites. For the former the future is 'objectively obstructed,' while for the latter it appears as the utopian evolution of technical rationality (Rabinbach, 1977: 7).

Bloch put down these thoughts as a way of explaining fascism and also as a commentary on the failure of Comintern strategy to come to terms with the ideological and aesthetic appeal of fascism and how what he called the 'fragment[s] of an old and romantic antagonism [towards] capitalism,' were utilized and deployed by fascism to provide a source of (misplaced) hope for the future through appeals to a past.[22] While Bloch was concerned with the specificities of fascism and German National Socialism, the key components of his argument are applicable and relevant in helping to account for the conjunctural appeals of the far-right over the *longue durée* in contexts of crisis. Thus, although social development has moved on such that the peasantry no longer exists as such, the ideational and aesthetic asynchronousity that he refers to is reproduced and continues to shape political appeals. So, even though the peasantry has disappeared as a social class and material reality, the idea and myth of the peasant and peasant life and the rural and romanticized idyll of the past associated with it continues to act, ideologically, to shape political consciousness and subjectivities. Such reactionary ideas exist and effect politics as disembodied forms of politics because of the ideological reproduction of the past in the present. More generally, Bloch's insights in reformulating uneven development reveal the complex sedimentation of historical lived experience of different social layers within the same Now.

This brings us to the second component of UCD, 'combined development' or 'combination'. For Anievas and Nişancioğlu (2015: 48, my emphasis), in a general sense combined development refers,

> to the ways in which the internal relations of any given society are determined by their *interactive* relations with other developmentally differentiated societies, while the very interactivity of these relations produces amalgamated sociopolitical institutions, socio-economic systems, ideologies, and material practices melding the native and foreign, the 'advanced' and 'backward', within any given social formation.

Combination recognizes the legacies and vestiges of the non – (and anti) capitalist past within the concrete amalgam of any society – even those purportedly the most technologically or politically, advanced. As Neil Davidson (2012: 300) posits, '[t]he archaic and modern, the settled and disruptive, overlap, fuse, and

---

22  Bloch was clear about the illusory and fetishized elements of this 'hope' via an appeal to the past – he saw the Nazi idea of labour as amounting to 'a "refeudalization", to a Medievalism in which labor is handicraft, [sic] proletariat gives way to the workers' estate (Arbeiterrum), and work itself is raised to a moral dimension and spirit of rejuvenation that preceded the age of capital' (Rabinbach, 1977: 13).

merge in all aspects of the social formations concerned ... in entirely new and unstable ways.'

Following Justin Rosenberg (2006: 324–5) we can see the significance of combined development playing out in three distinct ways. First, in that the internal development of any one social formation must be understood and explained through the manner of its integration into a wider international/ inter-societal social field of interacting patterns of development. Thus, the internal development of all state-society complexes is, to varying degrees, conditioned by the outcomes of the developmental consequences of those other societies it has relations with. Secondly, is the 'interdependence' of 'structures of social, material and cultural life' whereby relationships based on trade, migration and cultural connections traverse borders and intrude into the interiors of societies thus forming a part of that interior fabric of social life to varying degrees. Finally, it is revealed in how any single social formation is constituted as a hybrid based on the amalgams of the past to the present, the internal with the external and the particular with the general.

Combination, then, provides an additional source; indeed, it is the *actual, historical, and concrete means* through which uneven development plays out and is realized as the inter-societal relations derived from multiplicity and the material and spatial effects of uneven capitalist accumulation and the resulting concentrations are realized, mitigated, responded, and reacted to (see Peck, 2019). And this is evidenced in the varied and particular institutional and ideational expressions of politics within any one particular geopolitical context derived from the precise articulations of combination within each national jurisdiction. Through this we can see how the structural or generalized logic of capitalist development that operates across all those jurisdictions absorbed into it – the structural or general logic of capital – ends up giving expression to *particular* and unique expressions of capitalist development. Thus, as Jeremy Green (2012: 351 emphasis in original) suggests, UCD enables us to account for the *interactivity of international development*. This interactivity is both *produced by* and *productive of* the intended and unintended effects of developmental strategies and their outcomes. Further, its account of social development and its political effects 'conceives of both the particular and universal elements of [Europe] ... without unduly subordinating one aspect to the other' (Green, 2012: 352).

Because development – in all historical (and contemporary cases) – takes place within a unique and local historically-determined present it also means that legacies of the past impinge on and come to shape the actuality and consequences of development. The ideological significance of the past in determining the politics of the present was well-captured by Trotsky as something that operated within the most advanced capitalist societies not just those undergoing a process of transition. Thus,

> [t]oday, not only in peasant homes but also in city skyscrapers, there lives alongside of the twentieth century the tenth or the thirteenth. A hundred million people use electricity and still believe in the magic power of signs and exorcisms. The Pope of Rome broadcasts over the radio about the miraculous transformation of water into wine. Movie stars go to mediums. Aviators who pilot miraculous mechanisms created by man's genius wear amulets on their sweaters. What inexhaustible reserves they possess of darkness, ignorance, and savagery!
>
> TROTSKY, 1975: 413

It is here, then, that the past – be it a social structure or institution and mythical representations of it – are reproduced and *act on* the present. Indeed, as we saw with regard to Ernst Bloch's understanding of fascism, such a mythical and romanticized representation of past provided a source – if misplaced and corrupted – of hope for the construction of the future that came to determine the precise combination of capitalist development within Germany. And, as we have seen in recent political events in Britain and the United States (as reflected in slogans such as 'taking back control' and 'make America great again') such pasts continue to provide an important means with which to mobilize people around a political platform to address what are perceived as the problems of the present and create an alternative future. However, it goes beyond this form of mediated or 'amalgam' of development to involve instabilities, dislocations, crises, and conflicts as the horizontal (spatial expansion) and vertical (intensification) character of capitalist development works to weaken and break up existing socioeconomic arrangements triggering resistance and conflict. While such tendencies are not, *a priori*, hostile, or problematic for capitalism; as we have seen, pre-existing ideologies and institutions rooted in ideational structures such as racism can be utilized to help consolidate capitalism as uneven and combined development.

Combination also brings to bear the role of agency through the 'contradictory co-existence' (Peck, 2019: 50) that it reveals and generates within social forms and in mediating and responding to the structural imperatives of capitalist growth and competition. It is here where the ideologies, cultures and institutions of the past can be utilized and grafted on to the present to, on the one hand, realize economic or technological transformation whilst, on the other, cementing existing political or geopolitical arrangements of dominance. However, as was revealed in the varied political trajectories of the

European great powers on the eve of World War One, the outcomes of UCD are relatively open and not pre-ordained. Combination reveals a varied historical process connected to how different state-society forms reproduce themselves from distinct historical positions that were at one time or another pre-capitalist and, at the same time, the role of political agency within and outside the state in mediating, channelling, and directing such processes of transformation or, in some cases, resisting it.

It is here where the far-right can be seen to play a significant role within the politics of uneven and combined development. Thus, as noted by Bloch, the ideo-political current of the far-right is *continually* reproduced within capitalism as a defining dimension of its combined character because there is a past to recover and which provides an ideological means to offset the dislocations of the present. This is revealed in a romanticized anti-capitalism rooted in a pre-capitalist past and an attachment to religious and cultural symbols and sensibilities at odds with the present. In more contemporary contexts where there is no lived experience of or a direct connection with a bucolic rural idyll, idealized pasts continue to be reproduced – some within direct living memory if one is referring to secure, well-paid employment and/or relative racial homogeneity within a particular region or country. Likewise, the fabric of the urban/built environment and the sense of place within particular locales in terms of bustling high streets or pride in a community. And it is these references to the past – that have an historical objectivity – that are mythologized by far-right ideo-political forces in particular to offer hope for the construction of an alternative future. Such reproductions of the past advantage the far-right over that of the radical left because the left is implicated in the causes of capitalist crises through the centrality of labour and workers' struggle in capitalist development and because its vision of a better future is a pure ideal; that is, it is an unlived and wholly new future rather than the concrete or historical myths associated with the past.

The far-right's presence or role within combined development indicates a significant agency and ideological component in shaping the character of capitalist societies. In particular, it refers to a value system, a sense of belonging rooted in place, culture and race that provides an important form of moral economy and solidarity that tends to be particularly pronounced in moments of crisis and especially – as we shall see below – when the international/cosmopolitan dimensions of capitalist development are brought into view. Far-right ideo-political currents are, then, a *permanent* reservoir of recreated ideals, values and myths that problematize the onward 'progress' of capitalism reflecting the non-and-anti-capitalist pasts that capitalism emerged from and an important ideo-political means of exit from periods of crisis. And for Bloch these remnants, which he saw embodied in fascism, were not dangerous to capitalism,

> on the contrary, capital uses that which is nonsynchronously contrary, if not indeed disparate, as a distraction from its own strictly present-day contradictions: it uses the antagonism of a still living past as a means of separation and struggle against the future that is dialectically giving birth to itself in the capitalist antagonisms.
>
> BLOCH, 1977: 29, 32

### 3.2    *The International-Geopolitical Determinants of the Far-Right*

In much of what I have outlined so far, I have implicitly highlighted the importance of international factors and the structure, organizational and institutional dimensions of the international system in particular for thinking about and explaining how and why far-right forms of politics emerge, develop, and become politically significant. In stressing the significance of the international I have also tried to highlight the difference between context and conditioning from what actually *causes* the far-right. If then, we are to take UCD seriously it means that we have to recognize both the possibilities and empirical realities of unevenness with respect to the far-right in terms of both time and space. Thus, within the same historical moment – the late nineteenth century or the inter-war period – and within the same international context – new/social imperialism or inter-war hegemonic crisis – the inevitability of far-right outcomes is not pre-determined or universal; how else to explain the relatively marginal impact of fascism within some capitalist states and, at the same time its strength in others? However, in recognizing the local and national particularities of combined development that produce different political outcomes does not mean that we should discount or underestimate the way in which the evolving structure and political-institutional organization of the international system relates to the workings of UCD and the possibilities and openings for the far-right. In a word, some kinds of international order are more favourable to the far-right than others are.

In what ways, then, can the analytical and methodological vantage point of the international help us explain the nature of the far-right?[23] There are two ways in which we can see the international as *constitutive* of the far-right that, consequently, make an analysis of it through an *international* historical

---

23    Much of the following few paragraphs draws on Saull et al., (2015: 13–14).

sociology, essential. The first is through the ways in which far-right move-ments – in their rhetoric, propaganda, and programmatic positions – fixate on the international as the 'spectre' and source of fear, hostility, *and* opportu-nity. The international tends to be understood as consisting of those ethnic/ racial, ideological, geopolitical, and cultural forces deemed 'outside', 'separate' or 'inferior' to the 'people' or '*volk*' – which is assumed to be co-terminus with the geopolitical boundaries of the *nation*-state. The international is identified, then, as the primary reference or source of causation for the ills, fears, and insecurities that the far-right centres on and which it reduces domestic social and political problems to.

Unlike any other political current, the far-right tends to *internalize* the international as a permanent and existential threat to the spatial and racial integrity of 'the homeland'. This produces a political discourse that is secu-ritized with the international framed as the basis of threat and disorder and, consequently, results in the promotion of borders and exclusions as the means to address such threats. Thus, borders provide the spatial bulwarks protecting the homeland from a variety of (racialized) threats and exclusions thus ensur-ing the unity and cultural homogeneity of the homeland based on preventing or expunging cosmopolitan legal norms associated with international organ-izations, universalist ideologies, and transnational civil society organizations that are seen as promoters of social and cultural pluralism (Anievas and Saull, 2022: 6).

This spectre and the political and cultural imaginaries associated with it provide a permanent ideological reservoir for the far-right that sustains its propaganda and political mobilizations, and this can play out in contexts of international peace, geopolitical stability, and co-operation, as much as it does in contexts defined by geopolitical rivalry and aggression. Accordingly, attempts at international co-operation through the development of formalized legal and institutional structures can be ideologically constructed as a funda-mental threat to the homeland as much as the build-up to war. Indeed, it is the spectre of war and existential threat from outside that provides the permanent imaginary within which far-right discourse is located even if the actual political-geopolitical context reflects quite the opposite. This is obviously con-nected to the way in which spatial and racial tropes and discourse is so central to the far-right even if such framings may also constitute the language of other political currents. Thus, the uneven spatial dynamics of global capitalism and the shifting interactive nature of the authority and power of nation-states as constitutive of modern politics provides the far-right with a political imaginary that can always locate the spatial and racial properties of the international as a source of threat and insecurity. Thus, it is not just the material effects or geopolitical structure that determines the significance of the international for the far-right but how an ideological arsenal associated with the *imaginary* of the international provides the content for far-right discourse more than any other ideo-political current.

In Schmittian terms, it is the political basis for the friend/enemy distinction (Schmitt, 2007) and, consequently, the grounds for identifying the nature of sovereign power and the ethnos of which sovereign power is oriented towards protecting and promoting. Thus, while the politics of the far-right racializes or ethnicizes the world, it does this through projecting and sourcing local and domestic problems onto the international plane. In other words, far-right ideology internalizes the existing socioeconomic and geopolitical properties of the international *into* domestic politics thereby necessitating and demanding a reconstitution of the domestic-international relationship as the means to resolve the difficulties identified; be it through population expulsion, immigration controls, territorial annexation, disengagement from international cooperation, trade protectionism and/or what a contemporary writer has called 'welfare nativism' (Mudde, 2007: 132). In this way it is possible to see the far-right as constituted by the international,

> in that its localized articulations are always and necessarily products of the way in which the generalized properties of the international – at any given time – reveal themselves in the structuring and playing out of socio-economic and political relations within particularities of nation-states.
>
> ANIEVAS and SAULL, 2022: 5–6

Although all political currents – to varying degrees – refer to the international within their propaganda and programmes, it is the far-right that focuses a unique kind of attention towards the world outside the nation-state community. Accordingly, it is the structures, forces and processes associated with the international that are regarded as innately and pathologically inimical to the interests of 'the people' as articulated by the far-right and which results in the securitization of political discourse.

The second way in which the international can be regarded as constitutive of the politics of the far-right is in the methodological sense of how we study this type of politics. Simply put, any study of a far-right movement located within a particular national locale needs to recognize and explain how the domestic political spaces within which it operates provides both opportunities and openings based on how the international comes to constitute the material and ideological fabric of domestic political life. It is the evolving and historically distinct character and configuration of the international and, in

particular, the moments of internationally-derived transformations and crises associated with uneven capitalist development that explains the *general*
appearance and political momentum of the far-right at *particular* historical
conjunctures. Consequently, each temporally specific manifestation of a far-
right politics – be it the era of the new imperialism, the inter-war era or the
contemporary neoliberal epoch – is a *particular* expression of the *generalized*
properties of the international system at that particular time. Each expression
of far-right – in time and space – rests on this *interactive* relationship between
the international and domestic, where the politics of the latter are embedded
with and constituted by the structure and workings of the international system
in terms of the patterns and relations of capital accumulation and its geopolitical and institutional organization and governance. That these expressions are
variable rather than uniform – in strength and content – reflects the uneven
spatial properties of the international and it is the specific form of intercon-
nection between each locale and the international that determines the extent
to which each national far-right is enabled. And it is in moments of general or
international crisis – playing out across multiple jurisdictions as in the inter-
war era and post-2007–8 – where a *generalized pattern* of far-right revival is
visible.

The precise form of interactivity or connection between the 'domestic' and
the 'international' will vary within the same temporal moment as revealed in
the different possibilities for the advance of fascism within the leading capitalist states during the Great Depression of the early 1930s and, more broadly,
as the structure and relations that characterise the international system evolve
and change. We can see this in the case of explaining the rise of Nazism. Thus,
as Alexander Anievas (Anievas, 2014; see also Eley, 1983; Green, 2012; Saull,
2015b) has outlined, the domestic social, economic and political conditions
that enabled Nazism were a product of the way in which Germany's internal
development was shaped by its interaction with a *multiplicity* of unevenly
developing societies and it was this that contributed to the particularly inten-
sive and dislocating character of its capitalist-industrial development and the
singular impact of the global economic crisis on it. Therefore, the analytical
optic for explaining the rise of Nazism requires a perspective centred on the
international dimensions of Germany's internal social development[24] thus
situating its 'peculiarities' as one developmental trajectory among the many

---

24    Contrary to the Bielefeld school of German historiography (see Fischer, 1967; Wehler, 1985)
      that explains Nazism as deriving from Germany's singular and autochthonous domestic
      properties, the so-called 'Sonderweg' (or special path) that underplays the causal drivers
      derived from the inter-societal dimensions of German state formation.

variegated patterns of uneven and combined development characteristic of the conjuncture as a whole. Such a framing is based on a recognition of how Germany's internal development was inextricably conditioned by both the decisions and relative power of the other great powers – and Britain and the United States in particular – and how the social, ideological, and political fabric of the German interior was constituted by the international; be it economic investment, imports, capital flows, cultural symbols, literature, migrants, and 'alien' political ideologies such as socialism.

Approaching the far-right from this ontological perspective provides a framework for explaining and theorizing those moments when the far-right has been ascendant across a range of national locales because of the infusion or combination of the international – in its various features – in the domestic social and political fabric of states thus diluting, though not expunging, the singular *differentia specifica* we find when comparing different states. This also relates to the state given that the international – above all through the hierarchies associated with imperialism – can provide significant material and ideological resources for the reproduction of particular domestic socioeconomic and political orders conducive to the far-right.[25] The key, then, to unlocking those conjunctural moments of the far-right – of its relative quiescence and strength – is provided by an internationally-centred explanation of these movements.

What then is the relationship between capitalist development and the international political/geopolitical context that it takes place within? We have already discussed the particular – uneven and combined – pathologies of capitalist accumulation, which serves to particularize the generic properties or logic of capital revealed in its quest for its self-valorisation across territorial space based on the exploitation of wage labour. However, because this emerges and expands historically across international space we need to factor this into our account of the connections between the far-right and capital. In recognizing the essentially unequal and, thus, hierarchical features of capitalist development we necessarily invoke the politicized, competitive, and conflictual histories in the geographical spread of capitalism. This is because this history reveals how the spread of capitalism into the interiors of non-capitalist

---

25    In the sense that imperial structures – and especially those which are premised on the direct connection between geopolitical aggrandisement and material accumulation – are the basis of power for a ruling class such that the coercive machinery of the capitalist state is *directly* implicated in the reproduction of a ruling class. And, further, whereby such forms of political economy are promoted via populist far-right mobilizations of subaltern social layers (see Arendt, 1968).

spaces via economic or geopolitical pressures from without – what Trotsky referred to as the 'whip of external necessity' (Trotsky, 2008: 25) – highlights the material and productive superiority of one state or group of states over others. Consequently, this means that this leading state or hegemon will, in all likelihood, determine the geopolitical character of capitalist development and thus the spatial forms, constraints and opportunities within which the development of other (capitalist) states takes place within.

Viewed historically,[26] the actual socioeconomic process of capitalist development in Europe and elsewhere has, therefore, been *primarily* about how international or global structural socioeconomic forces organised around the capital social relation have permeated, de-stabilised and transformed the socioeconomic and political interiors of non-capitalist or developing capitalist states (Gourevitch, 1978; Hobsbawm, 1987; Rosenberg, 2006; Selwyn, 2011). A key driver of this was obviously imperialism – the forceful and coercive opening up of spaces and their reconfiguration and subordinate insertion into the developing world market – but it also concerned the policy responses to 'external competition and threat' by political and socioeconomic elites within other nation-states through programmes of state-promoted reform and modernisation (Green, 2012; Kemp, 1985; Selwyn, 2011; Skocpol, 1979; Trimberger, 1978). This latter case tended to characterise most of the European experience through the nineteenth century in response to the rise of industrial capitalism in Britain and beyond. The long and the short of this is that the reality of the encroachment of capitalism within different national locales – and its destabilising and destructive power – has always had a *foreign* or cosmopolitan dimension.

This is highly significant to the study of the far-right for two reasons: (1) that national economies have become integrated into a capitalist world market from an initial position of subordination to pre-existing structures of international capitalist power concentrated in one or more great powers, such that successful economic development has tended to require geopolitical facilitation – *contra* contemporary neoliberal myth-making – upon which far-right movements have played an important political role in alliance with ruling classes (Green, 2012; Hefferman, 1997; Kemp, 1985; Kennedy, 1980; Kennedy and Nicholls, 1981; Lebovics, 1988; Mayer, 1971; Semmel, 1960; Wehler, 1985); and (11) that, in consequence, the permeation and consolidation of capitalist social relations within the interiors of developing capitalist states has been regarded not as a purely economic phenomenon associated with value, economic

---

26    This and the next few paragraphs draw on Saull (2015b: 622).

growth and the reconstitution of society to best realise economic development, *qua* liberalism, but, rather as a 'foreign invasion' – at least for significant
sections of the populace – to overturn a 'natural' and 'organic socioeconomic
order'. And this is a recurring phenomenon given the enduring uneven and
combined character of capitalist development.

However, the international and geopolitical matrix within which state-
society complexes were originally inserted and integrated into capitalist development is not fixed. Indeed, the contradictions, crises and two world wars that
developed out of these contradictory and conflict-ridden international and
geopolitical dynamics resulted in a reconfiguration of the international order
and, in particular, after 1945, the partial decoupling of capitalist development –
even if it remained uneven and combined – from geopolitically-determined
circuits of accumulation and especially in the core geographical circuits of
global capitalism. Such a development – material, political and geopolitical in
equal measure –is suggestive of a fundamental break in the geopolitical organization of world capitalism from the 1870–1945 era and the historically distinct
workings of UCD within it, consequently altered the enabling conditions of
the far-right.

The political-institutional dimensions of capitalist development at the
international level also play an important role in conditioning the socioeconomic and ideo-political complexion of state forms. Simply put, imperial forms
of state premised on a political economy based on exclusive and expanding
geopolitical divisions – what some have described as 'territorial accumulation'
(see Teschke, 2003) – have tended to be constituted, at least to some degree,
by a far-right social constituency and a political orientation towards extreme
forms of nationalism and racism (Gourevitch, 1988). What follows from this
is that the international can be considered as determining for the internal
political, ideological, and cultural characteristics of states and the dominant
social and cultural forces within them, which helps to reinforce and reproduce
such an international arrangement. Domestic social forces and their political
allies within the state, therefore, not only emerge and evolve within a distinct
international milieu but such an environment may also provide *structural*
opportunities and advantages for the cultivation and promotion of such socioeconomic and political interests, particularly if such an international context
can be politically articulated via a narrative of threat and injustice. In such
circumstances, the international system provides a structural prop for specific
domestic social and political groupings over others, particularly through the
way in which such social forces are reproduced via specifically geopolitically-
determined socioeconomic arrangements.

### 3.3    *The Contradictions of Liberalism and Liberal Orders*

Thinking about a distinct political identity such as the far-right, necessarily, raises the question of the relationship between said ideo-political current and other, opposing ones. As already suggested – in the earlier discussion of existing scholarly treatments of the far-right – much of the definitional framing of the far-right has been centred on an assumed ideological antagonism towards liberalism, as if the far-right is the latter's nemesis and binary opposite. There is, obviously, much to be said in recognizing such an opposition and accounting for what drives such an enmity. Politically, some of the key moments in modern European history have been about this division from the destruction of liberal democracy in Germany with the dismantling of the Weimar Republic to the line-up of some of the main belligerents involved in World War Two pitting the liberal democracies of Britain, France and the United States against the fascist powers.

However, the ideo-political antagonism between the far-right and liberalism is more complex and politically ambiguous than many scholarly accounts sufficiently recognize (see Woodley, 2010: 1–3), even if there are sound reasons for clearly differentiating one from the other.[27] Liberalism's political ontology rooted in the 'sovereign' and 'abstract' individual, its ambivalence towards fixed territorial orders and the establishment of binding agreements and rules on international conduct, its commitment to universalism and human equality – if formal rather than substantive – its defence of representative rather than popular democracy, its commitment towards the limited constitutional state based on the rule of law, its assumption of progress based on material enrichment and its promotion of the spatial expansion of market exchange are demonstrative of an opposition and antagonism between it and the core features that tend to define the far-right. Yet, notwithstanding such oppositions, the workings of liberal democracy and the positions taken by liberal – not just conservative – political forces have shown themselves to be willing, if momentarily, to embrace the politics of the far-right since the mid-nineteenth century (see Saull, 2015a, 2015b).

Thus, although it is clear that there are theoretical and ideological positions that differentiate liberalism from the far-right and that, in many respects, these can be seen as mutually-oppositional within the political-institutional context of a historically evolving liberal democracy, the relationship between these two distinct sets of political forces and practices is more complex and,

---

27    Something that some contemporary critics (see Mishra, 2017; Mondon and Winter, 2020) of contemporary liberalism – as ideational schema or practical institutional framework – largely fail to do.

in some cases, *inter-twined*, than an insistence on their ideational and nominal oppositions would suggest. If this is the case, then we might argue that both liberalism and the far-right have operated in a more ambivalent manner, and especially in the case of the former's relations with the latter within contexts of crises in the reproduction of liberal *social* orders.

In the historical account that follows in subsequent chapters we will see how these two sets of ideo-political forces have interacted with each other in the history of the development of liberal democratic forms of state and politics and the political economy of capitalism. And while this history is both spatially and temporally uneven, we can identify the period from the middle of the nineteenth century as the moment when both the institutional arrangements and ideo-normative framing of politics have, or, were increasingly connected to both an institutional and practical reality and ideational imaginary centred on liberal democracy. If this is so, then it is clear that both liberalism and the far-right have been constitutive of liberal democracy across European nation-states and that the substantive character of liberal democratic politics has been influenced and conditioned by other ideo-political (including socialism) currents and practices, not just liberalism.

Thus, the actual politics of liberal democracies involves an amalgam of ideological forms and political currents, which means that those parties competing for political office and contributing to the political culture are not necessarily 'liberal' (or democratic) and this obviously conditions the specificities and content of one or other liberal democracy from another and, also, its direction and precise ideo-political content at any one time. The shock of Trump's election and his manner of governing – the trampling of constitutional norms and the racist and authoritarian rhetoric and practices that defined the Trump presidency – is but one recent exemplar of such possibilities. It is also the case that though far-right forces may be part of the permanent political fabric of liberal democracies, including sometimes gaining access to state power, such issues only tend to matter for the actual structures and the workings of the institutions of liberal democracies in those specific or extreme cases when the basic and fundamental conditions and institutional processes of liberal democracy have been terminated, as in the cases of fascism. As demonstrated by the Trump presidency and the current political system in Hungary associated with the regime of Viktor Orbán, there is a grey area when the authoritarian dimensions of the state, or when the content and discourse of politics is infused with illiberal, populist and racist invective, that undermines the *liberal* character of liberal democracies that not only serves to blur the boundaries between liberal democracy and illiberal or authoritarian forms of politics, but also raises the possibility of a qualitatively different form of political system emerging in place of *liberal* democracy (see Cooper, 2021).

The central point here[28] is that while the politics of liberal democracies reveal the interconnections between far-right and liberal socio-political forces over some key areas of public policy, it is also the case that because these two ideo-political positions are in many respects antagonistic towards each other, such *connections are unstable and contradictory*. So, even if we might accept that liberalism or, to be more accurate, the policies and decisions of some liberal political actors and forces have been, in some respects, 'responsible' for and have, historically, benefited from the mobilizations and advances of the far-right, this is not the same as asserting that the far-right is a supplicant of dominant class interests or political elites, or that the politics of the far-right is *functional* to the reproduction of liberal (international) orders.[29]

Thus, in the two historical cases where liberal international orders collapsed – with the moves towards nationalist protectionism and intensified geopolitical rivalry that preceded the outbreaks of the two world wars – far-right forces were central if not determining in producing such breakdowns. In these cases, then, the far-right was, ultimately destructive of the existing liberal *political-institutional* order at the domestic and international levels. And although the two renderings of far-right state forms that played out in the two world wars helped preserve the fundamentals of the *capitalist* order anchored in the sanctity of private property rights (see Bel, 2010, 2011; Tooze, 2007) they did so on the basis of the destruction of the liberal-democratic political and institutional frameworks associated with them. Such developments expose the contradictory dimensions and inter-connections between the theorization of, and the actual evolving historical political and geopolitical relationships between the political and economic within liberalism. So, while liberalism – as a theoretical framework and politics – cannot be solely defined by one or other, as its political *and* economic dimensions are co-constitutive in this respect, the differentiation between them and the tensions and contradictions in their inter-relationship permit and *promote* openings for the far-right. Further, this relationship – between the political and the economic within liberalism – also tends to be uneven and unstable as evident in that the economic crises that propel the advance of far-right movements and parties as a consequence of

---

28    The discussion that follows here draws on Saull, (2018: 591–3).

29    This, I hope, addresses any suggestion that my argument is either 'functionalist' in the sense that what I set out below could be read as the 'primary role of the far-right is to act as an agent of liberalism to rescue it from the revolutionary left', or that it conflates these two distinct ideo-political orientations.

capitalist development, can result in a radical reconstitution of the political as evidenced in the fascist experience and, more broadly the proliferation of right-wing dictatorships during the Cold War. Such instances of economic crisis in the reproduction of liberal orders have – through forms of far-right agency – resulted not in the reconfiguration of the economic sphere but, rather, a restructuring of the political and geopolitical spheres as the means to secure the fundaments of the economic.

The ideological positions and political currents of liberalism and the far-right have been a common feature of emerging liberal democracies since the nineteenth century. These positions are distinct resting on different political and ideological sources and modes of politics as evidenced in their differences over 'free trade', citizenship rights, the relationship between the individual and the community, borders and the spatial limits of market exchange and the idea of progress. Consequently, the far-right has been, and is, an enduring critic of liberalism and the 'liberal project' and liberals – thinkers and political parties – have consistently articulated political positions in opposition to the far-right. The most fundamental difference is an ontological one regarding the nature and boundaries of the social and political community. Thus, whereas the liberal position tends to be based on the universal individual rooted in an assumption of equality, the far-right one, is framed around the idea of an organic national community and associated limits on the rights and freedoms accorded to any individual, which is also framed around a 'natural inequality' between men and women and between different ethnic groups.

From this, we can extrapolate a further set of distinctions framing the politics of each. For the far-right, that cultural and racial difference is both organized through separate and organic national communities *qua* states that connect to political arrangements that are both hierarchical and where – for the European far-right – European/white nations are regarded as superior/atop of this hierarchy (see Balibar, 1991, 1999). This contrasts with a liberal position that subsumes the normative privileging of the historical nation-state according to its institutionalization of a set of liberal-universalist principles founded on individual rights and where political or moral supremacy is derived not from – at least explicitly – a cultural or racial particularity, but rather, to the degree to which any existing polity conforms to these normative principles that are, nominally, acultural and aracial.

In relation to political-economy, liberals tend to be flexible as to the political-institutional and spatial arrangements that facilitate economic development, in contrast to the far-right which inclines to prioritise racial homogeneity and socio-cultural cohesion grounded on relatively fixed conceptions of spatial order based on the nation-state. And although both regard private property as natural and sacrosanct, the far-right tends to advocate limits on the exercise of these rights according to nationality/ethnicity. This also relates to the operation of labour markets and the wider limits to the efficient allocation of the factors of production that invoke geopolitical imaginaries and zero-sum assumptions in trade relations and the costs of labour. Consequently, even in the cases of fascism the dismantling of the international-spatial arrangements of liberal order did not amount to a categorical break with liberalism *tout court*.

However, in spite of these differences, the political reality of actually existing liberalism as a political discourse and practice has been more complex, reflecting the inter-connections and correspondence between these two ideo-political imaginaries in the actual political practices of liberal democracies. Thus, in some moments – limited though they may be – these two opposing ideo-political currents have 'embraced' or come together; in effect, dissolving some of the key differences between them. In some respects, we can understand or even explain this inter-connection through differentiating the political and economic dimensions of liberal thought and practice and the *organic tensions* within liberalism itself that, arguably, are not resolvable from within the intellectual resources nor political-institutional frameworks associated with it.

Indeed, since the mid-nineteenth century, as the following chapters will demonstrate, it is possible to identify a pattern in terms of how such contradictions within liberal orders – between its political/democratic and economic/private property and domestic/international dimensions – have been resolved. This is revealed in the suspension or termination of the democratic political form which is specifically targeted at the weakening or destruction of the social power of organized labour and the institutions of working-class democracy – in many cases endorsed by either domestic and/or international liberal social and political forces – as the means through which to secure the economic bases of liberal order. Or, looked at another way, the securing of capitalism through the suspension of liberal *democracy*.[30] Further, in such cases the far-right has been the primary social base and political organization involved in such assaults on democracy, which suggests that the far-right has been a *necessary* political agent in securing economic liberalism anchored in private property rights.

---

30   As endorsed, publicly, by the leading neoliberal thinkers, Friedrich Hayek and Milton Friedman, in their support for the military dictatorship of Augusto Pinochet in Chile after the September 1973 *coup d'état* (Fischer, 2009; Slobidian, 2018) and as evidenced in the numerous covert and overt interventions against democratic forces committed to radical socioeconomic change by the main liberal powers during the Cold War (Saull, 2007, 2010).

This shared orientation as regards the workings of the liberal or capitalist economy contrasts with what appears to be a clearer distinction as to the understanding of what politics is, and the scope of its operations across the two ideo-political positions. Thus, in the case of liberalism there is a long-standing ambivalence and, in some cases, fear of democratic forms of politics and governance through an aversion to 'mass' or 'populist' politics. Such sentiments – originally articulated in the works of John Stuart Mill (2010) and Alexis de Tocqueville (2009) and more recent neo/liberal thinkers (see Kiely, 2017; Landa, 2012, 2018; Mullholland, 2012) provide the basis for the liberal account and critique of fascism, which is understood as a form of 'mob-rule', premised on the demagogic manipulations of the masses leading to dictatorship.[31]

This is an important distinction that separates a liberal from a far-right understanding of politics and the ideal-typical forms or methods of politics that we might associate with each. And such distinctions bring out a fundamental difference between the two as highlighted in what are seen as far-right-inspired tyrannies trampling on the rights of individuals and the protections afforded to minorities; arguably what are existential challenges to liberalism. However, as the historical development of liberal democratic societies seems to demonstrate, this distinction or opposition, has, at certain moments, broken down. Further, the actual operation and development of liberal democratic societies has exposed shortcomings in both the intellectual arguments and justifications derived from liberal political thought for the maintenance of liberal political order, and the historical and concrete institutional forms that actually existing liberalism has taken on.

We might regard this reconfiguration of the political – the (temporary) suspension of liberal-constitutional order – as the *temporal requirement* for ensuring the social order of private property, as exposing the liberal fiction regarding both the separation of powers and the democratic basis of and limits to state power (see Saull, 2015a, 2015d; Tomba, 2013). Such a fiction equally applies to the economic sphere in the ideological nostrums of the 'free market' and the 'natural tendency of markets towards equilibrium'. As the history of liberal political economy evidences, in periods of crisis the deceit of market self-adjustment quickly dissolves as the necessity of state intervention to resolve the crisis ensues. The significance of this for our concerns here is that such scenarios expose the core or organic features of liberal political economy to the necessity of external political resolution, which provides a permanent

---

31   The classical account of this – from a Republican theoretical perspective – is that of Hannah Arendt (1968) but also appears in more recent liberal commentary on populism (see Müller, 2017).

structural possibility for the far-right and, particularly, in contexts where the threat from the radical left appears strong. In short, liberal forms of political economy or social rule have, in key moments required rescue from without by the forces of the far-right.[32] This reveals an important dimension to both liberal political thought and practice and the actual operation of liberal democratic states in the shifting relationship between the spheres of economy (or market) and politics (or state). Further, it relates to who are recognized as *legitimate* or acceptable political subjects within liberal political orders that has a significant effect on the substantive workings of liberal democracy and where the mass or populist potential of the far-right has revealed itself throughout the histories of different liberal democracies.

The far-right operates as both oppositional current challenging and, when successful, displacing the left as a form of populist anti-capitalism – fascism being the exemplary though not the only case – and, at the same time, the political and popular means to overcoming crises on the basis of upholding capitalist social property relations. As first recognized by Marx in the *Eighteenth Brumaire* (Marx, 1934; see also Saull, 2015a) the mass and subaltern dimensions of the far-right – what distinguish it from the conservative or mainstream right – have provided the mass social base for the 'Party of Order' in the service of capital in moments of crisis, if not directed by it. It is these properties of the far-right as both antagonist *and* saviour that define it and provide it with its ideological ambivalence and political dexterity. That this comes at a price for liberalism and liberal democracy – in its domestic political-institutional properties as much as in its geopolitical arrangements – is enough to demonstrate that the far-right's subaltern and oppositional features should not be overlooked. Yet, because its opposition is both partial and rests on a degree of 'liberal embrace' its radical and subaltern features always tend to be moderated or displaced by its fixation with the racial and spatial dimensions of capitalism and liberal order.

---

32    The era of the Cold War after 1945 reflected such a connection at a global level where the upholding of a globalized regime of postcolonial private property rights and capitalist markets involved fascist legacies playing out in the liberal heartlands and beyond as a form of 'counter-revolutionary reserve army' employed – if not always directly controlled – against the forces of the left (social democratic as much as communist) and the perceived threat that they posed to capitalist social property relations from the (potential) outcomes of the workings of democratic processes. Consequently, viewed from this perspective, the far-right was an important, indeed, a constitutive, element within the broader 'liberal historical bloc' that waged the Cold War (see Anievas, and Saull. 2020 and forthcoming).

It is here where the coercive underside of the liberal democratic state is revealed, in its para-political dimensions (see Bale, 2017; Seymour, 2016; Wilson, 2009, 2012). Para-politics refers to 'the relationships between the public state and the political processes and arrangements operating outside and beyond conventional politics' (Wilson 2012: 3). And it draws our attention towards the political outcomes emergent from the relationships between the coercive apparatuses of the liberal state and those elements located within civil society – reflected in the ideo-political forces of the far-right – that are the most ideologically pre-disposed towards securitization and order. The para-political dimension of the liberal state is rarely commented upon in the existing literature on the far-right but it reflects not only the coercive or 'emergency properties' of the liberal state constituted in legislation such as Britain's Defence of the Realm Act of 1914 or the US Patriot Act of 2001, but also an aspect of liberal political orders that privilege the ideo-political forces of the far-right who may be co-opted to assist the state in the defence of private property rights and social order in moments of constitutional emergency or 'national security threat'.

The two fascist episodes in Italy and Germany revealed the role of para-politics in the periods before each fascist movement formally took over the state through the way in which the coercive apparatuses not only turned a blind eye to fascist violence against the mobilizations of the left, but also facilitated and encouraged fascist violence. Such proclivities also played out in the anti-communist liberalism of the Cold War under the aegis of US hegemony (Anievas and Saull, 2020, forthcoming) that – as we shall see in Volume 2 – extended to significant political connections between far-right terrorists such as the *Organisation armée secrète* (OAS) in France and *Ordine Nuevo* and *Avanguardia Nazionale* in Italy and elements within the state targeting the political left. Para-politics, then, highlights a sphere and form of conjuncturally produced political relations within the workings of liberal democracies that is not reducible to either state or civil society. Occupying an intermediate zone the para-political moment transfers, legitimizes and empowers far-right forces outside of the state into agents of the 'emergency state' and, in doing so, exposes the fundamental and deeply-internalized contradiction in liberalism's political-economic co-constitution.

More fundamentally, what the para-politics[33] of the liberal state reveals, then, is a structurally inscribed 'strategic selectivity' of the liberal state as 'a system whose structure and *modus operandi* are more open to some types

---

33   This and the following couple of paragraphs draw on Anievas and Saull (2020: passim).

of political strategy than others ... because of the modes of intervention and
resources which characterize that system' (Jessop, 1990: 260). Consequently,
the institutions of the state and especially its coercive apparatuses should be
seen as sites of strategic action, conditioned from within and without. Further,
such arrangements reflect a hierarchy of social forces within the state associated with different class fractions in relation to the hierarchical relations
of force and consent. And this means that the institutions and apparatuses
of the liberal-capitalist state come to display specific ideo-political biases
towards some ideo-political tendencies and strategies over others (Poulantzas,
1978: 125–6, 137, 140–5). And it is through such arrangements that what might
be termed 'authoritarian enclaves' of or for the far-right within the liberal state
are constituted.

Para-politics reveals the liberal fiction as to how the relationship between
the political and economic is co-constitutive of liberal order and *mutually reinforcing*. As the history of the emergence and evolution of the liberal international order has demonstrated over the *longue durée*, the relationship between
the political and economic has been far from mutually stabilizing. Thus, with
respect to the workings of international market exchange the history of capitalist development has been punctuated by moments of intense socioeconomic crisis where the maintenance of a private-property based-system – the
economic *sine qua non* of liberal order – has required external state and geopolitical intervention to secure it. It has been in these moments where the forces
of the far-right have come to take on a greater political significance, not only
in the sense of providing a political response to international economic crises
that helps secure the fundaments of private property and market exchange,
but also through providing an important ideo-political legitimation and
source of solidarity in suturing the social wounds and ideological dislocations
created by such crises. This is not to suggest that all liberals were accomplices
to fascism, but rather to highlight the contradictory – rather than the mutually
stabilizing and beneficial – possibilities contained within liberal democracy
produced from the interplay between its two constituent parts: the political
and the economic.

Indeed, it is the destabilizing geosocial consequences of the uneven and
combined character of capitalism as the actually existing form of liberal
political economy that helps shape the ideo-political conditions for liberal
international order construction. Thus, the concrete forms of uneven development undermine liberal assumptions about the complementarity of politics
and economics. Capitalism expands, spatially, and reproduces itself within
geographic locales – at the sub-state level as much as the state – defined
by the presence of significant social, ideological and political conditions

antithetical to the establishment and maintenance of liberal political order that serves to question and problematise the universalising pretensions of liberalism based on individual freedom, constitutional order and representative government, as complimentary to the workings of capitalist economy.

What flows from this is that the amalgam of combined development of which the ideo-political forces of the far-right are but one defining element are constitutive of liberal political order. Emerging within the globalizing crosshairs of capitalist development, the far-right offers a distinct political response to the social instabilities and crises engendered by it: a politics defined by articulating a mythical presentation of the past that idealises it in racial and cultural terms. This was revealed in the nineteenth century when a British-centred liberal international order struggled to consolidate itself as its combined development promoted a far-right politics that ultimately destroyed it in 1914 (cf. Anievas, 2014). And it remains the case today as demonstrated in the recent advances of the far-right out of the crisis conjuncture of the 2007–8 North Atlantic financial crisis.

The contradictory nature of liberalism in terms of both its spatializing properties and in the relationship between its political and economic forms that give rise to far-right political agency as an element in the construction and maintenance of liberal orders also points us towards the social and political complexes that underpin the construction and maintenance of liberal hegemony and, especially, the place of particular social layers and ideological forms in what Antonio Gramsci termed the 'historical bloc'. The concept of 'historical bloc' is relevant as it goes to the heart of the specific social layers, political forces and ideological imaginaries that conjoin to make up the concrete substance of liberal order and where the far-right – past and present – has been a significant component. For Gramsci, an historical bloc consists of a dialectical unity of 'structures and superstructures' that produces 'the complex, contradictory and discordant ensemble of the superstructures' which align with the assemblage of the social relations of production (Gramsci, 1988: 192). Thus, it is a socio-political arrangement that builds on the integration of different class interests organized both within and outside the state to realize a unified political and economic project based on the existing spatial and material basis of capital accumulation (Bieler and Morton, 2004: 90). In effect, the historical bloc is the political form of hegemony that determines the political orientation of the state and the precise arrangement of class power, and the dominant ideological character contained therein (Cox, 1987: 105).

What is significant about this rather complex conceptual formulation is that within a particular historical bloc – at any one time – there co-exist multiple ideological tendencies and different iterations of hegemonic projects within a single formation. Consequently, the development and overall character and orientation of the bloc is determined by the extent to which these assemblages of social forces cohere together in organizing, guaranteeing, and reproducing a particular set of productive relations (Thomas, 2009; 100). Further, it is the contradictory elements contained within the historical bloc that provides the dynamic for its development that play out in political struggles involving its different social layers and ideo-political components. And it is during moments of 'organic crisis' (Gramsci, 1973: 210–11) that subaltern or more marginalized ideo-political forces within the existing historical bloc can assert themselves through articulating a different ideological basis for either the maintenance or development of the productive forces and upon which a new historical bloc can be constructed.

Relating this to the history and politics of the far-right is suggestive of the presence of the far-right – to varying degrees – within the broader contours of the liberal historical bloc over the *longue durée*. In recognizing this and – as we shall see in the chapters that follow – emphasizing the contradictory and antagonistic as much as the complimentary and reinforcing properties of the far-right on and within liberal order construction and development, I will identity both the shifting dynamics within the evolving liberal historical bloc and the precise articulation of the far-right within it, and how both have acted together to mutually condition the political character of each.

The concept of the historical bloc allows us, then, to not only recognize the contradictory praxis of liberal political economy and politics but also the internal and external aspects of the far-right within the broader parameters of the exercise of liberal hegemony and the entwined contradictory unity of opposites – a *complexio oppositorum* (Anievas and Saull, 2020: 391) – that characterizes the workings of liberal order. As a fluid, contradictory and always incomplete project of political rule, the concept of historical bloc incorporates both the spatial, institutional, and distinct political and economic dimensions that define liberal state forms and liberal order and, in a way, that gives appropriate recognition as to the contradictory ideological currents and social forces contained within it, of which the far-right is the most significant.

In summary, the far-right has not only been a constitutive ideo-political current within the workings of liberal democratic politics and the broader liberal international order(s) that it exists within and works through, but has also, in key conjunctures, helped to supplement the economic basis of liberalism. It has done this through protecting private property from collectivist-democratic pressures and demands, even if such protections have come at a cost of its pre-existing spatial and institutional framings. That such a connection and role has been and is contradictory – as we see in the role of the far-right in the contemporary neoliberal era – does not negate the substantive limits on the far-right's antagonism towards actual existing liberalisms.

### 3.4    Race: Master Signifier of the Far-Right

In thinking about the far-right one is, inevitably, drawn to the question of race. Thus, for all of the explanations concerning who or what is the far-right and how we explain its genesis and development with reference to capitalism, class and/or geopolitics; above all else is it is race and racialized hierarchy that is the fundamental and necessary signifier or *explanan* of the far-right. Indeed, the social ontology of the far-right is based upon a racialization of the social: social and political problems are rooted in racial sensibilities and differences whereby nation-states are depicted as containers of racialized ideals of culturally homogenous 'natural' communities and where international relations reflect a 'natural hierarchy' ordered upon racial distinctions. In a world that does not reflect such racial ideals – the modern era gives birth to this racialized imaginary whilst, at the time, setting in motion dynamics and trajectories that help produce *and* subvert it – the far-right is the permanent source and propagator of a racialized *Weltanschauung*, making political interventions, particularly in contexts of crisis and widespread anxiety, to provide a means of ideological exit and renewal based on such racialized imaginaries.

However, in singling out racial difference and its accompanying social and political hierarchies as the defining quality of the far-right, we also need to be cognizant of how race and racism operates and is constitutive of ideo-political forces beyond the far-right. For, in trying to theorize the far-right over the *longue durée* we, necessarily, need to situate both the changing registers and focus of racism since the mid-nineteenth century and the role of other political currents in the articulation and reproduction of racism (See Allen, 2012a, 2012b; MacMaster, 2001). Necessarily then, race and racism need to be recognized as an embedded and substantive structure within liberal-capitalist modernity based on the structures and legacies of the history of European imperialism, colonialism, and Atlantic slavery (Césaire, 2000; Du Bois, 1935 Fanon, 2008; Mosse, 1985; Shilliam, 2012).

In this respect, the far-right pushes on a partially open door and where countervailing social forces and ideological imaginaries are not always strong enough to counter or limit its power 'to racialize'. This was certainly the case in the period of capitalist-imperialism between 1870 and 1945 and, despite the public sideling and delegitimization of a white supremacist and 'scientific racism' since the end of World War Two, racism continues to condition the workings of liberal democracies and inform the politics of parties beyond the far-right. Consequently, to some extent, the significance of race implicates the whole tradition of Western political thought and practice and the racialized dimensions within these traditions – including that of the socialist and Marxist lefts – that are not an exclusive identity of the far-right. So, while it is correct to single-out the far-right as a politics with a distinct and enduring racialized social and political ontology, we also need to recognize the way in which European imperialism and its associative cognate of white supremacism informed the politics of liberals and socialists up until 1945 and beyond. Thus, race and racism are fundamentally connected to political economy and the structure and workings of capitalism; it is also a key component of uneven and combined development (Anievas and Nişancioğlu, 2015; Shilliam, 2009) as revealed through the distinct spatialized dimensions within which racialized forms of politics play out, and how the ideological imaginaries connected to colonial and imperial legacies have continued to inform political identities and political debates well after the end of Empire.

In thinking about the significance of race in the politics of contemporary liberal democracies much is made in scholarly, political and popular commentary on the significance of the post-colonial context and the watershed of the Holocaust on the political role of racism. Thus, and following the associated idea of 'post-fascism,' World War Two is seen as the defining turning point for political racism in both the organization and reproduction of Western liberal state-society complexes and the wider international political order with the moves towards a systemic process of decolonization. In these respects two fundamental determinants of the historical far-right were dismantled: (I) racist public discourse as a basis of political judgement, policy and values was delegitimized as international politics moved towards a regime of formal (legal) equality between nation-states based on a process of decolonization; and (II) the political economy of capitalism was reconfigured such that colonial hierarchy and geopolitically-managed extraction and exploitation were dismantled removing a key ideological and material pillar of the historical far-right associated with capitalist-imperialism. This was particularly significant in working class formation in that the metropolitan privileges derived from imperial-colonial 'primitive accumulation' that European/Western workers benefited from no longer operated – at least in the same ways – alongside the important ideological role played by 'social imperialism' in facilitating social order and the political quiescence of workers in metropoles.[34]

---

34    One of the most important theorizations of race in the imperial epoch is that of W. E.
      B. Du Bois (1935, 2015) and his concept of the 'wages of whiteness'. Du Bois deploys this
      term to demonstrate the role of a compensatory psychological mechanism in the reproduction of capitalism as a necessary factor in its social stabilization and ideological

The transformation of capitalist political economy towards a liberal, as opposed to an imperialist one, after 1945 shifted the imaginary terrain of race across the liberal democratic world. For the politics of the far-right, the significance of this shift was revealed in both a political and economic dimension. In the case of the former, decolonization and, in particular, when it took on a form of violent struggle against colonial rule or imperial intervention – as in Algeria and Indo-China/Vietnam – re-opened up an ideological point of entry for the far-right. As the primary purveyor of white or European supremacy, the far-right was a key source of support for metropolitan states fighting anti-colonial forces through the utilization of racist tropes – still fresh in the mind – rooted in imperialist propaganda to justify the use of force and dispatch of troops (see Singh, 2017). While the far-right – in and out of the state – had been an important ideological source of imperialism, so it also played an important role in promoting support for European settler regimes and in opposing any concessions to 'militant' anti-colonial forces and especially those who were considered 'communist' or close to Moscow (Borstelmann, 2001).[35]

Indeed, although race was officially banished as a category of international political order after 1945, in the context of Cold War – and feeding off the original Western response to the 1917 Bolshevik Revolution in Russia – race and the figure of the black African in particular became entwined within the ideology of anti-communism. Anti-communist ideology pertained to a number of ideological tropes, but it was also racialized in the sense that it was seen as a doctrine inimical to the existing colonial order and its white supremacy. Relatedly, it was also viewed as a creed that was specifically targeted at blacks who were seen as being particularly susceptible to its temptations.[36] The

---

legitimation. This takes the form of an ideology of white privilege whereby the economic consequences of wage labour and the constitutive class inequalities of capitalism are mediated and obscured through the ideological-psychological compensations provided by the ideology and structures of white supremacy. As Du Bois detailed '[i]It must be remembered that the white group of laborers, while they received a low wage, were compensated in part by a sort of public and psychological wage. They were given public deference and titles of courtesy because they were white. They were admitted freely with all classes of white people to public functions, public parks, and the best schools. The police were drawn from their ranks, and the courts, dependent upon their votes, treated them with such leniency as to encourage lawlessness. Their vote selected public officials, and while this had small effect upon the economic situation, it had great effect upon their personal treatment and the deference shown them' (Du Bois, 1935: 700–701).

35  As Quinn Slobidian details (Slobidian, 2018; see also Kiely, 2018: 91) such a position was also shared by a significant number of neoliberal intellectuals.

36  As Heonik Kwon remarks (2010: 37), '[b]eing a white person or person of color was a major determining factor for an individual's life career for a significant part of the past

consequence of this for the post-war articulations of racism and their material effects was that the inculcation of anti-communism with racial signification was a potent force in the ideological and repressive repertoire of the American 'integral state' and its counter-subversive practices (see Anievas, forthcoming; Katagiri, 2014; Seymour, 2016; Woods, 2004) that not only re-charged the ideological arsenal of racism in a 'post-racist' context, but also provided a significant political opening for the far-right and the legacies of fascism even while liberal politicians and commentators were heralding the dawn of a post-fascist and liberal order. And not least in the US in the far-right mobilizations against the campaign for African-American Civil Rights.

In economic terms the shift played out in the geographical focus of racism particularly as de-colonization proceeded through to the 1960s. Here, it was not just the case that the far-right's imperial-geopolitical political economy had been over-turned after 1945 but that an important element in the post-war construction of the major centres of capitalist accumulation required immigration of post-colonial labour into the metropoles. In this sense the racialized Other was no longer 'over there' and ordered and managed through an imperial system of white supremacy, but was now, 'over here,' as a neighbour and co-worker or, in the eyes of the far-right, a competitor to national or white labour. Far-right racism – which had targeted the figure of the Jew as an 'internal Other' from the nineteenth century through to the 1940s – now shifted its orientation towards immigrants from Africa, the Caribbean and Asia. And the racism that it articulated was derived from the structure and workings of the capitalist political economy.

In the earlier period of capitalist imperialism between 1870 and 1945 racism was aligned with and a consequence of colonial relations of expropriation, dispossession and white supremacy, but after 1945 – and with the era of colonial rule all but over by the mid-1960s, and with immigrants from former colonies now visible on the streets and workplaces of metropoles – it came to be articulated as a politics of racial difference and separation based on the fundamental incompatibility and tension between Europeans and immigrants.[37] The workings of liberal political economy after the war, then, opened up a fissure with

---

century, but so was the relatively novel color classifications of being "Red" or "not Red" in many corners of the world including the United States and South Africa'.

37   As Neil MacMaster (2001: 172–3) notes, '[d]uring the period from 1945 to 1974, the age of mass labour immigration, European political racism switched its prime target from Jews to the "black" minorities' as reflected in the shift in Oswald Moseley's racism from Jews in the 1930s to non-white Commonwealth immigrants who were racialized as carriers of disease and criminals.

the far-right – that continues to this day – in terms of how the 'efficient work-ings of the economy' and economic growth have relied on the movement of economic resources such as labour, which not only rested on a reconstitution of the politics of the border as the line of security for the nation-state, but also in subverting the racial and cultural homogeneity of society because of the presence of new immigrants.

Yet, racial difference and associated hierarchies have continued to structure capitalist development in the post-war liberal era and, especially, through the way in which borders, and racialized constructions of citizenship have helped ensure the reproduction of a permanent 'Other' in the global reserve army of labour.[38] Migration – formal and informal – is the means by which the reserve army is channelled into capitalist metropoles for both super-exploitation and wage suppression and, in ideological terms, as racialized spectre to thwart working class solidarity (Balibar, 1991: 224, 1999; McCarthy, 2016). In this sense, then, the racialized international political economy of the liberal order con-tinues to rely on racial hierarchies as a means to spur capitalist accumulation and the management of metropolitan class relations through a racial ordering of the global working class and, up until the 1980s, privileging white/European workers within the core.

The continuing significance of race after 1945 within a very different geopo-litical and political-economic context and the different ways in which racism is both articulated and produces material effects highlights the difficulty of defining race/racism and identifying its key properties. Race has no material or physiological basis; consequently, 'scientific' or 'biological' racism based on phenotype or physiology was always connected – to varying degrees – with the supposed cultural or behavioural traits of different races and racist dis-course tended to switch inter-changeably across the two referents (Banton, 1998; Barkan, 1992; Ignatiev, 1995; Miles and Brown, 2003; Roediger, 2010b) as a basis for justifying racial hierarchies. And what follows from this is how ref-erence to race and racism is fundamentally about the naturalization of social inequality based on imaginaries of cultural *qua* racial difference (Müller-Uri and Opratko, 2014: 11). Further, as Müller-Uri and Opratko (2014: 10; see also Lentin and Titley, 2011: 69) emphasize,

> [i]t follows that there is always a cultural core in every form of racism: his-torically, the construction of racist difference has always been about

---

38    See a recent piece by Arun Kundnani (2021) for an interesting discussion of this in rela-tion to the contemporary globalized neoliberal economy.

the essentialization of socio-cultural differences that allegedly express themselves in biological characteristics, but only tendentially and always precariously. This brings us to see that while these cultural differences should tendentially be linked to bodily markers, racist discrimination does not stop where this isn't possible.

And as demonstrated in the examples of artificial visibilization of racial difference in the yellow badge/star of David or the hijab, racism can hinge on 'non-racial' signifiers (Müller-Uri and Opratko, 2014: 10).

Consequently, the ideology of racism based on culture was (and is) deeply embedded within the state-society complexes of the liberal order and continued to be reproduced even after the public disavowing of white supremacy (Barker, 1981; Balibar, 1991; Hall, 2000; Taguieff, 1993). Thus, although there are no races as such and the political meanings associated with race exist only within pre-existing racist discourses. Yet, this does not mean that racial differences – the treatment of people and their social experiences are not conditioned by racialized conditions and concepts. To be designated and socially and politically recognized as 'white' ensures fundamental differences in life experience than someone designated as 'black' in contemporary liberal democracies, and this is so even before we consider the significance and role of the far-right in the life experiences of non-whites within these societies (Bonilla-Silva, 2009).

The embeddedness of racial categories and distinctions within liberal democracies is such that in some respects race appears as a 'natural fact' even though this 'naturalness' is a discursive effect and social construct.[39] This is the strength of long-standing racial discourses whereby they determine or name, in effect, 'a series of imaginary characteristics to do with genetic inheritance, via which de facto positions of social domination and inferiority are perpetuated and legitimised in reference to the genealogy of differences within species' (Müller-Uri and Opratko, 2014: 7). The embeddedness of racialized tropes, stereotypes and their accompanying structures producing hierarchy, inequality, exclusion and, sometimes, violence within 'post-racial' liberal societies reflects what Eduardo Bonilla-Silva (Bonilla-Silva, 2009) calls, 'racism without

---

39    As Étienne Balibar (1991: 22) suggests, 'culture can also function like a nature, and it can in particular function as a way of locking individuals and groups *a priori* into a genealogy, into a determination that is immutable and intangible in origin.' And as Ali Rattansi (2007: 104–5) has argued, when such alleged cultural traits become stereotypes, they are also naturalized in a way that they become inherent to the group that is so defined.

race.' Moreover, as a social and ideological structure within liberal societies it provides a permanently open door for the far-right.

It is not only in the historical social and political fabric of liberalism that the far-right secures an ideological and political opening based on difference and inequality, but also in the basic workings of the states-system. Here it is the policing of borders and the separate and differentiated legal frameworks and codes that define citizens from non-citizens that is also coded into the DNA of the liberal state no matter how open it might be to economic migrants. The institutionalization of racialized difference through national citizenship means that a far-right imaginary is never too far away from the basic assumptions of statehood. It is clear then that the racialized structures of an evolving liberal order have provided a social and ideological context favourable to far-right political imaginaries. Indeed, the racialized character of liberalism reflects a structural condition or enabler of the far-right. Yet, at the same time, the evolution of liberal democracies has also, in effect, compelled the far-right to articulate its racism in a different way within the evolving and 'progressing' forms of liberalism (Traverso, 2019: 32).Consequently, liberalism and the advance of liberal democracy have also imposed political *conditions* on the far-right's ability to realize its political objectives. In this sense, the racism produced within liberal states and across the liberal order has had different effects – such that racial advances have been achieved in some domains – on racialized groups in the face of far-right opposition. This suggests a difference and unevenness in the politics of liberal states concerning race and what is at stake in organizing and campaigning for an anti-racist politics. It also suggests that the racialized character of liberalism is paradoxical and contradictory in terms of where and how racism is most pronounced, that reflects an important differentiation with the far-right.

The contradictory and differentiated nature of liberal racism is evidenced in the spatial dimensions of racism and far-right support. Thus, we can identify a geography of 'racial progress' in terms of the social relations between different racial groups, the formation of multi-racial anti-racist alliances and the relative weakness of far-right political appeals in larger cities defined by a more cosmopolitan cultural and a multi-racial working class. This conforms to the generalized spatialized political economy of capitalism as uneven development. Thus, whereas the far-right offers a permanent and uniform racialized imaginary that acts as a perpetual source of pressure and invective over the rest of the political system, the liberal order that it exists within generates – mainly through the workings of capitalist accumulation and the liberal defence of cultural pluralism and its formal commitment to equality – a set of socioeconomic dynamics and cultural norms that *undermine* racial and

cultural homogeneity and/or displaces the privileging of it to 'economic' considerations, that reveal important differences in the moral economy of liberalism from that of the far-right. In this, *qualified* sense, then, far-right racism
or the racism that distinguishes the far-right is not reducible to, or the same as
the racialized effects of liberalism. This is a subtle but, nevertheless, important
recognition in considering the racisms of liberal order.

## 4     Conclusions

This chapter has outlined the core theoretical framing of the substantive and
historical discussion that follows in the two volumes. Starting with an assessment of the existing academic literature in the fields of comparative politics
and the history of ideas, I provided a critique focused on the methodological internalism and positivist assumptions that dominate these perspectives.
While these approaches provide important empirical observations on the far-
right, they overlook the ways in which the evolving structure of the international political system and geopolitical order have constituted the politics of
the far-right and conditioned its development. This also relates to the structural dimensions of liberal modernity that facilitate and reproduce the politics
of the far-right over the *longue durée*.

This chapter has also provided an in-depth engagement with the Marxist
literature on the far-right and fascism. In this survey I outlined a number of
critical interventions concerning the problems in aspects of the existing class
analysis of fascism as well as the lack of a developed international historical
sociology of the far-right. However, I also identified some important elements
in the Marxist literature that continue to be useful in explaining the far-right
and its historical development. Indeed, my analysis is, in a fundamental
sense, aligned with Marxist assumptions regarding the political opportunities
afforded to the far-right from the uneven and combined character of capitalist development and the geopolitically-infused crises produced from within it.
Further, my theorization is based on an assumption that the far-right has distinct class characteristics in terms of its social base and where it draws support,
and in its relationship with the capitalist class and state; not least in its record
of upholding capitalist social property relations.

Finally, I mapped out the theoretical framing and general argument that
structures and directs the historical discussion. The main argument consists
of the following. First, the far-right should be seen as an evolving form of modern politics originating in a set of international political, economic and spatial transformations that has its origins in the construction of a liberalizing

international order in the middle of the nineteenth century. Thus, the far-right emerges out of the kinds of politics and crisis situations that develop in the evolving and internationally-mediated relationship between mass democracy and capitalist markets.

Secondly, the politics of the far-right and, specifically, the spaces and moments where it has gained most support and political influence are connected to the uneven and combined character of capitalist development. The far-right is reproduced within specific geopolitical spaces connected to the dislocations, instabilities and crises that punctuate the history of capitalist development.

Thirdly, the capitalist socioeconomic determinants of the far-right are closely associated with or conditioned by the international and geopolitical organization of capitalist development. In this way the evolution of the international system demonstrates how the far-right was constituted by the international in its capitalist imperialist form between 1870 and 1945, and also how the spectre or imaginary of the international provides the primary ideological resource for the far-right. Indeed, it is the precise character of the international political economy and geopolitical structure of capitalist development at any given moment that provides the ideological content of an evolving far-right politics. Thus, the far-right is a politics that reveals an antagonistic mirror-image of the precise spatial, institutional and ideological framing of an evolving capitalism.

Fourthly, the politics of the far-right are fundamentally related to the paradoxes and contradictions of liberalism and the evolving forms of liberal order, concretized in the politics of liberal democracies. It is the contradictions in the relationship between the political and economic aspects of liberal order in which the ideological, institutional, and political resources of liberalism are unable to resolve that provides a recurring 'crisis-opening' for the far-right. Finally, the far-right is distinguished as a distinct ideo-political current by its racialized social ontology and the over-determined nature of race in its politics and imaginary.

# The Politics of the 1848 Revolutions and the Origins of the Far-Right

This chapter seeks to answer the questions of how and why a distinctly modern form of far-right politics emerged in the nineteenth century. This is no straightforward task. As the previous chapter pointed out, the ideas or 'political thought' associated with a particular political perspective or practice are rarely singular or unique to a specific political tradition. Thus, the far-right reflects a form of politics – ideas and practices – that is connected to conservativism or 'the right' in general whilst, at the same time, being antagonistic to aspects of a conservative political sensibility in terms of the methods of its politics and some of the political objectives it seeks. Consequently, the emergence of a modern far-right politics develops, in part, out of pre-existing conservative ideological perspectives and political practice. However, its emergence also reflects a fundamental shift or discontinuity in the socio-political terrain that existing forms of conservative political thought and action related to; and this is particularly so with respect to the changes that the development of capitalist social relations unleashed across Europe from the late eighteenth century.

In many respects, conservative politics – since the late eighteenth century – has been defined as a response or reaction – hence 'reactionary' – to these socioeconomic changes. Consequently, conservatism, while committed to upholding private property rights – a fundamental mainstay of capitalism and liberalism – has also been uneasy about some of the disruptive social, cultural, and political developments that have accompanied the rise and spread of capitalism. Conservative political thought and politics obviously responded to the spread of capitalist social relations and, in some respects, promoted such changes. However, the challenge for conservatism has been how many of the changes that have accompanied capitalist development have eroded some of the core social, economic, political, and cultural structures and institutions that conservatives have valued. Further, these changes have also made it harder for the traditional political methods and technologies to respond to and shape these changes. In many respects, the emergence of a distinct far-right tradition of politics is a reflection or response to this.

By the late nineteenth century – and even more clearly by the eve of World War I – a distinct far-right form of politics was clearly visible across many, if not all, European states. These movements and parties – from the British Brothers

League, to *Action Française* and the *Alldeutscher Verband* (Pan-German League) – were products, or responses to the combined processes of socioeconomic, geographical, cultural, ideological and political transformations that had accelerated over the final decades of the nineteenth century as evidenced in industrialization, urbanization, imperialist expansion (and associated geopolitical rivalry) and democratization associated with the rise of the politics of organized labour. However, the emergence of these far-right movements was predicated on prior changes; that is, changes or shifts that were triggered earlier in the nineteenth century. These changes opened up the *possibilities* for a far-right politics to emerge where previously they had not existed and, in doing so, established an alternative ideo-political current on the right from the pre-existing or *ancien régime* conservatism that had developed in response to the 1789 French Revolution.

I identify the European revolutions of 1848–9 as the defining moment in the origins or creation of a modern far-right form of politics. I obviously do not mean that, suddenly, a set of people started to view the world through the prism of a coherent and singular far-right ideological perspective, establish distinct far-right parties and pursue a far-right politics either during or immediately after 1848. The far-right was not, then, literally, born in 1848. Rather, the significance of the 1848 revolutions reflected the original crystallization of a distinct set of socioeconomic and political problems connected to international capitalist development from which a far-right political sensibility originally emerged. Although it was clouded by and connected to pre-existing and, at the time, dominant, alternative forms of right-wing politics, it is possible to see a clear and distinct kind of far-right politics emerging in the responses to the revolutions of 1848–9 and in the political and state forms that developed after the period of revolutionary upheaval had subsided.

The revolutions and the responses to them did not produce uniform outcomes in terms of the kinds of politics that resulted from them. Thus, the relative significance of the far-right as an outcome of the revolutionary crisis that engulfed Europe over 1848–9 varied across different national or spatial locales. However, despite these important qualifications, my argument here is that in a general sense, and as demonstrated across several cases rooted in the conjuncture of 1848–9, we can see evidence of a distinct form of far-right politics emerging and that each of these national responses was connected to a set of similar processes or problems.

In focusing on 1848 as the point of origin for the far-right I emphasize the coming together of a confluence of forces and relations across a differentiated spatial field within the same conjuncture. As we shall see, 1848 marked a turning point or rupture in the history of Europe after which social relations,

politics and state forms were quickly transformed into new structures and relationships recognizable to a contemporary observer as modern and familiar.
It was this shift – an outcome of the revolutions – in the rearrangement of
state-society relations, politics, and economics and in the interactive relations
between the domestic and the international that provided the altered structural context which gave birth to and developed the politics of the far-right.
The reproduction of such structures premised on a newly established form of
inter-societal interaction and the ideo-political contexts that emerged out of
this transformation – which have been re-produced through the contradictions produced from such inter-connectivity after 1848 – demonstrate that the
far-right has a *longue durée* pedigree. Therefore, despite the distinct qualities
of each expression of the far-right across time and space since 1848, these different expressions also share much in common across these different locales
and temporalities and this is what connects the ideas and forces that emerged
in the 1848 revolutions with the formation of far-right movements in the 1870s
and 1880s to the contemporary far-right associated with the forces that voted
for Brexit and Trump.

The rest of the chapter is organized as follows. First, I map out what was
distinct about 1848 as a series of temporally and spatially framed political
events and how and why they are responsible or causal to the emergence of
the modern far-right. Secondly, I discuss the inter-connections and distinctive-
ness of the politics of the pre-existing conservative or *ancien régime* European
right with the emergent far-right. I then spend some time outlining what
actually happened over 1848–9 before ending the chapter with a discussion
of Bonapartism and its associated state form as a model for a far-right form of
authoritarian state.

1      Historicizing the 1848 Revolutions and the Contradictions of
       Liberal Modernity over the Longue Durée

What then was unique or causal about the 1848–9 revolutions for the emergence of a modern far-right? What did the revolutions reveal about the new
possibilities of politics bequeathed by the socioeconomic changes of the
preceding decades – which were to accelerate, broaden and deepen after
1848? While change is a constant of human societies – though its pace and
scope may vary – such changes in the social, economic, or political structures
of a society are not always self-evident until a socio-political eruption takes
place like a revolution to reveal them. The combined and multiple changes
affecting ever-larger numbers of people that take place at the micro-level may

only become visible and be recognized at a macro-level through an event like a revolution. This is what happened over 1848–9 and why it is defining. The 1848 revolutions reflected a watershed moment in the development of existing social, economic, and political trajectories associated with the reconfiguration of national economies, shifts in the complexities and relations within and between social classes and distinct articulations of politics. Yet, because these changes were compounded and accelerated by revolutions – doing what all revolutions do, moving people across political time with a supercharged velocity, within months if not days in some cases – a new social and political era was created. Consequently, the ruptures of 1848 and the counter-revolutionary responses to them realized a shift in the direction of political travel that combined with a reconstituted political geography from that which had existed before the revolutions. So, although the revolutions were, in most respects, thwarted or over-turned, the post-revolutionary era did not see the restoration of the *status quo ante*.

While the 1848 revolutions cannot be simply described as 'bourgeois revolutions' – indicating that moment whereby one mode of production is superseded by another and the concomitant rise of a new ruling class (Davidson, 2012: 133–51) – they can be considered, at least within the western half of Europe, as reflecting a watershed moment in the process of transformation towards societies increasingly dominated by the logic of capitalist social relations of production. In a word, the revolutions marked a tipping-point after which European state-societies became increasingly subject to, and moved towards opening themselves up to, the tentacles of an Anglo-centric internationalizing capitalist system. Thus, this was an international structure whose uneven and combined development was associated with British economic ascendancy – based on the advantages it had secured as the first capitalist industrial power – such that Britain and its Empire was the primary source of the geo-economically driven destabilization of the interiors of other European societies and the accompanying changes resultant from it.

More broadly, what 1848 revealed, then, in its blood, violence, sacrifice, heroism, hope and brutality was the forging of a set of internationally-framed structures and processes that, to a significant degree, continue to characterise modern politics. What I mean by this is that the consequences of 1848 in Europe marked out two defining paths for human social development thereafter. On the one hand, the spatial (or horizontal) expansion and vertical deepening of capitalist social relations over other forms of social life. Simply put, more and more people – at an accelerating pace as the rest of the nineteenth century wore on – became subjects of the capital-labour process, an arrangement that was fundamentally shaped by international forces and international-framed political and geopolitical structures. On the other hand, the spread of liberal democratic forms of governance and political legitimacy that rested on an engagement with an expanding democratic citizenry as the basis of political order.[1] Further, while these developmental paths were seen as complimentary and mutually reinforcing and stabilizing within the liberal imagination, in many cases they were contradictory and unstable; and it was out of this volatile connection and co-determination that the far-right has flourished. Finally, what marked out these developments, and which contributed to their unstable and contradictory – crisis-ridden – relationship was their international framing. This was significant already in terms of the socioeconomic causes of the 1848 revolutions but was to become much more pronounced as the nineteenth century wore on and as the twin processes of liberal modernity: capitalist development and democratization were conditioned by distinct international structures of uneven and combined development, imperialist geopolitical rivalry, and the growth of an international revolutionary workers movement.

This internationally-framed socio-political order was defined by new and distinct ideological fault lines, social imaginaries, and political possibilities from those that had preceded it. Not immediate or universal in scope, as the years and decades after 1848 passed they came to increasingly determine the nature and conduct of politics across the capitalist world. It was within this new set of socio-political structures – produced out of the peculiar dimensions of capitalist uneven and combined development – that the seeds of the far-right, planted in the turmoil, angst and hopes of 1848, began to germinate and fertilize. What 1848 originally reflected and which was to become much more manifest as the nineteenth century wore on, were societies defined by permanent socioeconomic insecurities (see Polanyi, 2001) with the imminent possibilities for the eruption of the kind of crisis that had sparked the 1848 revolutions as these societies became ever more deeply integrated into the capitalist world market. The 1848 revolutions can be seen, then, as the first episode of a modern form of social and political crisis that has been repeated over the *longue durée* of capitalist development thereafter.

This disruptive character of capitalist development was also evident and sourced in its distinct international properties. In this sense, the unevenness of capitalism was most manifest in the material and economic differences

---

1  As Eric Hobsbawm (1995: 25) recognized, '[t]he defenders of the social order had to learn the politics of the people. This was the major innovation brought about by the 1848 revolutions. Even the most arch reactionary Prussian Junkers discovered during that year that they required a newspaper capable of influencing "public opinion" – in itself, a concept linked with liberalism and incompatible with traditional hierarchical political forms.'

between Britain and the rest of Europe, as reflected in Britain's growing lead in industrial production, technological innovation and the competitive edge of the factory industrial system based on wage labour (Hobsbawm, 1995). This was not only significant in determining Britain's class formation, political development, and relative social stability over 1848–9, but also in the way that Britain's economic development, in effect, increasingly provided the international structural context that conditioned domestic economic and social developments within other European states; what Trotsky characterized as 'the whip of external necessity' (Trotsky 2008; 24). This was evident in the writing of the German economist Friedrich List (1966) among others, who outlined a strategy in response to Britain's industrial leadership and competitive advantage.

In concrete terms by the 1840s uneven and combined development revealed itself most clearly in the way in which British capitalist industrialization increasingly conditioned the socioeconomic interiors of other societies (Lafrance, 2019: 216). What became known in the far-right vernacular as 'Manchesterism' – the idea of unrestricted competitive free trade as the basis of international economic activity – was already conditioning production and class relations in France,[2] Germany and elsewhere. Hence, unevenness was revealed in the relative levels of capitalist-industrial development, factory-commodity production, the proportion of workers defined as wage labour, between Britain and other countries. And combination in the social and political amalgams that characterised European states – as reflected in the mix of *ancien régime* political and economic institutions, structures, and forms of social reproduction with emerging, if small, capitalist-industrial sectors increasingly entangled in internationalizing processes and characterized by a 'contradictory coexistence' (Peck, 2019: 50).

The developments taking place within France, Germany, and other European countries in the 1840s reflected the impact of this external competitive pressure both in terms of policy decisions that governments were making (for example in terms of supporting railway construction) and private economic actors in cities and the countryside having to respond to import competition and new production technologies and commodities. It was also revealed in the transport and communications revolution associated with

---

2   As Xavier Lafrance (2019: 179–80) notes, for the burgeoning French socialist movement of the 1830s and 1840s – that came to play a central role in the revolution of 1848 – developments in Britain were understood as reflecting 'free anarchic competition' and the 'permanent state of war' between workers and employers based on the 'crushing of small and middle-sized property' and which meant that the early French socialists were desperate to avoid developments in France replicating what had happened in Britain.

the expansion of railway construction from the mid-1830s onwards. The railways opened up local markets to external economic penetration and competition in an unprecedented manner transforming spatial relations. Indeed, in Germany there was growing concerns about the impact of cheaper imports from Belgium and Britain on the country's economic health and social fabric by the mid-1840s (Noyes, 1966: 27). The expansion of railway construction facilitated the 'external whip of necessity' as geographical distance no longer insulated local and protected markets from external competition and its dislocating consequences. Accordingly, the railways were a concrete expression of what Marx referred to in the *Grundrisse* of capitalism realizing the 'the annihilation of space by time' (Marx, 1973a: 524).

The international properties of UCD were central in conditioning the socioeconomic contexts within the interiors of European states and contributing to the local socioeconomic causes of the revolutions. Although this was not a universal transmission belt as unevenness works both ways – on the one hand revealing the social proximity and destabilizing effects of one interior to another outside of it and, on the other hand, revealing a weaker level of significance in other locales – the consequences of Britain's capitalist economic advance had a profound impact on the countries of Western Europe. This would continue through the rest of the century and up until 1914 and, in doing so, provide an ever more fertile terrain for the far-right.

In emphasizing the centrality of the disruptive and contradictory dimensions of capitalism, my argument does not reduce the pathology of the far-right to capitalism as the causal dynamics of the far-right extend beyond the economic imperatives of capital accumulation and growth. Instead, it is to emphasize the significance of the changes wrought by capitalist development over this period and the way that such changes – and their associated dislocations, insecurities, and crises – continue to provide socioeconomic openings for the far-right. Thus, in referring to or concentrating on capitalist development as the dominant driver of the type of changes that ushered in the politics of the far-right, I am obviously referring to the social or class structure of European societies prior to 1848 and international political economy; the precise relationship between political authorities and economic activities. Further, through the prism of UCD I am referring not only to the uneven, spatially different, and varied dynamics and consequences of economic growth and market activity/dependence that characterised this period, but also to the specific and localized national combinations that were emerging prior to 1848 as locales – cities, towns, villages, and hamlets – were affected by the increasing penetration and impact of commodity production and wage labour. What 1848 revealed then was the first wave of a type of socioeconomic crisis that has punctuated international capitalist development dissolving what might be regarded as the much more geopolitically-insulated determinations of social life that had framed the social relations and life chances of previous generations. Questions of place, identity, culture, and race were reconstituted – given new meaning and purchase – within the dislocating and crisis-ridden universe of capitalism in contrast to the more inert and less-disrupted and more insulated contexts of the past.

Such changes were revealing themselves in the two decades prior to 1848. As Jonathan Sperber (Sperber, 2005: 26) has observed, capitalist forms of market exchange had begun to determine the socioeconomic conditions of increasing numbers of people 'dissolving previously existing social and economic arrangements and exacerbating inequality,' whilst pre-existing forms of political economy based on the protections of the guild system and the remaining feudal or seigneurial agricultural tenures persisted to limit the encroachments of the capitalist market. The scope and impact of these socioeconomic dislocations were highly uneven[3] reflecting the continuing social and political power of the *ancien régime* and the delicate socio-political hierarchies involving the church and organized religion in preserving the existing order.

The simmering socioeconomic crisis expressed in the destruction of machinery and the houses of merchants and rioting by labourers and artisans alongside increasing demands for protection from competition – including from immigrant workers such as Belgians working in Paris and northern France – across different parts of Europe (Sperber, 2000: 402–3; Blackbourn, 1998: 145; Lafrance, 2019: 68, 179–80; Siemann, 1998: 13–34) provided a series of dress rehearsals for 1848. Depicted in E. P. Thompson's magisterial, *The Making of the English Working Class* (Thompson, 1963), the emergence of a collective working class political subject across much of Europe in the run-up to 1848 was imbued with a set of contradictory – both revolutionary and conservative – imaginaries. While the revolutions in France and Germany, in particular, revealed a concentrated and much more widespread continuation of subaltern responses to the birth pangs of capitalism that was most acutely felt by the urban labouring classes, the revolutions also saw the emergence, for

---

3    Thus. as Sperber (2005: 13) details, the distribution of steam-powered industry (an important element in factory production) in the 1840s was concentrated in a highly uneven way across continental Europe at this time: in northern and north-eastern France through Walloonia in Belgium; the Prussian provinces of the Rhineland and Westphalia in north-western Germany; further south and east including portions of the Kingdom of Saxony and of the neighbouring Austrian province of Bohemia; finally, parts of Alsace in eastern France, as well as neighbouring portions of south-western Germany and north-western Switzerland.

the first time, of a distinctly revolutionary democratic and socialist tradition with workers focusing on the need to combine the vote and their political representation with collectivized forms of social intervention to curb the inequities of capitalism (Geary, 1986; Noyes, 1966; Saville, 1987).

Whereas in Britain the spread and consolidation of a social order based on a capitalist market had gone furthest and intensified after the 1846 repeal of the Corn Laws inaugurating 'free trade,' in France and Germany, on the other hand, the impact of capitalist development was less a means of industrial expansion and more a set of competitive and destabilizing pressures undermining the social basis of the existing political order. So, although far from stable or harmonious, the synchronization of limited political reform – the 1832 'Great' Reform Act that extended political citizenship to a significant portion of an emerging middle class in Britain – alongside economic reform that broke the power of agricultural protectionism and the development of a legal regime to manage modern factory production with the factory acts of the 1840s, came together to help secure the foundations of capitalist development.[4]

In Germany, on the other hand, the impact of economic change was more troubling. Predictably, the greatest changes were in the countryside following on from the peasant emancipations triggered by the earlier impact and legacies of the French Revolution. Thus, with the dismantling of the *ancien régime* relationship between peasant and landlord and the failure to establish a fully commercialised model of landownership and production, a rural landless underclass grew, making up to half of the rural population across most of the German states (Blackbourn, 1998: 109–12; Siemann, 1998: 13–34). As the rural economic crisis grew in the years running up to 1848, increasing numbers of peasants migrated to cities where they also remained stuck in precarious and insecure work but in this case in a very different ideo-political context. For those traditional urban craft workers and producers – the artisanate working within the guild system – the situation was only marginally better. Thus, the numbers of textile workers were growing through the 1840s but the encroachments of international competitive pressure from Britain led to an increasing dependence on a 'putting-out system' that deprived more and more workers of not only decent pay but employment and thus social security (Blackbourn, 1998: 113, 120). The situation in Germany in the lead up to 1848 reflected a classic exemplar of UCD and its contradictions as evident in the construction

---

4   As Marc Mullholland (2012: 63–4) posits, the combination of the 1832 Great Reform Act and the 1846 Repeal of the Corn Laws effectively allied a large social constituency – including the middle and significant parts of the working classes – to the liberal constitutional state and economy.

of locomotives in the August Borsig factory in Berlin 'near the Oranienburg Gate, not far away from fields of beet growing in Luisenstadt'. And, yet, while improved transportation increasingly tied German towns and cities closer together, men and women still starved in those locales where the harvest failed (Blackbourn, 1998: 118).

In France, the destabilizing effects of the transition towards an increasingly capitalist economy were revealed in economic instability that fed into highly insecure living conditions for those who depended on selling their labour power even if some of these labourers remained organized within craft workshops and guilds. Hence, even though many of these workers 'may have "owned" their means of production ... their material life approximated wage labourers' (Haupt and Lenger, 2008: 631). More broadly, the workers in these trades were stuck in a context of an inflationary spiral that had gone on since the 1820s with their real wages having fallen between 10 and 15 percent between the 1820s and 1840s (Ellis, 2000: 30).

One of the key social dimensions of this playing out of UCD in the years preceding 1848 – and which would accelerate and intensify after it – was the recomposition of class and changing class relations within and across European societies. This was most notably revealed in the emergence of a bourgeoisie of financiers and industrialists who were pre-occupied with nurturing and expanding the realm of market exchange, investment, and trade which, in many respects, necessitated challenging the economic interests of those standing behind the political order of the *ancien régime* rooted in land, and who wanted limits on the scope of capitalist forms of market exchange. This reflected a political clash between the promises of liberalism and the traditional securities and certainties of conservatism. However, as we shall also see in the following section, some of the key sources of economic conservatism who participated in the revolutions demanding democratic representation and political transformation were craft and artisan workers fearful of the impact of free trade and economic competition on their livelihoods and ways of life. We might regard such a position as the original articulation of a kind of social and political orientation that is endemic to capitalism and which continues to reveal itself in the contemporary anti-globalization posture of many workers and other subaltern layers (see Frey, 2019). These workers, then, opposed both the traditional right of the *ancien régime* because it denied workers political rights and agency, as well as liberals and the growing bourgeoisie, who were committed to economic reform and the dismantling of the protective regimes of guilds that restricted trade practices, and offered some protection from competition.

In political terms, the competing interests and objectives of the bourgeoisie and landed interest were focused on growing demands – articulated in a
liberal vernacular – for legal and constitutional reform of political institutions
and the state in general. For liberal-minded reformers this focused on calls
for changes that would reduce, if not eliminate, most aspects of traditional
royal or executive privilege and political power, introduce the rule of law and
a reformed set of institutional arrangements that extended the scope of political citizenship; in some cases, with calls for universal manhood suffrage. Thus,
prior to 1848 some parts of Europe – and Britain and France in particular – had
seen some limited progress towards realizing liberal demands as revealed in
the 1832 'Great' Reform Act and the constitutional changes instituted under
the July Monarchy after 1830. In general, however, the traditional sources of
social and political power of the *ancien régime* remained in the ascendant.

The other major social development – a necessary concomitant of the
increasing significance of a bourgeoisie – was the growth of a working class,
that social layer defined by a dependence on the selling of their labour power
for a wage to produce goods and services as commodities for sale in a market.
Reflecting a changing set of economic circumstances in cities and towns – evidenced in increasing levels of economic activity in production and trade – as
well as the countryside, this uneven development began to rapidly alter the
spatial character of economic activities as the relationship or division between
town and countryside began to take on an increasing economic and political
significance. While relatively small with respect to the numbers comprising
an industrialized proletariat, the emergence of a working class quickly complicated the political objectives and methods of the liberal bourgeoisie. Thus,
whereas some liberals were formally committed to the principle of universal
manhood suffrage as the basis for a reconstructed political settlement through
which they could form alliances with the emerging socialist or workers' movement, they were also troubled by many of the demands beginning to emerge
from radical democrats that challenged the rights of private property and the
functioning of market exchange.

The rise of the working class brought with it the 'social question;' that is
how to manage the social and economic dislocations and cleavages associated
with increasing capitalist development reflected in the growing numbers of
the poor and destitute found on the streets of European cities. And the 1848–9
revolutions could be seen as revealing the centrality of the social question in
the transition to capitalism for the first time (Hobsbawm 1975, 1995: 23; Mann,
1993; Sperber, 2005). The political significance of the working class in the 1848
revolutions was not only its baptism as an autonomous revolutionary political
subject – a key factor in triggering the emergence of the far-right – but the

acceleration of its political development and collective political consciousness through the experience and consequences of 1848. So, although Marx and
Engels' *Communist Manifesto* call to arms was precipitous in terms of what
actually happened in 1848, it was visionary and insightful in recognizing the
political potential of working class political activity in the shaping of political
developments through the second half of the nineteenth century as the organization of European political order became increasingly pre-occupied with
and defined by responses to the rise of an organized and politically conscious
working class; a significant fraction of which was committed to the revolutionary overthrow of capitalism.

The 1848 revolutions exposed the fragility of the social bases for the construction of a liberal (democratic) political order as the alliance between a
liberal bourgeoisie and an urban working class quickly fractured in the momentum and turmoil of revolutionary politics. This breakdown was revealed in
the siding of the bulk of different bourgeois forces in France and the German
states with those of the reactionary right, as the revolution unfolded as workers became increasingly more assertive and threatening to the bases of social
order and the rights associated with the ownership of private property. Such
an outcome was a defining one, as we shall see in later chapters, in the history
of liberal political development in moments of structural or revolutionary crises. Indeed, the 1848 revolutions revealed, for the first time, one of liberalism's
'original sins' in the ambivalence of liberals towards the process of democratization thereafter[5] and the political tools required to manage the emergence
of a 'mass politics' which led them – in 1848 and thereafter – to embrace the
far-right (see Siemann, 1998: 219–20).

Though far from homogenous in terms of its social complexion and political
demands, the 1848 revolutions reflected the dawning of the democratic and
socialist eras with the entrance onto the European political stage of workers
as revolutionary political subjects. And although the revolutions did not result
in the victory of democratic forces the social fabric of the political sphere was
transformed. Consequently, whereas the politics of the *ancien régime* had
been based upon the idea of godly principles of rule centred on monarchy,
nobility and church, with subaltern layers occupying a 'natural' and inferior
place within this regimented socio-political hierarchy, after 1848 political elites
and ruling classes increasingly had to take notice of – and engage with – such
groups through institutions that were seen as representing the voices of 'the

---

5   As Hobsbawm (1995: 17) noted, '[f]rom the moment the barricades went up in Paris, all
    moderate liberals (and, as Cavour observed, a fair proportion of radicals) were potential
    conservatives.'

people' in the business of government and the prosecution of rule. The character and power of these proto-democratic institutions varied across different national locales reflecting the different dynamics of political transformation associated with the varying constellations of social forces – witness the differences in the relative power and influence of traditional landowning classes in the political workings of Britain, France, and Germany after 1848 – across Europe. Accordingly, the scope of political transformation was intimately connected to the pace, scope, and depth of capitalist industrialization and, with it, the increasingly urban focus of politics[6] involving the three classes that came to illuminate modern politics: bourgeoisie, proletariat, and petty bourgeoisie (Saull, 2015c: 23).

Through its participation in the 1848 revolutions, an embryonic European working class demonstrated the subversive and revolutionary possibilities of both capitalist development – creating a working class and subjecting it to a permanent experience of economic exploitation and social insecurity – and liberal democracy should workers gain the vote and realize their socioeconomic demands on the funeral pyre of private property rights. This was a major preoccupation of the leading liberal thinkers of the time such as John Stuart Mill (Mill, 2010) and Alexis de Tocqueville (Tocqueville, 2009) and has continued to pre-occupy liberals thereafter (see Hayek, 2001; Lukacs, 2005). Thus, the commitment of both Mill and de Tocqueville to representative government over that of the political arrangements of the *ancien régime, noblesse oblige* and aristocratic or elite power, implied and, in some senses, demanded, universal suffrage and workers gaining the vote. Yet, at the same time, the likely consequences of the working masses gaining the vote, in their view, was to most probably result in either the abolition or serious undermining of private property rights, which threatened to produce what they regarded as a form of majoritarian tyranny. As Beatrix Bouvier (2008: 893) suggests, after 1848 – indeed, *because* of the 1848 revolutions – the terms 'democracy' and 'socialism' became

---

6   Locating modern politics as a specifically urban phenomenon is a *sine qua non* of the modern political condition that not only spatializes the conduct of politics (see Harvey, 1989; Lefebvre, 2003) in particular ways – such as where key political institutions and sources of power are located and where the focus and communication of political debate play out – but also reveals the distinct spatial imaginaries associated with different political ideologies. Indeed, for the emerging far-right the city was imagined as the den of degeneration, depravity and barbarism providing the source of fear in terms of who were concentrated in the cities – workers and immigrants – and the kinds of social and cultural conduct that went on in cities that corroded 'natural inequality and hierarchy' bringing forth, as the century wore on racist and sexist tropes that continue to define the far-right.

inextricably connected with the latter being seen by conservatives and many liberals as the inevitable outcome of the expansion of former.

The contradictory dynamics of the social relations of the Western European states that burst out into the open in 1848 have defined the evolution and development of liberal-capitalist states ever since. What was first revealed by 1848 was the constitutive and imminent tension within the political and economic dimensions of liberalism deriving from the specific social character of capitalist development: the constitutive necessity of the exploitation of labour power which required the dismantling of pre-existing labour regimes and legal codes, and a redefinition of space and international relations as geopolitical borders and domestic interiors were mediated and conditioned by inter-societal connections, relations and forces. Further, such tensions were also centred on the creation and growth of a working class which, on the one hand, was ostensibly recognized as part of the citizenry by the liberal bourgeoisie but, on the other, was also regarded as the social agent with the capacity to subsume the economic into the political through utilizing the democratic process. In a world of mass politics and democratic demands and aspirations, the far-right emerged as a form of political agency that could help secure private property rights on the basis of an authoritarian politics. This has continued to be the solution and form of politics associated with the far-right ever since. To borrow Marx's words, a 'reserve army' for capital against workers' power.

On the eve of the 1848 revolutions we can identify two channels of growing socio-political antagonism that the existing socio-political settlement and state authorities were unable to manage and contain. The first was that within the ruling class, as evident in the struggles to determine the political economy of the state between the forces of the *ancien régime* – who continued to dominate the administrative and coercive apparatuses of states – and the rising industrial and financial bourgeoisie. The second was that between an emerging working class movement that, on the one hand, was defensive in outlook reflecting its concerns about the growing power and competition from largescale manufacturing, free trade and international competition, and, on the other hand, a smaller but growing strand of radicals and socialists who were committed to a more fundamental re-making of the social order through prioritizing the rights of labour over those of private property.

What the revolutions revealed were the consequences of an increasingly capitalist uneven and combined development with an emphasis on the latter, as the temporal and spatial unification of the revolutions were produced from the same kind of political and economic dynamics that had sourced the crisis and fueled the popular revolt across Europe. While these combined changes were uneven – displaying the different local and national levels of economic activity and scope for establishing and expanding the realms of market exchange – this uneven development also reflected a set of universal drivers based upon growing international trade flows and networks and the competitive pressures these imposed on pre-existing socioeconomic arrangements. And as I will demonstrate in the discussion that follows, '1848' should be understood as a watershed moment in the social and political transformation of the interiors of European states that revealed a fertile social topography for a far-right politics committed to engaging with and mobilizing the masses in a political struggle to determine the political response to the social, economic, and cultural transformations unleashed by the internationally-mediated spread of capitalist modernity. Consequently, without such socioeconomic changes connected to a wider international social and geopolitical dispensation, a far-right would not have emerged (Saull, 2015c: 23).

## 2     The Politics of the *Ancien Régime* Right before 1848

The far-right emerged within a political universe ideologically defined and socially structured by a pre-existing right. The right of the early nineteenth century and in the years before 1848 was a politics fundamentally formed and conditioned by the 1789 French Revolution and its impact in shaping European and world politics up until the final defeat of Napoleon in 1815. The conclusion of the French revolutionary wars, and the defeat of the final political instantiation of post-revolutionary France at the Battle of Waterloo, brought to an end an unprecedented period in European and world history (see Blackburn, 1988; Hobsbawm, 1975; Palmer, 1959, 1964). This period had seen not only the destruction of the remnants of feudalism and the dismantling of the power of royal absolutism and clerical authority in France, but also a wider transformation of the European *ancien régime* witnessed in a series of social and political reforms in many of the states that had opposed the revolution.

The defeat of the revolution and the restoration of royal authority in France and the wider international system after the peace settlement and the redrawing of territorial borders (including Prussia's annexation of the Rhineland) settled at the 1814–15 Congress of Vienna did not, then, restore European or French politics to the *status quo ante*. So, while the forces of conservatism in Europe ultimately prevailed, the social and political landscape that they came to administer and manage was fundamentally different from that which had existed prior to 1789. This, obviously, had a bearing on the character of right-wing politics; that which was to be conserved was no longer the social and political structure that had existed prior to 1789. Further, and more significantly, because the revolution had unleashed political forces and ideas focused on radical social and political change that could not be contained by force alone, traditional social elites and the conservative political class were, invariably, forced to make some level of accommodation. Indeed, this was to be the pattern through the rest of the nineteenth century. Conservatism, in practice – if not always in thought – was not 'reactionary' in the sense of reversing and turning back the changes unleashed by the revolution and the counter-revolutionary response to it but, rather, made attempts to limit the scope of these changes and minimise their impact on the traditional structures and institutions of rule.

Above all else, the politics of the right – across all of its shades from moderate to extreme – after 1815 was preoccupied with preventing another revolution. Consequently, the domestic political arrangements that individual states put in place alongside the counter-revolutionary dispensation of the new 'Concert system' after 1815 were concentrated on this objective. Internationally, the Concert system under the guidance of the Austrian statesman, Prince Klemens von Metternich, was set up to police the new conservative dispensation based on the centrality of monarchical authority (see Ikenberry, 2001: 80–116; Kissinger, 1973; Halliday, 1999: 212–3) and Christian values which 'legitimate' members of European international society needed to reflect. And while Britain quickly moved to limit its responsibilities for policing the new international dispensation, the other three main counter-revolutionary powers (Russia, Austria and Prussia) formed the Holy Alliance, thereby committing themselves to armed intervention in the domestic affairs of any European state where conservative political order appeared to be threatened (Halliday, 1999: 212–3; Lyons, 2006: 38–9).

These arrangements were firmly committed to reinforcing traditional sources of social and political authority and clamping down quickly on anything that they saw as threatening radical social and political change. However, the divisions within the conservative right as reflected in Britain's attitude towards the Concert system and the management of social and political change within individual states revealed a distinction between moderate and reactionary strands. The former demonstrated itself in reform-minded political elites, as was the case in the series of political and administrative changes introduced in Prussia over 1807–13 that were also replicated in Britain from the late 1820s with the repeal of the Test and Corporations Acts – that had prohibited non-Protestants from holding public office – in 1828 and the subsequent Catholic Emancipation in 1829 that culminated in the introduction of major political reform with the 1832 'Great' Reform Act. It was also revealed in the 1814 Charter that restored royal power in France, given that the return of the monarchy was now in association with a form of parliamentary government, even if it was based on a very small franchise (see Cobban, 1965; Craig, 1974: 46–9; Lyons, 2006: 29; Rapport, 2005: 61; Jardin and Tudesq, 1983: 10–13). These were modest changes and especially so with regard to the extension of the voting franchise – which remained a tiny property-owning elite – but they did reveal a particular pragmatic strand within the conservative-right (see Alexander, 2000: 29–47; Pilbeam, 1995: 117) that was willing to initiate political and economic reform, sometimes in the face of reactionary opposition.

It was the reactionary strand of the right that was most evident in the international politics of the Holy Alliance – closely connected to the social and political forces of the *ancien régime* – that provided the most important ideo-political influence on the far-right after 1848. The ideology of the reactionary right was most clearly and forcibly articulated in the writings of the French revolutionary exiles, Joseph de Maistre and Louis de Bonald (see Jennings, 2011: 44–7, 327–334; Wilson, 2011). These writers, along with Edmund Burke, outlined a reactionary condemnation of the revolution and the ideas and values that they regarded as having inspired it.[7] De Maistre and Bonald targeted the *Philosophes* of the Enlightenment and Jean Jacques Rousseau in particular as bearing a responsibility for creating the ideological conditions for the revolution based on the triumph of universal-secular reason and universal human rights connected to a doctrine of political equality.[8] Such ideas were, indeed, closely associated with both liberalism and socialism and, in this sense, these Conservative writers were correct to highlight what they saw as the dangers to traditional social order. However, even the most reactionary figures, such as Charles X – who came to the throne in 1824 – recognized that while he would push for the restoration of as much of the royal prerogative to rule as possible, there could be no return to the politics of the pre-1789 era (Roberts, 1990: 103).

_____

7   As Jeremy Jennings (2011: 327–8, 332–4) affirms, de Maistre 'was firmly of the opinion that it was the philosophers of the Enlightenment who had produced the revolutionary monster that had devastated France and Europe.' His fundamental source of critique was a Christian epistemology against secular and universal reason. After reading Locke's *Essay on the Human Understanding* for the first time in 1806 he concluded that, 'contempt for Locke is the beginning of wisdom' and 'Monarchy, he proclaimed, was the most ancient, the most universal, and the most natural form of government.'

8   In the words of de Maistre, '[t]here is a satanic element in the French Revolution which distinguishes it from any other revolution known or perhaps that will be known. Remember the great occasions – Robespierre's speech against the priesthood, the solemn apostasy of the priests, the desecration of the objects of worship, the inauguration of the goddess of Reason, and the many outrageous acts by which the provinces tried to surpass Paris: these all leave the ordinary sphere of crimes and seem to belong to a different world' (quoted in Davies, 2002: 14).

The reactionary right argued that the inevitable consequences of revolution were the Terror and political dictatorship (Richter, 1982: 192). Such views also informed conservative and liberal thinking on revolution and especially the work of Alexis de Tocqueville (2000: 106–17, 304–9). Thus, the destruction of traditional or pre-existing social and political institutions and constitutional arrangements would, inevitably, not only bring chaos, disorder, and violence, but would also lend itself to the establishment of dictatorship. The issue here – for both liberals like Tocqueville and reactionaries in the form of de Maistre and Bonald – was that authoritarian dictatorship from the right was regarded as the antidote to the threat of revolution from the left (Mulholland, 2012). For reactionaries, the re-establishment of an authoritarian political order and, with it, a rigid social hierarchy incorporating class, gender, and race, was seen as an unambiguous positive because it reinstated the bases for the *ancien régime* and the 'harmonious' arrangements of a 'natural' order based on hierarchy. In contrast, for liberals, it was a conjunctural and strategic decision that protected private property rights and elite forms of governing, even if such structures fell short of representative forms of government. It was not a permanent solution.

The tensions and conflicts within the right – between its reactionary and moderate strands – were evident within France after the return of royal power in 1814. The reactionaries were concentrated in the '*Ultras*' – royalist supporters drawn from the provincial medium and lower nobility and the clergy – who attacked those surrounding the new king, Louis XVIII, and their acceptance of the Charter and its limits on royal power and the traditional social and political privileges of the nobility. The *Ultras* reflected a distinct reactionary right-wing orientation in French politics (Remond, 1969: 44–7) until the July Revolution of 1830 that saw the overthrow of one of their number, Charles X.

As well as pressing for a return of the *ancien régime*, the *Ultras* also demonstrated a tendency for counter-revolutionary violence. Thus, in the immediate period after Napoleon's 'Hundred Days' when Napoleon made one final return to lead France before his defeat at Waterloo, they embarked on a 'White Terror'. Led by the new king's brother, the comte d'Artois, ultra-royalist organizations such as the *Chevaliers de la Foi* unleashed a wave of counter-revolutionary violence in the south of France targeted at republicans and Napoleonic administrators, killing scores in Marseilles and elsewhere (Craig, 1974: 49–50; Lyons, 2006: 26–8; Rapport, 2005: 61–2; Weiss, 1977: 45–50; Jardin and Tudesq, 1983: 23–5). By its end, between a quarter and a third of all French officials had been purged and thousands had been killed (Weis, 1977: 50). The *Ultras* also played an important role – through intimidation – in helping to ensure that a reactionary majority was elected to the new legislative assembly in 1815 (Roberts, 1990: 90).

The *Ultras* could be seen as reflecting the continuation of the counter-revolutionary violence that local nobles and clergy had helped organize in the Vendée (Davies, 2002: 41; Roberts, 1990) after the outbreak of the revolution in 1789. Further, the White Terror of the *Ultras* prefigured a generic characteristic of the far-right, and especially in its fascist form: a political willingness and ideological orientation to justify the utility of para-political violence to secure their political ends. Whereas conservativism was defined by its respect for existing political institutions including a reliance on the official organs of the state to maintain order, the far-right has been defined by an association with and willingness to use para-political violence, by-passing the official coercive organs of the state to promote disorder as a prelude to gaining power.

The politics of the reactionary right were, then, firmly rooted in not only opposition – if necessary, with force – to demands for liberal social and constitutional reform, but also in attempts to re-instate the institutional frameworks, political arrangements, and social relations of the *ancien régime*. Such arrangements centred on a political economy rooted in land and agricultural production based on the traditional landlord-peasant nexus, alongside restrictions on commercial activities and trade in towns and cities, and on international exchange that might undermine the delicate balance of the agrarian economy. Socially, it rested on a strict hierarchy based on customary rights and duties of the nobility as the governing class under the authority of royal power ordained by God and absent of democratic and representative institutions. Thus, in effect, eliminating any possibility for serious involvement in government by the bourgeoisie or popular classes. Alongside the restitution of royal power, the Church was to be the centre of social and cultural life helping to maintain social stability and remind the poor of their godly duty to obey.[9]

That these ideas and the politics that they inspired  realised few if any of their objectives after 1815 does not, in itself, reflect their insignificance. Their continued articulation meant that the ideas and myths of the *ancien régime* informed political discussion and provided a key reference point for the broader right in the immediate decades after 1815 (Halperin 2004; Mayer 1981). Indeed, even though the ideology of the reactionary right was opposed to the involvement of the masses in politics – instead, relying on a passive and compliant peasantry as their popular base – many of the core ideas of the reactionary right were to become part of the ideological and political armoury of

---

9   As de Maistre argued, Catholicism was a 'religion of obedience' (quoted in Jennings, 2011: 334).

the far-right in the decades after 1848. Thus, the modern far-right was hostile to liberal constitutionalism and doctrines of universalism and equality and was also committed to social hierarchy. Further, they were also opposed to free commercial exchange and open international trade networks, and they also provided an important political constituency for an imperialist geopolitics.

In this respect there was a disconnect between the social forces that had developed these ideas and the social forces and political actors that came to champion them later. After 1848, then, while the nobility and the landed interest continued to play an important role in government and economy – especially in Germany – the rise of the industrial and financial bourgeoisie, the workers movement, and the consequent transformations in the political economy of agriculture shifted the social and political topography that reactionary politics played out on. Specifically, a politics centred on royal authority and the privileges of the traditional ruling class would no longer wash and this provides an important characteristic of the far-right: an organizational framework *autonomous* of ruling classes and political elites. Hence their 'subaltern' and militant character, and a politics that aims to institutionalise new forms of authoritarian politics configured within the modern state and involving mass mobilization and participation, albeit in a hierarchical fashion.

The far-right emerged within an ideological context where it could draw on the ideological legacy and baggage of the *ancien régime* right whilst, at the same time, introducing its own ideological and political innovations that reflected the altered socioeconomic and geopolitical context. Above all else, however, what distinguished the far-right from the pre-existing reactionary right was that it was firmly rooted in and committed to a *mass politics* that fundamentally challenged some of the key ideological tropes and institutions of the *ancien régime* right with regard to the institution and political authority of monarchy and the social and cultural authority of the church. This was how the politics of the right would be characterized after 1848. And while some of its ideological tropes and hostility towards liberal democracy and socialism managed to engage with some social layers in the developing mass politics, its sociological basis and political organization became increasingly limited and redundant as the century wore on.

3      The Politics of the 1848 Revolutions and the Emergence of the Far-Right

The 1848-9 revolutions have been the subject of copious scholarly enquiry as to their causes, development and consequences (Dowe, 2008; Evans and

Pogge von Standmann, 2000; Price, 1989; Rapport 2009; Sperber 2005; Stearns, 1974), not least in the Marxist debate over the idea of 'bourgeois revolution' (Davidson, 2012). I obviously do not have the space here to offer a detailed historical survey of each of the constituent revolutions. Rather, I will outline and comment on some of the key developments connected to the causes, development, and outcomes of the revolutions for a consideration of my claim that the revolutions created the social and political terrain upon which the modern far-right subsequently emerged and grew.

Whether or not these revolutions were, strictly, 'bourgeois revolutions', the historical evidence of both the revolutions themselves and their longer-term consequences indicate that the encroaching logic of capitalism was a significant driver of the revolutionary upsurge. And this was especially so with respect to the revolutionary *dramatis personae* of a liberal bourgeoisie and labouring classes increasingly subjected to the disruptions and insecurities of market competition in their social reproduction. Thus, the revolutions concerned demands – if not universally registered across all national locales – for an opening up of the political system to wider participation beyond the social constituencies of the *ancien régime*, and demands for addressing the increasing concerns of the labouring classes in terms of either secure employment or reinforcing the social protections of masters and journeymen from the vicissitudes of their growing vulnerability to internationally-sourced market competition. As Sperber (2005: 26) nicely summarizes,

> [t]he general characteristics of social and economic development in the quarter century before 1850 could be summed up by saying that social wealth was visibly increasing, and yet poverty was increasing as well, and the living standards of the majority of the population seemed to be in decline. In many ways, it was an era in which the capitalist market economy showed its least attractive features. The market's disruptive force, dissolving previously existing social and economic arrangements and exacerbating inequality, outweighed its ability to create new wealth. At the same time, such non-market economic institutions as the guild system and feudal or seigneurial agricultural tenures, existing primarily in central and eastern Europe, did not so much counteract these market trends as amplify them.

What detonated these longer-term structural trends was the economic crisis triggered by the potato blight of 1845 and the shortage of cereals in 1846, which not only inflated the prices of the basic means of subsistence of the urban poor, but also contributed to wider falls in demand that urban-based manufacturing and trades relied on through 1847 (Gemie, 1999: 114; Hamerow, 1958: 75–96; Jardin and Tudesq, 1983: 192–5). Indeed, the food crisis was connected to and accentuated by the banking and trade crisis that had erupted over 1847. So, while the former could be seen as a product of the vicissitudes of the traditional agrarian economy, the later reflected a very modern capitalist crisis.

The financial and trade crises reflected the conjunctural expression of a longer term and structural dimension of uneven development – in the rise of the City of London as the leading source of international finance – that played out between the spring and autumn of 1847. The source of the crisis was in Britain and derived from the continuing instabilities in food production on the availability of credit, and the response to a change in banking law (Peel's Banking Act of 1844) that created a shock to the financial system resulting in a further squeeze on credit (see Dornbush and Frenkel, 1982; Ward-Perkins, 1950; Turner, 2014). This quickly reverberated across other European economies – reflecting how, in the realm of finance and credit, the boundaries between domestic and international were becoming increasingly blurred as national credit and financial systems of European states became ever more entangled with that of the City of London. The financial crisis resulted in the demise of a number of banks and the bankruptcies of firms adding a further layer of social misery to that caused by the rising prices of food stuffs. Thus, the confluence of a credit and agrarian crisis playing out across Europe through 1846–7 resulted in farm and business foreclosures because of the credit squeeze and levels of debt, which further contributed to a slow-down in economic activity in the manufacturing and handicraft sectors as consumption levels dropped. In some parts of Germany up to three-quarters of workers were unemployed (Blackbourn, 1998: 139).

The widespread – in spatial and class terms – socioeconomic crisis that engulfed agrarian and urban labourers ensured mass participation in the attack on the structures and institutions of the *ancien régime*. However, although these social layers provided the foot soldiers of the revolutions (Hobsbawm 1995: 15; Lévêque 2008: 100) it was the professional and commercial bourgeoisie (Blackbourn, 1998: 130–31; Mulholland 2012: 1–12) and their articulation of civil rights – of assembly, speech and the rule of law and extension of the franchise – that became the dominant ideological representation of the revolution.

However, the social coalition that triggered the revolution soon broke down, as the contradictions between the political and socioeconomic demands associated with each social layer quickly burst out into the open (Hamerow, 1958: 97–136; Hobsbawm, 1995; 9–26; Wallerstein, 2011: 77–142). Such contradictions played out – if unevenly – across Europe and they were given their most visible and dramatic expression in France, with the so-called 'June Days' of 23–26 June 1848, when large sections of the Parisian working class fought street battles with troops loyal to the newly baptized bourgeois republic under the command of General Eugène Cavaignac. This violent form of class conflict resulted in thousands of casualties and the mass slaughter and deportation of thousands of defeated 'insurgents'.[10] The 'June Days' brought out into bold relief the contradictory and antagonistic social demands of the labouring classes associated with the creation of the 'National Workshops' for the unemployed – which they saw as the first step in a fundamental reconstitution of the socioeconomic order (Lafrance, 2019: 208–9; Price, 1997: 13) – against the newly empowered bourgeoisie, as the new French government moved to terminate the social experiment of the state providing secure employment for the urban poor.

Indeed, the radicalism of the demands of Parisian workers and their willingness to use force propelled the liberal supporters of the February Revolution into the hands of the forces of reaction and social order. Thus, as Ellis (2000:) details,

> [t]he ranks of the counter-revolutionaries were swelled by large numbers of Parisian bourgeois, now willing to be counted on the streets, as they had not been in February. Equally significant, as eyewitness accounts testify, thousands of landowners from provincial France (apparently including peasants of only modest wealth) poured into the capital by train to play their part in what they saw as the defence of the propertied order, while massive reinforcements of troops and National Guards from the provinces were transported to Paris by the same means.

Further, as Immanuel Wallerstein (2011: 90) posits,

> the middle classes were not in the least prepared to accede to workers' demands for either a reversion to the artisanal mode of production or for substantial reforms of the emerging industrial mode. Not only did they baulk [sic!] at socialistic plans for cooperative ownership, but they were equally loath to grant even modest wage increases.

---

10    Ellis (2000: 41) suggests that as many as 40 to 50,000 workers were involved in the struggle with a combined figure of over 1,500 fatalities. An additional 3,000 captured insurgents were immediately executed with another 12,000 arrested of whom 4,500 were deported.

The 'brothers in arms' who had created the republic in February 1848 were 'at daggers drawn' by June. Thus, '[i]n every city affected by the insurrections of 1848 some sort of civilian militia was set up to protect the victors and their property. And in almost every case, once the first flush of euphoric enthusiasm had passed, the militia was used as a weapon against the lower classes' (Ellis, 1974, 39–40).

As Michael Rapport argues (2009: 191), '[w]orking class militancy and the radical left seemed to endanger not only nobles and well-heeled bourgeois, but anyone who had property including the landowning peasantry and the more prosperous artisans.' Such fears were evident in the thoughts of one of the liberal-republican scions of the age, Alexis de Tocqueville, who commented that the 'June Days' revealed a fundamental class division and conflict within France,

> I had suspected ... that the whole of the working class was engaged in the fight, either physically or morally ... In fact, the spirit of insurrection circulated from one end to the other of that vast class and in all its parts, like blood in a single body ... it had penetrated our houses, around, above, below us. Even the places where we thought we were masters were crawling with domestic enemies; it was as if an atmosphere of civil war enveloped the whole of Paris.
>
> cited in RAPPORT, 2009: 209

Across France a widespread fear enveloped the upper classes and property-owners encapsulated in the demonization of the workers in the Liberal newspapers, *Constitutionnel* and *Le National*, which exclaimed, 'on one side stood order, liberty, civilization, the decent Republic, France; and on the other, barbarians, desperados emerging from their lairs for massacre and looting' (cited in Rapport, 2009: 208). It was in this febrile context that republicans and monarchists alike embraced the army and the suppression of the workers.

The dramatic events in Paris were not replicated elsewhere in Europe, yet it was the tensions between the demands and priorities of the revolutionary forces that, ultimately, determined the outcomes of revolutions. Thus, with the perceived threat of socialism rapidly emerging from sections of the labouring poor in Germany, Austria, Hungary and elsewhere, bourgeois forces quickly moved to join the 'Party of Order' as the surest means of protecting their liberty and property rights. As Roger Price (2008: 27) opines,

> [q]uite clearly, for many moderate republicans in France and for liberals elsewhere, democracy and the threat of a redistribution of property,

which granting the vote to the propertyless seemed to imply, were terri-
fying prospects.

In this respect, while Britain remained largely immune to the revolutionary
contagion that spread through the continent, liberal and bourgeois opinion
throughout the country tended to replicate the *generic* fears of the European
liberal bourgeoisie of the social consequences of conceding to both the democratic demands of workers for the vote and the revolutionary possibilities
associated with working-class political organization. The social and material
contexts of Britain and Europe were quite different – paradoxically in the case
of Britain where the working class had developed an advanced form of class
organization and coverage in the Chartist movement but a rather underdeveloped political and ideological vision – yet the rising bourgeoisies across each
side of the English Channel tended to view the organized working class in
equally fearful and hostile terms.

Thus, although Tocqueville appeared to reluctantly endorse the suppression of the workers, his English contemporary, Walter Bagehot – a doyen of
nineteenth century constitutional liberalism – viewed the events in France
and their violent suppression, along with the emergence of the Bonaparte
dictatorship (see the following section) as a necessary and wholly appropriate
response to the demands of a social republic,

> You will, I imagine, concede to me that the first duty of a government
> is to ensure the security which is the condition of social life and civi-
> lized cultivation ... It is from this state of things, whether by fair means or
> foul, that Louis Napoleon has delivered France. The effect was magical ...
> Commerce instantly improved; New Year's Day, when all the boulevards
> are one continued fair, has not (I am told) been for some years so gay and
> splendid.
>
>          cited in LANDA, 2012: 41

The high-point of Chartism was reached some years before 1848, indicating not
only the distinct political temporality of Britain vis-a-vis the continent, but also
the maturing of a distinct form of working class politics and militancy ahead of
developments in Europe connected to the more advanced scope and penetration of capitalist social relations. As Wallerstein (2011: 84) notes, Chartism was
in decline after 1843 and this was not just a consequence of ruling class unity
and strategic acumen, but also something that was to blight working class formation and political development in Britain (and Europe) thereafter centred
on racialized identities. In this case, the question of race focused on both the

role of the Irish leaders of Chartism, such as Fergus O'Connor and Bronterre O'Brien, and the wider issue of Irish immigration and composition within the developing British working class.[11] Marx and Engels were acutely aware of the significance of the 'Irish factor' in both Britain's political development – there could be no hope of socialism in Britain until Ireland had been liberated from its colonial status (Marx, 1974) – and the development of a proletarian class consciousness required the overcoming of the racialized divisions that came to increasingly frame the depiction of Irish people across the Anglosphere throughout the nineteenth century.

Nevertheless, at the time – in the Spring and early summer of 1848 – elite and middle-class opinion were dominated by the fear of a workers' uprising led by the Chartists (Saville, 1987: 102–3). And while the main Chartist leadership remained committed to non-violent action, the recent past had also evidenced more militant and violent off-shoots of Chartism with armed insurrections in 1840 in parts of the English Midlands and the north (Mann, 1993: 528–9), as well as some less serious, but much more recent, rioting in Glasgow and London in March 1848 (Rapport, 2009: 94–6). Such fears ensured that the British state not only mobilized thousands from the urban middle-classes as special con-stables in preparation for the mass-demonstration called by the Chartists at Kennington Common in early April 1848, but its newspaper cheerleaders also unleashed a wave of anti-Chartist propaganda that emphasized its Irish con-nections – in a clear attempt to undermine workers' support for it through racializing its politics. While little came to pass – in terms of social disorder and violence – at the Kennington rally, the response of the British state and its key social allies indicated not only a deep fear of the organized working class but a willingness to mobilize a far-right form of para-politics to deal with any worker unrest that revealed not only the class character of the emerging bourgeois state but also its constitutive dispensation and 'strategic selectivity' (Jessop, 1990: 260) vis-à-vis the politics of the far-right.

The context of revolutionary crisis engulfing Europe over 1848–9 permitted socialist ideas that had once been the privilege of small groups of conspirators to be more widely articulated. For the first time, socialists could outline and demand the implementation of their ideas for the renewal of society (Lévêque 2008: 99). Yet in response, and especially when such demands were connected to a willingness to engage in extra-parliamentary struggle, the liberal bourgeoi-sie fled into the arms of the remnants of the *ancien régime* that continued to

---

11    Such that across much of English bourgeois opinion at the time, working class militancy
      was racialized as an Irish problem or a consequence of Irish contagion in contrast to the
      moderation of the English (see Mitchell, 2000: 93–6).

occupy the key coercive institutions of the state. Thus, although far from being clear or consistent, the demands of urban labour for socialism or a restoration of the 'social nostalgia' of the guild combined to enforce a liberal retreat from the revolution (Mulholland 2012: 79).

In what ways did these developments in the European revolutions matter for thinking about the origins of the modern far-right? The most significant development was that, for the first time, the revolutions brought out into the open the simmering social conflicts attendant on the growing pressures and influence of capitalism across Europe. The significance of this was two-fold: (1) the inability of the politics and ideology of the *ancien régime* right to offer a coherent and effective political counter to the growing discontent of an alienated and resentful peasantry and an increasingly self-conscious working class; and (11) the need of ruling layers – after 1848 increasingly constituted by a commercial, industrial and financial bourgeoisie – to establish a popular *qua* mass base to meet the challenge from the left, whilst still maintaining the social order of private property.

The social basis of this anti-socialist politics was obviously founded on significant parts of the peasantry (Mann 1993: 962–722) – which was to form an important element of the popular or subaltern far-right up until the fascist era, particularly in parts of Germany (Eley 1986; Larsen, et al., 1980; Hamilton, 1982). Another significant constituent came from some layers of urban labour and especially the self-employed petty bourgeois artisans. Artisans played an ambivalent role in the 1848–9 revolutions. On the one hand, many artisans – notably those of a lower status, who were economically more precarious – were at the forefront of the struggle for a social republic. On the other, 'masters' in particular remained committed to the defence of private property and, consequently, joined forces with the bourgeoisie to form a major part of the 'Party of Order.' Moreover, it was also the case that with the property qualification some artisans qualified to vote in the post-1848 political-constitutional dispensation, which was not only a political inducement to join the 'Party of Order,' but also helped to reinforce their social status – given that this social layer was particularly vexed by pre-capitalist status sensibilities and anxieties. Indeed, this sentiment has been a defining characteristic of the petty bourgeoisie, which has played an important role in their sympathies to far-right appeals caught, as they have been, between the bourgeoisie and proletariat (see Crossick and Haupt, 1995; Mayer, 1975).

In the German context this was to prove decisive, reflecting the strength of conservative and reactionary sentiments across wide swathes of the lower middle class in the run-up to the revolution. Thus, as Edward Shorter (1969) argued, what characterized a key social constituency – that of the small property owners – in the lead-up to the revolution was a 'middle class anxiety' centred on fears of demographic change as expressed in an increase in the numbers of the labouring poor, the mechanization of work and 'immorality'. In many respects, such sentiments reflected a contradictory fusion of social problems defining of the era: on the one hand a radical and revolutionary hostility to the economic situation that they confronted – a fear of mechanization and industrial competition[12] – and, on the other, worries over the growing numbers of urban poor and the economic costs of assisting them. The encroachment of capitalist modernity as expressed in economic competition *and* the rise of an urban working class were seen, then, as a fundamental threat to the social status and economic interests of German lower middle-class layers; a political expression that was to become even more pronounced in a far-right form as the century wore on (Saull, 2015b).

But this commitment to the 'Party of Order' and allying with the liberal bourgeoisie was highly contradictory, as these artisans were concerned with preserving their *traditional* guild privileges *in opposition* to the working of the capitalist market and free competition. Thus, as Haupt and Lenger (2008: 623–4) note, the anti-capitalism of many artisans (in the case of Frankfurt) was,

> primarily directed against commercial capital that had degraded a portion of the artisans into the dependence of outworkers, and furthermore against factory owners, whose production artisans were not able to compete with and whose competition was felt to [sic] 'dishonest'.

This anti-capitalism that informed significant strands of artisan opinion over 1848–9 across Germany reflected an embryonic far-right political economy that rested on a defence of private property rights that combined with a hostility towards big and international capital and free trade and competition that would form the backbone of organizations such as the *Bund der Landwirte* and the *Alldeutscher Verband* that emerged in the final decades of the nineteenth century. At this moment it meant that not only were many labourers looking and demanding to move 'backwards' as well as 'forwards' but that some of them ended up on the side of counter-revolutionary forces allying with the urban bourgeoisie and landlord class to help secure the social order and private property.

---

12 'Machines are ruining all classes, and especially the spinners ... [it] is the destroyer of households, the ruination of the youth, the inducer of luxury, the spoiler of the forests, the populator of the workhouse' (Johann Weinmann, a master artisan from Bavaria cited in Shorter, 1969: 206).

Yet within the revolutionary conjuncture of 1848, it was the *externalization* of the causes of the social contradictions and conflict that helped to maintain the coherence of the 'Party of Order' as embryonic of a recognizably modern far-right. Ruling class propaganda – which was explicitly targeted at the peasantry and artisans – painted working-class revolutionaries as 'blood thirsty communists and anarchists' fuelled by 'alien' and 'foreign' ideas led by degenerates and foreigners and Jews (see Price 2008: 36; Sperber 2005: 212) – a defining trope of the far-right. Such vitriol and, with it, a racialized animus, was also present in some of the liberal deliberations of the Frankfurt Parliament – the principal venue of liberal-bourgeois opinion and deliberation over the course of the German revolution. Here, there was evidence of a highly racialized idea of German identity and citizenship that focused on attacking the ethnic and Slav minorities resident within the German territories. Thus some members talked of a brewing (and necessary) conflict between Germans and Slavs as a key part of the process of forging German nationhood which made Wilhelm Jordan's (a German politician) dismissal of Poles as no more than "charming mazurka dancers" sound relatively benign; others spoke of a possible war of extermination in Central Europe between progressive Germany and the menacing Slav millions (see Lyons, 2006: 226).

What was also typical of the German case was the way in which dominant social and political elites played a key role in the founding of mass-based conservative and far-right political movements that mobilized peasants, artisans, and former servicemen, on the basis of the patriotic defence of 'king, fatherland and property'. One of the most important of these was the Association for King and Fatherland that had widespread support in the provinces of Brandenburg and Pomerania in particular, rapidly growing to over 20,000 members in July 1848 and reaching over 60,000 by the following summer; most of whom were drawn from the petty bourgeoisie (Blackbourn, 1998: 157). This was to establish an important pattern in Germany in the coming decades in terms of the role of some elite layers in the organization and leadership of far-right movements, as well as the heavy concentrations of mass support from the rural and urban petty bourgeoisie.

The 1848 revolutions reflected, for the first time, then, a crisis in the birth pangs of a liberal-capitalist order located in its co-constitutive pillars of politics and economics. Such crises have continued to punctuate the history of liberal modernity in the evolving relationship between societies ever more defined by and integrated into an internationalizing or globalizing capitalist economy and political rule anchored in forms of representative and democratic legitimacy. And although the far-right was not a clearly defined and independent actor in the counter-revolutions, both the specific class-based character of the social and political mobilizations against their most radical and socialist iterations and the ideological tropes deployed by anti-socialist actors in particular – elite and subaltern – reflected a distinct and emerging ideo-political current that was especially pronounced in France and Germany.

## 4 The Emergence of Bonapartism as a Model Far-Right State

The significance of the 1848 revolutions as the 'originating moment' for the emergence of the modern far-right politics is also associated with the type of state forms that developed out of the counter-revolutionary offensive that ultimately suppressed the revolutions. Such outcomes were most significant in Germany and France. In the former, the defeat of the liberal-democratic revolution re-emboldened the forces of conservative reaction, but it also pushed Prussia towards a project of unification based on an ideology of nationalism that was to be expertly guided by Otto von Bismarck through to the late 1880s. Post-1848 state formation was characterised by a number of issues that distinguished it as a model form of far-right state. Thus, German unification was a top-down and imperialist project based on geopolitical manoeuvring and war directed by the imperial chancellery with little representative let alone, democratic, input. Consequently, this project was a major source of geopolitical tension in Europe reflected in the wars that cemented it: the war with Denmark over Schleswig-Holstein in 1864, the Austro-Prussian War of 1866 and the Franco-Prussian War of 1870–71.

Ideologically, this was a political project framed in ethnic or racial terms defined by a nationalism that was specifically targeted at 'cleansing' Germany of its Polish and Slav minorities in the east, suspicious of religious minorities, and crushing the emerging socialist left and its associated politics of class solidarity. Thus, the *kulturkampf* waged against the Roman Catholic church that originated in the early 1860s followed by the attempts to suppress the rise of the socialist left and the organized working-class movement from the late 1870s – alongside a simmering anti-Semitism – defined it as a project of geopolitical, ethnic, religious, and social unification. Its characteristics of militant ethnic nationalism, anti-socialism, geopolitical rivalry, and militarism are typical features of a distinctly far-right form of politics.

Further, while this project had no place for the masses or the working class as autonomous political subjects – indeed it was constructed in direct opposition to such a goal – it also came to be defined by a paternalistic and authoritarian social imperialism that sought to appease the lower orders and labouring classes through the introduction of forms of social insurance and other welfare measures (Hennock, 1988; Wehler, 1979) that combined with an assertive nationalist geopolitical orientation. The objective, then, was to bind the growing working class to the established social order and political regime and offset the appeal of the Social Democrats through emphasizing the common ethnic identity of all classes in Germany and using the welfare state as a means to mimic the hierarchical social relations that characterised the basis of the traditional *ancien régime* with peasants (and now workers) 'knowing their place.' Thus, the objective was a reconfiguration of the social and political arrangements of the classical *ancien régime*; that is, a hierarchical social order flowing down from the Kaiser and legitimized through the duties and obligations of the upper classes towards the poor and lower orders. Such an arrangement can also be characterized as reflecting what is now termed – referring to the policy orientations of the contemporary far-right – a form of 'welfare nativism.' It was also a political dispensation that tried to bind the lower orders and the working class in particular into an ethno-nationalist political project that provided a mass-base to an aggressive geopolitics: a classic trope of what would later become fascism. The type of state that developed in the German lands after 1848 had, then, a considerable far-right pedigree even if the ruling class continued to be dominated by remnants of the *ancien régime*.

Developments in France could be seen to reflect – given the more advanced level of its social development and political contradictions – the emergence of the first modern far-right state model after Louis-Napoléon Bonaparte's *coup d'état* in December 1851. Bonaparte's coup resolved the stand-off between the two sets of political forces – conservatives and liberal republicans – that had emerged victorious after the crushing of the workers insurrection of the 'June days' in the summer of 1848. However, while the forces of the radical left had been crushed by the rifles and canon commanded by General Louis-Eugène Cavaignac, this had not returned France to political stability. The immediate threat to the ruling class had been seen off but the 'Party of Order' remained divided between a chastened liberal bourgeoisie wary of the masses, and a resurgent royalism associated with the forces of right-wing authoritarianism that the former was no longer willing to be governed by. In the period after June 1848 France was far from the state of social strife, political inertia and institutional gridlock and geopolitical tensions that characterized the final days that ushered fascism into power in Weimar Germany in 1933. However, the form of its post-revolutionary political regime remained far from settled and dominant social layers remained insecure and worried over when – rather than if – a new bout of social unrest would erupt.

It was in this context that the nephew of Napoleon Bonaparte, Louis-Napoléon, came to play a defining role in determining the future course of

French politics over the next twenty years. Prior to the electoral campaign for the French presidency in late 1848 Louis Napoléon Bonaparte was little known in France (Price, 1997, 2002). However, it was in this campaign that he proved himself to be a skilled political operator who took full advantage of the unsettled social and political context that the campaign took place within. Taking advantage of the insecurities of dominant social layers and presenting himself as willing to do the bidding of right-wing and royalist forces associated with the Orleanist politician, Adolphe Thiers – who apparently regarded him as an 'imbecile' who could be easily manipulated (Cobban, 1965: 150–1; Lyons, 2006: 221; Price, 2002: 149) – Bonaparte swept to victory winning almost 75% of the votes cast. Such a massive victory demonstrated that Bonaparte secured support from all sections of French society based on his campaign promises to protect private property and secure social order through reasserting the centrality of the church and the traditional family in social life, as well as indicating that he would be sympathetic to workers, peasants and the poor through improving employment conditions and promoting economic growth (Price, 1997; Plessis, 1979; Rapport, 2009). However, despite his appeal to the lower orders, none of the radical social reforms associated with the left that had been introduced by the previous Provisional Government survived after 1849 (Ellis, 2000: 45).

Bonaparte's strategy in the 1848 presidential election, which he would continue to deploy in subsequent elections, reflected a form of populism in terms of claiming to represent the 'ordinary man' against the prevailing elites and as casting himself as an 'outsider'. Indeed, he articulated the complexity and contradictions within French society as an undifferentiated mass in a manner that has been emblematic of the far-right over the *longue durée*.[13] He was obviously assisted by his name recognition and connection to his uncle. This assisted his appeal to the *'menu peuple'*. As Geoff Watkins (2002: 168–9) posits,

[a]s with religion, an iconographical tradition already existed which depicted Napoleon as the friend of the ordinary man, whether sharing a chicken leg with soldiers on the eve of battle or being lifted shoulder high on his return from Elba. Once again, Louis-Napoleon added political substance to these images by receiving Radical Republican leaders in prison, establishing links with the progressive artisanal journal *L'Atelier*

---

13    One of Bonaparte's key slogans was 'no more taxes, down with the rich, down with the Republic, long live the Emperor' (cited in Hobsbawm, 1995: 25–6).

and, above all, writing *The Extinction of Pauperism* in 1845. In this work he showed he was aware of the plight of the poor.

Bonaparte's victory produced an uneasy period of 'co-habitation' between a parliamentary assembly that remained under the influence of the liberal republicans wary of Bonaparte's mass and popular appeal and authoritarian tendencies, and a new president committed to centralizing executive power in his own hands and ruling by decree. In this respect, Bonaparte's election victory reflected a growing and unresolved division within the ruling class and political elite between those who wished to construct a liberal republic of elite-based representative government against those forces gathered around Bonaparte – royalist and others – who were committed to restoring the power of the state through reliance on a plebiscitary form of mass democratic engagement.[14] Indeed, Bonaparte appointed a number of right-wing figures with royalist and clerical sympathies (Price, 2008; 105) to lead his government, such as Odilon Barrot and the comte de Falloux. The splits within the ruling class alongside the differences as to what form of political rule should prevail – authoritarian presidentialism or liberal parliamentarianism – were suspended over ongoing social instability that continued to simmer after the June Days. The left re-emerged, securing major gains in the May 1849 parliamentary elections and with their hostility towards Bonaparte called for another workers' insurrection that was quickly suppressed. The workers' insurrection in Paris was linked to Bonaparte's military intervention in Rome to reinstate Papal authority after a republican revolution. The armed intervention delighted Bonaparte's Catholic supporters on the right but further alienated liberals and republicans and provided an early demonstration of Bonaparte's combination of political opportunism, authoritarianism, imperialism, and militarism.

The instability of France's political situation and where it was heading was reinforced the following year with victories for liberals and republicans in the parliamentary elections, which further reinforced the sense of political inertia and stalemate as neither faction of the 'Party of Order' (see Marx, 1934) appeared able to consolidate a political coalition to rule, and which further

---

14    In this sense the split in France reflected, for the first time, an enduring tension within the liberal democratic form of politics and, specifically, the institutionalization of democratic structures of governance. For the far-right – then and now – the preference has been for a form of populist form of democratic engagement that empowers an authoritarian form of executive power freed from constitutional and legal constraints whilst operating through a veneer of plebeian democracy, as opposed to elite-based representative structures based on protections on minority rights and constitutional limits on executive power.

compromised Bonaparte's authoritarian ambitions. Thus, soon after the election – and in response to the revival of the radical left and suspicions about Bonaparte's authoritarianism – the assembly passed a new restrictive voting law based on residency requirements and taxation that removed approximately a third of the existing electorate that was especially pronounced in the larger urban centres (Crook, 2015: 63; Lyons, 2006: 221; Thody, 1989: 51). Seeing the basis of his political legitimacy and authority being undercut by the assembly, Bonaparte responded by condemning parliamentarians as an 'undemocratic elite' and embarked on a national tour demanding that the legislation be overturned. Given that his single-term only presidential mandate expired at the end of 1852, it appeared that liberal-republican forces had out-manoeuvred the right and Bonaparte.

By the end of 1851, then, France remained engulfed in political turmoil resulting from the unfinished business of the 1848 revolution. The machinery of government was not functioning because of the impasse between the legislature and the Bonapartist presidency, and the democratic legitimacy of the Republic had been seriously weakened by the new voting restrictions. On top of this, dominant social layers and conservative-royalists and liberal-republicans alike remained deeply concerned about the long-term stability of the social order because of the unresolved status of the social question. Thus, despite repeated hammer blows after the June Days, the radical left maintained a political presence and an organizational network to mobilize workers and peasants. They had shown this in their protests against the imperialist intervention in Rome in May 1849 and, in spite of the subsequent repression that followed this – with the arrests of left-wing deputies, the closing down of political clubs and publications and the outlawing of political meetings (Rapport, 2009: 390–91) – an outspoken critic of the reactionary Falloux law (empowering the Catholic Church's supervision of education) was one of a slew of left-wing candidates who won a series of by-elections throughout 1850 (Rapport, 2005: 155). For the social and political elites, then, the threat from the left had not been properly extinguished and the potential remained for the masses to seize power.

This impasse was 'resolved' with the *coup d'état* of December 2, 1851. Leading parliamentarians were arrested, and the Assembly dissolved and universal manhood suffrage (for all men over the age of 25) was re-instated. The coup was met with resistance in Paris that was quickly suppressed by the army, but more significant resistance sprung up in the south of the country. Over 26,000 republicans were arrested (Price, 2002: 150) with thousands interned or exiled (Payne, 1966: 46–9; Thody, 1989: 53; Merriman, 1978: 215). The coup destroyed what remained of the republican and socialist lefts (Wright, 1975). The *démo-socs* that had provided the organizational structure and the ideological underpinnings of the left were broken up and the left (Merriman, 1978: xxi-xxii) would remain marginalized until the implosion of the regime in the debacle of the Franco-Prussian war in 1870–71. Thus, while the immediate trigger for coup had been Bonaparte's inability to get parliament to bend to his will and the breakdown in the republican political system, the context of the unresolved business of 1848 was key. Such a crisis – defined by the perception of a continuing threat from the left and in breakdown in the workings of the governing institutions – had a lot in common with the later crises that would immediately precede fascists coming to power in Italy and Germany. Consequently, again, the principal contradiction and focus of conflict was between those social and political forces concerned with order and political stability and those who continued to press for the realization of the possibilities unleashed in the revolutions of 1848. The primary victims of the coup and the regime that developed out of it were the forces of the radical left. The coup and the regime of Empire that emerged in 1852 – after the plebiscite endorsed Bonaparte's dismantling of the republican order – evicted the liberal bourgeoisie from the corridors of political power yet secured their core social interests with the restoration of stable, if authoritarian, government committed to the protection of private property rights.

The regime that emerged – the Second Empire – which was to last until 1870, began as a far-right authoritarian formation before moving towards phases of liberalization in terms of its representative and institutional character, as well as in aspects of its international relations.[15] Thus, by the late 1850s and thereafter, the regime began to tolerate some liberal and republican political currents,[16] as well as a greater plurality in the membership of the National Assembly. Further, in 1860 it signalled its willingness to engage in a liberal international free trade regime and promote inward foreign investment with the signing of the Cobden-Chevalier free trade treaty with Britain. By the mid-1860s an official opposition was permitted in the National Assembly and workers were allowed to form trade unions (Price, 1997: 39–58, 2002: 156; Thody,

---

15    Bonaparte also surrounded himself with liberal-minded reformers such as Michel Chevalier, the architect of the 1860 free trade treaty with Britain and prominent financiers such as Paulin Talabot and the Pereire brothers. Indeed, the regime was quickly defined by close connections between leading state officials and leading fractions of French capital even if this did not, always, translate into a consistent orientation towards liberalization (see Lafrance, 2019: 221).

16    However, it remained the case that official candidates tied to the regime had a distinct advantage in terms of the support provided by the state which helped secure the return of pro-regime candidates to parliament over opposition currents (Cobban, 1965: 159).

1989: 50–54; Price, 2002: 156; Hazareesingh, 2004: 129–52; Grenville, 2000: 288–96; Zeldin, 1958).

It is clear that the outcome of Louis-Napoléon's coup did not lead to the formation of a fundamentally different *species* of state or political regime.[17] In many respects, the reasons for this reflected the limited ideological ambitions of Bonaparte and his goal of securing legitimacy for his regime and the succession which required the support of the dominant social interests in France. It also reflected the incomplete character of both the politicization of French society at the time and the limited vision of and instruments by which the masses would be engaged or mobilized within the state, at least as compared with what characterized fascism.[18] Thus, while Bonapartism could be seen – in its campaigning and electoral modes – to reflect a form of para-politics as evidenced by the organization and activities of the militarized cadres of the Society of December 10, it did not create or rely on a permanent centrally-directed political party and militia that characterized fascism. This reflected the limits of its organizational form and ideological vision of establishing a 'mass politics' and state, as well as the limits of its radical and revolutionary character.

Nevertheless, Bonapartism – the term that Marxists in particular have used to describe the particular means by which Louis-Napoléon secured and maintained political power and the type of state that he created – can also be seen as the first exemplar of the process through which a far-right regime came to power and the specific political character of a far-right form of state.[19] Indeed, as suggested, there are many parallels in the case of Bonapartism that overlap

---

17    As Baeher and Richter (2004: 2) recognize, it was a regime that appealed to the masses through 'manipulating opinion and the use of censorship' and dominated them 'through a centralized state with police, military, and administrative controls at a level never before attained'.

18    Through the 1860s the regime played off workers and elites through social reforms and some liberalization that permitted a greater role for parliament in policy and law-making but this was all about managing power rather than a systematic move towards liberalism/constitutionalism or socialism. It was the frailty of the regime regarding its social base that provided the context of the disaster of 1870 as foreign policy and war had provided the *deus ex machina* for the regime in the past (see Rapport, 2005: 217).

19    One of the most important theorists of the right-wing authoritarian state form, Carl Schmitt, recognized the similarities in the social contexts and character of political crisis in France after 1848 with that of the final years of the Weimar Republic. Schmitt saw the momentum within mass revolutionary movements as *inevitably* resulting in a sovereign dictatorship in the name of the people, which, for him (and liberals like de Tocqueville), would then lead to revolutionary terror following the example of France after 1793. His solution in such contexts was the constitutional mechanism of 'commissarial dictatorship' that would permit a conjunctural suspension of constitutional and democratic order to both suppress the threat of the mass movement and overcome the inertia and

with the coming to power of fascist regimes in Italy and Germany decades later. Bonapartism could be seen to be reflective of a generic far-right, then, in that it emerged within a context of prolonged social and political crisis where the memory and fear of the revolutionary left provided the key ideological context informing the behaviour of dominant social interests. The fact that the revolutionary threat from the left had been defeated – in a similar way that Italian fascism and German Nazism came to power *after* the revolutionary aspirations of the working class had been quashed – and was no longer able to challenge the existing political regime is of secondary importance. Thus, it was the prevailing ideological fear – indeed, paranoia – and the knowledge of the possibility of a challenge based on this memory, combined with the inertia and failings of the existing political regime to move beyond the crisis conditions and establish political stability, that opened up the opportunity for a Bonapartists/far-right intervention.

In this respect, Bonaparte, like Mussolini and Hitler, was not the preferred choice of the ruling classes (Draper, 1977: 396–7); rather, the crisis situation and inability of existing elite actors to secure a widespread social basis to both anchor and *legitimize* the political regime pushed social and political elites to embrace populist, demagogic and authoritarian outsiders to rule, reassured that, in doing so, the fundamental tenets of the social order would be safeguarded.[20] In this sense, Bonapartism, like fascism, provided an ideological and aesthetical means of exiting the crisis and restoring social order upon a new authoritarian political dispensation, and its rituals and theatre were a prefiguring of what some scholars of fascism have described as the 'sacralization of politics' (Gentile, 1996). In the words of Hal Draper (1977: 398, original emphasis; see also Marx, 1934: 53, 57) the key to Bonapartism is that '[*i*]*n order to preserve the bourgeoisie's social power, its political power must be broken*'. Thus, Bonaparte presented himself as a national saviour beyond petty political or particular class interests. Further, in emphasizing the restoration of state power and national glory, Bonapartism reflected a form of authoritarian

---

stasis of representative government, and which would be legitimated through plebiscite. Bonapartism, to a significant degree, reflected this (see McCormick, 2004: 197–219).

20    In the words of Roger Price (2002: 150), '[t]he coup d'état required abdication from power by the social elites, the landowners, and wealthy businessmen, in return for the protection of their "vital" interests and most notably private property, against the threat of revolution. Subsequently, the popularity of the monarch was to be enhanced by the "invention" of ritual and by provincial tours ... which sought to personalise the bonds between ruler and people. Invariably wearing military uniform, the emperor posed as a symbol of national unity and as the supreme warlord. This resurgence of the monarchical state was glorified in school, church and in the developing mass media.'

nationalism and charismatic authority[21] particularly connected to the far-right. It was an authoritarian regime that actively sought the support of the population, through the state subsidizing Bonapartist newspapers and disseminating almanacs, songs, and Napoleonic prints, as a way of instilling loyalty and providing a direct connection between the masses and the emperor. Through this the myth was promoted that Napoleon III stood above the traditional elites and ruled for the common man (Rapport, 2005: 162).

The political economy of Bonapartism was also significant. So, though the regime ended up moving towards liberalization, it was also characterized by state intervention and made a great deal, in its propaganda, of the influence of Saint-Simonian (socialist) ideas in its economic thinking (Draper, 1977: 439–40). There was some evidence for this in infrastructure investments that benefited some workers through employment, and improvements to public spaces and the lay-out of cities through Baron von Haussmann's schemes. However, the overall character of the Bonapartist economy favoured big and finance capital in particular as state policy was directed towards building up France's banking and financial system (see Draper, 1977: 404–5; Grenville, 2000: 147; Thody, 1989: 150). Thus, the leading international financiers – and focus of anti-Semitic diatribes – the Rothschilds, were involved in the setting up of *Crédit Mobilier* that played a key role in financing railway construction (Thody, 1989: 59; Cobban, 1965: 442–4; 164–5; Draper, 1977). This obviously contributed to promoting social stability and reflected the regime's commitment to offering more than just spectacle and rhetoric to secure the allegiance of workers. At the same time, however, it created a class of financiers that approximated a form of 'financial monopoly capital,' wedding significant parts of the capitalist class to the political fortunes and wellbeing of the Bonapartist regime.

Bonaparte's reliance on the army as the mainstay of his regime and his connection to and articulation and defence of a mass politics were also significant. Almost immediately after the coup, the suffrage was returned to its mass coverage that the liberal and conservative elites had earlier restricted. Indeed, it was this that secured the regime's legitimacy and basis for the restoration of political order. It was something that the liberal and conservative elites could not achieve. The only other means through which this could have been possible was via the republican and socialist lefts, but these forces had been repeatedly hammered by the coercive forces of the state after June 1848 almost to the

---

21    Thus, as Michael Rapport (2009: 327) remarks, Bonaparte 'envisaged Bonapartism as a combination of the principle of popular sovereignty and authoritarianism: the Emperor would be the executor of the people's will'.

point of irrelevance by the time of the coup. Further, such forces were anathema to the political elite and the ruling class.

However, while Bonapartism rested on a mass base and deployed a mass-popular mechanism (referenda) to institutionalize and legitimize its rule, this was a use of democracy or embrace of mass politics that helped realize an authoritarian and repressive state that deprived the mass of people of their political rights (Payne, 1966: 56–7). This is typical of far-right and fascist forms of political regime and differentiates a far-right form of authoritarianism from that of the traditional or *ancien régime* right. Thus the masses – or at least those mobilized by the regime in part through forms of intimidation and terror – were complicit in their own political castration but this mass involvement is a necessary element in the consolidation of the far-right regime.

What was also significant, and which was directly linked to the manner through which the masses were mobilized, was that Bonapartism, like fascism, operated and was realized through a distinct kind of para-politics. Thus, Bonaparte's initial political breakthrough in winning the presidency in December 1848 relied, in part, on the role played by the Society of December 10. This was a para-political organization that drew on *déclassé* social layers, 'which functioned both as an approving claque simulating public enthusiasm and as a terrorist gang intimidating political opponents' (Linton, 1989: 107). Part political theatre and part violent thugs, the Society of the December 10 was not a political party as such, nor a para-military organization analogous to the Italian Blackshirts, yet it provided Bonaparte with a national political network that helped mobilize support for him and ensured that public spaces of debate existed under its intimidating shadow, if not the outright terrorist violence characteristic of fascism.

That Bonapartism did not develop into a fully-fledged authoritarian dictatorship reflected the limited para-political basis of the regime as compared to fascism and the greater significance of the army as its political backbone. Further, in a less challenging geopolitical context – indeed, with Britain offering a trade agreement and alliance against Russia in the Crimean War – the external pressures on the regime were of a very different order compared to the early 1930s. Yet, Bonapartism did reveal the emergence of a distinct political form of state that foreshadowed fascist dictatorship (Vajda 1976: 93; Poulantzas 1974). This political form was very much of the modern age in its use of sophisticated tools of propaganda and manipulation, and its direct appeal to a disembodied mass through a range of contradictory and populist appeals (Hobsbawm 1995: 25–6; Weiss 1977: 65). In its form, ideological content, and *modus operandi* Bonapartism approximated much of what was to come later in the inter-war fascist state. The Bonapartist state appeared to stand above society, free from dominance by one particular class, relying on the mobilization of *déclassé* social layers located in the peasantry and sections of the urban poor and embodied in the charismatic, populist, and demagogic leadership of Louis-Napoléon Bonaparte.

The Bonapartist state, then, appeared to and propagated itself as autonomous of dominant social layers – and the bourgeoisie in particular – based on its rhetoric of government and its appeal to 'the people', but in practice it consolidated the bourgeois counter-revolution after 1848 through facilitating the logic of capital as the basis of social order (Cobban 1965: 158–71; Plessis 1979: 78–91) and grinding down the remnants of the social republic. Consequently, Bonapartism could be seen to rest on the political disenfranchisement of the middle class – after their advances in 1848 – but they were compensated by the armed and coercive defence of private property rights and the deepening of a capitalist social order (Dülffer, 1976). It realized the social and political dynamic that the 'June Days' had revealed; that the only way that the bourgeoisie could be secure in their property rights was in a political order that had the capacity to rule by force without recourse to democratic or parliamentary sanction.[22] Bonapartism was not a form of fascism, as the recourse to systematic state terror that characterized fascism was absent. Nor in the latter's extra-legal mode of rule and the lack of formal representative institutions alongside its mobilization for war, all of which reflected the development of the specific contradictions of the 'high imperialist era' of liberal-capitalist development. So, while Bonapartism resembled the fascist model of state, its organizational, ideational, and geopolitical attributes were of a different order (Thalheimer 1983a).

## 5    Conclusions

The preceding discussion argued that a distinct and modern kind of far-right politics emerged within several European state-society complexes from the

---

22    In the words of Massimiliano Tomba's (2013: 34–5) exegesis of Marx's *Eighteenth Brumaire*, the political logic of liberal bourgeois social order amounts to '[p]arliamentary cretinism' whereby the belief holds 'in defending parliamentarianism from the proletariat by reinforcing the executive … [i]n order to neutralise conflicts and to suppress class struggle, parliamentary cretinism evokes the state of siege and paves the way for the destruction of parliament through the executive.' In a more general sense, we can say that constitutional liberalism is based on an internal contradiction, that of the requirement of a clause permitting 'its own violent suppression'. Liberal democracy therefore provides the constitutive basis and imminent political possibility for a far-right.

social crisis and political convulsions heralded and accelerated by the 1848 revolutions. The claim here was not that extant, visible, and independent far-right political movements were created by 1848 but, rather, that the 1848 revolutions introduced a political universe and ideological imaginary that was, to a significant extent, constituted by the far-right[23] in parallel to the more developed and visible political forces of traditional (or *ancien régime*) conservatism. Indeed, the development of the far-right after 1848 was, to a significant degree, conditioned by the development of these other ideo-political forces, particularly the traditional; or what remained of the *ancien régime* right.

The significance of the 1848 revolutions, then, for our understanding of the far-right, is that the revolutions – at least in France and Germany – brought into bold relief the social and political challenges of the existing political order. These were: (I) the social dislocations produced from encroaching and expanding capitalist development on pre-existing modes of production and, in particular, the place of private property rights within such arrangements and market forces in determining economic activity and social relations; and (II) the consequences of the ideological appeal of democratic citizenship across the labouring classes and the social and political effects of moving towards democratic citizenship. In a nutshell, the revolutions of 1848 concerned fundamental transitions in, or towards, modern political economy. That is the accelerated movement from one form of social reproduction to another and the precise relationship between a growing capitalist market and the political-administrative machinery and agencies of the state.

After 1848 and, arguably, up until the outbreak of World War One, the political development of European state-society complexes was determined by two sets of inter-connected processes. First, the expansion of industrialized capitalist social relations within different states via UCD, mediated within an international context framed around British 'hegemony'. Simply put, the trends and developmental trajectories that had been set in motion – and which had provided the dominant causal trigger for the 1848 revolutions – earlier in the century after Britain's 'industrial take-off' were accelerated and deepened. Consequently, the contradictions and socioeconomic dislocations – and resulting class frictions and restructurings – that had characterized the earlier period were also intensified as the industrial and financial bourgeoisie ascended and an urbanized working class grew.

---

23    To shift the gaze of and correct Marx and Engels' famous opening to the *Communist Manifesto* (2012) of '[a] spectre haunting Europe – the spectre of Communism,' the spectre that became material in determining the cause of European history was that of the far-right and not communism.

The transformation of politics bequeathed by 1848 was about governing for and engaging with a public that exposed the antimonies and contradictions of liberal thought and politics. And while the connection between liberalism and the rise of democracy was not realized in a singular pattern, the tensions in the relationship provided an important opening for the far-right. Indeed, the later development of fascism is unthinkable in a non-democratic context. This is not to suggest – as some republican and liberal-minded critics would have us believe (see Arendt, 1968; Hayek, 1944; Mosse, 1987) – that 'mass politics' or democracy inevitably leads to fascism, only that traditional social and political elites were not passive bystanders in democracy but engaged and used the new methods and ideologies associated with it, particularly the equation of people to 'nation' (see Balibar, 1991), to not only limit the possibilities of a socialist inspired democratic transformation, but to construct new hierarchies around race and 'Othering' in particular.

Further, the opening up of civil society for political spaces provided the roots of fascism (see Riley, 2010). What I mean by this is that the 1848 revolutions transformed the scope and ideological content and direction of politics. Henceforth, the vernacular of politics was oriented towards a mass audience – be they formally enfranchised or not. Accordingly, the legitimacy of existing political orders required and, indeed, rested on, reference to and institutions that reflected the 'will of the people' even if the people were not formally consulted through democratic processes. Consequently, as the decades after 1848 passed – in Western Europe at least – the breadth of the democratic citizenry increased, yet the bases of an authoritarian and reactionary political order were not diminished; instead, they grew. In this sense, democratization obviously threatened existing ruling classes and political elites and it was because of this that the precise political form of democracy was infused with a whole set of resentments, grievances and pathologies that came to direct and condition the precise ideological content of democracy. This obviously also included race and racisms. And a primary beneficiary of such developments which implicated; indeed, to some extent, was directed by ruling classes and state elites, was the far-right. This was because the far-right was conservative and reactionary in its ideological outlook, as well as being deeply hostile to socialism and Marxism in particular and also, more significantly, because it was organized around and rested on subaltern and non-ruling class forms of political agency. The far-right then emerged as a particular 'democratic' reaction to the twin changes of capitalist development and democratization.

In retrospect  we can see the socioeconomic dimensions and political consequences of the 1848 revolutions as a watershed in European politics centred on the shift towards social contradictions and conflict associated with capitalism as the primary driver of political developments that resulted in the emergence of new forms and modes of politics, and forms of state, to deal with the new social challenges. Thus, the spatial unevenness of capitalist development – a processed characterized by a structural dynamic of shifting locales of revolutionary socio-economic transformation – is reproduced through the combining of the new with existing and reactionary institutions, ideas and social and political arrangements that form the concrete amalgam of capitalism and are a key source of the ideological articulations of crisis and 'resistance' within it. The far-right emerged and grew out of this. Indeed, we might argue that it was to be the socio-political outcomes of 1848 in terms of forms of state and currents of social conflict that would come to – in the medium and longer term – determine European politics until the onset of World War II. The next chapter examines such developments as the internationalizing dimension of capitalist development – evident and causal of 1848 – became much more pronounced as the century wore on, helping to provide a set of enabling conditions all the more favourable to the growth of the modern far-right and, in many respects, laying down the basis for the subsequent emergence of fascism.

# The Rise of the Far-Right

By the final decades of the nineteenth century, a distinct and autonomous current of far-right politics was clearly visible across several major European states. Evident in organizations such as the *Alldeutscher Verband* (Pan-German League) and the *Bund der Landwirte* (Farmers' League) in Germany, the *Ligue des Patriotes* and *Action Française* in France and the Tariff Reform League and British Brothers in Britain, the far-right exercised a significant level of political influence in determining both the character of domestic and international politics concerning trade relations, immigration, citizenship, and geopolitics. While both the ideological fabric and political complexion of European states were far from homogenous, the period from the early 1870s onwards reflected a universal or generalized trend across different national locales suggestive of a common set of causal structures and dynamics in fostering the far-right.

This 'subaltern' far-right – developed through popular mass mobilizations outside of, and, in many cases, antagonistic to existing political-institutional arrangements and elites – operated in a political universe that was also defined by a far-right embedded within and part of the capitalist-imperialist state. This far-right was in some respects a legacy of the *ancien régime*, and notably so with regard to the landlord class – as exemplified by the Prussian Junkers – but it was also made up of a growing industrial bourgeoisie committed to geopolitically-driven economic expansion abroad and the repression of the workers' movement at home. The politics of the period up until 1914 were to be significantly coloured by the interaction of these two forms of authoritarian right: one of which remained – to varying degrees – anchored in the state and part of the ruling class and, the other, characterized by the mass politics of the age as evidenced in the street, propaganda and mass movements that challenged the traditional social and political prerogatives of the traditional political elites and ruling classes which laid the social and ideological foundations for what was to become fascism after 1918.

The temporality, number, strength, and significance of these movements varied from country to country, as well as their respective connections to traditional conservative ruling social and political interests based on land ownership. However, they shared some common features. They tended to draw support and membership from a range of social constituencies but particularly from farmers, landlords, small businessmen and the new petty bourgeois layers of low and medium grade white-collar employees of the modernizing state. Made cohesive through the ideology of racialized nationalism dominated by a universal anti-Semitism and an aggressive anti-socialism, they sought to provide a popular and mass alternative to the growing working-class movement of the time and, in consequence – and in spite of their rhetoric of transcending class divisions – largely failed to draw anything but fleeting or marginal working-class support. Further, they tended to support a nationalist-imperialist foreign policy based on geopolitical rivalry. Indeed, the economic health and prosperity of the nation were seen as being closely aligned with geopolitical strength and struggle. Growing geopolitical power was seen as a means of realizing economic prosperity.

They also had an ambivalent position towards capitalism. Committed to upholding private property rights and market-based economic transactions, these groups tended to oppose liberal doctrines of free trade – which in much of Europe was labelled 'Manchesterism' – calling for protectionism and the formation of imperial trading blocs as a means to secure social and racial protections from cosmopolitan forces. Finally, they were concerned with the growing encroachments of global and foreign capital within their respective economies and the way in which such developments were seen as undermining traditional social relations, and consequently, the overall 'health of the race' and the cultural fabric of the nation. Whether this was in the form of economic migrants present in cities and towns looking for work and sounding and appearing 'different' (Jews across Europe, Irish in Britain and Poles in Germany) – at odds with the racialized imaginary of the citizen that characterized this age – or the increasing presence of large scale and foreign firms and commodities within domestic markets. Their concern about the international or cosmopolitan dimensions of capitalist exchange was acute. And while not fascist, the ideological outlook and political concerns of many of these movements foreshadowed the fascist movements of the inter-war era and, to a not insignificant extent, the ideological predilections of the contemporary far-right (Saull, 2015b).

This chapter focuses on explaining the structural and conjunctural causes of the rise of the European far-right in the final decades of the nineteenth century. Focusing on developments within Germany, France, and Britain – the three most important capitalist-imperialist states of the era – I will outline how the evolving political economy of a globalizing capitalism contributed to the reconfiguring of the domestic socioeconomic and political interiors of these states and how the far-right came to prosper therein. Consequently, the discussion will assess class formation and class relations, the interactions between political elites and leading class fractions and the subaltern movements of the far-right. In doing so, I will demonstrate how the origins of the far-right that

I discussed in the previous chapter came to fruition and why. Further, I will also focus on how the emergence of these modern far-right movements set in place an international contextual, socioeconomic, and ideo-political template that continues to inform and characterize the contemporary far-right and the socioeconomic and political impulses that help generate it. Before focusing on each specific national case, I provide a general explanatory framework that outlines the wider context and impulses that these different national expressions existed within and where the broader methodological and theoretical framework centred on capital, race and space is mapped out.

## 1 Capitalist Imperialism and Geopolitics in the Rise of the European Far-Right

In many respects the changes that produced a fertile social terrain for the growth of the far-right were a product of the ever-increasing expansion and penetration of capitalism into the societies of Europe and, in consequence, how this undermined and led to the breakdown of pre-existing forms of moral economy and their associated social protections. It was this that triggered forms of collectivized response demanding the restoration of social protections (see Polanyi, 2001). However, there was something more to these developments than just the social and political consequences emergent from the contradictions between capital and labour and the opening up of ever more space to capitalist exploitation and the weakening of traditional sources of social obligation and protection. In this respect, the far-right was born out of the birth-pangs of an emerging *international* capitalist division of labour and the domestic (class) and international (geopolitical) contradictions and tensions that this process generated. Specifically, it was the working out of uneven and combined capitalist development over the course of the second half of the nineteenth century and the social, cultural, ideological, and political amalgams that were produced. In this respect, while the international and geopolitical context in conditioning and shaping the politics of the far-right at this time must be emphasized, these international determinants were not uniform, singular, or monolithic. This was because of the precise temporal and spatial aspects of unevenness that capitalism produces, as well as the agent-centred politics produced from the distinct – and nationally specific – forms of combination.

The global character of capitalist development and the geopolitical and political architecture that was associated with it was, then, a key source of the far-right, particularly through the way in which the reproduction of the global capitalist-imperialist order was allied with the continued reproduction of the domestic socioeconomic and political order within the leading European industrial states. In this regard two trends associated with capitalist development were particularly important in promoting the development of the far-right over this period: (I) the uneven geographical development of capitalism across and within European states and how this contributed to and intensified geopolitical rivalry; and (II) the concomitant rapid transformation of Europe's social structure which undermined existing – traditional – political institutional arrangements. Regarding the former, UCD was particularly apparent in the relations between town and countryside whereby – over the space of a couple of decades – particular regions were transformed from largely rural-agrarian to urban-industrial environments. The result was that European societies and Germany in particular (and Italy by 1914) were characterised by zones dominated by rapidly urbanizing and industrializing cities increasingly integrated into global networks of capital accumulation in contrast to stagnating and economically backward regions, such as southern Italy, the East Elbian parts of Prussia and the south-west of Germany (see Bessel, 1978: 199–210; Eley, 1983: 68–9; Pollard, 1981; Tipton and Aldrich, 1987: 21; Torp, 2014).

They key issue in these developments is that this uneven development was driven by an increasing penetration of a globalizing capitalism within these countries and that the geographically uneven impact of these trends triggered spatially-framed far-right responses. Thus, as much as the far-right was and is constituted by an uneven temporality, it also emerged and grew within specific geographical locales. In the case of late nineteenth century far-right mobilizations these tended to be concentrated in two locations: (I) those rural regions subject to the most acute contradictions of uneven capitalist development and especially where mobilizations from below were co-opted and/or linked to the machinations of landlord classes, which was typical of the German case; and (II) in those urban areas where the combination of the increasing presence of big and foreign capital and the recent arrival of ethnically or religiously distinct immigrants combined to trigger far-right responses based on a hostility to the rapid changes in the socioeconomic and cultural fabric of urban-life. Following Geoff Eley, we might say that 'the pace of social change outstripped the adaptive capabilities of existing political institutions' and especially so when these institutions were confronted with such a range of competing and conflicting social demands derived from the rapid transformations unleashed by capitalist development (Eley, 1983: 69).

This process of socioeconomic change was, as we shall see, hardwired into a pre-existing and evolving geopolitical framework which, at times, were inseparable. The working out and consequences of UCD on class relations and class formation, industrial development, and political stability, as well as the spatial distributions and concentrations of economic activity, were significantly driven and shaped by geopolitical networks, arrangements, and decisions (Arendt, 1968; Harvey, 2003: 33–49; Tooze, 2015b). After all, this was a capitalist imperialism whereby the 'pristine logic' of the capital-labour relation was, in various ways, imbued with a geopolitical dimension, reflected not only in forms of colonial plunder and trade arrangements, but also in the domestic reproduction of class fractions – ruling and subaltern (Halperin, 2004: 119–44; Hobsbawm, 1987; Weiss, 1977). The 'spatio-temporal fix' of capitalist development (Harvey, 2003: 43–4, 120–4) evident in the constant spatial expansion of capital into new geographical locales and the transformation of existing and new spaces – and how such spatial relations take on a specific temporality in moments of crisis (Bloch, 1977, 2009) – was integral to capitalist development at this time. Yet, as we shall see, the specific spatial arrangements and the working out of the spatio-temporal fix were intimately connected to both the territorial logics of nation and state formation that characterized the era and the broader context of an imperialist geopolitics that set limits, as much as opportunities, for the resolution of crises.

In consequence, the spatial arrangements that capitalist accumulation took place within meant that significant fractions of the industrial bourgeoisie (heavy industry, shipping and armaments etc.) were materially reproduced through such geopolitically-determined modes of accumulation. This resulted in a political or hegemonic 'common-sense' predisposed to maintaining and expanding such geopolitical circuits that, in some cases, made these class fractions favourable to the use of force and war as a means through which to preserve and expand such avenues of capital accumulation. Thus, capitalism was not just conditioned by space; it was also conditioned and organized, to a significant degree, through militarism and its associated ideo-political currents. Further, the elite-generated racialized nationalism that helped legitimate such arrangements filtered down – via propaganda – into subaltern layers through the idea of 'social imperialism' (Eley, 1976; Semmel, 1960; Wehler, 1985). The ideological and culture reservoirs of the far-right were, then, to a considerable extent embedded in the fabric of these societies through the orientations of ruling classes and state elites and, to varying degrees, in a popular 'common sense' (Halperin, 2004: 51–77; Mayer, 1981).

These arrangements and the intertwining of a geopolitical with an economic logic of capitalist accumulation continued up until 1945. Combination exerted itself over unevenness in the sense that, within the capital relation of value creation produced from the exchange relationship between capital and labour, the politics and state-forms that facilitated this reflected racialized and

militarized amalgams that asserted a powerful dynamic within the reproduction of capitalism. And, as we shall see, this organic relationship was constitutive of a far-right politics that saw the drawing together of social alliances
between reactionary ruling class fractions with subaltern layers whose social
security and reproduction was equally determined by such international
arrangements, thus producing a socio-political amalgam of the 'ancient and
the new' in the politics of the era. This was the original far-right social alliance;
but it is something that has continued to define the far-right in its relationship
with capitalist development even as capitalism has dissolved some of the class
layers – and its agrarian sources located in the 'landlord peasant nexus', specifically – that originally constituted it.

What is clear is that the actual process of constructing an international
capitalist order at this time reflected a set of very uneven and internationally-
sourced pressures and compulsions. Consequently, because capitalism has
spread unevenly and tended to bequeath superior material and productive
forces to the most advanced capitalist states (Arrighi, et al., 1999a; Rosenberg,
2006; Smith, 2008), its international spread into the interiors of other socioeconomic formations was realized via economic and geopolitical pressures
from without (Gerschenkron, 1962; Lafrance, 2019: 8). Trotsky described this as
the 'whip of external necessity' (Trotsky, 2008: 24) which reflected the external context that confronted all the major European powers over this period,
including Britain despite the advantages it accrued though its unique position
of being the first capitalist-industrial power. And, as Rosenberg (2006, 2016;
see also Anievas, 2014) has well-argued, methodologically, it means that the
understanding and explanation of the domestic social development (sociology) of any one state is, at the same time, a process that can only be explained
via a reference to the international and the mediating role provided by the
existence of multiple states and external relations and interactions operating
at the same time.

The historical process of capitalist development in Europe and elsewhere
has, accordingly, been primarily about how international or global structural
socioeconomic forces organized around the capital social relation have permeated, de-stabilized and transformed the socioeconomic and political interiors
of states (Hobsbawm, 1987; Rosenberg, 2006, 2010, 2016; Selwyn, 2011; Silver,
2003; Tooze, 2015b), or, at least, have come to exert powerful social and geopolitical pressures on national state elites and ruling classes to implement
reform or 'modernization' (see Halliday, 1999; Gerschenkron, 1962; Mann, 1993;
Skocpol. 1979; Trimberger, 1978). A key driver of this was obviously imperialism – the forceful and coercive opening up of spaces and their socioeconomic
reconfiguration and subordinate insertion into the developing world market.

However, it was also actualized through the policy responses to such an environment defined by 'the unevenness of multiplicity' by political elites within other sovereign states through programmes of state-promoted reform and modernization (Kemp, 1985; Selwyn, 2011). This latter case tended to typify the European experience throughout the nineteenth century in response to the rise of industrial capitalism in Britain and beyond. The long and the short of this is that the reality of the encroachment of capitalism within different national locales – and its destabilizing and destructive power – was very much understood at this time as having a foreign or cosmopolitan accent, which obviously nationalized and racialized the political and economic responses to it.

The varied and relative significance of both the imperialist geopolitics of the era and the reality and perception of international compulsion in shaping domestic socioeconomic locales and the organization of the state in responding to such compulsions reflected the different developmental trajectories that UCD produces within the same temporal moment (see Green, 2012; Pollard, 1981: 184–5). Thus, the structure and workings of the international economy were partially constituted by – and fractions of national (especially British) capitalist classes were reproduced through – liberal institutional forms and patterns of international economic exchange, as reflected in the operation of the Gold Standard, capital investment and international capital flows organized via the City of London.[1] It was these dimensions that provide the evidence of this period revealing a form of liberal international order under British hegemony (see Cox, 1987: 123–47; Gilpin, 1975: 79–84; Polanyi, 2001) and the positive contribution that British trade and finance – the main international economic public goods of the era – made to the economic development of other societies in Europe and elsewhere. Yet, paradoxically, such liberal arrangements also compelled illiberal and nationalist responses from developing capitalist states (see Gourevitch, 1978; Poulantzas, 1974) in Europe. This was in part because of the co-constitutive imperial geopolitics that defined British global power, but also because of the external economic pressures of the competitive liberal order and the political difficulties that developing capitalist powers such as

---

1   For some scholars in International Relations (IR) and International Political Economy (IPE) the final decades of the nineteenth century are considered as a *belle époque* and a precursor to post-Cold War globalization (see Held, et al., 1999; Hirst and Thompson, 1999; Hopkins, 2002). Such views capture something about the world economy, at this time, but they clearly overlook its imperial character and the centrality of geopolitics to its operations. Thus, this was a globalization with a distinct spatial framing heavily conditioned by imperial blocs and closed markets with militarized competition for control of strategic waterways and exploitation of minerals and natural resources based on monopoly privileges (see Harvey, 2003; Callinicos, 2009; Kiely, 2010).

France and Germany, amongst others, had in responding to them in a way that secured the basis of their existing domestic political orders and the class hierarchies attached to them.

Consequently, the model form of national capitalism that emerged in this hierarchical and competitive context within the later-developing economies such as Germany was one organized around monopoly capital. While monopoly capital was not the generic form of industrial-financial organization of the capitalist class as Lenin (Lenin, 2010) and others claimed, it had become the dominant form in Germany as industrial production was organized through the vertical integration of the production process and the combining of finance with industrial capital. Such an arrangement implicated both the character of the state as political elites were crucial in facilitating this arrangement and geopolitics as the vertical integration of the firm was premised on its monopoly privileges over vast spatial domains organized via geopolitical circuits and imperial trading blocs (Arrighi, et al., 1999b: 124–5; Bairoch, 1993: 24–9; Barratt Brown, 1974: 183–200; Jessop, 1982: 32–9; Silver, 2003:131–44). This form of political economy leant itself to a far-right politics; indeed, it was reproduced through it as revealed in nationalist protections and monopoly exclusions and the management of the economic contradictions between the backward agrarian sector and industry and finance by state elites – overlaid with nationalist propaganda that served to mobilize and promote far-right movements from the top via official state propaganda (Barratt Brown, 1974: 165).

The issue here, however, is that through the methodological prism of uneven and combined development these variable outcomes – relative stability and more limited openings for the far-right in one jurisdiction, compared to instabilities and crises giving rise to strong far-right movements in other states – were *inter*-connected. That is, the explanation of one cannot be insulated or isolated from the other, because the specific socioeconomic structure of capitalism is constituted by such international interactions as a mediated or *differentiated totality*. In the case of Germany, as Jeremy Green (2012: 352) explains, '[t]he particular course of German economic development was moulded by the conditioning force field of international development and the gradual universalization of capitalist social relations throughout Europe.' Further, and following Sydney Pollard (1981: 30–1, 184–5), we can see the wider international context conditioning the precise form of industrialization and the embedding of the capital social relation as amounting to 'the differential of contemporaneousness'. In other words, considered from the perspective of the system as a whole and its differentiated totality, we can recognize how the developmental processes of other societies within the same temporal moment shaped, to varying degrees, not only the individual pathways of late industrialisers, but also their subsequent development. And this is certainly what played out after the early 1870s as the imperialist form of the international capitalist economy began to solidify. And such variations in the geopolitical outcomes of the birth-pangs of this emerging liberal international economic order were intimately connected to the decisions of liberal political actors and social forces within Britain in particular. What we can take from this is that the liberalism of Britain over this period was, in part, a consequence of, or contingent on, a set of geopolitical international economic structures that helped foster a far-right politics *elsewhere*. And what this means methodologically is that seeking to explain the national specificity of how and why a far-right politics develops in one place compared to its absence in another *necessarily* invokes that absence and the causal drivers producing such varied but *co-constituted* outcomes in the same temporal moment in a way that a focus on the singular case cannot provide.

The externally-driven and geopolitically mediated dimension of international capitalist development creating a capitalist imperialism over this period was also conditioned through and constituted by the growth of an industrial working class. The significance of this was not just in a sociological and spatial sense as demonstrated in its emergence as a mass subaltern layer located in urban concentrations, but also political, with respect to its connection to democratization and mass politics. Workers were the primary social agents of democratization after 1848, which meant that democracy was directly connected to socialism and the possibility of revolutionary social transformation. This is something that Marx shared with his liberal and conservative critics and why democratization did not develop in the way or with the outcome that Marx had anticipated. Thus, while the struggle for democracy in the second half of the nineteenth century reflected the rise of the 'gravediggers' of capitalism in mass working class parties epitomized by the Social Democrats in Germany, alongside the emergence of a 'democratic public sphere' of political deliberation, it also provided a means for the consolidation and reinforcement of social hierarchies and ruling classes. So, although democracy was perceived by reactionary ideologues in particular (Bon, 2001; Gobineau, 1999) as a threat to the existing socio-political order – liberal or otherwise – it also offered novel ways of constructing new social and political hierarchies (see Arendt, 1968). And, as we shall see, far-right political forces were one of the primary agents and beneficiaries of such developments.

For political elites and ruling classes, the second half of the nineteenth century was defined by a duel set of political pressures and socioeconomic forces: on the one hand emanating from without through the competitive economic pressure of a globalizing capitalism and, on the other hand, from

within, as revealed in the growing organized and socialist working class movements that developed through the process of capitalist industrialization and
that  threatened the existing forms of social property relations and political
order. The far-right developed out of these contradictory arrangements as an
autonomous mass and subaltern actor that conditioned both domestic socioeconomic and political development and the character of international
relations and geopolitics. In the former it helped establish and drive a hyper-
nationalist and racialized mass politics that utilized the spaces, opportunities,
and structures of the emerging democratic universe and, in doing so, opposed
and frustrated the socialist left. And in the latter, it fed-off extant imperial hierarchies and geopolitical tensions and super-charged them, thereby contributing to the crisis of August 1914.

International arrangements for the management of the capitalist order
were far from being hegemonic. Thus the leading liberal power, Britain, had
not managed to establish a developed international institutional architecture
to manage relations and deal with crises (see Tooze, 2015b). And, further, there
was little or no acceptance by other industrializing states of the international
leadership privileges accruing to Britain based on a political-ideological consensus shaped around liberalism – as a basis for international or domestic
political order (Halperin, 2004; Mayer, 1981) and realized through the universalization of international public goods. Consequently, the imperialist character of capitalist development resulted not only in the weak, indeed, absent
socialization of other ruling class and elites into the British-led 'international
historical bloc,' but also in subaltern layers. This facilitated the development of
vertical forms of far-right mobilization which were co-ordinated by state elites
and framed around nationalist hostility to the existing Anglo-centric international order.

This was significant on its own terms, but it was particularly so in moments
of crisis, as demonstrated in the period of the deflationary spiral (especially
pronounced in agricultural and commodity prices) – as the full impact of the
railways revolution on opening up distant markets was finally felt[2] – and falling

---

2  The crisis revealed itself in falling profits and prices resulting from the technological innovations that facilitated increased competitive pressures in agriculture, in particular, as cheaper
   goods flooded into European markers from extra-continental sources. While the crisis
   resulted in fluctuating periods of economic stagnation triggering falling incomes and unemployment, this period also saw growth in production and international trade overall (though
   at a slower rate than before) which would – by the end of the century – see Germany and the
   US overtake Britain in their respective industrial capacities (Hobsbawm, 1995: 34–55; Landes,
   1969: 231).

profits over the course of the Long (or 'Great') Depression across the world economy between 1873 and 1896. The period, then – at a time when developing capitalist states such as Germany were being integrated into a world capitalist economy – was dominated by deflationary pressures and profit squeezes[3] that accentuated the already extant pressures derived from its existing structural hierarchies and inequities. Such a development reflected the working out of uneven and combined development as the technological advances associated with the railways and the production efficiencies of specific agricultural regions demonstrated the spatial and temporal unevenness of capitalist development alongside an intensification of the contradictions of combination within those economies on the receiving end of these competitive pressures.

The long depression of the late nineteenth century was an economic crisis that had a set of spatialized consequences determined by the existing geopolitical order of the time and which foreclosed, as much as it opened-up, the workings of the spatio-temporal fix. Indeed, such arrangements were central to the promotion of the nationalist and geopolitically-assertive responses that came to define the politics of this era. Thus, through the turn to trade protectionism and imperialist competition for new resources and markets for investment and exports (Barratt Brown, 1974: 183–200; Kiely, 2010: 69–90; Lenin, 2010; Saul, 1985) – highlighted by the 'scramble for Africa' in the 1880s – the Long Depression not only coincided with, but provided a major stimulus to, the fevered colonizing activity of European states that ended up provoking a series of geopolitical crises that were to lay the prelude to war in 1914.

The significance of the Long Depression was two-fold with respect to the growth of far-right movements. First, as we shall see later in this chapter, it tended to squeeze those social layers – especially small-scale farmers, small traders and property owners – that became the main foot soldiers of the far-right. Although not confined to these petty bourgeois layers, it was these groups, and especially those located in the districts of towns and cities where the logic of capital had most revealed itself, where far-right mobilizations were concentrated. In other words, the economic consequences of the Long Depression facilitated a particular socio-political response based on extreme nationalism and economic protectionism.[4] Secondly, because an imperialist geopolitics

---

3  Between 1873 and 1896 in general, the volume of sales in Europe grew on average by 2.3 percent per annum compared with growth levels more than double that of 5–6 percent in the preceding decades (Bairoch, 1993: 46).

4  Europe was flooded with cheap agricultural produce that had a dramatic impact on the most backward agrarian regions of Germany. The pressures of the growing capitalist world market in agriculture goods, and the way in which this undermined the economic livelihood of

was already embedded within the structure and workings of the world market – this was no flat borderless liberal spatial utopia but rather a much more
fractured, segmented and heterogenous space – that gave economic advantages to some states over others, the crisis intensified the developmental tendencies towards empire and imperialism for industrializing late-comers. It was
this which provided the second part of the 'virtuous circle' conducive to the
advance of the far-right and particularly as it unleashed a logic of militarism
and war into elite economic strategizing. In short, the existential nature of the
threat to the economic viability of some key ruling class – notably landlords –
fractions that the crisis caused helped supercharge a politics saturated with
the language, symbols and leitmotifs of angst, resentment and catastrophe
that added fuel to the fire of the far-right.

## 2      Race and Racialized Politics in the Developing Liberal
International Order

The development of an international capitalist economy in the nineteenth
century and the contradictions and crises that were produced within it were
also – as alluded to already – closely connected to the politics of race and the
centrality of racism in the projects of state formation, the maintenance of metropolitan social order and imperialism over the second half of the nineteenth
century. Race, then, was constitutive of the construction of liberal-capitalist
order in the spheres of domestic as much as international and colonial politics. Further, the issue of race was all-pervasive in the sense that it was central
to the framing of the varied political ideologies across the European political
spectrum from the left to the right. So, while the far-right occupied the most
entrenched, virulent, and violent position on race, it was also the case that the
world views and political arguments of liberals and, to some extent, socialists, were also informed by a distinct racialized sensibility. Indeed, European
working-class formation was fundamentally associated with and conditioned
by racialized structures and relationships through the material advantages
that European workers gained through racialized colonial labour regimes and
imperial trading relations, as well as by the ideologies of social imperialism
that were inflected by varying degrees of racialized nationalism based on a

---

German peasants and landowners (Eley, 1993; Kitchen, 1978: 163; Vascik, 1993) was a major
current in the development of the German far-right up to and including the fascist episode.

racial imaginary of whites as the dominant race with Africans at the bottom of the racial hierarchy.

Racial identities and forms of racism and racial (or white) supremacy had been part and parcel of European politics and culture for a long time, to some extent going back to the fifteenth century original colonial encounter, but the centrality of race and racialized identity had been more varied and fleeting in the determination of European domestic politics than it was to be after the 1870s. As Neil MacMaster (2001: 1–27; see also Mosse, 1985: 65–127) makes clear, across European countries in the final decades of the nineteenth century a much more systematic and constitutive form of racism came to be embedded into social structures and ideological imaginaries as race came to be connected to national identity and citizenship, to social order and politics and to militarism and geopolitical rivalry. In many respects, race became the over-determining category – in relation to gender and class – of social and political analysis (see Du Bois, 2015) in terms of the maintenance of the European colonial order and the domestic social and political stability of imperial metropoles.

The deployment of racial categories, racial hierarchies and the racialization of social issues and population groups were trends that cut across otherwise distinct and antagonist ideo-political currents in Europe at the time, such that a set of racialized attitudes dominated a popular common sense across large swathes of European publics and such attitudes were promoted and propagated through 'bottom-up' and popular sources (literature, theatre, arts and popular culture), as well as by elite-level or state-sponsored propaganda (MacMaster, 2001: 31–57; Malik, 1996: 101–48). Furthermore, as much as far-right movements centred on an ideology of anti-Semitism – as a core part of their propaganda and political appeal – so it was also the case that some currents on the left adopted anti-Semitic tropes as part of their anti-capitalist positions and notably with respect to the perceived connections between Jews and international finance (Holmes, 1979; McMaster, 2011: 86–114; Mosse, 1985: 150–56; Pulzer, 1988; Volkov, 1978).

The all-pervasive currency of race and racism that dominated society through these years makes clear that racism was not, solely, the *sine qua non* of the far-right. However, this does not mean that there were not important distinctions to be made between the racism that inflected liberal thinking (and some parts of the socialist left) and that of the right and its centrality in the political identity of each. Indeed, Alexis de Tocqueville as representative of European liberalism was critical of and opposed to the 'scientific racism'[5] of

---

5  Scientific racism refers to a distinct body of literature that originated out of the philosophical naturalism of the Eighteenth century and the attempt to classify the human race through

the leading French advocate of a global racial hierarchy, Arthur de Gobineau (Gobineau, 1999; see Mosse, 1985: 51–62 for a critical commentary), which he regarded as not only wrong but 'pernicious'. Such a view was also shared, to some degree, by John Stuart Mill (Varouxakis, 1998). So, although Mill's position on race and the racialized assumptions in his defence of colonialism have been singled out for critical commentary (Bell, 2010; Jahn, 2005), Mill was also a leading critic and opponent of the right-wing positions on race and, in particular, the views of Thomas Carlyle on slavery and Africans (Mill, 1984: 87–96). This was also evident in his role in the Jamaica Committee, and its (unsuccessful) attempt to have the Governor of Jamaica, Edward Eyre, tried for his role in the brutal suppression of the Morant Bay rebellion of former enslaved people in 1865.

Such distinctions were more than just symbolic or technical in significance for the type of politics and state that these different ideo-political positions articulated. At the time, they reflected important theoretical and political distinctions on race and racial equality that continue to inform the distinctions between liberals and the far-right on these issues in the contemporary political context. Further, specifically with regard to the socialist left in the nineteenth century, its anti-Semitism was clearly linked to a distinct, if crude and flawed, class analysis as to the workings of capitalism and the distinct role and power of financial interests, even if it did all too easily draw on a deep-seated anti-Semitism through racializing the properties of a particularly important international banking house – the Rothschilds. Further, as much as the left deployed anti-Semitic tropes to help forward its anti-capitalist agenda within

---

a taxonomy of race and racial differences across the human species based on a physical anthropology or biology. Thus, different racial groups were categorized based on physiological differences (hair, skin colour etc) that in nearly all cases were then grafted onto preexisting (within Europe) assumed social and cultural dispositions such that the cultural dispositions of said races were in effect, inherited and passed onto future generations. These taxonomies not only tended to *fix* particular racial groups with inherited and permanent social characteristics, but they also articulated a white supremacism based on the social and cultural 'achievements' – in part reflected in colonial domination – of Europeans. These ideas were re-articulated and re-packaged after the 1850s, in a number of publications involving racist propagandists (for example see Ernst Haeckel and Houston Stewart Chamberlain in Germany, Arthur de Gobineau and Vacher de Lapouge in France and Robert Knox and Francis Galton in Britain) within a very different social and political context. Thus, the 'science' of race was an important factor in helping to legitimate and propagate societal racism, but these ideas of inherited racial characteristics became so significant because of the way in which they came to be articulated as explanatory responses to the particular cultural, socioeconomic, and political changes and crises that European societies were passing though at this time (see MacMaster, 2011; Malik, 1996: 114–48; Mosse, 1985: 1–34, 77–93).

a popular discourse that continued to be saturated with anti-Semitic associations, it was forces on the left – both socialist and liberal – that had been in the forefront of promoting and realizing Jewish emancipation over the course of the nineteenth century in the face of reactionary opposition from the right. It was also the case that the most revolutionary layers of the European working class also participated in the struggle against plantation slavery with the involvement of significant numbers of German political refugees from the 1848 revolution joining up to fight for Union forces in the American Civil War. Indeed, Marx's writing on the American Civil War made clear his commitment to the overthrow of plantation slavery and racial equality (Marx, 1973b; see also Anderson, 2010; Blackburn, 2011).

In addressing the question of why, at this moment, did racism and racializing narratives become much more central to European social and political life, and deployed in a much more systematic and comprehensive fashion, we need to relate how ideas about race and, in particular, the prevailing scientific racism of the time filtered into and became attached to a number of social and political questions that confronted European societies in this period. In this sense, we can identify how the changing political and economic contexts – at both the domestic and international levels – were causal of a racialization of politics that was obviously favourable to a far-right *Weltanschauung*, as well as how far-right agency played such a key role in promoting and realizing such a racialized politics over other ideo-political currents.

As already noted, the period after 1870 through to the beginning of the twentieth century was dominated by a set of rapid social dislocations and transformations, much of which took place within a context of a severe economic downturn. The pace and depth of socioeconomic change and the apparent (and real) international sources of this change and associated instabilities provided an opportunity for anti-Semitism to re-emerge as a powerful mobilizing, scapegoating and 'explanatory' ideology. Thus, those social layers – landlords, peasants and small businessmen in particular as well as some workers – who were particularly affected by socioeconomic transformation and especially when their economic woes were connected to international competition and problems with accessing or maintaining credit flows, were particularly susceptible to anti-Semitic demagoguery given the long-standing stereotype of the Jew as money lender and the importance of a Jewish-owned bank, Rothschilds, in European finance.

Of course, much of this did not rest on any objective or material basis given the poverty and political marginalization of large numbers of Jews across Europe. But within a context of generalized economic crisis that was punctuated by episodes of banking failure and financial crisis as in France, unfounded rumours of Jewish involvement and benefit were enough to racialize such incidents and the wider economic malaise. The fact that these racist claims were often incoherent and contradictory, as well as lacking credible material support, did not weaken their – as now – political significance and appeal across a wide range of social layers. Instead, what mattered was how such 'anti-Semitic conspiracism' offered 'a total explanation of a supposed state of cosmic and social decadence by identifying Jews as the evil agents of that dislocation and decay' (Wilson, 1982: 738). Anti-Semitism provided a *universal* cause for the multiple contradictions of modernity (MacMaster, 2001: 88), making for a powerful ideological device that reflected a superficial and distorted reality based on the largely minor role of Jews in international finance and local money-lending, the depiction of socialism as a Jewish creed – based on its association with Marx and its anti-nationalist cosmopolitanism – and the presence of Jewish refugees and migrants in ghettos scrambling for employment and competing with the other, non-Jewish, poor.

However, the causal elements or sources of a racialized anti-Semitism went beyond such economic or material concerns. Religious-sourced anti-Semitism emanating from the Roman Catholic Church's hierarchy continued to promote anti-Semitism. In this way, the church's Judeophobia morphed into a racial anti-Semitism based on the idea that Jews were a fundamental threat to Europe's Christian civilization and the power of the Church within society through their association with secularist trends associated with materialism, economic development, and the extension of civil rights and socialism (MacMaster, 2001: 99; Mosse, 1985: 128–49). Here, it was the figure of the assimilated Jew who was perceived as the biggest threat; a figure that reflected, to some degree, the apotheosis of the liberal vision of politics (see Sartre, 1948).

Finally, the wider international context of insecurity, geopolitical rivalry and inter-imperialist conflict also played an important role in fostering anti-Semitism. Specifically, anti-Semitism was connected to nationalist ideas that were increasingly connected to eugenics, race and 'Social Darwinism'. Accordingly, who could be recognized as legitimate citizens of the state and, specifically, who could be counted on as loyal in a context of international threat and insecurity, came to be framed through the Jew as a 'nation within a nation' and, as such, genetically unreliable and treacherous. Such positions came to dominate French politics in the 'Dreyfus Affair'[6] at the end of the

---

6   It was in this context of intense anti-Semitic hysteria in France in the late 1890s – whipped up by far-right movements and elements within the French state – that the most infamous document of anti-Semitic conspiracy – the *Protocols of the Elders of Zion* – was drafted by the French far-right and agents of the Czarist secret police. For the former, it provided

nineteenth century, but they also appeared in some aspects of liberal and left-wing commentary on conspiracies behind armed conflicts and who would benefit from them.[7] In this sense, race and nation became inter-changeable (see Balibar, 1991) in part because the perceived insecurity of the nation rested on the strength and loyalty of the race and the extent to which the nation and its citizens were constituted by a singular and inherited racial group because the racial stock was seen as the fundamental martial quality of military preparedness and strength. This racism extended not just to Jews but also to religious and ethnic minorities: see the Irish in Britain, and to Catholics and Poles in the *Kaiserreich*.

Anti-Semitism, however, was not the only racist discourse and ideology that facilitated the growth of the far-right at this time. Drawing on some of the same causal sources as anti-Semitism, an anti-black racism also became much more central to political discourse and racial identity helping to reinforce a European and white identity based on white supremacism – or fears about the threats to it. Again, a long-standing anti-black racism had been part of the European cultural imaginary for centuries, but such attitudes became supercharged in the late nineteenth century to produce a set of developments that were to play an important role in the class politics within Europe and through laying the ideological foundations for brutal – and in some cases genocidal – violence perpetuated by European colonial forces in sub-Saharan Africa. In many respects, this anti-black racism appears contradictory when viewed through the prism of Britain's abolition of the slave trade and the deployment of the Royal Navy against the transatlantic slave trade earlier in the nineteenth century, as well as the Union's victory and the emancipation of enslaved African-Americans after 1865. Such developments provide grist to the mill of a liberal rendering of the advance of progress and racial healing and equality that paralleled the advance of liberalism and democracy throughout the century.

However, the contradictions within liberalism vis-à-vis race meant that not only did an anti-black racism come to be rearticulated in the latter decades of the nineteenth century but it came to play an important role in shoring up social hierarchies and class power within European metropoles, as well as helping to justify a new wave of colonial expansion across Africa. As Neil MacMaster (2001: 64) notes, an entrenched anti-black racism continued to be pronounced across Britain and Europe even after racial emancipation was supposedly progressing. Thus, in accounts of the American civil war, newspapers

---

'authenticity' of a worldwide Jewish conspiracy that Dreyfus was connected to and, for the Russians, support for anti-Semitic pogroms (see Mosse, 1985: 117).

7   As evidenced in John Hobson's *Imperialism* (Hobson, 1988).

expanded on alleged black atrocities of rape and violence denoting the 'savagery' of Africans. Moreover, an important variant of liberal-sourced anti-black racism also developed in response to slave emancipation. Thus, in the British case, the fact that many former enslaved people in Jamaica and elsewhere across the Caribbean did not willingly offer themselves up as wage labour to capital suggested a return to the 'idleness' and 'primitiveness' of the 'savage' (MacMaster, 2001: 65), which provided an important racialized understanding of the quality of wage labour and those who were willing to subject themselves to such conditions. Such views are not so far removed from contemporary neoliberal discourse on work and the 'undeserving poor' (see Shilliam, 2018).

When such resistance played itself out in the newly acquired colonies of sub-Saharan Africa and particularly in the Belgium Congo and German South-West Africa, as Africans rejected,  or resisted their coercive exploitation as 'wage labour,' the response was extreme violence and, in the latter case, genocidal violence against the Herero and Nama peoples (Conrad, 2012; Kühne, 2013; Zimmerer, 2008). And while such violence took place in locales some distance away from the metropoles, this violence obviously implicated and characterized the types of states involved in its prosecution. This is particularly so with reference to the racialized logics of class formation that characterized this period particularly with respect to the working class and its racial vigour and loyalty.

In this respect elements from within the working class, including trade unions and socialist parties, bought into aspects of the ideology of white supremacism of the time (see Virdee, 2015). Indeed, some layers of the European industrial working class identified their social position and material well-being with colonial exploitation and the maintenance of Empire. However, the growth of working-class movements and socialist parties calling for the vote and, in some cases, revolutionary forms of change facilitated a racialized re-imagining of workers by elites and assisted by far-right movements, as racially impure or 'degenerate'. Thus, racist tropes and images drawn from the colonial experience and justification for anti-black racism were applied to elements of the metropolitan working class – those that were deemed 'degenerate' because of illness or infirmity due to disease from malnutrition and/or poor housing conditions – and/or those that actively embraced 'unpatriotic' or 'alien' ideologies etc. In this respect, opponents of the exploitative rights and accumulative privileges of private property and the designation of wage labour were racially suspect and tarred with racial epitaphs. Such racialized images – these workers were like 'savages' (MacMaster, 2001: 35; Malik, 1996) – drew on the pre-existing racial vocabulary of the time. In Britain  this was most infamously associated with anti-Irish racism, with popular publications including *Punch* depicting Irish people as ape-like and as a way of reinforcing a racist stereotype about Irish people and promoting racial divisions within the urban working class (see Giley, 1978; Swift, 1987). Racialized imaginaries and racist tropes were deployed via a range of media to sow division within the working class through trying to embed a popular racist common sense based on anti-Irish racism.

The final element that contributed to the prevalence of racism at this time derived from Social Darwinism. Linked to and drawing on the pretensions of a scientific racism, Darwin's theory of natural selection and evolution was reconfigured and, in many respects, distorted, by several racist propagandists, some of whom – such as Ernst Haeckel – were leading voices in far-right movements – in his case the *Alldeutscher Bund* (see MacMaster, 2001: 41). Social Darwinism contained two elements that assisted the politics of the far-right: one, associated with domestic social insecurities and the other international. In the former, it was articulated as a way of responding to the consequences of capitalist development in the form of the growth of proletarian populations in cities living in slums and their associated health risks. Social Darwinism in this iteration amounted to a form of class racism bemoaning a degeneracy of the racial stock which, for many of its advocates, justified the working out of a Social Darwinist logic as reflected in the deaths of those who did not have the strength to survive through independently reproducing themselves as wage labour and citizens. Such a logic was obviously linked to eugenics and racialized fears as to the quality of the nation's racial stock that would, in the long-term, be better-off with the 'disappearance' or 'breeding out' of such poor and weak elements (Claeys, 2000; MacMaster, 2001: 34–40; Weikart, 2003). However, such views were also connected to a fear of the urban poor that, again, related to racialized narratives associating the 'criminal' European urban poor with the 'savagery' of Africans. Such racist depictions of the metropolitan (white) poor associated with their lived proximity with the racial Other and their embrace of the culture of the racial Other – be it in the form of dress, language or slang and music etc – continues to define the contemporary far-right's imaginary of the city.

The second element concerned the international context of geopolitical rivalry, militarism, and war-making capacity. Consequently, Social Darwinism was connected to an idea of race war and how the maintenance of colonial power over non-Europeans, and the competitive struggles within the white race demanded a strengthening and revitalization of the racial stock. The concern with the racial stock was both a physiological issue – to what extent the labouring classes were physically fit enough for war fighting in a context where conflict between the major powers seemed increasingly likely – but also a social and cultural one that was connected to the idea that workers were particularly vulnerable to subversion by ideological doctrines such as socialism that threatened the sociological and cultural basis of the race and the nationalist virtues associated with it. Such themes became particularly pronounced in the United States after 1918, as a combination of labour militancy, murmurings of a campaign for African-American civil rights and the growing spectre of revolutionary Bolshevism came together in the 'red-scares' of the early post-war period and which would continue to punctuate American politics and the politics of labour through to the 1960s (see Anievas, forthcoming).

I now move the discussion on by focusing on how the specific national dimensions of capitalist development and liberal political economy played out within this broader framing outlined above. This gave rise to a generic far-right political condition, but one which also reflected the distinct characteristics of how the contradictions within the articulations of capital, race and space played out in Germany, France, and Britain.

## 3    Germany: From Elite to Subaltern Far-Right

The emergence of distinct and independent far-right ideo-political currents in Germany in the latter part of the nineteenth century has been the subject of voluminous scholarly enquiry. Obviously, this stems from the subsequent history of Germany after 1918 and, specifically, the identification of the roots of what became National Socialism, as well as the role of the German far-right in the causes of World War One (see Anievas, 2014; Green, 2012; Halperin, 2004; Mayer, 1981). Indeed, there was something unique about the far-right in Germany in terms of its class basis, connections to the strategies of the ruling class and political elites, as well as the way in which geopolitics was central to both the institutional character of the German state and the material reproduction of dominant class interests.

For our purposes we can identify two overlapping strands to the development of the German far-right after 1848. On the one hand, a distinct form of state-led and ruling class endorsed strategy of social and political management that focused on the geopolitical consolidation of the newly formed *Kaiserreich*. This form of far-right was particularly associated with Otto von Bismarck, who was Imperial Chancellor and the key figure in this process between 1870 and 1890 (Arrighi and Silver, 1999: 124–5). On the other, a more subaltern and autonomous set of far-right movements that became much more pronounced in the 1890s; most notably through organizations such as the *Alldeutscher Verband* (Pan-German League) founded in 1891 and the *Bund der Landwirte* (Farmers' League) founded in 1893. In emphasizing the distinctions between the 'top-down' versus 'bottom-up' forms of far-right, I am not suggesting an independence and separation between these two strands of the far-right. Both were inter-connected to each other highlighting the enduring connections between far-right mobilizations from below and the strategies of dominant class interests in contexts of intense socioeconomic change, international rivalry, and revolutionary challenges from the left – real or imagined.

As we shall see, both dimensions of the far-right concentrated on and drew significant degrees of political support from urban and rural petty bourgeois social layers associated with small-scale farmers, traders and craftsmen commonly described as the *Mittelstand*. These inter-connections between the traditional or authoritarian right and the radical subaltern right have provided important social and ideological resources for elites to weather and negotiate the contradictions and challenges of uneven and combined development – we can see the far-right as a particular dimension of combined development – and specifically through the para-political dimensions of the liberal-constitutional state. Nevertheless, in contrast to developments in France and Britain after 1848, the connections between the state and ruling classes and far-right movements were unique and much more pervasive in the German case than elsewhere and this was a consequence of the distinct geopolitical context of late German state formation, alongside the particularly rapid and intense form of its capitalist modernization and the uneven and contradictory manner of its integration into the world economy.

Paradoxically, what was also significant about the structure of the German economy by the final two decades of the nineteenth century was that its rapid industrialization was connected to, and increasingly *dependent on*, its internationalization and *increasing* integration into the workings of the global economy (Torp, 2014: 20–36, 53, 115, 132, 252). This was not just about rising exports and how Germany's economic growth and industrialization were connected to penetrating overseas markets – including that of the British Empire[8] and the United States – but also how this relied on imports of raw materials, technology, and capital. Indeed, it was this exposure and increasing dependence in the reproduction of dominant fractions of the industrial capitalist class, as well as workers employed in export-facing and import-dependent sectors, that not only triggered far-right mobilizations from those social layers subject to internationally-driven economic disruption and change and competition,

---

8   By the early 1890s Germany was not only outproducing Britain in steel but was also increasingly eating into Britain's export and domestic markets. At the end of the century the world market in the new industries of chemicals, electronics and machines was dominated by German firms (Fremdling, 1997:352; Milward and Saul, 1977: 60; Torp, 2014: 47, 55, 63 1893).

but also acted as a countervailing socioeconomic force on these mobilizations because of the economic damage consequential on undermining these international connections.

The particularities of the German far-right in large part derived from the geopolitical challenges that confronted German state formation and economic development after 1848. This meant that German elites had to manage the challenge of national integration, or cohere the political and legal structures of a state geographically situated between two great powers – France and Russia – and, at the same time, do so through managing the socioeconomic and cultural dislocations attendant from uneven and combined development based on grafting capitalist industrialization onto a backward agrarian sector and the rapid development of what – by the 1880s – had become the world's most organized and militant working class. As noted by several scholars (Blackbourn, 1986; Blackbourn and Eley, 1984; Eley, 1980, 1983; Wehler, 1979, 1985), German state formation and capitalist development were particularly geopolitically determined (see Anievas, 2014: 71) in terms of both the creation of a coherent and unified capitalist industrialized society across a range of relatively autonomous jurisdictions after 1848 (and after the *Kaiserreich* was officially established in 1870) and secondly, in a wider international context where the access to markets and resources was determined by a material logic closely aligned with geopolitically-determined forms of economic exchange, trade, investment and market openings associated with more powerful imperial states.

In this regard, a distinct far-right, (or conservative-authoritarian and nationalist) form of politics came to dominate Germany after 1848 and was given a specific direction under Bismarck's leadership from the 1870s onwards. The sequencing or timing of the development of the German far-right was, however, determined by international developments, and specifically the long economic downturn – the 'Long Depression' of 1873 to 1896.[9] The Long Depression provided the determining international context for the development of the European far-right and in Germany in particular. The significance of this prolonged downturn was that the social reproduction of the Junker landlord class, as well as significant sections of the East Elbian peasantry, confronted a growing economic crisis from the mid-1870s as the world market in agricultural goods was transformed and as the basis of the agrarian social order was ripped

---

9   German industrial production dropped by almost a third over this period compared to the period from the early 1850s up until the early 1870s (Tylecote, 1992: 12, 214–20). Milward and Saul (1977: 22) note that it was not until 1880 that industrial production was to reach 1872–3 levels.

apart with the flooding of European markets with cheaper agrarian produce from the American and Russian bread-baskets (Hobsbawm, 1987; Kitchen, 1978; Torp, 2014: 49).[10] Further, as the crisis developed and metastasized into the domain of manufacturing production and trade, it also enveloped the *Mittelstand* – small and medium-sized manufacturing firms and traders – thereby contributing to a conjunctural social and political cocktail of radical and militant nationalism defined by an increasingly geopolitical orientation.

The far-right proclivities across the *Mittelstand* had been evident in the revolutionary crisis that gripped Germany over 1848–9 (as the previous chapter discussed), as revealed in the articulation of a politics based on social protection. Indeed, along with the peasantry, German political elites identified this social layer as the 'the best and strongest bulwark against the red flood' (Blackbourn, 1984a: 36). Consequently, throughout the post-1848 period, a concern with cultivating a distinct kind of '*Mittelstand* politics' was to be a key objective of German political elites that significantly conditioned Germany's political development – the ascent of a nominal democratic politics through the extension of the voting franchise after 1848[11] – and economic development through capitalist industrialization, as both were framed around accommodations towards the *Mittelstand* (Blackbourn, 1977; Blackbourn and Eley, 1984).

Thus one, if not the most significant, political outcomes of 1848 was the decision to incorporate this social constituency into a broader conservative coalition of the *conservative historical bloc* that included the traditional east-Elbian Junker aristocracy and the rising bourgeoisie of heavy industry (Blackbourn, 1977, 1984a: 36–7; Tipton, 1974: 953; Winkler, 1976: 2) because it was seen as providing an important element of popular legitimacy for the maintenance of the existing order that was central to the transformed political context unleashed by the 1848 revolutions. Further, and relatedly, these petty bourgeois layers

---

10   While in the early 1860s – before the impact of the transport revolution had been felt – Germany provided almost a third of Britain's wheat imports (thus helping to bolster the economic fortunes of Junker estates in the east), by the early 1880s – when cheaper grain and cereal imports from the New World and Russia were dominating European markets (the world market price of wheat fell by almost two-thirds between 1873 and 1894 with similar if slightly lower falls in other cereal crops; see Torp, 2014: 50) – these exports to Britain had dropped to less than four percent (Tipton, 1974: 958). The decline in the agrarian sector's export competitiveness was matched by it also being subject to increasing competition in its domestic market: between the early 1880s and 1913 wheat imports increased by four times and barley by eight times (Torp, 2014: 41).

11   In this respect, Bismarck closely followed political developments in France after Bonaparte's *coup d'état* of 1851 and, in particular, the mobilization of the masses and the role of democratic mechanisms – especially plebiscites – in helping to uphold a conservative and authoritarian social order (see Kitchen, 2012: 112–3).

formed the primary mass social bulwark against the growing working class, which became an explicit objective of state politics from 1878. Consequently, Germany's state formation and political economy had a distinct social dimension determined by its combined development. This was revealed through the particular character of its capitalist development and the relative autonomy of dominant classes. This also ensured that its political development was defined by an opening to a form of mass politics involving the integration of subaltern petty bourgeois social layers legitimized through both material concessions[12] and a radical and racialized nationalism, as well as an implacable opposition to the political advance of the industrial working class.

These tendencies – that had been visible in the 1848 revolutions – were to take some time to mature, politically. This was in part because of the more favourable economic climate of the 1850s, which saw a period of sustained growth in the international economy (Landes, 1969: 193–230)[13] that benefited Germany in particular (Böhme, 1978: 45–60; Henderson, 1975: 111–60; Hobsbawm, 1995; Kitchen, 1978: 87–160; Tipton, 2003: 97–9; Torp, 2014: 85) and especially Junker interests in the agrarian east (Schissler, 1986: 34). This situation was to change in the 1870s. The onset of the Long Depression after 1873 triggered several political shifts within Germany and the emergence of a more orchestrated top-down far-right politics (Blackbourn, 1984b: 49). Indeed, the move towards trade protectionism and an increasingly assertive geopolitics couched in the ideology and language of *völkisch* nationalism[14] continued through until the outbreak of World War One in August 1914, with a brief interlude during the early1890s associated with the administration of Leo von Caprivi.

---

12    One of the most innovative developments in this respect to tie workers to the state in a more paternalist direction was the social welfare legislation introduced by Bismarck from 1883 with a health insurance law covering workers which was soon followed by social insurance legislation which laid the foundations of a modern welfare state (see Beck, 1995; Hennock, 1998; Lerman, 2004: 182–4; Manow, 2020: 15–35; Steinberg, 2011: 416; Stienmetz, 1993).

13    World trade increased by 260 percent between 1850 and 1870 after almost doubling between 1800 and 1840 (Hobsbawm, 1995: 34). Andrew Tylecote (1992: 206) calculated that world industrial production grew at a rate of 7.6 percent per annum between 1850 and 1856 with all the major economies sharing in this period of expansion.

14    This shift was pushed as much by leading fractions of capital as the political elite. Thus, as Torp (2014: 91) posits, this nationalist and protectionist shift was also revealed in the creation of the *Central verband Deutscher Industrieller* (Central Association of German Industrialists or CVDI) in February 1876. The CVDI was primarily concerned to combat the 'doctrine of free trade' and the protection of national labour.

However, even before outbreak of and the economic consequences of the Long Depression began to be felt, the Imperial Chancellor, Bismarck, moved to consolidate a distinct conservative and nationalist cultural and ideological imprint on the recently established *Kaiserreich* with the initiation of anti-Catholic policies – the so-called *Kulturkampf* – that ran through to the late 1870s. This authoritarian strategy to help consolidate the newly-established and unified *Kaiserreich* was based upon fears as to the cultural and political autonomy of the Catholic Church and how both the authority of the Papacy in Rome (which had opposed German unification) and the religious observance and political sympathies of German Catholics might undermine the effective consolidation of the new state (Baranowski, 2011: 17–19; Gourevitch, 1977: 289; Hoyer, 2021: 180–6; Kitchen, 2012: 125–8; Lerman, 2004: 176–80). The strategy was specifically targeted at nullifying the political significance of the Centre Party – the primary political representative of German Catholicism.

The *Kulturkampf* reflected a tendency – of drawing on cultural tropes and identifying internal enemies, the so-called *Reichsfeinde* – of what would become a racialized nationalism, that became much more pronounced as the century wore on and as the challenges facing the German state and ruling class intensified. Thus, while Catholics were the principal focus of animus in the 1870s, this quickly shifted direction in the 1880s and thereafter towards the organized working class in the form of the Social Democratic Party (SPD) (Diehl, 1977: 4; Hoyer, 2021: 110–11). The SPD was founded in 1875 and quickly grew as the pace of German industrialization accelerated; by the mid-1880s it was already gaining almost ten percent of the national vote share, rising to over 20 percent by the 1890s, as it swiftly moved to become the biggest party in terms of popular support[15] by the early 1890s (Silver, 2003: 135; Sassoon, 1996: 9–12) and the principal source of political opposition to the *Kaiserreich's* social order. Even though it was still well below its peak – in terms of levels of support and social influence – Bismarck saw it as a threat and its official designation as *Reichsfeinde* with the passing of the 1878 anti-socialist law helped to reinforce the conservative and authoritarian character of the state, as well as

---

15    However, its representation in the Reichstag did not reflect this because of the way in which both the open voting and three-class franchise system (*Dreiklassenwahlrecht*) – that operated in the largest constituent state of the German Empire, Prussia – seriously diluted the electoral strength of the urban working class. Further, by the early 1890s the electoral system no longer reflected the urban-rural population distribution – consequent of industrialization and urbanization that had radically transformed German society – as parliamentary representation rested on an electoral map from the early 1870s (see Tirrell, 1951: 64) which produced a highly unequal distribution of constituencies that disproportionality favoured rural areas in the east in particular.

to stigmatize and racialize socialism as an un-German and treasonous political identity.[16]

While Bismarck attempted to suppress the left, the *Kaiserreich's* internal enemies also included the Polish minority east of the Elbe, who became an increasingly important element of the agrarian workforce as rural-urban migration picked up as industrialization accelerated.[17] The significance of the Polish minority within the political economy of the *Kaiserreich* became particularly pronounced in the early 1890s for two principal reasons. First, a growing reliance on Polish labour working on farms and the great Junker estates in the east challenged one of the idealized racial myths associated with the idea of a 'unified *volk*' working on and being part of the land. This myth – and its centrality in the upholding of the traditional social order – was closely associated with the direct and personalized relationships between lords and peasants (or tenants) in the countryside that the increasingly depersonalized nature of agrarian social relations of the final decades of the nineteenth century seriously undermined (Tipton, 1974: 956). Further, it also meant that the social reproduction of the Junker class – in the context of the agrarian crisis of the Long Depression – was increasingly dependent on a racial Other. Secondly, the Polish minority – and as a Slav people who were showing increasing signs of developing a nationalist political consciousness in the final decades of the nineteenth century – was also regarded as a potential geopolitical vulnerability in the 1880s and especially from the early 1890s onwards.[18] With diplomatic relations with Russia cooling after the *Kaiserreich* refused to renew the (secretive) so-called 'Reinsurance Treaty' with Russia (that provided Russia with

---

16    Bismarck introduced his attack on the socialists as a 'war of annihilation' on 'rats in the country' (cited in Baranowski, 2011: 20). The law stated that the SPD and any other 'revolutionary' movement was an enemy of the state, society, and the constitution, and resulted in the banning of all public activities by the SPD. Although draconian, a number of legal loopholes within it meant that individual SPD members could continue to campaign and be elected to parliament (Kitchen, 2012: 132).

17    Approximately two million people migrated westwards between 1880 and 1910 with nearly 60 percent of Berlin's population in 1910 having been born elsewhere (Tipton, 1974: 959, see also Bessel, 1978: 203 footnote 18).

18    As Shelley Baranowski (2011: 22) documents, between 1883 and 1885 the Prussian government expelled thousands of nonnaturalized Russian and Galician Poles; an unprecedent act during peacetime. Further, in 1886 non-Prussian Poles were expelled from Silesia and the border with Russia was sealed but this was to be short-lived as the dependence on Polish labour saw large landowners press for the return of Polish labour. Poles were re-admitted in 1890 with temporary work permits to work in the coal mines as much as on farms and, by the eve of World War One, over a million were employed across industry and agriculture in the east (Pollard, 1981: 247).

geopolitical guarantees in the context of the outbreak of wider European hostilities), the geopolitical security of the eastern borderlands became a much
greater security worry.[19] And this was especially so as the ethnic German population living there was falling due to westward migration, which meant that
ethnic Poles – whose loyalty to the Reich was seen as suspect and who were
also regarded, in some quarters, as a Russian 'fifth column' – remained as a
larger element within the population.[20] The working out of uneven and combined development, as reflected in the unevenness of the country's economic
geography and the dependence of its traditional conservative *ancien régime*
ruling class to reproduce itself on the back of the labour of an 'alien Other' –
who were widely stereotyped as 'primitive and anarchic, wallowing in filth and
unable to lift themselves out of poverty' (Baranowski, 2011: 23) – reinforced its
geopolitical vulnerability in the east.

Concerns around the integrity of the new German state were accentuated
with the long economic downturn that began in 1873. The downturn accelerated a number of developments that had already appeared on the horizon and
undermined the economic well-being of the three key sources of social order
after 1848. Further, it reflected a classic example of the workings of uneven and
combined development and how its socioeconomic consequences provided
important drivers for the development of a far-right politics. Thus, German
farmers and the Junkers in particular were threatened by the cheap agricultural imports that flooded into Europe from the Russian and American bread-
baskets resulting in grain prices falling by between 12 and 15 percent by 1875
and continuing to either fall or stagnate until the mid-1890s (Puhle, 1986: 87).
Such deflationary developments also played out in industry between 1873 and
1879 with average prices falling by 30 percent and with even steeper falls of

---

19 The place of geopolitical entanglements in Germany's capitalist development in the late
    nineteenth century did not concern Russia, exclusively. Indeed, the friction in Russo-
    German relations at the start of the 1890s was a key factor in the development of closer
    diplomatic, and then (by 1892), military relations between Russia and France. Further, the
    ending of the trade clauses of the 1871 Treaty of Frankfurt in 1892 – that concluded the
    Franco-Prussian War, and which constrained French trade policy and allowed Germany
    to benefit from 'Most Favoured Nation' aspects of any commercial treaty signed by
    France – (see Tirrell, 1951: 80) gave France more autonomy in determining its own trade
    policy, which is did with the introduction of widespread tariffs in 1892.
20 Bismarck had tried to address this issue with an internal colonization policy formally
    inaugurated with the 1886 Colonization Act, which saw the state purchase Polish
    owned estates in the east that were then sub-divided and distributed to Germans (see
    Baranowski, 2011: 23; Tirrell, 1951: 67), but this did not manage to alter, significantly, the
    demographic balance in the region.

60 percent or more in coal and iron as over-production became entrenched (Kitchen, 1978: 149, 157).

Furthermore, with agricultural production falling because of cheaper imports, urban migration accelerated (Schissler, 1986: 35), which ended up increasing the price of agrarian labour[21] producing a further cut in profit margins. With credit conditions tightening, there was also a shift towards monopolization – based on a growing concentration in industry with smaller producers across most sectors of the economy either going out of business[22] or being taken over by larger firms, reflecting the ability of these larger firms to respond to the impact of falling prices on profits (Blackbourn, 1977: 411; Kitchen, 1978: 168). The Long Depression terminated the so-called 'laissez faire' era of capitalist development (Bairoch, 1989: 41–8) and initiated what many regarded as the 'monopoly capital' era (Böhme, 1978: 63, 74–8; Kitchen, 1978: 138, 154–5) that was to last until World War Two, whereby domestic political stability and economic growth were increasingly dependent on a combination of the development of large national industrial conglomerates (Fremdling, 1997:359; Kocka, 1980:79–89; Lee, 1988: 359; Tipton and Aldrich, 1987: 21; Torp, 2014: 54–61)[23] closely connected to the big banks (such as the mining corporation Gelsenkirchner Bergwerks AG), access to international markets for exports and international sources of credit.

The challenges – domestic/social, international/geopolitical and economic in equal measure – that German industry confronted in the final two decades of the nineteenth century enforced a rapid capitalist industrialization directly involving the state in the production process through the re-structuring and integration of firms and the disciplining of labour (Blackbourn and Eley, 1984; Eley, 1986: 42–58) and, in geopolitical terms, through the search for export markets. Necessarily, then, the process of surplus extraction and capital

---

21   The upshot of which was that landlords in the east became increasingly dependent on importing Russian and Ukrainian labour (see Strikwerda, 1998: 219) which only served to stimulate anxieties in the east about the presence of foreign workers, thereby providing a major stimulous to the establishment of the Society for Eastern Marches in 1894, which campaigned against any softening of hostility towards Germany's ethnic minorities (Chickering, 1984: 47).

22   The Borsig locomotive factory in Berlin shed around a half of its labour between 1874 and 1876 which was typical of the sector as whole in the early years of the depression (Kitchen, 1978: 143).

23   Kitchen (1978: 155) provides an example of this tendency towards monopoly after 1873 focusing on the mining industry with 40 percent of mining companies ceasing to be independent entities between 1873 and 1890, while overall production trebled, and mining employment increased by two and a half times.

accumulation were politicized on two levels, helping to reinforce an authoritarian politics and a political opening to the subaltern far-right. On the one
hand, an authoritarian politics was directly implicated in responses to labour
militancy at home and, on the other, in crafting a political and mass mobilization for an imperialist geopolitics that necessitated a challenge to the British
Empire. In this way the far-right became deeply embedded in the reproduction
of German capitalism in a way that was much more pronounced than in any
other major capitalist power.

   However, monopoly capitalism provided a contradictory stimulus to the
growth of the far-right. Thus, while the increasing tendency towards the concentration and vertical integration of firms and the integration or absorption
of industrial into financial capital provided the ruling class basis of the far-
right that necessitated a more aggressive geopolitics, as Hobson and Lenin had
diagnosed (Hobson, 1988; Lenin, 2010), such a monopoly dynamic also undermined and destroyed the possibilities of the petty bourgeoisie – or its commercial, manufacturing and trading elements – from reproducing themselves.
Thus, despite the ruling class and political elites' attentiveness to a *Mittelstand*
politics, the compulsion of the 'whip of external necessity' and the accumulative drives of industrial capital pushed Germany towards the concentration
and vertical integration of industry to the cost of smaller producers (Arrighi,
et al., 1999b: 125; Böhme, 1978: 74–86).

   In this sense, significant elements of the (old) *Mittelstand* were increasingly
struggling to co-exist and prosper in a German economy ever more subject to
capitalist industrial imperatives. Consequently, for these major social layers –
which made up a significant portion of the working population – their lives
were dominated by a permanent state of anxiety and insecurity that crystal-
lized into the following features that provided a major opening for the subaltern far-right: (i) they were in constant need of credit and, because this was
difficult to access, they often had to mortgage their farms or shops to secure
credit, resulting in a deep resentment towards the existing sources of credit;
(ii) they suffered from the fluctuations of the market economy but were unable to secure enough favourable legislation or monopolies to allow them to
ride out the downturns in contrast to big capital and organized labour; (iii)
they were squeezed by larger firms and monopolies especially because they
could not buy and sell in bulk; and, finally, (iv) they were unable to match
the massive production and distribution systems of estate agriculture, efficient
factories, and large commercial enterprises (Lebovics, 1969: 6). It was out of the
cross-hairs of such developments that a far-right emerged and, with it, an 'anti-
capitalist' current within it that would continue through to National Socialism.
Accordingly, a key reactionary strand of the far-right and, subsequently, fascism

was based on the social protection of the petty bourgeoisie and the identification of those internal ('monopoly labour') and external (monopoly capital) forces identified as being responsible for its socioeconomic woes.

The response to the challenges posed by the Long Depression had two dimensions. First, Germany, like other countries (with the exception of Britain) moved towards protectionism, which would be the dominant trend up until 1914. Bismarck introduced tariffs in 1879 with duties attached to textile and heavy industry imports and to most agrarian imports at a lower rate. Through the 1880s until the end of his Chancellorship, tariffs were increased and extended to a wider range of imports and culminated in a significant increase of duties on cereal imports in 1887 (Torp, 2014: 106–7) to the joy of the agrarian sector. Thus, reflecting the continuing social and political power – if declining economic strength – of the Junkers, agricultural tariffs rose fivefold over the period (Kitchen, 1978: 167; Stern, 1977: 46–59),[24] inaugurating what scholars have called the alliance between 'Iron and Rye' (Blackbourn, 1977: 411; see also Webb, 1980; Torp, 2010).[25]

Tariffs, however, were more than just an economic measure; they had political significance too. Thus, they reflected a recognition on the part of the agricultural interest – that Bismarck was particularly associated with as a representative of Prussian Junkerdom – of the importance of industry and the need to give the industrial bourgeoisie a greater political stake in the stability and future of the *Kaiserreich*, hence the dawning of the coalition of 'Iron and Rye' – the classical ruling class rendering of a far-right. In many respects, this repeated the tendencies within German liberalism that had initially revealed themselves in 1848 when the threats to social order and private property saw them embrace the reactionary response to the revolution as the best way of preserving their own social interests even if it came at the cost of the constitutional and political reform that they had initially been committed to. Consequently, this alliance between the dominant class interests in industry and agriculture was also connected to a popular and mass politics that

---

24    The protective tariffs not only ensured an economic lifeblood for big landowners – around half of whom were Prussian Junkers – but also reflected and upheld their continuing political hold on the state. The economic writing, however, was clearly on the wall as they could no longer compete with grain and corn imports within their own domestic market, let alone compete internationally through an export offensive (Kitchen, 1978: 163).

25    As Martin Kitchen (1978: 145–8) further notes, the Central Association of German Industries (*Zentralverband Deutscher Industriellen*) formed in 1875 'declared total war on the pernicious theory of free trade, which it saw at the root of Germany's apparent economic distress, and called for a common front of industry, agriculture and handicrafts to revitalise the German economy.'

focused on the mobilization of the petty bourgeoisie or *Mittelstand*. And it was here where nationalist, authoritarian and racist ideological imaginaries were unleashed under the direction of public authorities. Thus, an Anglophobia emerged through the deployment of 'Manchesterism' as a pejorative term against the doctrine of free-trade and the corrosive impact it had on small producers – urban and rural – in equal measure.[26]

It was in this context, too, that a politics of empire and imperialism developed. Indeed, the connections between an international politics of empire and imperialism became explicitly connected to the management of Germany's political development and social order (Baranowski, 2011: 3, 13). We can identify here the foundations of the social and political basis of the German far-right that was to persist as a dominant feature within German state and class formation through to 1945. It was also the case here that the rising advocates of empire – the nationalist societies that emerged through the 1880s and thereafter – were relatively autonomous of the state. Thus, while Bismarck's turn to protectionism and nationalism in 1879 indicated a rightward turn in German foreign policy, this was not an embrace of an emerging far-right position *tout court*, as advocated by the Colonial Society or others (Smith, 1978: 15). However, this was the key opening that saw a confluence of social and ideological forces push Germany towards imperialism and, with it, a move by political elites towards fostering a far-right politics from below. Colonization would provide not only a protected market for German exports – industrial and agricultural – but also a means to deal with the social question highlighted by the growth of the left and the working class, through the export of 'surplus population' to found German colonial settlements. Indeed, by the mid-1890s the social and economic transformation of Germany was coming very close to a tipping point with employment in industry and mining almost equal the level of agricultural employment (by 1900 agriculture employed 9.7 million workers and industry and mining, 9.5 million; see Moeller, 1986: 4; see also Kitchen, 1978: 200; Puhle, 1986: 83), thus fundamentally changing the character of German politics and,

---

26    Bismarck's tariff policy was also closely connected to a domestic political strategy of
      reconstituting the political basis of the *Kaiserreich* through undermining the left/progres-
      sive wing of the National Liberals who were most closely associated with free trade. Thus,
      the 1878 election campaign – that laid the foundations for the shift towards protectionism
      in 1879 – focused on depicting the Liberals as agents of 'Manchesterism' and a threat to the
      Empire in a similar fashion to the threat posed by social democracy. While the election
      result was no watershed, it did see a major shift towards the right with advances made by
      Conservatives and the losses for the left wing of the National Liberals (Torp, 2014: 102; see
      also Webb, 1982: 309) cementing the political coalition upon which the *Kaiserreich* would
      be administered until 1890.

in consequence, the means through which the existing political order could be maintained in a context of the declining demographic weight of the peasantry.

The nationalist/imperialist pressure groups – such as the *Alldeutscher Verband* and the *Kolonialverein* (Colonial Society) that were founded in the midst of the Long Depression – saw the crisis as a problem of overproduction based on the incapacity of the German domestic market to absorb the products of its expanded industrial production. And rather than addressing this through increasing the consumption – and hence the social power – of workers, these movements saw colonial expansion and empire as the answer. This was seen as addressing the problem of production through the establishment of new/external markets for German goods and, at the same time, empire would reduce social tensions through exporting Germans (and those social layers most threatened by the pace and consequences of rapid industrialization) to settlement in new colonies. In short, empire was seen as a way of addressing social order and economic growth in a way that consolidated and expanded Germany's geopolitical strength (Chickering, 1984: 29–30; Wehler, 1972: 75–6).

Initiated at the same time as the alliance of 'Iron and Rye' – indeed it was an important legitimizing element of it – Bismarck and his successors promoted rounds of domestic protectionism through offering commercial concessions to craftsmen and artisans, thus limiting the combined encroachments most feared by farmers and the traditional petty bourgeoisie of either being destroyed by the power of big (and foreign) capital or being subsumed into the ranks of the proletariat. Thus, in 1881 craftsmen secured the legal recognition of their guilds and associated privileges in the training of apprentices. Further concessions were made to *Mittelstand* producers later in the 1880s and 1890s such as restrictions on peddlening in 1883 and 1896, and a handicraft law in 1897 which introduced the possibility of compulsory membership of guilds (Winkler, 1976: 2). Further, the *Mittelstand* were depicted in political pronouncements, newspapers, and literature as the personification of the *volk* – independent, hard-working, self-reliant, loyal, and conservative – thus providing the principal popular constituency of the *Kaiserreich*, in opposition to the growing strength of social democracy. Here, a distinct ideology of producerism was articulated as a form of virtue and moral economy aligned with specific cultural and racial tropes and, at the same time, anchored in the naturalization and protections and privileges of private property.

However, although the German state proved itself favourable towards the *Mittelstand*, major elements within this social layer also allied themselves as the primary constituency of the roll-call of German far-right movements that emerged from the 1880s onwards, many of whom were far from being pawns of the ruling class. Thus, as Geoff Eley has noted, although the traditional conservative parties in Germany referred to the *Mittelstand* as the core of the social order, many of the popular *Mittelstand* pressure groups that emerged were based on the repudiation of old traditions of hierarchy and deference; a *sine qua non* of the far-right as a distinct current of politics (Eley, 1986: 240; see also Blackbourn, 1984a: 50; see also Hunt, 1975: 520).

The character of German economic development in the final years of the nineteenth century was to be particularly significant for the development of the far-right. Even as the economy grew – by the 1880s Germany had come to overtake Britain in the production of iron and coal and had also moved to take a leading edge in the new industries of chemicals and electrical engineering (Hobsbawm, 1987: 34–55; Fremdling, 1997: 352; Kemp, 1985; Torp, 2014: 63) – the pace of this success came at the cost of large sections of industry, not to speak of agriculture, being left behind in terms of their ability to compete with factory production and to absorb new productive technologies. While not, then, quite comparable to the degree of uneven and combined development that Trotsky noted with regard to Tsarist Russia at this time (Trotsky, 2008), the contradictions and dislocations afflicting German society over these years were immense and profound. It was the traditional craft and artisan sectors of the *Mittelstand* that were particularly affected by these developments (see Arrighi, et al., 1999b: 125), despite legislative attempts to protect them as part of the '*Mittelstand* politics' that had been the focus of German political elites since the early 1880s.

To this sectoral imbalance was added a geographical one (see Lee, 1988: 355) with industry concentrated in a small number of regions around Berlin and in the West across the Ruhr, in contrast to the eastern provinces – where the traditional Junker ruling class was based – which continued to suffer and where approximately 35 percent of the work force continued to be concentrated up until the first decade of the twentieth century (Tipton and Aldrich, 1987: 21). This unevenness was revealed, as Tipton (1974: 960; see also Bessel, 1978: 203–9) details, in the increasing divergence in regional per capita incomes between the more urbanized and industrialized west compared to the more rural and agrarian east in the final two decades of the century. This regional unevenness was also reinforced by the combined character of Germany's social development as illustrated by the reactionary stance of sections of the Junker class in the east. Thus, assisted by the propaganda and agitation of the *Bund der Landwirte*, the popular commitment to a reactionary ideal of a rural *volk* saw farmers and Junkers oppose proposals by Gustav von Gossler (the head of the provincial administrator of West Prussia) to implement a policy to industrialize the east, which they saw as leading to the growth of social democracy with peasants turning into workers, and thus the embedding of what were regarded as 'alien' cultural and political ideas subversive of the existing hierarchical social order (see Tipton, 1974: 962).

By the mid-1890s the pace, success and social contradictions of Germany's capitalist industrialization posed immense strains on the stability of the political system giving rise to the distinct form of far-right moral economy that emerged out of this contradictory process. Indeed, the social and political situation had also come to be defined by the realization of the imminent possibilities of 1848, as with the rapid growth of industry came the concomitant and necessary growth of an industrial working class and socialist labour movement in the form of the SPD. And with the lapse of Bismarck's anti-socialist law in 1890, an emboldened and much bigger and more powerful SPD re-entered the political arena creating an additional headache for traditional elites that had, in effect, conceded the need to practice a form of democratic politics to legitimize the Reich (Chickering, 1984: 46).

These domestic developments took place within a wider international context increasingly marked by geopolitical rivalry and animosity. In Germany's case, this was in part connected to a resentment at not having a colonial system given that Germany had quickly become Europe's dominant industrial economy (Anievas, 2014: 71–2). Relatedly, the social repression that had characterized German economic development in terms of the failure to expand the consumption and social power of labour meant that over-production continued to haunt German capital. Stuck in a bind and not willing to increase labour's share of the social product, significant sections of both industry and agriculture advocated for empire as the only means to secure external markets, and as a way of dealing with the threat of overproduction and maintaining social and political order at home (Smith, 1978: 119). Such concerns even extended to Gustav Stresemann, a sage of German liberalism, who spoke of the inevitability of Germany having to create a closed economic bloc in the period before 1914 (Berghahn, 1996: 10–11).

The social and political costs resulting from rapid economic development were felt in the growing tensions and breakdown in the original alliance of Iron and Rye that Bismarck had orchestrated at the end of the 1870s. It was within this conjuncture that nationalist and far-right infused political and ideological imaginaries gained greater political traction and where, in spite of conservative attempts to re-create a new *Sammlungspolitik* uniting industry and agriculture and a popular mobilization of the *Mittelstand*, new and autonomous far-right movements emerged that came to play a formative role in taking Germany to war in 1914. Let me look at these top-down, ruling class strategies before examining some of the new far-right movements that emerged in the 1890s.

Top-down strategies of socio-political mobilization were infused with a far-right character and, particularly so, for the two that dominated the 1890s: social imperialism and *Weltpolitik*. In the words of Geoff Eley, the foremost historian of the *Kaiserreich*, social imperialism refers to the 'diversion outwards of internal tensions and forces of change in order to preserve the social and political status quo'. Consequently, it was a 'defensive ideology against the disruptive effects of industrialization on the social and economic structure of Germany'. It was also a principal means by which the dominant agrarian-industrial bloc secured its popular support because popular nationalism was consciously manipulated as a 'long-term integrative factor' for stabilizing the 'anachronistic social and power structure' (Eley, 1986: 4; see also Baranowski, 2011: 3). Social imperialism mixed ideological manipulation and enthusiasm for the *volk* and the aspirations of German nationalism. This had several dimensions that were connected to shoring up the existing socio-political order of heavy industry and agriculture through blaming Britain for domestic economic woes whilst articulating a *völkish* nationalism – through the educational system and propaganda and indoctrination carried out by public agencies and the nationalist *verbands* that proliferated at this time (see below). Such measures were combined with a series of welfare measures and social insurance to compensate and 'purchase' the loyalty of the industrial working class (Evans, 1978: 19; Manow, 2020: 15–35) from the growing strength of the SPD, which by the early 1890s had reached almost 25 percent of the vote share and had become the biggest single party based on voter support.

The social imperialism that had been originally initiated by Bismarck in the mid-1880s proved to be an ineffectual means to draw the industrial working class away from the SPD and for many conservatives it was a distraction or came at the cost of paying insufficient attention to the needs and political support of the *Mittelstand*. This was addressed with the move towards a policy of colonial empire in 1897 with the announcement of *Weltpolitik*. Looking towards the international and, to be more precise, a policy of geopolitical expansion and rivalry, allowed a temporary papering over of the on-going contradictions within Germany's political economy that reflected its combined development: that of a political ruling class drawn, disproportionately, from and oriented towards the cultural and political sensibilities of the Junker aristocracy that was economically stagnant, whilst the economic dynamism of the industrial bourgeoisie had not managed to realise its political ascendancy. And this arrangement was maintained up until the immediate period before 1914 – even as the social and economic significance of industry expanded – largely because of the mass, subaltern mobilizations of the Farmers' League and other nationalist organizations in opposition to the further encroachment of a liberal or bourgeoise modernity over German society in general.

The commitment to colonial empire was a major boost to heavy industry which would benefit from the construction of a fleet. As Evans (1978: 20, see also Kehr, 1977; Lowe, 1994: 145) notes, *Weltpolitik* reflected a bargain between heavy industry and the landlords with the former gaining from demand for iron and steel to build the fleet and the latter from higher import tariffs on agricultural goods as a way of boosting the revenues of the Junkers and reducing the threat from international competition. In addition, as Geoff Eley (1986: 49–50) has argued, this new settlement also witnessed an intensification of the disciplining of labour in the factory production process as evidenced by the behaviour of Krupp in the Ruhr, that reflected a distinctly modern approach to the capitalist production process and integrating labour with new technologies (Eley, 1986: 55). Such a distillation provides a perfect example of combined development in the combination and contradictory tendencies of shoring up a backward agrarian sector whilst, at the same, advancing the logic of capital and industry in a way that requires a set of geopolitical and ideological compensations to paper over such contradictions.

These developments in the late 1890s – that were based on an explicit attempt by social and political elites to mobilize a mass far-right from below (see Retallack, 1988) – did not, however, produce a singular and unified far-right position towards the international. Thus, even though heavy industry was enthused by the prospect of an intensification of geopolitical competition with Britain through a naval arms race which would, inevitably, promote an expansion of the dynamic of industrialization within Germany and the deeper permeation of the industrial logic of technological innovation and economic progress, far-right agrarian interests were worried over such industrial expansion and, with it, the continuing erosion of agriculture's centrality within German society and the survival of the peasant community (Baranowski, 2011: 57; Eley, 1986: 9–10; Hunt, 1975; Tipton, 1974: 956, 965; Tirrell, 1951). Consequently, although much of the agrarian bloc advocated a politics of economic isolation or autarchy conjoined with a geopolitics of territorial expansion and annexation towards central and eastern Europe (Puhle, 1986: 97) – as a way of dealing with the challenges of global capitalist competition – the industrial far-right wanted to combine industrial growth with global geopolitical rivalry and an extra-continental empire (Smith, 1980). The assumption here was that agriculture would sooner or later become the junior social partner and, furthermore, that Germany was moving, irrevocably, towards becoming an urban-industrial civilization.

It is clear that ruling class interests and political elites constituted a major part of the German far-right by the final decades of the nineteenth century. However, it is also important to emphasize the modern far-right qualities of the German subaltern far-right rather than exaggerating the role of political elites in the construction of a *Mittelstand* movement as the mass base and political driving force of the *Kaiserreich*, and especially so in relation to the origins of World War One (see Kehr, 1977; Wehler, 1985). Indeed, in the context of increasing worker militancy after the lifting of the anti-socialist law in 1890 and the growth of the SPD as *the* mass party of the *Kaiserreich*, such sharpened class conflict meant that elites saw the *Mittelstand* as a 'saviour of the social order, or *staatserhaltend*' (Blackbourn, 1977: 411). This was revealed in the announcement of the so-called 'Tivoli programme' of the Conservative Party that was adopted at its national congress in December 1892, which was dominated by anti-Semitic tropes and anti-Jewish sentiment associated with populist street movements alongside promises to roll-back the civil rights of Jews, as well as a return to Bismarckian authoritarianism with a new anti-socialist law (see Eley, 1993: 212–4; Mosse, 1985: 133–4; Tirrell, 1951: 150). For Retallack (1988: 393), the significance of the Tivoli congress also extended to what he regards as a fundamental break with the traditional *Honoratiorenpolitik* (the politics of notables) and an embrace of a politics explicitly targeted at a mass audience.[27] For the Christian Socialist agitator and notorious anti-Semite, Adolf Stocker – a key figure in the emergence of the modern far-right – the Tivoli congress realized a transformation of the Conservative Party, '[i]t was not a party conference in black tails and white gloves but in street clothes' (cited in Blackbourn, 1984b: 63) suggesting an embrace of a more plebian and populist form of politics.

However, while the petty bourgeois social layers of the *Mittelstand* provided the mass base for the subaltern far-right and the focus of the traditional and constitutional right, this was far from a unified or single class in

---

27    Retallack (1988) provides an excellent discussion of the growing prominence of anti-Semitism and populist propaganda attacking 'Manchesterism' and the figure of the Jew as the personification of high capitalism and free trade in the politics of the German Conservative Party from the early 1880s, as a way of trying to secure a wider mass base beyond its traditional Prussian heartlands. Thus, in quite a shocking articulation of an anti-Semitic *Weltanschauung* in 1881, prefiguring Nazism, one Conservative publication, the *Badische Landspost*, decried '[t]he Jews have our finances in their hands, the Jews have our newspapers in their hands, the Jews have our trade in their hands, the Jews have our farmers – in their pockets. In a word, the Jews have won superiority in our whole political and social life. That is the situation. How are we once again to escape it? That is the question, that is the Jewish question' (cited in Retallack, 1988: 389).

terms of the specificities in its material relations and social reproduction within German capitalism, and hence its political orientation. As Geoff Eley and David Blackbourn have noted, rather than being a homogeneous social layer, the *Mittelstand* was divided within itself and particularly between its 'old' (artisans, craft/guild workers and small farmers) and the 'new' (salaried white-collar workers in the lower levels of government and professional employment) strands. Indeed, the new strands were, to a significant degree, beneficiaries of monopoly capital, as reflected in industrial concentration and the lower consumer prices, which put them at odds with the older strand who were implacably opposed to monopoly capital and lower prices for their wares (Blackbourn, 1977: 412–3; see also Eley, 1986: 438–43).

The subaltern far-right – elements of which were found within the Conservative Party as evidenced by its shift towards a more radical nationalist and authoritarian direction in 1892 and in elite-led organizations such as the Navy League – emerged as relatively autonomous political actors in the early 1890s out of the anxieties and insecurities of the *Mittelstand*. Such fears were centred on the pace of industrialization, the spread of socialist doctrine, continuing degrees of social and economic insecurity linked to a cultural pessimism and a 'general alienation from the political establishment' (McGowan, 2002: 23–5). This alienation from the conservative political establishment was particularly associated with the administration of the new Imperial Chancellor, Leo von Caprivi, who was appointed by the Kaiser after the dismissal of Bismarck in 1890.

Shifting to a 'new course' in foreign and domestic policy, Caprivi attempted to move away from a dependence on parliamentary support from the traditional rightist bloc that had been the mainstay of the Bismarckian era. The shift was revealed in a less hostile approach to the SPD after the renewal of the anti-socialist law was defeated in early 1890 and the implementation of new trade and commercial policies favouring industrial development that reversed the protectionist turn inaugurated by Bismarck in 1879. It was this shift, revealed in the negotiation and passing of a series of trade treaties through the early 1890s – all of which depended on the support of the left and anti-conservative forces in the Reichstag – that saw tariff reductions on a range of agrarian imports, including cereals (see Farr, 1986: 121; Tirrell, 1951; Torp, 2014: 114), that made Caprivi the enemy of the agrarian interest. Indeed, these developments highlighted an important contradiction in the alliance of Iron and Rye: given the price sensitivity and tight profit margins in the heavy industrial sector, reducing the costs of labour – of which food consumption was an important ingredient – was a prevailing concern, and which meant that the material logic within the alliance rested on shaky foundations.[28] Caprivi's new course inaugurated a unique conjuncture in the politics of the *Kaiserreich* with the sense of economic crisis that had been building across the agrarian sector since the early 1870s combining, for the first time since its foundation, with a political crisis in an Imperial Chancellor not only deaf to the concerns of agriculture, but also reliant on the *Riechsfeinde* of the SPD to secure passage of new trade treaties.

Consequently, while these subaltern far-right movements continued to be influenced and have members drawn from the traditional conservative elite, they were no pawns of the traditional elites or the ruling class. Indeed, their emergence reflected the failure of traditional strategies of top-down mobilization (see Blackbourn, 1984b: 55–6; Eley, 1993; Retallack, 1988) and rule, alongside the depth of the crisis facing this particular social layer (Blackbourn, 1984b: 51–3). In many respects, the precise socioeconomic and geopolitical context of their emergence, and their relationship to existing structures and sources of political power, prefigured that of Nazism a generation later. Thus, this radical and subaltern far-right reflected a 'combined social-political mobilization from below' (Jones and Retallack, 1993: 11) whereby subaltern social forces came to play an important and relatively autonomous role in determining the politics of the range of far-right movements that emerged through the 1890s and thereafter. As Marilyn Coetzee (1990: 4; see also Puhle, 1986: 103) suggests, these new nationalist or patriotic societies represented 'a distinctive departure in German public life' particularly with regard to their respective size, national reach, social basis and militancy in criticizing traditional political elites, state leaders and policies.[29]

These organizations framed their propaganda in a moralistic terminology based on the central concept of fairness, and it was this that provided the basis for the questioning of established authority, including that of the Kaiser (Hunt, 1975; 520; Tirrell, 1951: 313). In the words of David Blackbourn (1984a: 51), they appealed to the state to 'intervene and restore (as it was imagined) conditions in which public life would resemble an idealized version of private family

---

28    Thus, while in February 1891 the CVDI publicly declared its continuing support for agriculture, in April 1891 it moved – as the economic situation deteriorated – to support Caprivi's new course towards shifting away from protectionism and subsequently supported the new trade treaty with Russia in 1894 (see Torp, 2014: 122, 133).

29    According to Coetzee's figures (1990: 4) by 1914 the key societies contained the following levels of membership: the Colonial Society (42,000), the Pan-German League (18,000), the Imperial League against Social Democracy (221,000), the Navy League (331,000) and the Army League (990,000). In some cases – such as the Pan-German League – membership was higher in the late 1890s.

life. But this same moralism and attachment to fairness provided a basis for questioning established authority' and this sense of injustice and moral outrage was also focused on the judgement of public spending, which produced 'a resentful and vengeful political radicalism whose precise form was unpredictable' that was infused with a widespread grievance towards officialdom (Blackbourn, 1984a: 51). This was a political orientation firmly on the right but linked to a sensibility and embrace of demagoguery quite alien to a traditional and patrician conservatism of a Bismarckian kind.

The two most important movements in Germany that reflected these characteristics – specifically drawing on petty bourgeois social constituencies and defined by a radical nationalism and subaltern far-right politics – were the *Alldeutscher Verband* and the *Bund der Landwirte*. Both articulated a vision of an idealized '*völkish* community' or *gemeinschaft* threatened by the encroachments of a cosmopolitan capitalist materialist universe embodied in the term 'Manchesterism,' and both also articulated an aggressive geopolitically driven form of political economy, as a way of resolving domestic and international problems. However, while the Farmers' League advocated a political economy of autarchy based on a geopolitics of territorial annexation and population expulsion in east and central Europe that also rested on an implicit hostility towards increasing industrialization (Eley, 1993; Vascik, 1993), the Pan-German League was committed to rapid industrial expansion based on naval construction, as a way of directly challenging British imperial power via a strategy of *Weltpolitik*. I will now look at each in turn.

### 3.1 The *Alldeutscher Verband*

While the social and economic dislocations of the Long Depression provided an important enabler for the emergence of the Alldeutscher Verband (ADV) or Pan-German League in the early 1890s, it was the way in which such dislocations were imbued with a geopolitics of capitalist imperialism that was, ultimately, determining. Thus, it was the popular uproar that greeted the decision of the government to concede to British pressure over the control of colonial territories in east Africa that triggered its creation in April 1891 (Feuchtwanger, 2001: 117; Henderson, 1944: 193; Urban, 2016: 65–6).[30] The quest for colonies and

---

30  A response by a founding member of the ADV published soon after the treaty was signed in two leading newspapers, the *Kölnische* and *Frankfurter Zeitung*, captured the essence of its position 'who can prevent such a nation from tearing up this treaty which clearly serves only to cheat the next generation out of its inherited share of the planet?! [...] We are ready upon the call of our Emperor to join the ranks and in silence and obediently be led to strike against the enemy fire, for which, however, we may ask a price worthy of

Germany's geopolitical predicament were then defining and central to the ideology and aims of the ADV and, consequently, the political economy it became associated with. Indeed, the ADV was not an untypical movement in the wider complexion of socio-political forces that emerged across several European powers in the final years of the nineteenth century. This reflected the inseparability of geography and territorial control from economic development and growth. It also demonstrated the deeper connections between industrialization and militarism as key parts of the industrial sector and profit streams – not least heavy industry – were increasingly associated with military technologies and militarism (Anievas, 2014: 68–9; Arrighi, et al., 1999b: 125; Urban, 2016: 67).

The developmental tendencies originally sourced in the 1848 revolution made the emergence of the kind of political movement that the ADV reflected highly likely, as the contradictions of Germany's late nation-state formation and political consolidation and the rapid and intense character of its capitalist industrialization produced inherent tendencies of over-production and class militancy that the absence of empire made difficult to manage, politically. Such contradictions – and especially the non-contiguousness of its borders with a dispersed '*volk*' outside of them (Baranowski, 2011: 43; Chickering, 1984: 76) – increased the demands for geopolitical expansion. However, the combined nature of international capitalist development was also central to its emergence and growth with respect to the geopolitical determinants of economic activity and expansion. As the 'humiliation' over east Africa at the hands of the British appeared to demonstrate, imperial power was not only a means of closing-off avenues of German economic growth; it also indicated that Germany's future and, in particular, the management of the social question within it, was to be determined, ultimately, by the policies of the British Empire – and this was not just about colonies but also about trade, markets, and credit. Simply put, for the ideologues of the ADV, the situation that Germany confronted by the early 1890s appeared to be one of an imminent 'strangulation for want of (external) outlets for surplus population and areas for economic growth' (Baranowski, 2011: 43–5; Chickering, 1984: 77).[31]

---

that sacrifice, and that price is affiliation to the master nation, which takes its share of the world and does not endeavour to acquire it through the grace and benevolence of some other nation. Germany, wake up!' (cited in Urban, 2016: 66).

31  This Anglophobia was also saturated with anti-Semitism with the ADV identifying Jews and an 'international Jewish conspiracy' – laying the seeds of what became central to Nazi ideology – as preventing Germany from becoming a world power (Baranowski, 2011: 45, 47).

In this respect, the politics of the ADV can be traced back to the lower middle-class anxieties evident across much of Germany that played out in the politics of the 1848 revolution. They were concerned about the consequences of rapid economic change and the social and demographic consequences thereof; specifically, the accommodation of the growing class of workers in the cities and the need to steer them away from socialism. For the ADV and other imperialist-minded movements such as the Colonial Society, Germany's economic health and social order necessitated a colonial empire, as a means to export the surplus population, and as a way of maintaining the social and democratic equilibrium. Consequently, like many of the other nationalist movements of the time, the ADV reflected a form of *Mittelstand* politics (Henderson, 1944: 194) that was an attempt to build a mass-based politics that drew on petty bourgeois social layers (Urban, 2016: 68) – in this case from more urban than rural settings – acting as a bulwark against the rising left. The *Mittelstand* was important not only because of the cultural conservatism of its members but also because of their attachment to property; that was seen as key to the preservation of social order. Indeed, though its membership did not exceed around 22,000 throughout the 1890s, because it had good access to newspapers through its members – whom Shelley Baranowski (2011: 44) describes as 'well-connected middle-classes' – its influence on national politics was well in excess of its rather modest membership.

Such a concern with social order did not make them passive or submissive to the interests of dominant social layers and so, while supportive of the hierarchical and authoritarian dimensions of the *Kaiserreich*, the ADV also demanded a reconfiguring of both economy and politics and so challenged the prerogatives and privileges of political and socioeconomic elites. Thus, as Chickering (1984: 91) suggests,

> many of the schemes that the Pan-Germans advocated reflected a concern about the evils of urbanization, rootlessness, and social disorder. In the Prussian east and in North Schleswig, they promoted what amounted to a program of land reform, the large-scale settlement of an independent German peasantry; to this end, they even advocated breaking up large estates in the east that were worked by a landless (and usually Polish) proletariat. Pan-Germans also advocated various programs to bail out small businessmen. And, in speaking of the need for colonies, most of them were unsympathetic to the claims of the companies which were turning profits: they subscribed instead to the emigrationist argument that settlements abroad were essential as future bases for an independent German peasantry.

There were two key inter-connected ideological drivers of the ADV: one domestic and the other international. The former was primarily concerned with the social and political threat from socialism.[32] Here, the articulation of a *völkisch* nationalism rooted in the mythical and timeless values of the *Mittelstand* and the German peasantry was linked to an aggressive nationalism that blamed international forces – 'Jewish liberalism' or 'free-trade' – for the socioeconomic distress across Germany. The rise of social democracy built on the back of rapid industrialization underlined the political significance accorded to geopolitics and empire, as a means to address the social question whilst preserving the fundaments of the existing order. Thus, colonial settlement of the *Kaiserreich's* 'surplus poor' would, for the ADV, reduce the population reservoir that socialism drew its support from whilst – at the same time – helping to maintain more of the traditional hierarchical social balance and reinforcing an anti-class ideology of national unity. On the other hand – yet intimately connected to these domestic socio-political concerns – was how the existing international political system and geopolitical order and Britain's dominance in particular, were seen as boxing in the possibilities for resolution of the economic contradictions that afflicted the ruling class alliance of Iron and Rye and its association and dependence on the mobilization of the *Mittelstand* as a means to deal with the social question. Thus, dealing with the threat posed by the growth of an organized working class and the rise of the left – developments that were ideologically disassociated from a social order based on private property – necessitated a confrontation with Britain. It was these combined problems that promoted an increasingly militant and racialized language. Indeed, as Chickering (1984: 122–3) notes, the ideology of the ADV,

> was a vision of fear ... [t]he symbolism of the flood, the premonitions of catastrophe, the obsession with enemies, the anxieties about disorder, about the failure of authority and loss of control, all suggest a world view, if not pathological, was at least psychologically problematic.

---

32   Quoting from ADV publications, Chickering (1984: 92) notes, that this threat was sourced in the 'rootlessness and temptations of the big city' with Social Democracy described as, 'simply the most ominous thing conceivable, the original evil, the repudiation of order. It was a Mephistophelian force, "the spirit of abnegation" ..., of indiscipline, dissension, destruction, and discontent, the mortal enemy not only of property and social order, but of the principle of ethnicity as well. For the Pan-Germans, Social Democracy was the most palpable manifestation of the flood; it was the very spirit of chaos.'

The significance of the ADV as an exemplar of a modern far-right politics was not only reflected in its impact on mainstream German conservatism in shifting it further to the right, but in its articulation of a militant and racialized nationalism that fostered a militarism that was central to the momentum that produced war in 1914. Further, it's identification of threats and proposals for how to deal with them and the social layers it mobilized revealed a politics that subverted traditional sources and institutions of the ruling order; an expression of the far-right as an agential form of combined development.

### 3.2    The *Bund der Landwirte*

The Farmers' or Agrarian League was founded in early 1893 in a context of profound disillusionment across much of the agricultural sector due to the longer-term transformation of the world market – that, simultaneously, eroded both traditional export markets (and especially for cereals producers) and intensified international competition in domestic markets, driving down prices. It was also a response to the trade policies associated with the Chancellor Leo von Caprivi. Within months it claimed 162,000 members, and in the elections later that year claimed to have the support of 140 Reichstag deputies (Eley, 1993: 194).[33] The main focus of the League's campaigning through the 1890s up until 1902 was on forcing the government to change course towards more nationalistic and protectionist international trade policies through exerting particular pressure on the Conservative Party (as well as the National Liberals in areas where the party relied on rural voters – see Blackbourn, 1984b: 64–5).[34] The League campaigned for guilds to set minimum prices, restrictions on advertising for department stores and mail-order houses, the taxing of department store turn-over and limits on membership of consumer co-operatives (Hunt, 1975: 521), all of which reflected a distinct set of petty bourgeois concerns. In doing so, it ended up transforming the political culture of German Conservatism giving it a much more militant and biologically-racist dimension infused with Social-Darwinist and anti-Semitic tropes (Hunt, 1975; Puhle, 1986: 93–6; Tipton, 1974) that not only laid the foundations for the populist mobilization behind the move towards war in 1914, but also a political context fertile for the planting of the seeds of fascism through the rhetorical

---

33    A year after its founding it had 200,000 members climbing to 250,000 by the turn of the century and peaked at 330,000 members in 1913 (see Puhle, 1986: 92).

34    Puhle (1986: 92) suggests that by 1898, over a quarter of Reichstag representatives (118/397) were League supporters and 76 of them were actual league members.

demagoguery and racist scapegoating by some of its key spokesmen and its commitment to a plebiscitary form of mass politics that was anti-liberal and anti-parliamentarian in equal measure (Eley, 1993: 187–8).

The Farmers' League – like many other *Mittelstand* groupings[35] – identified free-trade and liberal doctrines of political economy or 'Manchesterism' as alien and threatening to Germany and propounded the generic far-right narrative that domestic socioeconomic problems were a consequence of foreign and cosmopolitan conspiracies.[36] Through such a narrative, domestic minorities – Jews and Polish migrants in particular – were identified as the local conveyors of such foreign forces, be it from the economic competition of migrant labour and their cultural incompatibility with the *volk*, to the competition of foreign producers and the alien ways of doing business associated with Jews. This racialization and spatialization of social relations also extended to the nature of politics, with the Farmers' League identifying liberalism and socialism – the two ideologies of cosmopolitanism – as 'Jewish faiths' (Pulszer, 1988). In a manner, then, that foreshadowed Nazism, these far-right demagogues identified Jews as being both the agents of cosmopolitan finance-capital *and* socialism (Puhle, 1986: 96, 106).[37]

The economic woes of many small-scale farmers deteriorated significantly from the 1880s as continuing flows of cheaper imports increasingly undermined their market viability. In addition, this economic misery was over laden with accelerating social change in the countryside highlighted by the emergence of state agricultural bureaucracies – another dimension of modernization – which subverted the traditional peasant-landlord relationship. The impact of such changes and the identification of political elites and the state bureaucracy as complicit in them helped generate what Geoff Eley (1993: 205–15; see also Blackbourn, 1984b: 63; Farr, 1986: 113; Hunt, 1975: 524) describes

---

35   The Farmers' League was a national organization and the most politically influential, but there were also a number of other local leagues that were significant in state-level politics at this time – such as the Bavarian Peasants League – which also shared many of the far-right ideo-political characteristics of the Farmers' League (see Farr, 1986: 120–32; Hunt, 1975).

36   In the words of James Hunt (1975: 521) the League 'exploited the fears, snobbery, and social resentment of the *Mittelstand* by picturing it as threatened simultaneously by capitalism from above and organized labour from below, by liberal or Jewish plutocrats and social democracy [and the] single most frequent and constant theme of League agitation was anti-Semitism'.

37   Further, as George Vascik (1993: 242–3) also notes, one of the League's key propagandists and spokesmen, Diedrich Hahn, was also a militarist who advocated a large army in preparation for wars against France, Britain and Russia that combined with his calls for the internment of Social Democrats – a harbinger of fascism indeed.

as an 'anti-plutocratic populism' that targeted the aristocrat, the priest and civil servant as much as the usual suspects of far-right populist demagoguery. Consequently, the Farmers' League was no dupe or supplicant of the ruling class or political elite and challenged the existing social and political dispensation in the *Kaiserreich*. Further, some of its leading propagandists, such as Gustav Ruhland, fomented a dual resentment of small farmers towards the 'red and gold internationals' highlighted in the growing power of organized labour, on the one hand, and that of finance capital – banks, big corporations and the stock exchange, on the other. All were encapsulated in the idea of the Jew forming an international conspiracy of Marxism and 'bank capital' (Winkler, 1976: 4) – the classic formula of a fascist political economy.

In this respect, the politics of the Farmers' League – like the generic far-right over the *longue durée* – reflected a stark contradiction produced from UCD in that the compulsion towards concentration and monopoly stemming from the internationally-mediated and geopolitically-directed structural imperatives of consolidation and competition intensified the crisis confronting the traditional classes. This was, however, not just an economic crisis connected to the possibilities of material survival of both small farmers and the Junkers, but a social and cultural one, as the complexion and character of the future of German civilization and the disappearance of the rural idyll within it was all too apparent. Thus, on the one hand peasants and landlords faced the challenge of the international capitalist market that revealed itself in cheap imports, new technologies of production and the problem of credit and, on the other hand, the growing response to the challenge of capital revealed itself in socialism – a cultural, social and ideological outlook that was anathema to the naturalized hierarchy of a *völkisch* pastoralism. As Geoff Eley remarks,

> the animus and sense of grievance behind the peasantry's political activism were strengthened by the institutional effects of Germany's capitalist transformation on the social relations of the countryside. Smaller farmers confronted their problems not only at a time of accelerating social and economic change, but also when the institutional consolidation of the rural class structure was creating greater distance from the landowning notability through the growth of state agricultural bureaucracies, the cooption of agricultural associations, and the incorporation of chambers of agriculture. The peasants seemed to suffer most of the costs of economic transformation without any of the gains.
>
> ELEY, 1993: 205–6

Supporters of the Farmers' League denounced what they called 'Manchesterism,' which they saw as a liberal creed 'that goods and men should sink or rise to their natural market level, regardless of the damage that might be caused' (Stone, 1985: 181). Demanding protection from the vicissitudes of the workings of the world market based on government-backed guarantees of secure credit flows and low interest rates, their animosity was particularly fixated on Jews who they racialized as the purveyors of money-capital in general. And from this, as Stone (1985: 181) suggests, the Farmers' League went on to claim that German liberalism was alien and Jewish because some prominent liberal members of the Reichstag were also Jewish.

The politics of the Farmers' League reflected a new and distinctly far-right form of popular and mass mobilization. In this way, these kinds of movement broke with the remnants of *ancien régime* conservatism and the traditional *Honoratiorenpolitik* (Eley cited in Coetzee, 1990: 8; see also Blackbourn, 1984b; Farr, 1986: 114) and, instead, fostered the emergence of a new breed of political activists and agitators who sort to radicalise the nature of political debate within the public sphere through their rhetoric and demagoguery undermining the traditional codes and practices of Conservative politics that the ruling elites had, until then, monopolised (Blackbourn, 1984a: 50). In short, the politics of the Farmers' League and similar organizations reflected a radical break in the politics of the right by establishing a distinctly populist, mass-based, nationalist, authoritarian and racist politics. Imminent, if not fully or coherently articulated within the politics of the League, was an idea or concept of democratic politics that was anti-parliamentary and anti-traditionalist in equal measure. Indeed, the class tensions within the Farmers' League were revealed in the role of the anti-Polish agitation of some elements within it that was focused on securing a racialized ideal of the *volk* that clashed with the seasonal labour market that the east-Elbian Junkers relied on (Eley, 1993: 191).[38]

In sum, then, the Farmers' League played a leading role in the creation of a specific *Mittelstand* ideology and the subsequent establishment of the largest fighting organization of the *gewerblicher Mittelstand* as a whole, the *Reichsdeutscher Mittelstandsverband* (founded in 1911) that reflected an attempt to bridge the socioeconomic interests of the large Junker landlords with small-scale farmers (Winkler, 1976: 4). Drawing on the bedrock of far-right ideology

---

38   By 1914 there were at least one million Polish casual labourers in Germany many of them concentrated in the Junker estates in the east. Though subject to racist scapegoating and sometimes violence, the dependence of the agrarian ruling class on this migrant labour served to limit the possibilities of *völkisch* imaginaries being fulfilled (see Kitchen, 1978: 200–2).

in identifying the antagonistic class positions of the international labour solidarity of Marxism and that of cosmopolitan-finance capital as part of the red
and gold international, the League proffered an anti-cosmopolitanism rather
than an anti-capitalism with the figure of the Jew as the unifying racial signifier bringing Marxism and finance/corporate capital together. And in targeting their message at and mobilizing support from what they regarded as the
distinct social and racial qualities of the *Mittelstand*, it campaigned to limit
further industrialization and democratization, which were seen as the twin
wings of the cosmopolitan and racial threat.

## 4      France: The Rise of a 'Revolutionary' Right Prefiguring Fascism

The rise of the far-right in France mirrored developments in Germany both
with respect to the role of lower middle class social layers that came to be
mobilized by it in the closing decades of the nineteenth century, the binding
ideological glue of a nationalism infused with anti-Semitic racism, and the role
of geopolitics and empire in structuring far-right ideological imaginaries and
the developmental pathways open to French capitalism in the context of the
Long Depression. A growing working-class militancy – given added ideological
potency by the legacy of the Paris Commune still fresh in the minds of political
elites and dominant class forces – reflected the contradictory-laden consolidation of capitalist social property relations as the basis of social order. And,
internationally, the reproduction of that domestic social order was locked into
an environment defined by growing trade protection that helped foster a top-
down attempt within France to reorganize a new set of hegemonic arrangements based on a politics of 'national-social protection.' French politics from
the 1880s was infused with a modern far-right which was the product of ruling
class manoeuvring and political adjustment and a set of subaltern and militant
ideo-political forces enabled by the transformed international-geopolitical
context and the behaviour of ruling elites but that were far from loyal to the
institutions and workings of the Third Republic (Lebovics, 1988: 32).

   However, the absence in France of a key social pillar of *ancien régime* politics – the traditional agrarian landlord class – and its occupation and control
of key state institutions, obviously had an important impact on the character
of the French state and the possibilities for a 'top-down' state-directed far-right
infused authoritarian politics. This did not mean that far-right forces did not
benefit from contacts with and ideological influence and support from leading social forces rooted in the land and the church (see Griffiths, 1978: 724–5;
Fuller, 2012; Golob, 1944: 98–107), but, rather, that the relationship between

ruling class, political elite and popular far-right mobilization was more frac-tured and less coherent than was the case in Germany. The political develop-ment of liberal democracy – and the culture associated with it – within France and the legacies of the Revolution played an important part, then, in reducing the structural and institutional context conducive to a far-right politics (from above) than was the case in Germany thus reflecting the multiple and varied development trajectories of uneven and combined development (Green, 2012).

The main consequence of this was that the far-right that emerged in France was much more anti-state or anti-regime (the Third Republic) than was the case in Germany. Indeed, in a way quite distinct from the far-right in Germany, the French far-right that emerged in bouts of militancy from the 1880s onwards was much more 'revolutionary' in terms of its propensity for extra-parliamentary struggle and violence (see Weber, 1964, 1976) and in its commitment to the overthrow of the existing republican political system and its replacement with a new kind of political order centred on a centralized and autonomous executive power committed to authoritarian forms of gov-ernance. Consequently, this militant character that was reflected in its willing-ness to use violence and engage in street politics – drawing on the syndicalist and revolutionary (or Jacobin) traditions ingrained within French nineteenth century politics – was an important stepping-stone, alongside the virulent and popular anti-Semitism, in the later emergence of fascism.

This radicalism was, however, also connected to an ideo-political current of reactionary royalism. While not always or necessarily connected to one or other line – Bourbon or Orléanist – the commitment to a monarchical figure as the key unifying representation and institution of the French nation was counter-posed against the 'corruption' and 'divisiveness' of the Republic and parliamentarianism. Thus, royalism was an important element within the far-right in France and particularly associated with figures like Charles Maurras and organizations such as *Action Française* (Weber, 1962), even if it was articu-lated and organized largely outside of the republican state. Indeed, we can com-ment further on these connections between this elitist agency committed to the upholding of social order based on private property rights and the Catholic church and the subaltern and militant far-right of the street as reflected in the *Ligue des Patriotes*, the *Ligue Antisemitique* etc. – who pushed the boundaries of social and political order. In many respects, this relationship – which was far from harmonious or stable – reflects an enduring quality of a far-right politics in the ambivalent and contradictory connections between a popular or mass far-right defined by a 'revolutionary' potential and dynamic with those petri-fied at the thought of largescale social disorder, revolutionary violence, and the accompanying threats to private property.

What helped drive the development of the French far-right, as elsewhere at this time, was the transformation of the geopolitical and international economic context within which the political imaginaries of elites and masses were shaped by and to which they responded. In the French case, this geopolitical context was particularly significant given that the founding of the Third Republic occurred immediately after the annexation of one of its constituent parts – the province of Alsace – with France's defeat in the 1870–71 Franco-Prussian War. Revanchism, directed at Germany, came to play a defining role in the politics of the Third Republic and in the rise of the far-right. However, this revanchism and its association with an injured, resentful, and conspiratorial nationalism and militarism was also directed at Britain. Thus, even though Anglo-French relations had warmed under Bonaparte's Second Empire regime, the new political dispensation of the Third Republic and the impact of the Long Depression saw a return to geopolitical rivalry with Britain in North Africa, which was particularly intense in the 1890s prior to the 1904 *Entente Cordiale* (Lowe, 1994: 15). Consequently, the search for and identification of a political figure or movement that appeared to offer a way of restoring French military pride and national self-respect was a major mobilizing focus of the far-right that was directly connected to the settling of military accounts through the re-taking of Alsace-Lorraine (Craig, 1974: 293; Rutkoff, 1981: 33–5; Tint, 1964: 38–9).

In recognizing the importance of the geopolitical context that framed the political conditions for the French far-right from the 1880s onwards it is important to note, that during this period, the relationship between capitalist imperialism and the far-right was far from singular or straightforward. Indeed, through the 1880–90s some of the key, if not the dominant, drivers of imperialist adventure and colonial expansion were liberal and conservative republicans (Halperin, 2004: 100–1)[39] – the core political constituencies of the Third Republic – and not the far-right which, in many respects opposed such colonial adventures.[40] This had paradoxical consequences for the French far-right. Thus, the move towards overseas adventure and annexations raised

---

39   In particular, the administrations of the Opportunist politician, Jules Ferry, were a key driver of increased French imperialist activity in the 1880s. Ferry's colonialism was couched in the racialized liberalism of the time, declaring in an 1885 speech, that colonialism 'is a right for the superior races, because they have a duty. They have the duty to civilize the inferior races' (Ferry, 1885 cited in La Palme, 2014: 344–5, author translation).

40   One of the leading propagandists of the far-right, Édouard Drumont, was a vocal opponent of French colonialism, which he claimed was organized by and for the benefit of Jews. Likewise, Henri Rochefort – another leading figure (and a leading Anti-Dreyfusard) also opposed the colonization of Tunisia and Indo-China (Wilson, 1982: 469).

the spectre of geopolitical confrontations with Britain in Africa that not only reinforced the geopolitical spectre of competition and confrontation playing out within France's domestic politics (which also included Germany), but also underlined the rupture with free-trade policy cemented in 1892 – given that this was a relationship primarily with Britain and aligning with British imperial interests. In short, the form of assertive and, in many respects, racialized nationalism that emerged in the closing decades of the nineteenth century in France was, to some extent, authored by liberals and conservatives, as much as it was by the far-right. Moreover, while the former deployed it as the basis for managing the instabilities and crises of domestic politics, this top-down legitimization and use of nationalist ideology could only strengthen and help normalize and legitimize the far-right even whilst, at the same time, the far-right sought to super-charge such racialized nationalism as a means to mobilize a mass layer through which to overthrow the Republic.

This period was defined by a contradictory set of political dynamics and international developments that implicated liberal and conservative elites and social forces in equal measure and the ideo-political atmosphere that emerged problematized the continued stability of the Republican order. Imperialism, then, was a response to both economic (the Long Depression) and geopolitical (the rise of Germany and continuing competition with Britain) challenges but was also central to domestic strategies of rule and social order. And even though the far-right was implicated in the creation of this social imperialist historical bloc, it was also antagonistic to the spatial focus of French imperialism. For the far-right and figures such as Paul Déroulède of the *Ligue des Patriots* and Charles Maurras of *Action Française* – the two main far-right movements that emerged as the nineteenth century closed out – France's overseas colonial adventures were of a secondary concern to that of Alsace-Lorraine (Heffernan, 1997: 89–113). Thus, Déroulède regarded the Opportunists' quest for overseas empire as a means to distract from the ongoing humiliation of Sedan. As the *Ligue's* publication, *Drapeau* put it,

> [w]hen condemning faraway wars, the *Ligue* has had no motive other than its ardent desire to maintain in Europe the sole endeavour of French diplomacy and arms ... [i]t is not with great new supplies of African sand and Asiatic silt that we shall ever fill the gap in the Vosges.
>
> cited in TINT, 1964: 43

And, more explicitly from Déroulède, 'I have lost two children and you offer me twenty servants' (cited in Craig, 1974: 365) with reference to the government's programme of colonization in North Africa.

In sum, the general outlines of the causal forces conducive to the advance of a far-right politics in France at this time were connected to the uneven and combined nature of capitalist development and, in particular its international and spatial properties. This was evident, as will be demonstrated, below, in the spatially concentrated social contradictions – notably centred on Paris – derivative of the uneven capitalist development underlaid by the Long Depression that began to bite particularly deep during the 1880s. It was in these locales where far-right mobilizations were most evident. It was also reflected in the way in which the geopolitical openings afforded by capitalist imperialism were connected to a nationalist politics of 'national social protection' that was also tied to the ongoing nationalist sore and humiliation of the loss of Alsace-Lorraine. Consequently, geopolitics was a significant and toxic dimension of French domestic politics providing a dagger aimed at the heart of the Third Republic wielded by the far-right for as long as Alsace remained under German rule. In what follows, I elaborate on the importance of the international political economic milieu in conditioning the domestic context that was conducive to the development and strengthening of the far-right, after which I will focus on the politics and social bases of the principal late nineteenth century far-right movements.

Under Bonaparte's Second Empire regime, France's international economic posture had been framed around a policy of free trade as reflected in the 1860 Cobden-Chevalier Treaty which saw significant reductions on import duties of goods that helped to stimulate bilateral trade and France's economic growth (Smith, 1980: 28–34). However, with the onset of the Long Depression after 1873 the international economic context was radically transformed giving way to a generalized trend towards protectionism that also affected France throughout the 1880s culminating in the 1892 Méline tariff. In a similar pattern to that of Germany, the depressive impact on prices and profits (Sperber, 2009: 122–3; Milward and Saul, 1977: 106–7) saw an intensification of domestic political demands for protectionism and a reassertion of geopolitical dimensions in capitalist development. Indeed, as Paul Bairoch (1993: 25; see also Cobban, 1990: 43; Millward and Saul, 1977: 106) has noted, France pursued a more systematic policy of trade protectionism and export monopoly than any other major European power at this time, thus helping to fuel geopolitical rivalry contributing to far-right mobilizations elsewhere. Hence the relational and interactive qualities in the workings of UCD in creating the enabling global conditions for the advance of the far-right.

The move towards protectionism – which proceeded, incrementally, during the 1880s with tariff increases – reflected a coming together of agricultural and industrial interests after the steep decline in prices and profits (Golob,

1944: 62–82, 147–215; Lebovics, 1988: 21, 31, 38; Milward and Saul, 1977: 106–7; Pollard, 1981: 258; Rutkoff, 1981: 28–9, 41; Smith, 1980: 63–114). In agriculture, there was a systemic decline in the average prices across a range of goods[41] from 1882: 1882–86, 7.2 percent; 1887–91, 14.8 percent; 1882–91, 11 percent (Golob, 1944: 70–1).[42] One not insignificant political consequence – evident in some of those areas most acutely effected by the agrarian crisis, such as in the south-east of France – was the election of anti-Semitic representatives to the National Assembly (Wilson, 1982: 270). In industry, profits fell in heavy industry and in banking throughout the 1880s. According to Lebovics (Lebovics, 1988: 51), the general index of profits reached a high of 193.8 for the period 1860–64 but declined to 112.9 by 1880–1884 and sank to 100 in 1890–94. The 1880s, then, was a decade defined by economic stagnation and anaemic levels of growth (Cameron, 1975: 70–1; Golob, 1944: 62–82; Lévy-Leboyer and Bourguignon, 1990: 53; Rutkoff, 1981: 41; White, 2007: 115) as the internationally-sourced deflation of the Long Depression interacted on and accentuated the domestic vulnerabilities of the French economy.

This protectionist shift was not just reflective of an economic reaction to the depression but a broader social and political response to reshape the wider ideo-political context  of the *fin de siècle*. In this respect, while the primary incentive was economic – the need to secure a floor on commodity prices and an uplift in profits – the broader political shift that the protectionist turn invoked was connected to a much more nationalist and socially protectionist ideology. This was based on worries – across political elites and industrialists – of a growing militancy from workers (see Perrot, 1987; Silver, 2003; Shorter and Tilly, 1974); a militancy that derived, in large part, from the intensification of class conflict, as capital responded to the falls in profit levels by shifting the social burden of the depression onto workers.

A politics of 'national labour' (Lebovics, 1988: 46–7, 122–3; Smith, 1980)[43] emerged that attempted to shift the axis of social conflict from that between

---

41    Prior to the onset of the agricultural depression, a significant part of the rural economy – wine production – had been decimated by the Phylloxera disease – caused by an aphid – that destroyed vines and which affected wine production throughout the 1860s until the early 1870s (see Cameron, 1975: 70–71).

42    Cereal prices began to fall in the 1870s and by 1895 were 27 percent below their level in 1871; this was also 33 percent in the case of wheat, 14 percent for oats and 26 percent for rye. For potatoes the decline started in 1885 falling by 35 percent, with lesser declines in livestock and dairy (Price, 1981: 226).

43    The first issue of *Le Travail National* made clear the intentions of the captains of industry in reducing class conflict, '[o]ur guiding principle is the solidarity of employer and worker. We reject the categories of "capital" and of "labor", from the patron, like the worker, also

capital and labour within and across French firms to that of a national antagonisms between rival economies which was becoming all the more evident
with the rapid rise of Germany and the United States and the privileges that
Britain derived from its empire and Sterling.[44] Accordingly, it was the differential developmental trajectories and advantages produced from UCD that determined the wider geopolitical opportunities and limits open to French elites
as the nineteenth century closed out and the Long Depression only served to
narrow such geopolitical openings. Thus, during the 1880s, commercial pressures from British industry in the textile sector undermined France's domestic industrialization, capital formation and economic development, which
was paralleled by Britain's imperial superiority that limited the non-European
geopolitical options for French capital. And in the case of Germany, while the
annexation of Alsace provided a permanent indignity and source of resentment at the heart of French politics – galvanizing a militarist-infused nationalism – Germany's economic dynamism further narrowed both the commercial
and geopolitical options available to France.

Although the economic impact of national labour may have been more limited than its architects had hoped for (see Smith, 1980, 1992) its ideological
effect was significant in reorientating the discussion of political economy into
a vernacular that focused on a nationalist geopolitical narrative linked to an
understanding of international relations as a competitive and 'zero-sum' struggle. The fact that it did not resolve the tensions and conflicts within the capital-
labour relationship is secondary to its ideological significance in fostering a
far-right politics given that an anti-class politics resting on geopolitical asser-
tion and nationalist scapegoating and demagoguery was obviously helpful to
the growth of the far-right and its political respectability.

Moreover, the ideology of national labour and the protectionist political
economy upon which it was based also provided an important stimulus to
France's imperialist and geopolitical ambitions given that its colonial markets were relatively underdeveloped in their economic potential at this time

---

labours. Rather, we propose solidarity of all French workers before the threat of foreign
competition' (cited in Lebovics, 1988: 66).

44    In the words of Jules Méline, the principal architect of the 1892 tariff, '[w]hat we have to
defend by means of the tariffs is labor, that is, the jobs and bread of our workers ... To do
this, we have to maintain the prices of our products at a profitable level by thwarting the
excessive inroads of foreign competition. That is how customs duties are linked to the
social question itself in its most acute form' (cited in Smith, 1992: 231).

(Lebovics, 1986: 164).[45] Such ambitions provoked a major geopolitical confrontation with Britain over Fashoda on the White Nile in East Africa in 1898, as well as with Germany over Morocco in 1905 and 1911 (Lowe, 1994: 16). In the case of Fashoda, the crisis helped – if in a relatively short-lived fashion – to reinvigorate an Anglophobia that had long been a feature of French politics and which the far-right latched onto and connected to the Dreyfus crisis (see below) that was playing out at the same time as the Fashoda dispute erupted.

The significance of the Fashoda crisis was not only that the French government was forced into a humiliating climb-down after the British fleet mobilized and speculation over the possibility of war briefly gripped France, but also how it reflected an intense period of both a resentful and conspiratorial nationalism at home that was also directed against France's key international rivals. And, while it would be a short-time before such rivalry was overcome by the *Entente Cordiale* of 1904, it lingered after Fashoda through French sympathy for the Boers in their struggle with British forces in South Africa. The Boers became a *cause célèbre* for the far-right in which they played a key role in the dispatch of over 400 volunteers who fought with the Boers. With the French government remaining neutral and the war turning in Britain's favour by 1900, some elements on the far-right demanded a French invasion of Britain as a way of ending the 'British yoke and the Judeo-Masonic virus' over France (Fuller, 2012: 171, 172–3).

Thus, the expansion of colonies and their more effective integration into a French-centred international economic system – echoing the principle of an imperial bloc – became a popular and politically supported endeavour[46] under governments led by Jules Ferry's Opportunists that highlighted the Republican and liberal-conservative dynamics behind the intensification of French imperialism and geopolitical rivalry as the century came to a close. However, it also ensured a structural opening for the far-right through normalizing a political economy of geopolitical rivalry.[47] Of course, for the far-right, the politicians and parties of the Third Republic – indeed, the constitutional regime and

---

45 Though as Lafrance (2019: 254–5) details, Normandy's cotton industry, which had been devastated by the impact of British competition after 1860, only managed to survive through servicing protected colonial markets such as in Algeria.

46 Delegates at the general meeting in December 1884 of the primary organization of French industrial capital, the *Association de l'Industrie Française*, voted to demand that the government introduce a 'privileged position' for French business in the colonies and for wider protections against foreign competition in France's colonies (Lebovics, 1988: 144–5).

47 The ideology of social protection and national labour identified 'foreign invaders' and Prussians and English in particular as the enemies of French production that required a unified national response from capital and labour (Lebovics, 1988: 46–7).

form of state itself – were seen as being either ineffective in pursuing French interests with sufficient vigour and vision, or actually complicit in maintaining French weakness.

As Lebovics (1988: 31) notes, for the leaders of largescale industry and agriculture the shift to national social protection was not only a strategy to realize their economic objectives but also the nationalist ideological underpinning of social protection would also help stabilize or inoculate the political system and wider society from the threat from the revolutionary left and the extremes of the militant far-right thus securing the political hegemony of those social and political elites committed to the Third Republic. Thus, by the mid-1890s the Republic seemed to have secured itself, socially, through the combination of the policies of trade protectionism and the ideology of national production thereby ensuring the reproduction of capital and bringing together large and small-scale farmers under the aegis of the *Union Centrale des Syndicats des Agricoles* (see Golob, 1944) and in the pacification of working class militancy. In practice, however, as Lebovics recognized (Lebovics, 1988: 123), this was more a marriage of convenience that reflected both a temporary, unbalanced – in favour of big capital and large landlords – and, in consequence, limited ability to ensure longer-term social peace and an exit from the structural contradictions that France found itself within.

One of the key consequences of the agrarian stagnation was an acceleration of rural-urban migration that was particularly felt in Paris from the 1880s through to the late 1890s, which saw its population more than double (Rutkoff, 1981: 36). Given that these country-people settled in Paris in the midst of an economic crisis, this could not have been a less propitious time for the capital to successfully absorb these rural migrants whose traditional views were ripe for baiting and manipulation. Thus, as Pierre Rutkoff (1981: 30) argued,

> [w]ithin a generation, the 'new social groups' whose life was most disrupted by the financial and agricultural crises of 1881–1882 would see themselves as victims of both the overall recovery of the 1890s and the militant working class response to that recovery [reflected in intensified strike action]. The success of the department stores on the one hand and the socialists and syndicalists on the other, combined with the myths of parliamentary corruption and 'foreign' influence, created a political environment permeated with tensions and uncertainties.

Further, this rural-urban migration concentrating on Paris occurred at a time when Jewish migration to the capital (as well as towns in the north-east of the country and Lille in particular) was also significant. And this prescence of a visible alien 'Other' constituted an important focus of racialized scapegoating for the economic malaise.[48] Thus, after the German annexation of Alsace in 1871 the local Jewish population migrated to France, mainly settling in Paris and Lille, where they quickly became a focus of anti-Semitism through the claims that they were driving out existing French traders and artisans because of their unfair and cut-throat competition (Byrnes, 1950; 254).

However, it was the migration of Jews – escaping pogroms from the Jewish Pale of the Russian Empire – in the 1890s and who settled in the northern and eastern districts of the French capital that was to provide a powerful boost to the rise of the far-right and a defining aspect of its association with anti-Semitism and its geographical concentration in these particular parts of Paris. And especially so as these areas of the capital were most economically unstable and depressed with fluctuating employment and wage levels. Hence, it was not just the visible presence of newly-arrived Jews, and particularly Yiddish-speakers from eastern Europe, that triggered far-right mobilizations around the *Ligue des Patriots* and, later, Jules Guérin's more plebeian *Ligue Antisémitique*, but that many of the newly arrived Jewish migrants competed with the struggling petty bourgeoisie of salesmen, tailors, shoemakers and so forth living in these districts – such that economic competition in a context of economic volatility and hardship had a very 'foreign appearance' (Rutkoff, 1981: 115–7). The 'foreignness' of Jewish migrants was particularly significant in that it tied-in with a pervasive anti-Semitism channelled towards what was seen as corrupt and dominant big, foreign and finance capital 'controlled by Jews' who had been implicated in the two major financial scandals of the Third Republic in 1882 and 1892.

Such a context, defined by a transformed urban milieu associated with economic distress and culturally distinct migrants seen as both economic competitors and cultural outsiders, helped fuel the emergence of petty bourgeois producerist movements demanding national-social protection such as the far-right small shopkeepers' movement, *Ligue Syndicale*, that cultivated a distinct form of populist anti-cosmopolitanism. It defined itself as the defender of family and workplace based not on the logic of capitalist exchange relations but, rather, as 'little communities organized hierarchically and cemented by ties of sentiment' (Nord, 1984: 177), echoing the fetishized producerism that

---

48    And as in Paris it was petty bourgeois social layers in these towns who were particularly drawn to anti-Semitic political messaging at this time, through a combination of concern as to the growth of a socialist consciousness amongst industrial workers and the presence of Jewish refugees from Alsace-Lorraine (Byrnes, 1950: 254).

has lain at the basis of the far-right's political economy. Articulating an anti-cosmopolitanism, anti-monopoly and a national as opposed to collective socialism, the *Ligue Syndicale* defended the 'hard-working citizen' against the 'rapacious monopolist' and called for the expulsion of foreign workers and the expropriation of those who the *Ligue* described as 'horders' and 'monopolists' because these were Jewish-owned businesses (Nord, 1984: 179–84). Leading figures in the *Ligue* campaigned for General Georges Boulanger – the short-lived hope of the far-right in the late 1880s – and later, joined with other anti-Semites who took to the streets in 1898–99 as anti-Dreyfusards (see below).

The impact of the agricultural depression extended well beyond farming, contributing to and accelerating urbanization – even if employment prospects in the major cities did not pick until the early 1890s – and thus the social transformation of France. It also reflected a structural vulnerability and the particular inflection of combined development within France at this time as French agriculture had not undergone a major overhaul in terms of land ownership, production techniques or market access since the years of the French Revolution (Golob, 1944: 8, 17–61). Indeed, the force of change unleashed by the Long Depression effected a socioeconomic transformation that no French government was able to realize or risk prior to the 1880s given the vulnerabilities of the French political regime and the important social conservative role that the French peasantry had played in the period after 1815 in helping to prop-up the Republican order (Lafrance, 2019: 248).

The banking, or financial, crises that dove-tailed with the beginning and ending of the agricultural depression concerned the collapse of Union Générale bank in January 1882 and the Panama Canal Scandal in 1892; both were connected to France's geopolitical manoeuvrings and reflected the deepening entanglements and intertwining of international economic relations and geopolitics in the reproduction of French capitalism, exemplary of the era's spatio-temporal fixes. The sources of the two crises can be seen as contradictory outcomes of the workings of the 'external whip of necessity' associated with uneven development with regard to French attempts to establish and grow national banking champions, as a way of reducing France's dependence on securing credit from international banks and the financial power of the City of London in particular.

The collapse of Union Générale came after a period of speculative boom from 1878 onwards connected to its international investments in east-central Europe as French banks sought to break the 'Anglo-Jewish' (sic. Rothschild's) monopoly on international finance (Heywood, 1992: 35) and eek out profit streams and facilitate the furtherment of diplomatic alliances abroad and a geopolitical prop to France's domestic social order and economic dynamism.

The bank, itself, had emerged in the 1860s with the support of the Bonapartist state as an attempt to challenge the City of London's growing dominance of international finance and France's dependence on it. Its sudden collapse sent shock waves through the French economy (Cameron, 1975: 70–1, 198–9; Kindleberger, 2011: 74–6; Rutkoff, 1981: 28–9; White, 2007) given that it had quickly developed into a major part of the banking sector. The collapse was connected to its investments in east-central Europe that failed to maintain expected (and necessary) levels of returns that combined with the speculative hedging associated with the rapid and unprecedented rise in the valuation of the bank's stocks by 600 percent between 1879 and 1882 (Griffiths, 1978: 722; Rutkoff, 1981: 29).

The result was not only that a large number of small investors lost money but that credit conditions became much tighter through the rest of the decade, as bankers moved to a much more conservative and cautious approach to lending (Cameron, 1975: 70–1, 198–99, 457). Given the impact on Catholic small investors in particular – notably in the increased level of bankruptcies in small and medium-scale retail outlets and other businesses (Haupt, 1984: 102), as credit flows tightened up at the same time as demand slowed – the crisis was ripe for conspiratorial explanations given the perceived dominance of Jewish financiers in the international banking system because of the role of the Rothschild's bank in international credit markets. Consequently, the impact of the collapse of Union Générale went much further than the bank itself, and although it was not the primary cause of the economic stagnation of the 1880s, the tightening of credit played an important role in undermining the prospects for economic growth throughout the decade as industrial concerns found themselves short of funds.

As suggested, the consequences of the collapse of Union Générale had political as much as economic reverberations in the years that followed. The bank had styled itself as a 'Catholic bank' committed to not only financing French Catholics but challenging the 'Protestant' (read English) and 'Jewish' (read Rothschild's) dominance of European finance (White, 2007: 127). This framing of the bank as a form of 'racial finance' became even more pronounced after its failure with a conspiratorial narrative quickly emerging based on the attempt by its founder, Paul Eugène Bontoux, to blame the collapse on an international conspiracy (rather than bad investment decisions) involving Jews and Masonic lodges which a number of French newspapers were happy to disseminate (Fuller, 2012: 59; White, 2007). The collapse of the bank quickly became an anti-Semitic *cause célèbre* in France propagated by the Catholic and Royalist right – the original backers of the bank – serving to provide an important case amongst a number of others that followed in the construction of a popular and widespread anti-Semitic and nationalist conspiratorial politics that developed throughout the 1890s (Birnbaum, 1992, 2003; Byrnes, 1950; MacMaster, 2001; Wilson, 1982: 247–318). The crisis was seen as reflecting a more significant transformation in France's political economy, which was latched onto by the emerging far-right. And while the explanation and narrative that far-right demagogues propagated were far from the truth, it did refer and relate to a set of real and objective economic changes that French society was undergoing at the time. These changes were visible in the increasing significance of both the material reality of international economic exchange in the workings of the French economy and the ideological imaginaries that were deployed to explain it via a range of sources – literary and popular[49] as much as demagogic and conspiratorial.[50]

Coming relatively soon after the collapse of Union Générale, the Panama Canal scandal of 1892 not only accentuated the precariousness of the financing of the French economy, but also reinforced the popular anti-Semitic narrative within French politics. The scandal saw tens of thousands of small investors lose their money as the company overseeing the construction of the canal went bankrupt. However, though these losses were serious enough – thousands were financially ruined and economically desperate – it was the subsequent corruption scandal that soon emerged, involving senior French politicians, that proved to be politically explosive and an ideological gift and 'recruiting sergeant' for the far-right.

---

49   As Stephen Wilson (1982: 282; see also Kahan, 2003: 180) states, even the great novelist Émile Zola – one of the leading Dreyfusards – commented on these developments in his 1883 novel, *Au Bonheur des Dames*, which referred to changes in commercial society reflected in the rise of big department store shops and their negative impact on small traders but in a way which also deployed some notorious anti-Semitic tropes that reflected a widespread (but unfounded) suspicion that Jews were behind most of these new big stores.

50   Drumont's anti-Semitism was, then, connected to a genuine hostility to the French bourgeoisie whom he condemned as 'venal, corrupt, materialistic and unpatriotic' that contrasted with 'the people' who were defined by a natural and uncorrupted virtue. This was a form of populism in a very modern (and contemporary) sense and a view that also drew inspiration from the literature of a significant strand of French socialism. For Drumont and others, French workers were social victims of the existing social system through no fault of their own, and despite their honesty and hard work. While the blaming of Jews or the racial fetishization of the French bourgeoisie was wide of the mark, the symptoms that Drumont identified were very much real in terms of the poverty and suffering that many workers suffered at this time. Further, and as Stephen Wilson (1982: 321, 322–3; 324, 325) has argued, because it spoke to a real crisis, it resulted in anti-Semitism gaining a widespread acceptance because it appeared to confirm 'socialist truths'.

The scandal concerned the paying of bribes to politicians via a number of middle-men to cover-up the financial problems in the company as a rescuer for it was sought.[51] One of these middle-men, Jacques de Reinach, handed over documentation in September 1892 – suggesting corruption – to the leading anti-Semitic journalist, Édouard Drumont, who published a series of articles in his anti-Semitic mouthpiece, *La Libre Parole*, that alleged a conspiracy involving leading politicians and Jews. Another important nationalist (and founder of the *Ligue des Patriotes*), Paul Déroulède, accused the leading Republican, Georges Clemenceau, of accepting bribes and of protecting the 'little German Jew' Cornelius Herz – one of the middle-men (Fuller, 2012: 52).

The scandal that ensued – it dragged on through 1893 as the legal cases against leading figures in the company were heard, providing an open wound for the far-right to fester on – was not just about the losses that a large swathe of the French middle class suffered but that leading politicians involved in the government's support of the scheme were accused of having been directly involved in bribes to delay the firm's bankruptcy. The scandal's economic impact was less serious than the crisis of 1882 but, politically, it was arguably more so, and especially with regard to the development of the far-right. As in the political fall-out that greeted the collapse of Union Générale, a Jewish conspiracy was blamed for the scandal, reflecting both the influence of widespread and deeply in-grained anti-Semitic attitudes across much of the French elite and middle-class, as well as the way in which the shadow of the Rothschild's banking house continued to hover over financial affairs in France. Thus, in Drumont's portrayal, the Third Republic was not only rotten to the core based on the corruption of politicians, but it was also dominated by Jews, which connected to wider and longer-standing conspiracies associated with the role of Jewish finance in France going back to the collapse of Union Générale in 1882 and also the role of Rothschild's bank in the financial settlement after the France's defeat in the Franco-Prussian War (Arendt, 1968: 97).

The two crises were framed by the far-right as evidence not only of the continuing stranglehold of Jews over international finance but also the influence of

---

51   Here, the inter-connections between international financial capital and the French state were clearly evident. They highlighted the monopoly-tendencies within capitalist development at the time as – in the midst of an on-going economic depression – the French government looked for international sources of revenue (a form of spatio-temporal fix) through combining international speculative adventures such as this, with international finance. In short, the nature of the project and the form in which it was financed and managed through public and private collusion and corruption is inexplicable outside of the international economic and geopolitical context of the time.

Jewish interests at the heart of the French state and economy (Weiss, 1977: 95; Winnock, 1998: 91). That this had little material credibility – as Hannah Arendt (1968: 95–6) noted, no Jews were among the bribed members of parliament or on the board of the company (but two were identified as being involved in the distribution of the bribes) – did not matter. Almost overnight, the revelation that two Jews were involved in the scandal was enough to racialize it, with Édouard Drumont's anti-Semitic daily, *Libre Parole* dramatically increasing its circulation to over 300,000 as a result (Burns, 1984: 122).

The significance of the scandal was also due to its temporal setting within a political context where far-right and anti-Semitic forces had begun to organize in earnest and assert an important influence over French politics. The ability of anti-Semites, political opportunists, and far-right demagogues to take advantage of the scandal was closely connected to the existence of an already well-established, strong, and growing anti-Semitic politics associated with the broader right. The sources of this popular and political anti-Semitism were well-established across the French social and political elite[52] and particularly concentrated within the French Catholic hierarchy and royalism that saw the Third Republic – and the social and cultural changes taking place within it – as evidence of a materialism, egalitarianism, and cosmopolitanism that Catholic reactionaries and royalists blamed on a growing Jewish influence because of their cosmopolitan dimensions and apparent international origins.

As Stephen Wilson (1982) has documented in his monumental study of anti-Semitism in France at the end of the nineteenth century, the figure of the Jew provided an ideal construct for a reactionary and authoritarian politics at this time. The scandals plaguing Republican institutions and politicians alongside the weakening hold of Catholicism, as a basis of social order and driver of French politics, were regarded as the 'corruption' of French political life through the influence of 'alien' and 'cosmopolitan' political influences depicted in the figure of the Jew – the 'wandering' and 'nation-less race' – that also extended to free masons and Protestants, as similar, if lesser, incarnations of moral degradation and political subversion.[53] Further, the increasing

---

52    Indeed, one of the most vocal advocates of protection, the *Societe des Agriculteurs*, also articulated a strong anti-Semitic position. Thus, the Eastern Association weeks before the 1898 elections stated, '[w]e will only cast our votes for those candidates who pledge themselves to propose, support and vote for a law disenfranchising the Jews and banning them from public office, civil or military' (cited in Wilson, 1982: 19–20).

53    In this respect, the contradictory features of anti-Semitism were evident. Thus, as much as the crisis of capitalism was racialized as the fault of Jews or part of a Jewish conspiracy that reflected a bastardized form of anti-capitalism, figures on the right and far-right also argued that socialism and collectivism were Jewish ideas. Pierre Biétry a leading figure of

encroachment of money and commodified-exchange as the mediator of the life-chances of individuals and in structuring social relations was also articulated less as a problem of capitalism or private property and, instead, of Jewish economic domination.[54] In the Dreyfus Affair at the close of the century when the 'corruption' and 'decadence' of Jewish influence was seen by the French right as having extended into the heart of the military – one of the last bastions of 'honour' and 'patriotism' free of such 'Jewish influence' – and as exposing French military security to its primary foe, Germany, the narrative and popular appeal of this conspiratorial politics based on the idea of Jewish domination and betrayal was to reach unprecedented heights.

These economic developments – the stagnation of French agriculture and its contribution to a deflation across swathes of French industry and the two financial crises reflected the crisis-workings of a capitalist imperialist form of uneven and combined development in both its economic and (geo)political articulations. Thus, the impact of cheaper imports of grain and other agrarian commodities into the European market from the 1870s not only reflected the competitive pressures of new agrarian producers assisted by the technological transformations associated with steamships and a developed railway infrastructure, but also the legacies of the changes ushered by the French revolution in land ownership and agrarian production in France. The end of the agrarian *ancien régime* did not, then, result in a fundamental modernization of French agriculture with respect to the creation of a capitalist and export-oriented agrarian economy. That this did not occur was also, in part, a consequence of the delicate social balance within France after 1815 and the significance of the peasantry as a bastion of conservative social order that mitigated against any wholesale consolidation and reform from above. Thus, it was to be the pressures and the deflation of the 1880s that was to kick-start significant change in the French countryside; not least the squeezing of small farms resulting in

---

the far-right who was to play a leading role in the *syndicats jaunes* at the turn of the century, claimed, '[b]y the institution of common ownership of property (preached by the Socialists), the sedentary, rooted races would be at the mercy of the wandering races, the races without a homeland, that is to say the Jews, who treat all uncircumcised Gentiles as "the seed of cattle"' (cited in Wilson, 1982: 352).

54   For the leading anti-Semite, Édouard Drumont, '[s]mall workshops could not compete with the giant factories built and owned by Jews. In these giant factories honest French workers, who took pride in their craft, were chained to merciless machines that robbed them of their skills and produced cheap and shoddy goods. French workers were being enslaved by Jews' while the Catholic social theorist and leading figure in the *Oeuvre des cercles catholiques d'ouvriers*, the marquis Ren de La Tour du Pin, described free-masons as 'the general staff of the gilded international, Jewish high finance' (see Fuller, 2012: 58, 60).

significant rural-to-urban migration and a consolidation of agricultural production. Industry was trapped in the shadow and co-dependent on agriculture and with the deflation of the 1880s reducing profit levels, the possibility of
overcoming the crisis through a major increase in exports was frustrated by a
lack of viable developed colonial outlets and the growing commercial-export
power of Germany and the United States that were also eating into traditional
British export markets.

Further, the working out of UCD-generated crisis in finance reflected the
spatial-temporal fix (Harvey, 2003: 43–4) of attempts to carve out new streams
of capital accumulation via international financial speculation directed at the
Habsburg empire in east-central Europe (which defined the workings of Union
Générale) and the economic and geopolitical benefits connected to the construction of the Panama Canal that could be seen as an attempt to secure new
forms of geopolitical leverage in a similar way that the earlier construction
and opening of the Suez Canal had provided. These two financial crises were
a reflection of the growing pressures – both economic and geopolitical – that
France confronted over the last two decades of the nineteenth century as the
structure and workings of a globalizing capitalist economy advanced and, in
consequence, the character of its uneven and combined development became
more pronounced and entrenched.

In political terms combined development was to be encapsulated in the rising tide of anti-Semitism and the concurrent growth of the far-right. While
the rise of the far-right was not the singular ideo-political development of the
late nineteenth century – the growth of an organized and militant socialist
movement was also signal, and an important and paradoxical contributing
element to the growth of the former – it reflected a singular form of combination through its internal contradictory identity formation as a product of
internationally and geopolitically-mediated capitalist transformation that was
both conservative and revolutionary.[55] Such ambivalence and contradiction
reflected its distinct posture towards the internationalizing forces of capitalism, as reflected in its appeal to a form of 'national socialism' whereby socialism reflected a quasi-corporatist framework connected to trade protectionism
and nationalist economic exchange, but which left private property rights (of
French nationals) largely intact and the forces of an independent working

---

55    The geopolitics of the French far-right – at least with respect to the leaders of the *Ligue
      Antisémitique* – was also highly racialized in their attacks on what they saw as a 'cozying-
      up' to the 'Jewish-dominated states' of England and Germany, and their advocacy of an
      alliance with Russia defined by its authoritarian social conservatism and virulent and
      state-orchestrated anti-Semitism (Fuller, 2012: 65).

class suppressed and neutered. In this respect, anti-Semitism was an ideological structure that went well beyond the far-right, extending to some parts of the socialist left and the French ruling class, as the means through which scandals were managed and the Republic stabilized. So, although anti-Semitism was a dominant ideological leitmotif of the far-right and an important ideological basis through which the far-right attacked the Third Republic, it also provided an important set of ideological tropes that helped deflect and manage the social and political tensions within it, as well. Hence, the antinomies of the liberalism of French republicanism.

Consequently, the pervasive role of anti-Semitism, as both a defining ideological structure within French political culture and as a political instrument deployed by the ruling class and political elite in the management of scandals provided it – and its most rabid proselytizers in the far-right – with a veneer of political respectability and entrance into parts of the state apparatus that did not exist for the democratic left. Moreover, it also meant that the anti – Semitic political economy of the far-right as expressed by Édouard Drumont – who claimed that rich Jews had arrived from abroad, 'done no work, produced nothing, and yet made millions of francs through the financial system' (cited in Griffiths, 1978: 726) – was widely accepted as a form of popular common sense. Yet, despite such interconnections and commonalities, it is important to recognize the revolutionary and anti-system characteristics of the far-right. Because for all the commonalities across the elite, ruling class and far-right based on their shared anti-Semitism and how this connected to the ideology of national protectionism that targeted foreign money and foreign labour as responsible for France's economic ills (Tint, 1964: 109–10), for the far-right and politicians such as Maurice Barrès, the ultimate source of the problem was the Republic itself – its institutions and workings – which had to be overthrown.

Now that we have a grasp of the enabling conditions that helped produce a modern far-right in France from the 1880s, I will spend the rest of this section focusing on the principal political movements that emerged. Specifically, I will discuss Boulangism and the *Ligue des Patriotes* – arguably the dominant incarnation of a pre-fascist far-right in the closing decades of the nineteenth century and the most important movement associated with the rise of authoritarian and militarist right prior to 1914. The popular mobilization that coalesced around the political ambition of the former Minister of War, General Georges Boulanger, captured some key elements usually associated with the modern far-right. The core organization within Boulangism was the *Ligue des Patriotes* (founded in 1882) under the leadership of the nationalist poet and veteran of the Franco-Prussian War, Paul Déroulède. The *Ligue* was to quickly become the leading far-right movement in France up to the Dreyfus Affair at the close of the century before it was eclipsed by *Action Française*. Blessed with some level of governmental support at its inception (Tombs, 1996: 53), it defined itself as a non-partisan, patriotic organization dedicated to defending French political and military honour,[56] which ensured that it was fundamentally pre-occupied with the loss of Alsace. In its early years the *Ligue* did not take on the classical form of a far-right movement. Indeed, as a number of authors have argued (Payne, 1995: 43; Rutkof, 1981: 1–7, 33; Sternhell, 1986), the anti-Semitism and violent street militancy and political conspiracies for which it was to become infamous, were of much less significance in its early years. Instead, it had a Jacobin and almost socialist ideological character that reflected the prominence of a left-republican nationalism (Payne, 1995: 43) that continued to linger within French political culture after the destruction of the Commune.

However, early developments under Déroulède's leadership were to give a taste of what was to blossom later. Thus in 1884 it denounced the policies of Jules Ferry's Opportunist government as too pro-German and a betrayal of France (Rutkoff, 1981: 33). It also demonstrated an interest in socioeconomic issues – given the economic impact of the Long Depression which intensified in France from the early 1880s – with a particular worry over rising unemployment and the perceived increase in foreign workers in France (Seager, 1969: 175). The *Ligue* was also concerned with growing conflict between employers and workers signalled by the increases in the number and militancy of strikes,[57] which became particularly pronounced after 1892 (Halperin, 2004: 130; Perrot, 1987; Polanyi, 2001: 130; Smith, 1992: 232; Silver, 2003). This is significant in our understanding of the far-right, which tends to want to overcome class-conflict and especially when it involves, or is associated with, the rise of a socialist-type of consciousness within the labouring classes, as was feared by the *Ligue* and many others on the right and centre of French politics at this time.

Thus, the *Ligue* articulated a nationalist and protectionist position based on bringing workers and employers together in a form of corporatist arrangement that combined with preferential treatment for French workers (Rutkoff, 1981: 37; see also Arnold, 1999); a position generic to the far-right – then and now. As Stanley Payne (1995: 43) describes it,

---

56    As Edward Tannenbaum (1962: 7) noted, the *Ligue* was founded 'for the purpose of developing a military spirit in France, preparing Frenchmen morally and physically to be good soldiers, and preserving the cult of *revanche* in the public mind.'

57    Lebovics, (1988: 95; see also Kergoat, 1990: 171–5;) details a surge in strikes after 1892 – in spite of the passing of the Méline Tariff 45,900 workers participated in 268 strikes in 1892. That number jumped to 634 labour conflicts involving 172,500 employees by the end of 1893.

[a] central motif [of the *Ligue*] was national vengeance, based on the doctrine of militarism and a mystique of discipline and death rooted in the national soil and the culture of the people. Contemptuous of new parliamentary democracy, the League nonetheless directed its appeal to the masses, seeking to harmonize social interests within promises of new economic regulations that appealed especially to small shopkeepers and the lower middle classes.

Such a perspective was gaining ever more political traction as the 1880s proceeded and such a position was not just about promoting social stability through undermining the penetration of socialist ideas and methods across France but was also about ensuring that France was economically strong enough to deal with Germany. This reflected a classical far-right form of political economy: domestic social peace through a nationalist protectionism that would, on the one hand, help preserve the existing bourgeois social order and the institution of private property – partly through the scapegoating of migrant workers (upon which parts of French capital depended) – and, on the other hand, a nationalist politics focused on geopolitical concerns and security as another means of dissolving the ideological resonance of a socialist-form of class politics.

However, it was the decision by General Georges Boulanger – initially prompted by pro-Royalist patrons (Irvine, 1989: 7–8) – to run for political office and challenge the legitimacy of the Third Republic and its governing elites after 1887 that was to see a transformation in the size and influence of the *Ligue*, as well as shifting it in a more far-right ideological direction that would deepen through the 1890s. As John Weiss (1977: 93) has argued, Boulanger's entrance into politics could be seen as a moment of opportunism. Thus, while Boulanger, himself, may not have been the far-right or populist ideologue in the way that people who supported him – such as Paul Déroulède, Maurice Barrès and Édouard Drumont – wanted him to be, he was certainly a quasi-monarchical figure and potential authoritarian saviour who might rescue France from the Republic's decadence. Further, he also helped unleash and promote an authoritarian and populist politics founded on revanchism and militarism, as well as an abiding hostility towards the liberal democratic institutions of the Third Republic.[58]

---

58    Boulanger came to public prominence – and especially his identification with an anti-German militarism – in April 1887 in the so-called 'Schnaebelé Affair' named after the capture of a French customs official, Guillaume Schnaebelé by German authorities in April 1887 and his arrest as a spy. Even though the German Foreign Ministry quickly

Indeed, prior to his electoral campaign success in 1887, Boulanger reportedly had dealings with the Comte de Paris – the Orléanist pretender to the French throne – who issued a manifesto endorsed by Boulanger that called for the replacement of the democratic institutional arrangements of the Third Republic by a corporatist framework that would have resulted in a return to a quasi-monarchical system and a serious dilution of the political power of any elected body. For Weiss (1977: 93–4), this arrangement – taking heed of the situation in Germany that appeared to realize strong and effective government – meant 'Boulanger, presumably, would gain ... electoral victories, restore the pretender and play Bismarck to his William [the Kaiser]'. Boulanger's royalist inclinations were revealed in his election successes which tended to be confined to capturing support from traditional conservative-voting districts based on lower middle-class support (Irvine, 1989: 9; 119). Thus, although at the outset of his political campaign in early 1888 he managed to draw support from some left-republicans, Blanquists and Bonapartists (Burns, 1984: 58; Fuller, 2012: 30–46; Payne, 1995: 43–4; Wilson, 1982; Winnock, 1998: 213–28), which was assisted by the prevailing context of the economic crisis and his apparent sympathy towards parts of the labour movement (Burns, 1984: 7; Hutton, 1976: 85–7; Irvine, 1989: 5–7, 119; Rutkoff, 1962: 591; Seager, 1969: 174–5), he was never able to go beyond a rather marginal association with urban working class voters who saw him as 'another Louis Bonaparte' (Tint, 1964: 62–3).

No doubt Boulanger's politics hinted at appeals to both the radical left[59] and traditional and far-right. And while he did not articulate a public anti-Semitism[60] himself, he mobilized social and political forces that were increasingly targeting Jewish influence as the defining and catch-all narrative to account for France's malaise. Consequently, we are, I think, able to categorize Boulangism as a form of far-right politics in both its form and political methodology and its substantive positions, and particularly when we consider his reliance on the foot soldiers of the *Ligue des Patriotes* (that numbered around 100,000 with over a quarter in Paris alone over 1888–89; see Rutkoff,

---

released him and announced that he was not a spy, Boulanger demanded a 'vigorous response to German provocations and asked permission to send troops to the border' (Fuller, 2012: 28).

59   Drumont made effective use of the propaganda value of the memory of the Commune and its suppression by centrist Republican forces through which he tried to cultivate a socialist form of anti-Semitism (see Wilson, 1982: 247–318, 319–78).

60   Boulanger may have personally detested Drumont but that did not stop the representatives of the movement that bore his name from pursuing a vicious anti-Semitic campaign in the Marne targeting its Jewish population as a way of securing votes through appealing to base emotions and fear of a 'foreign menace' (Burns, 1984: 101–5).

1962: 586)[61] in helping to secure his electoral successes. Boulanger's political style, then, was based on a militarist form of charismatic leadership suspended above politics as parliamentary manoeuvre, compromise, and debate. Indeed, for many – desperate to find a saviour from deepening economic misery and seemingly official political negligence – Boulanger offered a way out of the malaise that would restore French pride[62] and economic well-being. For some workers, as described by Michael Burns (1984: 7), the General appeared to represent the 'hero of Decazeville: the enlightened War Minister whose troops had exchanged rations not bullets with striking workers in 1886'.

Accordingly, we should see Boulanger as part of that ambiguous Napoleonic or Bonapartist political tradition in France based on his ambivalent postures to the left and right, appearing to be a 'man for all seasons' and a saviour of the nation in a moment of economic, and geopolitical crisis. His direct appeal to the people, his anti-parliamentarism, and his hostility to the Third Republic suggested a classical plebiscitary and anti-parliamentary style of politics (Irivine, 1989: 6) centred on the charismatic leader; a *sine qua non* of a far-right form of politics. Further, the embrace of mass politics with a strong appeal and mobilization amongst the petty bourgeoisie in Paris and in parts of the countryside based on his promise of new economic reforms to ease the strain of the crisis on shopkeepers and small businesses in particular (Payne, 1995: 43) appeared to reflect a mirror of the subaltern and radical form of *Mittelstand* politics that characterised the *Bund der Landwirte* and *Allverband Deutsch* in Germany that while embedded in the defence of private property and social conservatism and hostile to socialism, was equally hostile to the political status quo and the political privileges of the ruling class.

Boulanger's appeal focused on speaking to the 'little man' – the classic figure in the imaginary of petty bourgeois militancy and popular reaction who, in today's political vernacular would be labelled 'the left behinds' (Tannenbaum, 1962: 8) – who were increasingly looking for political alternatives to Third Republic parliamentarianism as a means to address their socioeconomic anxieties and insecurity (Hutton, 1976: 88). In a short period of time Boulanger appeared to have uprooted French politics, gaining ever more momentum that reached its highpoint in January 1889 with the General taking a seat in

---

61    Support for the *Ligue*, and particularly in its provincial membership reflected economic as much as political concerns with members requesting financial assistance in support of small businesses. Many were military veterans who, in the words of Peter Rutkoff (1962: 588, 593–4) viewed the *Ligue* as 'a kind of unofficial Ministry of Veterans Affairs' and who joined it a as a way of 'ameliorating their status as the nation's forgotten men.'

62    He was popularly known as 'Le Général Révanche' (Payne, 1995: 43).

Paris having benefited from the support provided by the local committees of the *Ligue*. The significance of this for his more radical followers, including Déroulède, was that having gained power in a city not known for its support of the anti-parliamentary right, it appeared that Boulanger had the momentum to overthrow the republic via a military-backed coup on the back of popular support. Although he continued through February and March to make inflammatory speeches including calling for the end of the parliamentary system (Tannenbaum, 1962: 9), Boulanger, ultimately, wasn't willing to take the risk and with talk of a *coup d'état* circulating on the Parisian streets – indeed the crowds that greeted his victory chanted for Boulanger to seize power and put an end to the Republic (see Weiss, 1977: 94) – he fled to Belgium. The authorities took action against the *Ligue* arresting its leaders and charging Boulanger with treason.

With Boulanger disappointing many of his far-right supporters in the *Ligue* and the arrest of some of its leaders, the momentum behind the far-right soon evaporated and it was disbanded in 1891, only to re-emerge in 1897 amidst the Dreyfus Affair where it became, once again, a leading force in the coalition of right-wing nationalist and anti-Semitic movements – some of which were funded by wealthy landowners (Wilson, 1982: 272) – supporting the Army High Command. As we have seen, above, in our discussion of the move towards protectionism in France, this top-down shift to the right with an increased state-led nationalism along with the easing of the economic situation in the early 1890s helped reduce the socioeconomic and political context that movements such as the *Ligue* thrived in. In this respect, the Dreyfus Affair that came to dominate French political life from 1896 through to the early years of the twentieth century became a new rallying point for the far-right that saw the mobilization of tens of thousands in nationalist and anti-Semitic *ligues*.[63]

Alfred Dreyfus, an army captain, had been imprisoned in 1894 for treason – on what would later be revealed as a 'trumped-up' charge – for providing military intelligence to Germany. The fact that the secrets had been betrayed to France's primary geopolitical foe and by a Jew provided a perfect storm

---

63    Support for the army and condemnation of Dreyfus and his supporters also came from senior sections of the Catholic church. In the spirit of de Maistre and Bonald, the editors of the Assumptionist paper, *La Croix*, called for a restoration of the old unity of throne and altar. They also insisted that Dreyfus was part of an international conspiracy bent upon weakening the French army and seizing France's territories. The Jesuit Order called for political and economic sanctions against Jews and publicly expressed hope for the day when they might be banished from Europe altogether' (see Weiss, 1977: 100; Arendt, 1968: 116; Birnbaum, 1992, 2003; Byrnes, 1950; Fuller, 2012: 72–157; Wilson, 1982).

ideally-suited for far-right mobilizations. However, it was the public scandal that erupted in 1897 – when information entered the public domain after an internal military investigation that suggested that Dreyfus had been the victim of a grave miscarriage of justice – that was to provide the lightning rod for a renewed bout of far-right agitation. The 'Dreyfus Affair', as it became known, revealed the deep political and ideological divisions within France as a series of struggles took place – on a number of levels that involved various social and political actors – with one side dominated by anti-Semitic currents and movements[64] supporting the original conviction and the reputation of the French Army, and the other demanding justice and the freeing of Dreyfus. The case – as far as the far-right were concerned – revealed the corruption, weakness, and Jewish penetration of the Third Republic that these ideo-political forces had been pre-occupied with since the 1870s.

The far-right upsurge after 1897 saw a range of movements emerge from the reformed *Ligue des Patriotes* to the *Ligue de la Patrie Française* and the *Ligue Antisémitique de France*, as well as number of Royalist organizations. The new political movements were defined by a much more militant nationalism where a form of national socialism, connected to a virulent anti-Semitism, was the basis of their shared political identity.[65] In this respect, the seeds planted by Boulanger and the mobilization of the *Ligue des Patriotes* in the late 1880s were now super-charged in a more clear-cut far-right direction. Thus, while the French economy had stabilized from the doldrums of the Long Depression – benefitting from new technological and industrial developments in chemicals electronics and coal mining (see Price, 1981: 231) – such beneficial economic conditions did not naturally translate into social harmony or political stability (Rutkoff, 1981: 89). Indeed, economic growth ushered in further social transformation putting increased pressure on small-scale producers and the self-employed, as France became increasingly dominated by largescale capitalist production and the growth of working-class militancy with the intensification of strikes co-ordinated by the recently founded (1895) Confédération Générale

---

64    As John Weiss (1977: 95–9 emphasis added) states, for the many anti-Semites of the French right and especially one of their leading demagogues, Édouard Drumont, '[w]hether Dreyfus was guilty or innocent was not the point. Drumont argued that Jews were traitors *by nature* and that the army was all that stood between France and the Prussians, and must be defended at all costs.'

65    As Philip Nord (1984: 179) suggests, however, while many of those former Boulangists who re-joined the *Ligue* in 1898 saw themselves as socialists, their socialism 'was not collectivist, but national; they sought the salvation of the "worker", not in the abolition of private property, but rather, in the expulsion of foreign workers or the expropriation of a minority of accapareurs or in the extinction of exploiting Jews.'

du Travail (CGT) (see Griffiths, 1978: 732; Kergoat, 1990: 171–5; Lafrance, 2019: 265–6; Polanyi, 2001: 130).

With the campaign for Dreyfus's retrial gathering steam in 1897–8, Déroulède used this opportunity to revive the *Ligue* in the autumn of 1898. In contrast to its earlier incarnation as a source of voter mobilization and electoral propaganda for Boulanger, it was now focused on preventing Dreyfus's retrial and engaging in a violent form of anti-parliamentary street politics to help create a context of crisis as a way of opening up the possibility of a military-supported coup. In Hannah Arendt's (1968: 110–117; see also Fuller, 2012: 72–95; Wilson, 1982: 47–124) account, the anti-Dreyfusard coalition was based on interconnections and alliances of convenience between the leadership of the French military, the higher echelons of the Church and the anti-Semitic shock troops of Guérin's *Ligue Antisémitique*.[66] Arendt suggested that this co-ordination was directed at intimidating both the judiciary in its processing of Dreyfus's retrial after 1897 and at the violent attacks on Dreyfusard rallies. As she opined,

> [u]nder the leadership of Guérin the mob took on a military complexion. Antisemitic shock troops appeared on the streets and made certain that every pro-Dreyfus meeting should end in bloodshed. The complicity of the police was everywhere patent.
>
> ARENDT, 1968: 111

At its high point in early 1898 there were riots and violent demonstrations in over 70 towns, involving 4,000 people in Angers and Marseille, 3,000 in Nantes, 2,000 in Rouen (Birnbaum, 1992: 1) that resulted in financial losses to Jewish property-owners that were targeted, not counting the scores of injuries; though, incredibly, no fatalities were recorded by the authorities in spite of mobs chanting 'death to the Jews'.[67] The *Ligue*, then, like the other sources of anti-Dreyfusard agitation saw the defence of France's military honour and the

---

66    Stephen Wilson (1982: 184) notes the proto-fascist character of the 'shock troops' of the *Ligue Antisémitique*, who were uniformed, trained in martial arts and armed with clubs and iron-bars, primed for violence and intimidation in a way that foreshadowed Mussolini's Blackshirts and the Nazi SA.

67    The violence of the anti-Dreyfusard leagues was, ultimately, unsuccessful even if it did contribute to an electoral breakthrough for far-right candidates in the 1902 parliamentary elections with a fourfold increase in votes for the far-right to over 14 percent of the overall vote share (making up a third of the total right-wing vote) and doubling the number of deputies (Fuller, 2012: 194).

ideal of French national and racial honour as tied up with the fate of Alfred Dreyfus.[68]

The *Ligue*'s revival was to be short-lived. Though it quickly gained membership with sources indicating 60,000 members by early 1899 concentrated in the lower middle class areas of Paris, Déroulède's failed coup attempt at the funeral of the former French President Félix Faure in February 1899 saw the organization outlawed and its leadership arrested (Rutkoff, 1981: 128–36; Tannenbaum, 1962: 35; Vaiciulenas, 1991: 105). Short-lived though its revival and rapid growth were, it reflected the socioeconomic transformation of Paris over the closing years of the nineteenth century, which provided the beneficial social context that it was able to take advantage of, and which persisted in the support for other far-right movements that emerged after the *Ligue*'s demise (such as *Ligue de la Patrie Française* and the *Ligue de le Défense Nationale*). Thus, the *Ligue*'s membership in 1899 was concentrated in the districts of Paris that were undergoing a profound – and for many of their petty bourgeois inhabitants who joined the *Ligue*, a very unsettling and worrying – restructuring in its economy, geography, and demographic make-up. In addition to economic pressures, these areas were transformed in the late 1890s with the immigration of thousands of east European Jews. These new immigrants not only looked and sounded different – with Yiddish as their first language – but many of them ended up competing with existing locals in artisan trades such as tailoring, shoe-making and shop owners. And, as Peter Rutkoff (1981: 115) has noted, there was a clear causal relationship between the concentration of a new Jewish population in the north and east of the city and the *Ligue* as two-thirds of its members were located in these same districts.

Out of the ashes of the *Ligue*, *Action Française* was born. Although never as numerically large as the *Ligue* (Payne, 1995: 47), it was to be the dominant ideo-political force on the French far-right through to 1914, and the standard bearer of a militant authoritarian street politics that called for national social-ism. Propagating its views via a range of print media, *Action Française* – under the ideological direction of Charles Maurras and Maurice Barrès – sought to transform the consciousness of the French public through creating a new

---

68    As Arendt (1968: 117) argued, the anti-Semitism that engulfed the anti-Dreyfusard agita-
      tions against the Republic was also linked – via a number of Catholic journals – to impe-
      rialism and France's geopolitical rivalry with Britain. Given the humiliation of France
      after the stand-off with Britain at Fashoda in 1898 'the Jews were to blame' for England
      taking Egypt from France. Further, as Rutkoff (1981: 163) also notes, '[s]similarly, the same
      Déroulède who had vociferously opposed the new imperialism of Ferry eighteen years
      earlier was by 1899 one of the loudest trumpets supporting French forces at Fashoda.'

state of mind immune from and antagonistic towards what they saw as the un-French and unnatural abstractions of cosmopolitan rationalism and, in doing so, recreating a set of pre-modern social and cultural values across society commanding obedience throughout France in a way that echoed Gramsci's Marxian and revolutionary 'war of position'. At its founding, Henri Vaugeois its general secretary identified 'Jewish, Protestant, and Masonic value-systems' as sources of evil in France which was couched in a 'medieval Catholicism' hostile to 'financial manipulation and unfair profits,' that were racialized as the fault of Jews (Tannenbaum, 1962: 36–7). Like its counterparts in Germany, *Action Française* would continue to play an important role in informing public opinion throughout the early years of the new century and especially so in the immediate period before 1914.

5       Britain: Hegemonic Decline and the Structural Limits on the Rise of the Far-Right

The development of a distinct form of far-right politics in Britain over the final decades of the nineteenth century was quite different to the experiences in Germany and France. In the British case, though there was some popular far-right agitation that drew on racialized ideological tropes, including anti-Semitism and a mobilization of distinct social layers and campaigns for a more aggressive and militarist imperialism, such positions never secured any significant mass appeal and neither did they stir-up or were attached to significant support from dominant social interests or political elites. As we shall see, below, political support for protectionism and a more assertive geopolitics were concentrated in a particular wing of the Conservative Party, and while Britain did succumb to a militarist-inspired jingoism during the Boer War between 1899 and 1902 (Halperin, 2004: 114, 155; Hobsbawm, 1995: 310; Sykes, 2005: 11–33), this did not generate either a significant long-term popular base for the far-right over this period nor a major re-orientation of its political economy.[69]

---

69    The question of British militarism – usually contrasted with that of its Prussian variety – can be seen as a somewhat marginal issue at this time given the lack of compulsory military service and the ambivalence of the major political parties to it. However, as Anne Summers (1976) recognized, the mass and enthusiastic volunteering for the British Expeditionary Force after August 1914 suggested otherwise. Thus, British society was influenced by a popular militarism even if it was not directed by the organs of the state nor consistently connected to a far-right ideo-political imagination as was the case in Germany.

The paradox of this domestic marginalization of a British far-right was that the structural significance and wider place of the political economy and geo-politics of the British Empire at this time – through which Britain continued to secure major economic benefits as the leading imperial power – played an important and, in some cases, *constitutive* role, in fuelling far-right mobili-zations in *other* countries, and in Germany and France in particular. In this respect, then, a celebration of Britain's liberalism, 'moderation' or the consen-sual and progressive dimensions of what others have described as its 'hegem-onic leadership' (see Ferguson, 2003; Ikenberry, 2001; Cox, 1987), or seeing capitalist development in Britain as in some way immune or inoculated from the political virus of far-right politics, is to overlook Britain's significance in the overall structure, dynamics and drives of uneven and combined capitalist development that provided a *structural context* and political fuel to the far-right within the wider international capitalist system.

Understanding capitalism as a globalizing socioeconomic dynamic and, in systemic terms, as a differentiated totality ensures that the explanation for the weakness of the political phenomenon under observation – in this case the strength of the far-right in one country compared to others – is not reduced to the *differentia specifica* of the singular national case *à la* methodological internalism, but rather how such singular qualities require the vantage point that incorporates its inter-connected and inter-societal dimensions as part of a wider whole. Thus, as was outlined in chapter one, the far-right emerges and becomes a *constitutive* ideo-political current in an international context defined by or organized around a capitalist geopolitics. The structure, institu-tional arrangements and material dynamics of accumulation and crisis which characterised the international political economy over the late nineteenth cen-tury; but also the centrality of British power and British decisions and activities in determining its character and direction that were – in various ways – con-nected to Britain's domestic political economy and social order which were also causal of the domestic political contexts out of which far-rights in France, Germany and elsewhere emerged and grew. This is not to point the finger of blame at Britain as being, in some ways, responsible for the global far-right, but rather to qualify the domestic liberal characteristics of Britain's political econ-omy and politics as *causal* of the relative weakness of the far-right in Britain at this time and, instead, to emphasize both the international framing or causal-ity of the far-right and the uneven and combined character of capitalist devel-opment (see Green, 2012: 351–2).[70]

---

70    As encapsulated in the idea of 'free trade imperialism' (see Gallagher and Robinson, 1953), indicating the combined character of British capitalism – liberal in its growing economic

In many respects, the development of a far-right politics within Britain was stymied or limited through the *benefits and advantages* that Britain secured as the first industrializer. Consequently, some of the core and defining social and political transformations and cleavages that marked out the processes of capitalist development in subsequent industrializers did not trouble it because Britain's capitalist and industrial development occurred within a very different international political economic and spatial context; a context or structure that was to be fundamentally transformed through and because of Britain's capitalist development (see Hobsbawm, 1968, 1995; Kemp, 1985). As Jeremy Green (2012: 353) argues,

> [b]uilding upon the prior agrarian transformation, British industrial development occurred in a distinctly endogenous manner, without the intense pressures of world market competition experienced by late-industrializing societies. During the 18th century Britain utilized naval supremacy to capture and monopolize the export markets of other countries, destroying foreign competition in the process through war and colonization. Through this process it came to constitute and dominate a world market for goods. The achievement of world market dominance, at a very early stage of industrial development, was to cocoon Britain from serious competitive pressure until the last quarter of the 19th century.

These afflictions that conditioned the character of the subsequent capitalist development of the major powers through the nineteenth century (with the partial exception of the United States due to its relative geographical isolation and security) amounted to the intensity and speed of socioeconomic transformation in a context of precarious state formation, imperialist rivalry and geopolitical tensions; they owed much to the dynamics of the world economy that Britain and its growing empire did so much to contribute to.

Returning to the advantages of advancement or being first – to paraphrase Trotsky's famous phrase the 'privileges of backwardness' – by the mid-nineteenth century the peasantry had all but disappeared as a distinct and significant socioeconomic layer in Britain (Moore, Jr., 1967: 25–9; Gillis,

---

links with non-colonial economies whilst, at the same time, remaining an expanding (in a geopolitical sense) imperial power, as well as the structural significance of India to Britain's overall international economic and hegemonic position. This was an issue – as we will see in the following chapter – generative of Nazism as it was Germany's *Weltpolitik* at this time.

1983: 37; Floud and McClosky, 1994: 99)[71] *before* industrialization had made significant progress in the German lands of central Europe. This restructuring of Britain's class structure and class relations had an important bearing on the development of both Britain's political economy and class politics thereafter. For one, it made the social basis of politics more stable through reducing, if not eliminating, the opportunities for the establishment of a reactionary political coalition between landlords and peasants in opposition to the 'forces of progress' associated with a liberal urban bourgeoisie and working class. And, as scholars such as Gregory Luebbert (1991; see also Moore, Jr., 1967) argued, it helped facilitate the integration of the urban working class into a liberal democratic political order through alliances with parts of the bourgeoisie. The end of the peasantry resulted, then, in the absence of a social constituency that could play a reactionary role in the democratizing process by pushing it in an illiberal and authoritarian direction, as Marx recognized with respect to the mass basis of Bonapartism and, in Germany, providing an important mass basis for far-right mobilizations. Consequently, one of the major social pillars and political strands of the nineteenth century far-right – in contrast to the situation in Germany – did not exist in Britain.

Simply put, there was little or no social base for a movement such as the *Bund der Landwirte* to emerge because British agriculture did not have significant numbers of small-scale peasant producers and neither did it have a significant caste of landlords, geographically concentrated and with positions in the state administration affected by the deleterious consequences of international commodity trade.[72] This was significant, particularly in the context of the Long

---

71    Agricultural employment fell to 22 percent of the total labour force by 1851 which paralleled rapid urbanization with over half of the population living in towns of more than 2,500 inhabitants by the early 1850s (Rapport, 2005: 83–4). By 1891, 72 percent of the population were urbanized (Gillis, 1983: 173). Such figures, however, understate the profound socioeconomic differences in Britain (and England in particular) relating to land ownership. Thus, even by the end of the eighteenth century and at the start of the industrial revolution, agricultural production was concentrated in large-scale farming with large landlords owning 75 percent of cultivated land with approximately 20 percent owned by freeholders (or tenant-farmers) which meant that the peasantry in the usual sense of the word no longer existed (Hobsbawm, 1968: 78).

72    The transformation of British agriculture and the character of capitalist industrialist development had an impact on dominant agrarian class interests, as much as it did on peasants with the consolidation of a capitalist landlord class much more aligned with the rigours of bourgeois modernity than their Prussian counterparts. The earlier consolidation and security of British state formation (and victory/non-occupation in the struggle against Napoleon) also mitigated against the maintenance of a militarist culture across the aristocracy.

Depression after 1873. Thus, in contrast to both France and Germany – where the economic well-being and social reproduction of landlords and small-scale peasant producers were threatened by the influx of cheaper foodstuffs from Russia and the Western Hemisphere which helped to trigger a nationalist/protectionist response – Britain had, in effect, dealt with the problem or reconciled its agricultural sector to such developments decades earlier.

Although this 'reactionary nexus' rooted in the soil of agriculture and an idealized peasant past was not the sole or, necessarily, the most significant social axis of the late nineteenth century far-right, its absence from Britain was an important impediment for the development of a far-right because mass or democratic politics was not determined by the presence and role of this social nexus and ideology. Indeed, what defined the land or agrarian question in Britain was largely decided in 1846 with the repeal of the Corn Laws. While the repeal of the Corn Laws did not, overnight, shift Britain to a consistent or universal position of free trade – this was not possible in a context of an imperial political economy based on the Empire and the significance of India to Britain's economic fortunes in particular – it did amount to a fundamental structural difference vis-a-vis the other capitalist economies that were emerging.

The significance of this for the emergence of a far-right was twofold. First, *contra* Arno Mayer (1981) and Sandra Halperin (2004), the landed interest had lost its political veto in determining the direction of economic development within Britain as a growing number of landlords had embraced capitalist farming and/or moved into other forms of commercial activity including industry. The significance of this was that it meant that a dominant section of the landlord class moved away from lobbying for protectionism and the geopolitical tensions that accompanied such nationalist economic strategies – a key component of a far-right form of political economy. Secondly, the significance of the repeal of the Corn Laws – over the medium and longer term – served to consolidate the popular hold of the ideology of free-trade over the popular classes and many of their key social (in the form of trade unions) and political representatives. A key plank of liberal political economy – in the form of cheap food and the daily loaf in particular – was, then, embedded in the popular consciousness (Barratt-Brown, 1974: 163; Gourevitch, 1988: 205–6; Green, 2012: 352–5; Semmel, 1960: 97). This  helped to secure a structural and hegemonic hold for free trade (Brown, 1966: 36; Cain and Hopkins, 1993: 218) that was absent in nearly all other major capitalist economies of the time.

National class formation associated with capitalist development in Britain not only removed two key social constituencies of the European far-right, but also had a significant impact on the other core social layer of the far-right, the petty bourgeoisie. As Geoffrey Crossick (1984: 257) notes, significant sections of the petty bourgeoisie such as shop keepers and small traders also bought into the ideology of free trade in a way that contrasted with most of their European neighbours and thus formed an important element within the liberal hegemonic/historical bloc. The liberal character of British capitalism and the benefits that flowed from the Empire also conditioned the social development and ideo-political orientation of workers and the organized labour movement. In contrast to both Germany and France, the British working class developed in a distinctively non-revolutionary fashion encapsulated in the term 'labourism' (Stedman-Jones, 1988: 73–4). As John Saville (1988: 14; see also Daunton, 2000; Matthew, 1999: 536–44; MacRaild and Martin, 2000: 144–65; Price, 1990) noted,

> by the 1870s an ideology was developing that was common to most working men who were activist in some way or another [that] encompassed social and political attitudes whose horizons were firmly set within the boundaries of existing society ... Labourism was a theory and practice which recognized the possibilities of social change within existing society, and which had no vision beyond existing society ... [it] was the theory and practice of class collaboration.

This was not reflected in any significant lessening of the paranoia and hatred of major sections of the ruling class and political establishment – something which they shared with their European counterparts – regarding the possible social and political consequences of the full enfranchisement of the working class, however. Thus, while French workers were mobilizing to overthrow governments in 1848, the most significant British working class movement, Chartism, framed its class politics around a bourgeois recognition of the political right to vote. And, after the high point of Chartism in the 1840s, the political development of the British working class was fundamentally framed – despite Marx's best efforts – towards working within the confines and limits of bourgeois democracy. Although this was not, in itself, a reason for ruling class paranoia to be diluted, it did mean that the structural dynamics of British political development were very different to those in France and especially Germany.

In contrast, then, to Germany, the organizations of the British working class could be accommodated into the existing political framework and political economy. In the former, this was because the liberal bourgeoisie and the two dominant political parties of the late nineteenth century – the Liberals and Conservatives – actually *embraced* and courted working class support. Indeed, the 1867 Reform Act (or The Representation of the People Act) which enfranchised a significant number of working men appeared to reflect such an accommodation; the representatives of the working class – two decades after the high-point of Chartism – had shown themselves to be 'responsible' political citizens well-socialized as to the parameters of the scope of British parliamentary democracy and the political elites were now willing to permit (some) workers to vote and with little to fear. The two fractions of the capitalist ruling class did not confront an independent working-class political movement. Instead, by the final decades of the nineteenth century, the organized labour movement allied itself with the Liberal Party and it was not until the turn of the century that an independent workers party – the Labour Party – was to be established. Inter-class dynamics, in part a consequence of the specificities of British economic development, state and class formation, reflected a weakened impetus of class conflict playing out in the political sphere, which reflected a combination of working class political strategy and tactical compromises by political elites. The contrast with developments in Germany was stark. The significance for our concerns here though is that dominant social interest and political elites did not confront an independent, militant, and revolutionary – in an ideological sense – political movement that could count on the support of millions of voters, and which also dominated the culture and social consciousness of workers.

These domestic dimensions of Britain's political economy that were antithetical to the development of a mass-based far-right agitation in the late nineteenth century and leading up to 1914 were also reinforced through the way in which Britain's political economy and leading capitalist class fractions were integrated into the international capitalist economy at this time.[73] Indeed, as already alluded to, this domestic-international connection was mutually reinforcing and constitutive. Accordingly, the structure of the international capitalist order – in which Britain was at the centre – facilitated a domestic socioeconomic order built on a much greater level of consensus than anywhere else in Europe at the time. This also derived from a structural tendency within the existing international capitalist order and Britain's unique position within it. Unlike any other major capitalist power, the income streams of the

---

[73]   In the decade or so leading up to 1914, this internationalizing or globalizing trend within British capitalism and the reproduction of its leading class fractions continued. In 1913, one-third of Britain's net wealth was invested overseas as a result of annual flows of foreign investment, and one third of everything owned by Britons was located overseas (Floud 1997: 164; Halperin, 2004: 108). And in the immediate period before 1914, British finance centred on the City of London accounted for 44 percent of total overseas investments (Post, 1999: 108).

dominant fractions of the British capitalist class derived from *global* circuits of exchange and foreign investments.[74] Ironically, given the increase in the territory brought under the control of the British Empire between 1874 and 1914, these income streams were increasingly associated with exchange relationships separate from Britain's imperial commerce.[75] This not only meant that major sections of the ruling class and state managers were committed to Britain's continuing role as the centre of a liberal global economy, alongside the premier status of the City of London as the world's financial clearing house based on Sterling, but that there was also much less appetite amongst dominant social interests for militarism (Gourevitch, 1988: 205). This not only highlights the uneven character of capitalist development, but also its contrasting political consequences at the domestic and international levels. However, while capitalist development did not produce the socioeconomic dislocations that it did elsewhere, because of its uneven and globalizing logic it did produce tensions at the international level, which triggered a split within the British ruling class and state elite over tariff reform and protectionism.

The relative weakness or absence of a significant far-right within Britain in the final decades of the nineteenth century did not mean that British politics was immune to the generic trend of far-right development evident elsewhere. Nor that those impulses and tendencies were separate from international developments associated with the uneven and combined character of capitalist development. And, in this respect, the relative decline of Britain's industrial and technological dominance over the last two decades of the nineteenth century (see Post, 1999: 108) came to play an important role in not only promoting a split across the capitalist class, but also in influencing the discourse and character of domestic politics as nationalist calls for tariff-reform and protectionism arguably became the dominant political issue in the early years of the twentieth century. Concern at growing industrial competition and relative technological decline had become much more pronounced across Britain's industrial heartlands in the Midlands and Lancashire by the 1890s and became

---

74    In the words of Eric Hobsbawm (1987: 39), '[o]f all the major industrialized countries only Britain held fast to unrestricted free trade, in spite of powerful occasional challenges from protectionists. The reasons were obvious, quite apart from the absence of a large peasantry and therefore of a large built-in protectionist vote. Britain was by far the biggest exporter of industrial products, and had in the course of the century become increasingly export-oriented – probably never more so than in the 1870s and 1880s – much more so than her main rivals.'

75    By the end of the nineteenth century around 75 percent of British trade was with non-imperial countries (Brown, 1966: 126); see Hobsbawm (1987: 66) on the concentration of British capital exports to the dominions and non-colonial areas.

closely associated with geopolitical sentiments after a number of its key competitors had introduced protectionist measures.[76] A widely-shared perception
emerged within parts of the British capitalist class that not only was Britain's
industrial strength and advantage being eroded but that the protectionism of
other powers was accelerating it – through shutting out Britain's exports – and
encroaching on Britain's home markets given that Britain remained an open
economy. It was in this context – one defined by a sense of imperial or hegemonic decline – that both protectionist and nationalistic sentiments gained
political ground and thus opened up a channel for the growth of a far-right
politics.

In this respect, the key development, as elsewhere, was the Long Depression
with the emergence of a campaign for tariff reform and imperial protection
in the early 1880s in response to the rising production and trade threats from
Germany and the USA[77] to Britain's pre-eminent global economic and geopolitical position. This also reflected tendencies of UCD. Thus, as Cain and
Hopkins (1993: 210) in their history of British capitalism note,

> Chamberlain and the Tariff Reformers also stressed the link between
> free trade, low domestic investment, and a high rate of capital export.
> But they did so with a greater sense of urgency and with wider indus-
> trial support since, by 1900, the erosion of Britain's industrial superiority
> had gone further and the demand for protection, as well as for retaliatory
> tariffs, had become distinctly stronger. The Tariff Reformers raised the
> spectre of a de-industrialised Britain where crucial industries like steel ...
> were lost; they pointed to the time when Britain could no longer main-
> tain her position in the world and would be faced with a breakdown in
> social order as industry disintegrated.

---

76    By the mid-1890s the world industrial economy with the exception of Britain was man-
      aged via a range of competing levels of protectionism: German protectionism had begun
      in 1879 and deepened in 1885; France had moved towards protectionism in the 1880s cul-
      minating in the 1892 Méline tariff as had the US with the draconian McKinley tariff of
      1890 followed by Dingley tariff of 1897. The second tier of industrial powers in Europe –
      countries such as Italy, Austro-Hungary and Russia had also moved to protection by the
      early 1890s.

77    Britain's relative decline was evident in its declining share of world trade which fell by
      over a third from 1880 – 23 percent in 1880 to 14 percent in 1912. This was also reflected in
      its share of world industrial production – falling from 23.2 percent in 1880 to 13.6 percent
      by 1913; at this time Germany's rose to 15 percent and US production surged to 32 percent
      (Lowe, 1994: 6; see also Anievas, 2014: 64).

Thus, in the early 1880s British politics saw the short-lived emergence of an indigenous right-wing populism led by the Conservative-Unionist – and scion of the English bourgeoisie – Joseph Chamberlain. Chamberlain's populism identified the enemy of British workers as foreign workers, not British employers. Chamberlain – echoing the propagandists of European far-right movements – regarded economic development as a struggle between nations waged in the geopolitical domain, as much as in the commercial, such that the British worker had a common interest with the British employer in confronting a common enemy both at home – via immigration – and abroad in the foreign worker. Chamberlain presented tariffs and welfare legislation as two sides of the same collectivist approach as industrial legislation protecting working conditions,

> raised the costs of production ... If these foreign goods come in cheaper ... either you will take lower wages or you will lose your work. ... You cannot have free trade in goods and at the same time have protection of labour.
>
> cited in SYKES, 2005: 17; see also SEMMEL, 1960: 74–88, 89–117

This was a politics that echoed what was playing out in France and Germany at this time: a top-down attempt through the existing political framework and forms of representation (the imperialist-wing of the Liberal Party) to construct a nationalist-protectionist politics that bound the organized working class to big industrial capital and where domestic politics was couched in a language and sentiment based on the insertion of nationalist tropes connected to geopolitical rivalry that was specifically targeted at attacking Germany and German workers.[78]

To address this, Chamberlain called for imperial unity to ensure that Britain's dominions were not sucked into closer economic relationships with Britain's main challengers – Germany and the United States – which were seen as a threat to Britain's security as much as its economic well-being (Brown, 1966: 89; Cain, 1979: 36–42). And, in this respect, Germany's shift towards a geopolitics of *Weltpolitik* (connected to the construction of a significant fleet) poured fuel onto the flames that had been ignited by concerns of iron and steel producers in the Midlands. Indeed, this period – and the opening to a more

---

78    As Bernard Semmel (1968: 89–117) outlined in his comprehensive survey of English social-imperialist politics between the 1890s and 1914, the leading advocate of social imperialist protectionism, the Tariff Reform League, concentrated on and invested huge financial resources and political capital in trying to persuade British workers – hitherto over-whelmingly supportive of free-trade – to support protectionism.

nationalist strain of politics within Britain – reflected a confluence of three distinct but inter-related developments. First was the concern of industrial decline that was particularly felt by iron and steel producers centred in the Midlands based on the rise of Germany's industrial power (Semmel, 1968: 80–81; Lowe, 1994: 77). Second was the emergence of the so-called 'Anglo-German naval race' after the passing of the first Navy Law in Germany in 1898 committing the *Kaiserreich* to a policy of major naval expansion as a key part of its *Weltpolitik* strategy, which became a major source of geopolitical concern by the early 1900s. The third and final element concerned the debate on Irish Home Rule that emerged in the mid-1880s and continued on – to the point of almost triggering civil war in Ireland over 1912–14.[79] The significance of this issue was both political – opponents of Irish Home Rule on the British right opposed what they saw as the threat to Britain's national integrity – but also economic, in that some of the main opponents of Home Rule were industrialists who rallied behind Joseph Chamberlain and others who were worried about the possibility of losing more home market access (Semmel, 1968: 75–7).

Chamberlain called for an import tax on industrial goods produced from outside the Empire ensuring the likelihood that British manufactures would have a near monopoly across the Empire with the agricultural products of the Empire having a near monopoly on exports to Britain since there would be a tax on non-imperial agricultural imports. However, the expected result – and hence its lack of political appeal and widespread support – was that only a small proportion of the population dependent on the land would benefit, in contrast to other major capitalist economies, and it would not secure working-class support as the imported inflation would result in a more expensive loaf (Stone, 1985: 104–5).

---

79    Indeed, the most militant and potentially violent aspect of the right became fixated on the issue of home rule with Conservative-Unionist forces indulging Ulster Protestant 'loyalists' who were deeply opposed to it, and who, under Sir Edward Carson's leadership, established the Ulster Volunteer Force militia in 1912 to oppose the imposition of home rule by Westminster 'by all means necessary.' While such conflict did not come to pass – the outbreak of war in August 1914 just after the passing of the Home Rule Act meant that its implementation was temporarily suspended, the significance and implications of this issue were clearly evident with the so-called 'Curragh mutiny' of British Army officers in Ireland in March 1914. This incident saw several officers based in Ireland refuse to accept the possibility of using force against the Ulster Volunteers should the Irish Home Rule Act be implemented. The significance of the Curragh Mutiny was that a number of senior officers in London, including General Henry Wilson, had conveyed their support to the mutineers, thereby highlighting the deep fissures within parts of the British state on the matter of home rule and an endorsing of a position that not only undermined the rule of law and the will of parliament but gave succour to an armed militia.

For Chamberlain and the Tariff Reform League, 'true imperialism' was a policy about racial survival as much as territorial control, echoing the pervasive influence of 'scientific racism' across elite opinion and public discourse. Through focusing on empire over free trade, British economic policy would serve – argued Chamberlain and his supporters – the interests of both its capitalists and workers through protecting jobs and profits from foreign competition. This was, then, an attempt to craft a politics of national labour that mimicked developments that had been taking place in France from the late 1880s. Protectionism would secure the nation and having secured men, markets, raw materials, manufactured goods and food, Britain and her empire could remove itself from the world economy. As Chamberlain stated,

> [w]e shall be isolated ... but our isolation will be a splendid one ... [international relations is] a race for existence that has been going on ever since the world began ... [and] I want to prepare you, now ... while there is still time, for a struggle ... from which, if we emerge defeated, this country will lose its place, will no longer count among the great nations of the world.
>
> cited in SYKES, 1979: 17–18

Chamberlain's position revealed a major split within the British ruling class, which percolated down into parts of wider society and demonstrated the way in which uneven capitalist development could trigger populist right-wing responses even in state-society complexes that appeared to be much less vulnerable to the emergence and rise of such ideo-political currents. Chamberlain tapped into a growing concern of the vestiges of the traditional – landed – ruling class who saw that their real enemy was the 'plutocrat', a bogey figure of enormous wealth linked to cosmopolitan financial interests, identified as Jewish, or German, 'who had no stake in, or loyalty to, the country'; another echo of the far-right imaginary prevalent across the Channel at this time. And the apparent connection of some  members of the Liberal government, 'especially Lloyd George, with wealthy foreigners... made this a useful stick with which to beat the government' (Sykes, 1979: 289; see also Semmel, 1968: 81–2).

But this was short-lived – the British state responded to the concerns about its export competitiveness through moving towards a more aggressive policy of imperial expansion,[80] which was an important ingredient in increasing geopolitical tensions leading up to 1914. Indeed, Chamberlain returned in 1903

---

80    Between 1870 and 1914 the area of the empire increased in area by nearly two and a half
      times, but in economic terms this was expansion at the margin since the old territories
      remained dominant in imperial trade and finance (Alford, 1996: 7).

with the formation of the Tariff-Reform League (see Thompson, 1997: 1035–7) in a context of the Boer War, where Britain's military prowess and quality of its 'racial stock' – after the difficulty of recruiting healthy soldiers from its cities – had been seen to be found wanting, as well as the growing geopolitical threat from Germany through its decision to pursue a *Weltpolitik* after 1897.

Consequently, while the earlier attempt at tariff reform in the 1880s was largely devoid of the kind of popular and militant movements that had accompanied demands for protectionism on the continent, in this later case the campaign for tariff reform took place in a milieu where other movements of a far-right persuasion – the Navy League (1894), National Service League (1901), and the Imperial Maritime League (1908) – had appeared and where the discussion of imperial protectionism took on an increasingly racialized tone. To these movements we can add the more plebeian and proto-fascist British Brothers League, which agitated against Jewish immigration in the east-end of London and contributed to a wider xenophobia that lead to the 1905 Aliens Act to curb immigration (Sykes, 2005: 32). Again, this reflected the distinct geographical character within which UCD played out in enabling the politics of the far-right.

The campaign for tariff-reform failed, split the right and helped ensure a period of Liberal electoral ascendancy. However, it did contribute to a more xenophobic politics up to 1914 as concerns about economic competition, the rising left and Germany's geopolitical challenge poisoned political discussion.[81] While Britain did not, then, see the development of a coherent far-right mass movement in the final decades of the nineteenth century, the growing challenge to its imperialist ascendancy, geopolitical advantages and world economic leadership did contribute to a shifting orientation towards a domestic politics increasingly inflected by racialized and nationalist tropes, and where militarism took on a distinctly populist dimension after the Boer War[82] as evidenced in its influence on the outcome of the so-called 'khaki election' of 1900 (see Townshend, 1988: 16–17).

---

81    As Marilyn Shevin Coetzee (Coetzee, 1990: 51) argued, the cultural significance of war and militarism were all pervasive even in 'liberal England; as evidenced in propaganda of nationalist and imperialist leagues and in popular fiction such as the 'British invasion-scare novels,' and especially Erskine Childers' *Riddle of the Sands* (1902), and William le Quex's *The Invasion of 1910*.

82    The scene had been set for the Khaki election – held in the Autumn of 1900 that saw the re-election of Salisbury's Conservative government – with mob rioting and street celebrations after the news of the lifting of the Boer siege of Mafeking in South Africa in May (see Semmel, 1968: 44).

## 6    Conclusions

As the above survey has demonstrated, a distinct form of modern far-right politics came of age in the final decades of the nineteenth century. Uneven in its levels of mass mobilization and political impact (in the sense of determining the direction of state policy) its entry into the cauldron of a mass-democratic politics was one of the defining developments of the age. Each case examined above reflects the distinct political and economic structures of each country and, specifically, their geopolitical location within the broader dynamics of uneven and combined development. Consequently, the development of the far-right – its social bases, distinct ideo-politcal complexion, relationship to dominant social class and political elites and the specific forms of nationalism and geopolitical assertiveness associated with each case – reflected specific forms of combined development.

The defining structures that framed and promoted the far-right were located in the historical specificity of the embeddedness of geopolitical circuits and ideological assumptions in capitalist development. So, while capitalism always has distinct geopolitical characteristics, this period was defined specifically by an international politics of high imperialism that united domestic politics and class politics with geopolitical circuits of capitalist accumulation and geopolitical strategies to preserve and expand capitalist production and manage the social dislocation and conflicts produced by it. In this respect, this period was unique in that the politics of the far-right was both promoted by and drove the major capitalist powers towards geopolitical confrontation and war in 1914.

This period also reflected two other major structural socio-political continuities in the evolution of the European far-right. First, in the ambivalence of liberal elites and political forces in managing the rise of the far-right. The rise of the far-right at this time was intimately connected to the challenges of both existing (conservative) elites and liberals in maintaining social order in the midst of the rise of an organized working class. The degree of the challenge – or the perception thereof – posed to economic liberalism and the rights of private property played a defining role in the political strategy of liberal and conservative elites in a context of mass democratization and the willingness to embrace the lesser evil of the far-right. The significance of far-right, then, was not purely demonstrated in terms of what these movements and parties achieved in themselves, but also in terms of their role in wider political developments associated with challenges to the foundations of liberal order and the character of mass politics and democratization.

Consequently, the decisions of political elites at this time and, in particular, their willingness to integrate the organized working classes into the workings of the bourgeois state was to become a key factor in the subsequent development of fascism and its political success. And although this was an issue that played out in the specifics of domestic politics and the particularities of each country's organization of representative politics and the scope and workings of democratic processes, it also played out against a back-drop conditioned by international and geopolitical structures and impulses that advantaged and disadvantaged – in equal measure – the scope for accommodation and repression.

The second structural continuity concerns the politics of race within the reproduction of capitalist political economy at this time. While racism and anti-black racism in particular was constitutive of the form of liberal political economy – in the sense that the workings of an ostensible rules-based liberal international economic order were embedded within and, to some extent, conditional on colonized exploitation and the racialized structures associated with it – racism, as a determining and active political current within European metropoles, was primarily articulated via anti-Semitism. The far-right reflected the most pronounced and over-determined and entrenched form of racism that was much more widely and commonly articulated, including across segments of the political left. Structural or organic racism provided a political advantage for the far-right and a legitimizing and acceptable entry-point for its politics in a way that was distinct from the form of liberal politics after 1945 (even if its racism had mutated, not disappeared).

Anti-Semitism, then, provided a plausible and comprehensive ideological framing of the complex instabilities and transformations that swept across these societies at the time. Anti-Semitism could be seen as an ideological structure defining of this era, as much as the demand for the vote for the working man. Indeed, it provided a powerful ideological device for the management of both domestic class conflict and imperialist nationalism and geopolitical assertiveness (see Arendt, 1968: 54–120). These themes play out in the following chapter which concentrates on the fascist expression of a far-right politics during the inter-war period. It was in fascism that the racialized, authoritarian, anti-democratic and terroristic tendencies contained within a far-right politics alongside the generative mechanisms and impulses promoting such an ideo-political current within capitalist UCD were to reach their fullest expression.

# Fascism: 'Revolution' of the Right

The focus of this chapter is fascism – as ideology, politics and state form. Fascism can be seen as a particularly violent and 'revolutionary' manifestation of a far-right politics. Through its use of distinct and modern communications rituals and technologies, its appeal and idealization of a form of mass politics based on 'corporatist notions of social place' (Eley, 1983: 76), its animosity towards existing forms of political representation and practice and its embrace of the revolutionary potential of the crisis generated within capitalist social development that is connected to an uncompromising and racialized nationalism; fascism is the historical expression of the 'revolution of the right' (Griffin, 2000b: 187; Neocleous, 1997: IX–XII). Notwithstanding the levels of violence and revolutionary disruption to the international/geopolitical order associated with fascist movements and states, the discussion here understands fascism as a 'revolutionary' form of far-right rather than a genus of politics that is situated beyond the traditional left-right political axis, or a 'third way' (see Mosse, 1999; Sternhell, 1996). Further, in spite of its superficial similarities with Stalinism or revolutionary communism, fascism is not, as suggested by Cold War liberals and conservatives (see Arendt, 1968; Friedrich and Brzezinski, 1965; Hayek, 2001) a species of 'totalitarianism'; the half-sister of communism.

Fascism, like its broader far-right kindred, is a radical species of politics that is conjuncturally specific; based on its emergence and growth in those moments of the most intense and over-determined/inter-connected/multi-layered forms of crisis in the reproduction of bourgeois social and political hegemony. Thus, while it is an inherent possibility during those periodic moments of crisis in the normalized reproduction of the social regime of capital, its appearance has been temporally and spatially limited. Further, its connection to, or derivation from a crisis rooted in class-based politics – which is also associated with the defeat or inability of the radical left to engineer an overcoming of capitalist social property relations – means that a fascist politics remains embedded within a bourgeois social universe reflecting the organic connections between fascism and capital.

From this we can see the far-right as the permanent and fixed continuum within bourgeois politics that becomes more central and significant in determining the contours and substance of liberal orders in moments of crisis in the maintenance of capitalist social hegemony. Fascism becomes the *dominant* form of far-right in those more singular or unique moments of rupture where the social and geopolitical parameters associated with the maintenance of the capitalist state fundamentally break down – at the same time – at the domestic *and* international levels and, consequently, where the politics of the far-right is imbued with a specifically revolutionary dimension. Fascism's revolutionary character is then defined by the socio-political context within which it develops and grows out of and, crucially, by the absence or prior defeat of an *actual* revolutionary subject. So, while fascism is committed to a radical reconfiguration of state-society relations and the creation of a 'new man' (Eatwell, 2003; Griffin, 1993, 2000b: 198) – which, to some extent, it realizes – the 'fascist revolution' is also limited, through the enabling role of dominant social forces and existing political elites in its development and capture of state power, and in terms of the socioeconomic transformation it delivers.

The focus of the analysis developed in this chapter reflects the thrust of the preceding discussion throughout this volume: understanding and explaining how fascism, as a form of far-right politics, is framed or produced from within specific international and geopolitical determinants. My concern is to give explanatory emphasis to the international dimensions of the fascist far-right through situating its origins, development and 'triumph' in securing state power through the lens of a post-1918 international political order embedded within the dislocations and crises produced from an uneven and combined development associated with the geopolitics of the Versailles settlement.[1] In framing the origins of fascism in this way I give analytical and methodological primacy to how the enduring, destabilizing and crisis-ridden character of capitalism and its connection to and embeddedness within international institutional and geopolitical structures produced the social and political terrain that enabled a fascist politics to triumph. Thus, the historical expressions of fascism that emerged after 1918 are, in my view, inseparable from both the experience of industrialized total war, as exemplified by the carnage of World War One and its geopolitical settlement, and the attempts to construct a new geopolitical architecture for renewed capital accumulation.

Capitalism or, more precisely, capitalist crisis, provides the paternity of fascism, but what ultimately produced fascism was its co-determination through the way in which capitalist crisis was embedded within a set of international

---

1   Given that the broader focus of this volume is on the far-right it is important to note that the period under consideration here witnessed a generalized rise of the far-right across much of Europe (and elsewhere – see Finchelstein, 2017) where, in several states beyond the two most important cases of Italy and Germany – that I focus on in this chapter – other far-right forces came to power: in Spain, Greece, Hungary, Yugoslavia, Romania and Poland (see Mazower, 1999: 27–31), as well as Japan.

and geopolitical structures, processes and decisions that *actively* assisted and enabled fascist resolutions of the crisis. Consequently, the domestic causes of the fascist revolution – in the combined breakdown of the existing forms of capitalist accumulation and the workings of the liberal democratic political system and its forms of political representation (see Eley, 2015; Mazower, 1999) – are inseparable from the precise inter-connection and inter-active relationship between the domestic and the international which ultimately determined the ways in which each domestic fascist generating crisis could be resolved. Accordingly, both the causes of the domestic crisis and the opportunities for fascist political agency that it produced, as well the limits on the agency of existing political elites and dominant social forces, were intimately connected to the distinct geopolitical location of Italy and Germany within a capitalist-imperialist international order.

An emphasis on the centrality of the international and spatial drivers of fascism provides an important qualification to the suggestion – associated with the work of Timothy Mason in particular – of fascism revealing the 'primacy of politics' (Mason, 1968, 1995) and, as such, a unique form of 'relative autonomy' in the institutional structure and workings of the capitalist state. Thus, following Mason, if fascism is a genus of the capitalist state it is one whereby the typical arrangement and institutionalization of politics and economics associated with bourgeois order is radically reconstituted, in a manner and form that shares something in common with that of Bonapartism (see chapters one and two). And while the fascist political penetration of the economy was evident in Italy and Germany in the early years of each regime, it was the acceleration and intensification in the preparation and then prosecution of total war that shifted the arrangement between politics and economics in a fundamentally unique fashion. However, this re-alignment – that is suggestive of the 'primacy of politics' or the subordination of the class privileges and interests of capital and the wider structure of the capitalist state – took place and was mediated by the wider structure of international political economy and the openings and closures that this offered Nazi Germany in particular. What this suggests is that fascism is a unique form of internationally politically over-determined capitalism (see Anievas, 2014: 183) and a temporally contingent outcome of uneven and combined development. It is an attempt to re-order the general structure and dynamic of capitalist development through resolving its organic sources of crisis, spatially, through the conquest and re-ordering of geopolitical space – reflecting a distinct and racialized form of 'spatio-temporal fix' – and, socially, through the political destruction of organized or politicized labour. And it is race, or a hyper-racialized nationalism that provides the ideological means to realize these twin objectives.

In recognizing the distinct qualities of the fascist form of capitalist state we also need to acknowledge that not only was fascism a product of a *generalized* crisis of capitalist development affecting *all* of the major capitalist states, but that its specific geopolitically-directed resolution was reflective of a broader trend in the reconstitution of politics and economics that also occurred within and across liberal powers such as Britain and the United States. Thus, the dynamic that Mason concentrates on in the case of Nazi Germany also played out elsewhere with respect to the increasing statist and politicization of capitalist social relations (see Anievas, 2014: 162–4, 168–74) even if the Nazi case is recognized as the most radical. Yet, this radicalization was in its racialized geopolitics and not, as Mason (1995: 54) suggests, in its opposition towards the interests of capital. And the fact that it was the mobilization for war that ultimately terminated the cycle of stagnation in production and growth triggered by the 1929 Wall Street Crash is suggestive of a more generalized, if differentiated, pattern of capitalist militarization as decisive in overcoming the crisis of accumulation. The point here is that while there is much to accept in conceptualizing the fascist state as reflecting a 'primacy of politics' – that in practice served to reduce the scope and autonomy of capitalist agents to organize and determine production and the ultimate shape and structure of the economy – this primacy within Germany and Italy was itself conditioned and constrained by the international (geo)economic structure of the capitalist world economy.

Fascism reflects a particular outcome of uneven and combined development whereby a reactionary idealization of a past is grafted onto a future-oriented politics that seeks to overcome, ideologically and aesthetically, the material, socioeconomic and political crises of the moment. This ideological utilization through the reassurance and security of a concretized past (Bloch, 2009; Bloch and Ritter, 1977) is articulated through modern forms of communication, propaganda, and social mobilization. Fascist ideology and politics draw on and are connected to both a modern technological means that actually only manifests itself – as a particularly militant, violent and revolutionary form of far-right politics – within a context defined by the advances of a highly organized and vertically-integrated capitalist structure of production and the politics of mass democracy where the organized working class poses a fundamental threat to the dominant class interests who are the principal beneficiaries of such an arrangement. Fascism, then, is produced from the technological advances and competitive drives of capitalist accumulation within a geopolitically fractured context. Indeed, as I will suggest in the discussion that follows below, it is the international context and the decisions (and non-decisions) taken at the international level by other – primarily liberal – capitalist powers that provides the political context through which the fascist movements in Italy and Germany come to power.

The rest of the chapter is organized as follows. First, I outline a general argument as to the international political economy of crisis within which fascism developed after the end of World War I before moving on to an explanation of the individual case studies of fascism's path to power in Italy and Germany. I then assess the political economy and state forms of fascism. Here, I end up focusing more on the Nazi experience and, specifically, the *differentia specifica* of Nazism's *sui generis* capitalist war economy and follow this with a discussion of the nature of Nazism's form of imperialism which I describe as a 'bifurcated system' and where I also offer some discussion of the Holocaust. The chapter ends with an examination of the relationship between liberal order – as an institutional structure – and the decisions and actions of the key liberal powers (Britain and the United States) in the rise of fascism. However, before proceeding I will introduce the principle thematic points that provide the core analytical framing that informs the more detailed historical discussion in the rest of the chapter.

1     Framing Fascism as a Form of Far-Right

Fascism reveals – if in its most militant and extreme form – a number of key themes evident over the *longue durée* of the far-right; a temporally and spatially contingent expression of a set of generic pathologies within the organization and evolution of a liberal-capitalist modernity. Let me introduce these themes that will be addressed in much more detail in the rest of the chapter. First, and as I have already suggested, above, fascism expresses a form of combined development. What I mean by this is that fascism provides an ideological and aesthetic means of exit from a crisis situation that is articulated via a set of reactionary and backward-looking cultural, social, and political signifiers, references and images that reveal the distinct way in which capitalism reproduces an ideal of the past in the present. Further, the 'fascist combination' is connected to the structural – material and geopolitical – contours that are grounded in the deeper material structures of accumulation that pre-existing forms of capitalist-imperialism have generated and carved out and which, in effect, determine the possibilities of a fascist political economy. Fascism seeks a radical geopolitical reconfiguration of the way in which the capital social relation is spatially and politically organized – a new 'spatio-temporal fix' – but its ability to realize this as a solution to the crisis that brought it to power is limited by both the pre-existing material structures of (monopoly) capitalist accumulation and the geopolitical organization of world capitalism. This obviously invokes the capital-labour process, in terms of the ability to exploit labour and realize productivity gains in a context whereby organized labour has been destroyed as a social and political actor and also the agency of the capitalist class – or its leading fractions – in the politics of fascism.

Fascism's path to state power also brings the institutional workings of liberal democracy and the actions of liberal and conservative political forces under the analytical microscope. We can see this at two levels. First, within the domestic politics of Italy and Germany, in the role that liberal and conservative parties and elites played in facilitating fascist parties into the corridors of state power. Secondly, at the international level, and the way in which the fledgling post-war liberal order provided an international political economic structure conducive to fascism, as well as in the behaviour of the leading liberal powers – Britain and the United States – in shutting off alternative economic and geopolitical solutions to the crisis generated by the 1929 Wall Street Crash. The domestic non-fascist political options in Germany in particular for overcoming the social catastrophe of the Great Depression were all but extinguished by the actions of these two powers (Riley, 2014), which meant that this not only reinforced the fear and hostility towards the left but, in effect, insured that the political elites and key fractions of the ruling class were propelled towards embracing fascism. Examining the role played by non-fascist political forces in the rise of fascism in Italy and Germany reflects the analytical focus of this volume as outlined in the Introduction and Chapter One and which, as I have discussed elsewhere (see Saull, 2015b, 2015c, 2015d, 2018; and Anievas and Saull, 2020) follows a generalized pattern of behaviour by conservative and liberal forces in their ambiguous and shifting relationship with the far-right over the *longue durée*.[2]

---

2  This raises the broader question of the role of these elites and social forces in the other major capitalist powers – Britain, France, and the United States – that did not become fascist. So, while the ruling class in each of these states continued to have an interest in and commitment to existing geopolitical arrangements in contrast to Germany, what was also key was that the workings of their respective domestic liberal-constitutional political orders provided them with alternative political options to fascism, even if this was far from an inevitable outcome during the high-point of the global crisis in the early 1930s. Thus, the decision by the Labour government in 1931 to maintain Treasury orthodoxy rather than pursue a more interventionist and inflationary strategy, alongside the weakened power of organized labour after the 1926 General Strike meant that Britain's elite and dominant classes were not confronted with a radical political threat from the left nor a challenge to their class privileges as owners of capital. In the US, Roosevelt's New Deal was realized after the Democrats secured enough votes to allow Congress to deliver a legislative solution that whilst provoking some opposition was broadly welcomed by the capitalist class. Benefiting the South's capitalist

Reference to the enabling role played by liberal and conservative political forces – in the domestic and international spheres – in the rise of fascism also implicates the class forces that these ideo-political currents were connected to and the broader theme of the class basis of fascism. Originally seen as a reflecting the distinct ideological anxieties and material interests of petty bourgeois social layers (see Beetham, 1983; Renton, 1999: 63–76), by the time that Hitler came to power the orthodox Marxist position – at least with respect to official Comintern doctrine – described fascism as 'the open, terrorist dictatorship of the most reactionary, most chauvinistic, and most imperialist elements of finance capital' (Dimitrov, 1935). This shift in the understanding of the class basis of fascism demonstrated the distinct qualities of fascism as an ideology and social movement that revealed its 'subaltern' class character and the class basis of the fascist state and the political economy of fascism which reflected the dominance of monopoly capital.

The scholarly debate on the social basis and sources of support for fascism has tended to be framed around a Marxist position that tends to differentiate fascism as movement and state form, which also emphasizes the role of leading fractions of the capitalist and landlord classes in securing its path to power. This contrasts with non-Marxist accounts that emphasize the significance of cross-class support – including from significant parts of the working class (see Eatwell, 2003; Mann, 2004; Payne, 1995) – and the hesitation and opposition of capitalists to fascism's accession to state power (Beck, 2008; Turner, 1969, 1985). Fascism did appeal to a trans-class constituency in Italy and Germany in terms of the rhetoric of its leaders and fascist propaganda, and as reflected in the social layers it recruited and secured votes from. Fascists tended to tailor their propaganda, rhetoric and policy suggestions to the specific locales and social groupings that they were targeting (Paxton, 2004: 65–6) even if this meant that such rhetoric or policy promises were contradictory. Thus, while Hitler was desperately trying to reassure corporate leaders and bourgeois opinion formers in the early 1930s as to how they had nothing to fear from National Socialism, Nazi propagandists in the countryside were talking of expropriating large farms and other Nazis borrowed communist party rhetoric to try and gain

---

class alongside the racial exclusions that it maintained, the New Deal also revealed a form of liberal embrace of the far-right. In France, the possibility of a fascist solution was much greater in part due to the strength of fascist political forces but also because of the revolutionary possibilities bequeathed by the communist-aligned Popular Front government that came to power in 1936. Thus, it was, as Geoff Eley (1983: 81) suggests, the failure of the Popular Front to consolidate itself as a new hegemonic bloc that meant that the threat of a coup led by the authoritarian right and backed by the mobilization of the fascist street was avoided.

support from workers and the unemployed. Such flexible and contradictory messaging (Eley, 1983: 74; see also Beetham, 1983: 7) was replicated in Italian fascism in the period between 1920 and 1922, as fascists tried to win over support from workers, the petty bourgeoisie and peasants, before Mussolini consolidated his authority over the Fascist Party. Thus, whilst he was 'cozying-up' to the Italian bourgeoisie, some of his local fascist leaders' spoke of the need for radically transforming the existing economic system that had many capitalists worried over their future.

Fascist rhetoric and drawing sources of support from a plurality of social classes – including parts of the working class – aside; fascism can be seen as a form of class movement given its consistent hostility towards the ideology, social institutions, material interests and politics of the organized working class. Workers joined and voted for fascist parties, yet fascism was much more successful in building a voting bloc from those social layers that typify the core social constituencies of the far-right over the *longue durée*. Thus, the petty bourgeois in the countryside and smaller towns tended to provide the mass basis of fascism (Childers, 1976; Hamilton, 1982; Larsen, et al., 1980) as well as some workers – typically located in spatial and cultural contexts removed from any attachment to the social milieu of organized labour. So, although the left – in the form of the Social Democratic, Socialist and Communist parties – managed to maintain their urban and industrial working class support as class-parties, *par excellence*, fascists managed to be more successful in building a voting bloc that was much less limited to a single class layer (Mann, 2004: 18). And in the context of crisis – especially so in the German case – where the traditional sources of working class support and political mobilization had been most severely affected and undermined by the consequences of the Great Depression, this was to prove highly effective.

Fascism, then, was a form of class politics – even if its social base was not confined to one class constituency – because it was based on a fundamental antagonism to the working class as an autonomous social and political actor and the institutions and culture that defined it as such. Indeed, considering the revolutionary context within which fascism emerged and evolved within, such an ideological orientation was logical given that a politics committed to the material interests of the (industrial) working class was the primary mass alternative to fascism's resolution of the crisis of bourgeois hegemony within Italy and Germany before fascist parties gained state power. Further, and as we shall see below – when I examine the political economy of fascism – once in power, the class basis of fascism was revealed in not only the destruction of the working class as a collective political subject, but also in the meagre material benefits thatworkers and the petty bourgeoisie secured from fascism in contrast to that of the major fractions of the capitalist class.

## 2    The Crisis of the Bourgeois State and the Rise of Fascism

The inter-war episode of the fascist far-right brings out in bold relief the way in which social and political crises associated with the *longue durée* of capitalist development provided a highly favourable international context that conditioned the domestic politics of European states facilitating the fascist routes to power in Italy and Germany and the success of far-right movements elsewhere. World War One developed from a crisis generated out of the multiple and contradictory developmental trajectories of the capitalist great powers such that the existing international institutional framework and geopolitical order that had 'managed' and directed capitalist development through the long nineteenth century broke down (see Anievas, 2014: 57–106; Arrighi, 1994; Hobsbawm, 1987: 302–27). Viewed through the methodological-theoretical prism of uneven and combined development the crisis of August 1914 reflected a 'unity in separation or contradiction' in the totality of the workings of the capitalist world economy. Thus, while made up of discreet social formations and political jurisdictions and geopolitical spaces, the multiple socioeconomic interactions between them, from commodity trade, capital flows, investment and monetary/exchange relations based on the Gold Standard, ensured that the singular or domestic paths of each was influenced and conditioned by political and economic decisions and processes made elsewhere; hence revealing capitalism as a differentiated totality.

Consequently, the relative stability of Britain in the period leading up to 1914 was not something that is explicable through a focus on its singular domestic social and political properties but was, instead – contrariwise the instabilities and tensions within the *Kaiserreich* – related to the uneven and combined development of other capitalist powers. That is, Britain's path of development as much as that of France and Germany's was *relational* grounded on the socioeconomic and political connections that provided the micro and macro-structures and processes of capitalist development. Further, such relationships and the socioeconomic structures that they helped to reproduce were not purely economic or political because these economic processes – associated with trade, capital flows, monetary stability and international liquidity, access to markets, investment decisions and levels of economic growth and employment – were also intimately connected to geopolitical arrangements.

Such interconnections continued to be the case after 1918, even if the particular geopolitical framing had been transformed by the war. International relations continued to be organized around a dynamic of inter-imperial competition and rivalry and the workings of the capitalist world economy continued to be shaped by the problem of industrial over-capacity and over-production (Brenner, 2006; Riley 2018) – two of the key ingredients that had helped produce war in 1914. Consequently, despite the restructuring of the geopolitical order with the dismantling of the three empires that dominated central and eastern Europe and the re-drawing of borders and the creation of new nation-states, the basic impulses of capitalist political economy soon re-asserted themselves after 1918 (Hobsbawm, 1994: 85–108; Mazower, 1999: 106–40; Tooze, 2015a). The emergence of the USSR created a new and antagonistic geo-economy, but this did not – in terms of productive capacity, key raw materials, or source of demand – prevent the basic fundaments of international capitalism returning in terms of global commodity trade, capital flows and the centrality of the Gold Standard. What was different, was the much greater significance of the American economy and the financial centre of Wall Street as a key source of global liquidity – given the debts that Britain had racked up through the funding of its war effort – and as a geoeconomic space for both generating aggregate demand and, consequently, absorbing exports and mitigating global over-capacity. Further, a major difference was also revealed in that this new geopolitical framing of global capitalism was centred on the strictures of the Versailles Peace settlement which came to affect the victor powers such as Britain and France as much as it did Germany.

Thus, politics – both domestic and international – was to be fundamentally framed around the continuation of the *longue durée* pattern operative since the middle of the nineteenth century of an internationally and geopolitically mediated set of socio-political conflicts derived from the social transformations wrought by capitalist development (the rise of an organized proletariat and the death-throes of the agrarian-based *ancien regime*; see Jessop, 1990: 156–60; Halperin, 2004; Mayer, 1981). However, such structural and geopolitical continuities – empire and imperialism continued to be important and legitimate means, including for the war's liberal victors, by which to organize capitalist accumulation and order international politics – were accentuated or over-determined by a set of distinct vulnerabilities, frailties and divisions that the war and its settlement had bequeathed.

Such frailties were particularly pronounced in the following ways. First, the de-mobilization of millions of veterans provided a potentially explosive social and political constituency for violent and revolutionary political transformations. Such a potential had already revealed itself before 1918 with the

Bolshevik Revolution and the ensuing civil war across Russia that would lead to the creation of the USSR. In the context of the war's losers[3] in central Europe and Germany in particular, such a constituency could – and ultimately did – provide the basis for nationalist and revanchist movements, who were committed to gaining state power through which to overturn the geopolitical settlement of Versailles. Military veterans, then, became an important part of both the Italian fascist movement and its notorious *squadristi* (that emerged in 1919), as well as providing an important element of the early National Socialist movement in Germany and its street militia, the *Sturmabteilung* (Storm Detachment – SA) (Elazar, 1993; Gerwarth, 2008; Gerwarth and Horne, 2011; Jones, 2015: 14–30).

A related, if subordinate, phenomenon connected to this was the actual impact of the war in the domains of culture and aesthetics. Highlighted in the work and activities of the (Italian) Futurists in particular – and in spite of the horrors, trauma, and carnage – the war also contributed to new forms of cultural expression and aesthetic appreciation that celebrated the culture of war and its connection to framings of masculinity (see Falasca-Zamponi, 2008; Herf, 1984; Neocleous, 1997; Woods, 1996). This provided an important intellectual and cultural source for the revitalization of far-right imaginaries after the war and especially in its rendering as a 'cult of war' and sacrifice, thus reinforcing the place of militarism within the far-right's ideological landscape. Although this took an artistic expression in Italy – that also provided a vanguard and model for Mussolini to emulate after the seizure and occupation of the disputed port of Fiume by a group of Italian nationalists led by the poet Gabriele D'Annunzio[4] in September 1919 – in Germany it was expressed through the idea of 'conservative revolution.'[5]

---

3  As we shall see in the case of Italy, as a member of the victorious Allied coalition the combination of the acute social and political divisions that were created through the decision to enter the war and the impact of the fighting on Italian domestic politics and the failure of the Versailles settlement to meet the expectations of the Italian ruling class and popular opinion, made Italy see itself as a loser in the spoils of war *vis-a-vis* the major liberal powers (Row, 2002: 102–3).

4  Many scholars regard this occupation and the creation of the 'Italian Regency of Carnaro' under the leadership of D'Annunzio – who called himself '*Il Duce*' – as the precursor or ideological blueprint for Mussolini's fascist state (see Lyttelton, 2004a: 35).

5  Articulated in the work of Ernst Junger, Oswald Spengler and others, these writers sought to establish a cultural and political virtue based on the blood sacrifice of the war and an idea of 'national socialism' founded on a 'soldierly nationalism'. Through this, class divisions and conflicts would be erased, and a socialism grounded on the comradely experience of the war would provide the basis for Germany as antithesis to Bolshevism, the Weimar Republic

Secondly, the Bolshevik Revolution and the emergence of the Soviet Union as a 'workers' or 'socialist state' transformed the geopolitical structure and political horizons across the international capitalist order. The USSR quickly emerged as the existential 'Other' of liberal-capitalist civilization. Indeed, for many scholars, the Versailles settlement of 1919 was concerned with outlining a political response and geopolitical framework to contain the USSR and deal with the ideological menace of Bolshevism, as much as it was concerned with dealing with Germany (see Anievas, 2014: 126–38; Halperin, 2004: 204–6; Mayer, 1968; Tooze, 2015: 333–50).

This unique political development had a profound set of consequences that revitalized the far-right. First, as a geopolitical power the USSR represented a threat to capitalist social order whereby the ideological imaginary of socialism took on a concrete and geopolitical form for the first time. For ruling class ideologues and political elites across Europe and the capitalist world more broadly, the USSR was an intolerable harbinger of a possible future in moments of political and economic chaos and geopolitical conflict. Its continued existence provided a concrete expression of a possible future for workers in capitalist countries and with the establishment of the Communist International (or Comintern) in 1918, the USSR committed itself to internationalizing Bolshevism through the activities of local communist parties in capitalist states.

Further, given its geopolitical form it helped necessitate the calls for a military and geopolitical response. This emerged almost immediately after the Bolshevik seizure of power with Western armed intervention into the Russian civil war to assist local 'White' counter-revolutionary forces (Foglesong, 1995; Thompson, 1966) – many of which were imbued with far-right ideo-political sentiments associated with anti-Semitism, xenophobia and support for the restoration of the *ancien régime*. The intervention was fuelled by an increased level of social and ideological paranoia as to Bolshevik influence within the domestic political lefts that were now an important and, in some cases, the largest, most well-organized and most popular political parties across postwar liberal democratic Europe. The issue here, assisted by the establishment of the Comintern, was that the domestic radical lefts in France, Italy, Germany and elsewhere were now – in the eyes of much of the liberal establishment (let alone the far-right) – regarded as agents of a foreign and hostile revolutionary power. Such an ideo-political imaginary gave birth to what became

---

and liberal materialism, individualism, and hypocrisy. See Woods, (1996: 1–6; see also Mann, 2004: 68).

known as the Cold War after 1947 but the sentiments and politics that greeted the Bolshevik Revolution across the major capitalist powers almost immediately after 1917 demonstrated a Cold War ideological and psychological sensibility (Anievas, 2014; Carley, 2014; Leffler, 1994; Saull, 2007, 2010) reflected in the geopolitical counter-revolution and containment of the USSR alongside a set of domestic policies to contain and repress the radical left within liberal democracies. It was through this hostility that the far-right and – in the case of the *Freikorps* in Germany – proto-fascist paramilitary forces emerged to violently repress any radical impulses inspired by the Bolsheviks, as was the case in Germany and elsewhere across central Europe (Gerwarth, 2008; Gerwarth and Horne, 2011) in the period after World War One.

The emergence of the USSR reflected the inherent revolutionary potential contained within the logic of capitalist uneven and combined development that was causal of fascism through injecting a concrete revolutionary subject (socialist and communist parties) and object (the USSR) into the pre-existing political imaginaries of the right. In many respects, then, the immediate outcome of the war and the revolutionary crisis that engulfed Germany and other defeated powers in central and eastern Europe provided the scenario for counter-revolutionary paramilitary forces to emerge drawing on former soldiers who were quickly mobilized as fascists after the revolutionary crisis had passed.

There are two other elements of the post-war order associated with the Versailles settlement that are also connected to the contradictions of the *longue durée* of uneven and combined capitalist development that contributed to the historical enabling of fascism. The first was the establishment and/or extension – mainly through extending voting rights and reducing the political privileges of traditional sources of social power – of the political-institutional framework of liberal democracy (see Mazower, 1999: 1–39). The significance of this was twofold. On the one hand, it reflected the victory of social and political struggles led by the organized working class that had been waged since 1848. Such an outcome not only institutionalized political representation and discourse around the 'masses' thus undermining the political privileges of corporatist place-holders and elites, but it also placed an institutional limit on the power of capital through the extensions and deepening of regimes of taxation to fund the bases of a post-war social welfare state. Such developments were most pronounced in Germany with the creation of the Weimar Republic in 1919 after the failed November revolution. While the revolutionary left – and with two of its key leaders, Rosa Luxemburg and Karl Liebknecht assassinated – was crushed through the armed force of far-right *Freikorps* backed by the leadership of the SPD, the new constitutional settlement that emerged in

1919 reflected significant gains for the organized working class and concessions by big capital.[6]

The significance of this democratic transformation with the extension of the voting franchise to all (male) adults was not just the possibility it raised of placing limits on the powers of traditional political elites and the capitalist class via the ballot box; it also provided a spectre of a democratically-engineered radical social transformation that sowed a deep fear and mistrust across dominant social interests about their future. Consequently, it meant that for the social and political forces on the right, as well as many economic liberals,[7] such democratic arrangements could not be tolerated or accepted in the long term because as long as democracy remained the basis for determining who governed and controlled significant parts of the state there remained the possibility of the radical or revolutionary left coming to power. Democratic transformation, however, also reflected an ambivalence in the ideology of far-right that included fascists. Thus, on the one hand it institutionalized a social threat from the left and, in some respects, legitimated the political struggles of the working class through providing a legal-political means for the left to gain political power with which to address socioeconomic issues and transform the nature and workings of the state. On the other, democracy – and its relationship to the creation of mass political movements and mass parties – also provided a means for far-right socio-political forces to exercise influence over the political

---

6    These concessions (some of which were inscribed into the constitution of the new Republic) involved the introduction of welfare measures based on increased social spending and improved support for the unemployed – all of which contributed to significant increases in public expenditure to the benefit of workers and the poor and, in part, funded by taxes on capital. Further, and most contentious for capitalist interests, was the creation of the *zentralarbeitsgemeinschaft* or ZAG (Central Working Community) where trade unions were, for the first time, put on an equal legal footing with employers in industrial relations. The creation of the ZAG quickly led to the introduction of the eight-hour day and other concessions from employers over sick pay, job protection and collective bargaining. In addition to these developments a law establishing the *Betriebsrat* or works councils between the representatives of labour and capital reflected a further limit on the autonomy and power of capital over the labour process. Finally, a new law ensuring state arbitration of industry-wide disputes between capital and labour also weakened the power of capital through introducing a legal requirement of political interference in trade disputes. Such properties of the Weimar state were to prove highly significant and deeply unpopular for capital and conservative and liberal political opinion by the late 1920s (see Geary, 1990; Gluckstein, 1999: 41–2).

7    An important ideological current within Germany that reflected such a view were the Ordo-liberals who outlined an alternative justification and theory of dictatorship which, to some extent, was very similar to the justifications made by the 'crown jurist' of Nazism, Carl Schmitt (see the writings of Röpke, 1942, 1998 and Schmitt, 1985, 1988 and the critical commentary of Bonefeld, 2017a, 2017b; Kiely, 2018).

system and, possibly, to gain access to state power. Fascism, then, reflected the fulfilment of the 'democratic promise' of the mass politics that had emerged in the late nineteenth century and differentiated it (and the broader far-right) from the political methods of the traditional right.

In this way, the democratization of politics via the development of 'mass society' and 'mass politics' – developments that concerned and worried nine-teenth century liberals and conservatives (see Bon, 2001; Kahan, 2003: 3; Mill, 2010; Tocqueville, 2009) – reflected the longer-term tensions and rivalries between the forces of the conservative or *ancien régime* right and the sub-altern far-right. With their sources of political power rooted in pre and anti-democratic structures and political-institutional arrangements they were now at risk of political displacement by a far-right that drew on a mass base rooted in the transformations and dislocations of a developing industrial and mass society that included elements of the working class and petty bourgeoisie. Simply put, and as revealed in the growth of the fascist far-right, democracy – as institutional structure and its accompanying imaginary – offered a means for the realization of a more plebeian, militant, and radical far-right that could by-pass the power and privileges of the traditional or conservative right.

Thus, while fascists spoke a language, practiced a form of politics, and committed themselves to authoritarian and dictatorial solutions antitheti-cal to democratic procedures and structures (Eley, 2015), fascist movements gained political traction, momentum, and support through participating in and embracing the political opportunities and institutional structures of liberal democracy. Fascism is anti-democratic; it seeks to destroy the institu-tional forms, political mechanisms, and wider political culture of democracy, and especially the principle of equal citizenship that democracy is built upon. Yet, its emergence as a distinct and revolutionary current of the far-right and its ability to secure access to political power involved participation in elec-toral competition. Consequently, it was the combined social and political strengths – as reflected in vote share and political representation – of fascist movements/parties that made them seem as necessary or essential to govern-ment by political elites because they appeared to represent such a significant amount of political support across society and the only mass or 'democratic' antidote to the left – revolutionary or otherwise.

The other important issue associated with the spread and deepening of liberal-democratic forms of politics across Europe after 1918 was how such institutional arrangements based on party-systems provided the basis for effective government rooted in secure and stable parliamentary majorities and/or coherent coalition groupings (Mazower, 1999: 1–39). This issue became particularly significant in Germany after 1929 when the country was engulfed by the global economic crisis triggered by the 'Wall Street crash' at the end of October and where the social divisions within German society were replicated in the political representation in the Reichstag that made effective parliamentary government and law-making difficult if not impossible. While this problem of a divided or 'fractured centre' undermined the possibility of effective governing coalitions it was also much harder – given the rise of the political forces of the revolutionary left in the form of the Communist Party (KPD) and radical right. In short, the particular institutional arrangements that emerged in Germany (and elsewhere) of liberal-representative democracy, rested on delicate and unstable social constituencies which meant that effective and legitimate government required a reduction in class tensions and conflict. If, and when such tensions reappeared and intensified the result would be political stasis. Although this did not – in the case of Germany in the early 1930s – reflect a revolutionary crisis it did mean that the resolution of the capitalist crisis could not be achieved through pre-existing political-institutional arrangements.

The final development in the framing or situating of fascism concerns the political economy of capitalism and the accumulation strategies emergent from the war. As already discussed, above, the road to war in 1914 was intimately connected to the contradictions and conflicts that emerged from within the dynamics of uneven and combined capitalist development of the preceding decades and, specifically, how the differing accumulation strategies of the leading capitalist great powers were fundamentally connected to geopolitics – control of and access to space and the spatialized properties of capital accumulation. Relatedly, it also concerned the ability of the leading capitalist great power – the British Empire – to manage and regulate these contradictions.

The war had a profound impact on the structure of the world economy and the economic rankings of the major capitalist powers. The most significant were the following. First, the social and economic challenges that the *Kaiserreich* had confronted in the two decades leading up to 1914 that played an important role in causing the war were now further complicated and, to a significant extent, accentuated. The generalized logic of Germany's uneven and combined development that had provided the sources of the socioeconomic and geopolitical enabling of the far-right in the final decades of the nineteenth century were now reinforced and over-laden with the conjunctural impact of the Versailles settlement. Notably, the loss of territory and population and, in particular, raw material resources such as coal, all served to reduce the productive economic potential of the German economy after 1918 and, consequently, the wider economic vitality of Europe given Germany's significance as the leading European industrial power. Moreover, to these problems were added the economic dimensions of the Versailles settlement; consisting of the French occupation of the German industrial heartland of the Ruhr and the financial burden of reparations to the Allies. Consequently, the challenges and contradictions facing Germany after the war were unprecedented. In many respects, Germany's, and Europe's economic future and, therefore, its political and geopolitical stability were now to be increasingly contingent on the geopolitical and economic decisions of the Allied powers and especially Britain and the United States. Thus, it was these two powers that had the means to reconfigure the wider international terrain that Germany was located within, and the potential opportunities offered through international trade, investment, credit, and market opportunities to assist Germany's economy. Yet, it also went well beyond this because the actual basic fundamental workings of Germany's domestic economy – in terms of its fiscal and monetary policies – were also imbricated with international political considerations tied to the reparations regime and the financial diktats of the liberal powers.

To a significant degree the contradictions associated with Germany's uneven and combined development prior to 1914 continued to define German capitalism. Although labour had made some important gains in the immediate years after the war and in a form that socialized the majority of the working class into a more direct association with the new political system, the suspicion and hostility towards the organized working class and the SPD across dominant social layers – both agrarian and industrial – remained. Indeed, the connection between the gains of the left and the Versailles settlement provided a major reason why many on the German right viewed the left as traitors. This was to play an important role in undermining the stability of Weimar democracy in later years, and also provided an important opening for the far-right as it had done in the decades before 1914.

In many respects the class structure and class formation of the German political economy continued to be defined by a stark set of material divisions. The defining ones were those between different fractions of capital and notably between a heavy industry based on coal, iron, and steel production – that was particularly affected by the territorial and raw material losses – and that of a more export-oriented fraction of capital based on chemicals and electrical engineering. The issue here was the problem – that had plagued administrations of the late *Kaiserreich* – of how to construct a set of accumulation strategies for these different fractions when they had contradictory needs. So, while heavy industry with its major fixed capital and higher unit wage costs with much lower or precarious levels of profitability – in part connected to ongoing issues of overcapacity – required forms of trade protectionism, the export-oriented sector tended to be more competitive with the possibility for growing its international markets and with lower unit-level wage costs (Jessop, 1990: 157–8; Abraham, 1986: 13; Tooze, 2007: 1–33).

On top of this contradiction within industrial capital there remained severe developmental and structural problems within the agricultural sector. Hence, German agriculture remained relatively backward – in both a material and social sense – divided between small-scale producers who tended to be heavily indebted and subject to the vagaries of secure and stable credit flows and large Junker estates in the east that continued to demand and require agricultural protection from cheaper agrarian imports. Prior to 1914 these tensions revealed themselves in the emergence of militant far-right movements discussed in the previous chapter that provided an important subaltern and popular source for German imperialism focused on the east. Indeed, these tendencies provided the original basis of the *Lebensraum* policy and the geopolitical rivalry associated with it (Baranowski, 2011). Sooner or later these structural tensions would reveal themselves in an explosive political form within the Weimar Republic. And this is exactly what happened after 1929 as the collapse in international trade meant that Germany's domestic market – still significantly constituted by a backward agrarian sector – needed to soak up surplus industrial capacity, which it was unable to do. The consequence of which was the revival of the pre-1914 dynamic of territorial expansion (Riley, 2014: 341). Accordingly, the problem of Weimar reflected the consequences of the failure of the 1914 ruling class strategy of war to resolve these matters through a German hegemony or *Grossraum* across central and eastern Europe alongside the failure of the November Revolution to restructure class relations and, in particular, by finally removing the socioeconomic bases of agrarian reaction that continued to fester after 1918.[8]

The situation that Germany faced after 1918 was that if it was to remain as a capitalist society based on the continuing reproduction of its dominant class forces in the medium and longer term, it would have to overturn the Weimar constitutional settlement and/or the geopolitical arrangements bequeathed by Versailles. Thus, as Dylan Riley (2014: 337; see also, Tooze, 2007: 99–134) suggests, while the German capitalist class was far from universally committed to a policy of imperialism requiring geopolitical contestation

---

8  As Alexander Anievas (2014: 143) notes, it was the Allies' pre-occupation with Bolshevism and, in particular, its potential spread to Germany that was crucial in their decision to allow the most reactionary layers of the Wilhelmine elites to remain, thus ensuring their continued exercise of political influence over the new Germany. Such a posture also operated across central Europe in the social dispensations in the newly formed states that emerged that were seen in the *cordon sanitaire* to insulate western Europe from Bolshevism.

and domestic socio-political mobilization (involving an alliance with the far-right), unless sources of export-oriented capital accumulation could be found and developed, the imperialist temptation remained. And in the absence of any of the major capitalist economies and the liberal powers opening up their markets[9] – which none of them did – Germany remained bottled up in a mass of structural contradictions (see Kent, 1991).

Britain, or, more precisely, the British Empire had been the leading international economic power prior to 1914 and it was the breakdown of the bases of Britain's 'liberal hegemony' that was a key factor contributing to the world war. By 1918 Britain was exhausted and had rapidly moved from the world's primary creditor and source of international liquidity (centred on the city of London) to the world's biggest debtor – to the United States.[10] Though Britain benefitted from its imperial resources stretched throughout the Empire and, in particular, India's continuing contributions to its capital account and balance of payments, as well as the continuing centrality of Sterling as the unit of international credit and exchange, its economic freedom was also tied to the consequences of the war and the imperatives of servicing its debts to the United States. Indeed, while alternative models of capitalist political economy were articulated and sources of capital accumulation, Britain quickly reverted to the financial orthodoxy of 'sound money' secured through cuts to public spending and running consecutive budgetary surpluses. This was based on returning Sterling to the Gold Standard and maintaining its (pre-war) value – so making its exports much less competitive – as a source of international credit, confidence and means to meet its international financial obligations, even if this came at a cost of domestic deflation resulting in high unemployment and reduced potential for economic growth.

Alongside this financial orthodoxy Britain also maintained its pre-1914 commitment to free trade at least until the decision of the Ottawa Conference of 1932. The significance of these developments for our concerns here in terms of

9     Indeed, the short-lived period (between 1924 and 1928) when the economic prospects of the Weimar Republic improved significantly were based on a specific set of circumstances associated with the opening up of American-sourced capital flows into Germany facilitated by the Dawes Plan. The problem, however, which became manifest after 1929, was that the credit flows did not facilitate major structural reform; instead, they helped fragile coalition governments manage the contradictions and maintain some level of social peace but when the credit flows suddenly dried up – as they did, after October 1929 – when the US entered into a period of severe financial contraction, Germany found itself utterly exposed.

10    According to Eric Hobsbawm (1994: 97–8), Britain's financing of its war effort involved the liquidation of about a quarter of its global investments and by the end of hostilities British debts to the US amounted to around 50% of her national income.

how this helped enable the rise of fascism outside of Britain, was that Britain's post-war weakness meant that it was no longer able to stimulate global demand and pump liquidity into the international financial system in the way that it did prior to 1914. Accordingly, British economic strategy increasingly acted to undermine the accumulation strategies of other European capitalist states and the possibilities of carving out a path for sustained growth – and thus domestic political stability and geopolitical security – within the spatial arrangements confirmed by the Versailles settlement. The ramifications of this were not only felt within Britain, but also in countries such as Germany, Italy and elsewhere, as potential export markets were squeezed or shut-off and, in consequence, the possibility of breaking out of the post-war economic confinement reduced.

The most significant economic outcome of the war in terms of the shape and character of uneven and combined development was the emergence of the United States as the world's number one creditor and, potentially at least, the single most important source of world economic growth. While the US had grown to be the world's biggest industrial power before 1914, the war – and its 'gobbling up' of British economic and financial assets as Britain liquefied its overseas assets to help fund the war – saw the place of the US within the overall architecture of the world economy transformed. The global economic significance of the US was combined with its growing, if not quite hegemonic, geopolitical importance as reflected in the US contribution to the Allied war effort, its participation as a belligerent in the final year of the war and the role of President Wilson in the crafting of the Versailles settlement and the post-war international order (see Ikenberry, 2001: 117–62; Tooze, 2015a; Mayer, 1968; Gardner, 1984). Consequently, the decisions taken by the US government after 1918 and the impact of the American economy, and especially Wall Street, on the stabilization of the international financial system through the 1920s were to be pivotal in determining the character and direction of global capitalism after 1918 and the inter-connections between strategies of capital accumulation, political order, and geopolitics.

Thus, the increased post-war material weight of the US economy underlined and gave greater significance to US political leadership and whether or not it would act to construct a new set of institutional and geopolitical arrangements with which to facilitate geopolitical and political-economic stability based on a new structure for (post-imperial) global accumulation (see Tooze, 2015). That this did not happen reflected the underlying structure of uneven and combined development that that the war had intensified through widening the material bases and geopolitical character of uneven development as demonstrated by the rise of the United States, the weakening of Britain and the desperation of Germany. It was also reflected through the manner in which combined development operated and asserted itself on this uneven-ness, as revealed in the variegated ways that the major capitalist powers responded to the post-war dispensation: retreat into continental isolation by the US; a return to pre-war economic and financial orthodoxy by Britain; and Germany's desperation and dependence on the US for an expansion of its export market (see Anievas, 2014: 144–7).

What we can take from the transformation in the structure and workings of the world economy and geopolitical system after the war in explaining the rise of fascism, is that fascism emerges as a concomitant ideo-political current of a capitalist imperialism structured around the productive unit of monop-oly capital combined with the newly created social and political pathologies of militarized nationalism and anti-communism that were bequeathed by the war. In other words, the war had not only revealed the level of crisis in the international structure and governance of capitalism, but its ending and the 'peace' also made any long-term resolution of the sources of economic instability and geopolitical conflict that much more unlikely, as the continua-tion of nineteenth century currents of crisis were now over-determined by two new ones (see Tooze, 2015).

What fascism demonstrated, then, was the breakdown of post-war attempts to institutionalize bourgeois hegemony, as the generalized reproduction of capitalist social property relations was no longer possible through the existing political form and geopolitical order. Further, this failure to establish an inter-national historical (social) bloc was not just a domestic issue within Italy and Germany but was also fundamentally grounded in the post-1918 international political-economic architecture established after the war due to the inability to integrate German and Italian ruling classes and, more importantly, wider social layers into the institutions of that order. And this obviously implicates the ruling classes of the other major capitalist powers in failing to provide a basis for international co-operation and institutions that rested on a reason-able degree of political legitimacy. I will now move from the general to the specific, through addressing the genesis of fascist power in Italy and Germany after World War One, framing the analysis in relation to the broader theoretical architecture outlined above.

### 2.1    Italy: The Crisis of Liberal Hegemony and the Revolutionary Origins of Fascism

Italian fascism developed out of the specific context defined by the organic contradictions of its late developmental path as revealed in its fragile and fragmented form of national social and political integration after the Italian state was finally established in 1871 and in its late industrialization within an international context defined by imperialist-directed geopolitical competition and rivalry. Indeed, Poulantzas's observation as to the structural context or origins of fascism within particular forms of 'peripheral' capitalist state – drawing on Gramsci's earlier insights (Gramsci, 1971: 191–311) – is highly pertinent. For Poulantzas, fascism was a product or response to a national crisis within a wider imperial system of production and inter-state relations whereby the polities most susceptible to fascism were those who made up the weakest links within an imperialist system undergoing systemic crisis (Poulantzas, 1974: 17–24; see also Beetham, 1983: 10). Italy, like Germany, was such a state.

Paralleling social and political developments in France and Germany in the final two decades of the nineteenth century, fractions of Italian capital and landlords organized to press for a combination of trade protection and political authoritarianism. Thus, in 1885 landlords – in both the North and South of the country formed the 'League for Agrarian Defence' (Riley, 2010: 34) which demanded cuts in land tax, and higher tariffs on grain imports, as farmers in Italy, like elsewhere in Europe, suffered the consequences of cheap American grain imports flooding the market and driving down prices. They quickly forged an alliance with heavy industrial capital that resulted in the introduction of a general tariff in 1887 that saw significant increases in import duties on a range of manufactured goods and grain imports – the highest on wheat in Europe by 1894 (Clarke, 1996: 115–6, 118; Zamagni, 1993: 113–4). In addition to trade protectionism in response to the international economic vicissitudes of the Long Depression, the ruling class was also concerned by rising labour militancy in the countryside throughout the 1880s. And, following the generalized pattern elsewhere in Europe, the Italian state embarked on its first imperialist venture into Africa with the disastrous attempt to establish a protectorate in Abyssinia that culminated in the defeat of the Italian army at the Battle of Adowa in 1896 (Smith, 1997: 163–70). This battle – which was regarded as a national humiliation – brought down the government and ended this particular chapter of attempts to craft an Italian social imperialism based on nationalist protection and imperialist expansion. However, its memory lingered, coming to play a defining role in Mussolini's imperialist project in Africa, which was aimed at addressing this 'national humiliation'.

By the start of the twentieth century a militant socialist party had emerged concentrated in the industrial zones of the north that contrasted with the prevalence of a relatively backward and under-developed agricultural sector in the south (Smith, 1997: 135–42; Zamagni, 1993: 47–74, 81–2; Federico, 1996). The capitalist class was divided between an export sector specializing in textiles (especially silk) and food-stuffs and a state-organized heavy industrial sector based on shipping, iron and steel and heavy engineering (Zamagni, 1993: 87,

124–5). Mirroring the political economy of Germany, these fractions of capital argued for a protected domestic market and the creation of shielded external markets through imperialist policies of expansion and annexation and, in doing so, ended up supporting fascism (Adler, 1995: 22; Sarti, 1971: 7–40).

These contradictory dynamics of uneven and combined development were managed by a fledgling bourgeois state that, by 1911, was answerable to an adult male suffrage that gave considerable weight to the growing left.[11] Constructed out of the political struggles of the *Risorgimento*, the Italian liberal state struggled to maintain itself in terms of the upholding of social order across the country through integrating the masses into its constitutional arrangements and political culture given that the socioeconomic and geopolitical context within which the state was formed had radically altered by the early part of the twentieth century, most notably with respect to the growth of an urbanized and militant working class (Adler, 1995: 3–5; Riley, 2010:24–6, 34–41). It was in this context of a fractured capitalist class, rural stagnation in the South, the apparent exhaustion of the domestic sources of economic growth, and the spectre of a social revolutionary threat from the left that, in September 1911, saw the Liberal-led government of Giovanni Giolitti engage in another round of imperialist adventurism with an invasion of Ottoman-controlled Libya to set about establishing the bases of an Italian overseas colonial empire (Riley, 2010: 40; Smith, 1997: 241–9). This imperialist aggression could be seen as an attempt to address the multiple contradictions that confronted Italian liberalism at the time[12] through, on the one hand, opening up the potential for access to an external and protected market (as well as resources) and, on the other, integrating the masses into an Italian nationalism (see Adler, 1995: 5; Payne, 1995: 81; Riley and Desai, 2007: 823; Riley, 2010: 40) based on imperial success and nation-building. In doing so, helping to secure the existing political edifice; the kind of politics that had seemed to succeed in the other major European capitalist powers – an Italian variant of 'social imperialism'.

The significance of these developments for the subsequent emergence of Italian fascism in 1919 was that they inaugurated a left-nationalism within Italy

---

11    In the two elections that preceded 1914 the Socialist Party was capturing a vote share of just below 20 percent becoming the second largest political bloc in the National Assembly (Clarke, 1996: 157).

12    As Adler (1995: 24–5) notes, a key feature of Italy's specific variant of uneven and combined development was its simultaneous rather than sequential capital formation and industrialization with the growth of a workers' movement that could be seen to reflect, in Trotsky's words, the (revolutionary) 'privilege of historic backwardness' in relation to its organization and ideology (Trotsky, 2008: 24).

(Riley and Desai, 2007: 822–4) that ended up splitting the socialist and revolutionary lefts and providing a social revolutionary imaginary and social base for the anti-liberal and anti-socialist politics of Italian fascism. In this respect, the outbreak of World War One in August 1914 provided the conjunctural trigger that would end up intensifying and accelerating this nationalist impulse across the left and, assisted by the militarism, violence, and revolutionary aesthetics of the war, created the foundations of fascism at the war's end (Riley, 2010: 41–07). Thus, while fascism originated from the left in terms of its key intellectual influences and leaders, its foundational nationalist orientation became – through the intervention of the war – over-determining in its subsequent ideo-political formation. It was war – and its immediate social and political consequences – then, especially in providing the paternity to the two main protagonists in the birth of Italian fascism, that served to intensify and determine the outcome of the structural contradictions built up over the *longue durée* of Italian state and class formation.[13]

Italy entered the war on the side of the Allies over the summer of 1915 placing the government at odds with the socialist mainstream that remained committed to neutrality but did secure the support of the left-nationalist current and of Mussolini who was one of its main voices. It also reflected the continuation of the strategy on the part of the Italian ruling class revealed earlier in the invasion of Libya (and, before that the ill-fated intervention in Abyssinia). A hope of not only securing the social and political foundations of the state through a victorious war, but also being the beneficiary of imperial wartime spoils at the war's end (Smith, 1997: 276–82). Italy's involvement in the war, like its earlier invasion of Libya reflected Italian liberalism's loss of innocence as it struggled to manage the contradictions of its uneven and combined development, which was made all the more difficult with its participation in the war. Indeed, the decision to join the Allied war effort involved – to a much greater extent than the Libyan expedition – a gamble on the possibility of realizing a successful imperialist territorial expansion as the means to secure Italy's domestic political consolidation (see Riley, 2010: 41). In other words, a nationalist integration

---

13   Dylan Riley's account of the rise of Italian 'party fascism' gives particular emphasis to how the dominant social groups within Italy in the period after the *Risorgimento* were fragmented into sets of territorially-defined socio-political interests which continued to be the case up until 1914. This meant that not only did Italy not have a national ruling class but this also severely impeded the possibility of a wider national politics based on national parties and institutions (see Riley, 2010:23–71). In the immediate post-war context such shortcomings proved fatal to the liberal state, providing a key opening for fascism which offered such a national integrationist politics.

'from without' which also provided a political rationale for a kind of politics and state better equipped to realize such an outcome than its existing liberal form, as well as 'wetting the appetite' of significant fractions of its capitalist class over the prospect of post-war access and/or control of external markets (Adler, 1995; Sarti, 1971).

In the case of the former, then, while it would be an exaggeration to say that the strategic decisions of the Italian liberal elite *created* fascism, in opening up the 'Pandora's box' of a militarist nationalism focused on imperial adventures, Italian liberals helped create a political context and ideological imaginary with which they were quickly unable to realise or live up to. Thus, the contradictions of Italy's state formation and socioeconomic development pushed its ruling class towards such risky geopolitical endeavours even as they exposed and accentuated the fundamental frailties and weakness of the Italian state. And even though alternatives were beginning to emerge on the radical left, such ideological positions did not, at this stage, have sufficient levels of social mobilization behind them, nor a clear political-organizational framing, to see them realized.

Such a predicament was already evident in the early days of the war with the fragilities of the Italian political system playing out in the management of the war effort and in the fighting on the front line. As regards the economic interests of Italian capital and the future prospects for capital accumulation, the entry into war made clear that the Italian ruling class was expectant that its thwarted economic fortunes prior to 1914 would be turned around at the war's end with territorial annexations and imperial expansion to allow it to join the ranks of the other major industrial powers. Thus, what Italy had failed to do on her own prior to 1914 in forging herself as a distinct great power in the Mediterranean (Bosworth, 1979) – largely due to Britain's imperial incumbency – was now to be realized on the backs of the Allies with the opportunity provided by World War One. In a word, both politically and economically, the fateful decision of 1915, in effect, provided a political rationale perfectly suited to a fascist kind of politics.

Even before the war began to sow social and political division (Payne, 1995: 81–2) through its mismanagement and the casualties from fighting, the decision to participate triggered mass demonstrations and street-fighting between supporters and opponents of the war (Mann, 2004: 93). Although these war-time political conflicts had yet to congeal into a clear left-right binary they prepared the ground for a radicalization of the right into fascism as that expression of politics most closely aligned with a militant and violent nationalism. Thus, it was the Versailles settlement that provided the *coup de grâce* to the possibilities of Italy's fledgling liberal-bourgeois political order,

as the social, political and international foundations of liberal hegemony collapsed in the post-war crisis that Italy was quickly enveloped within.

What happened, then, in the immediate period after the war to seal the
fate of Italian liberal democracy through the growth of a fascist movement?
The ingredients for fascism were cultivated out of the contradictions within
Italy's political and economic development and, specifically, the way in which
Italy's late development and geopolitical insertion within a pre-existing imperial system fostered a particular variant of combined development conducive
to fascism. The war shattered what remained of the foundations of the liberal state, as its radicalizing impact destroyed the political culture that had
helped realize the maintenance of a liberal-bourgeois political ascendancy
even if the industrial bourgeoisie had ended the war strengthened by the way
that war had accelerated economic development (Dunnage, 2002: 46; Corner,
2002: 38). The war provided a key stimulant through the legacy of thousands of
disillusioned war veterans returning home who quickly became all the more
estranged from the political elites as the promises of national greatness – with
which they had entered and fought the war for – was denied the Italians as
the post-war settlement became clear. The significance of the failure to secure
territorial gains from Austria-Hungary in particular implanted a deep bitter-
ness that was focused on the weakness and betrayal of the government and the
liberal-imperial powers (Clark, 1996: 204; De Donno, 2006: 403; Mack Smith,
1997: 281). Mussolini was adamant, he denounced the machinations of the liberal powers as 'a solemn "swindle" of the rich' that was directed 'against the
proletarian nations' such as Italy by the rich powers who wanted 'to fix forever
the actual conditions of world equilibrium' (cited in Tooze, 2015: 10).

The failings of Italy's experiment with liberal imperialism – the last, dangerous, gamble of liberal hegemony – created a widespread anger across the
country that reflected the popular permeation of an ideology of left nationalism across all popular classes[14] in the towns and cities as well as the countryside. Such anger revealed itself in an eruption  of social militancy across the
subaltern classes with a wave of industrial strikes and the onset of land occupations and expropriations that ushered in the revolutionary moment of the
*biennio rosso*.[15] It was also demonstrated in the military occupation of Fiume

---

14    See Sarti (1971: 18–19) for the disillusionment of Italy's industrial capitalist fractions with
      the new post-war order with many of them supporting Gabriele D'Annunzio's description
      of the emerging post-war settlement as a 'mutilated victory.' Sarti states that this theme
      featured in the speech of one of Italy's leading industrialists, Enzo Ferrari.
15    As Stanley Payne (1995: 87) describes it, '[t]he years immediately after the war did not
      produce the triumphant and unified Italy promised by the wartime patriots but rather a
      major political and economic crisis, compounded by short-term economic depression.'

in 1919 and the proclamation of the Italian Regency of Camaro in September that year (lasting until 1920), after a band of veterans under the leadership of the nationalist poet, Gabriele D'Annunzio, seized the port city in response to the failure of the Versailles settlement to award Italy with any territorial gains. Such imperialist adventures were not limited to nationalist poets, but also capitalists, as seen in Ettore Conti's (the leading industrialist) sponsorship and direction of a warship and a detachment of Italian marines to the Caucuses in February 1920 – taking advantage of the breakdown of political order due to the Russian civil war – to carve out an opportunity for Italian commercial penetration (Sarti, 1971: 19).

However, it was the *biennio rosso* over 1919–20 and the revolutionary threat from the left that was to prove the final and, ultimately, determining factor in the rise and success of fascism. Thus, the simmering industrial and social conflicts that had been gradually growing in intensity in the immediate period up to 1914–15 returned in 1919 but in a much more widespread and systematic manner. Here, it was the faltering post-war economic situation and the absence of a peace-time economic fillip that was key. Adding to the militancy produced by the war-time mobilization and the geopolitical disappointments at the war's end the post-war inflation and mass unemployment – that had reached over two million by November 1919 (Clarke, 1996: 206; see also Mack Smith, 1997: 291) – saw Italy quickly move to a state of virtual ungovernability. As Dunnage (2002: 48) posits, in 1919 there were over 1,600 strikes involving over one million workers and 208 in the agricultural sector that mobilized over half a million peasants. In 1920 strike activity increased with nearly 1,900 strikes involving over 1.2 million workers and while the level of strike activity declined in agriculture the numbers participating more than doubled to over one million. As Riley and Desai (2007: 820–1; see also Adler, 1995: 617; Mann, 2004: 61; Sarti, 1971: 25–6) detail, from a low of 303 strikes in 1918 militancy massively increased to 1,663 recorded strikes in 1919 involving car workers, telegraph, and railway workers as well as those in the heavy industrial sector. This revolutionary militancy struck at the heart of the bourgeois social order and economy, and challenged the state's monopoly on 'legitimate violence' over large areas of the country. The significance of the strikes that echoed the telegraphed nature of the development of Italy's revolutionary working class was that the strikes were also paralleled by factory occupations that appeared to demonstrate the superfluousness of both the capitalist class and management cadres in industry, as workers asserted 'workers control' of production that was to reach a high point in the winter and early spring of 1920 (Morgan, 2004: 41–3; Riley and Desai, 2007: 821; Riley, 2010: 44–5).

The situation in the Italian countryside and in the Po Valley in particular reflected even greater dangers for the established landlord class and the privileges and legal protections for private property. Here, the Socialist Party organized Agrarian Leagues went about occupying land and seizing property. And benefiting from their political control of local governments – won through elections in November 1919 – socialists began to impose fundamental limits on the operations of agrarian capitalism through their interventions in the labour market. As Robert Paxton (2004: 60; see also Riley and Desai, 2007: 822; Corner, 1975: 89–90) opines, the socialist public authorities forced landlords to pay higher wages, improve working conditions and control the hiring of labour, as well as promoting the establishment of agricultural co-operatives. Accompanying these interventions, the more militant wings of Italian socialism encouraged and led land occupations of large landholdings; in some cases, burning the houses of landlords, as was the case near Turin in February and March of 1920 (Riley and Desai, 2007: 822; see also Snowden, 1979: 163–4).

These waves of revolutionary militancy raised the prospect and, in some cases, realized, revolutionary transformation in social relations suggesting the possibility of socialist revolution in Italy, or at least a state anchored in a form of social democracy.[16] In the context of a weak and discredited liberal state, the foundations of liberal hegemony based on the support of the bourgeoisie and middle classes collapsed, particularly as the evident weaknesses of the liberal state to deal with labour militancy (Dunnage, 1997: 64–6) was connected to the widespread perception that Italy had been humiliated in the Versailles settlement (Dunnage, 2002: 55); a variant of the 'stab in the back' myth that Hitler propagated in Germany. The democratic opening to socialism after 1912 appeared to suggest that the working class and peasants could not be socialized into liberal-constitutional democracy and the coercive apparatus of the state – fundamentally weakened after the war (Dunnage, 1997: 64–6) and the humiliation of the peace – did not have the political will or leadership to impose a crackdown from above. For a short-lived moment, then, it appeared that Italy was on the brink of socialist revolution, and it was this that is suggestive of fascism as reflecting of a form of counter-revolution.

16    In addition to the waves of strikes and land occupations the Socialist Party and its allies made major gains in the parliamentary elections of June 1919 – winning over 250 seats with the Socialists tripling their representation through securing around a third of the votes cast (Riley, 2010: 45–6; Grand, 1982: 24).

Capitalists and landlords, not the incapacitated state, moved to organize themselves against the left in place of the state.[17] Indeed, by 1920 – the high point of the *biennio rosso* – mainstream bourgeois opinion was increasingly reconciled to the need to deploy violence against the left (Maier, 1988: 306–7). Thus, leading industrialists were pressing elements within the state to consider a nationalist coup bringing in figures such as D'Annunzio, as a way of dealing with the 'red threat.' In the countryside, the black-shirted fascist *squadristi* – acting at this time with a high degree of local autonomy – became involved in strike breaking, attacking socialist co-operatives, and helping landlords reassert their class privileges (Paxton, 2004: 60–1; see also Mann, 2004: 129); in many cases with the connivance of local state officials weary of the radical left. For Sarti (1971: 20) the turning point in the rise of fascism, came in the second half of 1920 – just as the revolutionary wave (reflected in the factory occupations) was coming to its end – when the industrial leadership of Italian capital (organized in the recently created CGII – *Confederazione Generale dell'Industria Italiana*) moved to embrace fascism as a plebeian bulwark against the left and a 'revolutionary agency' capable of reconstituting the liberal state to re-ignite the fortunes of the Italian economy and capital. Significant sections of the capitalist class angered by the incapacity of the liberal state (Zamagni, 1993: 241) and frightened by the rhetoric and actions of the left searched for a political saviour. Fascism appeared to be it.[18]

In its movement phase the autonomous *squadristi* sections in the country-side flirted with talk of radical social transformation and its programme of June 1919 called for the eight-hour day, pensions and wider social security reforms, worker participation in management decisions and tax rises (Riley, 2010: 43–4; Sarti, 1971: 23).[19] Mussolini, ever the opportunist but also a clever observer of

---

17 Something that landlords, as Frank Snowden (Snowden, 1986: 143–4) documented, had been doing prior to the war using violent criminal elements in response to growing labour militancy and Socialist Party organizing.

18 The Fascist Party was created in Milan in March 1919, starting out as a loose coalition of different groupings rather than a well-organized and coherent formation in its first year of existence, and was initially made up of former revolutionary syndicalists, some former socialists (such as Mussolini), Filippo Marinetti and other Futurists and military veterans known as *arditi* (Payne, 1995: 90). Its proclivity for and connection to violence was almost immediate as evidenced in the involvement of armed fascists in the attack and destruction of the offices of the Socialist Party's official newspaper, *Avanti!* in April 1919 (Gentile, 2012: 89).

19 Reflecting its left-nationalist origins (in terms of ideology and personnel), the initial program of the fascist movement included a levy on capital, an 80 percent tax on war profits and confiscation of church property (Smith, 1997: 284; Morgan, 2004: 29). However, such promises were quickly abandoned.

the direction of the political wind, maintained fascist ambivalence towards capitalism and private property while the broader revolutionary forces and context appeared ascendant and which meant at least a rhetorical commitment to a radical posture that chastened bourgeois and business opinion and ensured that some subaltern layers could be drawn away from the revolutionary left.

At its foundation, Italian fascism drew on the support of small property holders and military veterans in particular. In part, this reflected the wider social milieu within which the left-national current was popularized and in other respects that class constituency – the petty bourgeoisie – most typically fearful and insecure about its future and outside the ideological appeals of the socialist left and ruling class forces. Although fascist ideology appealed to all social layers – including workers – it was only those in small towns and, in general, outside of the social and ideological contexts of organized labour that tended to be drawn to support fascism (Mann, 2004: 110–13). Indeed, it was in rural Italy where fascism secured its greatest support both in terms of political sympathizers and *squadristi* members but with a particular over-representation of petty bourgeois and middle-class social layers including lawyers, shopkeepers, teachers, and a significant number of students, in both its membership and leadership (Clarke, 1996: 218–9; De Felice, 1980: 314–5; see also Gentile, 2012: 91–2).

The failure of the revolutionary upsurge to capture state power through a co-ordinated national revolutionary strategy provided the opening in the second half of 1920 that Mussolini was quick to seize. With the liberal state inert and discredited and the left unable to conquer political power[20] Mussolini began to court ruling class opinion across industry and agriculture that the Fascist Party could provide the radical and popular-subaltern basis to deal with the revolutionary left and move Italy out of its post-war crisis (Mack Smith, 1997: 297–8).[21] At the same time as Mussolini was courting polite and ruling class opinion presenting fascism as a natural ally of a wider coalition of anti-Socialist forces,

---

20    In this respect the left, based on the Socialist Party and its cadres, was never able to agree on and deliver a clear national political strategy of either revolutionary transformation or a form of social democracy. Thus, it did not have the means, ultimately coercive and violent, to see through a revolution in the way that the Bolsheviks had done and the Spartacists and others in Germany attempted, and, on the other hand, its parliamentary bloc was unable to craft a national political strategy to govern Italy through working with other social political currents to create a new political-constitutional settlement based on parliamentary democracy (see Renton, 1999: 58).

21    In a major speech at U'dine in September 1921 and at a subsequent meeting in October, Mussolini stated that fascism in power would result in the termination of the 'statism' that they detested (see Maier, 1988: 339; see also Sarti, 1971: 36).

the *squadristi* were forging links with other right-wing and conservative and bourgeois self-defence formations (Riley and Desai, 2007: 825) creating the classic fascist political formula of a political party with its own, independent paramilitary forces (see Gentile, 2012: 85–103).

In this respect, as Riley (2010: 51) notes, the two key developments within Italian fascism after its founding were its rapid shift to a far-right ideological position and, secondly, its re-structuring as a party-militia. In the context of the *biennio rosso* and the revolutionary threat from the left – diminishing though it was through the second half of 1920 – both developments were inter-connected. Thus, the shift to the right reflected both the dominance of the Socialist Party in terms of the mobilization of workers and poorer peasants and the absence of a party of the right committed to radical social and political transformation through the overthrow of the liberal 'Giolittian system'. Accordingly, the alliance with landlords and fractions of big capital that emerged during 1920 reflected a coming together of mutual interests rather than fascism as a 'party of monopoly capital,' be it the fascist party as an 'instrument' of capital and/or a party that had given up on any commitment to radical change. Charles Maier (1988: 313) suitably captures the cocktail of social and political forces involved in the rise of fascism,

> [i]n this osmosis of terrorism, landlords, lawyers, and business leaders found a new striking force among the middle class and lower middle class ... [A] decaying small-town bourgeoisie and a rising rural one reinforced each other. Both were defensive, either about newly acquired or newly threatened status and property. Veterans and university youth who had migrated politically from syndicalist or republican radicalism via interventionism to fascism were ready to lead them. Major landlords were prepared to defray the costs of meetings and transport and to contribute to their local newspapers; lawyers and bankers in the provincial centers intervened to prevent police response; and even Rome was willing to delay any effective repression of the new violence.

This rightward and pro-capitalist shift was inevitably connected to the necessity of dealing with the left, which had, by 1920, become the primary social and political obstacle to the kind of radical transformation that the fascists desired – that of a national and 'mass' integration of Italy based on the overcoming of class conflict and its associated imaginary. The shift, or creation, of a paramilitary arm emerged from the connection between the initial *squadristi* sections and bourgeois self-defence groups that had sprung up after 1919 and a sense that this was the necessary way that the socialists should be dealt with – which its ruling class allies did not blush at – through violence and terrorism. Competing with the left democratically via an election would not have managed to do this because there was no guarantee that the Fascist Party and its electoral allies would secure a governing majority and, further, even if they did, the left would remain a significant political force and the organized working class a continuing threat to the existing social order and fascist programme.[22] Interestingly, as Gentile (2012: 90–91) details, the membership of the Fascist Party massively increased during the period of its anti-socialist violence, going from just over 20,000 members in December 1920 to 98,000 by April 1921 and then over 187,000 in May amounting to an almost ten-fold increase.

By 1921, Italian fascism had been transformed. It was now partly funded by elements within the ruling class (Guerin, 1973: 33–4; Beetham, 1983: 8; see also Mann, 2004: 118–20; Paxton, 2004: 60–1 and Adler, 1995: 171; 437–53) with several of its newspaper outlets now began promoting fascism as a party of government and a means to rescue Italy from crisis, while its real political significance was being secured through increasing waves of intimidation and violence against representatives and assumed supporters of the left and especially in the countryside (Riley, 2010: 52; Gentile, 2012: 89; see also Lyttelton, 1979: 104–35, 2004a: 50–60; Corner, 2002: 40–1). The significance of the urban-based *squadristi* 'expeditions' into the countryside – that concentrated on the areas where the socialist leagues had made their furthest social and political advances during the *biennio rosso* – saw fascist violence not only destroy the political structures that the left had created, but also their social base as agrarian labourers now confronted a choice of unemployment and destitution or work under the auspices of the fascist unions that had replaced the socialist leagues (see Corner, 2002: 41). Indeed, it was its violent dimensions[23] where

---

22    The Fascist Party failed to make inroads into Socialist support and political dominance in the national elections of November 1919 and the local ones a year later, which indicated not only that fascist propaganda could not break the Socialist Party's stranglehold over most of the Italian working class, but that its ideological appeals framed in the lexicon of the left were no way to increase fascist political support.

23    As Emilio Gentile argues, violence was the defining method of political action of fascism born from its proximity to World War One and its cult of speed and action. Gentile (2012: 95) quotes from the official newspaper of Italian fascism dated 20 November 1920 to convey the centrality of violence, '[t]hus the fascist smashes the socialist's head in and thereby inserts his ideas into the latter's skull. It's a guaranteed time-saving device, with all the virtues of a finely tuned and penetrating synthesis [that] acts directly on the opponentsbody both rapidly and definitively ... And what could be more of a synthesis than the shot of a pistol? ... Its efficiency lies in the fact that, with maximum economy and speed, it prevents debates from ever opening up again ... And then there's the synthesis of

Italian fascism's revolutionary character was most marked and where its radical appeal gained most traction (see Gentile, 2012: 85–103). This dynamic played out throughout 1921 until the 'fascist insurrection' of the so-called 'march on Rome' in October 1922 that brought Mussolini into power. During this period the left was violently intimidated and terrorized[24] – a form of one-sided civil war played out but where the coercive apparatus of the state was largely passive accept in some local cases assisting the fascists (see Maier, 1988: 316–7; Mack Smith, 1997: 303) – whilst the ruling class, at first the landlords but increasingly the leaders of industrial capital, pressed Giolitti to invite Mussolini into government as a way of finally bringing order to Italy.

In the months leading up to the 'march on Rome' of late October 1922 Italy was caught in a period of political stasis as the successive liberal governments of Giovanni Giolitti, Ivanoe Bonomi and Luigi Facta, respectively, struggled to maintain both parliamentary support to pass legislation and cohere a policy framework to deliver Italy out of its political and economic crisis that combined with the weakness and fragmentation of the key organs of the state to maintain the rule of law and social order across the north of the country in particular. Whereas the momentum had been with the radical left and the Socialist Party over 1919–1920, by 1921 with an economic recession undermining the strike weapon[25] and fascist black-shirts ever more on the offensive – and increasingly assisted by local agents of the state's security apparatuses in the countryside (Dunnage, 2002: 59)[26]– the tide was beginning to turn against

---

all syntheses and hence the favourite of fascists: the bomb. The fascist loves this weapon, which is more powerful than some unknown divinity or some woman one knows only too well. The bomb is adorably divine, and the fascist divinely adores it.'

24   Emilio Gentile (2012: 92) documents that in 1920, 172 socialists were killed and by mid-way through 1921 a further 89 had been murdered.

25   Thus, this material context significantly undermined the political effectiveness of the strike weapon as a means to realize a non-fascist future for Italy. And this was revealed with the failure of left's 'last shout' – with the lacklustre support for the national strike called on July 31, 1922. The aim of the strike was to put pressure on liberals to make concessions to the left as a basis for an anti-fascist reformist government. However, the shortfalls in support for the strike – even in some of the *Confederazione Generale del Lavoro's* (CGL) strongest branches – demonstrated the weakness of the left whilst, at the same time, highlighting the continuing challenge to industrial capital of a politically-militant working class. The outcome was the worst of both worlds for the Italian left and opened the door – that much wider – for Mussolini's entrance into power (see Clarke, 1996: 220).

26   After the mutiny of soldiers garrisoned at Ancona in June 1920, which drew on local working-class support, the Italian General Staff – worried over the loyalty of troops influenced by the rising left – issued a circular to officers recommending co-operating with local fascists as a possible ally in dealing with domestic disorder. By the summer of 1922 such sympathies were openly declared (Lyttelton, 2004a: 39).

the left. Thus, the revolutionary potential of the *biennio rosso* had exhausted itself (Morgan, 2004: 49) and, at the same time, the possibilities for constructing a left-centrist political and social coalition to secure political stability and deal with the violence and social disorder had also dissipated.

The failure of the Socialist Party's political strategy, however, only takes us so far in explaining Mussolini's accession to power. Indeed, as already suggested, the organs of the state had already declared their political and ideological preferences[27] – indicative of the para-political properties of the bourgeois state – in their failure to clamp-down on intensifying fascist violence. And even though the *biennio rosso* had also reflected social disorder and aspects of violence and intimidation, this paled in comparison with fascist violence in terms of attacks on the person and the killing of political opponents. The fact that fascist violence was not directed at the state but, rather, at the left and that ruling class opinion – conservative and liberal in equal measure – took comfort from this distinction and was a crucial element in the developing embrace between fascists and elites.

Indeed, the role of liberal and conservative forces in facilitating fascism soon became clear, as Giolitti invited Mussolini and the Fascist Party to join his National Bloc's electoral list in the May 1921 General Election that resulted in 35 fascists, (including Mussolini) being elected to parliament. Giolitti's decision was motivated by both the exigencies of parliamentary arithmetic and the attempt to construct a majority for governing, as well as the expectation that the experience would socialize Mussolini and fascism into the liberal-constitutional order ( Grand, 1982: 34; Morgan, 2004: 57–8). While Mussolini indicated a willingness to play the electoral game – which the result of the last free election revealed that the Fascist Party would never come close to winning on its own – he was forced to walk a delicate line given the strengths of local fascist chieftains or *Ras*. These local fascist leaders – whose local sources of power were based on mobilizations of *squadristi* – were much more committed to violence and paramilitarism and who also held the parliamentary system in contempt calling for a 'revolutionary transformation' into a new corporatist political order. In this respect, then, the liberal state's indulgence

---

27    As revealed with the outlawing of the communist paramilitary organization, *Arditi del Popolo* – that had been established in response to *Squadristi* violence – by the Bonomi government in the summer March 1921 while the fascist equivalent was not only tolerated but increasingly drew on active support from significant elements of the police force. And this kind of co-operation got official sanction in 1922 through the political favours granted to provincial fascists by the last non-fascist Prime Minister, Luigi Facta (see Dunnage, 1997: 67).

of the Fascist Party's militia – much of which was funded by local business and landlord elites (Morgan, 2004: 52) – demonstrated a clear diminution of the principles of liberal-constitutional order, as the Fascist Party was the only party that not only had its own militia but a militia that was engaging in regular acts of illegal violence.

This implicit endorsement of fascist paramilitarism and its ruling class funding and (localized) state-enabling brings the parapolitical dimensions of the liberal constitutional state into clear focus. Italian fascism not only benefited, then, from elite support in the form of newspaper commentary and propaganda and financial resources but was also advantaged by both the organization of the state and its overriding commitment to preserving the existing social order. Such tendencies and institutional spaces provide a generic advantage for and means of enabling of the far-right counter-posed, in most respects, to the forces of the radical left that tend to the be the target of the coercive and security apparatuses of the state. In the case of the rise and success of Italian fascism, the parapolitical dimensions of the liberal state were revealed through the inter-change of personnel across state institutions with the fascist *squadristi* – and not just the police – and also in terms of the legal and administrative workings of the state (something that also played out after the war with respect to the legal sanctions that former fascists were subject to compared to left and communist partisans). The fact, then, that fascist violence was treated differently to the violence of the left – and when the latter's violence was largely against private property and raised the spectacle of social breakdown and subversion of prevailing social hierarchies that implicated and undermined the state – was not just about an ideological affinity between fascists and the social and political elites, but that the liberal constitutional state was organized in a manner (and especially in moments of crisis), that institutionalized political opportunities for fascist-like agents.

The relationship between fascist violence and its principal agents – the locally organized *squadristi* – and the political leadership of the party centred on Mussolini, alongside the parallel tactics of anti-socialist terror and elite-level talks and parliamentary deal-making was far from smooth or without tensions. Such strains came to a highpoint in the internal crisis of fascism in the summer of 1921 when several *squadrisiti* leaders moved to sabotage Mussolini's elite-level strategy centred on the so-called 'pact of pacification' orchestrated by the liberal prime minister, Ivanoe Bonomi, to bring fascist para-legal violence to an end and as Mussolini tried to consolidate fascism as a political party. Denounced as a traitor by some of the provincial *Ras*, Mussolini not only had to quickly disown the pact, but the ordinances of the new national Fascist Party (founded in November 1921) included recognition of its own paramilitary organization; a price that Mussolini had to pay for acceptance of his continued leadership of the party at that time (see Clarke, 1996: 217; Gentile, 2012: 93–4). Such tensions continued to play out over the coming years and were not resolved until Mussolini managed to bring all of the local *squadristi* under his direction through the centrally-appointed fascist prefects in late October 1925, which was followed by a purge of large numbers of *squadristi* over 1928–9 (Morgan, 2004: 101–2).[28]

With the inability of liberals and conservatives to craft a governing majority, and the left not strong enough either and with the extra-parliamentary path evidently exhausted with the failure of the general strike in July 1922, Mussolini's Fascist Party looked to be the sole political actor that could bring the crisis to an end. Indeed, the fascists had played a crucial role in destroying the political and mobilizing capacities of the left and had also, in many respects, replaced the local agents of the state as the chief defenders of private property even as many of them talked of the need for corporatist revolution to reconstitute relations within the factory. It was in this context that the 'final act' of Mussolini's path to power played out.

The so-called 'march on Rome' when Mussolini and fascism purportedly 'seized power' in a show of fascist strength, could also be read as one of the greatest bluffs in political history. In the months leading up to late October 1922, local fascist *Ras* had been testing their power through continuing to prosecute violence against trade unions and socialists, as well as defying local state officials and, in some cases, forcing them from political office and thus, in effect, leaving local fascist chieftains in *de facto* control of some municipalities (Gentile, 2002: 148–9). In this respect, the tactics of the 'march on Rome' had been successively tested. But this case – the threat of armed fascists marching into the capital and seizing control of the offices of the state in a city with a sizeable and well-armed garrison – was of an altogether different magnitude. As it was, and despite the mobilization of fascist squads outside of Rome, it was the manoeuvring and lobbying from leading industrialists and military chiefs

---

28    One of the most notorious examples that reflected the dual character of fascism and Mussolini's duplicity and the complicity of liberal and conservative elites, concerned the murder of the socialist parliamentarian Giacomo Matteotti by a group of fascists in June 1924 after he had made a speech condemning fascist violence and fraud in the May election. The murder was widely condemned, and Mussolini's governing partners demanded that those implicated in the assassination be punished. As it was, while Mussolini allowed two leading fascists (Cesare Rossi and Giovanni Marinelli) to be arrested the crisis did not threaten the stability of the government as it easily survived a vote of no confidence (in which the liberal political philosopher, Benedetto Croce, supported the government); see Morgan (2004: 81–5); Grand (1982: 52); Lyttelton (2004a: 240–43).

pressing for Mussolini and the Fascist Party to be brought into government (Grand, 1982: 35–6) that smoothed the way of Mussolini's accession to power.

In this sense, while Mussolini and fascism's access to state power was realized through the constitutional formality of being invited to form a government after an audience with King Victor Emmanuel on October 29, the spectre of armed fascist squads only served to concentrate the minds of the key decision-makers around the King. The bluff worked. And the myth of fascist impregnability and supremacy was realized with the fascist squads allowed to march into Rome a couple of days later. Mussolini had taken a risk but the ultimate decision to indulge fascism had been taken some time before October 1922 through the connivance of elites to fascist terror. And the decision by the King to suspend the implementation of martial law, which would have, in all likelihood, called Mussolini's bluff (Lyttelton, 2004a: 85), was based on a political calculation that the time was right for fascism to govern.

The ambiguity of the way that fascism came to power in October 1922 – at this time as the leading element in a coalition government with conservatives, liberals, and nationalists – was reflected in the initial period of governance up until 1924–5 when the construction of a fascist dictatorship was initiated. Through this period the tensions within the Fascist Party between its revolutionary and paramilitary elements – many of whom were committed to the termination of parliamentary rule and the construction of a corporatist state – and those around Mussolini seeking to consolidate fascist power in the existing institutions of the state and its relationship with existing political elites and the ruling class continued.

The parliamentary elections that took place in April 1924 reflected the dual character that increasingly defined Italian politics as the constitutional normalities of parliamentary elections that reflected the fiction (by then) that an alternative to fascism (let alone the left) could come to power. Thus, the elections took place in a context of heightened fascist intimidation and violence. Consequently, the fascist-led National List was triumphant capturing over 60 percent of the vote share which secured Mussolini's constitutional authority (that was assisted by the Acerbo electoral – passed in July 1923 – which was introduced to support or favour the Fascist Party and lessening the requirement of parliamentary majorities based on multiple parties through disproportionately favouring the party that gained the most votes) alongside the continuing embrace of liberals and conservatives as part of the ruling coalition. However, the fiction of parliamentary democracy was not to last much longer.

Having secured the levers of power and facing continuing pressure from within the ranks of the Fascist Party, dictatorship was formalized over 1925–6 as fascist deputies in parliament voted for laws that instituted dictatorship with the ban on freedom of association (November 1926) – formalizing something that had become, in effect, a reality due to the impact of fascist violence – the banning of all political parties (other than the Fascist Party) at the end of 1926, the outlawing of strikes (April 1926) and Mussolini and the Fascist Grand Council increasingly taking centre stage as the seat of executive power. Draconian 'anti-subversive' legislation was introduced such as the 'law for the defence of the state' and state officials in the courts and in public administration were replaced by fascist appointees. However, the organization of much of the state apparatus remained in place alongside its leading personnel and, as we shall see in the discussion that follows, below, on fascist political economy, social property relations and the balance of social power between capital and labour continued to favour the former. Indeed, prior to the outbreak of the Great Depression fascist political economy remained largely orthodox in its monetary and fiscal arrangements and there was little evidence of a sustained commitment to statism or corporatism.

The means by which fascism came to power remained within the framework of a constitutional order even if the wider social and political context reflected a period defined by fascist-inspired terror and para-legal violence not only indulged by conservative and liberal elites but also, in many cases, financed by ruling class forces that severely corroded the basic principles and operational values of liberal democracy. Such a milieu and formula would be replicated to a significant degree in the case of Nazism. The immediate political context for fascism's entry into power was defined by a sustained period of social and political crisis that at first involved the radical left and which, in many respects, approximated a revolutionary crisis. The fact that revolution was not realized was crucial for the rise of fascism given that one of its generic features is its revolutionary dimension that derives from the existence of a revolutionary crisis that is unfulfilled by the left.

In this respect, Italian fascism's rise to power could be seen to reflect a form of *passive revolution* understood as a process whereby a modernization or reconfiguration of state society relations takes place through the leadership of a mass party drawing on extant revolutionary impulses but where the fundamental and structural character of the social order is left largely intact but where the political and administrative organization of the state is reshaped (Davis, 1979; Riley and Desai, 2007: 815–6; see also Morton, 2007, 2010). Fascism's emergence and the social and political context which allowed it to grow is inseparable from the revolutionary crisis that defined Italy over 1919–20. The crisis revealed the weakness of the existing state and the widespread appetite for radical change in Italy, but it was the weakness and failure of the left to take full political advantage of the situation that resulted in the revolutionary dynamic and mobilization manifesting into para-legal violence and the overturning of the liberal-constitutional order by fascists.

Fascism's entry into power was neither through a democratic mandate of winning an election – the election victory of April 1924 of the electoral bloc that the Fascist Party led was based on a combination of the Acerbo Law that assigned additional seats to the party that gained the most votes and widespread violence and intimidation of other parties – nor a revolutionary seizure of power. Consequently, the key structures and institutions of the state remained intact through the duration of fascist power up until 1943–4. Likewise, the class structure and the privileges accruing to agrarian landlords and industrial capital. Further, while the 'fascist masses' – and the petty bourgeois social backbone of fascism – were integrated into the state via their membership of the party and the establishment of some parallel fascist corporatist institutions, workers in the cities and the countryside secured few material benefits from fascist rule (Grazia, 1992: 9). Fascist Italy reflected a state-society construct that was distinct and different from both its liberal-constitutional predecessor and that of other European liberal democratic states. It pioneered some novel methods and institutional forms of governance centred on the Fascist Grand Council and plebiscites confirming and legitimizing dictatorship, but the institutions and personnel of the state were not remade, and the operations of capitalist industry and agriculture continued and largely conformed to the generalized properties of other capitalist states at the time. I now move on to look at developments in Germany after World War One.

## 2.2 Germany: Capitalist Crisis and the International Political-Economic Contradictions of the Weimar Republic

Like its Italian counterpart German fascism emerged out of the distinct conjunctural constellation produced by World War One and its immediate social and political aftermath. The Nazi Party emerged from several extreme nationalist currents after the war and initially in the formation of the Deutsche Arbeiterpartei (DAP) in early 1919 that morphed into the *National sozialistische Deutsche Arbeiter partei* (NSDAP) in February 1920. It came under Hitler's leadership from July 1921. The emergence, growth, and ultimate success of National Socialism – in gaining political power in 1933 – paralleled many of the particularities that defined Italian fascism. Thus, its social base and uneven geographical character – with respect to its concentrations of support – its organizational features around a dominant and charismatic personality holding together the contradictory ideological dynamics and tensions within the movement, the role of violence and terrorism in its political strategy and the ambivalence as to its revolutionary commitment, notably with respect to its anti-capitalist rhetoric and commitments,[29] which ensured an uneasy relationship with ruling class social forces.

While a fascist form of politics emerged in the immediate revolutionary context of the war's end in November 1918 as revealed in the *Freikorps* and their role in suppressing the revolution, the relationship between Nazism and the context of revolutionary crisis was quite different to that which characterized the Italian fascist experience. Thus, though the context of revolutionary crisis – as evidenced in the breakdown of state authority and social disorder alongside the strength of the left-wing and revolutionary forces – was a key stimulant for Nazism, indeed, it permeated and partially defined its inner characteristics as a mode of politics; what ultimately defined Nazism and determined its political dynamics and possibilities of growth and access to political power was the fragile and unstable international economic context that determined much of the politics of the Weimar Republic. And, specifically, the conjuncture of political and economic crisis that set in after 1929. So, although Nazism was baptized in the tumult of revolution after 1918 – something it shared with Italian fascism – its political relevance and 'triumph' was ultimately connected to the structural crisis of the regime of capital accumulation that emerged within Germany after 1918 and its terminal crisis over the course of 1929–33.

It was not then the prospect of social revolution that brought Nazism to power in January 1933. Rather, it was the desperation of ruling class forces within the conservative/reactionary echelons of the state and major fractions of the capitalist class to resolve the ongoing political-economic crisis of the Weimar regime's capacity to provide a social, political, *and* geopolitical framework for restored capital accumulation. In the words of David Abraham (1986: xvi),

---

29    The NSDAP's party programme of 1920 contained significant elements that suggested a commitment to a form of socialism reflecting the so-called 'brown current' associated with Gregor Strasser and Ernst Röhm, that continued to play an important role in Nazi propaganda, electoral strategies, and recruitment through to the early 1930s. Indeed, Röhm's leadership of the SA (*Sturmabteilung*) storm-troopers meant that the revolutionary-socialist pretensions of the NSDAP were an important basis of the internal ethos and recruitment of the SA. The pledges in the 1920 programme of the 'primacy of the worker over the exploiter' as well increased welfare spending, abolishing incomes unearned by work and a radical land reform programme (see Mann, 2004: 142) all complicated relationships with ruling class agents and ensured – that even in the midst of the crisis after 1929 – German capitalists did not, immediately, move to embrace Hitler or press for a Nazi-led solution to the crisis. Indeed, it was not until the 'night of the long knives' in the summer of 1934 when Röhm and other leaders of the 'brown faction' were murdered on Hitler's orders that the 'revolutionary socialist' current was ultimately cast-off by the NSDAP.

[n]o other force [other than the NSDAP] could claim genuine popular support while also demonstrating a credible commitment to eliminating Weimar's fragmented political democracy and generous welfare arrangements. Industrialists wanted class peace, an economy free to accumulate and generate profits, and a re-ascendant Germany.

And in this respect the political logic that the capitalist class demonstrated in the context of the revolutionary crisis of 1918–19 – that made it accept social and political concessions with the creation of the Weimar Republic – was replicated over 1932–3 when they moved to embrace Nazism as the last remaining political option, that offered the possibility of restoring profitability through the destruction of the Weimar settlement backed by mass support that the other anti-Weimar forces in the centre and right of German politics could not deliver.

Nazism also emerged out of a *longue durée* quite different from that of Italian fascism that was reflected in the longstanding organizations of far-right and extreme nationalist movements that had developed in the two decades prior to the outbreak of the First World War. Such movements had played a key role in promoting German militarism, a racialized nationalism and an imperialist model of political-economy grounded on geopolitical aggression. Indeed, the Nazi policy of *Lebensraum* (based on the creation of a German colonial empire in eastern Europe through annexing territories, population clearances, and ethnic German settlement in Poland and the western territories of the USSR) had been a longstanding imperial objective of significant fractions within the Wilhelmine ruling class (Baranowski, 2011; Friedrichsmeyer, 1998; Poiger, 2005; Smith, 1986) and the goal of far-right movements such as the of the *Bund der Landwirte* and *Alldeutscher Verband*. Such movements and ruling class sentiments continued after 1918 highlighted in figures such as Erich Ludendorff – the Prussian militarist, strategist and potential wartime putschist and dictator who was an early member/associate of Hitler in the NSDAP (who took part in the so-called Munich 'Beer Hall putsch' in November 1923) – and others such as Alfred von Hugenberg (a co-founder of the *Alldeutscher Verband* and leader of the *Deutsch nationale Volks partei* (DNVP)) which was a key ally (and rival) of the NSDAP.

Both the social forces of the far-right and their connection to elements within the state apparatus, notably the senior echelons of the army, judiciary, and parts of the civil service – the legacies of the *Kaiserreich* that remained in place after 1918[30]– meant that the far-right continued to be embedded within

---

30   Indeed, the East Elbian Junkers exercised a unique – in the context of post-1918 Europe – influence over and power within the Weimar state (Abraham, 1986: 10–11) compared to

the fabric of German society and state after 1918 to a significant degree, providing an important and positive contextual political milieu for Nazism to develop within. While this was the case, it was the Nazi variant of the German far-right that prospered most, becoming the dominant and, ultimately, most necessary strand of far-right by the early 1930s. In this sense, although Nazism undoubtedly benefited from both the structural context of the political-economic regime of the Weimar Republic and, especially, the crisis that engulfed it after 1929, it was also the case that it managed to carve out a distinct social and political position on the extreme right of German politics by the early 1930s that was reflected in its combination of a mass appeal and a political language and aesthetic that succeeded in responding to the particular grievances, insecurities (and hatreds) of a large swathe of the German public and across a wide range of social layers (Larsen, et al., 1980; Mann, 2004: 18–20, 26–7, 53, 161; Paxton, 2004: 64–8, 78, 83–4) more so than any other far-right current. In stating this, the rise and 'triumph' of Nazism was far from a foregone conclusion in 1918 and it is the task of what follows in this section to account for this turn of events.

Let us begin with an examination of the structural context – international/geopolitical and political and economic – that defined the Weimar Republic and the political context within which Nazism emerged and defined itself against. The first thing to note is that the establishment of the Weimar Republic reflected the interconnections between domestic social conflict (between capital and labour in particular) that exploded in the final days of the war and its immediate aftermath and the geopolitical position that Germany found itself within (Anievas, 2014: 143). This relationship, indeed, the geopolitical framing or determination of Weimar was to be crucial in shaping its subsequent evolution and possibilities for long-term survival and stability. We might see this as the structural determinant of Nazism. Further, the fact that Weimar's emergence was also intimately connected to the international political-economic order established by the Treaty of Versailles – which could be seen as the other parent of Weimar – meant that its legitimacy was severely undermined in the eyes of the German right.

The Weimar Republic emerged from the revolutionary turmoil that engulfed Germany at the war's end through a combination of increasing social strife on the domestic front, mutinies by military personnel and the government suing

---

other traditional landlord classes that not only reflected the partial or aborted character of the German Revolution and the class compromise of Weimar, but also the combined character of Germany's social and political development, which revealed itself in the reproduction of reactionary imaginaries and political strategies within the very modern and developed context of Germany's political economy.

for peace. Out of this context a revolutionary crisis emerged where radical-ized soldiers allied with workers seized government buildings and workplaces declaring 'socialist republics.' The German Revolution, however, was to be short-lived, crushed between the marshalling by state authorities of far-right paramilitary forces centred on the *Freikorps*[31] alongside a new constitutional and social settlement framed by the SPD that saw the end of the monarchy, the dismantling of the Prussian three class voting franchise and the creation of a parliamentary republican system of government based on universal suffrage. In addition to this political transformation the new state took on a distinct social complexion that reflected the strength of the organized working class and the relative weakness of capital helping to secure the allegiance of the working class and thereby extinguishing the flames of revolutionary temptation.[32]

The establishment of the Weimar Republic reflected a significant victory for the German working class and a major setback for the interests of big capi-tal. However, the balance of social forces and the broader international and geopolitical context that had helped produce Weimar were to be short-lived. Accordingly, the long-term contradictions of the German political economy soon began to reveal themselves reflecting the *conjuncturally-mediated* deter-minations of the structural dynamics of Germany's uneven and combined development, which was as much about decisions and structural forces ema-nating from without – and the Anglo-American powers in particular – as it was with decisions and processes located within Germany. Indeed, for the leaders of German industry the concessions – the limits on the length of the work-ing day (the Stinnes-Legien agreement),[33] the place of organized labour in the management decisions of firms (via the newly established ZAG (*zentralar-beitsgemeinschaft*) or Central Working Community) and the constitutional/legal clause enforcing compulsory state arbitration of industry-wide trade dis-putes – were all regarded as temporary measures that reflected the proximity of the revolutionary context that they were agreed within, and the balance of social forces at the time. Simply put, they were agreed for the sake of the fundamental class interests of capital given the balance of political forces and risks at the war's end. In the longer-term such arrangements could not be tol-erated (Gluckstein, 1999: 41; Geary, 1983, 1990: 99; James, 1986: 191) given the

---

31  Supported and financed by large landlords in the east (James, 1986: 253).

32  See note #6 above for detail.

33  However, a key element of the post-war 'class compromise' – the eight-hour working day – did not last long in heavy industry and was rolled back with the introduction by employers of a new working time regulation (Arbeitszeitverordnung) in December 1923 (see Weisbrod, 1979: 252, 256).

impact that they would have on the power of capital in the labour process and on profitability.[34]

The international conditioning of Weimar and its capitalist development was fundamentally linked to the reparations regime that was imposed on Germany in the 1919 Versailles settlement (see Kent, 1991). While this provided an important ideological leitmotif for the Nazis and the far-right in general, it was its economic consequences that were to prove to be of most signifi-cance in the rise of Nazism. The reparations settlement amounted to a bill of £6.6 billion – the equivalent of 1.5 times the sum of Germany's GNP in 1929 (Gluckstein, 1999: 39; Hobsbawm, 1994: 98). For most sensible observers – not just John Maynard Keynes (see Keynes, 2003) – at the time, this figure was a fantasy that would never be fully paid, but in the context of a post-war poli-tics defined by dashed hopes and false promises, politically, it made short-term sense in Paris and London and, for the US, if such an arrangement assisted in its debtors being able to service their debts to it, all the better (Kent, 1991: 103–38; Hobsbawm, 1994: 98–99).

The reparations burden was a permanent wound stabbing at the heart of Weimar, which meant the domestic political economy and the relations between capital and labour and possible sources and strategies for capital accumulation were tied to Germany's international legal obligations (and the geopolitical sanctions if such obligations were not met) associated with rep-arations. However, the reparations question went much further than the pol-itics of Weimar or how international economic diplomacy conditioned and framed the policy decisions – notably in public expenditure and taxation – of Weimar governments. Rather, the reparations issue and, in particular, its direct connection to the issue of inter-Allied war debt owed to the United States (see Costigliola, 1984; Hogan, 1991: 13–77; Leffler, 1979; Schuker, 1988) with respect to the two biggest debtors – Britain and France – meant that a substantial part of the world economy was affected by the diplomatic bickering, frustrations, short-term advantages and the obstinance of the US. The upshot of this is that the possibility of expanding global demand was fundamentally undermined by the international politics of reparations and because of this an important and, in some respects, only viable economic option for the stability and long-term viability of the Weimar Republic was closed off because the major capitalist

---

34    As Dick Geary (1990: 99) posits, by as early as 1922 business leaders in the RDI (*Reichsverband der Deutschen Industrie*) looked forward to a near future of cuts in social welfare and tax and the ending of the eight-hour working day and the other constitutionally-guaranteed 'privileges' secured by labour after 1918.

economies were not able and were not willing to prioritise demand after 1918 (see Kent, 1991).[35]

The fundamental economic problem for Weimar was that it confronted a need to find and develop sources of capital accumulation that would allow it to both service the debt regime imposed upon it by the liberal powers and grow its economy to ensure the profitability of German capital and the economic bases of social peace and the political and geopolitical stability of the regime through funding the Weimar socioeconomic settlement. To these problems were added the structural problem of Germany's uneven and combined development as illustrated by the divisions within capitalist industry between a protectionist-oriented heavy industry in coal, iron and steel, and an export-oriented cluster in chemicals and newer technologies alongside the continuing burden of an agricultural sector dominated by large unproductive estates which also clung to tariff-based protectionism (Bessel, 1978: 204–13; Tooze, 2007: 1–33). Such structural problems had been made worse by the post-war settlement as Germany lost both population, territory[36] and material resources[37] that further aggravated the weaknesses and vulnerabilities of heavy industry.

The early years of Weimar's history were marked by political instability reflected in the revolutionary challenges from the left[38] as well as the far-right with the Kapp putsch of March 1920 and the Hitler's Munich (Beer Hall) putsch of November 1923. However, in spite of these frailties the strong social

---

35    Further, Britain and France had also quickly moved – under the cover of war – to capture markets formerly dominated by German exports and were not willing to give up such gains at peace (Anievas, 2014: 148; see also Hehn, 2002: 9–41, 62–98; Newton, 1996: 17–34; Segal, 1987).

36    Ensuring that Weimar had a festering revanchism for the over-turning of the Versailles territorial settlement in Central and Eastern Europe (see Baranowski, 2011: 119–55; Bessel, 1978: 204–13).

37    Germany lost almost 80 percent of its iron ore production, just under half of its pig iron capacity, and about one-third of its steel plant and rolling mill capacity. It was also the case that the reparations settlement meant that about half of its coal production would be requisitioned for reparations (Weisbrod, 1979: 248; see also Abraham, 1986: 28).

38    After the November Revolution of 1918–19 was crushed the revolutionary left – organized within the Communist Party (KPD) and its off-shoots – made several attempts to seize power in the early years of the Weimar Republic. The most significant attempts took place in March 1921 and in October 1923. Both were crushed by state authorities that reflected the foundational split across the left between the KPD and the SPD that had partly determined the fate of the German Revolution, as well as the strength of the coercive apparatus of the Weimar state after the initial turmoil and state collapse in the immediate period after the war. In these two cases, unlike the 1918–19 German Revolution, it was the forces of the state and not the far-right *Freikorps* militia that suppressed these revolutionary attempts to seize power.

basis of support for the new Republic – not just reflected in strong working class support for it, but also the fact that ruling class forces and political elites had not, yet, moved to a position or implacable hostility towards it – and the commitment of enough of the political elite to maintain a faith with it, meant that it was able to see off these early challenges and contain the threat from the far-right and the fledgling Nazi movement.

It was to be the playing out of the longer-term and constitutive contra-dictions within the political economy of Weimar and its international/geo-political determination in particular that were to determine its fate and the possibilities of the far-right and Nazism within it. Indeed, as Adam Tooze (2007) notes in his monumental history of the political economy of Nazism, under the guidance of Gustav Stresemann[39] Weimar's political elite and dominant social forces embraced the possibilities of an international political and economic strategy focused on securing investment and market openings through a dip-lomatic relationship with the United States (Tooze, 2007: 4; see also Anievas, 2014: 14–7). Consequently, the possibilities for Germany's development after 1918 and its political stability and the wider international order were funda-mentally connected to decisions made in Washington and New York.[40] And, as Tooze notes in his analysis of the US role in the construction and manage-ment of the post-war international order, US policy was defined by a set of conceptual, cultural and institutional limitations and contradictions (Tooze, 2015a: 25–6), which meant that rather than helping to provide the basis for the long-term stability of Weimar, it ended up playing a major role in contributing to its instability and collapse.

The opening or possibility for an alternative historical path for Weimar came after 1924 with the overcoming of a combined economic and geopolitical crisis

---

39   An advocate of German imperialism prior to 1914, Stresemann served as Chancellor in 1923 (for just over three months) and as foreign minister between 1923 and 1929 where he was particularly associated with this 'Atlanticist' and liberal-internationalist strategy.

40   Britain continued to be a major source of foreign investment and overseas lending but because of the constraints imposed on it by debt-servicing and its return to the Gold Standard soon after the war, its role in stimulating global demand was significantly limited. Indeed, as Stephen Schuker (1988: 36) notes, Britain's commitment to the Gold Standard meant it placed an embargo on foreign loans for a year from the autumn of 1924 and even after this had ended financial legislation continued to ensure a preference for borrowers within the Empire (in a footnote #20, Schuker calculated that foreigners had obtained 75.6 percent of overseas new issues from Britain which shrank to 34.8 percent over 1925–29 and while the Empire accounted for only 47.3 percent of British overseas portfolio investment in 1913, its share rose to 58.7 percent by 1930). The consequence of this was that Germany was increasingly dependent on the US for sources of credit and investment.

that had engulfed Germany (and Europe more generally), and which provided a glimpse of a possible future for it. The crisis centred on Germany's default on its reparations payments in 1922 that was connected to the hyper-inflation that had surged across the German economy with the rapid and massive depreciation of the Mark – from an exchange rate of 32M to the US dollar in early 1922 the Mark plunged to 7,200 Marks to the dollar by the end of 1922.[41] The default on reparations (that took the form of coal and other commodity deliveries) triggered a Franco-Belgium military occupation of the Ruhr that highlighted the subordinate and weakened geopolitical position of Germany helping to fuel nationalist resentment. The consequent impact of the occupation on German industrial activity and the ongoing hyper-inflation reinforced the economic dilemma of Germany's inability to meet the reparations schedule (Kent, 1991: 220–42) and further undermined the longer-term prospects for a German industrial recovery due to the loss of capital stock. Much of the crisis – the hyper-inflation and the sabotaging of the reparations schedule – was a product of German political and diplomatic manoeuvring (see Feldman, 1977; Maier, 1988; Schuker, 1988); a means to engineer a crisis to provoke an Anglo-American intervention to revise or suspend reparations (Tooze, 2015: 365–71).[42] And, in this respect, it worked, as the US intervened to try to resolve the crisis through the implementation of the Dawes Plan in the autumn of 1924.[43]

The Dawes Plan provided a welcome resolution to the immediate international crisis centred on the military occupation of the Ruhr and Germany's hyper-inflation through re-establishing a revised schedule for reparations that the German government accepted thus facilitating the Franco-Belgium

41    Hobsbawm (1994: 89) noted that by 1923 the Mark had reduced to a level where it was worth one million millionth of its 1913 value, in effect, making it effectively worthless.

42    In the absence of the social and political forces to push through what would have been, in effect, a political counter-revolution after the social gains of 1918–19, there was only an international path for a 'double stabilization'. As Tooze (2015a: 371) describes it, '[i]t was this political impasse that drove the slide into disaster. Inflation was the path of least resistance. The Wirth government clung to the rhetoric of reparations fulfilment. But it did so by printing cash and dumping it on foreign exchanges. The result was a feverish domestic boom and a plunging exchange rate. By contrast with Britain and the US, up to the winter of 1922 unemployment in Weimar Germany was negligible. The bill was paid by the huge tax levied by inflation on Germany's savers. When that became unsustainable, the trigger was set for renewed confrontation.'

43    The fact that the US economy tipped into recession after May 1923 with a fall in exports (Costigliola, 1976: 482–4; Anievas, 2014: 147) obviously helped concentrate the minds of US policymakers given the continuing economic instability and reduced prospects for demand in Europe at the time.

evacuation of the Ruhr and the stabilization of the Mark based on Anglo-American loans. With the rebalancing of Germany's financial system with the backing of the main liberal international economic powers, for the first time since the end of the war a surge of foreign investment flowed into Germany (Abraham, 1986: 26). It was at this juncture – the resolution of the first major geopolitically framed international economic crisis centred on reparations – that the possibilities of stabilizing the Weimar Republic for the longer term suggested themselves.[44] Indeed, as the next four-to-five years were to show, the Weimar economy stabilized as the economy grew fuelled by a surge of US-led international investment.[45] An upswell that also contributed to a wave of speculative financing on Wall Street that came to play a major role in the crash of the US stock market and financial system in October 1929.

However, the Dawes Plan failed to address the fundamental, organic and long-term problem resultant from Germany's uneven and combined development that the Weimar and Versailles' settlements had supercharged through a conjuncturally-determined set of contradictions.[46] Although the Dawes Plan addressed the inflation problem and helped foster foreign investment and some export-led growth[47] it did not address, indeed, it brought out into a much bolder relief the structural problems of heavy industry in the form of 'a protracted crisis of overcapacity and low profits' (Anievas, 2014: 144; Abraham, 1986: 13; Mommsen, 1996: 220). The continuing problem of global industrial overcapacity – that had originated in the Long Depression of the final quarter of the nineteenth century – continued to structure the investment decisions

---

44    The geopolitical sequencing of the Dawes Plan was reflected in the signing of the Locarno Treaties in 1925, which aimed to re-stabilize and normalize the Versailles territorial settlement and Germany's place within the European geopolitical order, at least with respect to Germany's western borders. It opened the door to Germany's diplomatic normalization with its entry into the League the following year.

45    The surge in investment is well captured by Frank Costigliola (1976: 495), '[i]n the years after 1924, American investors put up 80 percent of the money borrowed by German public credit institutions, 75 percent of that borrowed by local governments, and 56 percent of the loans to large corporations. The market for foreign bonds, which American political and business leaders had so carefully nurtured, was already out of control.'

46    Thus, while the Dawes committee could and did recommend revisions to the scheduling (and content) of reparations, it did not have the legal power to reduce the total reparations figure established in 1921 (Tooze, 2015: 454).

47    Keynes suggested that for Germany to meet her reparation payments without incurring huge levels of international debt would require a 36 percent increase in the value of her exports, which, allowing for the imported raw materials embodied in the added exports, meant an actual increase of between 40–50 percent, something that was nigh-on impossible in the international trade context of the time (cited in Kent, 1991: 264).

and competitive strategies of heavy industry in particular (Riley, 2018: 9; Weisbrod, 1979). Further, an unintended consequence of the Dawes plan and subsequent surge of US sourced foreign direct investment (FDI) into Germany was that the deeply embedded developmental tendencies toward concentration, monopoly and cartelization of German industry were reinforced (Abraham, 1986: 12; see also Mommsen, 1996: 220) resulting in an intensification of the pathology of uneven development in the German economy and, politically, in the strengthening of the forces of protection and geopolitical revisionism. The significance of this was that a major fraction of the capitalist class became increasingly opposed to and determined to revise or overthrow the Weimar settlement at the international level. Given the difficulty of changing the domestic social and legal/constitutional context of capital accumulation – that would have required a constitutional amendment at least – the continuing inability of the agrarian sector to soak up spare or increased industrial capacity (James, 1986: 247; Riley, 2014: 341), ensured that demands for a radical revision of the geopolitics of the Versailles settlement began to gain traction (Weisbrod, 1990).[48] This meant that potentially explosive contradictions were ever-present within its functioning such that an internally-sourced crisis would have international and geopolitical effects[49] as occurred over 1922–23 and/or how any disruption in the functioning of the international economy and, in particular, trade relations or the flow of credit and capital to Germany, would fatally undermine the political stability within Germany that rested on the continuing suturing of the socioeconomic compromise between capital and labour.

---

48    This is particularly important because the Atlanticist strategy of pinning Germany's international orientation towards the United States was seen by Stresemann and others as a means to revise or overturn the geopolitical settlement of Versailles via an economic and diplomatic route. Thus, even amongst the more liberal fractions of the German ruling class and political elites, a revision of the 1919 geopolitical settlement was the ultimate goal; only the means – at this stage – differed (see Cohrs, 2006: 121–8; Tooze, 2007: 3–15).

49    For Stresemann, the key architect of Germany's international strategy at the time, the question of debt and its connections to reparations could now be used as a source of leverage to, once the (next crisis) moment came in the reparations schema, press for a final resolution of the issue through the use of the 'debt weapon'. Thus, in his own words from 1935, '[o]ne must simply have enough debts; one must have so many debts that, if the debtor collapses, the creditor sees his own existence jeopardized' (quoted in Tooze, 2015: 465).

Under the Dawes plan Anglo-American-backed international credit flowed into Germany after 1924,[50] but these flows of credit were not deployed to boost industrial productivity within Germany, nor to facilitate a restructuring of the contours of its political economy to ease or overcome its *longue durée* contradictions, notably with respect to the economic significance and political influence of heavy industry and the stagnation and burden of the agricultural sector.[51] The significance of agriculture for the growth of Nazism was more than just an issue around its economic significance in the vulnerabilities of the Weimar Republic, but how the structure and workings of the agrarian economy meant that the majority of popular agrarian social layers could not be incorporated into a broader cross-class alliance with the urban working class (as was the case in Scandinavia). And this meant that rural populations could be tempted by the radical if fanciful promises of the far-right (Farquharson, 1976; Luebbert, 1991:115–20,272–6; Mazower, 1999: 23–4).

This situation was partly a consequence of the political-institutional framework (and the failings of the Weimar party system) and the balance of social forces (based on the compromise between capital and labour) upon which the Weimar Republic was established. And while the Dawes settlement resolved the immediate crisis engulfing the German economy thus providing short-term relief and geopolitical stability, it did nothing to alter or overcome the structural international political-economic framework that German policy-makers and capitalists had to work within and which was, effectively, in the gift of the Anglo-American liberal powers and the US, in particular. In this sense, although it was a British-led liberal-imperialist 'hegemonic' system that conditioned and framed the political economy of the *Kaiserreich* in the two-to-three decades prior to 1914 and which, ultimately, framed the geopolitical options for Germany at this time, so it was the United States that did so after 1918. And it was this international framing – reflected in the decisions (and non-decisions), priorities and self-interests of the United States political leadership and capitalist class – that provided a key, if not defining structural determinant for the resolution of the organic contradictions of Weimar.[52]

---

50   William McNeil (1986: 1–2) calculated that between 1925 and 1930 US bankers lent nearly three billion dollars to German borrowers – over twice the $1.3 billion Germany received from the United States under the Marshall Plan.

51   After 1925 the economic outlook for the agricultural sector turned particularly negative with the new liberal-imperialist policy of Stresemann permitting increased imports and with continuing problems over access to capital and a widening 'price scissors' that culminated in the onset of an agricultural depression in 1928 (Abraham, 1986: 14).

52   See Adam Tooze (2015a) for an extended discussion and analysis of this.

The Dawes plan did manage, then, to provide short-term relief to Germany, but because its impetus and focus was limited to stabilizing the debt-transfer mechanism rather than addressing the broader deflationary tendencies operative within the post-war world economy it was not able to resolve the fundamental and structural contradictions that afflicted Germany. And as long as it restored the means of debt transfer from Paris and London to New York, then as far as US policy-makers were concerned, it was doing its job. Thus, while Germany secured some relief the US continued to prioritise international debt repayments as the bulk of the international credit that flowed into Germany after 1924 was recycled into reparation payments dispatched to France and Britain which helped fund their debt payments to the US. Further, the fact remained that unless the German economy managed to secure significant gains in its labour productivity in the near future and/or there was a massive expansion in international trade[53] the underlying contradictions and imminent sources of the next crisis remained in place. Consequently, one side of the Weimar social contract – capital or labour – would, one way or another and sooner or later, have to bear the costs of either maintaining the costs of domestic social consumption or slashing it via a major reduction on the social costs of capitalist production.

The spectre of crisis that hung over the Versailles order would soon reveal itself, but in terms of the strength of the far-right and Nazism within Germany it had not yet done so. There was a nationalist reaction to the terms of the Dawes Plan in May 1924 when the combined far-right gained over 25 percent of the votes cast (the DNVP with 19.4 percent and the Nazis, 6.6 percent), but with the short-term stabilization provided by Dawes the impetus of the far-right was, temporarily abated.[54] Indeed, between 1924 and 1928 – the period

---

53   This was undermined, if not deliberately so, by the consequences of US policy decisions through the 1920s. Thus, while the US insisted on the payment of inter-Allied war debt – which it continued to treat as a separate matter to that of reparations – it also pursed tariff polices that ended up denying increased access to the US domestic market; at the time, the largest consumer market (and in other areas of demand as well) in the world (see Tooze, 2015: 348–9, 440–61). The secondary impact of this went beyond ensuring the Anglo-French commitments to the reparations settlement, but also weakened any momentum towards expanding global demand through trade liberalization.

54   Another election followed in December 1924 that saw a slight fall in the combined far-right vote to 23.4 percent overall (DNVP, 20.4 percent and the NSDAP, 3 percent). The next national election to the Reichstag in May 1928, on the back of a decent period of economic stability and growth, and the maintenance of some degree of political stability suggested that the highpoint of the far-right had been reached, as it haemorrhaged a significant amount of support compared to the immediate period around the crisis of hyper-inflation and the Ruhr occupation, securing less than 17 percent in total (with the

of stabilization – Nazi electoral strength was weaker than the KPD polling between 2.5 and 6.5 percent (Abraham, 1986: 257).

The structural contradictions within Weimar re-emerged after 1928 and, in doing so, revitalized the far-right and the Nazis in particular. As already noted, what was to become a major social component of Nazism rooted in the German peasantry and small landholders – particularly in Schleswig-Holstein – began to suffer the consequences of both its longer-term backwardness and disarticulation within the overall political economy of Germany with the onset of an agricultural depression that began in 1928 (see Angress, 1959; Bessel, 1978: 213–15; James, 1986: 255–61; Paxton, 2004: 65). The depression, in part a consequence or legacy of the liberal-imperialist strategy of the bourgeois governments under the direction of Stresemann,[55] triggered massive peasant protest in the north of Germany in 1928 with demands for a banning of food imports, tax relief, cheap credit, reduced state bureaucratic interference and legal action against cartels. These calls combined with protests from some elements of the *Mittelstand* for protective measures to address their sense of marginalization and having been squeezed out of the social compromise and political prioritization of big (export-oriented) capital and organized labour (Abraham, 1986: 77–80). Indeed, the Nazis adopted many of these demands into their agrarian programme helping them to peel off large numbers of rural voters from their long-standing allegiance to the traditional conservative parties as well as the DNVP (Angress, 1959: 546–7; Bessel, 1978: 214–8; Farquharson, 1976: 1–42; Guerin, 1973: 55).

A key political development in 1928 was the electoral success of the SPD, which, as the largest party in the Reichstag (with 29.8 percent of the total vote) brought it back into government for the first time since 1923. Returning to power with its pledge to uphold and protect the 'daily interests of workers' as framed with the Weimar settlement and the social-welfare state, major fractions of capital and heavy industry found themselves on a collision course with the new government. Specifically, with a new Social Democratic Labour minister, heavy industrial fractions of capital were increasingly concerned about

---

NSDAP gaining only 2.6 percent of the vote – its worst ever performance) and the centre and left-wing parties (including the KPD) capturing over two-thirds of the votes and the SPD nearly 30 percent of the total.

55    As Herman Lebovics (1969: 29) argued, most of the peasant cultivators suffered from foreign competition despite some tariff protection. They also experienced a shortage of credit, and when they did get it, it was at very high rates of interest. Thus, by the mid-1920s around 52 percent of all farms were operating at a loss and in late June 1926 agricultural debt stood at RM3.7 billion, and by late March 1930 at RM7.66 billion. In that same year 2,554 farms were liquidated and in 1929 over 3,173 farms failed.

future wage arbitration disputes and their likely impact on profit rates after profitability had failed to pick-up significantly during the previous four years of general economic stability and under centre-right governments who had prioritized an industrial strategy based on the more competitive export sector. Consequently, a few months after the Hermann Müller-led coalition government came into power in October, heavy industry launched its offensive against organized labour with a lock-out of over 250,000 workers across the Ruhr heartland of heavy industry as 'an attempt by iron and steel industrialists to prevent a round of accelerated wage demands and simultaneously to attack the state arbitration mechanism' (Abraham, 1986: 246; Geary, 1990: 101; Weisbrod, 1979: 257–60).

This offensive was not, yet – by 1928–29 – a generalized verdict of German capital and its political representatives on the future of Weimar (and the Versailles settlement) republican-parliamentary order. While the SPD victory deeply worried conservative elites and significant fractions of capital, at a more fundamental level it exposed the inter-connected or co-constitutive vulnerability of the Weimar political economy because with the SPD in power it was likely that organized labour would press for increases in the social wage and put further pressure on rates of profitability. In so doing, the domestic social basis of the export-led strategy would be undermined, and a politics of class-conflict was likely to re-appear. In turn, this would (and did) have an impact on reparations payments, as the Dawes Plan had been established within a different social and political constellation. Indeed, it was premised on Germany securing a fiscal surplus.

Even before the October 1929 Wall Street crash, the contradictions began to concretize in political struggles and conflict at the domestic and international levels. In the latter, continuing German complaints about the reparations schedule led to the announcement of the Young Plan in 1929 that was formerly adopted – replacing the Dawes Plan –in January 1930. However, the arrangements and objectives of the Young Plan were quickly overtaken by the turn of international economic events. The plan itself was a modest revision to Dawes, marginally reducing the reparation annuities but it also opened up a vulnerability through abolishing the transfer protection clause[56] introduced by Dawes that was inserted to help create confidence in the scheduling of debt repayments. With this, the risk of default now exposed Germany's commercial creditors which helped to undermine the confidence in the long-term prospects

---

56    The transfer protection mechanism allowed the suspension of reparation payments if they threatened the stability of the German currency (Kent, 1991: 245).

of the scheme triggering an interest rate spike in New York (Anievas, 2014: 150; Tooze, 2007: 14). This, in turn, produced a fall in long-term capital outlays to Germany even before the October US stock-market collapse.[57]

The failure of the Young Plan to settle the reparations issue not only fuelled further nationalist resentment in Germany – exposing the SPD-led government to attacks from the nationalist right – but it also weakened a key pillar of the Atlanticist strategy that Weimar governments had relied on since 1924. The disappointments and limitations of the Young Plan reflected the limits of US hegemonic leadership in terms of stabilizing, let alone expanding, international trade relations. On the contrary, the US president Herbert Hoover's campaign pledge to voters in the mid-west to enact a policy of agrarian trade protectionism (see Tooze 2007: 14) reflected a broader political consensus with the US Congress moving to pass a major piece of trade protectionism in 1929 with the Smoot-Hawley Tariff Act, which came into force in June 1930. The tariff particularly focused on reducing European manufactured imports, which was bound to have deleterious effects on German industry and the survival of the Atlanticist-export-led strategy.[58]

US policy decisions over the course of 1929–30, in effect, severely undermined the post-1924 strategy of German capital and Weimar elites through dismantling the international institutional framework that German domestic political stability required. Inevitably, then, its harmful domestic consequences quickly followed. These became all the more significant as the leading representative of German industry, the RDI (*Reichsverband der Deutschen Industrie*), produced a memorandum in 1929 entitled 'Recovery or Collapse' which might be regarded as a general declaration by industrial capital of an offensive against the Weimar system. The significance of the memorandum was that a leading figure associated with the export-oriented fraction of German capital, Carl Duisberg, professed in January 1930 that the economic crisis in Germany was fundamentally about the burden of politically supported high taxation, high wages and social welfare costs whereby 'capital is being destroyed through the unproductive use of public funds' and where 'only an immediate and radical

---

57  After the Young Plan, France retained only 40 percent of its reparations payments, Britain barely 22 percent. The rest was passed to the United States for war debts. Tooze (2015a: 489) quotes Trotsky's verdict, '[f]rom the financial shackles on Germany's feet, there extend solid chains which encumber the hands of France, the feet of Italy and the neck of Britain.'

58  As Harold James (1990: 42) opines, '[a]n international consensus on budget stabilization – in practice deflation – as propagated from Herbert Hoover and Montagu Norman ...decided Germany's destiny during the world crisis.'

reversal in state policies' could address the issue (cited in Abraham, 1986: 254). Such interventions not only suggested that the domestic social basis of the Atlanticist strategy had broken down but that capital in general now saw the Weimar parliamentary system as little more than a means to enact social policy denouncing it as *Gewerschaftsstaat* or a 'union state' (Mommsen, 1996: 228; Geary, 1990: 103; James, 1986: 165).[59]

With the shift away from the Atlanticist strategy the representatives of heavy industry began to press the DVP (*Deutsche Volkspartei*) – its primary parliamentary interlocutor – to bring down the SPD-led coalition and, through it, open up the possibility of extra-parliamentary dictatorship. As Larry Jones (1988: 355; see also Anievas, 2014: 151; Kurlander, 2006, 2009; Mommsen, 1996: 263–8; Weisbrod, 1979: 260–1) notes, in his definitive history of the Weimar liberal parties, leaders of the DVP's right-wing (those most closely associated with heavy industry) began to mobilize party members and supporters to press the parliamentary delegation to exit the coalition government over the issue of unemployment benefits and industry's demands for tax cuts (James, 1986: 32, 178–9).[60] Indeed, this is what came to pass with the resignation of Müller and the collapse of the SPD-led coalition in March 1930.

The collapse of the SPD government pushed Weimar towards the political abyss. With its international prop cut away and, with the turmoil in the US financial system triggering the onset of the Great Depression, the international political economic context was about to shift onto a very different, indeed, catastrophic, plateau for the German economy over the next few months. In this scenario, the strain of reparations was to take Germany and the world economy towards breaking point. Domestically, however, in terms of the political management and governing within Germany, at this critical juncture, the country did not have a stable parliamentary government. The SPD would not govern to

---

59   At this stage capital and the leaders of heavy industry in particular had not moved to embrace Hitler and the Nazis but they had made a political commitment to overturning Weimar as evidenced in their role in the establishment of the League for the Renewal of the Reich (*Bund zur Erneuerung des Reichs*) in September 1927, as well as through their continuing support for Hugenberg's DNVP (Mommsen, 1996: 258).

60   As well as the growing disillusionment of the bourgeois centre with the Atlanticist strategy and the Weimar system, one of the key ideological and policy architects of Stresemann's policy, the Reichsbank president, Hjalmar Schacht, also moved towards the extreme right, denouncing the terms of the Young Plan and the policies of the Müller government, advocating abrogation of Germany's treaty obligations, and raising the issue of territorial revisions to Versailles (Tooze, 2007: 16). Indeed, the role of Schacht went beyond this as the Reichsbank was the driving force behind legislation passed in 1929 that limited the size of government deficits (James, 1986: 32), which closed off a temporary means of overcoming the impasse between capital and labour through deficit financing.

the tune of industrial capital and the centre and right – who could not muster sufficient votes to secure a parliamentary majority – were committed to slashing social-welfare spending and pushing through a range of other reforms to 'liberate capital'. However, the generalized opposition to the Social Democrats and the parliamentary system did not amount to a plan for government, nor a unified strategy for capitalist accumulation, let alone one that could unify the fractions of capital (and the Junkers) (see Abraham, 1986: 271–318) in the midst of the developing world economic crisis.

The immediate and short-term solution was the minority government of Heinrich Brüning of the (Catholic) Centre Party who succeeded Müller as Chancellor. Initially supported by significant sections of capital[61] who looked positively on Brüning's commitment to social welfare and tax reform, the government moved to impose deflationary policies as a means to secure the confidence of international capital markets as well as industry, as the social costs of accumulation began to be clipped back. Without a parliamentary majority Brüning was forced to resort to emergency powers under Article 48 of the constitution, authorized by President Paul von Hindenburg in July 1930. Government via emergency decree – what the leading ordo-liberal thinker, Wilhem Röpke referred to as a form of 'commissarial dictatorship' (cited in Bonefeld. 2013: 247)[62] – while legally permitted and politically legitimate within the Weimar constitutional system brought into bold relief the contradictions at the heart of the social basis of Weimar's parliamentary system that had been present at its creation. The move towards extra-parliamentary government meant, in effect, that until Germany was able to overcome the economic crisis

---

61    As Dick Geary (1990: 95–6) summarizes in his excellent analysis, '[i]n general the dynamic chemical, electrical and finishing industries remained more loyal to ... Brüning between 1930 and May 1932 than did heavy industry. Committed to international reconciliation [Atlanticism] to protect their exports and low prices for basic materials these sectors were less willing to cooperate with the agrarian lobby and bitterly opposed to agrarian protectionism.'

62    Röpke, alongside other ordo-liberals writing in the early 1930s (such as Alexander Rüstow, Walter Eucken, Franz Böhm and Alfred Müller-Armack), advocated the introduction of an authoritarian form of politics based on dictatorship as the political solution to what they regarded as, primarily, a political crisis that had engulfed the Weimar system in the early 1930s. The crisis afflicting the German economy was not, then, fundamentally about the economy but, rather, a crisis derived from the politicization of the capitalist economy which they associated with the social-democratic dimensions of the Weimar state. And while they were not Nazis their position overlapped with Carl Schmitt's critique of the Weimar Republic and endorsement of Nazi dictatorship. In short, the endorsement of dictatorship and the abolition of parliamentary democracy had become a widely-shared position across all shades of German elite opinion by the early 1930s.

that it now found itself enveloped within, there was very little prospect of a return to democratic or parliamentary government.

Brüning's austerity, socially destructive as it was, broke the back of organized labour as nation-wide wage cuts were imposed and unemployment rose.[63] With domestic sources of demand drying up because of austerity, Germany's only hope for a way out of the crisis and realizing the 'competitive logic' of Brüning's deflationary policies rested on the world market.[64] It was here where the Great Depression proved decisive. By 1931 the major capitalist powers were moving towards protectionist policies. Indeed, Britain's decision to exit the Gold Standard in September 1931 resulted in Sterling's depreciation by 20 percent making Britain's exports – in a shrinking world market – that much more competitive as Sterling's value was no longer fixed to gold via Bank of England international monetary interventions. The significance of Britain's departure was that it set-off a wave of currency devaluations as other countries exited reflecting the generalized trend towards 'beggar-thy-neighbour protectionism'.

It was within this context that Nazism emerged as a mass movement. Although Hitler and the Nazis had become a far from insignificant current in Weimar politics in the immediate period preceding the world economic crisis they were not seen as a favoured option by German capital to secure its long-term political and economic interests, nor were they seen as a means of overcoming the problems of Weimar. Indeed, their electoral strength and political significance prior to the onset of the Great Depression was marginal and they were a much less significant current of the far-right than Hugenberg's DNVP. By 1929 the NSDAP had become a mass party with approximately 130,000 members (Kershaw, 2008: 194)[65] yet it had not managed to affect a major political-electoral breakthrough. It was still the minority current on the far-right behind the DNVP, and especially so in electoral terms – gaining only 2.6 percent of

---

63  Patricia Clavin (2000: 112) gives the following figures on rising unemployment: 13.1 percent in 1929; 22.2 percent in 1930; and 33.7 percent in 1931 and a staggering over 40 percent of the labour force in 1932.

64  As Tooze (2007: 17) suggests, Brüning's policies did see a positive result in Germany's trade balance which moved into surplus in 1931, but this was not because of increased exports but, rather, due to a major fall in imports reflecting the decline of German industrial activity that required imported materials and goods. Within a year – as international protectionism generalized – Germany's exports fell by 30 percent. With Germany imposing exchange controls because of capital flight (as international investors withdrew after Brüning's demand for an end to reparations in June 1931), it accelerated towards becoming a closed economy, as there were dwindling sources to pay for imports and its exports were shut-out of international markets.

65  By early 1932 membership was estimated at 450,000 and, by the end of January 1933, 719,000, reaching over four million by the end of 1933 (see Remmling, 1989: 218).

votes in the 1928 election. And even as the party grew and its violence intensified, its paramilitary arm never challenged the state's monopoly on the means of violence and the SA was always careful about how it deployed its violence – overwhelmingly concentrated on the left – not to overly provoke state authorities (Bessel, 1986: 135).

The impact of the Great Depression, however, changed the rules of the game both in terms of international as much as domestic politics. And given how much the latter conditioned the scope of space for social and political compromises within the Weimar political system the intensification of the world economic crisis transformed the domestic political terrain that both the Nazis and the other principal opponent of Weimar, the KPD, operated within. In short, , without the Great Depression it is highly unlikely that the Nazis would have grown into a mass movement able to capture one-third of the popular vote across a range of social classes making them an indispensable political ally for capital in overcoming the crisis and dismantling Weimar (Hobsbawm, 1994: 130; Steiner, 2005: 810). This was because it was the economic impact of the crisis on petty bourgeois social layers in particular that drove them into the hands of the Nazis when, previously, they had remained loyal to the conservative and nationalist forces on the right and far-right (Jones, 1988: 396: Mommsen, 1996: ix, 241, 261–2).[66] The world depression intervened as a conjunctural crisis to break the Weimar political and economic system. Servicing reparations even whilst undergoing savage cut-backs in public spending and aggressive cost-cutting to make exports more competitive (the Reichsmark left the Gold Standard in July 1931) could not continue in a context of a massive contraction in global demand.[67]

Hoover's announcement of a debt moratorium in June 1931 on intergovernmental debts was too little too late and especially given that it was not until the following summer that its terms were finally agreed at the Lausanne conference. Interestingly, while this agreement formalized the end

---

66    What this suggests is that these social forces wanted to – sometime before the Nazi *Machtergreifung* – dismantle Weimar democracy, establish an authoritarian dictatorship and suppress the left. Equally, these forces were also committed to the active dismantling of the Versailles system and geopolitical aggression. While such orientations – domestically and internationally – did not mean that, in the counterfactual history, a far-right government would have pursued the same kinds of policies in the same way as the Nazis did (unlikely given the absence of the centrality of race war in the *Weltanschauung* of the far-right compared to Hitler's thinking and strategy), it would, in all likelihood, have resulted in great power conflict.

67    German exports fell from 12.7 RM billion in 1929 to 5.7 RM billion in 1932 and imports from 13.4 RM billion to 4.7 RM billion over the same period (Kent, 1991: 4).

of reparations the British and French also insisted – against Washington's wishes – that inter-Allied debts were also to be terminated.[68] The post-1918 financial stranglehold on the world economy had been finally loosened but far too late to have any meaningful impact. In the meantime, the crisis in Germany deepened with the unemployment level moving upwards to over four million workers over the winter of 1930–31. With the possibilities of exiting the crisis closed off through existing international economic and geopolitical arrangements and opposition to austerity mounting from sections of the bourgeoisie as much as the working class, Brüning began to search for alternative geopolitical remedies through the back-door of central Europe with an attempt to create an Austro-German customs union that potentially included the wider Balkan region (Anievas, 2014: 157) that breached the spirit if not the letter of the post-war treaties.[69]

The Weimar political system began to shift to the far-right as the key social and political pillars of the Republic began to weaken. Thus, in the September 1930 Reichstag election the Nazis captured 18.3 percent of the vote – a massive increase on their 1928 performance, securing over double the share of the DNVP – coming second to the SDP (26.4 percent). The fundamental breakthrough and tipping point came, however, in July 1932 when the Nazis topped the poll with 37.1 percent of the total vote beating the SPD into second place (with 21.6 percent). This weakening of the centre was also reflected in the rise of the KPD which had now moved to become the fourth largest party in the Reichstag after capturing 14.3 percent of the vote.

Indeed, Brüning's policies played a key role in assisting the rise of the Nazis. Politically, governing by decree he marginalized the Reichstag and introduced a quasi-authoritarian system.[70] His lack of popular mandate, the freezing out of the democratic deliberation of the parliamentary process and use of emergency decrees to push through laws were indicative of a classical bonapartist arrangement with an authoritarian leader suspended above opposing

---

68  This Anglo-French decision reflected ongoing despair over the attitude of the US Congress that continued to insist on the payment of war-debts. To that end, 'by the end of 1933 Britain and France had decided to suspend payment on billions of dollars of debt they owed to the people of the US' (Tooze, 2015a: 506–7).

69  The Minister for Occupied Territories in his administration, Gottfried Treviranus also called for an 'active revisionist policy in the east that amounted to a call for the return of German lands' (Mommsen, 1996: 299).

70  As Mark Mazower (1999: 19) outlines, '[t]he growing use of article 48, however, made it difficult to determine at what point democracy slid into dictatorship. Between 1925 and 1931 only sixteen emergency decrees were issued; in 1931 there were forty-two as against thirty-five laws passed by the Reichstag; in 1932 there were fifty-nine as against five.'

and mutually neutralizing social forces (Dülffer, 1976; Linton, 1989; Trotsky, 1975: 245–57) that suggested that parliamentary democracy and the Weimar party system were dysfunctional and/or undermining of attempts to deal with the economic crisis. This goes some way in describing the temporary situation within Germany between March 1930 and June 1932. In particular, it served to discredit existing governing parties and opened up possibilities for those on the political margins, such as the Nazis, to be taken more seriously. Thus, the fateful decision in the autumn of 1931 by the standard-bearer of German liberalism (and of its Atlanticist strategy), the DVP, to withdraw its parliamentary support for the Brüning government was very significant in contributing to this ideological shift towards the far-right. As Larry Jones (1988: 430) writes,

> not only did this turn of events spell the collapse of the efforts of a number of its leaders to unite the parties of the middle and moderate Right behind the policies of the Brüning government, but it also did much to blur the lines that separated the DVP from the more radical parties on the German Right.

And given the barely-concealed – which by the summer of 1932 was more or less out in the open – sympathy of the DVP's right-wing for an alliance with the so-called 'national opposition' grouped around the far-right, its subsequent support for Hitler's 'Enabling Act' in March 1933 could be seen as a 'logical' and inevitable outcome of the working out of the crisis dialectic playing out across both the political and economic and domestic and international spheres that overcame Weimar liberalism in the early 1930s.

In effect, Brüning's tenure terminated Weimar as a democratic-parliamentary system and, with the outcome of the July 1932 Reichstag election it was clear that there was no longer a democratic basis for governing rooted in the centre-left or centre-right.[71] A popular or mass basis for governing could now only

---

71    As Mommsen (1996: 261–2: see also Jones, 1988) recognizes, however, this rightward shift
      in Weimar politics was also reflected in liberal-conservative political opinion more gen-
      erally and the political standard bearers of German liberalism – the DVP, Centre Party
      and State Party. With regard to the Catholic Centre Party he notes, that its leader, Ludwig
      Kaas 'had repeatedly made disparaging comments about Stresemann's foreign policy
      [Locarno], which he now considered "finished" … Kaas was not merely an agent for the
      Confessionalization of the Center but favored a resolute nationalist and authoritarian
      course that would break with the democratic and social conditions of German political
      Catholicism and foster the trend toward a revision of the Weimar Constitution in a more
      authoritarian direction.' Such views were already evident in the DVP leadership by 1930
      as reflected in their decision to bring down the Müller government and move to hostility

come from a left partly constituted by the KPD – absolutely anathema to dominant social interests and political elites within the state apparatus (especially the *Wehrmacht*) – or the far-right dominated by the Nazis. The September 1930 elections demonstrated the growing popular verdict on Weimar and the Brüning government in particular with the KPD and Nazis becoming the second and third largest parties. This meant that whilst Brüning could rely on the passivity of the SPD at this stage and the support of the centre and right, sooner or later an alternative government would be required that could count on some measure of popular support. Indeed, as David Abraham (1986: 256) notes, the SPD was to some degree complicit in allowing Brüning's destruction of Weimar's social security state but Brüning's partial dependence on it (given the weakness of the right and their subsequent abandonment of him in the autumn of 1931) meant that the SPD was seen as obstructing a more radical (and necessary – in the eyes of capitalist interests) dismantling of the Weimar settlement that necessitated the exclusion of any SPD influence over governmental decision-making; including its bastions of social and political power at a local and regional level – especially Prussia. And it was this that, ultimately, led to elite and ruling class manoeuvring around Hindenburg to replace Brüning with a more right-wing and authoritarian government led by Franz von Papen in June 1932.

In economic terms, Brüning's policies certainly served to reinforce this dynamic. The social catastrophe of his austerity measures – even if they were driven by international political and economic developments – not only weakened the social basis of Weimar's key social constituency, the organized working class, and the SPD, but also aggravated the agrarian social crisis and fractured *Mittelstand* social layers. Thus, as credit was squeezed and economic activity seized up,[72] it was not just workers who suffered. Scores of small-traders and producers in towns as much as farmers in the countryside went bankrupt. Thus, those social layers and the German petty bourgeoisie, in particular, who had formerly voted for the liberal and/or conservative parties now began to shift towards the Nazis, as a party that could not be held responsible for the policy failures of recent years and, while characterized by aspects of political vulgarity and violence, was committed to radical economic measures and the

---

towards any government that had SPD influence. By late 1932 even the liberal daily, the *Frankfurter Zeitung* was expressing its willingness to accept a Hitler-led government (Gluckstein, 1999: 63).

72 After 1929 there was a catastrophic collapse in industrial production which, at its lowest point, fell to 61 percent of its 1929 level in 1932; the most severe contraction across the industrialized world with the exception of the USA (James, 1986: 6).

destruction of the social state, and foreign capital, what many of these voters blamed for their current malaise.

With the collapse of the centre and mainstream bourgeois parties (the DVP, Catholic Zentrum and DNVP), as liberal and conservative voters moved towards the far-right, capitalists faced a dilemma as to how to secure their social interests in the absence of a popular basis committed to the restoration of capitalist profitability.[73] In this respect, the final chapter of Weimar, between June 1932 and January 1933 reflected a move towards *de facto* authoritarian dictatorship under the provisions of Article 48 as Hindenburg and the coterie of advisers around him attempted to form a stable government that could govern without recourse to the Reichstag. Indeed, whilst governing, since 1930 had, in effect, been carried out via the use of emergency decrees, the parliamentary representatives of German bourgeois liberalism had largely reconciled themselves to the end of Weimar and political dictatorship (Geary, 1990: 97). This was already evident in the sabotaging of the SPD-led coalition over 1929–30 and, with it, the realization that given the continuing popular support for the SPD, parliamentary government or, rather, a government based on some degree of mass support and political legitimacy could only be realized with the Nazis forming part of the governing coalition if the SPD was to be kept out of power at all costs.

With the establishment of the so-called 'National Opposition' or the Harzburg Front in October 1931 the far-right, including the Nazis, had joined forces, to oppose Brüning and seek an alternative and far-right solution to the crisis. Although the leadership of the RDI was not directly present at the October meeting there was a significant industrial presence and representatives of heavy-industry had also been involved in providing financial support for this initiative (Geary, 1983, 1990; Mommsen, 1996; Abraham, 1986). It was in this political context of a unified nationalist opposition to Brüning,

---

73    As Henry Turner has argued (1969: 62, see also Turner, 1985) big business tended to fund the conservative opponents of Hitler even when, as he details, Hitler made explicit appeals for business support as in his Industrie Klub speech in the 1932 presidential election campaign. The Nazis were never the first choice of German business leaders, and we can agree with the thrust of Turner's general argument as to the suspicions towards Hitler of most of the leaders of German big industry. However, despite their proactive support for the non-fascist far-right as evidenced by the enthusiasm that greeted Franz von Papen becoming Chancellor in late 1932, these same business leaders encouraged and welcomed the inclusion of the Nazis into government in January 1933 and Hitler becoming Chancellor. And for that and contrary to Turner's claims, there is no question that they had a large degree of responsibility for Hitler coming to power (see Anievas, 2014: 168–9; Tooze, 2007: 100–1, 134; Volkmann, 1990: 187–8).

evaporating support from capital and the failure of his international strategy (the liberal powers had vetoed the proposal of a customs union with Austria) that his days in power were numbered. The coalescence of right-wing opposition to Brüning in late 1931 also reflected a coming together of an accumulation strategy that rested on the disavowing of any prospects of reviving the liberal-imperialist policy focused on cultivating a strategic-diplomatic and economic relationship with Washington. This now appeared dead and buried.[74]

Thus, through the auspices of the *Mitteleuropäischer Wirtschaftstag* (Central European Economic Congress) a strategy of capitalist accumulation and geo-political restructuring based on German hegemony over central and eastern Europe emerged (see James, 1986: 279; Anievas, 2014: 159). This turn to a form of imperial *grossraum* reflected a wider systemic trend across world capitalism given the direction of political travel in the US and Britain's decision to end free trade through the creation of an imperial preference trading bloc after the announcements made by the British Empire in the summer of 1932 at the Ottawa World (or Imperial) Economic Conference. In focusing on the specific geopolitical and economic possibilities offered by the countries of east and central Europe, in the final months of Weimar there was a shift in grand strategy that Alexander Anievas (2014: 158–60) suggests provides an important bridging or transition point between Weimar and the Nazi dictatorship and where the previously contradictory and conflictual relations across Germany's dominant social classes were, momentarily, resolved.[75] And it was this which provided the strategic economic foundations and thinking for a significant aspect of Nazi *Lebensraum* strategy.

---

74    Indeed, Roosevelt's decision in the summer of 1933 soon after being swept into office provided what Tooze (2015a: 506) describes as the *coup de grâce* to the possibilities of salvaging a liberal international economy with his decision that the 'dollar would float to whatever level suited the US economy, regardless of its impact on the rest of the world.'

75    Bob Jessop (1990: 158) provides a useful summary of the key elements of this *Mitteleuropa* strategy, '[t]he strategy involved cartellizing agriculture production and guaranteeing prices without altering property relations; holding down the costs of production while increasing public spending, especially on armaments, so satisfying heavy industry; and expanding trade, especially in middle and south-eastern Europe, thus benefitting the export industry without setting it against either the rural elite or heavy industry (as would occur if trade expanded with economies directly competitive with these groups). Pursuit of this strategy entailed "pacific" imperialism based on bilateral trade agreements in the middle and south-eastern European countries as a means of constituting an autarkic economic community preparatory to a strategy of "military" imperialism directed towards the Soviet Union. It also presupposed the destruction of the Weimar Republic in order to eliminate the power of organized labour and dismantle the *Sozialpolitik* system so that industrial costs could be reduced for both fractions of industry.'

In this respect, we might say that this geopolitical strategy based on a German *grossraum* over *mitteleuropa* reflected how the radical-nationalist and authoritarian ideological position of the heavy-industrial fraction of German capital became, in effect, hegemonic over the capitalist ruling class in general by mid-late 1932. This was a consequence of an 'organic crisis' of rule whereby the structural or long-term contradictions of Germany's uneven and com-bined development came together with a conjunctural crisis that dynamited the political foundations of Weimar's and capital's political legitimacy. And this meant that not only were the arrangements constitutionalized in the 1919 Weimar settlement no longer sustainable, but neither was the existing logic of capitalist production and accumulation. To paraphrase Lenin – but from a different perspective – the 'ruling class could no longer continue to rule in the old way' and, in consequence as, Tim Mason described it, the crisis and the inability of ruling class agents to guarantee the rule of capital and the stability of the state forced them to hand Hitler the reins of power (Mason, 1995: 58–9). Ultimately, while large sections of the capitalist class remained suspicious of Hitler and his intentions right up to the eve of Hitler being invited into government, such reservations were secondary to that of allowing the Social Democrats back into power and the return of parliamentary-based govern-ment based on the Weimar constitution. As Karl-Heinz Roth (Roth, 2014: 299; see also Riley, 2014: 341), summarizes,

> [i]n the end, the internal power struggle was won by groups whose eco-nomic and political survival-interests converged in the project of form-ing a new imperialist bloc by means of an alliance with the radicalised déclassé elements that the policies implemented in response to the eco-nomic crisis had produced throughout the social spectrum – the fascist mass movement.

The final months of Weimar reflected a kind of palace intrigue that was reminiscent of the plotting and interference of the Kaiser on high policy and the make-up of government in the hey-day of the Wilhelmine era. In this case, the plotting and manoeuvring centred on the President, Paul von Hindenburg – war hero and unimpeachable mythical figure – whereby dem-ocratic considerations based on vote share and the make-up of the Reichstag were marginal to the intrigue. In effect, after Brüning was forced from office in May 1932 the political and military elite around Hindenburg searched for a figure who could unite the social and political forces of the right but in a way that avoided any possibility of the reinstating of parliamentary government under the Weimar system. Further, the coterie around Hindenburg – sharing an ongoing concern across some fractions of the capitalist class – continued to be apprehensive as to the appropriateness of the Nazis as a party of government (based on Hitler's demands to be given the Chancellorship).[76] And it was Junker agrarian interests – of which Hindenburg had a personal stake in being one them – and the leadership of the *Wehrmacht* that played the key roles in influencing events. So, while the Nazis remained the most popular political force through 1932 and especially in the countryside[77] Hindenburg first turned to the Prussian aristocrat Franz von Papen through his 'military kingmaker' General Kurt von Schleicher. Papen had the support of heavy industry and the Junkers and demonstrated this with the introduction of unilateral import quotas at the behest of the agricultural interest. This alienated the more export-oriented industrial fraction of capital who quickly withdrew their support for Papen (Abraham, 1986: 162) and which meant that the German ruling class continued to be bedevilled by splits and the absence of a unified strategy of capital accumulation and, above all else, a mass, popular base.

In this respect it was only a matter of time before Hitler was invited to take the levers of power. Further, the impetus and dynamic that pushed Hitler to the precipice of power by the middle of 1932 was also connected to the fact that liberal and conservative elites alongside most fractions of capital and the landlord class were now committed to revising the geopolitical order bequeathed by the Versailles settlement with the acceptance that this would involve a major war with its architects – Britain and France (Roth, 2014: 300). Though the Nazis lost electoral support in November 1932 (securing 33 percent of the vote and down on the 37.1 percent they had gained in July) and, importantly, with the KPD increasing its share to 17 percent, there were no other forces on the right and far-right – let alone the bourgeois centre – that could provide the mass basis for

76    As Mommsen (1996: 346) outlines '[d]espite Hitler's overtures to big business, the NSDAP preserved the anti-capitalist rhetoric of its earliest days, which carried a distinctly anti-Semitic flavour with its polemics against big capital and stock market speculation. As late as the fall of 1931, the NSDAP Reichstag delegation resurrected the pseudo-socialistic idea of Gottfried Feder and demanded, among other things, nationalization of the major banks, a ban on trading on the stock market, a 5 percent limit on interest ..., and the confiscation of profits derived from war, inflation, and unjustifiable stock market transactions.' Nazi figures in the Reichstag delegation continued to use rhetoric to draw support from workers and the unemployed as well as poorer peasants that echoed some KPD sloganeering which made conservative political opinion fearful of the possibilities of Hitler gaining power.

77    It was in Schleswig-Holstien in the rural north that the Nazis gained their biggest vote share of 51 percent in the July 1932 election (Paxton, 2004: 1932) highlighting the strong basis of Nazi support across the peasantry and small farmers and highlighting the centrality of agricultural interests in the politics of their accession to power.

the final dismemberment of the Weimar settlement. By the end of 1932 the vast majority of centrist and right-wing political currents had moved to endorsing Hitler's inclusion in government even if this meant as Chancellor. So, although business representatives and liberal politicians may not have been directly responsible for handing over the keys to the Chancellorship in January 1933, they played a key strategic role in helping to define the political parameters for the resolution of Germany's political and economic crisis.[78] And in doing so they could not claim that they were in any way ignorant of Hitler's intentions and how he would carry these out as he was quite open about his primary objective of destroying the left (see Kershaw, 2000: 58; Tooze, 2007: 57–8).

The final manoeuvring over June 1932 to January 1933 with Papen[79] being appointed, soon to be replaced by Schleicher in December, reflected the final rolls of the dice of attempts to bring together the different and opposing ruling class fractions. And although Schleicher recognized the need to govern on the basis of engaging mass support his overtures to organized labour and his flirtation and attempts to work with the 'left-wing' Strasserite faction within the Nazi Party – through deploying reflationary policy instruments including repealing Papen's wage and benefit cuts, and hinting at threats to private property rights by nationalizing the steel industry and allowing peasants and unemployed workers to settle on bankrupt agrarian estates (Turner, 1969: 67; Abraham, 1986: 164, 210; Geary, 1983: 89, 98) – served to alienate and frighten ruling class forces about the possibility of 'bolshevism'.

The coming to power of Hitler and National Socialism in early 1933 was not an inevitable consequence of the contradictions of Germany's uneven and combined development, the so-called *sonderweg* that some historians have deployed to explain why Germany was susceptible to fascism (see

---

78    Indeed, as argued by Bernd Weisbrod (1979: 263, 260–3; see also James, 1986: 10) the actions of the leaders of heavy industry were instrumental in undermining the social compromise of Weimar sometime before the onset of the Great Depression, 'it was heavy industry that fundamentally disturbed this precarious stability even before the onset of the economic crisis and the success of the national socialists at the ballots.' Further, heavy industry not only aggravated the economic crisis but was also instrumental in destroying the basis for its economic resolution or mitigation within the existing political system. In sum, they opened the door to Hitler if they were not solely responsible for inviting him in.

79    Short-lived though von Papen's Chancellorship was, his government carried through one of the most important acts in the destruction of Weimar democracy with the coup against the SDP government in Prussia – the largest and most important länder in the country. Using the powers granted to him by the president, von Papen dismissed the Social Democrat Minister President and the head of the Prussian police ushering in the transformation of the Prussian police as an anti-leftist force (Baranowski, 2011: 161) and severely weakening any resistance from the left against Nazi violence and Hitler's accession to power.

Dahrendorf, 1967; Wehler, 1972; Winkler, 1976 and for a critique, Anievas, 2014: 17–21; Blackbourn and Eley, 1984). Nor was it an inevitable consequence of the conjunctural crisis provided by the particular tensions and contradictions of Germany's structural and organic socio-economic problems derived from the reparations settlement after World War One. The relationship between the reparations regime and the world economic crisis triggered by the 1929 Wall Street Crash cannot be rehearsed here (see Costiogliola, 1984; Leffler, 1979; Schuker, 1988). However, it seems clear that without the social and economic catastrophe produced by the Great Depression Hitler and the Nazis would not have gained the level of popular support that they achieved in 1932 in particular. Consequently, while a far-right solution to the constitutive problems of Weimar may have been a strong possibility by the late 1920s, the success of Nazism required the international political intervention of the Great Depression.

In this respect, even though the immediate and direct political responsibility for handing power to the Nazis lay with that of Hindenburg, Papen, and others across the German political and social elite – especially in their refusal to countenance a government involving the Social Democrats – the role played by the liberal powers is not without significance or some level of responsibility. We will turn to this in a subsequent section, below, when we look at the relationship between the main liberal powers and the international and geo-politics of the fascist states. However, with respect to the determination of the context and options that Germany confronted in the early 1930s, the actions of Britain and, in particular, the US were, as suggested above, central. The claim then that the *causal* responsibility or context for the rise and success of fascism cannot be found in capitalism in general because the main capitalist powers – even when they also succumbed to a grave economic and social catastrophe during the Great Depression, did not surrender to fascism (see Luebbert, 1991; Mann, 2004: 20–4) – only takes us so far. Rather, the organic contradictions of Germany's uneven and combined development and the conjunctural crisis that it confronted in the early 1930s reflected the *differentiated totality of a capitalist world system* that involves the structures, processes decisions and actions associated with and directed by the leading capitalist powers as part of this totality. The decisions and situations that Germany's political system had to deal with were, then, the flip-side of what confronted the liberal powers and the decisions that they made. Further, the ideology of Hitler can only be properly understood from the perspective of the structure and workings of a world socioeconomic system defined by contradiction and conflict. Indeed, while the United States did not succumb to fascism, the New Deal response to the crisis, as recognized in Ira Katznelson's (2013) magisterial account of it, was based on a revitalization of Southern racism and Jim Crow as key constituencies of the New Deal. Likewise, Britain's imperial preference system resting on an imperial geopolitics helped determine the path that Germany would soon follow. The far-right then, was evident and significant in the *liberal* resolution of the crisis of the Great Depression even if it did not take on a fascist form. We might say that a far-right-infused politics framed around trade protectionism, nationalist assertiveness – based on attempts to dilute and overcome class identities and conflict – defined the era. German fascism was the particular expression of the generalized trend in this regard.

### 2.3    *The Social Bases of Fascism*

Fascist movements spoke and appealed to, recruited and secured votes from, a variety of social layers which challenges the idea that inter-war fascism represented a particular kind of class movement. Fascists tended to tailor their propaganda, rhetoric and policy suggestions to the specific locales and social groupings that they were targeting (Paxton, 2004: 65–6) even if this meant – as in many respects it did – that such rhetoric or policy promises were contradictory or antagonistic. In spite of these attempts to go beyond class forms of political identity through an appeal to what Michael Mann (2004: 3) calls 'class transcendence' based on a 'cleansing nation-statism,' inevitably, these appeals had a varied impact in terms of securing support across different social constituencies and spatial locales.

In this way fascism reflected a generalized set of properties characteristic of the generic far-right over the *longue durée*. Consequently, some social layers were much more susceptible to fascist ideology and appeals than others and especially in moments of intense political and economic crisis. Indeed, in both the Italian and German cases it was in such contexts of crisis – in Italy between 1919 and 1922 and in Germany between 1930 and 1933 – where popular or mass support for fascism was actually significant. Outside of these periods, support was either marginal and thus electorally and politically insignificant, or elections took place under proto-fascist conditions as reflected in the banning of the Communist Party and the widespread intimidation and violence against the parties of the left undermining any sense that voters were exercising anything like a free choice.

Fascists succeeded – and especially in the case of Nazism – in building a multi-class voting bloc (Mann, 2004: 18; see also Childers, 1983) that provided their mass base, political significance and, ultimately, the reason why they were invited into power. This social plurality qualifies Marxist arguments that fascist parties were dominated by the petty bourgeoisie in terms of their electoral support (see Trotsky, 1975: 258–324, 406–15; Poulantzas, 1974: 261). In both cases

the *core* of their support tended to replicate the social profile of party membership and leadership – coming from white-collar workers, the self-employed
and small producers (see Geary, 1990: 106–7; Kater, 1983; Lyttelton, 2004a: 49–
50). Working class involvement was marginal other than the more 'lumpen'
elements who joined the Nazi SA in particular (Fischer, 1982). However, the
political success of fascism – in coming to power – involved an expansion in
their levels of support beyond the petty bourgeoisie and including workers and
rural labourers (Childers, 1983; Eley, 1983: 74), if less so in Italy (Lyttleton, 2004;
Mann, 2004: 107–11) as well as bourgeois social layers in cities (see Hamilton,
1982). Thus, an important source of votes for fascists came from workers.
Such support tended to be found within distinct spatial locations – smaller
towns and in the countryside (and in the German case, Protestant rather
than Catholic – see Hamilton, 1982) – and workers who tended to be younger,
unemployed and with little or no experience of the culture and institutions of
organized labour (Geary, 1990: 108–9; Hamilton, 1982: 38; Mann, 2004: 107–11).
In contrast, the socialist and communist parties were, overwhelmingly, parties
of the working class and especially so in the larger urban areas and most industrialized zones (Mann, 2004: 159; Mommsen, 1996: 352).

The widening of support for fascism and especially in the case of Nazism
was, then, directly connected to the playing out of the combined – economic
and political – crisis that engulfed Italy and Germany in the immediate periods before the fascist parties came to power. This not only intensified electoral
volatility (see Childers, 1983: 268–9), as traditional voting blocs haemorrhaged
(with the exception of the left parties) – in a fashion that realized Gramsci's
notion of 'organic crisis' (Gramsci, 1973: 210–1) – but also revealed a greater
willingness of voters to support extremist and anti-system parties. In short,
the political circumstances in which voters were choosing to vote for fascists
were, in many respects, unprecedented and where, as Geoff Eley (2015: 101)
has emphasized, both the workings of political institutions and the traditional party systems and modes of political representation had broken down.
However, despite these caveats as to the widening scope of support for fascism,
in terms of the significance of their proportionality as part of the overall population, workers were much less likely to vote fascist, while members of the
petty bourgeoisie were much more so (Eley, 1983: 72–3; Hamilton, 1982: 37–63).
It was the haemorrhaging of support from the traditional centrist and right-
wing parties that provided fascism with its mass votes and not votes from the
parties of the left.

The crisis-dynamic evident in the expansion of the fascist vote was also relevant with respect to the attitude and actions by ruling classes in Italy and
Germany towards fascists. In Italy, big capitalists and large landlords played

an important role in providing financial support and political legitimacy to fascists *and* fascist violence from 1920 (Guerin, 1973: 33–4; Beetham, 1983: 8; see also Adler, 1995; Mann, 2004: 118–20; Paxton, 2004: 60–1). This was largely driven by the revolutionary crisis context that fascism emerged within and responded to, and most notably in the activities of *squadristi* in the country-side in deploying violence against the left to overturn Socialist Party electoral victories and labour mobilizations against landlords and in defence of capi-talist property rights. The situation in Germany was rather different. As Henry Turner's (see Turner, 1969, 1985) exhaustive survey of business archives demon-strated, German capital did not provide financial or other significant support for the Nazis until the very final stages of the Weimar Republic.[80] Indeed, German capital not only tended to fund other parties of the right and far-right against the left,[81] it was also concerned about the 'socialist' dimensions of the left-wing of the NSDAP associated with Gregor Strasser.

In both cases capitalists and landlords preferred other right-wing and anti-socialist options in part because of the way in which the political and eco-nomic crises within both countries developed after the war and because they had reservations as to the degree to which fascists were sympathetic to a social order based on private property.[82] In spite of these reservations, and contrary to Henry Turner's account, increasing numbers of capitalists moved closer to Hitler after 1930 and especially from the middle of 1932, pressed Hindenburg for the Nazis to be included in the government (Remmling, 1989: 215–30). The structural context of the depression with little chance of restoring profitability until the domestic and international constraints on accumulation – the power of organized labour connected to the Weimar constitution in the former and the geopolitics of the post-war 1919 settlement in the latter – made this all but

---

80    The relationship changed through 1932: at the start of the year Hitler spoke at the Dusseldorf Industrial Club encouraged by the steel magnate Fritz Thyssen, while in the spring sections of heavy industrial capital began to move closer to the Nazis. By November, 38 industrial leaders wrote to President Hindenburg recommending Hitler as Chancellor (Remmling, 1989: 218–9).

81    This is an important point that qualifies any critique of Marxist explanations for the rise of fascism. Thus, the hesitancy towards Hitler was not replicated in ruling class uncertainty in support of other far-right currents who were committed to both a domestic political solution based on the dismantling of Weimar democracy and the establishment of an authoritarian dictatorship and an external one based on the tearing up of the Versailles settlement.

82    Indeed, as Trotsky noted 'the representatives of big business preferred a quiet and more stable solution to the crisis: "they want no convulsions no long and severe civil war. If they chose Hitler, it was only because of the depth of the crisis made a stable bourgeois democracy unsustainable"' (Trotsky cited in Renton, 1999: 71).

inevitable. And for a viable and 'legitimate' political solution it required the involvement and support of a non-left party with mass support. The Nazis were the only ones who could deliver this.

### 2.4    The Political Character of Fascism

Fascism came to power in Italy and Germany in moments of extreme crisis. In both cases the existing liberal political order – in the shape of its institutional set-up and forms of political representation – were unable to manage or resolve the crises that had engulfed each state. In the Italian case the crisis of liberal order centred on the long-standing centrifugal forces that had defined Italian nation-state formation and the inability to construct a national political culture and framework in the short period between unification and the trauma inflicted by Italy's participation in World War One. This structural problem, conditioned by the geopolitical context and relative weakness of Italy in the immediate post-war period, was super-charged by the revolutionary crisis that quickly consumed and overwhelmed the liberal state in the immediate post-war period. It was this that drove ruling class forces to consider an alternative political-institutional framework involving fascism, as a way of securing the basic tenements of the capitalist social order.

In Germany the source or context of the crisis was not that of a revolutionary kind where the revolutionary left appeared as a genuine threat to the maintenance of the existing social order. Indeed, the success of the appeal of Nazism in the early 1930s in many respects reflected the relative weakness of revolutionary forces in contrast to the period between 1918 and 1922. Rather, the crisis was centred on German capitalism reflected in a crisis of profitability that combined with an organic crisis within the social formation of the different fractions of German capital. Again, this was connected to a longer-term or structural problem in Germany associated with its uneven and combined development and, specifically, the difficulties of constructing a strategy of capitalist accumulation across the three major fractions of the capitalist class (heavy industry, export-oriented industries, and the large Junker agricultural estates) within the geopolitical framework that limited the international pathways of economic expansion. This longer-term contradiction was magnified or overlaid with that of the Weimar state that established a social (industrial working class) presence within the state that, politically and constitutionally, limited the possibilities for German capital to manage its contradictions and increase the rate of profit. When the Great Depression intensified this crisis bringing the overall capitalist economy to the verge of collapse and with the traditional political representatives of ruling class interests lacking the popular or mass base for dismantling the Weimar Republic and pursuing a radically new international strategy that included the possibility of war, dominant social forces and the traditional political elite moved to embrace Hitler: the only possible political option.

In both cases international structures and social forces played determining roles in the rise and success of fascism. Indeed, the period after 1918 saw a wave of militant far-right movements gaining political power out of the crises that developed from within liberal forms (or attempts to establish) of rule that were connected to an international context of newly created borders, poorly integrated populations and social layers and concerns about the state's ability to secure borders and its domestic political authority. In Italy the specificities of the international determinants of fascism were sourced in the post-war crisis and the geopolitical limits that confronted the Italian liberal state at the war's end. In particular, its inability to force geopolitical concessions from the great powers, as a way of helping to consolidate its nation-state formation and weather the trauma inflicted by its participation in the war. Italian fascism was, then, a logical political development given the momentum and limits of liberal imperialism within a geopolitical context that rested on imperial hierarchy.

In Germany's case fascism was incubated within the Versailles order as reflected in the nationalist grievances connected to the re-drawing of its borders after 1918 and the international presence within the functioning and stability of its domestic political-economy through the reparations regime that was imposed on it. However, it was the impact of the world economic crisis after 1929 that provided the *primary* determinant for Nazism, as it was the combined economic impact that drove social layers formerly unenthused by Nazism towards it, and the key decisions of the other major liberal capitalist powers that, in effect, pushed Germany towards a nationalist autarchy associated with geopolitical aggression. In this sense, a shift towards a nationalist and geopolitically revisionist political orientation was already on the way in Germany *before* Hitler came to power such that far-right social and political forces had become ascendant within the state after 1930. The significance of Nazism was that it reflected the most radical strand of this ideo-political shift and, further, that it was defined by a popular-mass base which, in turn, was directly connected to the international environment that emerged after 1930.

In both of these cases fascism emerged from *within* liberal democracy. Further, fascists gained the levers of state power with the *active* support and facilitation of ruling class interests and their political representatives including liberal forces. In other words, fascism was gifted political power as conservative and liberal forces (see Kershaw, 1998: 377–428) either actively facilitated the accession to power or remained passive and indifferent to the significance and the inevitable outcomes of fascists gaining control of the levers of the state apparatus. Fascism did *not* seize power or take control of the state through an external revolutionary assault on it after the disintegration of the administrative and coercive power of the state in the way that the Bolsheviks did in Russia in 1917. This is not to suggest that fascism's accession to state power was an ordinary or unexceptional development within liberal order. Indeed, the formal constitutional trappings – in Italy the king inviting Mussolini to lead a coalition government in October 1922, in Germany, the President, Paul von Hindenburg, asking Hitler to form a coalition government at the end of January 1933 – occurred in a context where both fascist movements had been deploying violence and intimidation against their main political opponents on the left and where, after the formalities of gaining control of the state, they continued to use violence against anyone who opposed them.[83] These fateful constitutional decisions revealed, then, how bourgeois political opinion was willing to accept fascism and its associated violence – even if they assumed that the 'responsibility' of governing would, necessarily, 'moderate' them – sometime before the fascist dictatorship was established.[84]

The only political opponents to this process – who were the first principal victims of fascist *state* terror and violence – were the different strands of the

---

83  The significance of this violence particularly in the Nazi case is suggestive of the revolutionary dimensions of Nazism and the means by which it consolidated state power. Further, because some of the victims of Nazi intimidation and violence were liberals and conservatives – including members of its coalition ally, the DNVP – some scholars (see Beck, 2008 in particular but also Nolte, 1965) have sought to characterise Nazism as a broader anti-conservative and anti-bourgeois form of politics. While it is certainly true that Nazis did use threats, intimidation, and violence against *some* conservatives and DNVP members after March 1933, this was limited to those that actively opposed Nazism. Further, it is also clear that the focus of Nazi violence was *overwhelmingly* targeted on the socialist and communist lefts and the representatives of organized labour who became the first concentration camp internees. And though some conservatives felt the brunt of Nazi intimidation and were disgusted and concerned by it, conservative opinion, and conservative forces within Germany at the time overwhelmingly supported Nazi actions in destroying the left and establishing an authoritarian dictatorship. After all, it was their votes that propelled Hitler into power.

84  As Tooze (2007: 100–1) notes, however, once Hitler had been invited into power and made clear his intention of destroying the left and terminating parliamentary government, leading representatives of the capitalist class began to fund the Nazi Party. Thus, during the March 1933 election the Nazis – via their interlocutor, Hjalmar Schacht – received donations from seventeen different business groups amounting to three million Reichsmarks. It is clear then that German business knew what it was getting itself into when it embraced Hitler and these contributions provided a 'substantial down payment' towards realizing the 'end of parliamentary democracy and the destruction of the German left'.

organized left. Consequently, there was a transition moment or basis within the constitutional framework of each liberal state that laid the authoritarian foundations for the creation of the fascist state out of the liberal order. In Germany it was the passing of the Enabling Act in March 1933 that provided the legal-constitutional veneer for the establishment of the Nazi dictatorship after Hindenburg had suspended the key civil liberties of German citizens in late February (after the Reichstag Fire) with the Decree of the Reich President for the Protection of People and State. The transition to dictatorship was, then, legally enacted; it was not created through an extra-legal assault on the state from without.

In Italy the shift from liberal democracy to fascist dictatorship took longer and involved many more twists that, arguably, implicated liberals and conservatives to a much greater extent. The 'march on Rome' expressed the dynamic at work in the establishment of dictatorship: a period of illegal but politically acquiesced fascist violence against the left that culminated in the political theatre of the massing of fascist black-shirts to intimidate traditional political elites but where fascism's entry into government was sanctioned by constitutionally-mandated royal authority on October 29, 1922 (Grand, 1982: 41; Riley, 2010: 56) and where Mussolini governed in coalition with conservative and liberal elements (Grand, 1982: 41). After this, with the pressure – fuelled by the continuing violence and terror of the provincial *Ras* – from the fascist movement that was balanced with the objective of maintaining the support of the state bureaucracy and conservative and liberal political forces, Mussolini gradually moved to impose dictatorship culminating in the decision of October 1926 to ban all opposition parties and formally establish a (fascist) one-party state (Lyttelton, 2004a: 267–8).[85]

---

85    In his closely argued summary of the move towards dictatorship, Dylan Riley (2010: 59) argues that the timing of the creation of the dictatorship emerged out of a crisis within fascism based on Mussolini's attempt to rule with the support of traditional political elites and the ruling class whilst maintaining the loyalty of the fascist movement's most radical elements in the provincial *Ras*. This arrangement collapsed in the context of the abduction and then murder of the leading socialist politician, Giacomo Matteotti, in June 1924 which triggered the so-called 'Aventine Secession' of the opposition from parliament with conservative and liberal allies deserting Mussolini (and who demanded that the *squadristi* be disciplined). At the same time the so-called 'intransigents' within the Fascist syndicats embarked on a series of strikes to challenge the existing framework for managing labour relations and a number of fascist squads embarked on a new wave of terror in parts of the countryside. As Riley notes, '[b]y December 1924 this wing of the party was in open revolt and Mussolini's speech in December took place in a context

Thus, while fascist states were defined by and realized revolutionary forms of change – they came to power via liberal *and* constitutional means. In this respect the two fascist states were *not* revolutionary;[86] they were part of a continuum within the existing liberal-capitalist political order, exceptional – especially in the case of Nazism – though they were to become. Indeed, while the capitalist states that the fascist parties inherited and worked through were changed in significant ways by fascism, it was also the case that many, if not most, of the key institutions of the state remained in place (alongside their bureaucracies) and carried on working as they had done in the past and where key conservative-bourgeois figures of the Weimar era such Hjalmar Schacht returned to lead the Reichsbank and act as the Nazi Minister for Economics until the late 1930s.

The most significant changes were in two respects. First, the termination of parliamentary-representative government and its replacement by the organs and rituals and theatre of the Fascist Party as an alternative way of integrating the masses into the new political order. In many respects this mass-based integrative feature – that had a *corporatist* gloss in Italy in particular reflected the 'dual state' (see Fraenkel, 2017) like character of fascist regimes where the continuation of pre-existing state institutions and practices (that continued to involve non-fascist elements) within the state apparatus operated alongside the creation of a number of party-based para-state institutions (see Paxton, 2004: 119–27).[87] The dual-state aspect of fascist regimes also relates to their

---

where the squads were saying radicalize the regime (abolish parliamentary government) or step down as fascist leader.' The result saw Mussolini forced to move to 'establish a new, much more authoritarian state while not fully adopting the intransigent fascist line. The instrument of this transformation was the police structure: the prefects of the old liberal state. Immediately after Mussolini's speech of January 1925, Luigi Federzoni, the conservative nationalist minister of the interior ... sent notes to the prefects, demanding the immediate closure of all opposition party organizations.'

86   The contradictions between the 'revolutionary' aspects of Nazism as mass movement and the emerging Nazi regime had been simmering for some time but it was in the context of a threat delivered by the army leadership and President von Hindenburg on June 21, 1934 to impose martial law unless Hitler acted to deal with the SA 'revolutionary trouble-makers' that forced Hitler's hand. Jane Caplan (1977: 89) describes this as such, '[t]he liquidation at Hitler's orders of the SA leadership (by the SS, with army connivance), and the elimination of the SA as an effective political force, must be seen primarily as a consequence of Hitler's early weakness vis-a-vis the old bourgeois power bloc (especially the army). The purge of the SA represented the terms of this initial compromise into which Hitler was forced, though the relationship was, to be sure, a complex one: a coup by Hitler against the fascist movement as such, in order to forestall a possible conservative-military coup against the new regime.'

87   As Riley and Desai (2007: 826) state in regard to fascist Italy, '[fascism] led neither to a rapid alteration of the class structure nor a rapid alteration in the state. The fascist party

respective ideological character and legitimation. Here, both states drew on a set of long-standing extreme nationalist symbols and tropes associated with a conspiratorial politics blaming Jews, communists, free-masons, and others for their political and economic ills, alongside the cultivation of ideas focused on the unity, purity and vitality of the nation expressed through mobilization for struggle and war.

Such ideological positions were aimed at breaking the hold and influence of both liberal individualism and materialism and bourgeois cultural sensibilities that fascists detested, thus radically re-drawing the boundaries – to the point of collapse in some cases – between the public and private spheres and the politics of class and its associated ideological imaginaries and cultural representations. Consequently, fascism repudiated liberalism and conservatism as much as it vilified socialism and communism. In Italy, Mussolini invoked the spirit of the Roman Empire as the basis for Italy's quest for national glory and strength providing a reactionary backdrop that contrasted with its fetishization of the power of modern industry and technology (Herf, 1984; Neocleous, 1997). After the invasion and annexation of Abyssinia in 1935, the ideological character of the regime became much more enthused through racialized and racist propaganda including increasing anti-Semitism (Bernardini, 1977; Sarfatti, 2005).

The role of race and racism within the ideological legitimation of Nazism needs little exaggeration. Such an ideological framework drew on ideological framings – and not just anti-Semitism – that had been a mainstay of the German right and far-right for decades, as framed in the idea of *Volkgemeinschaft*. However, it was Hitler's combining of this racism with a politics of total/aggressive war that super-charged the racist ideology of Nazism as something unique to it, and distinct from the traditional German far-right, as well as the generalized racism that characterized the politics of the broader liberal imperialist milieu of the time. The Nazi state defined itself immediately on its creation as a *racial* state committed to upholding the purity and interests of the *volk* and removing and destroying all those elements that were seen as 'contaminating' or undermining the *volk's* racial stock and vitality. Nazi propaganda drew on a reactionary imaginary of a pastoral rural idyll that combined with an iconography and political theatre of *'führer*-worship' that also became the basis for the ideological legitimation of state policy (see Broszat, 1981; Eley, 2013: 59–90). However, the significance and singularity of Nazi racism went beyond the realm of legitimizing the Nazi state. Indeed, it was Nazism's racist

---

instead carved out some areas of control (such as the union organizations, and the corporative bureaucracy), while pre-fascist elites maintained their dominance in most areas.'

ideology – that included anti-Slavism as much as anti-Semitism – that played a critical role in its geopolitics and war strategies, as well as providing the basis for one of the defining characteristics of the Nazi political economy, the 'annihilation by labour' (Herbert, 1993).

The ideological justifications of the fascist states played an important role in legitimizing and promoting the second element of the exceptionality of the fascist state in the development and augmentation of the machineries of state violence, terror, and military power through which it violently smashed any independent sources of social and political power. This augmentation in the apparatuses of terror played a central role in the domestic politics of fascism, as much as it defined its international and geopolitical orientation. In the former, Italy and Germany quickly moved to become police-states where any signs of public dissent to the regime and its ideology would lead to arrest, internment, torture and, all too often, death. And while these regimes, particularly Nazi Germany, generated an atmosphere of all-pervasive fear and terror, they never amounted to a form of totalitarianism – understood as the coherent and wholesale absorption of the state by the Nazi Party into a singular and unified political structure – given the fragmented, diffused and overlapping nature of the Nazi infrastructure of power that permitted and facilitated both corruption and, in some respects, spaces of relative autonomy and internal conflict (see Broszat, 1981; Caplan, 1977; Kershaw, 2000: 74–92). Obviously, such qualifications did not relate to the racialized *feindbild* of the Third Reich and Jews in particular.

Fascism, then, reflected a revolutionary *form* of politics, even if its substantive revolutionary outcomes and 'achievements' were more muted. And while the experiences of fascism in Italy and Germany can be considered exceptional forms of capitalist state (Poulantzas, 1974: 11)[88] they remained within the *genus* of the capitalist state and its political economy. Fascism's strength and success was a product of a shift in the politics of liberal order to one defined by internationally-framed instability that undermined existing political and institutional arrangements and the abilities of traditional political representatives

---

88    But not in a functionalist sense – as Poulantzas' account can be read as (see Mann, 2004: 20), but rather exceptional in the sense of a unique category produced from the most intense crisis of the capitalist state that is not resolved by revolution. Fascist states pushed the workings of capitalism to their limits; indeed, their connections to war provided the means of their ultimate destruction, but in spite of the changes unleashed and the over-determining role of terror and violence in their reproduction, these states never overcame their capitalist characteristics in terms of the production process and the wider structural constraints of a capitalist world economy.

and forms of politics connected to liberal-constitutional and parliamentary government. Fascism was a politics outside the norms of traditional liberal order even if it emerged and thrived within it. However, in taking seriously the revolutionary pretensions of fascism we also need to recognize the distinctions between fascism as politics or movement and the fascist state. So, although fascist movements emerged from within and, to some extent, contributed to a wider political imaginary that questioned and challenged existing socioeconomic arrangements through their so-called 'anti-capitalism,' fascist movements – when they acceded to power – *governed* capitalist states. While radical changes were made to some of the institutions and operations of the Italian and German capitalist states, they continued to be based on the organization of capitalist forms of production and the accompanying privileges and protections of the capitalist class.

## 3     The Political Economy of the Fascist State

The scholarly debate on the character of the two European fascist regimes encompasses a huge literature involving several  key controversies including the degree to which these states reflected totalitarian forms (see Arendt, 1968; Friedrich and Brzezinski, 1965; Bullock, 1991; Hayek, 2001) of politics (suggesting that they had significant overlaps and commonalities with Stalinism), that they represented a distinct revolutionary form of politics outside of the typical left-right conceptualization of politics (see Eatwell, 2003; Gregor, 1974; Griffin, 2000b; Mosse, 1999) and/or that they are best understood as reflecting a form of socialism (Hayek, 2001; Sternhell, 1996).[89] My concerns in this section will touch on some of these controversies but my main focus will be on an examination of the political-economic structures and relations of the two fascist states – for an excellent survey of the academic debate the nature of the Nazi economy see Kershaw (2000: 47–68). Specifically, how each fascist economy was organized and how it evolved; the class structure and dynamics within each state and also how the evolving international context, including war, shaped the character of fascist political economy.

The commentary on, or the attempt to conceptualize, the political economy of fascism comparable to that of liberalism, socialism or communism, is beset by a number of challenges that makes any definitive assessment, necessarily

---

89     Hayek famously opened his anti-collectivist work, *The Road to Serfdom*, addressing it to 'socialists of all parties' where he described the Nazi economy as a form of socialism. Likewise see Peter Temin (1991) and Richard Overy (1994: 118).

provisional. The short-lived nature of fascist regimes, their limited number (Italy and Germany as the most important cases), the absence of a clear and coherent ideological framework connected to the economics of fascism and the centrality of war – both as a political objective of fascist states in peacetime and as a material reality in terms of the way in which the prosecution of war conditioned the structure and working of the fascist economies of Italy and Germany – all contribute to the limiting any definitive assessment.

What I intend to do in the rest of this section is to address some of these challenges and, in doing so, outline an argument that fascist political economy reflects a particular, indeed, *exceptional,* and *crisis*-driven form of capitalist state (see Poulantzas, 1974; Caplan, 1977). Indeed, in part because of the connection between the structure and workings of the economy and war, while war was the primary objective of the fascist economy (rather than welfare, consumption, freedom, or profits), it was also both a source of crisis within each political economy and, necessarily, its short-term means to overcome crisis. It was war and race war in particular that provided the substantive basis for what Tim Mason (Mason, 1968) described as 'the primacy of politics'. What this means is that fascist political economy never really – and especially though not exclusively in the German case – managed to realize or reproduce itself as a political economy of peacetime. It was never a 'normal' or conventional form of capitalist economy. Rather, fascist political economy in historical terms was a form of capitalist economy fundamentally oriented towards and/or distorted by race war.

Thus, the history of actually-existing fascist political economy as exemplified by the experiences of Italy and Germany were economies in peacetime that were organized and directed towards war[90] and, when war broke out, they became war economies. As Neil Davidson (2015: 132–3) highlighted, this challenges the idea that fascism was *functional* to the needs of German or Italian capital as a whole. In retrospect, it seems all too self-evident that the interests of the capitalist class were fundamentally at odds with the ideology and politics of fascism and especially Nazism given the destructive consequences of the Nazi race war. However, the benefit of hindsight is not an appropriate historical or analytical way of assessing the relationship between capital and the fascist state, as we shall see below. Indeed, such a position assumes that there is a singular capitalist viewpoint or perspective as to the organization of the political economy and, further, largely ignores the real material benefits

---

90    Adrian Lyttelton (2004b) suggests that what marks out fascist political economy as distinctive was its 'creation of a wartime economy in peacetime' which he goes on to define as a ... 'consortialist state'.

that significant fractions of the capitalist class realized under fascist rule and, to a significant degree through war, and its associated imperialist plunder and exploitation of resources. It also overlooks the wider context of crisis that engulfed global capitalism at the time – before and after fascists came to power – and the generic similarities between the fascist and liberal models of political economy that emerged throughout the 1930s. Indeed, in this respect it was the mobilization for war after 1938–39 in the main liberal states of Britain and the United States when these two economies finally removed themselves from the accumulation drag that had set in after 1929.

The question of what would have happened or what would have characterized fascist political economy outside of the context of war is, obviously, quite speculative. And the two cases offer contrasting possibilities. In the case of Italy, up until 1929 its political economy – though it had introduced some protectionist measures[91] and moved towards cartelization in some sectors – remained wedded to the conventions of the liberal international economic order. Thus, Mussolini – reflecting both the domestic and international precariousness of his new-found power – made 'a conscious effort to maintain and improve [Italy's] status as a partner in the international economy', by stabilizing the lira and returning to the gold standard (Lyttelton, 2004a: 441). In particular, Mussolini and his ministers did all they could to win the favour of the great banks of the United States. Thomas Lamont and the Morgan bank played an indispensable role in the stabilization of the lira and American capital helped to re-equip Italian industry (Lyttelton, 2004a: 441). After Germany, Italy was the leading borrower from the USA among European states. Dependence on the good opinion of Wall Street and the City of London was an important restraint on Mussolini's adventurism in foreign policy (Lyttelton, 2004a: 441).

Ergo, the reproduction of Italian fascism up to that point had been realized within and, to some extent, complemented, by the workings of the international capitalist order. And although Italy moved towards much greater levels of protectionism that demonstrated a shift towards autarchy and 'organized capitalism' through cartelization and the creation of state-industrial combines, such developments were hardly exceptional across the capitalist world

---

91    In the initial period of fascist power between 1922 and 1925 economic policy was largely deferred to the liberal Finance Minister, Alberto de Stefani, who presided over a deflationary policy based on controlling inflation, stabilizing the exchange rate, cutting some taxes, and privatizing a number of public utilities, as well as resisting calls for increased protectionism from heavy industrial and agrarian interests up until June 1925. De Stefani also presided over a systematic process of privatizing state utilities (see Lyttelton, 2004a: 336–7, 338–40; Bel, 2011).

after 1930 given similar shifts in the United States and the British Empire. It was Mussolini's move towards Hitler after 1936 and the onset of war that fundamentally shifted Italy's political economy, as it became a war economy as well as, in effect, a supplicant of the Third Reich. What the Italian experience tells us is that Italian fascism realized a more statist and interventionist form of political economy that reflected the longer-term consequences of Italy's uneven and combined development alongside the role of some fascist predilections towards supporting some parts of the economy over others. The onset of the Great Depression deepened and extended some of these trends with the emergence of significant state-industrial monopolies and direction of the credit system, but Italy remained, fundamentally, a capitalist state and its capitalist class (and agrarian landlords) materially benefited from its workings and played a much greater role in determining state policies than other social layers. With the onset of war, Italy became increasingly dependent on Nazi Germany and a German victory and the secure establishment of a Nazi *Grossraum* would, in all likelihood, have continued that dependency and subordination to the much more economically and geopolitically stronger fascist state.

The case of Nazi Germany suggests something else. From the outset, the Nazi economy was a capitalist economy fundamentally oriented and/or distorted by the preparation for war. War – the way to realize territorial expansion and, with it, increased material resources and economic capacities – was seen as the means to address Germany's fundamental economic problems – both structural and conjunctural, as well as realizing Hitler's racial *Weltanschauung* and, as Adam Tooze (2007) has argued, provide the geopolitical platform to compete with the US imperium. The Nazi war economy in the occupied east was an economy of racial plunder, slavery and genocide and this provided the basis of what, in all likelihood, would have characterized the Nazi empire of *Lebensraum*: a space cleared of 'racial undesirables', and a settler colony allowing the Reich to feed itself and draw on reservoirs of slave labour and where German capital could plunder and appropriate its material resources.

In the west, the occupied zones reflected something different, suggesting an alternative future within the Nazi *Grossraum*. Here, the ideology of racial hierarchy would have played out – as it did during the short-lived period of Nazi occupation – but in a quite different way to that which characterized the Nazi occupation of the east. Thus, under the occupation, while there were expropriations of private property and elements of plunder, as well as the recruitment of forced labour for the Nazi war economy, capitalist property rights were, to a significant degree, respected, and forms of market relations continued. Of course, the prospect of global war with the United States would have continued to structure the economic workings of the *Grossraum*.

Any assessment of the specificities of fascist political economy, obviously, need to be considered in the context of war; both as a political objective of fascist states in peacetime and as a material reality in terms of the way in which the prosecution of war conditioned the structure and working of the fascist economies. To some degree this makes any definitive assessment of fascist political economy – with an emphasis on the economics of fascism – provisional, or, qualified because of the way in which the Italian and German economies under fascist rule existed within a wider international and political context defined by war.

While fascism does not have an intellectual or theoretical framework located in political economy or a materialist ontology of the social world in the way that liberalism and socialism do, its emergence as a distinct ideological current after 1918 was connected to a number of ideological strands that addressed economic questions even if they refused to use or recognize economic categories. In many respects the whole category of the economic both as an analytical framework (political economy or economics) and as a social reality was refuted by these thinkers (see Baker, 2006; James, 1986: 347; Maier, 1987: 86–7; Woolf, 1968).[92] The malaise and 'degeneration' of European societies, culture and civilization that they diagnosed from the 1880s onwards reflected what they regarded as the economization of life that they saw as responsible for the malignant consequences of liberal individualism and Marxist materialism. Turning against these influences, these thinkers – from Georges Sorel to Vilfredo Pareto and Oswald Spengler among a number of others (see Gregor, 2005; Sternhell, 1994) – sought to offer a set of ideological positions for reconfiguring society. In such imaginings the economy and its structure and workings would be subordinated to the national popular will and individualism and class divisions (and conflict) would be overcome through corporate structures of social order that would replace both capitalist markets and democratic and parliamentary systems of government rooted in an idealized vision of the people or 'volk' associated with a hierarchical and racialized ontology of the social world.[93]

---

92   As Lyttelton (2004a: 333) notes, '[f]ascism had no consistent theory about the economic system. The beliefs typical of fascism were not so much economic theories as what might be called anti-economic theories. The fascist belief in "will", in the capacity of the strong man with faith to triumph over natural obstacles, implied a devaluation of the whole sphere of economic action and utilitarian motive.'

93   In his masterful account of fascist political economy, Charles Maier (1987: 79–87) emphasizes how the concept of productivism defined fascist economic thinking. For Maier, productivism combined a defence of a conservative conception of work, industry and production that side-lined the organizational and financial circuits of capitalism *as a*

These ideological positions realized degrees of political influence prior to 1914 and, in some respects – notably in Wilhelmine Germany – played an important role in the development of the radical nationalism that fuelled the geopolitical rivalry that was to lead to the outbreak of war in 1914. Such ideas remained significant immediately after the war and, in a context defined by the weakness and fragility of liberal-democratic institutions and the continuing instabilities and social conflict that continued to plague the workings of the capitalist economy, provided a significant ideo-political outlet that became even more significant after the 1917 Bolshevik Revolution. These ideological influences were also evident in the initial platforms of Italian fascism and German National Socialism. Thus, while remaining anti-Marxist, both fascisms put forward electoral positions that, on the surface, looked decidedly anti-capitalist and 'national socialist'. Thus, the 1919 Italian fascist programme referred to restrictions on capital, a levy on war profits, a national minimum wage, and the need for workers to be involved in industrial decision-making that was given a post-capitalist gloss through the *leitmotif* of corporatism (Morgan, 2004: 29; Woolf, 1968: 127). In Germany, the 1920 programme of the Nazi Party (which at the time was led by Anton Drexler not Hitler) called for land reform, the abolition of unearned income (interest), nationalization of the banks, and confiscation of war profits (see Baker, 2006: 231; James, 1986: 346; Mann, 2004: 142). In both cases, fascists articulated a profound mistrust and hostility towards big and financial capital – the latter providing an important element to their anti-Semitism. Indeed, because fascism understood and focused on politics as about 'will', 'struggle' and 'overcoming' its orientation towards agency and voluntarism rather than structures lent itself to an analysis of economics such that when an 'economy failed or succeeded, "someone", not "something", was responsible' (Baker, 2006: 229). This obviously lent itself to both a conspiratorial politics of agency/blame that was graphed onto its racism; thus, Jews were identified as the primary agents responsible for economic failure and crisis, which could only be overcome through the will of heroic counter-agency.

Such ideological commitments would continue to be associated with both fascist movements for some years thereafter. However, they were soon eclipsed by a political orientation and strategy that focused on cultivating contacts and

---

*social system* whilst, at the same time, fetishizing individualist producer genius and autonomy associated with technological innovation. It also appeared to align with a broader corporative structure of producers through outlining a hierarchy of tasks and responsibilities within the production process. In a word, productivism conceded autonomy for capitalists at the level of the workplace and ignored the class dimensions of ownership.

support from ruling class interests in the capitalist and landlord classes of each state. In Italy the weak performance of the party in the 1919 elections demonstrated the limits and problems of an electoral and political strategy that professed to an anti-capitalist position based on courting the votes of workers. This was particularly so in a political context where the organized working class was overwhelmingly identified with the socialist left. This was also replicated in Germany. It was only when the Nazis began to focus on concentrating resources towards cultivating particular social (and geographical) layers that it developed into a genuinely mass party and successful electoral vehicle that downplayed its anti-capitalist or socialist pretensions. In this respect, both Mussolini and Hitler moved to reposition both movements as decidedly anti-socialist organizations in terms of their ideology and propaganda through a politics defined by violence and intimidation targeted at the social and political organizations of the organized working class. Consequently, the distinct ideological orientation of early fascism as regards political economy now had to be reshaped to accommodate the political acceptance of ruling class interests and those of the traditional political elites. This did not mean that these ideological currents that had helped create the basis of fascist movements were irrelevant or that we can understand and explain fascist political economy without reference to them, but that examining and accounting for the specificities of fascist political economy via ideas or ideology alone can only take us so far.

The character of fascist political economy was also, like any other, conditioned by the structure and workings of the international capitalist economy more broadly and, from the perspective of the argument outlined in this book, also by the uneven and combined character of capitalism. So, while fascism emerged and triumphed out of a political context determined, to a significant extent, by UCD, so the contradictions of UCD structured the possibilities of fascist political agency once fascists had gained power. As we shall see, below, the structure of the international political economy and UCD allow a nuance to Tim Mason's conceptualization of the fascist state as reflecting the 'primacy of politics' (Mason, 1968; see Anievas, 2014: 183).

Indeed, although the ideas and prejudices and anti-economic impulses of fascist ideology did influence the political economy of fascism both fascisms culminated in a political economy fundamentally directed towards and shaped by war. War provided the strategic logic for the organization of the capitalist economy and, after its outbreak, the contradictions, and limits on its operations, setting the parameters for the precise determination of how the economy was organized and functioned based on the individual decisions of Mussolini and Hitler. In this respect, the specificities of each political economy exhibited the opportunism, inconsistencies, paranoia, and racist ideology of the two fascist leaders reflecting the significance of their respective roles within each regime and how, ultimately, the importance of fascist ideology was determined by the decisions of each leader. The ideological coherence of fascism was, ultimately, then, about the political coherence and shifts in the actions of Hitler and Mussolini rather than the way a set of core ideological principles and positions were revealed in the policies of each state.

In the Nazi case this was determining of the regime at the outset as soon as it gained state power. While we cannot and should not ignore the ideological bases or influences in the determination of fascist political economy because they do provide a way of ideologically framing the policy decisions and organization of the Italian and German economies, the material and geopolitical imperatives imposed by war supersede such ideationally-driven accounts in the same way an overwhelming attention to liberal ideological nostrums are likely to be lost in the political economy of liberal states in contexts of war. However, as we shall see below, the historical evidence as to what fascist states actually did – and especially in the case of Italy prior to the world economic crisis – indicate that in spite of the distinct ideological justifications for fascist policies and what such policies were desired to achieve in practice, the social and material outcomes were limited to the extent that they revealed a very different set of structures or dynamics prevailing within international capitalism at the time.

Fascist political economy can be seen to reflect the most extreme form of a more generalized tendency across the capitalist world after the onset of the Great Depression towards a set of internal drives towards concentration and centralization in capital and the establishment of state-monopoly capitalist cartels as a way of organizing producer relations and stabilizing both prices and profits for capital. As David Beetham (1983: 53) noted, the greater role of the state in the workings of the capitalist economy was particularly focused on restoring production, growth, and profitability in a context of world depression where the possibilities of international trade as a source of growth had been squeezed dry. This involved the state not only taking on responsibility for production but also consumption in terms of infrastructure investments and rearmament. Such developments took place *across* the capitalist world as the capitalist class was reproduced through increasingly politically-mediated structures – giving rise to the notion of 'state capitalism' (see Pollock, 1982) – and processes whereby production levels, prices and profits were, to a significant degree, politically determined. Such developments were most advanced in Nazi Germany through the war economy's encouragement of such tendencies assisted by the issuance of credit (i.e., industrial debt) that would not need to be paid off due to the consequences of economic plunder.[94]

Alongside the internal reorganization of capitalisms, the international context – through which production and profitability could be realized – were radically reconfigured. In this respect the fascist powers were geopolitically disadvantaged and, ultimately, dependent on the decisions of the two largest international trading areas: the United States and the British Empire. While neither of these states embarked on geopolitical aggression after 1930 their respective turns towards protectionism accentuated the prevailing nationalist and imperialist mind-sets regarding the spatial organization of the world economy. Both Mussolini and Hitler were consistently clear about this; the geopolitical disadvantages that they identified in Italy and Germany's political economy and how the world economic crisis made it instrumentally and economically rational to consider geopolitical aggression as a way of overcoming it. Indeed, it was the foreclosure of any prospect of a liberal internationalist option after 1930 that made fascism a strategic necessity for Italian and German capital at the time. It was this international and geopolitical context – that was largely a consequence of the decisions of the main liberal powers – that helped move the fascist states towards an extreme nationalist framework committed to a reordering of the geopolitical configuration of capitalism as a closed economic system of which war – the preparation and prosecution of – provided the means to achieve. So, while capitalist crisis – in the form of political order in the case of Italy and profitability and growth in the case of Germany – gave rise to fascism, fascist regimes sought to overcome and reconstitute capitalism as a politically-directed system centred on securing interest representation within the fascist party-state and a spatio-temporal – fix based on new geopolitical arrangements that provided the basis for a new regime of accumulation achieved through war and racial extermination.

### 3.1    Organization of the Economy

In spite of fascist ideology and political campaigning and propaganda, once in power, both fascist regimes were defined by an increasing tendency towards centralization, consolidation and cartelization of the economy.[95] Organized

---

94    That is, the logical working out of the credit system in Nazism – whereby increasing levels of debt resulting in higher costs of borrowing – were, in effect, postponed and managed via the economic plunder of occupied territories. In other words, geopolitical plunder became the means to circumvent the normal workings of the capitalist credit system.

95    In the Nazi case this was realized via the Economic Ministry soon after Hitler came to power with the imposition of compulsory cartels as a way of controlling production and

labour was almost immediately destroyed as an independent social and political force, and those petty bourgeois social layers (especially in the Reich) who
had been so crucial in contributing to the mass base of fascism and its political
legitimacy as a government in waiting were largely neglected in the framing
and development of economic policy. There were exceptions for those who
had particular positions or skills serviceable for armaments production, but
it is remarkable that those social layers that had been instrumental in helping to secure fascism into state power failed to see significant material gains
or the restructuring of the political economy to reflect their specific concerns
(Volkmann, 1990: 206). In this respect, Nazism reflected a distinct kind of political economy from that of the far-right coalition of the Wilhelmine era.[96]

There were attempts in both regimes to reconstitute capital-labour relations to reflect the new ideological dispensation and modification of capitalism through forms of corporatist systems of compulsory sectoral organisation
and government of industry that, in theory, were supposed to integrate both
capital and labour as a way of overcoming antagonistic class identities. In fascist Italy this only occurred after an initial phase (1922–25) where the management of the economy was very much driven by the importance of the need
to reassure business interests whose support – via the non-fascist (conservative, nationalist and liberal) elements within the coalition government – was
crucial in consolidating Mussolini's grip on power and continued leadership
of the fascist movement. The initial phase of fascist political economy was,
then, characterized by orthodox liberal fiscal, monetary and economic policies
under the direction of the liberal finance minister, Alberto de Stefani that produced a budget surplus in 1924–25 alongside a number of privatizations (Bel,
2011). Such policies were consistent with Mussolini's shift in 1919 towards an
explicitly pro-business orientation even if it rubbed up against the demands of
a number of provincial *Ras* who insisted on the dismantling of parliamentary
government and the construction of a corporatist framework.

This dynamic played out in the crisis of 1924 that resulted in what most
scholars see as the inauguration of dictatorship. Here, the contradictions of
'liberal fascism' burst out in the open after the abduction and murder of the

---

prices. In the first three years of the regime, 1,600 voluntary cartels were established
alongside the imposition of 120 agreements (Tooze, 2007: 108).

96  As Volkmann (1990: 204–5; see also Milward, 1980: 58) posits, rather than promoting and
protecting the craft and corporate associations of the *Mittelstand* the Nazi shift towards
a political economy of rearmament very much favoured big capital reducing the number
of independent artisans by over 153,000 between 1936 and 1938 as many were, in effect,
forced into working for larger industrial units.

socialist parliamentarian, Giacomo Matteotti, by fascists in June that threatened to bring down Mussolini's coalition government. A little later the *Ras*
and the syndicals went on the offensive – the former through launching a programme of intimidation and violence in the countryside, the latter through a
wave of strikes demanding increased bargaining rights with employers – pressing Mussolini to break with the parliamentary regime. This is what happened
in January 1925 with the move towards the dismantling of parliamentary
government. While in the political sphere fascism move to eliminate opposition and any independent sources of political power, in the economic sphere
Mussolini outlined a corporatist platform whereby 'all economic forces of the
nation [were to be] integrated into the life of the state' (Bel, 2011: 951).

However, in Italy the attempts to establish an equality between the different
producer interests – capital and labour – within the corporate structure as a
basis for managing the economy quickly floundered. Organized labour as an
independent political actor was broken from above through the introduction
of new industrial relations codes that legally sanctioned the universal coverage of fascist unions in place of the independent ones that already existed,
and, from below, through the continuing intimidation and violence that workers and trade unionists suffered at the hands of the Blackshirts (Abse, 1996).
This weakening of labour, regardless of the formal trappings of equality that
supposedly reflected the respect accorded to the corporate-producer interests of workers,[97] in effect, meant that employers had gained not only greater
confidence, but also the political means to impose their will on the factory
floor and over industrial production in general (Grand, 1982: 69–71; Lyttelton,
2004a: 334).

In contrast to workers, the employers' organization *Confindustria* became
the exclusive representative of all industrial employers through the 1926
Vindoni agreement giving it exclusive negotiating rights, a place on the Fascist
Grand Council and a role in government planning agencies (Sarti, 1971: 75). In
spite of attempts by fascist syndical leaders to assert authority in the formal
corporate structure of the state, in practice the official corporate structures
were often by-passed, and key decisions were taken by other state organs.
Indeed, with the intensification of cartelization after 1930 it was direct state
ownership in key industrial sectors that tended to set the conditions of production (see Baker, 2006: 233–4), which only served to reinforce the influence

---

97    The break-up of the fascist labour union in 1928 into smaller – sector-wide – federations
      accentuated the power imbalance between capital and labour through checking the
      political ambitions of the syndicate within the fascist state and weakening the collective
      bargaining power of workers (Grand, 1982: 71).

and power of existing industrial cartels and the elimination of any sources of competition (Sarti, 1971: 137).

Although the fascist syndicals didn't disappear and never gave up their claims to represent the legitimate producer interests of labour, they failed to realize any significant material gains for workers during the course of the regime. Thus, in October 1927 the government announced a general reduction of wages from ten to twenty percent as part of its campaign – the co-called 'quota 90' – for the stabilization of the lira's exchange rate that affected over two million industrial workers and over 500,000 in agriculture (Lyttelton, 2004a: 345). There were further wage cuts in December 1930 (of eight percent) and May 1934 (of seven percent) on the basis, again, of maintaining Italy's export competitiveness (Sarti, 1971: 91–2). Indeed, Grazia (1992: 9) notes, 'Italy was the only industrialized country in which wages fell continuously from the start of the 1920s through to the outbreak of World War II'. Further, and particularly relevant in light of the context for the rise of Italian fascism after the successes of the agrarian red leagues over 1919–20, the wage increases secured over this period of labour militancy and landlord concessions were clawed back after 1922; by 1938 the real incomes of farm labourers were lower than they had been in 1919 (Riley and Desai, 2007: 826). What we can take from this is that the inevitable consequence of fascism's anti-labour orientation and legacy – that was how, ultimately, it came to be accepted into power – was that employers benefited because both their material ownership of the factors of production largely remained in place and with the elimination of organized labour, they had much greater coercive autonomy to determine production (Adler, 1995: 439–40).

In Nazi Germany a similar dynamic operated though with a more brutal character with the outlawing of independent trade unions soon after Hitler came to power in May 1933 and the compulsory registration of all workers as members of the DAF (the *Deutsche Arbeitsfront*). Although the DAF was not completely free of some of the anti-capitalist sentiments that characterized elements of the early Nazi Party it signally failed to represent the interests of workers as real wage growth stagnated throughout the course of the Third Reich. As Milward (1980: 57) noted, over a period when the annual average rate of growth amounted to more than eight percent, the comparable growth of real wages was less than three percent and it was also the case that deflationary wage controls were put in place soon after Hitler came to power until the end of the decade and at a level based on the lowest level reached in the depths of the economic depression (Overy, 1994: 57).[98] This contrasted with the much

---

98  As Richard Overy (1994: 192; 263–4) suggests, the economy of the Reich – even before the outbreak of war – was defined by a sustained and systematic squeeze on consumption,

more favourable dispensation towards the agricultural sector, reflecting the
ideological orientation of the Nazis and the goal of securing self-sufficiency
in food production, with the earnings of self-employed farmers being over
three times that of the increase in weekly wage rates between 1933 and 1938
(Milward, 1980: 58).

However, even this needs some qualification to reflect the class differentiation in this division of spoils. Thus, as Riley (2014: 338–9; see also Neumann,
2009: 392–6) outlines, while the Nazis did implement polices favourable to
agrarian small-holders – their primary mass base – through debt protections,
the establishment of patriarchal systems of impartible inheritance and the
foundation of the Reich Food Estate (the *Reichsnaehrstand*) which purchased
food at fixed prices, they also 'retained the legal device of entailment that protected large estates, and made no serious moves to break them up' and the 'so-
called Hereditary Estate Act of 1933 was aimed at consolidating the position of
an already privileged stratum of rich peasants.'

It is in this context that we need to consider the significance and the successes of fascist regimes in securing full employment. At a time of massive levels of unemployment, the success of fascist states in realizing full-employment
soon after coming to power, particularly in Germany, was a significant achieve-
ment.[99] However, and as we shall see in the discussion of the political economy of rearmament, below, this success was directly connected to, indeed,
inseparable from the militarization of the economy and the subordination of
consumption and welfare to that of rearmament. Full employment in the economic structure that emerged within Germany – a capitalist economy organized for warfare production – meant that workers were treated as producers
rather than consumers. Consequently, living standards in general fell and the
economic boom associated with rearmament in terms of growth was not distributed to workers but to capitalists because of compulsory wage freezes as

---

'[r]eal earnings, after allowance for increased taxation and party levies, as well as declining quality of goods, failed to regain the levels of the late 1920s, even though GNP per head
was 31 percent higher. Consumption as a share of National Income declined from 71 percent in 1928 to 59 percent in 1938, while consumer industries came bottom of the list in
the allocation of raw materials and capital. The deliberate containment of consumption
encouraged higher levels of saving, which was then channelled via the banks and savings
institutions into government loans for the war economy.'

99    The official unemployment level reached over six million in early 1933; a massive hike from
the one and a quarter million registered unemployed in mid-1929. The rise in the employment rate, though impressive, did not match that for the shedding of labour between 1929
and the end of 1932 as full employment based on official records was not reached until
1938 and the level only went below that of 1928–29 in 1936 (Overy, 1994: 38–43).

reflected in profits taking a larger share of industrial income after 1933 than before (Overy, 1994: 57, 95).

As much as the conditions created out of the instabilities and contradictions in the structure and workings of the international political economy helped precipitate the fascist path to state power, so it was this conditioning context that provided the directing impulses for fascist economic strategy. This played itself out in several areas and with the seizing up of transnational capital flows and foreign investment after 1929 and throughout the 1930s, meant that each state had to introduce forms of state debt-financing alongside exchange and capital controls to secure the financial bases of each regime. In Italy, with several banks financially exposed through their holdings in heavy industry, the state was forced to inject capital into the banks in December 1931 with the formation of the Istituto Mobiliare Italiano (IMI). This intervention was later surpassed with the establishment of the principal agency of fascist state capitalism, the IRI (Istituto per la Ricostruzione Industriale) in 1933 that became a key holding agency over a range of industries and especially in iron, steel and shipping, (Grand, 1982: 83, 2004: 52; Baker, 2006: 234). It also extended to the banking sector where 71 percent of banking assets were held in government securities by the end of the war compared with 20 percent in the early 1930s (Baker, 2006: 233–4) and where the three largest banks came under IRI control (Bel, 2011: 952). However, such extensions of state influence over parts of the economy did not necessarily amount to a squeezing out of private capital investment as private economic power continued to prosper as reflected in the growth of major concentrations of private power in the electricity sectors (Edison, SADE), chemicals (Montecatini, Pirelli), and automobiles (Fiat) (Lyttelton, 2004a: 439–40).

In Germany the credit squeeze was overcome through the creation of state-backed forms of credit (Meo), the *Metallurgichen-Forschungs GmbH* that were used as a form of payment associated with government orders and production, and also provided a source of credit for banks that helped stabilize the financial system during the 1930s (Baker 2006: 233). Further, as we shall see below, in the context of a war economy the Nazi state took extraordinary steps to maintain stable flows of credit to industry but at the cost of building up huge levels of debt that would have produced a financial reckoning with likely political consequences even if the Nazis had won the war.

The extension of state control and debt-financing in Italy and Germany also extended to research and production especially in sectors connected to armaments production. Indeed, in these cases, most notoriously that of the German chemicals combine, I. G. Farben, major firms and their corporate leaders became key architects of production (Hayes, 1987; Kershaw, 2000: 60;

Müller, 2003: 468, Tooze, 2007: 227–9, 389, 527). This encouraged bureaucratic in-fighting for control of resources and profits – fuelling rampant corruption – (see Milward, 1965; 8–10, 155–6; Overy, 1994: 144–5) that reflected the way in which production and accumulation were increasingly connected to access to or control of political influence within the fascist state, which revealed itself with the creation of 'mini' or 'local empires' within particular industries or regions such as Bavaria or parts of southern Italy. It also meant that some firms were at the heart of the fascist state complex where production, capital accumulation and the architecture of violence, war and genocide came together. Thus, as Alan Milward (1980: 59; see also Kershaw, 2000: 58–60) noted, I. G. Farben was highly successful in promoting its commercial interests throughout the history of the Reich including the way in which it plundered foreign assets in the occupied areas. More significantly though was the decisive role of its personnel in staffing the Four-Year Plan Office  and in determining industrial policy in the areas where the company dominated (Diarmuid, 2007; Hayes, 1987: 213–375; Kershaw, 2000: 60; Riley, 2014: 336–7; Tooze, 2007: 227; Volkmann, 1990: 328).

While state control was extended, the dominant ideological assumption that operated and played out across both regimes – even as war economies after 1939/40 – was that private ownership and capitalist forms of production based on the autonomy of owners and managers to determine forms of production and the accumulation of profits would continue.[100] These economies were certainly state-directed and, with the closing down of international sources of investment, markets and capital flows the state stepped in – as elsewhere across the international capitalist economy in the liberal states. In this respect, the primacy of politics played out via profit and investment levels being determined by Nazi state managers and competition amongst firms was reduced via cartelization and monopoly taking place via political connections and lobbying within and across the Nazi party-state machine, which had a deleterious effect on some of the traditional sources of social power (Overy, 1994: 106). And while there were obviously distinctive characteristics to the primacy of politics in fascism based on the peculiarities of each fascist party-state's corporatist structure, such issues and class dynamics also played out within the liberal-capitalist states to some extent in a context of the mobilizations and prosecutions of war (see Mandel, 2011).

---

100   Indeed, even as late as 1940 privatization of industrial concerns continued as with the Daimler-Benz taking over the private ownership of the aircraft engine maker, Genshagen (Baker, 2006: 235–6; Gregor, 1998).

It is clear then that although the locus of strategic decision-making effecting the structure and workings of each regime's political economy increasingly shifted towards political authorities and, in many respects, Mussolini and Hitler, personally, the organization and workings of each political economy continued to reflect the structural power of fractions of the capitalist class. So, while the initiative and the parameters and focus of production – where the greatest economic rewards lay – were determined by political authorities this did not mean that capitalists had no autonomy in how they responded to such directions, including, in some cases resisting them. Above all else, as Adam Tooze (2007: 134) demonstrates in the case of Nazi Germany, the regime did not have to look far or work hard to find active and enthusiastic partners and collaborators in fulfilling the production directives of the regime.[101] Indeed, it went beyond this. Thus, because of the way in which fascist ideology conceived of the economic sphere and the dynamics of economics and production they paid little attention to the specificities of the organization of the firm and of the actual processes and management of production; inside the firm capital was still king. Further, as Karl-Heinz Roth (2014: 304) has argued, the legal framework that firms worked within in fulfilling state contracts facilitated forms of profit-gouging based on the creation of a number of family businesses that worked alongside the cartels. Controlled by the Flick, Oetker, Schickedanz, Grundig, Reemtsma, Quadt and Bertelmann families these corporate concerns 'inserted themselves into the innovation processes that were subsidised by the military economy, using these processes to maximise their returns on investment'.[102]

---

101    For Ian Kershaw (2000: 66, original emphasis) '[a]bove all, *all* sections of the "power cartel" [including big business] worked to bring about the barbarous war of conquest which made genocide an attainable reality rather than a lunatic vision.' Further, the representatives of big business – in contrast to some of the other elements of the traditional and pre-Nazi elite – were largely absent from the 'internal resistance' to Hitler that had developed by 1943–44.

102    Roth (2014: 304; see also Offner, 1977: 376; Kolko, 1962: 724–5) also notes how the Nazi war economy was also bolstered through the co-operation of American multinational firms working in the Reich, 'General Motors presented the Wehrmacht with the most effective motor truck; the Nazi economy's mass statistics could not have been compiled without IBM's punch-card technology; the Ford plant in River Rouge provided the blueprint for the Volkswagen plant in Fallersleben; I.G. Farben secured for itself the economic options associated with the petrochemical sector by cooperating with Standard Oil of New Jersey [see also Borkin, 1978: 76–94]; the German-Dutch branch of Unilever corporation provided the organisational framework by which the deficit-driven European food industry was regulated.'

In this respect, though the form and mechanisms for the reproduction of capital and the capitalist class were reconfigured under fascism – as they were for capital *tout le monde* – through forms of circulation mediated and determined by state agencies that reduced the autonomy of capital, nevertheless, capitalism remained. In this respect as Franz Neumann (2009: 361) remarked in his classical account of Nazism, *Behemoth*, both capitalists and the Nazi leadership had,

> identical interests … . National Socialism utilized the daring, the knowledge, the aggressiveness of the industrial leadership, while the industrial leadership utilized the anti-democracy, anti-liberalism, and anti-unionism of the National Socialist party, which had fully developed the techniques by which the masses can be controlled and dominated.

Both regimes largely reproduced the class structure that they inherited. Accordingly, in Italy and Germany the key social layers – at least those working in the self-employed sectors[103] – that had provided the mass base of fascism did not materially benefit from fascism in power; in Italy, farm labourers and peasants particularly suffered. Workers had jobs but living standards were stagnant and as war increasingly dominated societal concerns and key shortages of consumption goods increased. This was not the case for capital – both agrarian and financial-industrial. Thus, as Renton (1999: 39; see also Müller, 2003) notes, the income of major employers in Italy rose by an average of 148 percent between 1932 and 1938 and between 1933 and the end of 1936, average profits surged by an astonishing 433 percent. The profits of one major firm – if the most integrated into the party-state nexus – I. G. Farben, increased from 74 million Reichsmarks in 1933 to 244 million in 1939 allowing it to contribute millions of marks to the NSDAP. Further, as Tooze (2005: 6) suggests, in his dismantling of the arguments of Richard Overy (1994) and Götz Aly (2007)

> there is no reason to doubt the well-established picture, which is that income was redistributed sharply away from the working population and in favour of capital in the course of the 1930s [and that while] Hitler's

---

103    The increase in the size and operations of the state did open up opportunities for white-collar employment and material advances – sometimes through networks of corruption – suggesting that the newer petty bourgeois layers, guardedly jealous of their status but not dependent on direct participation in market relations did secure some material (and other) gains through the structure and workings of fascist political economy.

economic recovery brought benefits for the entire population [the] owners of capital were disproportionately favoured.

In both regimes the complexion of the economy changed even if the fundaments of class relations and class power remained in place. These were not capitalisms based on international trade and transnational capital flows. Nor were
they capitalisms based on mass consumer markets. Rather, and to a significant
degree – like the liberal versions of the time – they were state-directed and,
increasingly based on state consumption and state-directed economic activity.
What distinguished the fascist variant of 'state capitalism' as we will see below
was its unique relationship to the *control and expansion of space* and, consequently, its relationship to war and the material means to wage industrial war.
This had consequences beyond the organization of the capitalist economy and
the distortions that it produced in the regular functioning of capitalism and
especially in the Nazi case with respect to Nazi imperialism and the connection
between capitalism and race war.

In recognizing the uniqueness of the fascist/Nazi political economy and the
unprecedented role of state and coercive power in its functioning and reproduction – this was no liberal capitalism – we also, however, need to recognize
the continuities of its capitalist class structure and the continuing sources of
autonomy and advantage that was hard-wired into it.[104] Thus, even in the final
months of the Nazi war effort the fundaments of private property rights and
the autonomy of capitalists[105] to control the production process remained in

---

104    The Nazis made little or no attempt to create alternative ownership structures of firms.
       Likewise, there was never any serious consideration of distributing a portion of a firm's
       profits to workers. For Albert Pietzsch, the president of the Reich chamber of the econ-
       omy, one reason for this was to ensure that workers never lost an interest in working
       harder as a means to serve the Reich (cited in Müller, 2003: 506).

105    Bucheim and Scherner (2006: 397) note that even during the war some firms that were
       integral to the war effort rejected some state contracts to prioritize exports. The fact that
       the regime tolerated such autonomy reflected the significance of the structural context of
       the international political economy that even the Nazi Empire had to work within and the
       need to balance – at some level – the production of war materials based on the resources
       of the 'domestic' economy of the Reichsmark and that of securing foreign exchange
       that necessitated exports without which raw material imports that were crucial to the
       war economy might not be secured. The authors document a range of examples where
       major firms that were integrated into and vital to the armament economy refused to pro-
       cess particular military orders, areas of investment or the prioritization of research to
       secure military objectives and the deployment of their resources and production facili-
       ties for non-military and strategic purposes. Further, rather than resorting to force or the
       'nationalization' of firms the economics and armaments ministries, instead, incentivized

place alongside the accumulation of vast profits. In this respect, as Christoph Buchheim and Jonas Scherner (2006: 393–4) have argued, the autonomy of capital went beyond the formalities or 'the shell of private of ownership' and, instead, amounted to the reproduction of the capital-labour relation within an economy increasingly organized around state-monopoly consumption.

This provides an important qualification to Mason's insight as to fascism reflecting the 'primacy of politics' within the capitalist state and the relationship between state and capital as one based on inequality. While this affected circulation – through guaranteeing sale/consumption – it also rested on politically-determined price fixing thus removing the logic of market competition from the functioning of the economy and the organization of the firm. It meant that new firms could not – or only with state assistance – enter the market, thus undermining some of the associated efficiencies of capitalist-*market* economies. The state direction of production and access to resources – through the rationing of raw materials – also meant that significant sections of the capitalist class withered and disappeared; but this is a *permanent* feature of capitalism. So, even though the complexion of the capitalist class and the wider economy altered, the fundamentals of the production process, the subordination and coercion; indeed, terrorism over labour, and the accumulation of profits remained. And while there were taxes on profit levels in Germany from 1935, the Nazis encouraged capital accumulation as a means to spur productivity and efficiency, as well as rationalization in production and to ensure the strongest firms were involved in meeting the Reich's needs; Hitler and the regime saw no contradiction here. Official profit levels were capped[106] but this did not stop firms from using their autonomy to actually conceal them[107] from the authorities (Müller, 2003: 507).[108] Indeed, even

---

contracts and production orders through offering a range of contracts and other incentives based on risk-sharing.

106   Early into the regime, the Economics Ministry imposed a cap on profits in response to the regime's unease at the (massive) profit levels reported by firms such that shareholder dividends should not exceed a rate of six percent of capital (see Tooze, 2007: 109).

107   As Müller (2003: 506) notes, '[e]arly in 1945, ...the Reich's audit office identified a whole range of hitherto tolerated practices for concealing excess profits that had led "to losses to the Reich treasury, with at the same time benefits to companies and groups of companies that are unjustified in wartime", that amounted to billions of Reichsmarks.'

108   Given the likelihood that officially recorded profit rates concealed the reality of actual profit levels accurate figures are hard to find but it seems clear from a number of sources that the Nazi war economy realized huge levels of profit for the major firms involved in military production. For Müller (2003: 507) 'medium-sized firms, where they were involved in manufacturing armaments, made enormous profits. In some cases, up to 65 percent of turnover can be found, with increases in turnover of 639 percent and

in an industry as vital to the war economy as iron and steel, firms could and did act in a way that prioritized their individual economic concerns over that of Nazi strategy. Thus, in the case of Krupp between 1932 and 1938 its earnings of 251 million Reichmarks saw only limited spending (of 45 million Reichsmarks) on the future enlargement of its production capacity – a key concern of the Reich – and money being accumulated as liquid assets and invested in other companies (Bucheim and Scherner, 2006: 398).

### 3.2     *A Sui Generis Capitalist War Economy*

Both fascist states saw war as the basis of politics; not only in terms of how the spectre of war and violence was a core element of fascist ideology and aesthetics, but also in how the realization of fascism *necessitated* war to secure the regeneration and revitalization of the 'ultranationalist palingenesis' (Griffin, 1995: 4). As we have already noted, fascist political economy was very much oriented towards self-sufficiency and autarchy organized through an imperial geopolitics. Although this was, to a significant extent, based on its ideological suspicions towards international trade – or what they saw as 'dependency' and subordination to other/larger economies – it was also connected to a fundamental concern to restore, reinvigorate and glorify the nation or *volk*, which, in some cases, led them to introduce policies that protected particular economic sectors such as agriculture that were both integral to the ideological myths that these regimes promoted and also central to their political-economic objectives of self-sufficiency. And, in preparation for war this became even more significant. Autarchy and self-sufficiency were, then, hard-wired into fascism and, in this respect, these positions reflected the particular fascist response to the structure and workings of uneven and combined development: a recognition of the inherent structural hierarchies within the world economy, the uneven distribution of economic resources – both natural and geopolitical – and the competitive and conflictual logics operating in the access and advantages accrued from the workings of the world economy.

Focusing on autarchy, however, only takes us so far in understanding the nature of fascist political economy. Thus, in a conjunctural sense, autarchy, or a turn towards reduced international trade exposure and dependence, became the default position; indeed, it was the shift towards imperial or geopolitical protectionism of the two major liberal economies – Britain and the United

---

increases in income of over 2,000 percent.' And '[o]n a rough estimate, the increase in profits of private industry due to the war is put at between 70 and 80 billion Reichsmarks. This order of magnitude matches the entire amount spent on arming the *Wehrmacht* up to 1939 or the *Wehrmacht*'s total expenditure in the fourth year of the war, 1942/3.'

States – after 1930 that provided the circumstances within which fascism came to thrive. In the context of the world economic crisis autarchy became a generalized phenomenon in the reproduction of capitalism – and part of it – in a way that trade liberalization and transnational capital flows had been so in the nineteenth century. The logic of capital was the same, the difference was in its spatial configuration and geographical dimensions.

The autarchy of fascism, however, was something other than that of the liberal powers. Fascist autarchy was a prelude to and a basis for a war economy. And it is this which provides the *differentia specifica* of fascist political economy within the genus of capitalism and the specific forms of crisis generated from within it. Both Italy and Germany were insurgent powers after 1918 and the fascist hostility to both the domestic and international social and political re-ordering that occurred at Versailles reflected a broader antagonism to the status quo of the right in general. In both states, and particularly after the onset of the world economic crisis, the urgency of the need for a revision of the geopolitical terms of the Versailles settlement asserted themselves. However, it was to be in the Nazi case where this would play out in its most extreme and horrific form. Accordingly, while both Italy and Germany became highly militarized economies in peacetime, it was Nazi Germany that will be forever associated with the deployment of economic resources within and outside of the Reich and the subordination of all other political demands for the preparation and prosecution of war and, specifically, *race* war. It was this that made Nazism, to quote Nicos Poulantzas (1974), an *exceptional* form of capitalist state in relation to the broader conceptualization of the capitalist state form with respect to Bonapartism and military dictatorship. And its exceptional character was such that the type of organized violence that came to dominate its structure and workings was also the source of its ultimate destruction from within or without.

Adam Tooze's masterpiece on the Nazi economy, *The Wages of Destruction* (2007), anchors his examination and narration of the evolution of the Nazi economy from this viewpoint, differentiating the Nazi experience from that of fascist Italy. In this respect, National Socialism revealed – as far as possible and in a historically unprecedented way (that it is unlikely ever to be surpassed) – the extent to which an industrial-capitalist economy can be organized and structured for war. This is the awful and horrific distinction of *fascist* political economy and its singularity within the genus of capitalism: a capitalist economy subordinated to the production of war materials and the exigencies of total and industrial war where all of the material resources of Nazi Germany and its empire of occupied territories and allies were subordinated to this objective. However, it went beyond this. The objective and means of the Nazi war economy were to service – and was organized as such – for *race* war: the unprecedented combination of the resources and agencies of capital and state for racialized mass murder and genocide which stands as unique in the history of imperialism. Indeed, as the logic of war and terror became ever more pronounced in the functioning of the regime – as evidenced in the coercion involved in the economic mobilization and prosecution of a war on two fronts and in the orchestrating of the 'final solution' – the contradictions of Nazism fully revealed themselves with the ss acting in an increasingly autonomous manner in terms of economic plunder and violence and the coherent workings of the different parts of the state breaking down.

Although the significance of the genocidal character of the regime was a defining marker of German fascism, the significance of race also extends to the organization and workings of the Nazi economy with respect to the key contradictions that emerged within it concerning the management of labour shortages, as well as the 'irrationality' (see Callinicos, 2001; Davidson, 2015: 133–7) or 'wasted economic resources' associated with the Holocaust. It wasn't the case then that Hitler's regime was typically racist in a way comparable to the racist imperialism of the other capitalist industrial powers of the time or, indeed, before. And this provides an important qualification as to the precise character of Nazi racism vis-à-vis European colonial racism in general and the distinct role of violence and the practicalities of genocide compared to the racist atrocities of the colonial era. Consequently, Nazi racism operated in a much more over-determined manner, in a way that, effectively, ended up *undermining* a more efficient employment of the factors of production of the war economy that, in a more *instrumentally* rationalist framing, (i.e., to win the war and secure *Lebensraum*), would have involved nullifying the logic of genocidal racism that came to fuel and direct Nazi policy. The Nazi economy was, then, a capitalist economy over-determined by race war: a capitalist economy where the organization of production and accumulation was mediated by a form of existential racial fear, and an economy organized for race war as an end (to secure *Lebensraum*) and a means, through the mass extermination of millions of Jews and other groups of 'racial inferiors.' In this respect, the (instrumental) rationalism, or political logic of Hitler's political economy of using war and the establishment of *Lebensraum* as part of a vision for a *Grossraum* over continental Europe to overcome the structural and organic problem of Germany's economic development and geopolitical security (see Tooze, 2007: xxiv-xxv), combined with a racist *Weltanschauung* that necessitated genocide. And which became a source of multiple contradictions that undermined the regime's geopolitical objectives of expanding and securing its external frontiers.

Nazism was a political response to the organic uneven and combined character of the Germany economy and state as revealed by the crisis of the early 1930s. This is not to suggest that Nazism was in-built into the DNA of Germany at its inception as a nation-state in the mid-nineteenth century; the so-called *sonderweg* or unique and special path or pathology that defined German political development up until 1945. The 'German problem,' if it can be put that way, is intimately connected to, and inseparable from, the broader global transformations associated with the emergence of a capitalist *world* economy. So, to get from 1848 to 1933 or 1939 is by way of a series of mediations that, nevertheless, implicate the broader structural dynamics of uneven and combined development: from the contradictions of 'iron and rye' prior to 1914, to the incompleteness of the German Revolution of 1918–19, to the contradictions unleashed by the Versailles settlement and the immediacy of the crisis unleashed after 1929. Such moments and decisions saw the ever narrowing of the prospects of alternative paths of capitalist development and, at the same time, the reinforcing and strengthening of the possibilities for and the tendencies towards fascism, but only because of the decisions and behaviour of *other* (liberal) capitalist states.[109] In this respect, the search for an internal or national explanation for fascism not only reveals the analytical weaknesses of methodological internalism; it fundamentally distorts and neglects the actuality of real historical processes and decision-making and the relationship between structure and agency.

In the case of Hitler and the Nazi economy there was a fundamental clarity about its nature and orientation that revealed itself almost immediately. This was the objective of preparing for war and it was the commitment behind this strategic decision towards armaments production that the structure and social relations of all the other aspects of the German economy after 1933 have to be viewed through. Armaments production and war never replaced or overcame

---

109   Tooze (2007: 41, 50–1) singles out two involving the principal liberal powers, the United States and Britain just before and after Hitler came to power and which destroyed any prospect of international economic co-operation. In the case of Britain, he quotes Sir Frederick Philips of the British Treasury on Britain's decision to implement imperial preference and exit the Gold Standard, '[n]o country ever administered a more severe shock to international trade than we did when we both (1) depreciated the £. (2) almost simultaneously turned from free trade to protectionism.' And with respect to the US, Roosevelt's announcement in April 1933 of a unilateral suspension of the dollar's gold convertibility and its subsequent depreciation. The US position was reinforced and with it, the last rites were read on the liberal international economy with the collapse of the London World Economic Conference in June 1933 that effectively closed off any possibility of Germany's economic salvation via international trade.

the working of the value-relation within the German economy; one way or another, sooner or later, the crisis that was building within it because of the focus on the accelerated preparation for war, would explode. And in this respect the 'success' of Nazism in 'resolving' both the political/representational and economic/profitability elements of crisis that had created the conditions for its entry into power must be regarded as highly qualified in the sense of establishing a strong social basis and a stable set of political-institutional arrangements for the longer-term organization and management of capitalism.

And as the months and years passed after 1933 and the window narrowed on the 'ideal' time for the regime to launch its war – when its preparations and economic mobilization had reached peak capacity and when its enemies were most unprepared – with the best chance of securing a quick victory, so the diplomatic and geopolitical opportunities and risk-taking accumulated alongside instabilities and ruptures within the regime itself. This resulted in not only the inevitability of world war – and the acceleration and intensification of Nazi militarization that this produced – but also meant that the ultimate timing of when Germany went to war with the Western powers was when its economy and army were far from ready; hence, triggering a further dynamic of crisis.

Much has been made of the Nazi's success in rapidly reducing the high levels of unemployed workers after coming to power. Indeed, one of the first initiatives was the announcement of the so-called 'Reinhardt programme' in June 1933 – based on a plan drawn up by the previous Schleicher administration – to spend one billion Reichsmarks from the state treasury to finance a works programme through housing and infrastructure construction. While this initiative did have an impact on reducing the number of unemployed, what ultimately accounts for the falls in unemployment in the months that followed was the massive and unprecedented rearmament programme that Hitler launched in June 1933 based on an initial outlay of 35 billion Reichsmarks (Tooze, 2007: 54). As Tooze makes clear, the resources channelled into civilian work programmes explicitly targeted at creating new employment opportunities were not only paltry compared to the sums that began to be lavished on rearmament after 1933[110] but the funds, in effect, dried up after 1934 (Tooze, 2007: 61). Unemployment fell, not as a direct consequence of the introduction of the works programme, but as an indirect consequence of rearmament which would soon contribute to the emergence of a labour shortage within the Reich

---

110    By 1934 military spending made up over 50 percent of central government expenditure on
        goods and services and by 1935 73 percent (Tooze, 2007: 62).

that only got more severe as the intensification of rearmament increased and, especially after 1939.

Rearmament succeeded in quickly realizing full employment as an indirect consequence of increasing levels of state expenditure on military procurement. However, this success was connected to a number of contradictions that be-devilled the rearmament programme and, after 1939, Germany's ability to wage war and meet the material exigencies of total war, especially when the economic resources of its enemies came to be fully realized after 1943. The first and immediate contradiction and constraint concerned the problem of maintaining a rapid programme of rearmament within the limited material resources of the Reich. This was obviously a spur towards innovation to realize self-sufficiency in key strategic resources that would otherwise have to be imported and thus funded through securing sources of foreign exchange that were particularly vulnerable in an international context where international trade was stagnating under the weight of the consequences of the world economic crisis. It was not only felt in industry, however; it also related to the long-standing weakness of the backwardness of German agriculture that never went away during the history of the Third Reich.

The national limits that Hitler confronted spurred on geopolitical risk-taking as well as opportunism. In the former, the re-occupation of the Rhineland in 1935, followed by the *Anschluss* with Austria in 1938 and then the dismemberment of Czechoslovakia in 1939. In the case of the latter, the regime sought out alternative sources of raw material imports crucial to the wartime economy, as well as foodstuffs through a number of bilateral trade treaties with its growing sphere of influence in south-eastern Europe (Berghahn, 1996; Kaiser, 1980: 57–80; 100–169; 218–62; Leitz, 2004: 92–104). However, the regime was not able to overcome its dependence on the international economy, in spite of its commitment to autarchy. As early as 1934 it faced its first crisis with its foreign exchange reserves falling dramatically, as a consequence of the rise in imports to meet the demands of the developing boom in the arms economy. The immediate result was the introduction of the rationing of foreign exchange allocations to importers to a level that was five percent what it had been prior to the crisis in July 1931 (Tooze, 2007: 69).

The crisis demonstrated the constraints that the regime was forced to work within. This reflected both the international structural vulnerabilities of the regime and its armaments programme derived from the uneven and combined character (see Anievas, 2014:164–83) of its development and the conjuncture that produced fascism, as well as the influence of political and economic decisions taken outside of Germany on its ability to realize its rearmament objectives and, ultimately, the future security of the Reich. In this respect it was the willingness of the British authorities to co-operate with the Nazi regime – and especially through the agreement to establish an Anglo-German Payments Agreement in November 1934 – that not only helped the regime weather the crisis, but also avoid a set of alternative policy options that would have had serious and negative consequences on the German economy and the regime. Thus, having been in power for less than two years Hitler's position was far from fully secure and given that Britain was Germany's primary export market and source of foreign exchange (Tooze, 2007: 70, 87; Wendt, 1983: 168) the way in which the crisis was favourably resolved for the regime was crucial to its longer term security and future prospects.

The regime's ability to navigate crises and maintain the momentum of its rearmament was then, *conditional* on the international economy. Thus, up until 1940 its ability to feed itself and prepare for major or world war continued to depend on working within the structural constraints imposed by Germany's position within the broader contours of the world economy and, specifically its continued dependence on the contributions of raw materials imports – that required foreign exchange from rising levels of exports – to the arms economy, and in spite of the huge investments and advances made in developing synthetic alternatives to rubber and fuel in particular. So, while Hitler's goal was self-sufficiency and the termination of Germany's dependence on exports through the establishment of a continental *Grossraum*, the means for achieving this end required, in the medium term – or until the *Wehrmacht* was ready to wage and win a major war – continuing engagement with the international economy.[111] The significance of this is that Hitler's actual decision to embark on war in 1939 – after he had purged the leadership of the Wehrmacht in early 1938 in response to their reservations about the timing of war – was determined by the exigencies of the structure and operations of the world economy (Kershaw, 2000: 62). With the shifting diplomatic and geopolitical context after 1938, as reflected in the inauguration of major programmes of rearmament in the West (alongside that of the USSR), Hitler knew that the timeframe to secure maximum military advantage based on Germany's rapid programme

---

111 Such engagement was, however, increasingly narrowly focused on securing Germany's military preparedness even when the broader prospects of the international economy looked more favourable towards German exports and the development of international trade as they did in 1936 based on decisions by the main liberal trading powers, including the United States. In this case, some elements within the regime looked favourably disposed towards such openings and a possible shift and rebalancing – away from rapid rearmament – in the direction of the German economy that Hitler refused to countenance (see Tooze, 2007: 216).

of rearmament was incredibly narrow. However, as Tooze (2007: 300–1) reveals the momentum of rearmament and the objective of having enough sufficiently equipped divisions was also contingent on paying for raw material imports and restructuring the Nazi economy to maximise the possibility of realizing such objectives. This is what drove the economic decisions of the regime and ensured that it went further than any other capitalist economy has gone in directing resources to the goals of rearmament and war.

A permanent feature of Nazi capitalism was that consumption was squeezed[112] both as a part of the economy and the population were made to endure sacrifices early on with the introduction of rationing of butter and meat in 1935 (Tooze, 2007: 659). The squeeze on consumption only intensified as the regime moved ever closer to war and once war broke out. Indeed, pressing down on consumption was a necessity for non-inflationary funding of armaments production which came via securing war financing through the 'syphoning off the money accumulated in the coffers of local government, the insurance funds and local savings banks' that saw eight billion Reichmarks worth of savings in 1940 and 12.8 billion in 1941 pumped into the Nazi war economy without any consultation with savers (Tooze, 2007: 354).[113] The Nazi trick here was that cutting back on consumption – combined with an ideological enforcement of a bounty to come at the war's end, alongside keeping a lid on inflation – meant that wages that would have otherwise purchased consumer goods were deposited in the savings banks. The capitalist economy was significantly reconfigured in that state policy increasingly limited the prospects of other forms and sectors of economic activity in terms of access to credit, resources for production (any material related to war production especially steel, rubber and so forth was prioritized for the armament sector with the consumer sector living off any crumbs left over) and access to a market – given wage repression and very high levels of savings – were severely

---

112    After 1935 consumption fell from 70 percent of total economic activity to only contributing 25 percent of growth by 1938 (see Tooze, 2007: 206–7).

113    According to Rolf-Dieter Müller (2003: 500–1) the regime's ballooning expenditure of RM1,471bn was not financed from tax receipts but rather debt which made up 55 percent of the outlays. This resulted in domestic debt rising tenfold from RM33 bn in September 1939 to about RM390 bn by the end of the war. The regime's debt was increasingly financed through short-term instruments that by the spring of 1942 had already outstripped long-term loans with German savings banks and insurance companies being 'silently expropriated' to provide the main sources of credit as savings grew by over 300 percent between 1939 and 1944 as there were fewer and fewer goods available to buy.

circumscribed.[114] This went well beyond any other capitalist economy preparing for and waging war at the time.

In spite of the state-enforced economic rationalization and concentration on armaments and moves towards import-substitution policies to promote self-sufficiency, the regime was unable to overcome the limits of national economy. Thus, while accelerating the pace of rearmament and increasing the capacity of the *Wehrmacht* were the primary goals of policy, the actual workings of the economy did not replicate a centrally-planned model based on the exclusive discretion of party cadres or bureaucrats, as steel – like other resources – continued to be used in non-armament production. Thus, indicating the continuing autonomy of capital and the limits of the 'primacy of the political.' Indeed, this was a factor in the decision to ration steel use in 1937, but this did not solve the problem; production quotas for military equipment slowed resulting in falls in the production of aircraft between 1937 and the summer of 1938 with the army informing Hitler that the four-year targets set in 1936 for the fighting strength of the army would not be met in time (Tooze, 2007: 231–2). The constraints imposed by the international economy continued to condition the workings of the Nazi economy and its ability to meet Hitler's objectives in the time set. And with foreign exchange reserves again falling precipitately low in late 1938 the regime was forced to deploy additional resources to the export sector at a cost to the rearmament drive. And with the steel ration for army goods cut from 530,000 tons to 300,000 in November 1938 the impact was felt on the equipping of approximately a third of the army's divisions in 1939 (Tooze, 2007: 301–3).

In summary, the militarized character of Nazi capitalism was riven with contradictions, of which the regime's responses to and management of, were key to the timing of the attack on Poland in September 1939 and the regime's war strategy thereafter. While committed to autarchy and self-sufficiency, this could only be realized with the establishment of the *Grossraum*, but this required a major war and defeat of the Western Allies and the USSR. And such an outcome could only be realized (successfully) with the rapid strengthening of its military power that necessitated engagement with and, to some extent, continued *dependence* on economic resources derived from international trade and the workings of the wider world economy (see Anievas, 2014: 178–9). It was these contradictions that ended up determining Hitler's diplomacy and risk-taking – notably the annexation of Czechoslovakia in March 1939 that brought much-needed access to and the plundering of Czech industry and

---

114    Tooze (2007: 353) offers figures of an 11 percent fall in civilian consumption levels in the first year of the war which were down by 18 percent on the 1938 level in 1941.

economic resources – and which, up until 1938 at least, also concerned the domestic security and stability of the Nazi regime. Furthermore, because of the regime's continuing entanglements with the international economy and the liberal powers, the role of and decisions taken by these powers were, by association and in how they, to some degree, enabled German rearmament, implicated in the momentum towards war.

Nazism revealed the most militarized form of capitalism and this was not just in terms of production, but also in terms of the coercive and terroristic character of its labour regime. Yet, it was not a centrally-planned war economy. This meant that in some respects there were organizational inefficiencies in production, as much as the realizing of the regime's war economy objectives were constrained by its need to engage with the international economy and, as we shall see below, the distortions and problems derived from Nazi racism.

### 3.3    Nazi Imperialism: A Provisional and Bifurcated System

The material constraints on the Nazi war economy and the ability of the regime to realize its ideological and geopolitical objectives shifted with its initial military successes in both Poland and the West. By the summer of 1940 Nazi Germany was an imperial-colonial power with the means to extract tribute and resources – material, technological, plant and labour – from the occupied zones. Again, the key economic and strategic objectives were the same: the building up and reinforcement of its military capacity at sea, in the air and on land. And this became even more important with the emergence of a two-front war after June 1941. The Nazi imperial system was short-lived with the period when it was not integrated into war-fighting incredibly short – around twelve months between the defeat of France in June 1940 and the launching of Operation Barbarossa in June 1941. However, while the regime was not fighting over this time it was preparing for a future military conflict and thus the structure and relations across the Nazi Empire were fundamentally rooted in and oriented towards war.

Nazi rule and Nazi imperialism have, obviously, generated a huge amount of commentary and, in particular, over how far Nazi imperialism should be situated and framed within a broader concept and history of European imperialism. Indeed, many of the features of European imperialism, land seizure, population expulsion, the use of slave labour, the establishment of racialized social orders based on racist ideology and genocide were replicated in the Nazi case. Consequently, for some scholars[115] Nazism reflected the organic, racist and violence of European imperialism such that there was a direct and organic

---

115    See Hannah Arendt (1968: 123–57, 185–221) and Aimé Césaire (2000: 36) in particular, 'the very Christian bourgeois of the twentieth century ... has Hitler inside him ... what he

connection between it and Nazism; the former was causal and revealed the substantive essence of the latter.

Speculation as to the longer-term or 'normalized' character of Nazi imperialism and its relationship to the German metropole, consequently, can only be speculative. However, what is clear is the evident bifurcation of the Nazi Empire between east and west, and while the differences began to break down as the war moved to its conclusion and as resistance in the West and south/south-east triggered a wave of Nazi terror, there continued to remain fundamental differences in the nature of Nazi imperial power across the two zones. The differences and the reasons for them are not difficult to identify and explain given the racist character of Nazi ideology and the economic and geopolitical goals of traditional German imperialism and Nazism (see Baranowski, 2011: 233–95; Mazower, 2008:15–30). The east was the area marked out for *Lebensraum*. It was also the location of those people who the Nazis identified as 'racial inferiors' and *Untermensch*, Slavs in particular. It was also the location of Europe's largest populations of Jews and, further east, the geopolitical home of Bolshevism, which the Nazis viewed as the ultimate political manifestation of international Jewry (Hitler, 1992: 631 661–64, 671–2).[116] In the west, Nazi racism privileged Western and Northern Europeans as 'Aryan kin' or racial associates thereof. These areas were also the most economically developed. As we shall see, Nazi imperialism operated within a genocidal racist and geopolitically imperative framework whilst also maintaining some key attributes of capitalist political economy, even within the context of genocide in the east.

Although the occupied zones in the east were the subject of intense and detailed considerations as to how they would be organized and governed and how the populations would be treated (see Dallin, 1957; Kay, 2006; Mazower, 2008: 137–258; Tooze, 2007: 461–85), Nazi policy towards the West was very different. Indeed, there was little clarity as to what the future would hold for the occupied countries of the West and any firm and permanent decisions were to wait until the end of the war. Instead, what characterized the Western zone was a mixture of military occupation and government as in northern France, forms of civilian rule by local collaborationist elites as in Denmark[117] and the

---

cannot forgive Hitler for is not the crime in itself, the crime against man, it is not the humiliation of man as such, it is the crime against the white man, and the fact that he applied to Europe colonialist procedures which until then had been reserved exclusively for the Arabs of Algeria, the "coolies" of India'.

116   In the words of Nazism's chief ideologist, Alfred Rosenberg, 'Russia = Bolshevism = Jewry' cited in Dallin (1957: 9).

117   Of all the Nazi occupied territories Denmark was the least scarred by Nazi rule. The military occupation was minimal, and an elected parliament continued to operate with

Netherlands and an ostensible independent state in Vichy France. All, however, were subject to the exigencies of war.

With respect to the political economy of empire, the Nazis quickly seized military equipment and prioritized control of resources and industries connected to armaments production. In this sense, the western empire replicated the German metropolitan economy with firms such as IG Farben that were integrated into the state, alongside the state conglomerate, *Reichswerke Hermann Goering*, taking control of assets that were either formerly state owned or regarded as of strategic necessity by the Reich (see Overy, 1994: 144–74; Tooze, 2007: 390). Other than these types of expropriation of foreign property, the seizures of private-property were limited with the obvious exception of Jewish-owned assets. Indeed, in France – the most important industrial power within the *Grossraum* outside of the Reich – other than major expropriations of assets in the Lothringen industrial regions there was no systematic or wholesale take-overs (Tooze, 2007: 389).[118]

Maintaining a generalized formal commitment to private property rights underscored the *class* dimensions of German imperialism in the West given the increasing resort to coercion and terror to secure skilled labour within the Reich for the war economy that became more pressing after 1942.[119] In this respect, capitalists were allowed – as they were within the Reich – to carry on organizing and managing the production process, disciplining labour in the firm – which became that much easier with the destruction of the institutions of organized labour – and to secure returns for shareholders. Indeed, most studies have concluded that the Nazis failed to penetrate the economies of the Western occupied zone to any significant extent (Umbreit, 2003: 206;

---

relatively free elections (highlighted by the fact that the local Nazi Party could only gain a paltry 2 percent of the vote in national elections in 1943). However, the longer term goal was its inauguration into the Reich (see Umbriet, 2003: 18; Mazower, 2008: 103).

118    As Tooze notes, 'Holland's great multinationals – Phillips, Uniliver and Shell – all evaded German penetration, by transferring ownership to offshore offices. Neither in Belgium nor in unoccupied France did German capital make significant inroads' (Tooze, 2007: 390; see also Mazower, 2008: 268–9).

119    This was most evident in Denmark where the limited Nazi-imperial incursions into the political administration of occupied Denmark paralleled that of its control of the Danish economy, which was 'largely left to "run itself" and whilst the Reich secured resources it didn't get beyond 10 percent of the overall economy compared to 30–40 percent in the case of France' (see Mazower. 2008: 266–7). Mazower (2008: 271) also notes that '[b]y March 1944, according to OKW [Supreme Command of the Reich's Armed Forces] calculations, France – easily the single largest contributor – had paid 35.1 milliard Reichsmarks, amounting to between a quarter and a third of its national income over that period.' For how this played out in the Netherlands see Warmbrunn (1963: 77–82).

Mazower, 2008: 259–93; Warmbrunn, 1963, 1993). This did not mean that the economy was largely autonomous of the Reich's power; key resources were prioritized for the Reich's economy that, obviously, had deleterious consequences for some firms in the occupied West, but this did not mean that there was no class differentiation within it, and, further, that the generalized logic of capitalist production and accumulation did not operate there. Rather, these were subordinate capitalist economies (and class fractions – again mediated by political connections) that, nevertheless, offered openings and institutional and legal privileges for significant, if not all, fractions of the capitalist class in the Western occupied zone.[120]

If subordination and exploitation were, to some extent, muted due to the limits of Nazi ideological zeal combined with pragmatic considerations over minimizing resentment and possible resistance in the West, this did not mean that the Reich did not extract tribute from the Western zone. As Tooze (2007: 391–2) highlights, the principal means for transferring resources and incorporating these economies into the Nazi war economy was via directly political means that, obviously, connected to coercion and force. These 'occupation costs' went beyond the funding of the administrative and military infrastructure of Nazi occupation, being based on a political calculation, as to what the occupied territories could tolerate in terms of the flow of resources towards the Reich. The Nazis also tempered such 'political accumulation' with offers of exchanging direct monetary transfers to the Nazi Treasury for share ownership of privately-owned firms and, in the case of French capital – with its longstanding economic connections and investments – taking over French-owned firms in east and south-east of the country, which were absorbed into German-owned companies, including the *Reichswerke Hermann Goering* (Tooze, 2007: 389).[121]

---

120   As reflected in the Belgian banker Baron de Launoit – described by a German admirer as 'a veritable Euro-visionary' – who was keen to build on and promote international economic co-op under the Reich, '[t]he Ruhr, South Holland, Belgium, Luxemburg, Lorraine and North France ... constitute a natural economic unit with regard to coal and steel ... We businessmen should burst state borders and learn to cooperate' (cited in Mazower, 2008: 268; see also Gillingham, 1974; Warmbrunn, 1963: 69–82, 1993: 191–3, 198–214).

121   Mazower (2008: 261) calculates that '[b]etween 1940 and 1944 the contribution of the conquered territories to overall German steel consumption rose from 3 to 27 percent, and the proportion of foreign workers in the Reich's labour force rose from 3 to 19 percent ... at the same time, German consumption increased by one-eighth as a result of contributions from the occupied lands – not including the crucial role of foreign labour ... [and] [b]y 1943 more than half of the French workforce was employed for the German war effort, and more than one-third of its national income was siphoned off for German benefit.'

Nazi economic imperialism also operated through the mechanism of international trade with the occupied economies increasingly organized and integrated into the needs of the Nazi war economy reflecting a typical 'hub and spokes' framework of imperial domination of a periphery. In this sense, the distortions of the armaments economy within Germany were also manifested in the relations between the Reich and its western economic periphery. The organizational form for this was the centralized clearing system organized through the *Reichsbank* that was imposed in August 1940. This framework provides a way of assessing the longer-term potential for the Reich's international economic arrangements with other developed capitalist areas. Accordingly, this arrangement facilitated international trade and also allowed Germany to run what was – for the course of its existence – an unlimited trade deficit (Tooze, 2007: 387). This worked through the political dominance of the Reich and reflected the temporary suspension of conventional market relations in the settling of current account (im)balances between countries. Thus, firms in the occupied zones supplying goods to the Reich were not paid by the consumer or direct purchaser via foreign exchange transactions but, rather, by their own central banks, which accumulated the debt on the balance sheet of the *Reichsbank*'s clearing account. While this allowed trade to take place and the needs of the Nazi economy to be met alongside assisting the circulation of capital so that capitalists received a return, hence ensuring continued production; the German account was never settled.[122]

At the end of war (1944 to be precise) the *Reichsbank* recorded almost 30 billion *Reichsmarks* owing to the combined national banks of the clearing system (Tooze, 2007: 388; see also Umbreit, 2003: 222–9).[123] The exigencies of the war and the provisional nature of the structure of the occupation meant that this arrangement allowed the Reich to meet its armament commitments without provoking a generalized economic crisis through production cuts and/

---

122  Such an arrangement based on the design of the Nazi Minister for Economic Affairs, Walther Funk, shared something in common with British proposals framed by John Maynard Keynes for the workings of a post-war international financial system. There were significant differences – beyond the centrality of Nazi racism in its workings – to be sure, as reflected in the geopolitical subordination of east-central Europe as a source of the Reich's foodstuffs and slave labour – but the centrality of Berlin in the clearing system and the financial and borrowing privileges that followed this paralleled those within Keynes' design for Britain (see van Dormael, 1978: 5–10, 33–6).

123  Foreign contributions to the financing of Germany's war economy added up to RM119bn, enough to cover 28 percent of the *Wehrmacht's* documented expenditure – a subsidy from foreign national economies of a kind none of the other warring states obtained (Müller, 2003: 502).

or hyper-inflation, but it obviously begs the question of how the imbalance would have been managed in the longer-term. In this respect, Nazi thinking was based as much on racial ideological tropes as economic considerations with the expected and anticipated absorption of countries such as Denmark and the Netherlands into the political structure of the Reich (Baranowski, 2011: 290; Mazower, 2008: 102–36; Umbreit, 2003: 24; Warmbrunn, 1963: 21-68). In the case of France – the biggest and most important element within this system – this was not a possibility, suggesting that the burden for any future adjustment would have fallen on the shoulders of the French economy, specifically labour. What this arrangement demonstrates, however, was the crisis-ridden and exceptional character of the Nazi state and imperial system.

Nazism as political statecraft was fundamentally about implementing a racialized vision through wars of conquest (and annihilation) whereby the contradictions within both the Reich and between the Reich and its subordi-nated periphery were put on hold or incubated within the exigencies of war. A context defined by peace does not seem to have been considered or thought through in terms of the relations between the Nazi metropole and its western and southern subordinates other than the considerations of absorbing par-ticular – 'Aryan-like' – countries into the Reich. Accordingly, there remains a fundamental gap in our knowledge as to what would have characterized the Nazi Empire let alone the Nazi political economy outside the context of war, given that the consolidation and extension of Nazi power was fundamentally connected to war – its preparation and prosecution. Indeed, outside of this context it is difficult to be definitive about the nature of the Nazi economy other than that these wartime arrangements and the distortions and contra-dictions within them could not have lasted in the long-term. Nazi imperialism in the West, then, rested on coercion and the threat of force and – in its class dimensions – replicated the kind of social power-relations between capitalists and workers within the Reich; but it did not amount to a systematic and per-manent organization of terror in the way that Nazi power reproduced itself in the East.

The situation in the occupied east was of an altogether different order of magnitude and violence. And it is here, in this geographical context, where the specificities of Nazi racism and imperialism vis-à-vis the *longue durée* of European racism and imperialism are comparable (Césaire, 2000; Fanon, 2001; Olusoga and Erichson, 2010; Zimmerer, 2008; Gerwarth and Malinowski, 2009; King and Stone, 2007; Kühne, 2013). What then characterized Nazi rule in the occupied east, the zone of both *Lebensraum* and Bolshevism? There are a num-ber of elements to be considered here. In the first place from June 1941 until 1944–45 this was a zone of warfare as much as occupation and colonization.

Further, while it became a zone defined by genocide it was also an area that provided important material resources and especially labour into the Reich's war economy (Umbreit, 2003: 107). So, although the east, first Poland and then the western and south-western parts of the USSR, were systematically plundered and – in contrast to the West – the genocide and 'annihilation by labour' that defined Nazi imperialism were juxtaposed to an increasing reliance on '*Untermensch* labour' to maintain the Nazi war economy that peaked at a figure of 7.8 million in the summer of 1944 (Baranowski, 2011: 292; Herbert, 1993: 149; see also Dallin, 1957:428–53; Tooze, 2007: 417; Roth, 204: 308). This not only mediated the playing out of genocide, producing antagonisms within different parts of the Reich's occupation machinery, but also problematized the Nazis' racist vision[124] with the need to import foreign labour from the east to work within the confines of the Reich metropole.

However, although the demand for foreign and slave labour increased as the pressures on the war economy intensified (Herbert, 1993: 151, 165–66, 180), while one part of the Nazi state (under the direction of Gauleiter Fritz Sauckel) sought to address this through deploying foreign workers, at the same time, other parts, (notably the *Wehrmacht* and SS) were carrying out the mass murder of millions, reflecting the awful contradiction and tension at the heart of Nazi imperialism and its political economy (Milward, 1980: 63; Mazower, 2008: 223–56, 303–12). And when one considers the organizational and material resources involved in the carrying out of the genocide as the war in the east moved against the Reich, the fact that so many resources were devoted to seeing through this ideological objective of race war is indicative of the over-determining role of Nazi racism and *race* war on its overall structure and workings, even when it came at a material cost to the effective prosecution of the geopolitical struggle against the Red Army (Mazower, 2008: 317; Milward, 1965: 113–15; Tooze, 2007: 524).

Consequently, while Hitler and the regime did implement a politics of race war in the east that suggested a primacy of ideology in Nazi rule – which meant that the organization of the capitalist economy was subordinated to racist imperatives – it also meant that economic imperatives associated with the efficient use of the factors of production and, in particular, labour, encroached

---

124    The contradictions in the Nazi race economy are illustrated in the regime's commitment to ensure that the Reich was '*Judenfrei*'. Thus, because of labour shortages – that were affecting armaments' production targets – Göring endorsed the lifting of race protocols to permit deploying Jews as forced labourers to work for Siemens and other firms in early 1941. However, only three weeks after Göring approved this, Hitler intervened to prevent the Polish Jews being brought into the Reich in spite of the labour needs that they would fulfil (Herbert, 1993: 157–8).

on and mediated the workings of Nazi racial capitalism, even if they never fully imposed themselves on the Nazi regime (see Herbert, 1993: 189–95). Thus, while Nazi imperialism was not defined by an absolutist genocidal imperative – the constraints of the war economy did impose themselves on the ideological logic of racial extermination – this was a constantly fluctuating, contradictory and tension-ridden process that never resolved itself. Indeed, what was ultimately determining was the question of labour in that, after 1942, it remained a weakness in the working of the Nazi economy because of the constant shortages in key areas and, in consequence, ended up undermining the ability of the regime to realize its military and geopolitical objectives (see Woolf, 1968: 143). Of course, it was the resilience and scale of the USSR that defeated Nazi military power in the east – it did not collapse from its own internal contradictions – but, nevertheless, the contradictions at the heart of the regime and its ideology increased the likelihood of defeat.

The Nazi political economy was defined by the imperative of war mediated by the ideology and practice of race-war; indeed, the material means – machinery and manpower – were focused on realizing a racialized resolution of the economic and geopolitical challenges that the regime faced. With these twin imperatives it is not difficult to see why the Nazi regime was the most coercive and repressive form of capitalist industrial economy in history and a qualitatively different form of imperialism. This raises the question of the relationship between the capitalist class or big business and the imperialism and political economy of Nazism. With the qualifications that have featured in the preceding discussion regarding those fractions of capital that were starved of resources[125] and/or operated in sectors (particularly parts of the export and consumer-facing sectors) that lost out because of the re-orientation of the economy towards autarchy and arms production, significant sections of capital, including banking, grew and benefited from the workings of the Nazi war economy. Thus, as has been well-documented, many key figures across the German capitalist class played crucial roles within the administration of the Nazi economy. Firms such as IG Farben and others showed themselves all too willing to participate in the economic plunder that came with conquest and occupation and, as Adam Tooze (2007: 99–134; see also Diarmuid, 2007; Hayes, 1987; Kershaw, 2000: 66–7; Overy, 1994: 315–42; Roth, 2014; Soth-Rethel, 1987: 89–110) has demonstrated beyond doubt, German capital in many respects enthusiastically embraced the Third Reich and race war.

---

125   By 1944 the goods available to the civilian population were down by 50–60 percent the pre-war level (Müller, 2003: 519).

While German capital was never in the driving seat in terms of the direction that the economy took after 1933 and even though the framework for production, exchange, circulation, and accumulation were reconfigured with the increasing mediation of political processes and state machinery to navigate, capitalists continued to own and manage their property and accumulate profit. And while it would be an exaggeration to claim that the capitalist class *in toto* was a 'willing partner' of the regime – this is seldom the case in any capitalist economy – the capitalist class and its class power and privileges continued to be reproduced through National Socialism and Nazi imperialism was integral to this. In this respect, capital was integrated into the race war of plunder and annihilation in the east. Capital may not have been the directing agent or instigator of these processes, but it willingly acted through and made the most of the opportunities presented by Nazi violence (Kershaw, 2000: 57–67; see also Anievas, 2014: 168–9; Callinicos, 2001: 401–6; Davidson, 2015: 135–7).

There was, then, obviously a difference in the operational or 'instrumental rationality' of capital and Nazism and neither one is reducible to the other. Thus, racism and its exterminatory consequences were 'value rational' for the Nazis (Davidson, 2015: 134; Mason, 1995: 74), in the sense that such actions and goals were 'rational political objectives' within their racial *Weltanschauung*. Accordingly, in Ulrich Herbert's (1993: 195) words, '[r]acism was not a "mistaken belief" serving to conceal the true interests of the regime, which were essentially economic. It was the fixed point of the whole system.' And, in this sense as, Neil Davidson (2015: 134–6) posited, there was a difference and, at some level and at some moments, a contradiction between the *value* rationality of capital accumulation and racial annihilation. German capitalism could have carried on without Nazism as it did prior to 1933 and after 1945 and neither did it 'need' or desire the Holocaust. But this is beside the point, or begs the question, because, even if we recognize the autonomy of the *logic* of capital abstracted from the historical and concrete moment of Germany after 1933 (and even those fractions such as IG Farben most implicated in the war economy), nevertheless, they each became enmeshed together in the workings and pathology of Nazism.

Indeed, the origins of Nazism (and fascism in general) and its essential political relevance was in its ability to reconstitute capitalism as a way out of the world economic crisis without recourse either to its revolutionary overthrow or, a social compromise that involved a place for the class interests of workers. Instead, private property rights would be secured and the class interests of capital, and a new path of capital accumulation established through a spatio-temporal fix based on geopolitical conquest and plunder that also *required* the squeezing out through coercion and terror of surplus value from the super-exploitation of labour. This was Hitler's service to German capital and their political debt to Nazism was because, from the outset, it amounted to a political intervention that, above all else, rested on smashing what were regarded at the time as the twin impediments to capital accumulation: the organized working class and the geopolitical settlement of Versailles.

Yet, at the same time as the capitalist crisis was 'resolved' or reconstituted onto a different geopolitical level (see Caplan, 1977) characterized by a new logic of crisis defined in racial and geopolitical rather than material terms, it brought into being the annihilationist and genocidal logic of Nazism, as *embedded within* the reproduction of actually existing German capitalism and Nazi imperialism. This relationship is suggestive of a set of complimentary interests in the context of the world economic crisis: Nazism was complimentary to capitalism in removing the obstacles to renewed accumulation and opening up the possibilities for a new hegemonic bloc based on *Lebensraum* in the east; capitalism was complimentary to Nazism in providing the innovative and dynamic means and organizational skills and material resources to provide the material bases for the regime's objectives (see Anievas, 2014: 169; Davidson, 2015: 135–7). And while the structure of the international political economy had conditioned and, in some respects, undermined the realization of Nazi political and economic objectives between 1933 and 1940, it was to be geopolitical pressures and constraints imposed by the two-front war after 1942 that would determine the workings of the Nazi economy, ultimately, leading to its collapse through wartime defeat. However, in stating this, and in spite of the levels of political conflict, corruption, and political pressure on the economy, it continued to remain capitalist in its broad outlines.

## 4      Liberal Order and the Rise of Fascism

In this final part of the chapter I want to discuss the relationship between the liberal international order and the rise of fascism and, specifically, the behaviour of the principal liberal democratic powers in the post-1918 period up until 1939. As I outlined in the theoretical discussion and framing of the argument at the start of this book the relationship between far-right forms of politics and liberalism – both as a set of political ideas and as a form of political practice, structure, and state – has been ambiguous, but also, in some moments much closer than the distinct and antagonist ideational features underpinning each would otherwise suggest. This has already been outlined in the previous discussion with respect to the involvement of liberal political actors and political forces in the facilitation of fascist movements coming to power in Italy and

Germany. And, in a different sense, the behaviour of the leading liberal states regarding the management of the international economy after 1918 and especially after the onset of the world economic crisis in 1929. Indeed, it was their decisions that were crucial in providing a set of structural geo-economic conditions advantageous to fascist propaganda and political mobilization.

In the case of the rise of Nazism in Germany, it was the *decisions* of the liberal powers *before* Hitler came to power that, in effect, served to dismantle and foreclose the possibilities of international economic co-operation – based on opening up global trade and capital flows – that ensured Hitler's relevance in resolving the crisis that confronted Germany after 1932. As Adam Tooze (2015a: 26) concludes in his survey of the post-1918 international order, it was, ultimately, the failure of the United States to work with the other main liberal powers to craft a multi-lateral and co-operative and burden-sharing order that opened the door to fascism.[126] Consequently, it was the failure of the US to offer the Weimar republic an international political-economic lifeline and liberal internationalist alternative to nationalist revanchism that destroyed the possibilities of a fascist alternative in Germany. Furthermore, viewing the rise of fascism through such a vantage point – seeing capitalism as a differentiated totality – is suggestive as to how the limits of fascist advance (or other radical system alternatives) within the Anglo-American liberal heartlands could be seen to some extent at least, as *causal* of fascist success elsewhere and especially Germany; the developments in each were inter-connected.

In this section I will focus on the relations between the main liberal powers and those of the two fascist states with a specific focus on Anglo-German relations – arguably the most important one in the build-up to World War Two – and the inter-connections between capitalist political economy and imperialist geopolitics through the ideological prism of anti-communism. The main point that I want to convey is that the ambivalences of the liberal powers in the face of fascism is inseparable from the fears and insecurities of the social and political elites in these powers towards their own domestic political situations – consequent from the global economic crisis – and the possibilities for the advance of the radical left therein, and how such fears corresponded to their geopolitical insecurities *vis-a-vis* the USSR.

Such concerns are part of the ideo-political imaginaries connected to the *longue durée* of liberal order construction and the role of the far-right in this

---

126   In Tooze's (2015: 26) words, '[w]hen all is said and done, the answer must be sought in the failure of the United States to cooperate with the efforts of the French, British, Germans and Japanese to stabilize a viable world economy and to establish new institutions of collective security.'

historical process. And with respect to the inter-war period, this was the key political difference that the governing elites and ruling classes of the liberal powers projected onto the two forms of dictatorship that they confronted in the 1930s. So, while on the one hand, the fascist states threatened to destabilize the post-war geopolitical settlement, but in a way that posed no significant threat to the domestic political and socioeconomic order of the liberal states; nor, in many respects their respective imperial possessions. This contrasted, on the other hand, with a communist state that combined both a geopolitical threat that extended beyond Europe to the imperial interests of the liberal powers and, of even more significance, a perceived threat to their respective domestic social and political orders through the activities of home-grown communist movements that were allied to Moscow, that also, to varying degrees, also extended to the broader and non-communist lefts. Further, such fears were seen as most likely to be realized should Europe be plunged into another major war – the precise circumstances that had produced revolutionary chaos across Europe and Eurasia between 1914 and 1919 and which had also brought the USSR into the world. The fascist dictatorships challenged the geopolitical status quo and – because of their autarkic tendencies – also made a resuscitation of a liberal trading system and international economy that much harder than otherwise would have been the case, but they did not threaten the fundamental pillars of the social and political arrangements of the leading liberal powers – at the domestic and international levels. Indeed, the imperial *economic* logic of fascism replicated the hierarchical and exploitative imperialism of the other major capitalist powers to a significant extent.

This differentiation in how the liberal powers understood and treated the two forms of dictatorship also rested on a further set of ideologically-tainted assumptions. The first was that the outbreak of another war in Europe – either triggered through German aggression or by the liberal powers acting to contain or deter the German geopolitical challenge through a rapid and massive programme of rearmament – would only benefit the USSR through splitting the major capitalist powers and, in the ensuing chaos and destruction of war, might result in communist revolution thus expanding Soviet power westwards (Anievas, 2011: 625; Carley, 1993, 1999: 256–7; MacDonald, 1981: 8; Schmitz, 1988: 1).[127]

The second one reflected the way in which Western elites and ruling classes viewed fascism as a form of politics and state. Until 1938 the liberal powers saw

---

127   Thus, a widespread view across ruling elites was that another European war should be avoided because it would 'hasten world revolution' (Stanley Baldwin cited in Niedhart, 1983: 290).

fascism as divided between 'moderate' and 'extremist' factions (MacDonald, 1981: 5, 9–10; Schmitz, 1988: 6, 61–2, 75, 141). The consequence of this was that their policies tended to focus on securing and supporting who they saw as the 'moderate' elements within the fascist state. Indeed, well into the Nazi dictatorship British and American state managers assumed that Hitler was part of the moderate faction.[128] Fascist dictatorship was viewed as a form of authoritarian politics well-suited to the instability and challenges that confronted first Italy and then Germany. That they were authoritarian and had dismantled the workings of liberal democracy was disagreeable, but the liberal powers regarded such developments as necessary and understandable political responses to the combination of domestic social and political crises and the threat of communism.[129] Accordingly, in the case of Italy, the violence that characterized Mussolini's accession to power and which continued to punctuate the dictatorship thereafter tended to be blamed on 'Bolshevik conspiracies' rather than the actions of the fascist state (Schmitz, 1988: 6, 36–7, 76). Thus, in spite of the brutal repression that marked out both of these regimes, it was only when they moved to forcefully reconfigure territorial borders in Europe did the liberal powers move to treat fascism as a form of politics fundamentally antagonistic to liberal and politically acceptable norms.

The final element that conditioned the liberal response concerns Britain in particular and how its ability to respond to the growing geopolitical threat of Nazi Germany – that was increasingly evident by the late 1930s – was severely hamstrung by a fear across the political elite that the domestic socioeconomic consequences of the rearmament required to deal with it and the possibility of war would irrevocably shatter the structure of the British economy and realize an unprecedented social and political advance for organized labour. So, although British policy was fearful of communism in its geopolitical and

---

128  As the American *charge d'affairs* in Berlin, George A. Gordon, opined in early 1933, 'there is no doubt that a very definite struggle is going on between the violent radical wing of the Nazi Party ... and what may be termed the more moderate section of the party, headed by Hitler himself ... which appeals to all civilized and reasonable people' (cited in Schmitz, 1988: 140).

129  For a significant, if not dominant, portion of the British political elite, 'fascism was not an unmitigated evil', but 'an effective weapon against communism and socialism and a barrier to the expansion of bolshevism beyond the borders of the Soviet Union' (Carley 1999: 3–4). Indeed, as the former British prime minister David Lloyd George recognized in his speech to the House of Commons in November 1934 when he asserted, 'that in a very short time, perhaps in a year, perhaps in two, the Conservative elements in this country will be looking to Germany as the bulwark against Communism in Europe' (quoted in Hansard, 1934, column 920).

domestic ideo-political manifestations, leading government figures and the wider milieu of the ruling class were willing to continue engaging fascism for as long as they did because they did not want to implement a series of political decisions that would damage their own social interests and the social layers that they represented. As it turned out, such concerns were highly prescient, as rearmament and the mobilization and then prosecution of war did lead to an unprecedented transformation of Britain's economy, social order, and politics, and in a direction that much of the British ruling class and political elite, prior to the war, were opposed to.

What follows from these observations is that it is possible to view; and, in many respects, it is undeniable, that the inter-war period reflected a form of *cold war*, as the major liberal powers viewed the USSR as a greater geopolitical threat than the fascist dictatorships and the ideology and politics of communism as a much greater worry for the maintenance of the liberal-capitalist social order at home and the wider liberal international order than fascism.[130] Consequently, until 1939 fascism was seen as a necessary response to the challenge of the revolutionary left and an international ally against the USSR.[131] It was this hostility towards international communism which was shared with fascism that brought these two ideological positions into a shared geopolitical orbit premised on an antagonism towards Moscow throughout the 1930s (Anievas, 2011, 2014; Carley, 2014; Halperin, 2004; Little, 1983; Shaw, 2003). The significance of this obviously has a bearing on the geopolitical confrontation between the liberal powers and the USSR after 1945 that came to structure world politics and, with it, as we shall see in the following volume, the way in which fascist legacies played out in the consolidation and development of the post-war liberal international order (Anievas and Saull, 2020, forthcoming).

In many respects, and especially in its framing within the discipline of International Relations, the period after 1918 is seen as a period or moment of 'thwarted liberalism', or, at least, an opportunity lost to construct a liberal international order out of the ashes of great power war. That the liberal order was compromised at birth – as evidenced in the punitive character of the

---

130  Indicative of such sentiments – that went well beyond reactionaries in the Conservative Party – the MP, Nancy Astor, in a speech to the House of Commons in 1937 opined that, 'when we talk about rearming it is absurd only to talk about the menace of Germany ... Russia has an army far greater than Germany's, and she has an air force far greater than Germany's, and furthermore Russia has a policy of international war. An international world war is what she wants' (cited in Crowson, 1997: 36–7).

131  Even one of the strongest opponents of appeasement, the Conservative MP Leo Amery, did not support an alliance with Moscow even after the debacle of Munich (Crowson, 1997: 116–7).

Versailles settlement, the fragility of many of the new states created out of the collapsed European empires, the continuation of imperial geopolitics and US non-participation in the newly created League of Nations – did not mean that international liberalism was doomed from the outset. Therefore, even with the establishment of the fascist dictatorships in Italy and Germany and the destruction of liberal democracy and the violent suppressions of the left, the ending of liberal order 'at home' did not, at this stage, signal the death of the post-war *international* liberal order. The establishment of dictatorship within these states did not automatically equate to a breakdown of the liberal international order given that the principal architects of the Versailles settlement continued to be liberal in their domestic political arrangements and remained committed to upholding the arrangements agreed in 1919. Further, the fundamental challenge to the post-war international order would only come if and when: (1) its international economic foundations collapsed; and (2) the geopolitical settlement was overturned through force.[132] In the case of the former, we have already seen how the world economic crisis after 1929 was crucial if not determining for the establishment of Nazi dictatorship. Moreover, it was the generalized breakdown and dismantling of the economic pillar of the post-war liberal order – in large part due to the actions of the two main liberal powers – that ultimately brought Hitler to the cusp of power. Such developments – both the global economic crisis and the way that the principal liberal powers responded to it – revealed the inherent tensions and contradictions within the architecture of liberal order of which fascism was a symptom.

The question that needs to be addressed is why the liberal powers permitted the post-war liberal international order to be destroyed. More specifically, is what explains the behaviour of the principal liberal powers in response to the emergence of fascist states and fascist *geopolitical aggression*, because this was how and why the liberal international order was, ultimately, dismantled. To understand the degeneration of the post-1918 liberal international order we have to go back to its origins or the context within which it emerged and the kind of compromises that defined it as a particular kind of liberal order that was already infused with proto-fascist qualities. This issue, as we shall see, is common to the formation of all liberal orders throughout history. In this sense the liberal-democratic bases of the post-1918 Versailles order were complemented

132  Even when Italy demonstrated an appetite for international aggression and re-drawing territorial boundaries – as exemplified by the shelling of the Greek island of Corfu in 1923 and the absorption of Fiume in 1924 after signing a treaty with Yugoslavia – it continued to be regarded as stable and loyal member of the post-war international order (see Schmitz, 1988: 101; Cassels, 1970: 91–43).

by the ideology and forces of the far-right. The liberal and democratic bases of the post-1918 international order were compromised at birth and, particularly so in relation to the domestic liberal characteristics of some of its main constituent states. This was because while the Versailles settlement rested on the defeat of Wilhelmine imperialism and the collapse of three empires that had dominated central, eastern, and south-eastern Europe, the actual legal settlement was also drafted with a concern as much with the Soviet Union in mind, as it was with dealing with German militarism. Versailles was, then, both a liberal *and* counter-revolutionary or anti-Bolshevik peace (Mayer, 1968; Anievas, 2014: 128–38; Halperin, 2004: 175–96; Saull, 2007: 25–35).

Indeed, at the war's end, for the key policy-makers of the liberal powers Bolshevism was regarded as not limited to the newly established USSR but also as having already 'infected' the body politic of the new German Republic. Consequently, in the words of Anievas (2014: 12 original emphasis), '[o]f all the dilemmas facing Versailles policymakers, the *social* problems of revolution and disorder at home and abroad were the most decisive in the making of the peace.' The post-war liberal international order was created out of a combined geopolitical and revolutionary context whereby the geopolitical settlement created by Versailles was as much about consolidating the bases of liberal democracy and national self-determination in the newly established states in the east and south-east of Europe as it was with stopping Bolshevism and Soviet power from seeping westwards into the wider body-politic of Europe. And what was significant about the newly created states in east and central Europe was not just that some of them bordered the USSR but that they also bore social, economic and political similarities associated with it as 'analogous forms of combined development' (Anievas, 2014: 129). In a word, they looked ripe for 'Bolshevization'. And the US president, Woodrow Wilson, as much as the French and British leaders at Versailles – Georges Clemenceau and David Lloyd-George – was preoccupied with ensuring that the settlement contained geopolitical measures to contain and overturn the potential of revolutionary expansion (Mayer, 1968; Rosenberg 1996: 11–12).

Accordingly, it was the Bolshevik Revolution itself which was the primary basis of liberal anxiety because it was seen as the main source of social and political disorder. Thus, when Bolshevism threatened to overwhelm Europe in late October 1918, President Wilson favoured maintaining the Kaiser in power in Germany to 'keep it [the Bolsheviks] down – to keep some order'. This position was echoed by the fiercely anti-Bolshevik Secretary of State, Robert Lansing, who continually asserted that of the 'two great evils at work in the world today' (i.e., German absolutism and Bolshevism) the latter was to be feared the most as it was 'destructive of law, order' and private property (quotes in Levin, 1968: 133–134; Foglesong, 1995: 44–45; see also Baranowski, 2011: 109).

For all its ambiguities and hesitations, the Wilson administration's response to the Bolshevik seizure of power, in effect, set the precedent for future US policies towards the USSR including in the period after 1945. Thus, fluctuating between a hope of restoring the liberal-constitutional possibilities associated with the March revolution that overthrew Czarism and the possibility of needing to rely on a far-right authoritarian figure (such as General Kaledin) to restore order and crush Bolshevism, the framing and direction of US intervention through 1918 and the early post-war period prefigured what would become the main stay of US Cold War diplomacy after 1945 (Fogglesong, 1995: 85–88, 104–5, 294–5; Saull, 2007: 25–27). The generalized Western and liberal response to the Bolshevik Revolution was one of counter-revolutionary intervention and it was the progress of these interventions over the course of 1918–19 that cast a shadow over the deliberations at Versailles and informed the substance and orientation of the final settlement. The intervention saw the Western powers provide support to a range of far-right forces across east and central Europe, as well as for the 'White' counter-revolutionaries inside the former Czarist Empire. The objectives were the same: to eliminate Bolshevism as a political threat and overthrow the new Soviet government before it could secure itself and become a geopolitical menace to Europe and the world. While Britain, France and the United States dispatched military forces to Russia and provided military aid to counter-revolutionary armies they also gave licence to Romanian troops to crush the short-lived Hungarian Soviet Republic based in Budapest in August 1919.

This also extended to tolerating anti-Bolshevik and anti-Semitic pogroms carried out by remnants of the German army – what became known as *Freikorps* – in the east, most notoriously in the Baltic states to prevent any possibility of Bolshevism spreading westwards. The significance of these *Freikorps* operations in the east is that such forces were also deployed within Germany itself over 1918 and 1919 to crush the workers' uprising and military mutinies ensuring that Germany was safe for the establishment of bourgeois democracy (Gerwarth, 2008). In short, the response of the Western Allies to the Bolshevik Revolution and the prospect of revolutionary disturbances elsewhere was not only diplomatic hostility, but an acceptance of and acquiescence to quasi-fascist violence that extended to include Jews and other minorities that went well beyond the supposed targets of Bolshevik revolutionary militants. The methods of violence, the agents that carried it out and the principal targets and victims of it in the immediate post-war period were to provide a template for much of what would play out later under the auspices of Operation Barbarossa in 1941 (Baranowski, 2011: 93–115; Traverso, 2007).

The significance of these developments for the determination of the post-1918 liberal international order was that its construction through the framing of Versailles involved an important far-right and quasi-fascist dimension across east and central Europe and Germany. In some respects, the role of violence – and its inter-ethnic dimension in particular – can be attributed to the generic convulsions and instabilities that have tended to accompany the formation of new borders and the movements (and expulsions) of populations in response to the new geopolitical dispensation, and this was certainly the case in the immediate post-war period under consideration here. However, the violence in terms of its political and geopolitical objectives and its intended targets and victims, also reflected a distinct anti-Bolshevik and *class* animus that was also heavily tainted by a racialized view of communism as a distinct international-ist or cosmopolitan ideological creed associated with and created by Jews. In many respects Jews were singled out *as* Bolsheviks regardless of their political sympathies, hence the racialized character of anti-Bolshevism. Consequently, the settling of territorial borders and the political-institutional arrangements that emerged after 1918 bore the imprint of the far-right even if far-right forces were not holding the actual reins of state power. Above all else, the forging of the liberal international order rested, as it did after 1945, on the geopolitical exclusion and containment of the USSR, which had become, by the early 1920s, the settled policy of the Western powers after the failure of Western-backed counter-revolution to overthrow the Bolsheviks.

The hostility towards Bolshevism and, in consequence, the tolerance and embrace of the far-right and proto-fascists in these years was informed by a widespread perception that Bolshevism reflected an ideology and politics that was 'racially Other' to Western and Liberal civilization, which continued to be self-understood in racial terms. Thus, the newly emerged Soviet state was regarded by many US (and European) policymakers as the 'half Asiatic' racial antithesis of the white, Christian West[133] and Bolshevism as a 'mongrel' political form characterized by its Asiatic and Jewish parentage (Fogglesong, 1995: 40; Niedhart, 1983: 291 fn 40; Wendt 1983: 164). This racial Othering that saw Bolshevism as a negation of Western civilization (in contrast to fascist Italy) would also, as we shall see in the next volume, play an important role

---

133   One of earliest and most notorious racial responses to Bolshevism was by the American eugenicist Lothrup Stoddard in his *The Rising Tide of Color Against White World-Supremacy* published in 1921.

in the politics of the post-1945 US far-right and particularly in its campaign against Civil Rights for African-Americans.

This hostility towards the USSR and the forces and ideas of international communism carried on up until the outbreak of war with Germany in September 1939. This is not to suggest that fascist aggression, especially German behaviour after 1936, was not regarded as of geopolitical concern – it evidently was with the move towards rearmament in response to Nazi aggression – but the policy of the Western liberal powers, and Britain and France in particular, towards Nazi Germany was framed in relation to what was seen as the more serious and fundamental threat from the Soviet Union. In the 1930s, then – as before and after – the attitude and behaviour of the liberal centre reflected a mutual unease towards both the fascist/far-right and radical left, but also ended up, until 1939, viewing fascism as both a possible ally against Bolshevism and the USSR, and as a secondary threat to the prevailing international order.

While the main liberal powers either turned a blind eye to or actively encouraged far-right violence at the end of the war and in the early post-war period they also showed themselves to be very much at ease with a fascist movement actually coming to power as was the case in Italy in October 1922 (see Diggins, 1966; Schmitz, 1988: 9–35; Little, 1983: 385). In Italy, as we have seen, the formal trappings of constitutional process overlooked the widespread and continuing role of fascist violence. And as much as the leading liberal and conservative politicians in Italy assumed that such violence was, to some extent, necessary, to suppress the revolutionary left, as well as the expectation that holding the reins of state power would make them 'more responsible', this was also the view shared by the main liberal powers (see Diggins, 1966; Lyttelton, 2004a: 425; Schmitz, 1988: 36–84). The response to and the relations with fascist Italy were in no sense based on ideological or diplomatic rupture or a sense that Italy was – at least until the late 1930s – outside of the liberal system.[134] Italian fascism was regarded as having not only brought stability to Italy but did so through crushing the radical left and preventing the possibility of Soviet access to the Mediterranean. Consequently, as much as Mussolini had helped secure the property rights and social future of the Italian ruling class, likewise, Mussolini was regarded as having done so for the wider interests of 'Western' or 'Liberal civilization'.[135]

---

134   As David Schmitz (1988: 160–61) argues, even after a clear-cut act of international aggression when Italy invaded Abyssinia in October 1935, the US was notable amongst the other main liberal powers for failing to take any significant diplomatic or economic action against Italy.

135   Up until the start of the Great Depression the US developed close economic relations with fascist Italy via forms of foreign direct investment with more than half concentrated in

Such attitudes continued as the prospect of European war increased and as fascist aggression against sovereign democratic states continued. Thus, with the military coup against the newly elected left-wing republican government in Spain, the Anglo-American liberal powers not only failed to assist the democratic government[136] but turned a blind-eye to the military intervention of the two fascist powers in support of Franco's forces (Ramsay, 2019), which played a crucial role in turning the tide in favour of Franco in the civil war. Long suspicious of the left-republican government, the US and Britain saw the civil war as less an armed right-wing assault on a democracy and more of a nationalist response to an attempt at communist expansion (Schmitz, 1988: 165–70; Little, 1985, 1988). Consequently, viewed through this ideological prism – and given that the Spanish republican government had shown itself to be committed to a democratic and social transformation of Spain that had already challenged the traditional powers and privileges of the church and the capitalist class – the liberal powers regarded a victory for Franco's forces in the civil war as preferable to the continuation of the politics of the Popular Front.[137]

While the relationship between fascist Italy and the liberal powers after 1922 suggested the existence of overlapping political, economic and, to some extent, geopolitical interests – that helped reinforce the broader foundations and continuities of liberal international order – the emergence of the Nazi dictatorship, for a number of reasons, posed a much greater threat.[138] This was

---

public utilities. Schmitz calculates that by the start of the Depression the US had invested or lent Italy over $860 million (Schmitz, 1988: 100).

136   The position of the Labour Party on support for the Republic and, more broadly, in relation to how to respond to fascism was equally passive, if for different reasons and Gustav Schmidt's (Schmidt, 1986: 9–10) conclusion that Labour did not offer a genuine alternative policy to the National Government's appeasement policy is largely accurate. Even though the party's pacifist wing became increasingly marginalized after the remilitarization of the Rhineland in 1936, it was not until the Autumn of 1937 that the party voted to support the Spanish Republic's call for the international supply of arms. Overall, even though some leading Labour MPs such as the party leader, Clement Attlee and Herbert Morrison were disposed to an alliance with Moscow against the fascist states, the overwhelming suspicion of Labour MPs and supporters as to the intentions of the National government towards the fascist states meant that Labour was not convinced that rearmament would be used to stand against fascism but, rather, to promote British imperial aggression and/or the suppression of the left at home (see Callaghan, 2007: 129–39; Wichert, 1983).

137   Indeed, Churchill initially focused on the threat of communist expansion consequent on a Republican victory and only changed his mind by mid-1938 when it looked like Franco's forces would prevail (Crowson, 1997: 79).

138   Although Italy's attempts at subverting the Versailles order were, in part, a consequence of its nationalist ideologically-based grievances and the impact of the world economic crisis after 1929, its ability to geopolitically act on them given its relative weaknesses vis-a-vis Britain and France was fundamentally connected to the geopolitical opportunities that

partly to do with Germany's geographical position in the centre of Europe and the significance of Germany to the overall workings of the European and international economies. Indeed, for both Britain and the United States, the revival of their own economies and, with it, the longer-term stabilization of their domestic class relations required an opening up of Germany as an export market. Thus, while the British deployed bilateral economic inducements to appease Hitler and avert a European war, the Americans engaged in economic diplomacy as much to help revive the US economy as it was aimed at maintaining peace in Europe.[139] It was this, and the competing strategies of London and Washington to realise this end which not only meant that they were unwilling to recognize the seriousness of Hitler's geopolitical threat, but also ensured that their respective policies ended up working against each other to Berlin's benefit. Further, it was also the case that the context of world economic crisis and the immediate default of a nationalist and protectionist response to it meant that both the context and language of international diplomacy had become much terser and more combative. Consequently, while fascism was not the generic response, all of the major capitalist states were much more assertive in a nationalist vernacular than they had been in the past and increasingly viewed the world and the workings of the international economy in 'zero-sum' terms.

However, the significance of the Nazi dictatorship lies, more fundamentally, in its radical and aggressive character as regards its international diplomacy after Hitler came to power and in its actions leading up to the invasion of Poland on September 1, 1939. Nazism, from the outset, was committed to not only radical and aggressive geopolitical revisionism, but also a fundamentally and antithetical international political outlook *vis-a-vis* the liberal democratic powers. Hitler's speeches and the course of German policy – both domestic

---

emerged in its relations with the liberal powers after Hitler came to power. Consequently, in the absence of German geopolitical revisionism there are strong grounds to suggest that Italian fascism would have had very limited international consequences on the stability and reproduction of the wider liberal international order.

139   As Callum MacDonald (MacDonald, 1981: 10) notes, 'American interest in "the expansion of international trade" conditioned American interest in appeasement. Cordell Hull [US Secretary of State] had always believed that the restoration of prosperity and full employment within the United States depended upon trade expansion ... As long as Hitler maintained autarky, however, world trade, deprived of the German internal market, would not revive. In the interests of escaping its own depression therefore, the United States had a vested interest in encouraging the German "moderates" who wished to replace autarky with a more traditional economic system.'

and international – suggested as much soon after the Nazis came to power.[140] In spite of this – Hitler did little to hide his obvious intentions vis-à-vis the future of the Versailles settlement – the actions of the Nazi state did not trigger a 'revolutionary' or geopolitical rupture with respect to the responses of the main liberal powers in the way that the Bolshevik Revolution and establishment of the Soviet Union had done.

What is striking about the relationship between Nazi Germany and the two main liberal powers, is how relations did *not* radically alter. Indeed, in many respects in the sphere of the workings of capitalist economy and international economic diplomacy the two liberal states made numerous overtures to engage the Nazi regime and to try and offer economic and geopolitical concessions to Hitler as a way of: (I) avoiding war; (II) engaging with and forming an alliance with the USSR; and (III) avoiding or delaying the implementation of rearmament policies that would have radically reconfigured class relations within their own societies (see Anievas, 2011; MacDonald, 1981, 1983; Offner, 1977, 1983; Schröder, 1983).[141] Both liberal powers tried to deal with Germany through forms of economic diplomacy; what they saw as the best way of protecting the dominant class interests within their own states and avoiding any engagement with the USSR. Further, though there were some dissenters (such as George Messersmith and William Dodd, the US Ambassadors to Austria and Germany, respectively and Sir Robert Vansittart, the permanent undersecretary in the British Foreign Office) policy-elites within both states were overwhelmingly opposed to dealing with Germany via geopolitical sanctions. These elites believed that such a shift would cause – as it did when it subsequently happened – a significant threat to the existing socioeconomic basis of capitalist order within their own societies; notably through greater state-direction of the economy, the politicization of labour relations and the likely social empowerment of organized labour.

The policies – what came to de encapsulated in the term 'appeasement,' – can be seen, then, as a rational and ideologically consistent response to the ideological, security and geopolitical threat posed by the *Soviet Union* rather than Nazi Germany (see Anievas, 2011) and how each state's geopolitical relations were directly connected to the stability of their respective domestic social

---

140 Within months of Hitler taking office, Germany had pulled out of multilateral disarmament talks and withdrawn from the League of Nations.

141 Even after the annexation of the Czech lands and Hitler's humiliation of the British government, the Anglo-German Dusseldorf agreements of March 1939 demonstrated how far Britain was willing to go to maintain the possibility of keeping Nazi Germany within the orbit of what remained of the international trading system (see MacDonald, 1983: 407).

orders. British and American policies were primarily concerned with keeping Nazi Germany within the 'western and capitalist fold'. For Washington this was to be achieved through attempts to draw Germany back into world trade, as this was seen as essential to reviving the liberal world economy to the benefit of the United States. This was done via a combination of commercial and trade inducements and threats of sanctions. Arguably, US policy – at least until late 1938 – was primarily concerned with addressing US *domestic* economic problems through gaining greater access to Germany's market for its exporters rather than treating Germany as first and foremost a geopolitical threat (Schröder, 1983: 392). For Britain, the goal was to use economic inducements to tie Hitler and the German economy into an Anglo-centric international trade order, which was seen as crucial for the maintenance of both Britain's domestic social and political dispensation, and the longer-term stability of the Empire. Such a position put Britain at odds with the US which was committed to weakening Britain's imperialist system that it saw as undermining the longer-term prospects of the US economy.

The relationship between the liberal powers and Nazi Germany was not just about their mutual hostility towards communism and the USSR, but also their contrasting and, to some extent, opposing strategies to secure the longer-term interests of the dominant fractions of the capitalist class within each of the liberal states. In this respect, appeasement was the mirror image of the strategy of the dominant class fractions in Germany (and Italy) in response to the global crisis. The only difference was that whereas the liberal powers required the preservation of geopolitical order, the German ruling class was committed, by the early 1930s – and before Hitler became Chancellor – to overturning it. Appeasement was as much a strategy of political economy as it was of geopolitical management and international diplomacy and to a significant degree it was the domestic socioeconomic and ruling class interests associated with it that prevailed in the reckoning with Nazism. In short, it was a *class* strategy concerned to bolster and reinforce the global economic interests of the dominant – international and imperial – fractions of each ruling class and, at the same time, to minimize the possibilities for the social and political advance of organized labour; hence it was also a strategy of accumulation in a context of crisis.

Regarding the former, as Alexander Anievas (2011) has persuasively argued, British appeasement policy was fundamentally connected to a 'Treasury world view' that reflected the strategic interests of the Bank of England – guardian of the Sterling Area, the City of London and Britain's key export industries. Foreign policy and geopolitical strategy were, then, fundamentally concerned with ensuring the maintenance of Britain's hegemonic position vis-a-vis global

finance and the Empire. Such a strategy recognized Britain's geopolitical vulnerabilities from rival great powers – Japan in the far-east, the US in the Western
Hemisphere and, after 1933, a re-assertive Germany in Europe. The response,
however, privileged political economy and the short-term interests of capital accumulation over that of geopolitical security.[142] Thus, when Britain did
move towards rearmament after 1936 it was done so within the existing macro-
economic framework that was based on the stabilization of Sterling's exchange
rate, the security of the Sterling Area and the maintenance of its international
markets. And, in this respect, the ability of Britain to re-arm was *contingent*
on a set of international economic arrangements that were inimical to US
international trading and economic interests. Consequently, a more effective
strategy of rearmament necessitated coming to terms with Washington and
sacrificing aspects of imperial preference and the wider macro-economic or
Treasury orthodoxy. Indeed, the US was quite clear about this with regard to
Britain's bilateral economic diplomacy. Thus, in its turn towards imperial preference, Britain moved to carve out trade concessions and advantages, in some
cases, challenging US economic interests, as reflected in its bilateral trade
agreement with Argentina that resulted in an increase in British exports at
the expense of US producers between 1930 and 1936 (MacDonald, 1983: 400).
The issue here reflected the rival class interests of the capitalist classes in
Britain and the United States vis-à-vis their respective international strategies of accumulation and the maintenance of the domestic structures of class
power.

Yet, it also went beyond this. While the US was not willing to wage war
to secure its geopolitical objectives it was, like, Germany, a revisionist power
(MacDonald, 1981: 31, 1983: 400), in the sense of its commitment to the dismantling of the British Empire – or at least the system of imperial preference
that had served to close-off large areas of the world economy for American
exports.[143] And given that this arrangement was a key element in Britain's
economic strategy after 1931 which, necessarily, combined with the broader
context of the geopolitics of the Empire, the US, as London was fully aware,
was, to a significant degree, also regarded as a geopolitical rival. Consequently,

---

142   As Anievas (2011: 612) outlines, 'in 1934, the Defence Requirement Committee (DRC)
      identified Germany as Britain's main potential long-term enemy, while further recognis-
      ing Italy and Japan as potential opponents. Despite the identification of these multiple
      threats, the necessary pace and direction of rearmament, as recommended by the DRC's
      November 1935 'Ideal Scheme', was continually stalled by the Treasury.'
143   Cordell Hull was particularly opposed to imperial preference which he regarded as a form
      of 'economic aggression' towards the United States (see MacDonald, 1983: 401).

London's dealings with Berlin reflected both its concerns about German geopolitical revisionism in Europe *and* US global revisionism, and its appeasement policies can be seen as an attempt to 'buy off' Germany – securing its prized economic and trading relationship with it – as a way of managing the growing challenge from the United States. This reached a high-point in March 1939 with the so-called 'Düsseldorf Agreements' between the main representatives of British and German industrial capital which the Americans saw as an attempt to create an Anglo-German imperial trading bloc[144] directed against the possibility of an 'open door' in world markets and at a direct cost to US industry and the prospects of peace (Holland, 1981: 297–8; MacDonald, 1983: 407; Orzack, 1950).

What further complicated or problematized British strategy was how this management of rising geopolitical challenges threatened to undermine the core tenets of Britain's domestic socioeconomic order, and, specifically, the political hierarchy within the capitalist class and the relative power of labour in the wider political economy and the nature of the state. In short, the kind of liberal-capitalist order that defined Britain was at risk. Appeasement policy reflected the dominance of a set of distinct and hegemonic ruling class social interests that prevented an earlier and more effective policy of rearmament. Consequently, class power, at least until 1938, prevailed over geopolitical security. And when geopolitics ultimately proved decisive in shifting the British elite – not least through the pressure of public opinion – the economic measures required for both rearmament and then war-fighting did necessitate and result in a major restructuring of Britain's political economy (Anievas, 2011: 614–5; Schmidt, 1986).

Rearmament – had it been implemented earlier instead of appeasement – would have struck at the heart of the delicate balance that the Treasury/appeasement policy rested on and which policy towards Nazi Germany was framed around. This was not just about a re-drawing of the geopolitical perimeter of imperial security (i.e., if Nazi Germany was the primary threat, then that meant privileging security and economic concerns closer to the British Isles

---

144    The agreement signed by the representatives of the Federation of British Industries and the Reichsgruppe Industrie in March 1939 – with the support of their respective governments – established a framework for industries to negotiate mutually beneficial bilateral cartels to protect and expand their export opportunities to the disadvantage of third party competition through the use of quotas, price fixing, market sharing and joint development schemes (see Orzack, 1950). The public outrage caused by Germany's invasion of the Czech lands whilst the agreement was being celebrated meant that the British government almost immediately disowned it and it was never implemented.

and Europe rather than the far-east), but also about the structure of the British economy: rearmament would come with debt-financing and higher taxes and resulting inflation that would have undermined Sterling's exchange rate and the wider Sterling Area. Further, it would have also resulted in an unprecedented state-political intervention into the workings of the market economy, infringing on property rights and opening up a space for organized labour and the political left to make political inroads on the workings of British capitalism (see Anievas, 2011: 614–5; Schmidt, 1983: 101–9, 1986: 23; Wendt, 1983: 160–1).

While this was not always viewed through an ideological prism distorted by a pronounced anti-Bolshevism it did, nevertheless, concern the potential threat posed by a re-invigorated Labour Party. As Anievas emphasizes, even after British perceptions of Hitler began to shift after 1936 the governing elite was unable to address its increasing geopolitical vulnerability because it continued to prioritise its domestic class foundations that combined with the continuing differentiation as to the threat posed by the USSR in contrast to Nazi Germany. Thus, fears over the reinvigoration of organized labour and the possibility of industrial conflict associated with a move towards rapid rearmament were widespread across the political elite, as revealed in the diary of Oliver Harvey, Lord Halifax's (British Foreign Secretary) private secretary,

> [t]he real opposition to re-arming comes from the rich classes in the [Conservative] Party who fear taxation and believe Nazis on the whole are more conservative than Communists and Socialists: any war, whether we win or not, would destroy the rich idle classes and so they are for peace at any price.
>
> cited in ANIEVAS, 2011: 616

The issue could not be more clearly stated: rearmament as either deterrence or preparation for war would signal the end of the political status quo and social structure that British elites were so desperately trying to save.

The concerns over the wider political and economic ramifications of rearmament – which were well-founded given what occurred after 1945 – of the British ruling class were also buttressed by a particular focus on the German economy and its continued participation in the international economy as integral to the commercial and political interests of Britain through the 1930s.[145]

---

145    As Bernd-Jurgen Wendt makes clear, '[m]any Britons – including those in the highest echelons of government – were prepared to turn a blind eye to the clearly criminal aspects of the Third Reich and Germany's internal affairs so long as Germany, in the heart of Europe, avoided socialist experiments, guaranteed reliability in business, inspired a certain degree

Specifically, it was the role of the City of London in the financing of German trade and as a source of credit for Germany that brought the two economies much closer together and, consequently, provided a substantial lobbying interest within Britain for the maintenance and preference towards Anglo-German economic relations. Indeed, at the time, the view from Washington was that Chamberlain was a 'City man' and that it was the economic interests of the City of London that were driving British appeasement policy.

We came across an important element, or moment, in the development of this relationship earlier in our discussion of the balance of payments crisis that Hitler confronted in 1934 and the role of the Anglo-German payments agreement in helping Nazi Germany overcome this. The agreement not only prevented a major rupture in Anglo-German trade relations, but also *assisted* Hitler's rearmament programme through allowing Berlin to use a significant part of its export surplus from Anglo-German trade to purchase raw materials rather than paying off its external debts to the City of London. While the British interest in the agreement concerned avoiding possible exposure of some British banks to a potential German debt default, it also maintained the contemporary blinkered ruling class fiction of Germany's continuing participation and stake in the liberal international economy (Anievas, 2011: 618).[146] This economic dimension of British appeasement reflected both a means to moderate German behaviour through offering economic inducements and concessions, as well as securing the fundamental bases of Britain's capitalist political economy and the leading class fractions that were dependent on it. Accordingly, in the context of the ongoing effects of the protectionist turn in the world economy the maintenance of Britain's financial and trading relationships with Germany were regarded as of existential significance.

While British policy could be seen as facilitating the economic basis of Nazi imperialism, US economic relations with Germany were hardly less significant. Thus, although US exports to Germany after 1933 fell behind those of other countries, the kind of exports and their particular significance and value to

---

of confidence in British business partners in exports, in the City, in shipping and insurance, and assured prospects of profit for private enterprise' (Wendt, 1983: 165).

146   This was also connected to shoring up international sources of support for the so-called 'pragmatists' or 'liberals' within the Nazi regime such as the Reich Minister for Economics and Reichsbank President, Hjalmar Schacht. As Anievas (2011: 619) notes, '[t]he Payments Agreement was thus designed to ultimately strengthen the Nazi regime from internal socio-economic shocks while protecting Britain's socio-economic interests. This was explicitly recognised by Montague Norman who, during a meeting with British bankers in early 1934, pledged the Bank of England to the Agreement citing the "stabilization of the Nazi regime" as its key objective.'

German rearmament mattered more. The US exported key goods such as petroleum, fertilizer, copper, copper alloys and iron between 1934 and 1938 and the sales of motor fuel and lubricating oil nearly tripled in quantity – and in value, from $12 to $34 million – and constituted between 22 and 32 percent in value of the total of German imports of these items. Such trends were replicated in other products such uranium, vanadium and scrap steel as well as a massive increase in wheat and corn exports in 1938. And, in addition to this, between 1936 and 1940 American direct investments in manufacturing production in Germany rose by 36 percent, from $151 to $206 million (Offner, 1977: 374–6).[147]

As well as working to help stabilize Nazi Germany's external trade and financing position, Britain, like the United States also accepted the terms upon which Hitler invoked revisions to the Versailles settlement (Crowson, 1997: 11; MacDonald, 1981: 31, 40). In this respect, British policy – and its indulgence of German imperialism in central and eastern Europe[148] – reflected a continuity with British attitudes towards the territorial integrity and political independence of the newly created states at the end of World War One. Consequently, as their primary function was as a geopolitical barrier against Bolshevism, they were, ultimately, expendable given the need to maintain Germany's commitment to limited rather than fundamental revisions to Versailles and because Nazi imperial expansion eastwards was regarded as strengthening the West's geopolitical defences against Bolshevism (Anievas, 2011: 619–20). Further, prior to 1938, US policy viewed the prospect of war in Europe as more likely a consequence of the geopolitical encirclement of Germany rather than because of German aggression (Schmitz, 1988: 155). And this obviously informed US thinking about any geopolitical response to German actions including the pressure put on France during the crisis over Czechoslovakia in 1938, less that any confrontation with Berlin over the sanctity of Czechoslovakia's borders might work to Moscow's benefit (MacDonald, 1981: 87). And when Hitler demonstrated that Germany was not interested in playing to Britain's (or America's) tune after the Munich conference with the dismemberment of Czechoslovakia

---

147  It also extended well beyond this as Offner (1977: 416; see also Kolko, 1962) notes, as the unrepatriated profits of US multinationals such as Standard Oil, General Motors, and Du Pont, were used to buy materials and construct transport and storage facilities that assisted the Reich's rearmament programme and assisted the regime in accessing strategic materials such as rubber, chemicals, and aviation fuel through to 1941.

148  British appeasement towards Berlin was also the case in its relations with Italy. Thus, after the 'flip-flopping' in its response to Italy's invasion and annexation of Abyssinia in 1935–6, in 1938 Britain granted de jure recognition of Italian aggression ratifying the agreement even before Italy had enacted its commitments to withdraw its troops from Spain (Crowson, 1997: 13–14).

in March 1939, Britain continued to stand-by its creditor agreement with the Reich which was signed-off in May 1939 (Anievas, 2011: 620).

The benefit of hindsight is a wonderful thing but, in many respects, it was popular and public pressure in Britain that forced the shift in British policy towards Germany, but even this was not fully confirmed until Churchill – the most outspoken and consistent opponent of Nazi aggression – was confirmed as Prime Minister in May 1940. Prior to this there was a possibility after the defeat of France and the humiliation inflicted on the British Expeditionary Force (BEF) that Britain might have sued for peace on the basis that the Empire would be saved. That this did not happen was a reflection of the collapse of public faith in those fractions of the ruling class and political elite resultant from the obvious failure to rein in Nazi aggression and the threat that Nazism all too clearly posed to the independence of Britain.

To reflect on and accept that British appeasement policy ended in ignominy is, however, to overlook the ideological and geopolitical consistency within it that went back to 1917. British policy and the ideological worldview of the ruling class and political elite were shot-through with a visceral hostility towards communism and the USSR and a paranoid fear that: (I) Moscow would manipulate social forces and benefit from any major conflict between Britain and Germany (MacDonald, 1981: 8; Shaw, 2003: 18); and (II) that any mobilization towards confronting Germany would necessitate a self-inflicted dismantling of the existing class order within Britain and which held the Empire together; and that (III) Germany's geographical proximity to the USSR alongside Hitler's unambiguous hostility towards Moscow and communism were of major strategic benefit to Britain. Indeed, prior to 1939, the widespread perception across British (and French) elites was not only that Moscow would benefit from an inter-capitalist war, but it actively wanted it as this would be the means by which communism would spread westwards (Anievas, 2011: 325). And, in this respect, there was an ideological myopia informing British policy that was reflected in an inability to recognize the primary drives of the two dictatorships.

Thus, for far too long Britain's elites treated Nazism and Hitler as both 'rational' and broadly committed to or part of 'Western Civilization'. This contrasted with the USSR and communism – which was understood through a racialized ideological prism – that implied that it was defined by a messianic worldview that prevented the conclusion of any agreement based on shared interests (see Carley, 1999; Shaw, 2003: 1–4, 5–30). Fascism was seen as an element and, in some respects, a necessary ideo-political sentiment within the broader framework of Western civilization in contrast to Bolshevism which was seen as an existential threat based on its Otherness. Such an understanding and differentiation is organic to a liberal *Weltanschauung* – as demonstrated in the ambivalent relationship of liberal and conservative political currents vis-à-vis those of the far-right after 1848 and, as we will see in the following volume, during the Cold War. While this perception of ideological messianism and fanaticism was far from the Soviet reality under Stalin's leadership it was the case, however, that any agreement and co-operation with Moscow would have come with associated costs – both domestic and international – that were far from insignificant for British imperialism and notably with regard to the security of India.

And in this sense, a preference for Nazism did have an obvious appeal from the perspective of the Treasury/Whitehall, the Bank of England, and the City of London. This was quite evident when comparing the social and economic impacts of the two dictatorships and the ramifications of any embrace of the USSR on British domestic and imperial politics. In short, the logic that informed British and Western policy towards the fascist dictatorships until 1939 was reflective of an organic and *longue durée* ambivalence over the relationship between liberalism and the far-right and a consistent anxiety and hostility towards the historical forms of the socialist threat to capitalist social property relations. Ultimately, the institutions and workings of the Western liberal democracies did ensure a shift in policy towards the fascist states with the acknowledgment that Nazi Germany was the primary geopolitical threat that had to be confronted, if necessary, with force. And, in doing so, the shift in political opinion in Britain and France appeared to rest on a recognition of the importance of maintaining and protecting the political *as much as* the economic foundations of liberalism and liberal order. Thus, the destruction of the former by the forces of the fascist far right could have existential costs and consequences of a kind that required looking beyond the short-term interests of those social forces most concerned about protecting their existing class interests based on private property.

## 5      Conclusions

Fascism reflects the most radicalized ideological articulation and state-political incarnation of the far-right. While it revealed some historically unique characteristics that differentiated it from the wider constellation of the far-right that it emerged out of and politically competed with, it was, nevertheless, a species of the generic far-right. This is revealed with respect to its racialized *Weltanschauung*, its hostility towards liberalism and socialism, its social conservatism, its distrust of traditional elites and its ambivalence towards capitalism; and all of these elements were concretized in the politics of the fascist state.

Fascism was also a product of its time and, in consequence, some of its defining characteristics are, to some extent, fixed in that conjuncture. Thus, its emergence and political significance were a direct consequence of the histor-ically distinct forms of both *unevenness* and *combination* that emerged after 1918 with the confluence of the spectre of revolutionary crisis, capitalist crisis, hyper-nationalism, militarism, and the vulnerabilities of liberal democracy. Fascism was the most extreme and radicalized outcome of uneven and com-bined development in the sense of the contradictions within the combination of the past and the present/future. Fascism revealed a conjuncturally specific but generalized trend within liberal order making with respect to the uneven geosocial consequences of capitalist development as revealed in the social layers produced from it and the degree to which they provide the necessary social foundations for the construction of a stable liberal order. Fascism, like Bolshevism was produced from within the contradictory dynamics of an inter-nationalizing liberal order. It exposed the varied and contradictory domes-tic sources of liberal order construction and the disruptive and destabilizing dynamics between the political and economic and national and international dimensions of liberal order construction and maintenance.

Consequently, the era that produced fascism reflected a confluence of structural determinants – ideational, political, economic, social, and geopo-litical – that had been building in the final decades of the nineteenth century and which needed the Great War and the Great Depression to finally reveal them as forms of capitalist state. Fascism was both antithetical to liberalism – it crushed liberal democracy at home and destroyed the liberal international order from without. Yet, in both respects, non-fascist forces and liberals and conservatives specifically – at the domestic and international levels – were complicit in its triumph. In this respect, fascism was compatible with the economic form of liberalism or, more precisely, an economy based on private property rights, the exploitation of labour, capital accumulation and market exchange organized around geopolitical hierarchy. That this involved geopolit-ical re-ordering through war was not, in itself, inimical to, or in contradiction with capitalist economy, nor the social interests of most, if not all, fractions of the capitalist class in a context of crisis.

While the Bolshevik revolution was another contradictory or combined outcome of uneven capitalist development that reflected its varied and con-tradictory geosocial consequences, whereas revolution sought and aspired to overcome the contradictions of historical combination through constructing a radical and future-oriented alternative, the fascist states repackaged the historical contradictions of combination in the amalgam of the reactionary past with the future and, in doing so, super-charged it in a way that created a politics that necessitated aggressive war and the most destructive and horrific form of modern imperialism. Fascism, then, revealed the destructive possibilities contained within the contradictions of capitalist combination. The significance of this is that although a fascist politics was a product of a set of structural conditions, its ultimate success was a product of *acts of historical and specific social and political agency*; decisions that sacrificed liberal democratic order – and the political possibilities and (subaltern) social constituencies therein – on the altar of capital and class. In this respect, fascism had distinct class consequences and can be understood as a form of class politics.

In recognizing the distinct historical features of fascism and its connection to the international and geopolitical structures and processes of the time, I am not suggesting that the significance of fascism is purely, historical. Only that to take the process of UCD seriously requires consideration of the evolving concrete forms that it takes and the kinds of political avenues and opportunities it opens up within any prevailing social and geopolitical structure. Thus, the kinds of crises today that approximate the 'fascist-producing crisis' of the early twentieth century (see Eley, 2015: 93) are largely devoid of the kind of historical structures – geopolitical, material and ideational – that produced fascism. Thus, fascism did not exist as a congealed political idea and movement until the termination of World War I, and while its emergence and experience can never – *post-hoc* – be erased from historical memory or political consciousness, its ability to be reproduced as a kind of replica of the past is fanciful. Yet, the criteria of fascism; the things that we associate with the fascist experience continue to be necessary in assessing the contemporary far-right and the possibilities for its metamorphosis into a political form that replicates aspects of the fascist condition. Indeed, in the second volume that addresses the rise of the neoliberal far-right after the 2007–8 North Atlantic financial crisis and, specifically, the election and support for Donald Trump in the United States after 2016, we return to the debate on fascism in a contemporary context.

# References

Abraham, David (1986) *The Collapse of the Weimar Republic: Political Economy and Crisis* 2nd ed., New York: Holmes and Meier.

Abse, Tobias (1996) 'Italian Workers and Italian Fascism,' in R. Bessel (ed.) *Fascist Italy and Nazi Germany: Comparisons and Contrasts*, Cambridge: Cambridge University Press, pp. 40–60.

Adamson, Walter (1980) 'Gramsci's Interpretation of Fascism,' *Journal of the History of Ideas*, 41/4: 615–633.

Adler, Franklin H. (1979) 'Thalheimer, Bonapartism and National Socialism', *Telos* 40: 95–108.

Adler, Franklin H. (1995) *Italian Industrialists from Liberalism to Fascism: The Political Development of the Industrial Bourgeoisie, 1906–1934*, Cambridge: Cambridge University Press.

Adorno, Theodor, Frenkel-Brunswik, Else, Levinson, Daniel and Sanford, Nevitt (1950) *The Authoritarian Personality*, New York: Harper.

Albertizi, Daniele and McDonnell, Duncan (eds.) (2008) *Twenty-First Century Populism; The Spectre of Western European Democracy*, Baingstoke: Palgrave Macmillan.

Albright, Madeleine (2019) *Fascism: A Warning*, New York: William Collins.

Alexander, Robert (2000) '"No, Minister": French Restoration Rejection of Authoritarianism,' in D. Laven and L. Riall (eds.) *Napoleon's Legacy: Problems of Government Restoration in Europe*, Oxford: Berg, pp. 29–47.

Alford, B. W. E (1996) *Britain in the World Economy since 1880*, London: Longman.

Allen, Theodore (2012a) *The Invention of the White Race, Volume I: Racial Oppression and Social Control*, London: Verso Books.

Allen, Theodore (2012b) *The Invention of the White Race, Volume II: The Origin of Racial Oppression in Anglo-America*, London: Verso Books.

Allinson, Jamie and Anievas, Alexander (2010) 'The Uneven and Combined Development of the Meiji Restoration: A Passive Revolutionary Road to Capitalist Modernity,' *Capital and Class* 34/3: 469–90.

Allinson, Jamie and Anievas, Alexander (2009) 'The Uses and Misuses of Uneven and Combined Development: An Anatomy of a Concept,' *Cambridge Review of International Affairs* 22/1: 47–67.

Aly, Götz (2007) *Hitler's Beneficiaries: Plunder, Racial War and the Nazi Welfare State*, New York: Metropolitan.

Anderson, Kevin (2010) *Marx at the Margins: On Nationalism, Ethnicity, and Non-Western Societies*, Chicago: University of Chicago Press.

Angress, Werner (1959) 'The Political Role of the Peasantry in the Weimar Republic,' *Review of Politics*, 21/3: 530–49.

Anievas, Alexander (2011) 'The International Political Economy of Appeasement: The Social Sources of British Foreign Policy during the 1930s', *Review of International Studies*, 37/2: 601–629.

Anievas, Alexander (2013) '1914 in World Historical Perspective: The "Uneven" and "Combined" Origins of the First World War,' *European Journal of International Relations*, 19/4: 721–46.

Anievas, Alexander (2014) *Capital, the State and War: Class Conflict and Geopolitics in the Thirty Years Crisis, 1914–1945*, Ann Arbor: University of Michigan Press.

Anievas, Alexander (forthcoming) *The Flaming Sword*.

Anievas, Alexander and Nişancioğlu, Kerem (2015) *How the West came to Rule: The Geopolitical Origins of Capitalism*, London: Pluto Press.

Anievas, Alexander and Saull, Richard (2020) 'Reassessing the Cold War and the Far-Right: Fascist Legacies and the Making of the Liberal International Order after 1945,' *International Studies Review,* 22/3: 370–95.

Anievas, Alexander and Saull, Richard (2022) 'The Far-Right in World Politics/World Politics in the Far-Right,' *Globalizations – Special Issue: The Far-Right in World Politics*, online first, https://doi.org/10.1080/14747731.2022.2035061.

Anievas, Alexander and Saull, Richard (forthcoming) *Fascist Legacies in the Making of Liberal Order*.

Arendt, Hannah (1968) *The Origins of Totalitarianism*, New York: Harcourt Inc.

Arnold, Edward (1999) 'Counter-Revolutionary Themes and the Working Class in France of the Bell Epoque: The Case of the Syndicats Jaunes, 1899–1912,' *French History* 13/2: 99–133.

Arrighi, Giovanni (1994) *The Long Twentieth Century: Money, Power and the Origins of Our Times,* London: Verso.

Arrighi, Giovanni, Hui, Po-keung, Krishnendu, Ray and Reifer, Thomas Erlich (1999a) 'Geopolitics and High Finance,' in G. Arrighi and B. Silver, et al., *Chaos and Governance in the Modern World System*, Minneapolis: University of Minnesota Press, pp. 37–96.

Arrighi, Giovanni, Barr, Kenneth and Hisaeda, Shuji (1999b) 'The Transformation of Business Enterprise' in G. Arrighi and B. Silver, et al., *Chaos and Governance in the Modern World System*, Minneapolis: University of Minnesota Press, pp.97–150.

Arrighi, Giovanni and Silver, Beverly (1999) *Chaos and Governance in the Modern World System*, Minneapolis: University of Minnesota Press.

Arzheimer, Kai (2013) 'Working-Class Parties 2.0? Competition between Centre-Left and Extreme-Right Parties,' in J. Rydgren (ed.) *Class Politics and the Radical Right* London: Routledge, pp.75–90.

Baeher, Peter and Richter, Melvin (2004) 'Introduction,' in P. Baeher and M. Richter (eds.) *Dictatorship in History and Theory: Bonapartism, Caesarism, and Totalitarianism*, Cambridge: Cambridge University Press, pp.1–26.

Bairoch, Paul (1989) 'European Trade Policy, 1815–1914,' in P. Mathias and S. Pollard (eds.) *Cambridge Economic History of Europe*, Volume XIII, Cambridge: Cambridge University Press, pp.55–8.

Bairoch, Paul (1993) *Economics and World History: Myths and Paradoxes*, London: Harvester Wheatsheaf.

Baker, David (2006) 'The Political Economy of Fascism: Myth or Reality, or Myth and Reality?' *New Political Economy*, 11/2: 227–50.

Bale, Jeffrey (2017) *The Darkest Side of Politics. Volume I*, London: Routledge.

Balibar, Étienne (1991) 'Racism and Nationalism' in E. Balibar and I. Wallerstein (eds.) *Race, Nation, Class: Ambiguous Identities*, London: Verso, pp. 37–67.

Balibar, Étienne (1999) 'Et Gibt Keinen Staat in Europa: Racism and Politics in Europe Today,' *New Left Review*, 186: 5–19.

Bambery, Chris (1993) 'Euro-Fascism: The Lessons of the Past and Current Tasks' *International Socialism* 60: 3–75.

Banton, Michael (1998) *Racial Theories*, Cambridge: Cambridge University Press.

Baranowski, Shelley (2011) *Nazi Empire: German Colonialism and Imperialism from Bismarck to Hitler*, New York: Cambridge University Press.

Barkan, Elazar (1992) *The Retreat of Scientific Racism*, Cambridge: Cambridge University Press.

Barker, Martin (1981) *The New Racism: Conservatives and the Ideology of the Tribe*, London: Junction Books.

Barratt Brown, Michael (1974) *The Economics of Imperialism*, Harmondsworth: Penguin.

Bataille, Georges and Lovitt, Carl (1979) 'The Psychological Structure of Fascism,' *New German Critique*, 16: 64–87.

Beck, Hermann (1995) *The Origins of the Authoritarian Welfare State in Prussia: Conservatives, Bureaucracy, and the Social Question, 1815–70*, Ann Arbor: University of Michigan Press.

Beck, Hermann (2008) *Fateful Alliance: German Conservatives and the Nazis in 1933*, New York: Berghahn Books.

Beetham, David (ed.) (1983) *Marxists in the Face of Fascism*, Manchester: Manchester University Press.

Bel, Germà (2010) Against the Mainstream: Nazi privatization in 1930s Germany,' *Economic History Review*, 63/1: 34–55.

Bel, Germà (2011) 'The First Privatisation: Selling SOEs and Privatising Public Monopolies in Fascist Italy (1922–1925)' *Cambridge Journal of Economics*, 35/5: 937–956.

Bell, Duncan (2010) 'Mill on Colonies,' *Political Theory*, 38/1:34–64.

Benjamin, Walter ([1935] 2008) *The Work of Art in the Age of Mechanical Reproduction*, Harmondsworth: Penguin Books.

Berghahn, Volker (1996) 'German Big Business and the Quest for a European Economic Empire in the Twentieth Century,' in V. Berghan (ed.) *Quest for Economic Empire: European Strategies of German Big Business in the Twentieth Century*, Providence, RI.: Berghahn, pp. 1–33.

Bernardini, Gene (1977) 'The Origins and Development of Racial Anti-Semitism in Fascist Italy,' *Journal of Modern History*, 49/3: 431–53.

Bessel, Richard (1978) 'Eastern Germany as a Structural Problem in the Weimar Republic,' *Social History*, 3/2: 199–218.

Bessel, Richard (1986) 'Violence as Propaganda: The Role of the Stormtroopers in the Rise of National Socialism' in T. Childers (ed.) *The Formation of the Nazi Constituency 1919–1933*, London: Routledge, pp.131–46.

Betz, Hans-Georg (1994) *Radical Right-Wing Populism in Western Europe*, New York: St Martin's Press.

Betz, Hans-Georg and Immerfall, Stefan (eds.) (1998) *The New Politics of the Right: Neo – Populist Parties and Movements in Established Democracies*, Basingstoke: Macmillan.

Betz, Hans-Georg and Meret, Susi (2009) 'Revisiting Lepanto: The Political Mobilization against Islam in Contemporary Western Europe,' *Patterns of Prejudice*, 43/3–4: 313–34.

Bieler, Andreas and Morton, Adam (2004) 'A Critical Theory Route to Hegemony, World Order and Historical Change: Neo-Gramscian Perspectives in International Relations,' *Capital and Class*, 28/1: 85–113.

Birnbaum, Pierre (1992) *Anti-Semitism in France: A Political History from Leon Blum to the Present* translated by Miriam Kochan, Oxford: Blackwell.

Birnbaum, Pierre (2003) *The Anti-Semitic Moment: A Tour of France in 1898*, translated by Jane Marie Todd, Chicago: University of Chicago Press.

Blackbourn, David (1977) 'The Mittelstand in German Society and Politics, 1871–1914,' *Social History* 1/3: 409–33.

Blackbourn, David (1984a) 'Between Resignation and Volatility: The German Petite Bourgeoisie in the Nineteenth Century' in G. Crossickand H-G. Haupt (eds.) *Shopkeepers and Master Artisans in Nineteenth Century Europe*, London: Methuen, pp. 35–61.

Blackbourn, David (1984b) 'Peasants and Politics in Germany, 1871–1914,' *European History Quarterly* 14/1: 47–75.

Blackbourn, David (1986) 'The Politics of Demagogy in Imperial Germany,' *Past and Present* 113/1: 152–184.

Blackbourn, David (1998) *The Long Nineteenth Century: A History of Germany, 1780–1918*, New York: Oxford University Press.

Blackbourn, David and Eley, Geoff (1984) *The Peculiarities of German History: Bourgeois Society and Politics in Nineteenth Germany*, Oxford: Oxford University Press.

Blackburn, Robin (1988) *The Overthrow of Colonial Slavery, 1776–1848*, London: Verso.

Blackburn, Robin (2011) 'Karl Marx and Abraham Lincoln: A Curious Convergence,' *Historical Materialism: Research in Critical Marxist Theory*, 19/4: 99–128.

Bloch, Ernst ([1935] 2009) *The Heritage of Our Times*, Cambridge: Polity.

Bloch, Ernst and Ritter, Mark (1977) 'Nonsynchronism and the Obligation to Its Dialectics,' *New German Critique*, 11: 22–38.

Böhme, Hemut (1978) *An Introduction to the Social and Economic History of Germany: Politics and Economic Challenge in the Nineteenth and Twentieth Centuries*, translated with an introduction by W. R. Lee, Oxford: Basil Blackwell.

Bon, Gustave Le ([1895] 2001) *The Crowd: A Study of the Popular Mind,* Mineola, NY: Dover Publications.

Bonefeld, Werner (2004) 'Nationalism and Anti-Semitism in Anti-Globalization Perspective,' in W. Bonefeld and K. Psychopedis (eds.) *Human Dignity: Social Autonomy and the Critique of Capitalism*, Aldershot: Ashgate, pp. 147–71.

Bonefeld, Werner (2013) 'Adam Smith and Ordoliberalism: On the Political Form of Market Liberty,' *Review of International Studies*, 39/2: 233–50.

Bonefeld, Werner (2017a) 'Authoritarian Liberalism: From Schmitt via Ordoliberalism to the Euro,' *Critical Sociology* 43/4–5: 747–61.

Bonefeld, Werner (2017b) *The Strong State and the Free Economy*, London: Rowman and Littlefield.

Bonilla-Silva, Eduardo (2009) *Racism Without Racists*, 3rd ed., Lanham, MD: Rowman & Littlefield.

Borkin, Joseph (1978) *The Crime and Punishment of I.G. Farben*, New York: The Free Press.

Borstelmann, Thomas (2001) *The Cold War and the Color Line: American Race Relations in the Global Arena*, Cambridge, MA: Harvard University Press.

Bosworth, R. B. J. (1979) *Italy, the Least of the Great Powers: Italian Foreign Policy before the First World War*, Cambridge: Cambridge University Press.

Botz, Gerhard (1976) 'Austro-Marxist Interpretation of Fascism,' *Journal of Contemporary History*, 11/4: 129–156.

Bouvier, Beatrix (2008) 'On the Tradition of 1848 in Socialism,' in D. Dowe, H-G. Haupt, D. Langewiesche and J. Sperber (eds.) *Europe in 1848: Revolution and Reform* translated by D. Higgins, Oxford: Berghahn Books, pp. 891–915.

Brenner, Robert (2006) *The Economics of Global Turbulence: The Advanced Capitalist Economies from Long Boom to Long Downturn, 1945–2005*, London: Verso.

Broszat, Martin (1981) *The Hitler State: The Foundation and Development of the Internal Structure of the Third Reich*, London: Routledge.

Brown, Benjamin (1966) *The Tariff Reform Movement in Great Britain 1881–1895*, New York: AMS Press, Inc.

Buchheim, Christoph and Scherner, Jonas (2006) 'The Role of Private Property in the Nazi Economy: The Case of Industry,' *Economic History Association*, 66/2: 390–416.

Bullock, Alan (1991) *Hitler and Stalin: Parallel Lives,* London: Harper Collins.

Burns, Michael (1984) *Rural Society and French Politics: Boulangism and the Dreyfus Affair, 1866–1900*, Princeton: Princeton University Press.

Byrnes, Robert (1950) *Anti-Semitism in Modern France, Volume 1: The Prologue to the Dreyfus Affair,* New Brunswick, NJ: Rutgers University Press.

Cain, P. J. (1979) 'Political Economy in Edwardian England: The Tariff-Reform Controversy,' in A. O'Day (ed.) *The Edwardian Age: Conflict and Stability 1900–1914*, London: Macmillan, pp. 35–59.

Cain, P. J. and Hopkins, A. G. (1993) *British Imperialism: Innovation and Expansion 1688–1914*, London: Longman.

Caiani, Manuela, della Porta, Donatella and Wagemann, Claudius (2012) *Mobilizing on the Extreme Right: Germany, Italy, and the United States*, Oxford, Oxford University Press.

Callaghan, John (2007) *The Labour Party and Foreign Policy: A History*, London: Routledge.

Callinicos, Alex (2001) 'Plumbing the Depths: Marxism and the Holocaust,' *Yale Journal of Criticism* 14/2: 385–414.

Callinicos, Alex (2007) 'Does Capitalism Need the State System?' *Cambridge Review of International Affairs*, 20/4: 533–49.

Callinicos, Alex (2009) *Imperialism and Global Political Economy*, Cambridge: Polity.

Callinicos, Alex and Rosenberg, Justin (2008) 'Uneven and Combined Development: The Social – Relational Substratum of "the International"?: An Exchange of Letters', *Cambridge Review of International Affairs*, 21/1: 77–112.

Cameron, Rondo (1975) *France and the Economic Development of Europe, 1800–1914: Conquests of Peace and Seeds of War*, New York: Octagon Books.

Cammet, John (1967) 'Communist Theories of Fascism, 1920–1935,' *Science and Society*, 31/2: 149–63.

Camus, Jean-Yves and Lebourg, Nicolas (2017) *Far-Right Politics in Europe*, Cambridge, MA: Harvard University Press.

Caplan, Jane (1977) 'Theories of Fascism: Nicos Poulantzas as Historian,' *History Workshop* 3: 83–100.

Caplan, Jane (1979) 'Female Sexuality in Fascist Ideology,' *Feminist Review* 1/1: 59–66.

Carley, Michael (1993) 'End of the 'Low, Dishonest Decade': Failure of the Anglo-Franco – Soviet Alliance in 1939,' *Europe-Asia Studies* 45/2: 303–341.

Carley, Michael (1999) *1939: The Alliance that Never Was and the Coming of World War II*, Chicago, IL: I.R. Dee.

Carley, Michael (2014) *Silent Conflict: A Hidden History of Early Soviet-Western Relations*, Lanham, MD, Rowan & Littlefield.

Carter, Elisabeth (2018) 'Right-Wing Extremism/Radicalism: Reconstructing the Concept,' *Journal of Political Ideologies*, 23/2: 157–82.

Cassels, Alan (1970) *Mussolini's Early Diplomacy*, Princeton: Princeton University Press.

Ceplair, Larry (1987) *Under the Shadow of War: Fascism, Anti-Fascism, and Marxists, 1918–1939*, New York: Columbia University Press.

Césaire, Aimé ([1950] 2000) *Discourse on Colonialism*, New York: Monthly Review Press.

Chickering, Roger (1984) *We Men Who Feel Most German: A Cultural Study of the Pan – German League, 1886–1914*, Winchester, Mass: Allen and Unwin.

Childers, Thomas (1976) 'The Social Bases of the National Socialist Vote,' *Journal of Contemporary History* 11/4: 17–42.

Childers, Thomas (1983) *The Nazi Voter: The Social Foundations of Fascism in Germany, 1919–1933*, Chapel Hill, NC: University of North Carolina Press.

Claeys, Gregory (2000) 'The "Survival of the Fittest" and the Origins of Social Darwinism,' *Journal of the History of Ideas*, 61/2: 223–240.

Clark, Martin (1996) *Modern Italy: 1871–1995*, Harlow: Pearson Education.

Clavin, Patricia (2000) *The Great Depression in Europe, 1929–1939*, Basingstoke: Macmillan Press.

Cobban, Alfred (1965) *A History of Modern France Volume II: From the First Empire to the Second Empire, 1799–1871*, Harmondsworth: Penguin Books.

Cobban, Alfred (1990) *A History of Modern France Volume III: France of the Republics, 1871–1962*, London: Penguin.

Coetzee, Marilyn Shevin (1990) *The German Army League: Popular Nationalism in Wilhelmine Germany*, Oxford: Oxford University Press.

Cohrs, Patrick (2006) *The Unfinished Peace after World War I: America, Britain and the Stabilization of Europe, 1919–1932*, Cambridge: Cambridge University Press.

Conrad, Sebastian (2012) *German Colonialism: A Short History*, Cambridge: Cambridge University Press.

Cooper, Luke (2021) *The Authoritarian Contagion: The Global Threat to Democracy*, Bristol: Bristol University Press.

Corner, Paul (1975) *Fascism in Ferrara: 1915–1925*, Oxford: Oxford University Press.

Corner, Paul (2002) 'State and Society, 1901–1922' in A. Lyttleton (ed.) *Liberal and Fascist Italy*, Oxford: Oxford University Press, pp.17–43.

Costigliola, Frank (1976) 'The United States and the Reconstruction of Germany in the 1920s,' *Business History Review* 50/4: 477–502.

Costigliola, Frank (1984) *Awkward Dominion: American Political, Economic, and Cultural Relations with Europe, 1919–1933*, Ithaca: Cornel University Press.

Cox, Robert (1987) *Production, Power and World Order*, New York: Columbia University Press.

Craig, Gordon (1974) *Europe since 1815*, New York: Harcourt Brace Jovanovich.

Crook, Malcolm (2015) 'Universal Suffrage as Counter-Revolution? Electoral Mobilisation under the Second Republic in France, 1848–1851,' *Journal of Historical Sociology* 28/1: 49–66.

Crossick, Geoffrey (1984) 'Shopkeepers and the State in Britain, 1870–1914,' in G. Crossick and H-G. Haupt (eds.) *Shopkeepers and Master Artisans in Nineteenth Century Europe,* London: Methuen, pp. 239–69.

Crossick, Geoffrey and Haupt, Heinz-Gerhard (1995) *The Petite-Bourgeoisie in Europe, 1780–1914,* London: Routledge.

Crowson, N. J. (1997) *Facing Fascism: The Conservative Party and the European Dictators 1935–1940,* London: Routledge.

Dahrendorf, Ralf (1967) *Society and Democracy in Germany,* London: Weidenfeld & Nicolson.

Dallin, Alexander (1957) *German Rule in Russia, 1941–1945: A Study of Occupation Policies,* London: Macmillan & Co. Ltd.

Daunton, Martin (2000) 'Society and Economic Life,' in C. Matthew (ed.) *The Nineteenth Century: 1815–1901, The Short Oxford History of the British Isles, 1815–1901,* Oxford: Oxford University Press, pp. 41–85.

Davidson, Neil (2006) 'From Uneven to Combined Development,' in B. Dunn and H. Radice (eds.) *100 Years of Permanent Revolution: Results and Prospects* London: Pluto Press, pp. 10–26.

Davidson, Neil (2009) 'Putting the Nation back into "the International"', *Cambridge Review of International Affairs,* 22/1: 9–28.

Davidson, Neil (2012) *How Revolutionary Were the Bourgeois Revolutions?* Chicago: Haymarket Books.

Davidson, Neil (2015) 'The Far-Right and the "Needs of Capital"', in R.G. Saull, A. Anievas, N. Davidson and A. Fabry (eds.) *The Longue Durée of the Far-Right: An International Historical Sociology,* London: Routledge, pp. 129–52.

Davidson, Neil and Saull, Richard (2017) 'Neoliberalism and the Far-Right: A Contradictory Embrace,' *Critical Sociology* 43/4–5: 707–24.

Davies, Peter (2002) *The Extreme Right in France, 1789 to the Present,* London: Routledge.

Davis, John A. (1979) 'Introduction: Antonio Gramsci and Italy's Passive Revolution,' in J. A. Davis (ed.) *Gramsci and Italy's Passive Revolution,* London: Routledge, pp. 11–30.

Davison, Sally and Shire, George (2015) 'Race, Migration and Neoliberalism,' *Soundings,* 59: 81–95.

De Felice, Renzo (1977) *Interpretations of Fascism,* Cambridge, MA: Harvard University Press.

De Felice, Renzo (1980) 'Italian Fascism and the Middle Classes,' in S. U. Larsen, B. Hagtvet, and J. P. Myklebust (eds.) *Who were the Fascists? Social Roots of European Fascism,* Bergen: Universitesforlaget, pp. 312–17.

De Hart, Jane Sherron (1991) 'Gender on the Right: Meanings Behind the Existential Scream,' *Gender and History,* 3/3: 246–267.

Diarmuid Jeffreys (2007) *Hell's Cartel: IG Farben and the Making of Hitler's War Machine,* New York: Metropolitan Books.

Diehl, James (1977) *Paramilitary Politics in Weimar Germany*, Bloomington: Indiana University Press.

Diggins, John (1966) 'Flirtation with Fascism: American Pragmatic Liberals and Mussolini's Italy,' *The American Historical Review*, 71/2: 487–506.

Dimitrov, Georgi (1935) 'The Fascist Offensive and the Tasks of the Communist International in the Struggle of the Working Class against Fascism,' *Main Report Delivered at the Seventh Congress of the Communist International*, August 2 https://www.marxists.org/reference/archive/dimitrov/works/1935/08_02.htm.

Donno, Fabrizio de (2006) 'La Razza Ario Mediterranea: Ideas of Race and Citizenship in Colonial and Fascist Italy, 1885–1941,' *Interventions* 8/3: 394–412.

Dormael, Armand van (1978) *Bretton Woods: Birth of a Monetary System*, Basingstoke: Macmillan Press Ltd.

Dornbusch, Rudiger and Frenkel, Jacob (1982) 'The Gold Standard and the Bank of England in the Crisis of 1847,' *National Bureau of Economic Research* Working Paper No.1039, December http://www.nber.org/papers/w1039.pdf.

Dowe, Dieter, Haupt, Heinz-Gerhard, Langewiesche, Dieter and Sperber, Jonathan (eds.) (2008) *Europe in 1848: Revolution and Reform* translated by D. Higgins, Oxford: Berghahn Books.

Draper, Hal (1977) *Karl Marx's Theory of Revolution: Volume 1 State and Bureaucracy*, New York: Monthly Review Press.

Draper, Theodore (1969) 'The Ghost of Social Fascism,' *Commentary* https://www.commentarymagazine.com/articles/the-ghost-of-social-fascism/#47.47.

Drolet, Jean-Francois and Williams, Michael (2018) 'Radical Conservatism and Global Order: International Theory and the New Right', *International Theory*, 10/3: 285–313.

Du Bois, W. E. B. (1935) *Black Reconstruction: An Essay Toward a History of the Part which Black Folk Played in the Attempt to Reconstruct Democracy in America, 1860–1880*, New York: Harcourt, Brace and Company, Inc.

Du Bois, W. E. B. (2015) *The Problem of the Color Line at the Turn of the Twentieth Century: The Essential Early Essays*, New York: Fordham University Press.

Dülffer, Joseph (1976 'Bonapartism, Fascism and National Socialism,' *Journal of Contemporary History* 11/4: 109–28.

Dunnage, Jonathan (1997) 'Continuity in Policing Politics in Italy, 1920–1960,' in M. Mazower (ed.) *The Policing of Politics in the Twentieth Century*, Oxford: Berghahn Books pp.57–90.

Dunnage, Jonathan (2002) *Twentieth Century Italy: A Social History*, London: Pearson Education.

Eatwell, Roger (1992) 'Towards a New Model of Generic Fascism,' *Journal of Theoretical Politics* 4/2: 161–94.

Eatwell, Roger (1996) 'On Defining the Fascist Minimum: The Centrality of Ideology,' *Journal of Political Ideologies* 1/3: 303–19.

Eatwell, Roger (2000) 'The Rebirth of the 'Extreme Right' in Western Europe?' *Parliamentary Affairs*, 53/3: 407–25.

Eatwell, Roger (2003) *Fascism: A History*, London: Pimlico.

Eatwell, Roger (2004) 'Introduction: The New Extreme Right Challenge,' in R. Eatwell and C. Mudde (eds.) *Western Democracies and the New Extreme Right*, London: Routledge.

Eatwell, Roger (2017) 'Populism and Fascism,' in C. Rovira Kaltwasser, P. Taggart, P. Ochoa Espejo, and P. Ostiguy (eds.) *The Oxford Handbook of Populism*, Oxford: Oxford University Press, pp. 363–83.

Eatwell, Roger and Goodwin, Matthew (2018) *National Populism: The Revolt Against Liberal Democracy*, London: Pelican Books.

Elazar, Dahlia (1993) 'The Making of Italian Fascism: The Seizure of Power, 1919–1922,' *Political Power and Social Theory* 8: 173–217.

Eley, Geoff (1976) 'Defining Social Imperialism: The Use and Abuse of an Idea' *Social History* 3: 265–290.

Eley, Geoff (1980) *Reshaping the German Right: Radical Nationalism and Political Change after Bismarck*, New Haven, CT: Yale University Press.

Eley, Geoff (1983) 'What Produces Fascism: Pre-Industrial Traditions or the Capitalist State?' *Politics and Society* 12/1: 53–82.

Eley, Geoff (1986) *From Unification to Nazism: Reinterpreting the German Past*, London: Allen & Unwin.

Eley, Geoff (1993) 'Anti-Semitism, Agrarian Mobilization, and the Conservative Party: Radicalism and Containment in the Founding of the Agrarian League 1890–93,' in L. Jones and J. Retallack (eds.) *Between Reform, Reaction, and Resistance: Studies in the History of German Conservatism from 1789 to 1945*, Oxford: Berg, pp. 187 227.

Eley, Geoff (2013) *Nazism as Fascism*, London: Routledge.

Eley, Geoff (2015) 'Fascism: Then and Now,' in L. Panitch and G. Albo (eds.) *Socialist Register 2016: The Politics of the Right*, London: Merlin Press, pp. 91–117.

Eley, Geoff (2021) 'What is Fascism and Where Does It Come From?' *History Workshop Journal*, 91/1: 1–28.

Ellis, Geoffrey (2000) 'The Revolution in France 1848–1849,' in R. Evans and H. Pogge von Strandmann (eds.) *The Revolutions in Europe, 1848–1849: From Reform to Reaction*, Oxford: Oxford University Press, pp. 27–53.

Ellis, John (1974) *Armies in Revolution*, Oxford: Oxford University Press.

Evans, Richard (1978) 'Introduction' in R. Evans (ed.) *Society and Politics in Willhelmine Germany*, London: Croom Helm, pp. 11–39.

Evans, Richard and Pogge von Strandmann, Hartmut (eds.) (2000) *The Revolutions in Europe, 1848–1849: From Reform to Reaction*, Oxford: Oxford University Press.

Falasca-Zamponi, Simonetta (2008) 'Fascism and Aesthetics,' *Constellations* 15/3: 361–65.

Fanon, Frantz ([1952] 2008) *Black Skin, White Masks*, London: Pluto Press.

Fanon, Frantz ([1961]2001) *The Wretched of the Earth*, Harmondsworth: Penguin Books.

Farquharson, John (1976) *The Plough and the Swastika: The NSDAP and Agriculture in Germany 1928–45*, London: Sage.

Farr, Ian (1986) 'Peasant Protest in the Empire – The Bavarian Example,' in R. Moeller (ed.) *Peasants and Lords in Modern Germany: Recent Studies in Agricultural History*, Boston: Allen and Unwin, pp. 110–39.

Federico, Giovanni (1996) 'Italy, 1860–1940: A Little Known Success Story' *Economic History Review* 49/4: 764–827.

Feldman, Gerald (1977) *Iron and Steel in the German Inflation, 1916–1923*, Princeton: Princeton University Press.

Ferguson, Niall (2003) *Empire*, London: Penguin.

Feuchtwanger, Edgar (2001) *Imperial Germany, 1850–1918*, London: Routledge.

Finchelstein, Federico (2017) *From Fascism to Populism in History*, Oakland: University of California Press.

Finchelstein, Federico (2018) 'Jair Bolsonaro's Model Isn't Berlusconi. It's Goebbels,' *Foreign Policy*, October 5 https://foreignpolicy.com/2018/10/05/bolsonaros-model -its-goebbels-fascism-nazism-brazil-latin-america-populism-argentina-venezuela/.

Fischer, Conan (1982) 'The SA of the NSDAP: Social Background and Ideology in the Rank and File in the Early 1930s,' *Journal of Contemporary History*, 17/4: 651–70.

Fischer, Fritz (1967) *Germany's Aims in the First World War*, London: Chatto & Windus.

Fischer, Karin (2009) 'The Influence of Neoliberals in Chile, Before, During and After Pinochet', in P. Mirowski and D. Plehwe (eds.) *The Road from Mont Pelerin*, Cambridge: Harvard University Press, pp. 305–46.

Floud, Roderick (1997) *The People and the British Economy, 1830–1914*, New York: Oxford University Press.

Floud, Roderick and McCloskey, Donald (1994) *The Economic History of Britain since 1700: Volume I, 1700–1860*, Cambridge: Cambridge University Press.

Foglesong, David (1995) *America's Secret War against Bolshevism: U. S. Intervention in the Russian Civil War, 1917–1920*, Chapel Hill: University of North Carolina Press.

Ford, Robert and Goodwin Matthew (2014) *Revolt on the Right: Explaining Support for the Radical Right in Britain*, London: Routledge.

Fraenkel, Ernst ([1941]2017) *The Dual State: A Contribution to the Theory of Dictatorship*, Oxford: Oxford University Press.

Fremdling, Rainer (1997) 'The German Iron and Steel Industry in the 19th Century,' in W. Fischer (ed.) *The Economic Development of Germany since 1870, Volume I*, Cheltenham: Elgar, pp. 352–75.

Frey, Carl Benedikt (2019) *The Technology Trap: Capital, Labor, and Power in the Age of Automation*, Princeton: Princeton University Press.

Friedrich, Carl and Brzezinski, Zbigniew (1965) *Totalitarian Dictatorship and Autocracy*, Cambridge, MA: Harvard University Press.

Friedrichsmeyer, Sara, Lennox, Sara and Zantop, Susanne (eds.) (1998) *The Imperialist Imagination: German Colonialism and Its Legacy*, Ann Arbor: University of Michigan Press.

Fromm, Erich ([1941] 1994) *Escape from Freedom*, New York: Holt.

Fuller, Robert (2012) *The Origins of the French Nationalist Movement, 1886–1914*, London: McFarland.

Gallagher, John and Robinson, Ronald (1953) 'The Imperialism of Free Trade,' *Economic History Review* VI/I: 1–15.

Gardner, Lloyd (1964) *Economic Aspects of New Deal Diplomacy*, Madison: University of Wisconsin Press.

Gardner, Lloyd (1984) *Safe for Democracy: The Anglo-American Response to Revolution*, Oxford: Oxford University Press.

Geary, Dick (1983) 'The Industrial Elite and the Nazis in the Weimar Republic,' in P. Stachura (ed.) *The Nazi Machtergreifung*, London: Allen & Unwin, pp. 85–100.

Geary, Dick (1986) 'Artisans, Protest and Labour Organization in Germany 1815–1870,' *European History Quarterly* 16: 369–77.

Geary, Dick (1990) 'Employers, Workers, and the Collapse of the Weimar Republic,' in I. Kershaw (ed.) *Weimar: Why did German Democracy Fail?* London: Weidenfeld and Nicoloson, pp. 92–119.

Gemie, Sharif (1999) *French Revolutions, 1815–1914: An Introduction*, Edinburgh: Edinburgh University Press.

Gentile, Emilio (1996) *The Sacralization of Politics in Fascist Italy*, translated by Keith Botsford, Cambridge, MA: Harvard University Press.

Gentile, Emilio (2002) 'Fascism in Power: The Totalitarian Experiment,' in A. Lyttleton (ed.) *Liberal and Fascist Italy*, Oxford: Oxford University Press, pp. 139–74.

Gentile, Emilio (2012) 'Paramilitary Violence in Italy: The Rationale of Fascism and the Origins of Totalitarianism,' in R. Gerwarth and J. Horne (eds.) *War in Peace: Paramilitary Violence in Europe after the Great War*, Oxford: Oxford University Press, pp.85–103.

Gerschenkron, Alexander (1962) *Economic Backwardness in Historical Perspective: A Book of Essays*, Cambridge MA.: Belknap Press.

Gerwarth, Robert (2008) 'The Central European Counter-Revolution: Paramilitary Violence in Germany, Austria and Hungary after the Great War,' *Past and Present* 200: 75–209.

Gerwarth, Robert and Horne, John (2011) 'Vectors of Violence: Paramilitarism in Europe after the Great War, 1917–1923,' *Journal of Modern History* 83/3: 489–512.

Gerwarth, Robert and Malinowski, Stephen (2009) 'Hannah Arendt's Ghosts: Reflections on the Disputable Path from Windhoek to Auschwitz,' *Central European History*, 42/ 2: 279–300.

Gill, Stephen and Law, David (1989) 'Global Hegemony and the Structural Power of Capital,' *International Studies Quarterly* 33/4: 475–99.

Gilley, Sheridan (1978) 'English Attitudes to the Irish in England, 1789–1900,' in C. Holmes (ed.) *Immigrants and Minorities in British Society*, London: Allen and Unwin, pp. 81–110.

Gillingham, John (1974) 'The Baron de Launoit: A Case Study in the "Politics of Production" of Belgian Industry during Nazi Occupation,' *Journal of Belgian History* https://www.journalbelgianhistory.be/nl/journal/belgisch-tijdschrift-voor-nieuwste-geschiedenis-1974-1-2/baron-launoit-case-study-politics.

Gillis, John (1983) *The Development of European Society, 1770–1870*, Washington D. C.: University Press of America.

Gilpin, Robert (1975) *U.S. Power and the Multinational Corporation: The Political Economy of Foreign Direct Investment*, New York: Basic Books.

Gluckstein, Donny (1999) *The Nazis, Capitalism and the Working Class*, Chicago: Haymarket Books.

Glyn, Andrew (2006) *Capitalism Unleashed: Finance, Globalization, and Welfare*, Oxford: Oxford University Press.

Gobineau, Arthur de ([1853] 1999) *The Inequality of Human Races*, New York: H. Fertig.

Goldberg, Joshua (2018) *Suicide of the West: How the Rebirth of Tribalism, Populism, Nationalism, and Identity Politics Is Destroying American Democracy*, New York: Crown Forum.

Golob, Eugene (1944) *The Méline Tariff: French Agriculture and Nationalist Economic Policy*, New York: Columbia University Press.

Gourevitch, Peter (1977) 'International Trade, Domestic Coalitions and Liberty: Comparative Responses to Crisis of 1873–96', *Journal of Interdisciplinary History* 8: 281–313.

Gourevitch, Peter (1978) 'The Second Image Reversed: The International Sources of Domestic Politics,' *International Organization* 32/4: 881–912.

Gourevitch, Peter (1988) 'Fascism and Economic Policy Controversies: National Responses to the Global Crisis of the Division of Labor,' in E. Burke *Global Crises and Social Movements: Artisans, Peasants, Populists and the World Economy*, Boulder: Westview Press, pp. 183–217.

Gramsci, Antonio (1971) *Selections from the Prison Notebooks*, edited and translated by Q. Hoare and G. Nowell Smith, London: Lawrence and Wishart.

Gramsci, Antonio (1973) *Selection from the Prison Notebooks*, edited and translated by Q. Hoare and G. Nowell-Smith, London: Lawrence and Wishart.

Gramsci, Antoni (1983a) 'Democracy and Fascism,' in D. Beetham (ed.) *Marxists in the Face of Fascism*, Manchester: Manchester University Press, pp. 121–4.

Gramsci, Antonio (1983b) 'The International Situation and the Struggle against Fascism,' in D. Beetham (ed.) *Marxists in the Face of Fascism*, Manchester: Manchester University Press, pp. 124–7.

Gramsci, Antonio (1988) *The Antonio Gramsci Reader: Selected Writings 1916–1936*, New York, NY: New York University Press.

Grand, Alexander de (1982) *Italian Fascism: Its Origins and Development*, London: University of Nebraska Press.

Grand, Alexander de (2004) *Fascist Italy and Nazi Germany: The 'Fascist Style' of Rule*, 2nd ed., New York, Routledge.

Grazia, Victoria de (1992) *How Fascism Ruled Women: Italy 1922–1945*, Berkeley: University of California Press.

Green, Jeremy (2012) 'Uneven and Combined Development and the Anglo-German Prelude to World War I,' *European Journal of International Relations* 18/2: 345–368.

Gregor, A. James (1974) *The Fascist Persuasion in Radical Politics*, Princeton: Princeton University Press.

Gregor, A. James (2005) *Mussolini's Intellectuals: Fascist Social and Political Thought*, Princeton: Princeton University Press.

Gregor, Neil (1998) *Daimler-Benz in the Third Reich,* New Haven: Yale University Press.

Grenville, J. A. S. (2000) *Europe Reshaped 1848–1878*, 2nd ed., Oxford: Blackwell Publishers.

Griffin, Roger (1993) *The Nature of Fascism*, London: Pinter.

Griffin, Roger (ed.) (1995) *Fascism*, Oxford: Oxford University Press.

Griffin, Roger (2000a) 'Interregnum or Endgame? The Radical Right in the "Post-Fascist" Era,' *Journal of Political Ideologies* 5/2: 163–78.

Griffin, Roger (2000b) 'Revolution from the Right: Fascism,' in D. Parker (ed.) *Revolutions and the Revolutionary Tradition in the West 1560–1991*, London: Routledge, pp. 185–201.

Griffiths, Richard (1978) 'Anticapitalism and the French Extra-Parliamentary Right, 1870–1940,' *Journal of Contemporary History* 13/4: 721–40.

Guerin, Daniel (1973) *Fascism and Big Business*, New York: Pathfinder Press.

Hainsworth, Paul (2008) *The Extreme Right in Western Europe*, London: Routledge.

Hall, Stuart (2000) 'Old and New Identities, Old and New Ethnicities,' in L. Black and J. Solomos (eds.) *Theories of Race and Racism* London: Routledge, pp. 199–208.

Halliday, Fred (1999) *Revolution and World Politics: The Rise and Fall of the Sixth Great Power*, Basingstoke: Palgrave.

Halperin, Sandra (2004) *War and Social Change in Modern Europe: The Great Transformation Revisited*, Cambridge: Cambridge University Press.

Hamerow, Theodore (1958) *Restoration Reaction Revolution: Economics and Politics in Germany 1815–1871*, Princeton: Princeton University Press.

Hamilton, Richard (1982) *Who Voted for Hitler?* Princeton: Princeton University Press.

Hansard (1934) Debate on the Address, House of Commons, Volume 295, November 28 https://hansard.parliament.uk/Commons/1934-11-28/debates/6d3c50e5-b67c-4907 -bb0a-7865e569bfa3/DebateOnTheAddress.

Harvey, David (1989) *The Urban Experience*, Baltimore: Johns Hopkins University Press.

Harvey, David (2003) *The New Imperialism*, Oxford: Oxford University Press.

Harvey, David (2005) *A Brief History of Neoliberalism*, Oxford: Oxford University Press.

Harvey, David (2006a) *The Limits to Capital*, London: Verso.

Harvey, David (2006b) *Spaces of Global Capitalism*, London: Verso.

Haupt, Heinz-Gerhard (1984) 'The Petite-Bourgeoisie in France, 1850–1914: In Search of the Juste Milieu?' in G. Crossick and H-G. Haupt (eds.) *Shopkeepers and Master Artisans in Nineteenth Century Europe*, London: Methuen, pp. 95–119.

Haupt, Heinz-Gerhard and Lenger, Friedrich (2008) 'Bourgeoisie, Petite Bourgeoisie, Workers: Class Formation and Social Reform in Germany and France', in D. Dowe, H-G. Haupt and J. Sperber (eds.) *Europe in 1848: Revolution and Reform*, translated by D. Higgins, Oxford: Berghahn Books, pp. 619–83.

Hayek, Friedrich ([1944] 2001) *The Road to Serfdom*, London: Routledge.

Hayes, Peter (1987) *Industry and Ideology: IG Farben in the Nazi Era*, Cambridge: Cambridge University Press.

Hazareesingh, Sudhir (2004) 'Bonapartism as the Progenitor of Democracy', in P. Baeher and M. Richter (eds.) *Dictatorship in History and Theory: Bonapartism, Caesarism, and Totalitarianism*, Cambridge: Cambridge University Press, pp. 129–52.

Heffernan, Michael (1997) 'The French Right and the Overseas Empire,' in N. Atkin, (ed.) *The Right in France: Nationalism and the State, 1789–1996*, London: Tauris Academic Studies, pp. 89–113.

Hehn, Paul (2002) *A Low Dishonest Decade: The Great Powers, Eastern Europe and the Economic Origins of World War II, 1930–1941*, New York: Continuum.

Held, David (1999) *Global Transformations: Politics, Economics and Culture*, Cambridge: Polity.

Henderson, W. O. (1944) 'The Pan-German Movement,' *History*, 26/103: 188–98.

Henderson, W. O. (1975) *The Rise of German Industrial Power, 1834–1914*, London: Temple Smith.

Hennock, E. P. (1988) 'Social Policy under the Empire: Myths and Evidence,' *German History*, 16/1: 58–74.

Herbert, Ulrich (1993) 'Labour and Extermination: Economic Interest and the Primacy of Weltanschauung in National Socialism' *Past and Present* 183/1: 144–95.

Herf, Jeffrey (1984) *Reactionary Modernism: Technology, Culture and Politics in Weimar and the Third Reich*, Cambridge: Cambridge University Press.

Hesketh, Chris (2017) 'Passive Revolution: A Universal Concept with Geographical Seats,' *Review of International Studies*, 43/3: 389–408.

Heywood, Colin (1992) *The Development of the French Economy, 1750–1914*, Basingstoke, Macmillan Press.

Hillach, Ansgar, Wikoff, Jerold and Zimmerman, Ulf (1979) 'The Aesthetics of Politics: Walter Benjamin's "Theories of German Fascism",' *New German Critique* 17: 99–119.

Hirst, Paul and Thompson, Graheme (1999) *Globalization in Question: The International Economy and the Possibilities of Governance*, 2nd ed., Cambridge: Polity.

Hitler, Adolf ([1925] 1992) *Mein Kampf*, London: Pimlico.

Hobsbawm, Eric (1968) *Industry and Empire: An Economic History of Britain since 1750*, London: Weidenfeld & Nicolson.

Hobsbawm, Eric (1975) *The Age of Revolution 1789–1848*, London: Weidenfeld & Nicolson.

Hobsbawm, Eric (1987) *The Age of Empire 1875–1914*, London: Weidenfeld & Nicolson.

Hobsbawm, Eric (1994) *Age of Extremes: The Short Twentieth Century, 1914–1991*, London: Weidenfeld & Nicolson.

Hobsbawm, Eric (1995) *The Age of Capital 1848–1875*, London: Weidenfeld & Nicolson.

Hobson, J. A. ([1902] 1988) *Imperialism: A Study*, London: Allen & Unwin.

Hogan, Michael (1991) *Informal Entente: The Private Structure of Cooperation in Anglo – American Economic Diplomacy, 1918–1928*, Columbia, MI: University of Missouri Press.

Holland, R. F. (1981) 'The Federation of British Industries and the International Economy, 1929–39,' *The Economic History Review*, 2nd Series 34/2: 287–300.

Holmes, Colin (1979) *Anti-Semitism in British Society 1876–1939*, London: Edward Arnold.

Hopkins, A. G. (2002) *Globalization in World History*, London: Pimlico.

Horkheimer, Max and Adorno, Theodor ([1944] 2002) *Dialectic of Enlightenment: Philosophical Fragments*, Stanford: Stanford University Press.

Hoyer, Katja (2021) *Blood and Iron: The Rise and Fall of the German Empire, 1871–1918*, Cheltenham: History Press.

Hunt, James (1975) 'The "Egalitarianism" of the Right: The Agrarian League in South-West Germany, 1893–1914,' *Journal of Contemporary History*, 10/3: 513–30.

Hutton, Patrick (1976) 'Popular Boulangism and the Advent of Mass Politics in France, 1886–90,' *Journal of Contemporary History*, 11/1: 85–106.

Ignatiev, Noel (1995) *How the Irish Became White*, London: Routledge.

Ignazi, Pierro (2003) *Extreme Right Parties in Western Europe*, Oxford: Oxford University Press.

Ikenberry, G. John (2001) *After Victory: Institutions, Strategic Restraint, and the Rebuilding of Order After Major Wars*, Princeton: Princeton University Press.

Inglehart, Ronald and Norris, Pippa (2019) *Cultural Backlash: Trump, Brexit and Authoritarian Populism*, Cambridge: Cambridge University Press.

Irvine, William (1989) *The Boulanger Affair Reconsidered: Royalism, Boulangism, and the Origins of the Right in France*, Oxford: Oxford University Press.

Jacobs, Susie (2011) 'Globalisation, Anti-Globalisation and the Jewish "Question,"' *European Review of History* 18/1: 45–56.

James, Harold (1986) *The German Slump: Politics and Economics, 1924–1936*, Oxford: Clarendon Press.

James, Harold (1990) 'Economic Reasons for the Collapse of the Weimar Republic' in I. Kershaw (ed.) *Weimar: Why Did German Democracy Fail?* London: Weidenfeld & Nicolson, pp. 30–57.

Jahn, Beate (2005) 'Barbarian Thoughts: Imperialism in the Philosophy of Jon Stuart Mill,' *Review of International Studies* 31/3: 599–618.

Jardin, André and Tudesq, André-Jean (1983) *Restoration and Reaction, 1815–1848*, translated by Elborg Foster, Cambridge: Cambridge University Press.

Jennings, Jeremy (2011) *Revolution and Republic: A History of Political Thought in France since the Eighteenth Century*, Oxford: Oxford University Press.

Jessop, Bob (1982) *The Capitalist State: Marxist Theories and Methods*, Oxford: Martin Robertson.

Jessop, Bob (1990) *State Theory: Putting the Capitalist State in its Place*, Cambridge: Polity.

Jones, Larry (1988) *German Liberalism and the Dissolution of the Weimar Party System, 1918–1933*, Chapel Hill: University of North Carolina Press.

Jones, Larry and Retallack, James (1993) 'German Conservatism Reconsidered: Old Problems and New Directions' in L. Jones and J. Retallack (eds.) *Between Reform, Reaction, and Resistance: Studies in the History of German Conservatism from 1789 to 1945*, Oxford: Berg, pp. 1–30.

Jones, Mark (2015) 'Political Violence in Italy and Germany after the First World War,' in C. Millington and K. Passmore (eds.) *Political Violence and Democracy in Western Europe, 1918–1940*, Basingstoke: Palgrave, pp. 14–30.

Judaken, Jonathan (2008) 'So What's New? Rethinking the new "Anti-Semitism" in the Global Age,' *Patterns of Prejudice* 42/4–5: 531–560.

Kahan, Alan (2003) *Liberalism in Nineteenth Century Europe: The Political Culture of Limited Suffrage*, Basingstoke: Palgrave Macmillan.

Kaiser, David (1980) *Economic Diplomacy and the Origins of the Second World War: Germany, Britain, France, and Eastern Europe, 1930–1939*, Princeton: Princeton University Press.

Katagiri, Yasuhiro (2014) *Black Freedom, White Resistance, and Red Menace: Civil Rights and Anticommunism in the Jim Crow South*, Baton Rouge, LA: Louisiana State University Press.

Kater, Michael (1983) *The Nazi Party: A Social Profile of Members and Leaders, 1919–1945*, Oxford: Blackwell.

Katznelson, Ira (2013) *Fear Itself: The New Deal and the Origins of Our Time*, New York: Liveright Publishing Corp.

Kay, Alex G. (2006) *Exploitation, Resettlement, Mass Murder: Political Economy and Planning for German Occupation Policy in the Soviet Union, 1940–1941*, New York: Berghahn.

Kehr, Eckart (1977) *Economic Interest, Militarism, and Foreign Policy: Essays on German History*, translated by Grete Heinz, Berkeley: University of California Press.

Kemp, Tom (1985) *Industrialization in Nineteenth Century Europe*, 2nd ed., London: Longman.

Kennedy, Paul (1980) *The Rise of Anglo-German Antagonism 1860–1914*, London: George Allen & Unwin.

Kennedy, Paul and Nicholls, Angus (eds.) (1981) *Nationalist and Racialist Movements in Britain and Germany before 1914*, London: Macmillan.

Kent, Bruce (1991) *The Spoils of War: The Politics, Economics and Diplomacy of Reparations, 1918–1932*, Oxford: Oxford University Press.

Kergoat, Jacques (1990) 'France,' in M. van der Linden and J. Rojahn (eds.) *The Formation of Labour Movements 1870–1914: An International Perspective*, New York: E.J. Brill, pp. 163–90.

Kershaw, Ian (1998) *Hitler, 1889–1936: Hubris*, London: Allen Lane.

Kershaw, Ian (2000) *The Nazi Dictatorship: Problems and Perspectives of Interpretation*, 4th ed., London: Bloomsbury.

Kershaw, Ian (2008) *Hitler: A Biography*, New York: W. W. Norton.

Keynes, John Maynard ([1919] 2003) *The Economic Consequences of the Peace*, New Brunswick, NJ.: Transaction Publishers.

Kiely, Ray (2010) *Rethinking Imperialism*, Basingstoke: Palgrave.

Kiely, Ray (2017) 'From Authoritarian Liberalism to Economic Technocracy: Neoliberalism, Politics and "De-democratization",' *Critical Sociology* 43/4–5: 725–45.

Kiely, Ray (2018) *The Neoliberal Paradox*, Cheltenham: Edward Elgar.

Kindleberger, Charles (2011) *Manias, Panics and Crashes: A History of Financial Crises* Basingstoke: Palgrave Macmillan.

King, Richard H. and Stone, Dan (eds.) (2007) *Hannah Arendt and the Uses of History: Imperialism, Nation, Race, and Genocide*, New York: Berghahn Books.

Kissinger, Henry (1973) *A World Restored,* London: Gollancz.

Kitchen, Martin (1973) 'August Thalheimer's Theory of Fascism,' *Journal of the History of Ideas* 34/1: 67–78.

Kitchen, Martin (1975) 'Trotsky's Theory of Fascism,' *Social Praxis* 21/2: 113–33.

Kitchen, Martin (1976) *Fascism*, Basingstoke: Macmillan.

Kitchen, Martin (1978) *The Political Economy of Germany 1815–1914*, London: Croom Helm.

Kitchen, Martin (2012) *A History of Modern Germany: 1800 to the Present*, Chichester: Wiley-Blackwell.

Kitschelt, Herbert (1995) *The Radical Right in Western Europe: A Comparative Analysis*, Ann Arbor: University of Michigan Press.

Kocka, Jürgen (1980) 'The Rise of the Modern Industrial Enterprise in Germany,' in A. Chandler and H. Daems (eds.) *Managerial Hierarchies: Comparative Perspectives on the Rise of Modern Enterprise*, Cambridge, MA: Harvard University Press, pp. 77–116.

Kolko, Gabriel (1962) 'American Business and Germany, 1930–1941,' *Political Research Quarterly*, 15/4: 713–28.

Knei-Paz, Baruch (1978) *The Social and Political Thought of Leon Trotsky*, Oxford: Clarendon Press.

Kühnl, Reinhard (1972–73) 'Problems of a Theory of International Fascism,' *International Journal of Politics*, 2/4: 47–81.

Kühnl, Reinhard and Rabinbach, Anson (1975) 'Problems of a Theory of German Fascism: A Critique of the Dominant Interpretations,' *New German Critique*, 4: 26–50.

Kühne, Thomas (2013) 'Colonialism and the Holocaust: Continuities, Causations, Complexities' *Journal of Genocide Research*, 15/3: 339–62.

Kundnani, Arun (2021) 'The Racial Constitution of Neoliberalism,' *Race and Class*, 63/1: 51–69.

Kurlander, Eric (2006) *The Price of Exclusion: Ethnicity, National Identity and the Decline of German Liberalism, 1898–1933*, Oxford: Berghahn Books.

Kurlander, Eric (2009) *Living with Hitler: Liberal Democrats in the Third Reich*, New Haven: Yale University Press.

Kwon, Heonik (2010) *The Other Cold War*, New York: Columbia University Press.

Laclau, Ernesto (2005) *On Populist Reason*, London: Verso.

Lafrance, Xavier (2019) *The Making of Capitalism in France: Class Structures, Economic Development, the State and the Formation of the French Working Class, 1750–1914*, Leiden: Brill.

Landa, Ishay (2012) *The Apprentice's Sorcerer: Liberal Tradition and Fascism*, Chicago: Haymarket Books.

Landa, Ishay (2018) *Fascism and the Masses: The Revolt Against the Last Humans, 1848–1945*, London: Routledge.

Landes, David (1969) *The Unbound Prometheus: Technological Change and Industrial Development in Western Europe from 1750 to the Present*, Cambridge: Cambridge University Press.

La Palme, Bruno de (2014) *100 Ans D'erreurs de la Gauche Française: Va-t-elle Recommencer?* Paris: La Boîte à Pandore.

Larsen, Stein Ugelvik, Hagtvet, Bernt and Myklebust, Jan Peter (eds.) (1980) *Who Were the Fascists: Social Roots of European Fascism*, Bergen: Universitesforlaget.

Lebovics, Herman (1969) *Social Conservatism and the Middle Classes in Germany, 1914–1933*, Princeton: Princeton University Press.

Lebovics, Herman (1986) 'Protection against Labor Troubles: The Campaign of the Association de l'Industrie Franchise for Economic Stability and Social Peace during the Great Depression, 1880–1896,' *International Review of Social History* 31/2: 147–165.

Lebovics, Herman (1988) *The Alliance of Iron and Wheat in the Third Republic, 1860–1914*, Baton Rouge, LA: Louisiana State University Press.

Lee, W. R. (1988) 'Economic Development and the State in Nineteenth-Century Germany,' *Economic History Review*, 2nd ser., XLI/3: 346–67.

Lefebvre, Henri ([1970] 2003) *The Urban Revolution*, translated by Robert Bononno, Minneapolis: University of Minnesota Press.

Leffler, Mervyn (1979) *The Elusive Quest: America's Pursuit of European Stability and French Security, 1919–1933*, Chapel Hill: University of North Carolina Press.

Leffler, Melvyn (1994) *The Specter of Communism: The United States and the Origins of the Cold War, 1917–1953*, New York: Hill & Wang.

Leitz, Christian (2004) *Nazi Foreign Policy, 1933–1941: The Road to Global War*, London: Routledge.

Lenin, V. I. ([1917] 2010) *Imperialism: The Highest Stage of Capitalism*, Harmondsworth: Penguin.

Lentin, Alana (2004) 'Racial States, Anti-Racist Responses: Picking Holes in "Culture" and "Human Rights",' *European Journal of Social Theory*, 7/4: 427–443.

Lentin, Alana and Titley, Gavin (2011) *The Crisis of Multiculturalism: Racism in a Neoliberal Age*, London: Zed Books.

Lerman, Katherine Anne (2004) *Bismarck, Profiles in Power*, London: Routledge.

Lévêque, Pierre (2008) 'The Revolutionary Crisis of 1848/51 in France', in D. Dowe, H-G. Haupt, D. Langewiesche and J. Sperber (eds.) *Europe in 1848: Revolution and Reform* translated by D. Higgins, Oxford: Berghahn Books, pp. 91–119.

Levin, Norman (1968) *Woodrow Wilson and World Politics: America's Response to War and Revolution*, Oxford: Oxford University Press.

Lévy-Leboyer, Maurice and Bourguignon, François (1990) *The French Economy in the Nineteenth Century*, Cambridge: Cambridge University Press.

Linton, Derek (1989) 'Bonapartism, Fascism and the Collapse of the Weimar Republic,' in M. Dobkowski and I. Wallimann (eds.) *Radical Perspectives on the Rise of Fascism in Germany, 1919–1945*, New York: Monthly Review Press, pp. 100–27.

List, Frederich ([1841] 1966) *The National System of Political Economy*, New York: Kelley.

Lilla, Mark (2018) *The Once and Future Liberal: After Identity Politics*, London: Hurst and Co.

Little, Douglas (1983) 'Antibolshevism and American Foreign Policy, 1919–1939: The Diplomacy of Self-Delusion,' *American Quarterly* 35/4: 376–90.

Little, Douglas (1985) *Malevolent Neutrality: The United States, Great Britain and the Origins of the Spanish Civil War*, Ithaca: Cornell University Press.

Little, Douglas (1988) 'Red Scare, 1936: Anti-Bolshevism and the Origins of British Non-Intervention in the Spanish Civil War', *Journal of Contemporary History*, 23/2: 291–311.

Lowe, John (1994) *The Great Powers, Imperialism, and the German Problem, 1865–1925*, London: Routledge.

Luebbert, Gregory (1991) *Liberalism, Fascism, or Social Democracy: Social Classes and the Political Origins of Regimes in Interwar Europe*, New York: Oxford University Press.

Lukacs, John (2005) *Democracy and Populism: Fear and Hatred*, New Haven: Yale University Press.

Lyons, Martin (2006) *Post-Revolutionary Europe, 1815–1856*, Basingstoke: Palgrave Macmillan.

Lyttelton, Adrian (1979) 'Landlords, Peasants and the Limits of Liberalism' in J. A. Davis (ed.) *Gramsci and Italy's Passive Revolution,* New York: Barnes & Noble, pp. 104–35.

Lyttelton, Adrian (2004a) *The Seizure of Power: Fascism in Italy, 1919–1929*, London: Routledge.

Lyttelton, Adrian (2004b) 'What Was Fascism?' *New York Review of Books*, 51/16, pp. 1–4.

MacDonald, Callum (1981) *The United States, Britain and Appeasement, 1936–1939*, London: Macmillan Press Ltd.

MacDonald, Callum (1983) 'The United States, Appeasement and the Open Door' in W. Mommsen and L. Kettenacker (eds.) *The Fascist Challenge and the Policy of Appeasement,* London: George Allen & Unwin, pp. 400–12.

MacMaster, Neil (2001) *Racism in Europe, 1870–2000*, Basingstoke: Palgrave.

MacRaild, Donald and Martin, David (2000) *Labour in British Society 1830–1914*, Basingstoke: Palgrave-Macmillan.

Maier, Charles (1987) *In Search of Stability: Explorations in Historical Political Economy*, Cambridge: Cambridge University Press.

Maier, Charles (1988) *Recasting Bourgeois Europe: Stabilization in France, Germany, and Italy in the Decade after World War I*, Princeton: Princeton University Press.

Malik, Kenan (1996) *The Meaning of Race: Race, History and Culture in Western Society*, New York: New York University Press.

Mammone, Andrea, Godin, Emmanuel and Jenkins, Brian (eds.) (2012) *Mapping the Extreme Right in Contemporary Europe: From Local to Transnational*, London: Routledge.

Mandel, Ernest (2011) *The Meaning of the Second World War*, London: Verso.

Mann, Michael (1993) *Sources of Social Power Volume II 1760–1914: The Rise of Classes and Nation-States,* Cambridge: Cambridge University Press.

Mann, Michael (2004) *Fascists,* Cambridge: Cambridge University Press.

Manow, Philip (2020) *Social Protection, Capitalist Production: The Bismarckian Welfare State in the German Political Economy, 1880–2015*, Oxford: Oxford University Press.

Marcuse, Herbert ([1964] 2002) *One-Dimensional Man: Studies in the Ideology of Advanced Industrial Society,* London: Routledge.

Marx, Karl ([1852] 1934) *The Eighteenth Brumaire of Louis Bonaparte*, London: Lawrence and Wishart.

Marx, Karl ([1857–61] 1973a) *Grundrisse: Foundations of the Critique of Political Economy*, Harmondsworth: Penguin Books.

Marx, Karl (1973b) 'Articles on the North American Civil War,' in *Surveys from Exile, Political Writings Volume II*, Harmondsworth: Penguin Books, pp.334–53.

Marx, Karl (1974) 'Letters on Ireland,' in *The First International and After, Political Writings Volume III*, Harmondsworth: Penguin Books, pp. 158–71.

Marx, Karl and Engels, Fredrich ([1848] 2012) *The Communist Manifesto*, New Haven: Yale University Press.

Mason, Timothy (1968) 'The Primacy of Politics – Politics and Economics in National Socialist Germany,' in S. J. Woolf (ed.), *The Nature of Fascism*, London: Weidenfeld and Nicolson, pp. 165–95.

Mason, Timothy (1995) *Nazism, Fascism and the Working Class*, Cambridge: Cambridge University Press.

Matthew, H. C. G. (1999) 'The Liberal Age,' in K. Morgan (ed.) *The Oxford History of Britain*, Oxford: Oxford University Press, pp. 518–81.

Matin, Kamran (2007) 'Uneven and Combined Development in World History: The International Relations of State-formation in Pre-Modern Iran,' *European Journal of International Relations*, 13/3: 419–447.

Mayer, Arno (1968) *Politics and Diplomacy of Peacemaking: Containment and Counterrevolution at Versailles, 1918–1919*, London: Weidenfeld & Nicolson.

Mayer, Arno (1971) *Dynamics of Counterrevolution in Europe, 1870–1956: An Analytical Framework*, New York, NY: Harper Torchbooks.

Mayer, Arno (1975) 'The Lower Middle Classes as a Historical Problem', *Journal of Modern History* 47/3: 409–36.

Mayer, Arno (1981) *The Persistence of the Old Regime: Europe to the Great War*, New York: Pantheon Books.

Mazower, Mark (1999) *Dark Continent: Europe's Twentieth Century*, London: Penguin.

Mazower, Mark (2008) *Hitler's Empire: How the Nazis Ruled Europe*, New York: Penguin.

McCarthy, Michael (2016) 'Silent Compulsions: Capitalist Markets and Race,' *Studies in Political Economy: A Socialist Review*, 97/2: 195–205.

McCormick, John (2004) 'From Constitutional Technique to Caesarist Ploy,' in P. Baeher and M. Richter (eds.) *Dictatorship in History and Theory: Bonapartism, Caesarism, and Totalitarianism*, Cambridge: Cambridge University Press, pp. 197–219.

McGowan, Lee (2002) *The Radical Right in Germany: 1870 to the Present*, London: Pearson Education.

McNeil, William (1986) *American Money and the Weimar Republic: Economics and Politics on the Eve of the Great Depression*, New York: Columbia University Press.

Merriman, John (1978) *The Agony of the Republic: The Suppression of the Left in Revolutionary France 1848–1851*, New Haven: Yale University Press.

Miles, Robert and Brown, Malcolm (2003) *Racism*, London: Routledge.

Mill, John Stuart Mill (1984) 'On the Negro Question,' in Mill, John Stuart *Essays on Equality, Education and Law*, ed., J. Robson, London: Routledge and Kegan Paul, pp. 87–96.

Mill, John Stuart ([1861] 2010) *Considerations on Representative Government*, Cambridge: Cambridge University Press.

Milward, Alan (1965) *The German Economy at War*, London: Athlone Press.

Milward, Alan (1980) 'Towards a Political Economy of Fascism' in S. U. Larsen, B. Hagtvet and J. P. Myklebust(eds.) *Who were the Fascists? Social Roots of European Fascism*, Bergen: Universitetsforlaget, pp. 56–65.

Milward, Alan and Saul, S. B. (1977) *The Development of the Economies of Continental Europe 1850–1914*, London: George Allen and Unwin.

Mishra, Prankaj (2017) *Age of Anger: A History of the Present*, London: Penguin.

Mitchell, Leslie (2000) 'Britain's Reaction to the Revolutions' in R. Evans and H. Pogge von Strandmann (eds.) *The Revolutions in Europe, 1848–1849: From Reform to Reaction*, Oxford: Oxford University Press, pp. 83–98.

Moeller, Robert (1986) 'Introduction: Locating Peasants and Lords in Modern German Historiography,' in R. Moeller (ed.) *Peasants and Lords in Modern Germany: Recent Studies in Agricultural History*, Boston: Allen & Unwin pp. 1–23.

Mommsen, Hans (1996) *The Rise and Fall of Weimar Democracy*, Chapel Hill, NC: University of North Carolina Press.

Mondon, Aurelien and Winter, Aaron (2020) *Reactionary Democracy: How Racism and the Populist Far-Right became Mainstream*, London: Verso.

Morgan, Philip (2004) *Italian Fascism, 1915–1945*, Basingstoke: Palgrave Macmillan.

Morton, Adam (2007) *Unravelling Gramsci: Hegemony and Passive Revolution in the Global Political Economy*, London: Pluto.

Morton, Adam (2010) 'The Continuum of Passive Revolution,' *Capital and Class*, 34/3: 315–42.

Moore, Jr, Barrington (1967) *Social Origins of Dictatorship and Development*, London: Penguin Books.

Mosse, George (1985) *Toward the Final Solution: A History of European Racism*, Madison: University of Wisconsin Press.

Mosse, George (1987) *Masses and Man: Nationalist and Fascist Perceptions of Reality*, Detroit: Wayne University Press.

Mosse, George (1999) *The Fascist Revolution: Toward a General Theory of Fascism*, New York: Howard Fertig.

Mounk, Yascha (2019) *The People vs. Democracy: Why Our Freedom Is in Danger and How to Save It*, Cambridge, MA: Harvard University Press.

Mudde, Cas (2000) *The Ideology of the Extreme Right,* Manchester: Manchester University Press.

Mudde, Cas (2007) *Populist Radical Right Parties in Europe*, New York: Cambridge University Press.

Mulholland, Marc (2012) *Bourgeois Liberty and the Politics of Fear: From Absolutism to Neo-Conservatism*, Oxford: Oxford University Press.

Müller, Jan-Werner (2003) *A Dangerous Mind: Carl Schmitt in Post-War European Thought*, New Haven: Yale University Press.

Müller, Jan-Werner (2017) *What is Populism?* Harmondsworth: Penguin.

Müller, Rolf-Dieter (2003) 'Albert Speer and Armaments Policy in Total War,' in B. R. Kroener, R-D. Müller and H. Umbreit (eds.) *Germany and the Second World War, Volume v, Organization and Mobilization of the German Sphere of Power, Part 2, Wartime Administration, Economy, and Manpower Resources 1942–1944/5*, Oxford: Clarendon Press, pp. 295–831.

Müller-Uri, Fanny and Opratko, Benjamin (2014) 'What's in a Name? The Challenge of 'Islamophobia' and Critical Theories of Racism,' unpublished paper presented at the Historical Materialism Annual Conference, London, November 5–8.

Neocleous, Mark (1997) *Fascism*, Buckingham: Open University Press.

Neumann, Franz ([1942] 2009) *Behemoth: The Structure and Practice of National Socialism, 1933–1944*, Chicago: Ivan R. Dee.

Newton, Scott (1996) *Profits of Peace: The Political Economy of Anglo-German Appeasement*, Oxford: Clarendon Press.

Niedhart, Gottfried (1983) 'British Attitudes and Polices towards the Soviet Union and International Communism, 1933–39,' in W. Mommsen and L. Kettenacker (eds.) *The Fascist Challenge and the Policy of Appeasement*, London: George & Unwin, pp. 286–96.

Nolte, Ernst (1965) *Three Faces of Fascism: Action Française, Italian Fascism, National Socialism*, London: Weidenfeld & Nicolson.

Nord, Philip (1984) 'The Small Shopkeepers' Movement and Politics in France, 1880–1914' in G. Crossick and H-G. Haupt (eds.) *Shopkeepers and Master Artisans in Nineteenth Century Europe*, London: Methuen, pp. 175–94.

Noyes, P. H. (1966) *Organization and Revolution: Working Class Associations in the German Revolutions 1848–1849*, Princeton: Princeton University Press.

Oesch, Daniel (2008) 'Explaining Workers' Support for Right-Wing Populist Parties in Western Europe', *International Political Science Review* 29/3: 349–373.

Offner, Arnold (1977) 'Appeasement Revisited: The United States, Great Britain, and Germany, 1933–1940,' *Journal of American History* 64/2: 373–93.

Offner, Arnold (1983) 'The United States and National Socialist Germany' in W. Mommsen and L. Kettenacker (eds.) *The Fascist Challenge and the Policy of Appeasement*, London: George Allen & Unwin, pp. 413–27.

Olusoga, David and Erichson, Casper W. (2010) *The Kaiser's Holocaust: Germany's Forgotten Genocide and the Colonial Roots of Nazism*, London: Faber & Faber.

Orzack, Louis (1950) 'The Düsseldorf Agreement: A Study of the Organization of Power and Planning,' *Political Science Quarterly*, 65/3: 393–414.

Overy, Richard (1994) *War and Economy in the Third Reich*, Oxford: Clarendon Press.

Palmer, Ronald R. (1959) *The Age of the Democratic Revolution: A Political History of Europe and America, 1760–1800 Volume I: The Challenge*, Princeton: Princeton University Press.

Palmer, Ronald R. (1964) *The Age of the Democratic Revolution: A Political History of Europe and America, 1760–1800 Volume II: The Struggle*, Princeton: Princeton University Press.

Panitch, Leo and Gindin, Sam (2012) *The Making of Global Capitalism: The Political Economy Of American Empire*, London: Verso.

Paxton, Robert (2004) *The Anatomy of Fascism*, London: Penguin Books.

Payne, Howard (1966) *The Police State of Louis Napoleon Bonaparte, 1851–1860*, Seattle: University of Washington Press.

Payne, Stanley (1983) *Fascism: A Comparative Approach Toward a Definition*, Madison: University of Wisconsin Press.

Payne, Stanley (1995) *A History of Fascism, 1914–1945*, Madison: University of Wisconsin Press.

Peck, Jamie (2019) 'Combination' in Antipode (eds.) *Keywords in Radical Geography: Antipode at 50*, Oxford: Wiley, pp. 50–55.

Perrot, Michelle (1987) *Workers on Strike: France 1871–1890* translated by Chris Turner, Leamington Spa: Berg.

Pilbeam, Pamela (1995) 'The "Restoration" of Western Europe, 1814–15,' in P. Pilbeam (ed.) *Themes in Modern European History 1780–1830*, London: Routledge, pp. 107–24.

Plessis, Alain (1979) *The Rise and Fall of the Second Empire, 1852–1871* translated by Jonathan Mandelbaum, Cambridge: Cambridge University Press.

Poiger, Uta (2005) 'Imperialism and Empire in Twentieth-Century Germany,' *History and Memory*, 17/1–2: 117–143.

Polanyi, Karl ([1944] 2001) *The Great Transformation: The Political and Economic Origins of Our Time*, Boston, MA: Beacon Press.

Pollard, Sidney (1981) *Peaceful Conquest: The Industrialization of Europe 1760–1970*, Oxford: Oxford University Press.

Pollock, Friedrich (1982) 'State Capitalism: Its Possibilities and Limitations', in A. Arato and E. Gebhardt (eds.) *The Essential Frankfurt School Reader*, New York: Continuum, pp. 71–94.

Post, Ken (1999) *Revolution and the European Experience, 1789–1914*, New York: St. Martin's Press.

Postone, Moishe (2003) 'The Holocaust and the Trajectory of the Twentieth Century' in M. Postone and E. Santner (eds.) *Catastrophe and Meaning: The Holocaust and the Twentieth Century*, Chicago: University of Chicago Press, pp. 81–114.

Postone, Moishe (2006) 'History and Helplessness: Mass Mobilization and Contemporary Forms of Anticapitalism,' *Public Culture* 18/1: 93–110.

Poulantzas, Nicos (1974) *Fascism and Dictatorship: The Third International and the Problem of Fascism*, London: New Left Books.

Poulantzas, Nicos (1978) *State, Power, Socialism*, London: New Left Books.

Price Richard (1990) 'Britain,' in M. van der Linden and J. Rojahn (eds.) *The Formation of Labour Movements 1870–1914: An International Perspective*, New York: E.J. Brill, pp. 3–24.

Price, Roger (1981) *An Economic History of Modern France, 1730–1914*, London: Palgrave Macmillan.

Price, Roger (1989) *The Revolutions of 1848*, Atlantic Highlands, N. J.: Humanities Press International.

Price, Roger (1997) *Napoleon III and the Second Empire*, London: Routledge.

Price, Roger (2002) 'Louis-Napoléon Bonaparte: "Hero" or "Grotesque Mediocrity"?' in M. Cowling and J. Martin (eds.) *Marx's Eighteenth Brumaire: (Post)modern Interpretations,* London: Pluto Press, pp. 145–62.

Price, Roger (2008) 'The Holy Struggle Against Anarchy: The Development of Counter – Revolution in 1848', in D. Dowe, H-G. Haupt and J. Sperber (eds.) *Europe in 1848: Revolution and Reform*, translated by D. Higgins, Oxford: Berghahn Books, pp. 25–54.

Prowe, Diethelm (1994) 'Classic Fascism' and the New Radical Right in Western Europe: Comparisons and Contrasts,' *Contemporary European History*, 3/3: 289–313.

Prowe, Diethelm (2004) 'Classic' Fascism and the New Radical Right, The Fascist Phantom and Anti-Immigrant Violence: The Power of (False) Equation,' in A. Fenner and E. Weitz (eds.) *Fascism and Neofascism: Critical Writings on the Radical Right in Europe*, Basingstoke: Palgrave-Macmillan, pp. 125–40.

Puhle, Hans-Jürgen (1986) 'Lords and Peasants in the Kaiserreich,' in R. Moeller (ed.) *Peasants and Lords in Modern Germany: Recent Studies in Agricultural History*, Boston: Allen & Unwin, pp. 81–109.

Pulszer, Peter (1988) *The Rise of Political Anti-Semitism in Germany and Austria*, Cambridge, Mass. Harvard University Press.

Rabinbach, Anson (1974) 'Toward a Marxist Theory of Fascism and National Socialism: A Report on Developments in West Germany,' *New German Critique*, 3: 127–153.

Rabinbach, Anson (1977) 'Unclaimed Heritage: Ernst Bloch's Heritage of Our Times and the Theory of Fascism,' *New German Critique*, 11: 5–21.

Ramsay, Scott (2019) 'Ensuring Benevolent Neutrality: The British Government's Appeasement of General Franco during the Spanish Civil War, 1936–1939' *International History Review*, 41/3: 604–623.

Rapport, Michael (2005) *Nineteenth-Century Europe*, Basingstoke: Palgrave-Macmillan.

Rapport, Michael (2009) *1848 Year of Revolution*, London: Abacus.

Rattansi, Ali (2007) *Racism. A Very Short introduction*, Oxford: Oxford University Press.

Reich, Wilhelm ([1933] 1970) *The Mass Psychology of Fascism*, New York: Farrar, Straus & Giroux.

Remmling, Gunter (1989) 'The Destruction of the Workers' Mass Movements in Nazi Germany' in I. Dobkowski and I. Wallimann (eds.) *Radical Perspectives on the Rise of Fascism in Germany, 1919–1945,* New York: Monthly Review Press, pp. 215–30.

Remond, Réne (1969) *The Right Wing in France: From 1815 to De Gaulle*, Philadelphia: University of Pennsylvania Press.

Renton, Dave (1999) *Fascism: Theory and Practice*, London: Pluto Press.

Retallack, James (1988) 'Anti-Semitism, Conservative Propaganda, and Regional Politics in Late Nineteenth Century Germany,' *German Studies Review*, 11/3: 377–403.

Richter, Melvin (1982) 'Toward a Concept of Political Illegitimacy: Bonapartist Dictatorship and Democratic Legitimacy,' *Political Theory* 10/2: 185–214.

Riley, Dylan (2004) 'Enigmas of Fascism', *New Left Review* II, 30: 134–47.

Riley, Dylan (2010) *The Civic Foundations of Fascism in Europe: Italy, Spain and Romania 1870–1945*, Baltimore: Johns Hopkins University Press.

Riley, Dylan (2014) 'The Third Reich as Rogue Regime,' *Historical Materialism: Research in Critical Marxist Theory*, 22/3–4: 330–50.

Riley, Dylan (2018) 'Editorial: What is Trump?' *New Left Review* II, 114: 5–31.

Riley, Dylan and Desai, Manali (2007) 'The Passive Revolutionary Route to the Modern World: Italy and India in Comparative Perspective,' *Comparative Studies in Society and History* 49/4: 815–47.

Roberts, David (2011) 'Reconsidering Gramsci's Interpretation of Fascism,' *Journal of Modern Italian Studies* 16/2: 239–55.

Roberts, James (1990) *The Counter-Revolution in France 1787–1830*, Basingstoke: Macmillan.

Robinson, William I. (2004) *A Theory of Global Capitalism: Production, Class and State in a Transnational World*, Baltimore: Johns Hopkins University Press.

Roediger David (1991) *The Wages of Whiteness: Race and the Making of the American Working Class*, London: Verso.

Roediger, David (2010a) 'Accounting for the Wages of Whiteness,' in W. D. Hund, J. Krikler and D. Roediger (eds.) *Wages of Whiteness and Racist Symbolic Capital*, Berlin: Lit Verlag, pp. 10–36.

Roediger, David (2010b) *How Race Survived US History: From Settlement and Slavery to the Obama Phenomenon*, London: Verso.

Röpke Wilhelm (1942) *International Economic Disintegration*, London: W. Hodge.

Röpke, Wilhelm ([1958] 1998) *A Humane Economy*, Wilmington, DE: ISI.

Rosenberg Alfred ([1934] 2012) 'Fascism as a Mass Movement.' *Historical Materialism: Research in Critical Marxist Theory* 20/1: 143–89.

Rosenberg, Justin (1996) 'Isaac Deutscher and the Lost History of International Relations,' *New Left Review* 215: 3–15.

Rosenberg, Justin (2006) 'Why is there No International Historical Sociology?' *European Journal of International Relations* 12/3: 307–340.

Rosenberg, Justin (2010) 'Basic Problems in the Theory of Uneven and Combined Development, Part II: Unevenness and Political Multiplicity,' *Cambridge Review of International Affairs*, 23/1: 165–89.

Rosenberg, Justin (2016) 'Uneven and Combined Development in Theory and History', in A. Anievas and K. Matin (eds.) *Historical Sociology and World History: Uneven and Combined Development over the Longue Durée*, Lanham, MD: Rowman & Littlefield, pp. 17–30.

Roth, Karl-Heinz (2014) 'Wages of Destruction: A Reappraisal,' *Historical Materialism: Research in Critical Marxist Theory*, 22/3–4: 298–311.

Row, Thomas (2002) 'Italy in the International System, 1900–1922,' in A. Lyttleton (ed.) *Liberal and Fascist Italy*, Oxford: Oxford University Press, pp. 83–104.

Rupert, Mark (1995) *Producing Hegemony: The Politics of Mass Production and American Global Power*, Cambridge: Cambridge University Press.

Rutkoff, Peter (1962) 'The Ligue des Patriotes: The Nature of the Radical Right and the Dreyfus Affair,' *French Historical Studies* 8/4: 585–603.

Rutkoff, Peter (1981) *Revanche and Revision: The Ligue des Patriotes and the Origins of the Radical Right in France, 1882–1900*, Athens, OH: Ohio University Press.

Rydgren, Jens (2007) 'The Sociology of the Radical Right,' *Annual Review of Sociology*, 33: 241–62.

Rydgren, Jens (ed.) (2013) *Class Politics and the Radical Right*, London: Routledge.

Sarfatti, Michele (2005) 'Characteristics and Objectives of the Anti-Jewish Racial Laws in Fascist Italy, 1938–1943,' in J. Zimmerman (ed.) *Jews in Italy under Fascist and Nazi Rule, 1922–1945*, Cambridge: Cambridge University Press, pp. 71–80.

Sarti, Roland (1971) *Fascism and the Industrial Leadership in Italy, 1919–1940*, Berkeley: University of California Press.

Sartre, Jean-Paul (1948) *Anti-Semite and Jew*, New York: Schocken Books.

Sassoon, Donald (1996) *One Hundred Years of Socialism: The West European Left in the Twentieth Century*, London: I. B. Tauris.

Saul, S. B. (1985) *The Myth of the Great Depression, 1873–1896*, Basingstoke: Macmillan.

Saull, Richard (2007) *The Cold War and After: Capitalism, Revolution and Superpower Politics*, London: Pluto Press.

Saull, Richard (2011) 'Social Conflict and the Global Cold War', *International Affairs*, 87/5: 1123–40.

Saull, Richard (2015a) 'Capitalism, Crisis and the Far-Right in the Neoliberal Era,' *Journal of International Relations and Development* 18/1: 25–51.

Saull, Richard (2015b) 'Capitalist Development and the Rise and "Fall" of the Far-Right,' *Critical Sociology* 41/4–5: 619–39.

Saull, Richard (2015c) 'The Origins and Persistence of the Far-Right: Capital, Class and the Pathologies of Liberal Politics,' in R.G. Saull, A. Anievas, N. Davidson and A. Fabry (eds.) *The Longue Durée of the Far-Right: An International Historical Sociology*, London: Routledge, pp. 21–43.

Saull, Richard (2015d) 'Capitalism and the Politics of the Far-Right,' in L. Panitch and G. Albo (eds.) *Socialist Register 2016: The Politics of the Right*, London: Merlin, pp. 136–53.

Saull, Richard (2018) 'Racism and Far-Right Imaginaries within Neoliberal Political Economy,' *New Political Economy*, 23/5: 588–608.

Saull, Richard, Alexander Anievas, Neil Davidson and Adam Fabry (2015) 'The *Longue Durée* of the Far-Right: An Introduction,' in R. G. Saull, A. Anievas, N. Davidson and A. Fabry (eds.) *The Longue Durée of the Far-Right: An International Historical Sociology*, London: Routledge, pp. 1–20.

Saville, John (1987) *1848: The British State and the Chartist Movement*, Cambridge: Cambridge University Press.

Saville, John (1988) *The Labour Movement in Britain: A Commentary*, London: Faber and Faber.

Schissler, Hanna (1986) 'The Junkers: Notes on the Social and Historical Significance of the Agrarian Elite in Prussia,' in R. Moeller (ed.) *Peasants and Lords in Modern Germany: Recent Studies in Agricultural History*, Boston: Allen & Unwin, pp. 24–51.

Schivelbusch, Wolfgang (2006) *Three New Deals: Reflections on Roosevelt's America, Mussolini's Italy and Hitler's Germany 1933–1939*, New York: Picador.

Schmidt, Gustav (1983) 'The Domestic Background to British Appeasement Policy' in W. Mommsen and L. Kettenacker (eds.) *The Fascist Challenge and the Policy of Appeasement*, London: George Allen & Unwin, pp. 101–24.

Schmidt, Gustav (1986) *The Politics and Economics of Appeasement: British Foreign Policy in the 1930s*, Leamington Spa: Berg.

Schmitt, Carl ([1922] 1985) *Political Theology. Four Chapters on the Concept of Sovereignty*. Chicago, IL: University of Chicago Press.

Schmitt, Carl ([1923] 1988) *The Crisis of Parliamentary Democracy*, Cambridge, MA: MIT Press.

Schmitt, Carl ([1927] 2007) *The Concept of the Political*, Chicago: University of Chicago Press.

Schmitz, David (1988) *The United States and Fascist Italy, 1922–1940*, Chapel Hill: The University of North Carolina Press.

Schröder, Hans-Jürgen (1983) 'The Ambiguities of Appeasement: Great Britain, the United States and Germany, 1937–9' in W. Mommsen and L. Kettenacker (eds.) *The Fascist Challenge and the Policy of Appeasement*, London: George Allen & Unwin, pp. 390–99.

Schuker, Stephen (1988) *American Reparations to Germany, 1919–33: Implications for the Third World Debt Crisis*, Princeton: Princeton University Press.

Seager, Frederic (1969) *The Boulanger Affair: Political Crossroads of France 1886–1889*, Ithaca: Cornell University Press.

Segal, Paul (1987) *The French State and French Private Investment in Czechoslovakia, 1918–1938: A Study of Economic Diplomacy,* New York: Garland Publishing Inc.

Selwyn, Ben (2011) 'Trotsky, Gerschenkron and the Political Economy of Late Capitalist Development,' *Economy and Society* 40/3: 421–450.

Semmel, Bernard (1960) *Imperialism and Social Reform: English Social-Imperial Thought 1895–1914,* London: Allen & Unwin.

Seymour, Richard (2016) 'Cold War Anticommunism and the Defence of White Supremacy in the Southern United States,' PhD thesis, London School of Economics, UK.

Shaw, Louise G. (2003) *The British Political Elite and the Soviet Union, 1937–1939*, London, Frank Cass.

Shilliam, Robbie (2009) 'The Atlantic as a Vector of Uneven and Combined Development,' *Cambridge Review of International Affairs*, 22/1: 69–88.

Shilliam, Robbie (2012) 'Forget English Freedom, Remember Atlantic Slavery: Common Law, Commercial Law and the Significance of Slavery for Classical Political Economy,' *New Political Economy*, 7/5: 591–609.

Shilliam, Robbie (2018) *Race and the Undeserving Poor: From Abolition to Brexit*, London: Agenda Publishing.

Short, Nicola (2017) 'On the Subject of Far-Right-Wing Politics,' *Critical Sociology*, 43/4–5: 763–77.

Shorter, Edward (1969) 'Middle Class Anxiety in the German Revolution of 1848,' *Journal of Social History* 2/3: 189–215.

Shorter, Edward and Tilly, Charles (1974) *Strikes in France, 1830–1968*, Cambridge: Cambridge University Press.

Siemann, Wolfram (1998) *The German Revolution of 1848–49* translated by Christine Banerji, Basingstoke: Macmillan.

Silver, Beverly (2003) *Forces of Labour: Workers' Movements and Globalization since 1870*, Cambridge: Cambridge University Press.

Silone, Ignazio (1983) 'What is Fascism?' in D. Beetham (ed.) *Marxists in the Face of Fascism*, Manchester: Manchester University Press, pp. 236–44.

Singh, Nikhil Pal (2017) *Race and America's Long War*, Oakland: University of California Press.

Skocpol, Theda (1979) *States and Social Revolutions: A Comparative Analysis of France, Russia and China*, Cambridge: Cambridge University Press.

Slobidian, Quinn (2018) *Globalists: The End of Empire and the Birth of Neoliberalism*, Cambridge: Harvard University Press.

Smith, Dennis Mack (1997) *Modern Italy: A Political History*, New Haven: Yale University Press.

Smith, Michael (1980) *Tariff Reform in France, 1860–1900: The Politics of Economic Interest*, Ithaca: Cornell University Press.

Smith, Michael (1992) 'The Méline Tariff as Social Protection: Rhetoric or Reality?' *International Review of Social History*, XXXVII: 230–243.

Smith, Neil (2006) 'The Geography of Uneven Development,' in B. Dunn and H. Radice (eds.) *100 Years of Permanent Revolution: Results and Prospects*, London: Pluto Press, pp. 180–195.

Smith, Neil (2008) *Uneven Development: Nature, Capital and the Production of Space*, Oxford: Blackwell.

Smith, Woodruff (1978) *The German Colonial Empire*, Chapel Hill: University of North Carolina Press.

Smith, Woodruff (1986) *The Ideological Origins of Nazi Imperialism*, New York: Oxford University Press.

Snowden, Frank (1979) 'From Sharecropper to Proletarian: The Background to Fascism in Rural Tuscany, 1880–1920,' in J. A. Davis (ed.) *Gramsci and Italy's Passive Revolution*, New York: Barnes & Noble Books, pp. 136–71.

Snowden, Frank (1986) *Violence and Great Estates in the South of Italy: Apulia, 1900–1922*, Cambridge University Press.

Sohn-Rethel, Alfred (1987) *Economy and Class Structure of German Fascism*, London: Free Association Books.

Sperber, Jonathan (2000) *Revolutionary Europe 1780–1850*, Harlow: Longman.

Sperber, Jonathan (2005) *The European Revolutions, 1848–1851* 2nd edition, Cambridge: Cambridge University Press.

Sperber, Jonathan (2009) *Europe, 1850–1914: Progress, Participation and Apprehension*, Harlow: Pearson Longman.

Stearns, Peter (1974) *The Revolutions of 1848*, London: Weidenfeld & Nicolson.

Stedman-Jones, Gareth (1988) 'The Mid-Century Crisis and the 1848 Revolutions: The Case of England,' in E. Burke (ed.) *Global Crises and Social Movements: Artisans, Peasants, Populists and the World Economy*, Boulder: Westview Press, pp. 72–85.

Steinberg, Jonathan (2011) *Bismarck: A Life*, Oxford: Oxford University Press.

Steiner, Zara (2005) *The Lights that Failed: European International History, 1919–1933*, Oxford: Oxford University Press.

Steinmetz, George (1993) *Regulating the Social: The Welfare State and Local Politics in Imperial Germany*, Princeton: Princeton university Press.

Stern, Fritz (1974) *The Politics of Cultural Despair*, Berkeley: University of California Press.

Stern, Fritz (1977) 'Prussia' in D. Spring (ed.) *European Landed Elites in the Nineteenth Century*, Baltimore: Johns Hopkins University Press, pp. 45–67.

Sternhell, Zeev (1986) *Neither Right nor Left: Fascist Ideology in France*, Berkeley: University of California Press.

Sternhell, Zeev (1996) *The Birth of Fascist Ideology: From Cultural Rebellion to Political Revolution*, Princeton: Princeton University Press.

Sternhell, Zeev, with Sznajder, Maria and Ashéri, Maia (1994) *The Birth of Fascist Ideology: From Cultural Rebellion to Political Revolution*, Princeton: Princeton University Press.

Stoddard, Lothrop (1921) *The Rising Tide of Color Against White World-Supremacy*, New York: Charles Scribner's Sons.

Stone, Norman (1985) *Europe Transformed, 1878–1919*, London: Fontana Press.

Strikwerda, Carl (1998) 'Capitalists, Immigrants, and Populists: The Impact of Social Conflict on the Origins of World War I,' in M. Hanagan, L. P. Moch and W. te Brake(eds.) *Challenging Authority: The Historical Study of Contentious Politics*, Minneapolis: University of Minnesota Press, pp. 213–27.

Summers, Anne (1976) 'Militarism in Britain before the Great War,' *History Workshop Journal*, 2/1: 104–123.

Swift, Roger (1987) 'The Outcast Irish in the British Victorian City: Problems and Perspectives,' *Irish Historical Studies*, 25/99: 264–276.

Sykes, Alan (1979) *Tariff Reform in British Politics 1903–1913*, Oxford: Clarendon Press.

Sykes, Alan (2005) *The Radical Right in Britain: Social Imperialism to the BNP*, Basingstoke: Macmillan.

Taguieff, Pierre (1993) 'From Race to Culture: The New Right's view of European Identity,' *Telos*, 98–99: 99–125.

Tannenbaum, Edward (1962) *The Action Française: Die-Hard Reactionaries in Twentieth Century France*, New York: John Wiley.

Temin, Peter (1991) 'Soviet and Nazi Economic Planning in the 1930s,' *Economic History Review* 44/4: 573–93.

Teschke, Benno (2003) *The Myth of 1648: Class, Geopolitics and the Making of Modern International Relations*, London: Verso.

Thalheimer, August (1973) 'Die Krise des Parliamentarismus – das Vorspiel zur Krise der bürgerlichen Herrschaft,' in Gruppe Arbeiterpolitik, *Der Faschismus in Deutschland*, Frankfurt: Europäische Verlag, pp. 49–51.

Thalheimer, August (1983a) 'On Fascism,' in D. Beetham (ed.) *Marxists in the Face of Fascism*, Manchester: Manchester University Press, pp. 187–95.

Thalheimer, August (1983b) 'The Development of Fascism in Germany,' in D. Beetham (ed.) *Marxists in the Face of Fascism*, Manchester: Manchester University Press, pp. 197–204.

Thody, Philip (1989) *French Caesarism from Napoleon I to Charles de Gaulle*, New York: St. Martin's Press.

Thomas, Peter (2009) *The Gramscian Moment: Philosophy, Hegemony and Marxism*, Leiden: Brill.

Thompson, Andrew (1997) 'Tariff Reform: An Imperial Strategy, 1903–1913' *The Historical Journal* 40/4: 1033–1054.

Thompson, Edward (1963) *The Making of the English Working Class*, London: Victor Gollancancz.

Thompson, John (1966) *Russia, Bolshevism and the Versailles Peace*, Princeton: Princeton University Press.

Thurlow, Richard (1998) *Fascism in Britain*, London: I. B. Tauris.

Tint, Herbert (1964) *The Decline of French Patriotism, 1870–1914*, London: Wiedenfeld & Nicolson.

Tipton, Frank (1974) 'Farm Labor and Power Politics; Germany, 1850–1914,' *Journal of Economic History*, 34/4: 951–79.

Tipton, Frank (2003) *A History of Modern Germany since 1815*, Berkeley: University of California Press.

Tipton, Robert and Aldrich, Robert (1987) *An Economic and Social History of Europe, 1890–1939*, Basingstoke: Macmillan.

Tirrell, Sarah (1951) *German Agrarian Politics After Bismarck's Fall: The Formation of the Farmers' League*, New York: Columbia University Press.

Tocqueville, Alexis de ([1835/40] 2000) *Democracy in America*, Indianapolis: Hackett Publishing Co.

Tocqueville, Alexis de ([1851] 2009) *Recollections of the French Revolution of 1848*, ed. J. Mayer and A. Q. Kerr, New Brunswick, NJ: Transaction Books.

Togliatti, Palmiro (1983) 'On the Question of Fascism,' in D. Beetham (ed.) *Marxists in the Face of Fascism*, Manchester: Manchester University Press, pp. 136–48.

Tomba. Massimiliano (2013) 'Marx as the Historical Materialist: Re-Reading the Eighteenth Brumaire', *Historical Materialism: Research in Critical Marxist Theory* 21/2: 21–46.

Tombs, Robert (1996) *A New Order: France 1814–1914*, London: Longman.

Tooze, Adam (2005) 'Economics, Ideology and Cohesion in the Third Reich: A Critique of Goetz Aly's Hitlers *Volksstaat*,' adamtooze.com https://www.adamtooze.com/wp -content/uploads/2017/01/Tooze-Review-of-Aly-for-Dapim-2005-.pdf.

Tooze, Adam (2007) *The Wages of Destruction: The Making and Breaking of the Nazi Economy*, London: Penguin Books.

Tooze, Adam (2015a) *The Deluge: The Great War and the Remaking of Global Order*, London: Penguin Books.

Tooze, Adam (2015b) 'Capitalist Peace or Capitalist War? The July Crisis Revisited,' in A. Anievas (ed.) *Cataclysm 1914: The First World War and the Making of Modern Politics*, Brill: Leiden, pp. 66–95.

Torp, Cornelius (2010) 'The "Coalition of Rye and Iron" under the Pressure of Globalization: A Reinterpretation of Germany's Political Economy before 1914,' *Central European History*, 43/3: 401–27.

Torp, Cornelius (2014) *The Challenges of Globalization: Economy and Politics in Germany, 1860–1914*, New York: Berghahn.

Toscano, Alberto (2017) 'Notes on Late Fascism,' *Historical Materialism Blog*, 2 April https://www.historicalmaterialism.org/blog/notes-late-fascism.

Toscano, Alberto (2021) 'Fascists, Freedom and the Anti-State State,' *Historical Materialism: Research in Critical Marxist Theory*, 29/4: 3–21.

Townsend, Jules (1988) 'Introduction,' in Hobson, J. A. *Imperialism: A Study*, London: Unwin & Hyman, pp. 9–41.

Traverso, Enzo (2007) *Fire and Blood: The European Civil War, 1914–1945*, London: Verso.

Traverso, Enzo (2019) *The New Faces of Fascism: Populism and the Far-Right*, translated by David Broder, London: Verso.

Trimberger, Ellen (1978) *Revolution from Above. Military Bureaucrats and Development in Japan, Turkey, Egypt, and Peru*, New Brunswick, NJ.: Transaction Books.

Trotsky, Leon ([1906/1930] 1962) *The Permanent Revolution and Results and Prospects*, London: New Park Publications.

Trotsky, Leon ([1930–34] 1975) *The Struggle Against Fascism in Germany*, Harmonds-worth: Penguin Books.

Trotsky, Leon ([1932] 2008) *History of the Russian Revolution*, translated by Max Eastman, Chicago: Haymarket Books.

Turner, Henry A. (1969) 'Big Business and Rise of Hitler,' *The American Historical Review* 75/1: 56–70.

Turner, Henry A. (1985) *Big Business and the Rise of Hitler*, New York: Oxford University Press.

Turner, John (2014) *Banking in Crisis: The Rise and Fall of British Banking Stability, 1800 to the Present*, Cambridge: Cambridge University Press.

Tylecote, Andrew (1992) *The Long Wave in the World Economy: The Present Crisis in Historical Perspective,* London: Routledge.

Urban, Martin (2016) 'The Pan-German League at the End of the 19th Century,' *Prague Papers on the History of International Relations*, 1: 60–71 http://cejsh.icm.edu.pl/cejsh /element/bwmeta1.element.desklight-4f8cefdc-9894-4d2f-afb1-fbeda924e8ce.

Umbreit, Hans (2003) 'German Rule in the Occupied Territories 1942–1945,' in B. R. Kroener, R-D. Müller and H. Umbreit (eds.) *Germany and the Second World War, Volume V, Organization and Mobilization of the German Sphere of Power, Part 2, Wartime Administration, Economy, and Manpower Resources 1942–1944/5*, Oxford: Clarendon Press, pp. 8–291.

Vaiciulenas, Albert (1991) 'Introduction' [to section on Nationalism and Politics] in R. Tombs (ed.) *Nationhood and Nationalism in France: From Boulangism to the Great War 1889–1918*, London: Harper Collins, pp. 103–7.

Vajda, Mihaly (1972) 'Crisis and the Way Out: The Rise of Fascism in Italy and Germany,' *Telos*, 12: 3–26.

Vadja, Mihaly (1976) *Fascism as a Mass Movement*, London: Allison and Busby.

Varouxakis, George (1998) 'John Stuart Mill on Race,' *Utilitas* 10/1: 17–32.

Vascik, George (1993) 'Agrarian Conservatism in Wilhelmine Germany,' in L. Jones and J. Retallack (eds) *Between Reform, Reaction, and Resistance: Studies in the History of German Conservatism from 1789 to 1945*, Oxford: Berg, pp. 229–60.

Virdee, Satnam (2015) *Racism, Class and the Racialized Outsider*, Basingstoke: Palgrave.

Volkmann, Hans-Erich (1990) 'The National Socialist Economy in Preparation for War', in W. Deist (ed.) *Germany and the Second World War. Vol. 1: The Build-up of German Aggression*, Oxford: Clarendon Press, pp. 159–372.

Volkov, Shulamit (1978) *The Rise of Popular Anti-Semitism: The Urban Master Artisans, 1873–1896*, Princeton: Princeton University Press.

Vajda, Mihaly (1976) *Fascism as a Mass Movement*, London: Allison & Busby.

Wallerstein, Immanuel (2011) *The Modern World-System IV: Centrist Liberalism Triumphant, 1789–1914*, Berkeley: University of California Press.

Ward-Perkins, C. N. (1950) 'The Commercial Crisis of 1847,' *Oxford Economic Papers*, New Series, 2/1: 75–94.

Warmbrunn, Werner (1963) *The Dutch Under German Occupation, 1940–45*, Stanford: Stanford University Press.

Warmbrunn, Werner (1993) *The German Occupation of Belgium 1940–44*, New York: Peter Lang.

Watkins, Geoff (2002) 'The Appeal of Bonapartism,' in M. Cowling and J. Martin (eds.) *Marx's Eighteenth Brumaire: (Post)modern Interpretations*, London: Pluto Press, pp. 163–76.

Webb, Steven (1980) 'Tariffs, Cartels, Technology, and Growth in the German Steel Industry, 1879 to 1914,' *Journal of Economic History*, 40/2: 309–30.

Webb Steven (1982) 'Agricultural Protection in Wilhelminian Germany: Forging an Empire with Pork and Rye,' *Journal of Economic History* XLII/2: 309–26.

Weber, Eugen (1962) *Action Française: Royalism and Reaction in Twentieth-Century France*, Stanford: Stanford University Press.

Weber, Eugen (1964) *Varieties of Fascism: Doctrines of Revolution in the Twentieth Century*, New York: Van Nostrand Reinhold Company.

Weber, Eugen (1976) *Peasants into Frenchmen: The Modernization of Rural France, 1870–1914*, Stanford: Stanford University Press.

Wehler, Hans-Ulrich (1972) 'Industrial Growth and Early German Imperialism,' in R. Owen and R. B. Sutcliffle(eds.) *Studies in the Theory of Imperialism*, London: Longman, pp. 71–90.

Wehler, Hans-Ulrich (1979) 'Bismarck's Imperialism' *Past and Present* 48: 19–55.

Wehler, Hans-Ulrich (1985) *The German Empire 1871–1918*, Leamington Spa: Berg.

Weikart, Richard (2003) 'Progress Through Racial Extermination: Social Darwinism, Eugenics, and Pacifism in Germany, 1860–1918,' *German Studies Review*, 26/2: 273–294.

Weisbrod, Bernd (1979) 'Economic Power and Political Stability Reconsidered: Heavy Industry in Weimar Germany,' *Social History* 4/2: 241–63.

Weisbrod, Bernd (1990) 'Industrial Crisis Strategy in the Great Depression,' in J. V. Kruedner (ed.) *Economics Crisis and Political Collapse: The Weimar Republic, 1924–1933*, Oxford: Oxford University Press, pp. 45–62.

Weiss, John (1977) *Conservatism in Europe 1770–1945: Traditionalism, Reaction, and Counter-Revolution*, London: Thames & Hudson.

Wendt, Bernd-Jurgen (1983) 'Economic Appeasement – A Crisis Strategy' in W. Mommsen and L. Kettenacker (eds.) *The Fascist Challenge and the Policy of Appeasement*, London: George Allen & Unwin, pp. 157–72.

White, Eugene N. (2007) 'The Crash of 1882 and the Bailout of the Paris Bourse,' *Cliometrica* 1: 115–44.

Wilson, Bee (2011) 'Counter-Revolutionary Thought' in G. Stedman-Jones and G. Claeys (eds.) *The Cambridge History of Nineteenth-Century Political Thought*, Cambridge: Cambridge University Press, pp. 9–38.

Wilson, Eric (ed.) (2009) *Government of the Shadows: Parapolitics and Criminal Sovereignty*, London: Pluto Press.

Wilson, Eric (2012) 'The Concept of the Parapolitical,' in E. Wilson (ed.) *The Dual State: Parapolitics, Carl Schmitt and the National Security Complex*, Burlington, VT: Ashgate, pp. 1–38.

Wilson, Stephen (1982) *Ideology and Experience: Anti-Semitism in France at the Time of the Dreyfus Affair*, Rutherford, NJ: Fairleigh Dickinson University Press.

Winkler, Heinrich (1976) 'From Social Protectionism to National Socialism: The German Small Business Movement in Comparative Perspective,' *Journal of Modern History*, 48/1: 1–18.

Winock, Michel (1998) *Nationalism, Anti-Semitism, and Fascism in France*, Stanford, CA: Stanford University Press.

Wistrich, Robert. S. (1976) 'Leon Trotsky's Theory of Fascism,' *Journal of Contemporary History*, 11/4: 157–84.

Wichert, Sabine (1983) 'The British Left and Appeasement: Political Tactics or Alternative Policies?' in W. Mommsen and L. Kettenacker (eds.) *The Fascist Challenge and the Policy of Appeasement*, London: George & Unwin, pp. 125–41.

Wodack Ruth, KhosraviNik, Majid and Mral, Brigitte (eds.) (2013) *Right Wing Populism in Europe: Politics and Discourse*, London: Bloomsbury Academic.

Woodley, Daniel (2010) *Fascism and Political Theory*, London: Routledge.

Woods, Jeff (2004) *Black Struggle, Red Scare: Segregation and Anti-Communism in the South, 1948–1968*, Baton Rouge: Louisiana State University Press.

Woods, Roger (1996) *The Conservative Revolution in the Weimar Republic*, Basingstoke: Macmillan.

Woolf, S. J. (1968) 'Did a Fascist Economic System Exist?' in S. J. Woolf (ed.), *The Nature of Fascism*, London: Weidenfeld & Nicolson, pp. 119–51.

Wright, Vincent (1975) 'The Coup d'état of December 1851: Repression and Its Limits,' in R. Price (ed.) *Revolution and Reaction: 1848 and the Second French Republic*, London: Croom Helm, pp. 303–33.

Zamagni, Vera (1993) *The Economic History of Italy 1860–1990*, Oxford: Clarendon Press.

Zeldin, Theodore (1958) *The Political System of Napoleon III*, London: Macmillan.

Zimmerer, Jürgen (2008) 'Colonialism and the Holocaust: Towards an Archaeology of Genocide', *Development Dialogue*, 50: 95–123.

# Index

·